HISTORICAL
POEMS

of the

XIVth and XVth Centuries

EDITED BY

Rossell Hope Robbins

George F. Johnson Library
St. Peter's College
Jersey City, N. J. 07306

NEW YORK
COLUMBIA UNIVERSITY PRESS
1959

Published 1959, Columbia University Press, New York
Published in Great Britain, Canada, India, and Pakistan
by the Oxford University Press
London, Toronto, Bombay, and Karachi
Library of Congress Catalog Card Number: 59-6661
Manufactured in the Netherlands

Saint Peter's University Library
Withdrawn

HISTORICAL POEMS

of the

XIVth and XVth Centuries

For H. A. M. R.

PREFACE

Historical Poems of the XIVth and XVth Centuries now completes the assembly in modern editions of the best of the Middle English lyrics, begun in 1924 by Carleton Brown and continued in his anthologies of 1932 and 1939, and in my own *Secular Lyrics of the XIVth and XVth Centuries* of 1952. In general, it follows the principles established in these earlier collections; however, "lyric" has been replaced by the wider term, "poem."

All the shorter historical and political poems in Middle English number not more than 250 items. Of these, 100 from 65 different manuscripts are presented here.

I have excluded thirteenth-century material. There is, in fact, very little, and the best has been published in Brown's *English Lyrics of the XIIIth Century.*[1] The scraps of verse quoted in Langtoft are omitted, because of their presumed date; vigorous, crude little pieces, they may conveniently be read in Wilson's *Lost Literature.* Second, I have excluded (with the exception of Nos. 20 and 55) any politico-religious or politico-moral poem already printed in Brown's religious anthologies[2] or in my *Secular Lyrics.*[3] Third, I have generally excluded poems over 150 lines long;[4] because of their prime

---

[1] No. 5, A Prisoner's Prayer; No. 20, Warning to Sir Eode; No. 72, A Song of Lewes, and No. 74, On the Follies of Fashion, both from Harley MS. 2253; and a few moral laments such as Nos. 11 and 12.

[2] *Religious Lyrics of the XVth Century* (Oxford, 1939): Nos. 130 and 131, prayers for Henry VI on his expedition to France in 1430, similar to Nos. 41 and 98 of this collection; No. 159, Skelton's Lamentation of the Soul of Edward IV; and the moral pieces on the decadence of virtue, Nos. 171-77, and 181-83.

[3] *Secular Lyrics of the XIVth and XVth Centuries* (Oxford, 1952): Nos. 120-23, the mummings and pageants; and Nos. 57-60, the "money" songs. A variant of No. 47 (here) is printed in the notes, p. 241.

[4] *Richard the Redeles* or *Mum and the Sothsegger* (*Index,* No. *6); Jack Upland's Complaint; the *Libelle of Englyshe Polycye* (*Index,* No. 3491); Lyarde (*Index,* No. 2026); *Wynnere and Wastoure*

importance, however, nine longer poems are included here.[5]
Fourth, since this is intended as only a selection of the best
and most representative poems, I have not given all poems
from a series, such as Minot's poems or the Digby MS. 102
group. Four poems by Lydgate are sufficient representation
of his forty or fifty political productions.

Little of much consequence has been omitted,[6] and the
above exceptions account for most of the other 150 texts.
All the poems (Nos. 53 and 57 only excepted) have been
printed previously; but they are scattered throughout historical works, rare books, and scholarly journals, available
only to a student in a major library. Even Wright's pioneer
work, now nearly a hundred years old, has only twenty-five
of the hundred poems in this anthology.

In my research I have been in communication with many
scholars in England, on the continent, and in the United
States. Such friendly intercourse is perhaps the most rewarding aspect of the scholar's life. To those who have in any
way helped me with this anthology go my sincere thanks.
In the latter stages of my work, the Research Committee of
the Modern Language Association of America made a liberal
grant-in-aid for manuscripts and rare books otherwise in-
accessible to me: to the Committee members I am appropri-

(*Index*, No. 3137); and, perhaps less inportant, Adam Davy's
Dreams (*Index*, No. 3763); Ashby's Reflections (*Index*, No. 437);
Edward IV's Recovery of the Throne (*Index*, No. 2808); Gower's
Praise of Peace to Henry VI (*Index*, No. 2587); and some of the
longer prophecies (*Index*, Nos. 365, 1112, 3665).

[5] Nos. 4, 13, 26, 28, 48, 64, 65, 70, 89.

[6] If space were of no consideration, there might have been included another of the carols on money (*Index*, No. 3959); the attack
on Bishop Booth from the already well-represented Cotton Rolls
ii.23 (*Index*, No. 544); the revised and much longer redaction of
Lydgate's Kings (*Index*, No. 882); another poem on "Galaunt"
(*Index*, No. 1874); Hoccleve's attacks on fashions (*Index*, No.
1398) and his ballades to Henry V (such as *Index*, Nos. 3402,
3788, 3853, 3854); and Lydgate's Praise of Peace (*Index*, No. 2156,
very similar to No. 99 printed here.

ately grateful. The whole scholarly community must thank the Columbia University Press, which has so generously undertaken the publication of this volume. In a far more specific sense than is customary in prefatory acknowledgments, I am in debt to my wife, Helen Ann Mins Robbins, who has not only acted as my amanuensis, but, at considerable personal sacrifice, has made possible that freedom from academic responsibilities necessary for any prolonged literary research. Without her, this book could not have been written.

R. H. R.

KATSBAAN ONDERHEUGEL, SAUGERTIES
Feast of St. George, 1958

CONTENTS

PREFACE   vii

INTRODUCTION   xvii

AN OUTLINE OF DYNASTIC HISTORY

1. The Kings of England, by Lydgate, *MS. Rawlinson* C.48   3

POEMS FROM HARLEY MS. 2253

2. Song of the Husbandman (1300)   7
3. The Flemish Insurrection (1302)   9
4. The Execution of Sir Simon Fraser (1306)   14
5. The Death of Edward I (1307)   21
6. Satire on the Consistory Courts (1307)   24
7. Satire on the Retinues of the Great (1307)   27
8. Thomas of Erceldoune's Prophecy   29

WAR POEMS BY LAWRENCE MINOT FROM COTTON MS. GALBA E.IX

9. Bannockburn Avenged (1333)   30
10. The Battle of Neville's Cross (1346)   31
11. The Siege of Calais (1347)   34
12. The Taking of Guines (1352)   37

POEMS FROM DIGBY MS. 102

13. What Profits a Kingdom (1401)   39
14. God Save King Henry V (1413)   45
15. The Follies of the Duke of Burgundy (1419)   50

POPULAR STRUGGLES I: THE GREAT REVOLT

16. On the Evil State of England (1381), *Cambridge Univ. MS. Dd.* 14.2   54
17. John Ball's Letters, I (1381), Stow, *Annales*   54
18. John Ball's Letters, II (1381), *Royal MS.* 13.E.ix   55
19. The Course of Revolt (1381), *MS. Digby* 196   55
20. The Insurrection and Earthquake (1382), *MS. Vernon*   57

POPULAR STRUGGLES II: LATER DISCONTENT

21. The Yorkshire Partisans (1392), *Stowe MS.* 393   60
22. A Song of Freedom (1434), *MS. Lat. theol. d.*1   62
23. The Day Will Dawn (1445), *B. M. Addit. MS.* 40166   62
24. The Kentish Insurrection (1450), *Magdalen Coll. Oxford Charter Misc.* 306   63
25. Injustices at Coventry (1496), *Coventry Corp. MS.*   63

POPULAR BALLADS

26. The Battle of Otterburn (1388), *Cotton MS. Cleop. C.*iv   64
27. The Battle of Agincourt (1415), *Cotton MS. Cleop. C.*iv   74
28. The Siege of Calais (1436), *English Coll. Rome MS.* 1306   78
29. Mockery of the Flemings (1436), *Lambeth Palace MS.* 6   83
30. Scorn of the Duke of Burgundy (1436), *English Coll. Rome MS.* 1306   86

POLITICS IN SONG

31. The Death of Archbishop Scrope (1405), *Trinity Coll. Camb. MS.* 652   90
32. The Agincourt Carol (1415), *MS. Arch. Selden B.*26   91
33. The Rose on Branch (1415), *B. M. Addit. MS.* 31042   92
34. The Lily White Rose (1486), *B. M. Addit. MS.* 5465   93
35. The Roses Entwined (1486), *B. M. Addit. MS.* 5465   94
36. For Victory in France (1492), *Cotton MS. Domitianus* xviii   96
37. God Speed the Plough, *MS. Arch. Selden B.*26   97

COMMEMORATION OF KINGS

38. Summer Sunday: A Lament for Edward II (1327), *MS. Laud Misc.* 108   98
39. The Death of Edward III (1377), *MS. Vernon*   102
40. Richard II Interred in Westminster (1413), by Hoccleve, *Huntington MS. HM* 111   106
41. A Recollection of Henry V (1429), by Audelay, *MS. Douce* 302   108
42. The Death of Edward IV (1483), *Rylands Lib. Manchester Eng. MS.* 113   111

POLITICAL PROPHECIES

43. Geoffrey of Monmouth's Prophecy, *MS. Rawlinson K.*42   113
44. The Cock in the North, *Cotton Rolls* ii.23   115
45. When Rome Is Removed, *Cambridge Univ. MS. Kk.*1.5   118
46. A Political Prophecy by the Dice, *Trinity Coll. Dublin MS.* 516   120
47. Merlin's Prophecy, *Trinity Coll. Dublin MS.* 516   121

THE FIRST UTOPIA

48. The Land of Cokaygne, *Harley MS.* 913   121

THE WICKED AGE

49. The Bisson Leads the Blind (1456), *Harley MS.* 5396   127
50. London Lickpenny, *Harley MS.* 367   130
51. Money, Money, *Royal MS.* 17.*B.*xlvii   134
52. Huff! A Galaunt, *MS. Rawlinson poet.* 34   138
53. The Pride of Women's Horns, *MS. Ashmole* 59   139
54. The Sayings of the Four Philosophers (1311), *Advocates MS.* 19.2.1   140
55. The Twelve Abuses, *St. John's Coll. Camb. MS.* 37   143
56. Abuses of the Age, I, *Harley MS.* 913   144
57. Abuses of the Age, II, *MS. Bodley* 416   144
58. England May Sing Alas, *Caius Coll. Camb. MS.* 71   145
59. Truth Is Unpopular, *Sloane MS.* 2593   146
60. How Goes This World About, *Sloane MS.* 2593   147
61. This World Is Variable, *MS. Eng. poet. e.*1   148
62. Now Is England Perished, *Cambridge Univ. MS. Hh.*2.6   149
63. The World Upside Down, *Bodl. MS. Eng. poet. b.*4   150

CRITICS OF THE LOLLARDS

64. Defend Us from All Lollardry, *Cotton MS. Vespasian B.*xvi   152

CRITICS OF THE FRIARS

65. The Orders of Cain (1382), *Cotton MS. Cleop. B.*ii   157
66. On the Minorites (1382), *Cotton MS. Cleop. B.*ii   163

67. Friars, *Ministri Malorum, Trinity Coll. Camb. MS.* 1144   **164**
68. The Layman's Complaint, *St. John's Coll. Camb. MS.* 195   166
69. The Friar's Answer, *St. John's Coll. Camb. MS.* 195   166

ENGLAND'S COMMERCE

70. A Trade Policy, *Lansdowne MS.* 796   168

THE FALLS OF PRINCES

71. The Sudden Fall of Princes, by Lydgate, *Trinity Coll. Camb. MS.* 600   174
72. The Lament of the Duchess of Gloucester (1441), *Cambridge Univ. MS. Hh.*4.12   176
73. Epitaph for the Duke of Gloucester (1447), *Harley MS.* 2251   180
74. Examples of Mutability, *MS. Rawlinson C.*813   184
75. Arrest of the Duke of Suffolk (1450), *Cotton Rolls* ii.23   186
76. The Death of the Duke of Suffolk (1450), *Cotton MS. Vespasian B.*xvi   187

THE RED ROSE OF LANCASTER

77. The Five Dogs of London (1456), *Trinity Coll. Dublin MS.* 516   189
78. The Ship of State (1458), *Trinity Coll. Dublin MS.* 516   191
79. Reconciliation of Henry VI and the Yorkists (1458), *Cotton MS. Vespasian B.*xvi   194
80. A Prayer for Victory, *MS. Ashmole* 59   196
81. God Amend Wicked Counsel (1464), *Bodl. MS. Lat. misc. e.*85   196
82. Willikin's Return (1470), *B. M. Addit. MS.* 19046   198
83. A Remembrance of Henry VI (1492), by Ryman, *Cambridge Univ. Ee.*1.12   199

THE WHITE ROSE OF YORK

84. Prelude to the Wars (1449), *Cotton Rolls ii.*23   201
85. Advice to the Court, I (1450), *Cotton Rolls* ii.23   203
86. Advice to the Court, II (1450), *Cotton Rolls* ii.23   203

87. Take Good Heed, *Trinity Coll. Dublin MS.* 432   206
88. Ballade Set on the Gates of Canterbury (1460), *Davies MS.*   207
89. The Battle of Northampton (1460), *Trinity Coll. Dublin MS.* 432   210
90. The Battle of Towton (1461), *Trinity Coll. Dublin MS.* 432   215
91. Twelve Letters Save England (1461), *Trinity Coll. Dublin MS.* 432   218
92. Edward, Dei Gratia, *Lambeth Palace MS.* 306   221
93. A Political Retrospect (1462), *Soc. of Antiquaries MS.* 101   222
94. The Battle of Barnet (1471), *Trinity Coll. Camb. MS.* 601   226

THE WELL-ORDERED KINGDOM

95. The Crowned King: On the Art of Governing (1415), *MS. Douce* 95   227
96. Advice to the Several Estates, I, by Lydgate, *Temple of Glas*   232
97. Advice to the Several Estates, II, *Sloane MS.* 4031   233

THE WILL FOR PEACE

98. A Prayer for England, by Lydgate, *MS. Fairfax* 16   235
99. That Peace May Stand, *Advocates MS.* 19.3.1   239
100. Send Us Peace (1499), *B. M. Addit. MS.* 5665   242

SELECT LIST OF ABBREVIATED TITLES CITED   243
NOTES TO POEMS   248
GLOSSARY   392
INDEX OF FIRST LINES   438

INTRODUCTION

The present anthology of historical poems reveals literary qualities that bear comparison with those of similar collections of religious and secular lyrics. Its poetic level seldom sinks so low as some of the formal exercises of devotion to a heavenly or earthly maiden that cluttered manuscripts in the later fifteenth century, although I have exhumed one counterpart in boredom (No. 73) to illustrate the genre at its worst. On the other hand, it must be admitted that there is nothing here so charming as "I sing of a maiden" or "Maiden in the moor lay." Generally, however, within a narrower range, these historical and political poems are competent, invigorating, and lively, if only because they deal with issues of vital pertinence to the people who wrote and used them.

The venom of Minot against the Scots and the French during the wars of Edward recalls the songs of scorn preserved in the chronicles of Langtoft and de Brunne and voices the clear-cut exultation of the professional patriot (No. 9):

> Rughfute riueling, now kindels þi care,
> berebag with þi boste, þi biging es bare;
> fals wretche and forsworn, whider wiltou fare?
> busk þe into brig, and abide þare.
>   þare, wretche, saltou won and wery þe while;
>   þi dwelling in donde es done for þi gile.

Few readers would agree with the late eighteenth-century judgment that Minot "is, perhaps, equal, if not superior to any English poet before the sixteenth, or even, with very few exceptions, before the seventeenth century."[1] But most would praise his power of evoking striking images in simple language.

The struggle of battle makes this historical verse dynamic.

[1] Joseph Ritson, *Poems by Laurence Minot* (London, 1795), p. xiv.

At Agincourt the horsemen fall panoramically to the flight of the arrows (No. 27):

> Stedes þer stumbelyd in þat stownde,
>   þat stod stere stuffed vnder stele;
> With gronyng grete þei felle to grownde,
>   Here sydes federed whan þei gone fele.

Townsfolk repulse the besiegers at Calais in 1436 (No. 28):

> The women, bothe yonge and olde,
> With stones stuffed euery scaffolde —
>   They spared no swete ne swynk;
> With boilled caudrons, grete and smale,
> Yif thay wolde haue sawted the wall,
>   Al hote to gif hem drynke.

His enemies gloat over the arrest of the Duke of Suffolk in 1450 (No. 75):

> Now is the fox drevin to hole! hoo to hym, hoo, hoo;
> For and he crepe out, he will yow alle vndo.

Simple punning on the fate of Lord Scales enlivens a somewhat routine account of the battle of Northampton in 1460 (No. 89):

> All þei had scaped vpon a nyght,
>   Saue þeire scales were plucked away;
> þan had þe fissh lost all here might,
>   And litel ioy in watyr to play.

Here, too, will be found such realistic poems as "The Battle of Otterburn" (No. 26), the story of the Douglas and Percy, which in one version or another moved Sidney and Addison; the verses against the Flemings, "the best and most spirited of all the fifteenth-century ballads"[2] (No. 29); the execution of Sir Simon Fraser, from the well-known Harley MS. 2253 (No. 4); the rollicking satire of the "Land of Cokaygne" (No. 48), half concealing the yearnings of the humble for a better way of life; and the vivid account of

---

[2] *Eng. Hist. Lit.*, p. 241.

"London Lickpenny," looking forward to Ben Jonson's portrayal of London's seamy side (No. 50):

> Then I hyed me Into Estchepe.
>   One cryes, "rybbes of befe, & many a pye!"
> Pewter pottes they clattered on a heape;
>   There was harpe, pype, and mynstrelsye.
>   "Yea, by cock!" "nay, by cock!" some began crye;
>   Some songe of "Ienkyn and Iulyan" for there mede.
>   But for lack of money I myght not spede.

Nor is song lacking.[3] The Agincourt carol (No. 32) is part of England's heritage and deservedly popular. The song for Henry VII's success in France in 1492 (No. 36), the romantically idealized Plowman's Song (No. 37), the lyrical moralizations from the "portable" MSS., Sloane 2593 (Nos. 59 and 60), and Eng. poet. e.1 (No. 61), along with the carols, "Willikin's Return" (No. 82) and "Edward Dei Gratia" (No. 92) enliven any anthology of Middle English poetry.

Since these historical and political poems were composed by men in the same walks of life as those who wrote the religious and secular poems, they show comparable technical skills. "Summer Sunday" (No. 38), for example, the lament for Edward II, is exceptionally contrived, having a *chanson d'aventure* gambit, an involved stanzaic pattern of bob and wheel, "crown" or stanza linking, an envelope form, and the specialized alliterative vocabulary. No. 66 illustrates the "O and I" refrain; No. 95 a *chanson d'aventure* dream allegory, frequently reminiscent of Langland; No. 40 a ballade with interlocking rhymes. "The World Upside Down" (No. 63) is a little squib cleverly uniting two devices, the "destroying" refrain and an inverted catalogue of the evils of the age.[4]

In less accomplished verses, the clichés of religious and secular poems find their political counterparts. The rose imagery of the Virgin, for example (*Index,* No. 1914):

[3] Music is preserved for Nos. 32, 34, 35, 37, 100.
[4] For a full discussion of the poem and its techniques see Robbins, *Anglia,* lxxii. 385-89.

> Herkyn to me boþe old & yonge,
>> How a rose began to sprynge.
> A fayerer rose to my lykyng
>> Sprong þer neuer in kyngis lond

paralleled in love poems:[5]

> Farewell pured pris presiable,
> Farewell ryall Rose in the ryse

is transferred to historical lyrics (No. 33):

> The rose it es þe fairest flour,
> þe rose es swetteste of odoure,
> þe rose in care it es comforthetur,
> þe rose in seknes it es saluoure.

Such commonplaces are perhaps most appropriate in homely verses that tell tales of men-at-arms.

Although rich as a source of historical evidence, this collection is not a consecutive history of England from 1300 to 1499, the opening and closing dates represented here (Nos. 2 and 100). Fewer than two dozen poems antedate 1400;[6] political poems became inevitably more numerous later, and by the time of the Wars of the Roses the conscious manipulation of public opinion was widely practiced.

These poems aid historical research by confirming and amplifying the chronicles, and by giving corroborative details.[7] The carol (No. 31) on the execution of Archbishop Scrope concludes its painful description:

> Here I wyll the commende,
> þou gyff me fyue strokys with thy hende,
> And than my wayes þou latt me wende,
>> To hevyns blys that lastys ay.

The *English Chronicle* reports the incident in similar fashion:[8]

[5] *Sec. Lyrics,* No. 205.
[6] Nos. 2-12, 16-21, 26, 38, 39, 65, 66.
[7] There are occasional lapses; cf. Notes to No. 10, l. 31; No. 41, l. 9; No. 90, l. 63. For close parallels with the chronicles cf. Nos. 72 and 90.
[8] *English Chronicle,* p. 33.

Thanne saide tharchebishoppe to him that sholde smyte of his hed, "For His loue that suffrid v woundes for alle mankynde, yeue me v strokis, and I foryeve the me dethe." And so he dede; and thus thay deide.

No. 42 alludes to Edward IV's love of the chase, repeatedly mentioned by most of the chronicles.[9] For the heated disputes which set off the civil wars, No. 76 confirms much in the chronicles, as for example the support of the court (or Lancastrian) faction by the clergy. Of the thirty-three "endited at Rowchestre," seven names appear in the Cotton Vespasian text printed here, and a further nine in its Lambeth variant; many other high clergymen not noted elsewhere are implicated in this poem by their friendship to Suffolk. No. 79, on the 1458 reconciliation between the two parties, describes the procession to St. Paul's:

> At Poules in london, with gret renoun,
>   On oure ladi day in lente this peas was wrought;
> The kyng, the Quene, with lordes many oone,
>   To worshyp that virgine as thei ought,
> Wenten a procession, and spariden right nought,
>   In sighte of alle the Comynalte,
> In token that love was in herte and thought.
>   Reioise, Anglond, in concorde & vnite.

Grafton, summarizing the earlier chronicles, almost paraphrases in prose:[10]

for the open apparaunce, and demonstracion of this goodly concord, publike Processions were appoynted, to be solempnly celebrate within the Church of Saint Paule, in the Citie of London, on the day of the Conception of our Ladie, in the Moneth of Marche. At which solempne feast, the king in habite royall hauyng his Diademe on his heade, kept his estate in Procession, before whome went hande in hande, the Duke of Sommerset, the Erle of Sarisburie, the Duke of Excester and the Erle of Warwike, and so one of the one faction, and another of the other

---

[9] Warkworth, pp. 24-25; Fabyan, p. 512; Madden, *Archaeologia* xxvi.278 ("Narrative of ... Seigneur de la Gruthuyse" in BM. MS. Addit. 6113).
[10] Grafton, i.659.

sect, and behinde the king the Duke of Yorke led the Queene, with great familiaritie to all mens sightes.

Four poems (Nos. 28-30; *Index,* No. 2657) deride the flight of Philip, Duke of Burgundy, from the siege of Calais in 1436. This victory came at a low ebb in England's military history, and perhaps for that reason the chroniclers and balladers made the most of it. No. 28, for example, describes the preparations for the siege, with the Burgundian camp at night brightened by cressets, and alerted by many "cokkes to crow anyght"—"ich cart had his cokke to crawe amonges the host," as the *Brut* chronicle records. Then the ballad names the defenders of the various gates: Lord Cameux at Boleyn Gate and Sir John (mistakenly called William) Assheton at the Millgate—details not found elsewhere. The poem resumes, as in the *Brut,* with an invocation to St. Barbara for help against the gunmen:

> Seynt Barbara than was the crie,
> Whan stones in the tovn did flye,
> They cowde noon other charme.

No. 29 reveals how verse became incorporated into the fifteenth-century vernacular chronicles and became part of accepted history. It occurs in a beautifully illuminated St. Albans chronicle in Lambeth Palace MS. 6, and elaborates a preceding prose account of the behavior of the besiegers around Calais. The chronicle introduces the poem thus: "Wherefore amonges Englisshmen were made many rymes of þe flemmynges, among the which one is here sette for a remembraunce, that saith on this wise." *Index,* No. 2657 also occurs in a prose *Brut* (in Lambeth MS. 84), introduced similarly: "And in despyte of þe fflemynges an Englissh man made this english yn Baladdys." [11]

[11] Other popular ballads are incorporated as poems into the chronicles: *Index,* Nos. 297 (Cotton MS., and *olim* Harmsworth MS., Sotheby Sale, Oct. 15, 1945, Lot 1951), and 979, on the Fall of Rouen in 1418; also No. 3539 on Halidon Hill.

In all four poems, as well as in the various prose chronicles, there is a general uniformity of presentation—not so much in exact words as in attitude and content.[12] Whether a man read an English or Latin (or French) chronicle, or whether he listened to a metrical version recited in public, he would be acquiring part of a common heritage of accepted facts, differing only slightly according to the partisan coloring of the writer, scribe, or ballad-monger.[13]

One of the reasons for this uniformity is graphically illustrated in No. 27, which, save for the laziness of the compiler, might have been submerged in a chronicle in Cotton MS. Cleopatra C.iv. The writer describes the events preceding the battle of Agincourt, and uses a contemporary ballad to fill out the battle scenes, at first transposing it into prose, and then, as he wearied, gradually allowing a few rhythmical and then a few rhymed phrases to creep in. Henry is speaking:

for as I am trew kynge & knyght, for me þis day schall neuer Inglond rawnsome pay. erste many a wyght man schall leue is weddes, for here erste to deth I wil be dyght; & þerfore lordynges, for the love of swete Ihesu, helpe mayntene Inglondes ryght þis day. Allso, archers, to yow I praye, no fote þat ȝe fle away, erste be we all beten in þis felde . . .

Finally, the writer discards pretense, since he was merely transferring lines into prose, and honestly copies what is left of the ballad as verse.

But the value of these poems is not just as the handmaiden of History. Admitting the importance of literature for historical research, one must place equal or greater reliance on documents—charters, parish records, wills, inventories, and so forth—and suggest that History illuminates Literature. This approach can produce rewarding results.

[12] For a detailed comparison see Robbins, *Neophilologus,* xxxix.142-46.
[13] Kingsford, however, in *Chronicles of London,* p. xxv, notes that relatively few ballads were incorporated into the chronicles.

It can, for example, help towards precise dating even of general moralizing pieces. In a seemingly apolitical composition (*Index,* No. 3608), three of the stanzas condemn those who clip money, use false weights and measures, "storble" the rights of the poor, and take bribes and pervert the law. These are not unusual charges, but the fact that they were all publicly discussed in Parliament just before Easter, 1410 ("This holy time" of the poem) enabled Kail, the editor of the series, to establish the year of the poem's composition.[14] Somewhat less spectacular evidence provides the dating of the other poems of Digby MS. 102 included here (Nos. 13-15).

Another example to which an exact year can be assigned is No. 49, a typical catalogue of corrupt practices: "gloserys full gayly þey go"; "mayntenerys be made Iustys"; "þe dred of god ys al todrawe"; "þer werld is turnyd up so doun among"; "wymmonis wyttes ar full of wynd"; and so forth. Among the listings of evils are two lines:

> He ys louyd þat wele can lye;
> And theuys tru men honge.

This couplet is not the conventional "þey louyn trewþe in non plas" (*Index,* No. 72), but points to a specific happening. Under 1456 in *Gregory's Chronicle,* is the shocking story of a thief turned state informer.[15] Thomas Whytehorn, about to be hanged for stealing, secured pardon by falsely accusing of treason men with whom he had at some time been acquainted. On his word alone, those "appealed" were put in prison and hanged (save a few who could buy their freedom). For this service, he not only avoided his own punishment, but received a bounty from the king, who himself profited by confiscating the property of the "traitors." The date assumed from the correspondence of the poetic allusion and the historical fact is confirmed by a reckoning

---

14 J. Kail, *EETS* 124.xiv-xvi.
15 *Gregory's Chronicle,* pp. 199-202.

in the same hand as the poem, dated "Monday aftyr seynt barthylmeweys day the xxxiiij ʒere of Kyng Harry the vj," that is, the Monday following August 24, 1456.[16]

Internal evidence can date other poems, some not always so precisely. No. 22, a song of freedom, occurs in a sermon manuscript, which can be placed between 1430 and 1436. During these years there was great discontent at the lawlessness prevalent throughout the land, the cost of the unpopular war in France, and the rising prices following a series of bad harvests. A suitable approximation is 1434, the only famine period to fall within these six years.[17] Another complaint (No. 23) can be roughly identified by the manuscript as mid-fifteenth century; here the suggested date of 1445, another famine year, is tentative, for any time towards the end of the Hundred Years War would be appropriate. The long prayer for peace (No. 99) is about 1440. No. 81, a lament put in the mouth of Henry VI, could be ascribed to almost any year after 1460 and before Henry's brief restoration. One line, "Alas I dare nowth schewe now my hede," gives a clue to the date of composition. The line could, of course, apply to the time between Henry's flight after Mortimer's Cross in 1461 until his comfortable reception in Scotland early in 1462; but, more likely, to his year in hiding, between the Yorkist victories at Hedgeley Moor and Hexham in the spring of 1464 and his capture at Clitheroe in July, 1465. During this time, "he and other liued in caues full hardly, vnknown more than a yeere";[18] and "where kyng Henry was become cowde not be knowen."[19] One further possibility is that the line is more literary than historical; once imprisoned, there would be little point in not "daring" to appear in the open. Henry's words in the poem:

---

[16] For a detailed discussion see Robbins, *MLN*, lxx.473-76.
[17] Cf. *Gregory's Chronicle*, pp. 150, 181; *English Chronicle*, p. 55.
[18] Stow, *Annales*, p. 418.
[19] *Chronicles of London*, p. 178.

> Of the bledde ryall I am kom;
> Kynge herry of Monmowthe me beforn,
> He was my fadir & I his sone,
> And of qwen katereyn was I born

are akin to a speech of the King while imprisoned by
Edward IV. Blacman, Henry's biographer, quotes:[20]

My father was king of England, and peaceably possessed the crown
of England for the whole time of his realm. And I, a child in the
cradle, was peaceably and without any protest crowned and ap-
proved as king by the whole realm, and wore the crown of England
some forty years, and each and all of my lords did me royal homage
and plighted me their faith, as was also done to other my predecessors.

The poem may belong to this slightly later period.[21]

The arrangement of poems in this anthology cannot be
based primarily on manuscripts, for the historical and
political poems are not concentrated in any one group of
manuscripts. However, a cursory review of the chief manuscripts will help toward a better understanding of the verses.

A few individual manuscripts are represented by groups
of poems—Harley MS. 2253 (seven); Cotton MS. Galba E.ix
(Minot, four); and Digby MS. 102 (three). Other manuscripts represented by several items include Cotton Rolls
ii.23 (Nos. 44, 75, 84, 85, 86); Lambeth MS. 306 (No. 92;
copies of Nos. 1 and 91); Trinity College Dublin MS. 432
(Nos. 87, 89, 90, 91); and Trinity College Dublin MS. 516
(Nos. 46, 47, 77, 78). These manuscripts[22] account for
almost a third of the hundred texts.

The manuscript of Minot's poems (Nos. 9-12) postdates
the events they describe by more than half a century. Cotton

---

[20] Blacman, p. 44.

[21] For complete documentation and discussion see Robbins, *Neu-
philologische Mitteilungen*, lvi.94-102.

[22] With Cotton MS. Vespasian B.xvi; Nos. 64, 76, and 79 are
third-quarter fifteenth-century additions to a *Piers Plowman*, and are
not further discussed here.

MS. Galba E.ix is a careful copy of these and other English poems—the romances of *Ywain and Gawain* and the *Seven Sages,* the *Gospel of Nicodemus,* and the *Pricke of Conscience.* In addition, there are three other short poems, including the lively satire, "Narratio de domino denario" (similar to No. 51).[23] Minot added rubrics to his poems to provide continuity, and, at the time of writing the last, apparently revised the whole series; for a poem on the naval Battle of Sluys (*Index,* No. 2189) which took place in 1340 refers to Henry, Duke of Lancaster. Henry became Earl in 1345 and Duke in 1352.

Douglas Stedman, expanding Hall's comments, has attempted to identify Minot with an ancient and noble family at Carlton Miniot in Yorkshire, and as a court poet of Edward II.[24] Yet two allusions in the poems to his name (*Index,* Nos. 2149 and 2189), a generally Northern dialect,[25] and a forced interpretation of commonplace epithets are insufficient documentation.[26] The limited evidence in fact suggests the contrary. Rubrics and lines in the fabric of the poems themselves contain typically minstrel admonitions, for example (No. 11):

> Lystens now and ȝe may lere,
> als men þe suth may vnderstand.

Such stereotyped appeals confirm the *Cambridge History of English Literature,*[27] following Wright, which regards Minot as "a professional gleeman, who earned his living by following the camp and entertaining soldiers with the recitation of their own heroic deeds."

[23] *Sec. Lyrics,* No. 58.
[24] Douglas C. Stedman, *The War Ballads of Laurence Minot* (Dublin, 1917), pp. xi-xxiv.
[25] Hall (ed. 1914), p. xvi suggests the scribe copied a Midland text; Oakden, *Allit. Poetry,* i.106-7, suggests a Mid-Lincs, rather than a Norfolk original.
[26] Moore, *MLN,* xxxv.78-81, prints several documents relating to the purchase of land in Cressy Forest by a Laurence Minot in 1331.
[27] ii.359.

From the literary view, Minot is important because at an early date he expressed a fervid nationalism, and an unswerving devotion to "gude king Edward." The omission of English defeats or English trickery, the rancor against the Scots and French, and the spirit of "my country right or wrong" assured these poems their popularity. From the historical view, the date of the manuscript is important: by the early fifteenth century the need for the unity of England behind the crown had crystallized, and the political value of these earlier accounts was recognized. The myth which Froissart constructed for the rich and highborn was duplicated for the humble by Laurence Minot.

Digby MS. 102 can be dated about the first quarter of the fifteenth century. All its twenty-four poems (bound with a copy of *Piers Plowman*) show a consistent attitude; deeply moral, church-supporting, gentry-favoring, monarchy-loving, they address the King (No. 13) or "a kyngis chaunceller," "a kyngis counselere," "lordis," those "that ouer puple han gouernaunce"; they deal with false justices and erring religious. One poem is especially outspoken in its defense of the poor (*Index*, No. 2763).

> Then cursed is he þat ful is fylde,
>   Wiþ wrong take pore mennys thrift,
> þat makeþ pore men be spilde,
>   For synguler profyt is sotyll theft;
> Make gulteles folk presoned and kylde,
>   Of house and land make wrongwys gyft;
> Wiþ hunger and þirst his hous is bylde.
>   In helle is shewed euell-sponnen wyft.

One example of their correspondence to the Rolls of Parliament, which permits close dating, has already been given (p. xxiv). From this evidence Kail assumed that their author was "most probably an abbot or prior," who "as such, occupied a seat in parliament, and voted with the Commons." The proposal is at least tenable.[28]

---

[28] Kail, *EETS* 124.ix.

It seems likely that the "prior" (if such he were) wrote the series over a period of years, one or two a year, for the poems successively deal with events ranging from 1401 to 1421. The present manuscript is a fair copy, neatly rubricated in red and blue. The whole series can best be regarded as occasional closet verse, written by some lesser religious dignitary for circulation among sober-minded laity and clergy who had a special interest and voice in practical politics. At times he turns to direct invocation of Henry V to resume the French wars; some lines have the air of a jingo editorial: we have the arms, tear up the treaties! [29]

> Stuffe ʒoure castels in eche coost,
>   Warnestor & folk þeder sende;
> So mow ʒe abate ʒoure enemys bost,
>   But not in trete, in wast to spende.
>   Wheþer ʒe assayle or defende,
>   On see or land, god ʒow spede!
>   Wiþ word of wynd, mad neuere werre ende,
>   But dent of swerd endid þe dede.

In their religious-political subject matter and their form (refrain, wheel and bob), the Digby series suggests the more numerous and better known Vernon-Simeon poems (No. 20).

Cotton Rolls ii.23 is a small roll containing various political items,[30] written about 1450 or 1451,[31] including articles against the Duke of Suffolk, the Duke of York's declaration to the King, lists of persons indicted at Rochester, and the demands of Jack Cade; in addition, there are political prophecies (No. 44 and three others), and a series of six poems (Nos. 75, 84, 85, 86; *Index,* Nos. 544 and 1138) favorable to the Yorkists. They are contemporary pieces, written amidst the tension of the halfway mark in the century, when the protagonists of the Wars of the Roses were jockeying

---

[29] *Index,* No. 3924; Kail, p. 59.
[30] Fully described in *Eng. Hist. Lit.,* pp. 358-68.
[31] The latest date is May, 1452. Art. 22 is a prophecy by the Dominical Letters for 1449, 1450, and 1451.

for position and lining up allies. Some of these poems can be dated by internal evidence. Thus No. 84 was written after November, 1449, but before February, 1450; No. 75 written in February, 1450. The prophecy (No. 44) could be satisfactorily interpreted about this time. The scribe cannot be identified, but the poems hint at the group to which he might have belonged. Nos. 84, 85, and 86 all mention with approbation "the commyns." No. 85 instructs the confidants of the king, "Duke, Iwge, baron, Archebisshop," not, for fear or favour of the Duke of Suffolk, to lose "the loue of alle þe commynalte." No. 86, having attacked Lord Say as well as Suffolk, points out to those "that haue the kyng to demene," that

> But yif the commyns of Englond
> Helpe þe kyng in his fond,
> Suffolk woll bere þe crown.

While leading noblemen themselves were much aware of the need of support of the commons—the rich London merchants who were daily gaining in political power—these poems reflect the attitude of the commons themselves. The list of commercial grievances (Art. 12) and the notes on taxes (Art. 11) suggest a London citizen.

Further clues about origin are suggested by the duplication of texts. No. 76 occurs in Trinity College Dublin MS. 516 and in Lambeth MS. 306. The Lambeth MS. contains many religious and secular lyrics, poems, romances, domestic, medical, and historical notes, including the Proclamation of the Kentish Rebels (f. 49r), the christening of Prince Arthur (f. 53r), the retinue of Edward III at Calais (f. 139r), and, in addition to No. 76, several other historical poems (Nos. 1 and 91; *Index,* No. 3880). No. 76 is erroneously headed (in Stow's hand): "Here folowythe a dyrge made by the comens of Kent in the tyme of ther rysynge when Iake Cade was theyr Cappitayn." The Lambeth MS. also contains a pro-

Yorkist *Short English Chronicle* (f. 1r),[32] and some late sixteenth-century chronicles (f. 204v).

One item from Lambeth MS. is duplicated in Trinity College Dublin MS. 432 (No. 91). This Dublin MS. gives as well Nos. 87, 89, and 90, all dealing with the events of 1460 and 1461; at least one poem (No. 89) was written within two months of the battle it recounts. This manuscript is another miscellany, written in two hands, forming ff. 59-87 of the complete volume, bound with various Latin, English, and French items from the thirteenth century. It includes a *Palamon and Ersyte* (*Index*, No. 3636), Robert of Sicily (*Index*, No. 2780), a King Palaan, a miracle play of Abraham and Isaac (*Index*, No. 2617), and a list of mayors and aldermen of Northampton.

Like the two previously mentioned manuscripts, it is strongly pro-Yorkist. Brotanek, who has made a comprehensive study of the manuscript, believes that the poems were composed by a partisan of some Yorkist lord, presumably living in the Warwick-Coventry-Northampton triangle.[33] As with the Cotton text of No. 84, so No. 90 of the Dublin MS. could have been written only by an intimate, familiar with the chief personages involved: the casual allusions to twenty-seven various ensigns would no doubt have been recognized by contemporaries similarly informed, but even modern research has as yet failed to identify all of them. The dominant aim of these poems was to influence people, whether it was the lords set high on Fortune's wheel (No. 87), or "þe trewe comynerys of Kent," and the upper-class citizens of "london þat fayre cyte" (No. 89).

The other Trinity College Dublin MS.—No. 516—provides two short prophecies: No. 46 (known in three other manuscripts, including Cotton Rolls) and No. 47 (in fifteen other manuscripts); and Nos. 77 and 78. Like the Lambeth and

[32] *Short Eng. Chronicle*, pp. i-xv, discusses this MS.
[33] Rudolf Brotanek, *Mittelenglische Dichtungen* (Halle, 1940), pp. 6, 192-93, 198.

Dublin 432 MSS., it is a typical mid-fifteenth-century commonplace book; but unlike them, though written by a Londoner, it is pro-Lancastrian. No. 78 is a catalogue of the chief Lancastrian nobles (comparable to the Yorkist lists in Nos. 84 and 90). The chief interest of the manuscript is No. 77, one of the most curious poems of this anthology, an early example of subtle semiofficial propaganda.

"The Five Dogs of London" (No. 77) was apparently designed to isolate Edward, Duke of York, from his London supporters. In the early spring of 1456, an apparently trivial incident, in which a young London mercer assaulted an Italian merchant, was blown up into a major riot involving the whole city. Committed to Newgate on the Italian's complaints, the Londoner was freed by his friends, who thereupon proceeded to attack the houses of the Italians. Many influential citizens either encouraged the rioters or at least winked at their activities. The Lancastrians had about this time removed the Duke of York from the protectorship, causing "sodain alteracions and sedicious commociouns, to spring and arise in the commonaltie, and in especiall, within the citee of London." [34] The Yorkists apparently seized the rioting of the mercers as a further opportunity to embarrass the government.

Against this background should be read the unique account in Bale's *Chronicle* of the circumstances surrounding the use of this poem:[35]

Item the xix day of September in the nyght tyme wer sett upon the Standard in ffletestrete a fore the duk of york being þer than lodged in the Bisshop of Salisbury place certein dogges hedes with Scriptures in their mouthes balade wise which dogges wer slayn vengeably the same nyght.

These bills clearly reflect on the integrity of the Duke of York. Each "dog" complains in turn how he was sacrificed

[34] Hall, p. 234.
[35] Flenley, *Six Town Chronicles*, p. 144. For a full discussion see Robbins, *PMLA*, lxx. 264-68.

to the ambitions of the Duke of York, and that it is Edward who should be punished. The moral is implied: such is the reward of those who support the treacherous Yorkists—how much better to uphold Henry VI!

Of the other major manuscripts drawn on here, Harley MS. 2253 is the most famous. It presents problems far too involved to be broached in this brief introduction. It is a large handsome volume of some 141 leaves, written in two hands, the first a late thirteenth-century which has written Anglo-Norman religious poems on the first forty-eight folios, and the second, an early fourteenth-century hand (probably about 1320) which has copied the mass of religious and secular Latin, Anglo-Norman, and English prose and verse. The earliest of the datable poems is that on the Battle of Lewes in 1264 and the latest that on the death of Edward I (No. 5), since the later allusion to Bannockburn in No. 8 may not be historical. The dialect of the poems indicates many sources (cf. Nos. 6 and 8), but it is largely West Midland, and the allusions on the flyleaves to St. Ethelbert suggest Hereford.

The historical poems of this manuscript reinforce some views suggested by its secular and religious contents. First, there was considerable interchange of texts between this and other early fourteenth-century manuscripts: No. 5 exists in a superior text in the Cambridge fragments,[36] and is, furthermore, a paraphrase of a French original in another manuscript.[37] Second, the stylistic evidence of the historical and political poems indicates a long established poetic tradition, not of sophisticated court poetry,[38] but of professional min-

---

[36] See Notes to No. 5, l. 28.

[37] Camb. Un. MS. Gg.1. 1, printed by Wright, *Pol. Songs*, pp. 241-45.

[38] The secular love lyrics show a technical vocabulary of love and a fascination for its psychological analysis, the two most distinguishing features of the established troubadour lyric. These features are especially apparent in *Index*, Nos. 2005, 2009, and 3222. Conventions such as these did not grow overnight.

strelsy. No. 5 is an excellent illustration of a professional composition, from its opening invocation for attention to the repetition of ballad commonplaces, as well as the usual kennings and the typical final ascription to "god ant oure lady." Admittedly, the result is not an inspired poem. Further evidence of minstrel origin for the political poems occurs in No. 4:

> Nou ichulle fonge þer ich er let,
> Ant tellen ou of frisel, ase ic ou by-het.

In Minot, who is certainly early fourteenth-century, there are similar stock phrases—"wight in wede," "suth for to say," "loud or still," "fers and fell," "mirth on mold." The absence of any large body of earlier thirteenth-century ballads, in which the conventions could have been worked out, is puzzling.

The variety of poems in the Harley MS. shows how artificial is any classification of Middle English lyrics into religious, secular, or historical; such a division separates the inseparable. The historical poems, quite unlike the secular, set the tone for nearly all the later pieces,[39] and there is surprisingly little intrusion of new types throughout the two following centuries.

The remaining texts in this anthology come from the usual variety of sources. Fifteen are found on flyleaves or are added to otherwise blank leaves.[40] Fourteen are included in the later fifteenth-century large Lydgate-type anthologies.[41] Five come from song-books,[42] three from large col-

[39] No. 2, the complaint of the oppressed, followed in Nos. 21-25, 60, 61; No. 3, battle descriptions, in Nos. 9-12, 26-30, 89, 90, 94; No. 4, death plaints, in Nos. 38-42; No. 5, personal abuse, in Nos. 65-69, 75-76; No. 6, satire on law courts, in Nos. 13, 14, 50, 51; No. 7, satire on extravagance and dress, in Nos. 52-63; No. 8, prophecy, in Nos. 43-47.
[40] Nos. 16, 19, 23, 36, 42, 43, 51, 62, 63, 64, 68, 69, 76, 80, 97.
[41] Nos. 1, 28, 30, 31, 50, 53, 54, 71, 72, 73, 80, 94, 98, 99.
[42] Nos. 32, 34, 35, 37, 100.

lections of religious materials such as the Vernon MS. (Nos. 20, 38, 39). Other sources (for one or two poems) include sermon manuscripts (Nos. 22, 58), charters (Nos. 24, 25), children's teaching books (Nos. 1, 82), medical collections (No. 55), religious treatises (No. 57), early friar miscellanies (Nos. 48, 56), and chronicles (No. 29). For the most part, these poems exist in unique texts, but some had extensive distribution. No. 1 is found in 46 manuscripts; No. 45 in eighteen; No. 47 in sixteen; No. 55 in fifteen; No. 44 in thirteen; No. 56 in ten; No. 58 in at least nine; and Nos. 46 and 98 in five manuscripts each. Three poems occur in three manuscripts each,[43] and seventeen in two manuscripts each.[44]

It is, of course, impossible to give more than a few names of authors of political lyrics, for the vast majority are anonymous. Two of the prolific known writers of religious verse are represented here by their sole political poems. Audelay, a chantry priest who ended his days on a corrody at Hagmond Abbey, near Shrewsbury, wrote fifty-six poems, including twenty-five "carols," all in Douce MS. 302. In a colophon, Audelay says he wrote as an example to the other members of his monastery. His recollection of Henry V (No. 41) was written about 1429. James Ryman, a Franciscan, produced a comparable poem on Henry VI (No. 83), a retrospective review composed thirty years after his deposition in 1461. Ryman wrote over 160 religious songs, including about 120 carols, in Cambridge University MS. Ee.1.12. He, too, gave his name, status, and date of composition (1492) in a colophon:

Explicit liber ympnorum et canticorum quem composuit Frater Iacobus Ryman ordinis Minorum ad laudem omnipotentis dei et sanctissime matris eius Marie omniumque sanctorum anno domini millesimo cccc*mo* lxxxxii*o*.

---

[43] Nos. 20, 71, 76.
[44] Nos. 16, 18, 19, 21, 24, 26, 28, 30, 32, 39, 50, 72, 73, 79, 91; and (fragments) 5, 54.

But religious rarely wrote political poems in the fifteenth century, unless they were only technically in orders and actually served as secretaries to noblemen or were attached to government service.

Lydgate (Nos. 1, 71, 96, 98) assumed a kind of un-authorized poet-laureateship, and wrote his verses for patrons on every possible occasion, using the monastery at Bury St. Edmunds as his base of operations. His poems are better des-cribed as "official" rather than poetical; the commemoration of the entry of Henry VI into London (*Index*, No. 3799), for example, found in six manuscripts, occurs also in three prose paraphrases as a kind of semi-official programme of the ceremonies.[45] Gower wrote mainly in Latin and French; his attractive 385-line praise of peace (*Index*, No. 2587) is his sole English political poem. Gower was apparently of good family; he is described as "esquire," he possessed two manors, and his elaborate tomb in Southwark bears family arms. The other famous name in political writing, because of his *De Regimine Principum*, c.1412 (*Index*, No. 2229), is Thomas Hoccleve—a clerk in a government office (the Privy Seal), not in orders, but with enough connections to receive church pensions and corrodies most of his life. Hoccleve penned pedestrian ballades to Henry V, pleas for gratuities, and a vicious attack in 512 lines on Sir John Oldcastle (*Index*, No. 3407).

In general, writers of political poems were employed like any other craftsmen or technicians to serve and promote the special interests of those classes with power or money. Con-sequently whatever other qualities they have, political poems seldom show any deep poetic vision or profound insight. Inevitably they become a public poetry—written to order and technically competent and emotionally satisfying; a Lydgate or a Gower could turn out such a piece for the

---

[45] MSS. Cotton Vitellius A.xvi; Egerton 1995; College of Arms XIX.

court circles, and a Minot for the people. Most of Nos. 71 to 100 are of this nature.

The "Ballade Set on the Gates of Canterbury" (No. 88) is a good illustration of the poetic commission. That this piece circulated, at least among Yorkist adherents, is seen by the verbal echoes in two later political poems, Nos. 89 and 91. These versified pamphlets were no doubt spread by Yorkists as a means of influencing the public with their supposed successes and proposed platforms.

This "Ballade" was written just before the Yorkist invasion of June 28, 1460. The leaders, routed at Ludlow in September 1459, had fled to Ireland and Calais; the packed Lancastrian Parliament, which met in January, 1460, attainted York, Salisbury, Warwick, and twenty others of treason. In the consequent suppression of the Yorkists, the Earl of Wiltshire was especially active. The pro-Yorkist *English Chronicle* continues the story:[46]

Ferthermore, the commones of Kent, dredyng the malyce and the tyranny of the forseyde erlle of Wylshyre and of other, lest he wolde exercyse his vengeaunce vppon thaym, as he had done vppon thaym at Newbery, and sent priuyly messangers and letters to Caleys to the forseyde erles, besechyng thaym that they wolde in alle haste possible come and socour thaym fro theyre enemyes, promytting that they wolde assyste theym with alle thayre power.

The sayde erles wold nat anone yeue credence to theyre wrytyng and wordes, but send ouer in to Kent the lord Fauconbrege, to know whether theyre promys and theyre dedes sholde accorde: and anone the peple of Kent and of other shyres aboute resorted to the sayde lorde Fauconbrege in grete nombre, abydyng the commyng of the erles.

Whan the erles knew the trew hertes of the peple, they dysposed theyme dayly for to com in to thys londe. And nat longe before theyre commyng, thys balat that folowethe was sette vppon the yates of the cyte of Caunterbury.

Brotanek suggests that the writer of this handbill was a cleric of Canterbury, disposed to the Yorkists, and, from the

---

[46] *English Chronicle*, p. 91.

irony of his epilogue (ll. 81-86) that he had escaped Wiltshire's purge and had been given up as dead.[47] The chroni-
cler "may have copied this Yorkist effusion from the city
gates." [48]

There are a number of other public "bills" in Middle
English verse. The lampoon (*Index,* No. 1934) affixed to
St. Peter's church in York by the Scots in 1337, contrasting
their simplicity with the better armed and luxurious English,
is probably the earliest:[49]

> longe berde herteles,
> peyntede hood wytles,
> Gay cote graceles,
> maketh englond þriftles.

Verses by the students abusing the Mayor of Cambridge in
1418 are extant,[50] as well as a tag against the Earl of Suffolk
in 1448:[51]

> But Suthfolke, Salesbury, and Say
> Be don to deathe by May,
>   England may synge well away!

Fabyan gives another celebrated couplet posted on the doors
of St. Paul's:[52]

> The Cat, the Rat, and Lovel our dog
> Rule all England under a hog.

Other verses were written on handbills and thrown "in the
wey," as when Emperor Sigismund thanked "Blessed Inglond,

[47] Brotanek, *Mittelenglische Dichtungen,* p. 204.

[48] *English Chronicle,* p. 201.

[49] The *Brut* gives this tag under 1327; Fabyan 1328. Trinity Dublin MS. 516, printed here, assigns it to 1441.

[50] Not in *Index;* printed by Coulton, *Social Life in Britain,* p. 66;
and by Wilson, *Lost Lit.,* p. 200.

[51] Not in *Index;* from Piggot's *Chronicle,* repr. *Eng. Hist. Lit.,* p.
370, and Wilson, *Lost Lit.,* p. 199.

[52] Not in *Index;* Fabyan, p. 672; repr. Wilson, *Lost Lit.,* p. 199.

ful of melody" after his visit in 1416. This method of publicity recalls the "Outlaw's Song of Traillebaston" in the Harley MS. 2253:[53]

> Cest rym fust fet al bois desouz un lorer,
> La chaunte merle, russinole, e eyre l'esperver;
> Escrit estoit en parchemyn pur mout remembrer,
> E gitte en haut chemyn, qe um le dust trover.

Rhymed proclamations included in this anthology, in addition to No. 88, are No. 25, the Coventry protest against enclosures; probably No. 86; and very probably No. 73, the Epitaph for the Duke of Gloucester, ascribed to Lydgate in Stow's *Siege of Thebes*. The refrain, "Have mercy on hym buryed in this sepulture," strongly suggests the poem may have been written on a scroll exhibited near the tomb at the time of the burial, just as Claudio left his elegy on the supposed tomb of Hero:

> Hang thou there upon the tomb,
> Praising her when I am dumb.

"The Kings of England" (No. 1) was also used as a "bill," and in its forty-six manuscripts must have been known to very many people. Children learned its conspectus of history by rote: in one manuscript (Rawlinson C.86) it is added on flyleaves, with the marginal names (circled in red) of the kings and their wives and children linked by lines to show descent; while on the preceding folio are pen-trials of a child copying: "The myghti William Duke of Normandy hath rythg tytl / The myghte Willm Duke of Normandy het rythg tytl." Adults too must have studied the ancestry of their rulers: MS. Douce g.2 is a roll, and so are the later redactions of the poem, MS. Ashmole 25 (*Index*, No. 444) and MS. Addit. E.7 (*Index*, No. 3431). The former is very carefully written and illustrated, and shows signs of much use. The latter is not the little roll a ballad singer might

---

[53] The story of Sigismund in Capgrave, p. 314; Traillebaston in Wright, *Pol. Songs*, pp. 231-36.

carry with him, but a long scroll with the lines of descent (as in Ashmole MS.) very clearly indicated by strokes and circles. No doubt it served only a slightly less direct purpose than the poem commissioned in 1423 by the Regent of France, the Duke of Bedford, from Lawrence Calot, a royal notary, to explain a pictorial genealogy which hung in Notre Dame.[54] "The picture is in fact a perfect interpretation of the Treaty of Troyes, and if hung in the churches might easily have helped to persuade a simple people that Henry's claim was just."[55] Lydgate, incidentally, commissioned in 1426 by the Duke of Warwick, "durst not withsey," translated the French, and added a rambling introduction and conclusion (*Index,* No. 3808); some lines are incorporated into "The Kings of England." In this Bodleian Addit. MS., "the titull of Fraunce," a prose justification of the claims of Henry VI to that country, follows the poem.

The employment by noblemen of poets as political propagandists is an old tradition. Long before Lydgate, Henry II employed Jordan Fantosme to pen an eye-witness report of the battle against the Scots, in which William the Lion was defeated in 1174.[56] Edward II employed a Carmelite prior, Roger Baston, famous as a minstrel, to celebrate the expected victories of his expedition for the relief of Stirling. When the English were defeated at Bannockburn, Baston was captured. The Scots exacted true poetic justice, for as his ransom Baston had to compose praises of the English defeat.[57]

A few writers, however, were not thus commissioned, and their verses, less polished perhaps, are consequently more genuine and direct. The popular rhymes of the Peasants'

[54] *Revue des études historiques,* July, 1909.

[55] Rowe, *Library,* xiii. 82.

[56] *Chronique de la Guerre entre les Anglais et les Écossais,* ed. R. Howlett, in *Chronicles of Stephen* (London, 1886), Rolls Series 82, vol. 3.

[57] *Scotichronicon,* xii, C.22.

Revolt (Nos. 16-18) and a few others (Nos. 21-25, 70) are in this category. No. 25, for example, graphically shows the folly of judging by outward appearances:

> We may speke feir & bid you good morowe,
> But luff with our hertes shul ye haue non!

Otherwise, the views of the middle or lower classes seldom enter into manuscripts, written almost exclusively by those whose training and interests lie with one of the ruling groups; when their doings are reported, it is through hostile and biased tongues.

The Great Revolt of 1381 came as a bombshell. No. 19 roundly condemns the churls who set themselves up as equals of the nobles, its hostility expressed both in English and Latin:

> On rowtes þo Rebawdes þey ran,
>   sua turpida arma ferentes.
> ffoles þey dred no man,
>   Regni Regem, neque gentes;
> laddes þey were þer cheveteyns,
>   sine iure fere superantes.

No. 20, a little more tolerant, views the uprising as "a warnyng to be ware" for the evil ways of the lords. Yet the poem gives the nobles no credit for any change of heart; had they not been in sin but in a state of grace, they might very easily have prevented the rebellion. God's allowing the rebellion to take place was a reminder to the mighty to observe God's lordship. The rising was one of several manifestations of divine displeasure, along with the plague (which still cropped up sporadically), and the earthquake of 1382.

It was inevitable that what the middle class "commons" were saying about their own position in society should be taken literally by the "inferiores" or "simple." The claims of "laddes" to be "Anglorum corpora viua" (No. 19) shocked the "comouns" in Parliament, who claimed they were "þe fayrest flour, þat euere god sette on erþely crown" (*Index*, No. 910). In 1450, the rebels of Kent were proclaiming they were the "comyns" (No. 24). On the surface, the unacceptable heresy of John Ball (No. 17) is indistinguishable from the acceptable orthodoxy of *Index*, No. 2356:

No. 17	*Index*, No. 2356
now raygneth pride in price,	Now pride ys yn pris,
couetise is holden wise,	Now couetyse ys wyse,
lechery without shame,	Now lechery ys schameles,
gluttonie without blame,	Now gloteny ys lawles,
enuie raygneth with reason,	Now slewþe ys yn seson,
and sloth is taken in great season.	In envie & wreþe ys treson;
God doe bote for nowe is time.	Now haþ god enchesyn
Amen	to dystrie þys worle by reson.

When does criticism become subversion? In these two poems, the distinction consists of a single line at the end of No. 17: "God doe bote for nowe is time." Previously, many had regretted evils; Ball wanted to remove them. In Ball's words, a typical complaint which could be found in the books of any law-abiding layman or cleric (such as the Digby MS. protest on p. xxviii) was turned into a call for action, breathing "the deep and gallant feeling that led the noblest among the rebels to defy gallows and quartering block in the cause of freedom." [58]

One other poem lies outside those works ordered by the lords. The so-called "Abstract" (No. 70) of the well-known *Libelle of Englyshe Polycye* (*Index*, No. 3491) is a unique example of a poorer man, perhaps a yeoman in one of the clothing guilds, trying to advance the ends of his own class. It is obviously derived from the *Libelle*, but it is much more than a redaction of this work. The "Abstract" compresses the main ideas into a Latin couplet, omits all the original illustrations and digressions, and introduces many quatrains

[58] G. M. Trevelyan, *England in the Age of Wycliffe* (London, 1948), p. 203, referring to No. 18.

with completely new problems. The *Libelle*[59] was originally (c. 1436) addressed to the Lords of the Privy Council; in the second version (c. 1438) to three in particular—William de la Pole, Earl of Suffolk; Ralph, Lord Cromwell, Treasurer of England; and "the grete prelate, the highest confessour."[60] For such statesmen, it dealt with broad policies, and gave detailed political analyses (as for Ireland).

The redaction, however, is addressed partly to the manufacturers of cloth and sellers of wool,[61] almost as if to provide arguments to influence national policy (ll. 53-68) and, surprisingly enough, argues against any victimization of "þe pore pepyll" or "poreyl." The poem exposes (ll. 77-104) the dishonest tricks by which the rich merchants and cloth makers fleeced the "spynners, carders, wevers," and other workmen:

> þat they take for vjd, yt ys dere ynow of iij;
> And thus þei be defrawdyd in euery contre;
> The pore haue þe labur, the ryche the wynnyng.
> This acordythe nowзte, it is a heuy partyng.

In its conclusion, the poem presents a plan for increasing the output of silver and then reverts to its major theme of wool.

What is curious, however, and has hitherto escaped observation, is that these demands for regulation of the woolen trade, and, moreover, for the protection of the workers were accepted. In 1463 Parliament passed legislation forbidding merchants to export wool, inasmuch as English weavers were

[59] Warner suggests written by the Clerk to the Council, Adam Moleyns; but disputed by Taylor, *Bull. John Rylands Lib.*, xxiv.376-418.

[60] Identified by Wright as Cardinal Henry Beaufort; by Warner as John Stafford, Bishop of Bath and Wells, the Chancellor; and by a note, post 1441, in Rylands MS. 995 as Archbishop Chichele.

[61] The changed audience is confirmed by the MS. (tempus Edw. IV), which includes lists of "syses" of various occupations (regulations governing weight, size, etc. of bread, cloth, wine) useful to members of the guilds.

short of raw materials, forbidding the importation of foreign woolens, and forbidding payment in kind to cloth workers. It is not too fanciful to see pressure for these regulations as the justification for this poem, just as the original *Libelle* produced the trade regulations of 1439-1440, re-enacted in 1453.

In writing or circulating political verses, there was always a certain amount of risk, intensified, of course, for those critical of the regime. The fate of John Holton in 1456 demonstrated what happened to those who offended the great; for his attacks "per scripturam billarum" on the King's person, he was drawn, hanged, and quartered.[62] For the composition of the couplet deriding Catesby, Ratcliff, and Lord Lovell, noted previously as a public "bill" (p. xxxviii), its author, Wyllyam Colyngbourne was, in 1484,

> put to the most cruel deth at the Tower Hylle, where for hym were made a newe payer of galowes. Vpon the whiche, after he hadde hangyd a shorte season, he was cutte down, beynge alyue, & his bowellys rypped out of his bely, and cast into the fyre there by hym, and lyued tyll the bowcher put his hande into the bulke of his body; insomuch that he sayd in the same instant, "O Lorde Ihesu, yet more trowble," & so dyed to the great compassion of moche people.[63]

The writers of political prophecies (Nos. 8, 43-47, 91) were the only class to suffer total repression, and legislation was passed to forbid the circulation of their subversive writings. In 1402 laws were directed against the Welsh bards, "the cause of the insurrection and rebellion in Wales"; in 1406, against the Lollards, who, among other crimes, had falsely predicted the overthrow of the King. By the early sixteenth century, Henry VIII had prohibited prophesying as a felonious act "to declare any false prophecy upon occasion of arms, fields, names, cognizances, or badges." In 1568, Elizabeth reinforced this law and explained how "fantastical or false" prophecies on "arms, fields, beasts,

[62] Whethamstede, i.247-48.
[63] Fabyan, p. 672.

badges" might be used "to make any rebellion, insurrection, dissension, loss of life or other disturbance." [64]

This repression is indicative of the effectiveness of the prophecies; they were regarded with extreme respect, as many chronicles record. John de Courcy was so convinced of the truth of Merlin's prophecies that he always carried a copy with him and tried to identify the prognostications with his own fortunes.[65] Henry II, in 1170, disinterred two bodies at Glastonbury "in order to shatter the Welsh belief in the return of Arthur. These bodies were supposed to be those of Arthur and Gwenhwyfor." [66] Llewelyn ap Gryffyth in 1279 was persuaded to meet Edward I in battle, because he was destined "to be crowned with the diadem of Brutus." [67] Adam de Usk used Bridlington's prophecy as evidence against excessive taxation in 1372.[68]

While the manuscripts of these prophecies are largely late fifteenth-century, the composition is of the mid-fourteenth. Prophecies increase their currency in time of trouble or stress, so that the frequent relation of symbols to the combattants in the Scottish wars of Edward III is not wholly unexpected. In the middle of the following century, prophecies were again revived, and old forms received new interpretations from the Wars of the Roses (for example, No. 44).

Where the historical and political poems reflect only the interests of a special class, they seldom make for great poetry, no matter whether it is the genuine plaint of an oppressed man speaking for his group or the semiofficial

---

[64] Rupert Taylor, *The Political Prophecy in England* (New York, 1911), p. 105.

[65] Ordericus Vitalis, *The Ecclesiastical History of England and Normandy*, tr. Thomas Forester (London, 1856), iv.101, fn. 1.

[66] Margaret Enid Griffiths, *Early Vaticination in Welsh with English Parallels* (Cardiff, 1937), p. 37.

[67] *Flores Hist.,* iii.57.

[68] Adae de Usk, p. 8.

pronouncements of a political faction. The prophecies are
at once the most political and the least poetic of the poems
in this anthology. Only where the interests of the poet
coincide with those of his patrons, and where both coincide
with the national welfare of England at any given time, is
there likely to be a political and literary fusion which may
produce great poetry. At times when it was to the English
advantage to beat back the Scots who were apt to ravage
England, lively verse results, as for example in Minot's
poems. Agincourt, an unexpected victory, produced good
verses, both in ballad and carol, not because the defeat of
the French could solve British military and financial problems (the English did not yet realize that France was a
separate nation), but because the country was uniting behind
a king, and this was one step forward in the necessary dis-
integration of feudalism. The towns generally tried to avoid
participation in the Wars of the Roses, but on the whole
(especially London) favored the Yorkists, because the
leading Lancastrians were marcher lords and more attached
to feudal ways. The pro-Yorkist verses, therefore, have a
potentially wider appeal; they are generally superior to the
Lancastrian efforts.

The fifteenth century was truly an age of transition, but
few of its contemporaries realized it as such. In so many
ways it looks forward to the Tudor period. But Lydgate and
his imitators with their dull lines and stereotyped formulae
do not foreshadow the Renaissance. It is rather the popular
ballads, the mystery cycles, the carols, and the conversational
and devotional prose that lay the groundwork and establish
the patterns for the sixteenth century. Nor is this dynamic
accidental; these forms were the literature of the middle
classes, the stratum of society that already in the fifteenth
century was becoming decisive in the political and economic
control of England, and by the seventeenth century was
dominant. De Worde printed eighteen works of Lydgate;
the Elizabethans knew him as an Appendix to Chaucer; the

Carolinians forgot him. Lydgate was a monk, and a spokes-
man for the feudal nobility and church, a dying force, no
longer the vital part of the nation; rarely is great literature
(except that which follows a long cultural tradition, such as
the Latin Silver poetry or the European *fin de siècle* decadence) the product of a waning class. The contrast between
the literature of those who live on the labors of others and
those who produce and help a country function may be seen
in Lydgate's translation of de Guileville and in Bunyan's
Pilgrim's Progress: the latter can still profitably be read
today, even though its "mythology" is no longer current coin.
It is the merchants, the yeomen, the new adventuring aristo-
crats—not monks and courtiers—who are the *Kulturträger*
of the fifteenth century. When they aped, or commissioned
others to ape, the conventions of cloister and court, the
resultant pieces became meaningless cant. When they dis-
carded these outworn traditions, and wrote verse of wider
appeal, the result, as may be seen in many of the poems of
this anthology, is fresh and enduring.

HISTORICAL POEMS

of the

XIVth and XVth Centuries

THE TEXTS

The texts printed here have been transcribed from the original manuscripts or photostats (with the exception of No. 88, the MS. of which is lost). They follow the originals in orthography and capitalization, and retain the Middle English characters þ and ȝ. Contractions have been expanded without the use of italics. The punctuation is editorial. Where components of words are separated in the manuscripts, they have been joined by hyphens. Obvious scribal errors have been corrected, the original reading being recorded at the foot of the page, but the editorial policy is conservative.

AN OUTLINE OF
DYNASTIC HISTORY

1. *THE KINGS OF ENGLAND*

BY JOHN LYDGATE

MS. Rawlinson C.48
(Sum. Cat. No. 11914)

This mythi William, Duke of Normandie,	[f. 78*v*]
As bookis old make mencion,	William
Bi iust title and bi his cheualrie,	Conqueror
Maade kyng bi conquest of Brutis albion,	4
Put out Harald, took possession,	
Bare his crowne ful xxj yeer,	
Buried at Cane; thus seith the Cronicler.	

Next in ordre bi succession,	8
William Rufus, his sone, crowned Kyng;	William Rufus
Which to godward hadde no deuocion,	
Distroid chirches of new and old bildyng	
To make a forest plesaunt for huntyng;	12
xiiij yeer bare his crowne in-deede;	
Buried at Wynchestir; the cronycle ye may reede.	

His brothir next, callid the first Herrye,	Herre the first
Was at London crowned, as I fynde,	16
Whos brothir Robert, Duke of Normandie,	
Gan hym werrey, the cronycle makith mynde;	

---

1. Norma MS. *torn.*   7. thus MS. this.

Reconciled, al rancour sett behynde,
   Ful xxxv yeer, bi record of writyng,   20
   He Regned; buryed at Redyng.

His cosyn Stephen, whan first Herry was deede,   Stephen
   Toward ynglond gan to crosse his sail;
Th'erchebisshop sett vpon his hed   24
   A riche crowne — beyng of his consail.
   xix yeer with sorwe and grete trauail
     He bare his crowne, had neuer reste;
     Att Feuersham lith buried in a chest.   28

Herry the secunde, sonne of the Emperesse,   [f. 79*r*]
   Was crowned next — a full manli knyht,   Herry þe ij*e*
As bookis old pleynli do expresse;
   This seid Herry bi froward force & myht   32
   Slouh seynt Thomas for holy cherchis riht!
     Yeers xxxv Regned, as it is maade mynde,
     Atte Font-euerad Lith buried, as I fynde.

Richard his sonne, Next bi succession,   Richard
   First of that name, strong, hardy, & notable,   the first
Was crowned Kyng; Callid Cuer de leon —
   With sarsyn heedis serued was at his table!
   Slayn at Gaylard, bi dethe lamentable —   40
     The space Regned fulli of ix yeer;
     His herte buried atte Rone the hih auter.

Next Kyng Richard Regned his brothir Iohn,   Kyng Iohn
   Afftir soone entrid into France;   44
Lost al Ange and Normandie a-non,
   This Lond entirdited bi his gouernaunce.
   And as it is put in remembraunce,

20. MS. xxxj.   28. *Catchwords at foot of page* Herry the secund.
40. Gaylard MS. *rubbed.*

xviij yeer kyng of this Region;   48
   Lith atte Wercestre; deid of poison.

Herry the thridde, his sone, of ix yeer Age   Herry
   Was atte Glocestre crowned, as I reede;   þe thridde
Long werre he hadde with his baronage;   52
   Greteli dilited in Almosse deede.
   lvj*ti* yeer he regned her in-deede;
      Buried att Westmenstre, bi record of writyng,
      Day of seynt Edmund, marter, maide & kyng.   56

Edward the First, With the shankis Long,   [f. 79*v*]
   Was aftir crowned, that was so good a knyht;   Edward
Wan Scotland maugre the scottis strong,   þe Firste
   And al Walis despite of al ther myht.   60
   Duryng his liff meyntened trouthe & riht;
      xxxv*ti* yeer he was heer kyng;
      Lith att Westmenstre: this trouth & no Lesyng.

Edward His sone, callid Carnarvan,   64
   Svccedyng aftir, to make his alliaunce,
As the cronycle weel reherse can,   Edward of
   Weddid the douhtir of the Kyng of Fraunce;   Carnarvan
   On Thomas Lancastre bi deth he took vengaunce;   68
      xix yeer heeld heer hes regalie;
      Buried atte Gloucestre, bookis specifie.

The thridde Edward borne atte Wyndesore,   Edwarde the iij
   Which in knyhthod hadde so grete a pris,   72
Enheritour off Fraunce, Withoute more
   Bare in his Armys quarterle iij flourelys;
   And he gate Caleys bi his prudent deuys.
      Regned in ynglond lj yeer,   76
      Lith at Westmenstre; thus seith the Cronycler.

64. MS. Carn.

Sone of prince Edward, Richard the seconde,   Richard the ij*d*
   In whos tyme was pes & gret plente,
Weddid queen Anne of bewme, as it is founde,   80
   Isabell, aftir, of Fraunce — who list see.
   xxij yeer he regned her, pardee;
     Att Langley Buried first, so stood the cas,
     Aftir to Westmenstre Hys body caried was.   84

Herry the iiij*te* next crowned, in certeyn,   [f. 80*r*]
   A famous knyht, and of grete semlynesse;   Herry the iiij*te*
From his exil whan he cam hom a-geyn,
     Traueilid aftir with werre and grete seknesse.   88
     xiiij yeer he regned in sothnesse;
       Lith at Canturbury in that holy place —
       God of his mercy do his soule grace!

The fifte Herry, of knyhthode Lodesterre,   Herry the v*te*
   Wise and ryht manly, pleynli to termyne,
Riht fortunat, preeued in pes and werre,
     Gretely expert in marcial discipline,
     Able to stond among the worthy nyne;   96
       Regned x yeer, who-so liste haue rewarde,
       Lith at Westmenstre not far from seynt edwarde.

The vj*te* Herry, Brouht forthe in alle vertu,   Herry the vj*te*
   Bi iuste title borne bi enheritaunce,   100
Afforne prouydyd bi grace of crist Iesu
   To weer too crownes in Ynglond & Fraunce,
   To whom god hath goue souereyne suffisaunce
     Off vertuous liff, and chose hym for his knyht,   104
     Long to reioisshe and regne heer in his riht.

Explicit.

86. MS. fomous.   98. MS. nat for.   103. MS. suffiaunce.

2. SONG OF THE HUSBANDMAN (1300)

Harley MS. 2253

Ich herde men vpo mold make muche mon,   [f. 64r]
  hou he beþ itened of here tilyynge:
gode ȝeres & corn boþe beþ agon;
  ne kepeþ here no sawe ne no song synge.   4
Nou we mote worche, nis þer non oþer won,
  mai ich no lengore lyue wiþ mi lesinge;
ȝet þer is a bitterore bid to þe bon,
  for euer þe furþe peni mot to þe kynge.   8

þus we carpeþ for þe kyng, & carieþ ful colde,
  & weneþ forte keuere, & euer buþ a-cast;
whose haþ eny god, hopeþ he nout to holde,
  bote euer þe leuest we leoseþ alast.   12

Luþer is to leosen þer-ase lutel ys,
  & haueþ monie hynen þat hopieþ þer-to:
þe hayward heteþ vs harm to habben of his;
  þe bailif bockneþ vs bale & weneþ wel do;   16
þe wodeward waiteþ vs wo, þat lokeþ vnder rys;
  ne mai vs ryse no rest, rycheis ne ro.
þus me pileþ þe pore, þat is of lute pris.
  nede in swot & in swynk swynde mot swo.   20

Nede he mot swynde, þah he hade swore,
  þat naþ nout en hod his hed forte hude.
þus wil walkeþ in lond, & lawe is forlore,
  & al is piked of þe pore, þe prikyares prude.   24

Written in long lines.

þus me pileþ þe pore and pykeþ ful clene,
    þe ryche me raymeþ wiþ-outen eny ryht;
ar londes & ar leodes liggeþ fol lene,
    þorh biddyng of baylyfs such harm hem haþ hiht.   28
Meni of religioun me halt hem ful hene,
    baroun & bonde, þe clerc & þe knyht.
þus wil walkeþ in lond, & wondred ys wene,
    falsshipe fatteþ and marreþ wyþ myht.   32

Stont stille y þe stude, & halt him ful sturne,
    þat makeþ beggares go wiþ bordon & bagges.
þus we beþ honted from hale to hurne;
    þat er werede robes, nou wereþ ragges.   36

ȝet comeþ budeles, wiþ ful muche bost:
    "greyþe me seluer to þe grene wax;
þou art writen y my writ, þat þou wel wost!"
    mo þen ten siþen told y my tax.   40
þenne mot ych habbe hennen arost,
    feyr on fyhsh day launprey & lax;
forþ to þe chepyn geyneþ ne chost,
    þah y sulle mi bil & my borstax.   44

Ich mot legge my wed wel ȝef y wolle,
    oþer sulle mi corn on gras þat is grene.
ȝet I shal be foul cherl, þah he han þe fulle;
    þat ich alle ȝer spare, þenne y mot spene.   48

Nede y mot spene þat y spared ȝore,
    aȝeyn þis cachereles comeþ þus y mot care;
comeþ þe maister budel brust ase a bore;
    seiþ he wole mi bugging bringe ful bare.   52
Mede y mot munten a mark oþer more,
    þah ich at þe set dey sulle mi mare.
þus þe grene wax vs greueþ vnder gore,
    þat me vs honteþ ase hound doþ þe hare.   56

28. MS. bddyng.

he vs honteþe ase hound hare doþ on hulle;
   seþþe y tek to þe lond such tene me wes taht.
nabbeþ ner budeles boded ar sulle,
   for he may scape & we aren euer caht.   60

þus y kippe & cacche cares ful colde,
   seþþe y counte & cot hade to kepe;
to seche seluer to þe kyng y mi seed solde,
   forþi mi lond leye liþ & leorneþ to slepe.   64
seþþe he mi feire feh fatte y my folde,
   when y þenk o mi weole wel neh y wepe;
þus bredeþ monie beggares bolde,
   & vre ruȝe ys roted & ruls er we repe.   68

Ruls ys oure ruȝe & roted in þe stre,
   for wickede wederes by brokes & by brynke.
þer wakeneþ in þe world wondred & wee,
   ase god in swynden anon as so forte swynke.   72

3. *THE FLEMISH INSURRECTION (1302)*

Harley MS. 2253

Lustneþ, lordinges, boþe ȝonge ant olde,   [f. 73*v*)
of þe freynsshe-men þat were so proude ant bolde,
hou þe flemmysshe men bohten hem ant solde
         vpon a wednesday.   4
betere hem were at home in huere londe
þen forte seche flemmysshe by þe see stronde,
whareþourh moni frenshe wyf wryngeþ hire honde,
        ant singeþ "weylaway!"   8

57. doþ MS. doh.

þe kyng of fraunce made statuȝ newe
in þe lond of flaundres, among false ant trewe,
þat þe commun of bruges ful sore con arewe,
        ant seiden amonges hem: 12
"gedere we vs to-gedere hardilyche at ene;
take we þe bailifs bi tuenty ant by tene,
clappe we of the heuedes an-ouen o þe grene,
        ant caste we y þe fen."   16

þe webbes ant þe fullaris assembleden hem alle,
ant makeden huere consail in huere commune halle;
token Peter Conyng huere kyng to calle,
        ant beo huere cheueuteyn.   20
hue nomen huere rouncyns out of þe stalle,
ant closeden þe toun wiþ-inne þe walle;
sixti baylies ant ten hue maden a-doun falle,
        ant moni an-oþer sweyn.   24

þo wolde þe baylies, þat were come from fraunce,
dryue þe flemisshe þat made þe destaunce;
hue turnden hem aȝeynes wiþ suerd & wiþ launce,
        stronge men ant lyht.   28
y telle ou for soþe, for al huere bobaunce,
ne for þe auowerie of þe kyng of fraunce,
tuenti score ant fyue haden þer meschaunce,
        by day ant eke by nyht.   32

Sire Iakes de seint poul yherde hou hit was,   [f. 74r]
sixtene hundred of horsmen asemblede o þe gras;
he wende toward bruges pas pur pas,
        wiþ swiþe gret mounde.   36
þe flemmysshe yherden telle þe cas,
a-gynneþ to clynken huere basyns of bras,
ant al hem to-dryuen ase ston doþ þe glas,
        ant fellen hem to grounde.   40

21. of *inserted above line*.   33. MS. hout.
40. when *expunged for deletion before* ant.

sixtene hundred of horsmen hede þer here fyn;
hue leyȝen y þe stretes y-styked ase swyn;
þer hue loren huere stedes any mony rouncyn
       þourh huere oune prude.   44
sire Iakes ascapede by a coynte gyn,
out at one posterne þer me solde wyn,
out of þe fyhte hom to ys yn,
       in wel muchele drede.   48

þo þe kyng of fraunce y-herde þis, anon
assemblede he is dousse pers eueruchon,
þe proude eorl of artoys ant oþer mony on,
       to come to paris.   52
þe barouns of fraunce þider conne gon,
Into þe paleis þat paued is wiþ ston,
to iugge þe flemmisshe to bernen ant to slon,
       þourh þe flour-de-lis.   56

þenne seide þe kyng Phelip, "lustneþ nou to me,
Myn eorles ant my barouns gentil ant fre,
goþ, faccheþ me þe traytours y-bounde to my kne,
       hastifliche ant blyue."   60
þo suor þe eorl of seint Poul, "par la goule de!
we shule facche þe rybaus wher þi wille be,
ant drawen hem wiþ wilde hors out of þe countre,
       by þousendes fyue!"   64

"sire Rauf de nel," sayþ þe eorl of boloyne,
"nus ne lerrum en vie chanoun ne moyne,
wende we forþ anon riþt wiþoute eny assoygne,
       Ne no lyues man.   68
we shule flo þe Conyng, & make roste is loyne;
þe word shal springen of him in-to coloyne,
so hit shal to Acres, & in-to sesoyne,
       ant maken him ful wan."   72

48. MS. mucheled *with* d *expunged*.   63. wiþ *supplied*.

seuene eorles ant fourti barouns y-tolde,
fyftene hundred knyhtes proude & swyþe bolde,
sixti þousent swyers among ȝunge ant olde,
           flemmisshe to take.   76
þe flemmisshe hardeliche hem com to-ȝeynes;
þis proude freinsshe eorles, huere knyhtes, & huere sweynes
aquelleden ant slowen by hulles & by pleynes,
           al for huere kynges sake.   80

þis frenshe come to flaundres so liht so þe hare,
er hit were mydnyht hit fel hem to care;
hue were laht by þe net so bryd is in snare,
           wiþ rouncin & wiþ stede.   84
þe flemmisshe hem dabbeþ o þe het bare;
hue nolden take for huem raunsoun ne ware;
hue doddeþ of huere heuedes, fare so hit fare,
           Ant þare-to haueþ hue nede.   88

þenne seyþ þe eorl of Artois, "y ȝelde me to þe,   [f. 74v]
Peter Conyng by þi nome, ȝef þou art hende ant fre,
þat y ne haue no shame ne no vylte,
           þat y ne be noud ded."   92
þenne swor a bocher, "by my leaute!
shalt þou ner more þe kyng of fraunce se,
ne in þe toun of bruges in prisone be,
           þou woldest spene bred."   96

þer hy were knulled y þe put-falle,
þis eorles ant barouns & huere knyhtes alle;
huere ledies huem mowe abide in boure & in halle
           wel longe.   100
for hem mot huere kyng oþer knyhtes calle,
oþer stedes taken out of huere stalle;
þer hi habbeþ dronke bittrere þen þe galle,
           vpon þe drue londe.   104

when þe kyng of fraunce y-herde þis tydynge,
he smot doun is heued, is honden gon he wrynge;
þourhout al fraunce þe word bygon to springe.
   wo wes huem þo!   108
Muche wes þe sorewe ant þe wepinge
þat wes in al fraunce among olde ant ȝynge;
þe meste part of þe lond bygon forte synge,
   "alas, ant weylawo!"   112

awey, þou ȝunge pope! whet shal þe to rede?
þou hast lore þin cardinals at þi meste nede;
ne keuerest þou hem neuere for nones kunnes mede,
   for soþe y þe telle.   116
do þe forþ to rome to amende þi misdede;
bide gode halewen hue lete þe betere spede;
bote þou worche wysloker, þou losest lond & lede,
   þe coroune wel þe felle.   120

Alas! þou seli fraunce, for þe may þunche shome,
þat ane fewe fullaris makeþ ou so tome;
sixti þousent on a day hue maden fot-lome,
   wiþ eorl & knyht.   124
her-of habbeþ þe flemysshe suiþe god game,
ant suereþ bi seint omer & eke bi seint Iame,
ȝef hy þer more comeþ hit falleþ huem to shame,
   wiþ huem forte fyht.   128

I telle ou for soþe, þe bataille þus bigon
bituene fraunce ant flaundres, hou hue weren fon;
vor vrenshe þe eorl of flaundres in prison heden y-don,
   wiþ tresoun vntrewe.   132
ȝef þe prince of walis his lyf habbe mote,
hit falleþ þe kyng of fraunce bittrore þen þe sote,
bote he þe raþere þer-of welle do bote,
   wel sore hit shal hym rewe.   136

131. heden *inserted above line.*   133. MS. ȝe.

4. THE EXECUTION OF SIR SIMON FRASER
(1306)

Harley MS. 2253

Lystneþ, lordynges, a newe song ichulle bigynne   [f. 59v]
of þe traytours of scotlond þat take beþ wyþ gynne.
Mon þat loueþ falsnesse & nule neuer blynne,
sore may him drede þe lyf þat he is ynne,   4
       Ich vnderstonde.
         Selde wes he glad,
         þat neuer nes a-sad
       of nyþe ant of onde.   8

þat y sugge by þis scottes þat bueþ nou to-drawe —
þe heuedes o londone brugge whose con y-knawe;
he wenden han buen kynges, ant seiden so in sawe;
betere hem were han y-be barouns ant libbe in godes lawe, 12
       wyþ loue.
         whose hateþ soth ant ryht,
         lutel he douteþ godes myht,
       þe heye kyng aboue.   16

To warny alle þe gentilmen þat bueþ in scotlonde,
þe waleis wos to-drawe, seþþe he wos an-honge,
al quic biheueded, ys bowels y-brend,
þe heued to londone brugge wos send   20
       To abyde.
         after simond frysel,
         þat wes traytour ant fykel,
       ant y-cud ful wyde.   24

The last three lines of each stanza written in MS. as one long line.

Sire edward oure kyng, þat ful ys of piete,
þe waleis quarters sende to is oune contre,
on four half to honge, huere myrour to be,
þer-opon to þenche, þat monie myhten se   28
          Ant drede.
               why nolden he be war
               of þe bataile of donbar,
          hou euele hem con spede?   32

Bysshopes ant barouns come to þe kynges pes,   [f. 60r]
ase men þat weren fals, fykel, ant les,
oþes hue him sworen in stude þer he wes,
to buen him hold ant trewe for alles cunnes res,   36
          þryes.
               þat hue ne shulden aȝeyn him go,
               so hue were temed þo.
          weht halt hit to lye?   40

To þe kyng edward hii fasten huere fay;
fals wes here foreward so forst is in may,
þat sonne from þe southward wypeþ away:
Moni proud scot þer-of mene may   44
          to ȝere.
               Nes neuer scot-lond
               wiþ dunt of monnes hond
          allinge aboht so duere.   48

þe bisshop of glascou, ychot he was ylaht;
þe bisshop of seint Andre, boþe, he beþ ycaht;
þe abbot of scon wiþ þe kyng nis nouht saht;
al here purpos ycome hit ys to naht,   52
          þurh ryhte.
               hii were vnwis,
               when hii þohte pris
          aȝeyn huere kyng to fyhte.   56

þourh consail of þes bisshopes y-nemned byfore,
sire Robert þe bruyc3 furst kyng wes y-core.
he mai eueruche day ys fon him se byfore;
3ef hee mowen him hente, ichot he biþ forlore,   60
       saunt3 fayle.
         soht forte sugge,
         duere he shal abugge
       þat he bigon batayle.   64

hii þat him crounede proude were ant bolde;
hii maden kyng of somere, so hii ner ne sholde;
hii setten on ys heued a croune of rede golde,
Ant token a kyne-3erde (so me kyng sholde)   68
       to deme.
         þo he wes set in see,
         lutel god couþe he,
         kyne-riche to 3eme.   72

Nou kyng hobbe in þe mures 3ongeþ,
forte come to toune nout him ne longeþ.
þe barouns of engelond, myhte hue him gripe,
he him wolde techen on englysshe to pype,   76
       þourh streynþe.
         Ne be he ner so stout,
         3et he biþ y-soht out
         o brede ant o leynþe.   80

sire Edward of carnaruan — iesu him saue and see —
sire Emer de valence, gentil knyht ant free,
habbeþ y-suore huere oht þat par la grace dee
hee wolleþ ous delyuren of þat false contre,   84
       3ef hii conne.
         Muche haþ scotlond forlore,
         whet a-last, whet bifore,
         ant lutel pris wonne.   88

Nou ichulle fonge þer ich er let,
ant tellen ou of frisel, ase ich ou by-het.
In þe batayle of kyrkenclyf ffrysel was ytake —
ys continaunce abatede eny bost to make   92
       biside striuelyn —
          knyhtes ant sweynes,
          ffremen ant þeynes,
       monye wiþ hym.   96

so hii weren byset on eueruche halue,   [f. 60v]
somme slaye were, ant somme dreynte hem-selue.
sire Iohan of lyndeseye nolde nout abyde,
he wod into þe water, his feren him bysyde,   100
       to adrenche.
          whi nolden hii be war?
          þer nis non aȝeyn star,
       why nolden hii hem by-þenche?   104

þis wes byfore seint bartholomeus masse,
þat ffrysel wes y-take, were hit more oþer lasse;
To sire Thomas of Multone, gentil baroun ant fre,
ant to sire Iohan Iose, by-take þo wes he   108
       to honde.
          he wes yfetered weel,
          boþe wiþ yrn ant wyþ steel,
       to bringen of scotlonde.   112

Sone þer-after þe tydynge to þe kyng com.
he him sende to londone wiþ mony armed grom;
he com yn at newegate, y telle yt ou a-plyht,
a gerland of leues on ys hed y-dyht   116
       of grene;
          ffor he shulde ben yknowe,
          boþe of heȝe ant of lowe,
       for treytour, y wene.   120

113. com *expunged for deletion after* tydynge.

y-fetered were ys legges vnder his horse wombe;
boþe wiþ yrn ant wiþ stel mankled were ys honde;
A gerland of peruenke set on ys heued;
Muche wes þe poer þat him wes byreued   124
   In londe.
    so god me amende,
    lutel he wende
   so be broht in honde.   128

sire herbert of Morham, feyr knyht ant bold,
for þe loue of frysel ys lyf wes y-sold;
a waiour he made, so hit wes y-told,
ys heued of to smhyte ȝef me him brohte in hold,   132
   wat so bytyde.
    sory wos he þenne,
    þo he myhte him kenne
   þourh þe toun ryde.   136

þenne seide ys scwyer a word anon ryht,
"sire, we beþ ded, ne helpeþ hit no wyht!"
(Thomas de boys þe scwyer wes to nome)
"Nou ychot oure waiour turneþ ous to grome,   140
   so y bate."
    y do ou to wyte,
    here heued wes of smyte
   byfore þe tour gate.   144

þis wes on oure leuedy euen, for sothe ych understonde,
þe iustices seten for þe knyhtes of scotlonde:
sire Thomas of Multone, an hendy knyht ant wys,
ant sire Rauf of sondwych, þat muchel is told in pris,   148
   ant sire Iohan Abel,
    Mo y mihte telle by tale,
    boþe of grete ant of smale,
   ȝe knowen suyþe wel.   152

þenne saide þe iustice, þat gentil is ant fre,
"sire simond ffrysel, þe kynges traytour hast þou be,
In water ant in londe, þat monie myhten se.
what sayst þou þareto? hou wolt þou quite þe?   156
     do say!"
        so foul he him wiste,
        nede waron truste,
      forto segge nay.   160

þer he wes ydemed, so hit wes londes lawe,   [f. 61r]
for þat he wes lord-swyke; furst, he wes to-drawe;
vpon a reþeres hude forþ he wes ytuht,
sum while in ys time he wes a modi knyht   164
     In huerte.
        wickednesse & sunne —
        hit is lutel wunne
      þat makeþ þe body smerte.   168

ffor al is grete poer, ӡet he wes ylaht;
ffalsnesse & swykedom al hit geþ to naht.
þo he wes in scotlond, lutel wes ys þoht
of þe harde iugement þat him wes bysoht   172
     In stounde.
        he wes four siþe for-swore
        to þe kyng þer bifore,
      & þat him brohte to grounde.   176

wiþ feteres & wiþ gyues ichot he wes to-drowe,
ffrom þe tour of londone, þat monie myhte knowe,
In a curtel of burel a selkeþe wyse,
ant a gerland on ys heued of þe newe guyse,   180
     þurh cheepe.
        Moni mon of engelond
        forto se symond
      þideward con lepe.   184

þo he com to galewes, furst he wes an-honge
al quic byheueded, þah him þohte longe.
seþþe he wes y-opened, is boweles ybrend;
þe heued to londone brugge wes send   188
        to shonde.
            so ich euer mote þe,
            sum while wende he
        þer lutel to stonde.   192

he rideþ þourh þe site, as y telle may,
wiþ gomen & wyþ solas, þat wes here play;
to londone brugge hee nome þe way —
Moni wes þe wyues chil þat þer-on lokeþ a day,   196
        Ant seide alas,
            þat he wes ibore
            & so villiche forlore,
        so feir mon ase he was.   200

Nou stont þe heued aboue þe tubrugge,
ffaste bi waleis, soþ forte sugge;
after socour of scotlond longe he mowe prye,
ant after help of fraunce wet halt hit to lye,   204
        Ich wene.
            betere him were in scotlond
            wiþ is ax in ys hond,
        to pleyen o þe grene.   208

Ant þe body hongeþ at þe galewes faste,
wiþ yrnene claspes longe to laste;
fforte wyte wel þe body, & scottysh to gaste,
foure ant tuenti þer beoþ to soþe ate laste   212
        by nyhte,
            ȝef eny were so hardi
            þe body to remuy,
        also to dyhte.   216

211. MS. garste.

were sire robert þe bruycჳ y-come to þis londe,
ant þe erl of asseles, þat harde is an honde,
alle þe oþer pouraille, forsoþe ich vnderstonde,
mihten be ful blyþe ant þonke godes sonde   220
        wyþ ryhte.
           þenne myhte vch mon
           boþ riden & gon
        in pes wiþ-oute vyhte.   224

þe traytours of scotlond token hem to rede,   [f. 61v]
þe barouns of engelond to brynge to dede;
Charles of fraunce, so moni mon tolde,
wiþ myht & wiþ streynþe hem helpe wolde,   228
        his þonkes!
           Tprot, scot, for þi strif!
           hang vp þyn hachet ant þi knyf,
           whil him lasteþ þe lyf   232
        wiþ þe longe shonkes.

5. THE DEATH OF EDWARD I (1307)

Harley MS. 2253

Alle þat beoþ of huerte trewe,   [f. 73r]
  a stounde herkneþ to my song,
of duel þat deþ haþ diht vs newe,
  þat makeþ me syke ant sorewe among;   4
of a knyht þat wes so strong,
  of wham god haþ don ys wille;
me þuncheþ þat deþ haþ don vs wrong,
  þat he so sone shal ligge stille.   8

No. 5. *MS. written in long lines.*

SAINT PETER'S COLLEGE LIBRARY
JERSEY CITY, NEW JERSEY 07306

al englond ahte forte knowe
 of wham þat song is þat y synge —
of edward kyng þat liþ so lowe,
 ȝent al þis world is nome con springe.   12
 trewest mon of alle þinge,
  ant in werre war ant wys,
 for him we ahte oure honden wrynge,
  of cristendome he ber þe pris.   16

byfore þat oure kyng wes ded,
 he spek ase mon þat wes in care.
"Clerkes, knyhtes, barouns," he sayde,
 "y charge ou by oure sware,   20
 þat ȝe to engelonde be trewe.
  y deȝe, y ne may lyuen na more;
 helpeþ mi sone & crouneþ him newe,
  for he is nest to buen y-core.   24

"Ich bi-queþe myn herte aryht,
 þat hit be write at mi deuys,
ouer þe see þat hue be diht,
 wiþ four-score knyhtes al of pris,   28
 In werre þat buen war & wys,
  aȝein þe heþene forte fyhte,
 to wynne þe croiȝ þat lowe lys.
  myself ycholde ȝef þat y myhte."   32

kyng of fraunce, þou heuedest sunne,
 þat þou þe counsail woldest fonde,
to latte þe wille of kyng edward
 to wende to þe holy londe;   36
 þat oure kyng hede take on honde
  al engelond to ȝeme & wysse,
 to wenden in-to þe holy londe,
  to wynnen vs heuenriche blisse.   40

40. MS. heueriche.

þe messager to þe pope com,
  & seyde þat oure kyng wes ded;
ys oune hond þe lettre he nom,
    y-wis is herte wes ful gret.   44
    þe pope him-self þe lettre redde,
      ant spec a word of gret honour —
  "alas!" he seide, "is Edward ded?
    of cristendome he ber þe flour!"   48

þe pope to is chaumbre wende,
  for del ne mihte he speke na more;
ant after cardinals he sende,
  þat muche couþen of cristes lore,   52
  boþe þe lasse ant eke þe more,
    bed hem boþe rede & synge;
  gret deol me myhte se þore,
    mony mon is honde wrynge.   56

þe pope of peyters stod at is masse,   [f. 73v]
  wiþ ful gret solempnete;
þer me con þe soule blesse:
  "kyng edward, honoured þou be!   60
  god lene þi sone come after þe
    bringe to ende þat þou hast bygonne;
  þe holy crois y-mad of tre,
    so fain þou woldest hit han y-wonne. 64

"Ierusalem, þou hast i-lore
  þe flour of al chiualerie!
Nou kyng edward liueþ na more,
  alas! þat he ȝet shulde deye!   68
  he wolde ha rered vp fol heyȝe
    oure baners, þat bueþ broht to grounde;
  wel longe we mowe clepe & crie
    er we a such kyng han y-founde!"   72

Nou is Edward of Carnaruan
 king of engelond al aplyht,
god lete him ner be worse man
  þen is fader, ne lasse of myht   76
  to holden is pore men to ryht,
   ant vnderstonde good consail,
  al engeland forte wisse ant diht,
   of gode knyhtes darh him nout fail.   80

þah mi tonge were mad of stel,
 ant min herte y-ȝote of bras,
þe godnesse myht y neuer telle
  þat wiþ kyng edward was.   84
   kyng, as þou art cleped conquerour,
    in vch bataille þou hadest pris;
   god bringe þi soule to þe honour
    þat euer wes & euer ys,   88
     þat lesteþ ay wiþ-outen ende!
      bidde we god ant oure ledy,
     to þilke blisse iesus vs sende.

      Amen.

6. SATIRE ON THE CONSISTORY COURTS
(1307)

Harley MS. 2253

Ne mai no lewed lued libben in londe,   [f. 70v]
be he neuer in hyrt so hauer of honde,
 so lerede vs biledes;

ȝef ich on molde mote wiþ a mai,   4
y shal falle hem byfore & lurnen huere lay,
   ant rewen alle huere redes.
ah bote y be þe furme day on folde hem byfore,
ne shal y nout so skere scapan of huere score;   8
   so grimly he on me gredes,
þat y ne mot me lede þer wiþ mi lawe,
on alle maner oþes þat heo me wulleþ awe,
   heore boc ase vn-bredes.   12
      heo wendeþ bokes vn-brad,
      ant makeþ men a moneþ a-mad;
        of scaþe y wol me skere,
        ant fleo from my fere;   16
        ne rohte he whet yt were,
      boten heo hit had.

ffurst þer sit an old cherl in a blake hure,
of alle þat þer sitteþ semeþ best syre,   20
   ant leyþ ys leg o-lonke.
An heme in an herygoud wiþ honginde sleuen,
& mo þen fourti him by-fore my bales to breuen,
   In sunnes ȝef y songe.   24
heo pynkes wiþ heore penne on heore parchemyn,
ant sayen y am breued ant y-broht yn
   of al my weole wlonke.
Alle heo bueþ redy myn rouþes to rede,   28
þer y mot for menske munte sum mede,
   ant þonkfulliche hem þonke.
      shal y þonke hem þer er y go?
      ȝe, þe maister ant ys men bo.   32
        ȝef y am wreint in heore write,
        þenne am y bac-bite;
        for moni mon heo makeþ wyte
      Of wymmene wo.   36

5. & MS. e.

ʒet þer sitteþ somenours syexe oþer seuene,
mys-motinde men alle by here euene,
   ant recheþ forþ heore rolle.
Hyrdmen hem hatieþ, ant vch mones hyne,   [f. 71r col. i]
for eueruch a parosshe heo polkeþ in pyne,
   and clastreþ wyþ heore colle.
Nou wol vch fol clerc þat is fayly,
wende to þe bysshop ant bugge bayly —   44
   nys no wyt in is nolle —
come to countene court, couren in a cope,
ant suggen he haþ priuilegie proud of þe pope —
   swart ant al to-swolle.   48
      aren heo to-swolle, for-swore?
       ʒe, þe hatred of helle beo heore!
        for þer heo beodeþ a bok,
        to sugge ase y folht tok;   52
        heo shulen in helle on an hok
      honge þere-fore!

þer stont vp a ʒeolumon, ʒeʒeþ wiþ a ʒerde,
ant hat out an heh þat al þe hyrt herde,   56
   ant cleopeþ Magge ant Malle.
ant heo comeþ bymodered ase a mor-hen,
ant scrynkeþ for shome, & shomeþ for men,
   vncomely vnder calle.   60
heo biginneþ to shryke, & scremeþ anon,
ant saiþ, "by my gabbyng, ne shal hit so gon,
   ant þat beo on ou alle;
þat þou shalt me wedde & welde to wyf."   64
ah me were leuere wiþ lawe leose my lyf
   þen so to fote hem falle.
      shal y to fote falle for mi fo?
      ʒe, monie byswykeþ heo swo.   68
        of þralles y am þer þrat,
        þat sitteþ swart & for-swat;
        þer y mot hente me en hat
      er ich hom go.   **72**

such chaffare y chepe at þe chapitre,
þat makeþ moni þryue mon vn-þeufol to be,
  wiþ þonkes ful þunne;
ant seþþe y go coure at constory,   76
ant falle to fote vch a fayly —
  heore is þis worldes wynne.
seþþen y pleide at bisshopes plee,
ah me were leuere be sonken y þe see,   80
  In sor wiþouten synne.
At chirche ant þourh cheping, ase dogge y am dryue,[f. 71v]
þat me were leuere of lyue þen so forte lyue,
  to care of al my kynne.   84
      atte constorie heo kenneþ vs care,
      ant whissheþ vs euele & worse to fare.
        a pruest proud ase a po
        seþþe weddeþ vs bo;   88
        Wyde heo worcheþ vs wo
      for wymmene ware.

7. *SATIRE ON THE RETINUES OF THE GREAT (1307)*

Harley MS. 2253

Of rybaudȝ y ryme ant rede o mi rolle,   [f. 124v col. i]
of gedelynges, gromes, of colyn & of Colle,
harlotes, hors-knaues, bi pate & bi polle —
to deuel ich hem to-lyure ant take to tolle!   4

þe gedelynges were gedered of gonnylde gnoste; [col. ii]
palefreiours & pages, ant boyes wiþ boste;
alle were y-haht of an horse þoste —
þe deuel huem afretye, Rau oþer a-roste!   8

No. 7. 1-23. MS. *written in short lines.*

þe shuppare þat huem shupte, to shome he huem shadde,
to fles ant to fleye, to tyke ant to tadde.
so seyþ romaunȝ, whose ryht radde:
ffleh com of flore, ant lous com of ladde.   12

þe harlotes bueth horlynges ant haunteþ þe plawe;
þe gedelynges bueþ glotouns ant drynkeþ er hit dawe.
sathanas huere syre seyde on is sawe:
gobelyn made is gerner of gromene mawe.   16

þe knaue crommeþ is crop er þe cok crawe;
he momeleþe & moccheþ ant marreþ is mawe.
when he is al for-laped ant lad ouer lawe,
a doseyn of doggen ne myhte hyre drawe.   20

þe rybaudȝ a-ryseþ er þe day rewe.
he shrapeþ on is shabbes ant draweþ huem to dewe;
sene is on is browe ant on is eȝe-brewe,
þat he louseth a losynger, & shoyeþ a shrewe.   [f. 125r]

Nou beþ capel-claweres wiþ shome to-shrude;
hue boskeþ huem wyþ botouns, ase hit were a brude,
wiþ lowe lacede shon of an hayfre hude,
hue pykeþ of here prouendre al huere prude.   28

whose rykeneþ wiþ knaues huere coustage,
þe luþernesse of þe ladde, þe prude of þe page,
þah he ȝeue hem cattes dryt to huere companage,
ȝet hym shulde a-rewen of þe arrerage.   32

whil god wes on erthe & wondrede wyde,
whet wes þe resoun why he nolde ryde?
for he nolde no grom to go by ys syde,
ne grucchyng of no gedelyng to chaule ne to chyde.   36

spedeþ ou to spewen, ase me doþ to spelle;
þe fend ou afretie wiþ fleis & wiþ felle!
herkneþ hideward, horsmen, a tidyng ich ou telle,
þat ȝe shulen hongen & herbarewen in helle!   40

8. THOMAS OF ERCELDOUNE'S PROPHECY

Harley MS. 2253

La countesse de Donbar demanda a Thomas de Essedoune   [f. 127r
quant la guere descoce prendreit fyn e yl la respoundy e dyt: col. ii]

When man as mad a kyng of a capped man;
When mon is leuere oþermones þyng þen is owen;
When londyon ys forest, ant forest ys felde;
When hares kendles o þe herston;   4
When wyt & wille werres togedere;
When mon makes stables of kyrkes, & steles castles wyþ styes;
When rokesbourh nys no burgh ant market is at fforweleye;
When þe alde is gan ant þe newe is come þat don noþt;   8
When bambourne is donged wyþ dede men;
When men ledes men in ropes to buyen & to sellen;
When a quarter of whaty whete is chaunged for a colt
                                    of ten markes;
When prude prikes & pees is leyd in prisoun;   12
When a scot ne may hym hude ase hare in forme þat
                          þe englysshe ne shal hym fynde;
When ryþt ant Wrong ascenteþ to-gedere;
When laddes weddeþ louedis;
When scottes flen so faste, þat for faute of ship, hy drouneþ
                                    hem-selue.   16
Whenne shal þis be? Nouþer in þine tyme ne in myne,
ah comen & gon wiþ-inne twenty wynter ant on.

No. 8. 3. y *inserted in* londyon.   9. MS. dedemen.

WAR POEMS
BY LAURENCE MINOT

9. *BANNOCKBURN AVENGED (1333)*

BY LAURENCE MINOT

Cotton MS. Galba E.ix

> Now forto tell ȝow will I turn   [f. 52*v* col. i]
> of batayl of banocburn.

Skottes out of berwik and of abirdene,
at þe bannok burn war ȝe to kene.
þare slogh ȝe many sakles, als it was sene,
and now has king Edward wroken it, I wene.   4
  It es wrokin, I wene, wele wurth þe while;
  war ȝe with þe skottes, for þai er ful of gile.

Whare er ȝe, skottes of saint Iohnes toune?
þe boste of ȝowre baner es betin all doune;   8
when ȝe bosting will bede, sir Edward es boune
forto kindel ȝow care and crak ȝowre crowne.
  he has crakked ȝowre croune, wele worth þe while;
  schame bityde þe skottes, for þai er full of gile.   12

Skottes of striflin war steren and stout,
of god ne of gude men had þai no dout;
now haue þai, þe pelers, priked obout,
bot at þe last sir Edward rifild þaire rout.   16
  he has rifild þaire rout, wele wurth þe while,
  bot euer er þai vnder, bot gaudes and gile.

6. ȝe MS. ȝit.

Rughfute riueling, now kindels þi care,
berebag with þi boste, þi biging es bare;   20
fals wretche and forsworn, whider wiltou fare?
busk þe into brig, and abide þare.
    þare, wretche, saltou won and wery þe while;
    þi dwelling in donde es done for þi gile.   24

Þe skotte gase in burghes and betes þe stretes,
all þise inglis men harmes he hetes;
fast makes he his mone to men þat he metes,
bot fone frendes he findes þat his bale betes.   28
    fune betes his bale, wele wurth þe while,
    he vses all threting with gaudes and gile.

Bot many man thretes and spekes ful ill,
þat sum tyme war better to be stane-still;   32
þe skot in his wordes has wind for to spill,
for at þe last Edward sall haue al his will.
    he had his will at berwik, wele wurth þe while,
    skottes broght him þe kayes, bot get for þaire gile.   36

10. *THE BATTLE OF NEVILLE'S CROSS (1346)*

BY LAURENCE MINOT

Cotton MS. Galba E.ix

> Sir dauid had of his men grete loss,   [f. 56r col. i]
> with sir Edward, at þe neuil cross.

Sir Dauid þe bruse was at distance,
when Edward þe baliolfe rade with his lance;
þe north end of ingland teched him to daunce,
when he was met on þe more with mekill mischance.   4

25. MS. skottes.   No. 10. *Written in short lines (except* l. 38).

Sir philip þe valayse may him noght avance;
þe flowres þat faire war, er fallen in ffraunce.
    þe floures er now fallen, þat fers war and fell,
    A bare with his bataille has done þam to dwell.   8

Sir dauid þe Bruse said he suld fonde   [col. ii]
to ride thurgh all ingland, wald he noght wonde;
at þe west-minster hall suld his stedes stonde,
whils oure king Edward war out of þe londe.   12
    bot now has sir dauid missed of his merkes,
    and philip þe valays, with all þaire grete clerkes.

Sir philip þe valais, suth forto say,
Sent vnto sir dauid and faire gan him pray;   16
at ride thurgh ingland þaire fo-men to flay,
and said none es at home to let hym þe way.
    none letes him þe way to wende whore he will,
    bot with schipherd staues fand he his fill.   20

Fro philip þe valais was sir dauid sent,
all ingland to win fro twede vnto trent.
he broght mani berebag with bow redy bent;
þai robbed and þai reued and held þat þai hent.   24
it was in þe waniand þat þai furth went;
for couaitise of cataile þo schrewes war schent.
    Schent war þo schrewes, and ailed vnsele,
    for at þe neuil cros nedes bud þam knele.   28

At þe Erchbisschop of ȝork now will I bigyn,
for he may with his right hand assoyl vs of syn.
both Dorem and Carlele þai wald neuer blin
þe wirschip of ingland with wappen to win.   32
    Mekill wirschip þai wan, and wele haue þai waken, [f. 56v
    for syr dauid þe Bruse was in þat tyme taken.   col. i]

When Sir Dauid þe Bruse satt on his stede,
he said of all ingland haued he no drede;   36
bot hinde Iohn of Coupland, a wight man in wede,
talked to Dauid and kend him his crede.
þare was sir dauid, so dughty in his dede,
þe faire toure of londen haued he to mede.   40

Sone þan was sir dauid broght vnto þe toure,
and william þe dowglas with men of honowre.
full swith redy seruis fand þai þare a schowre;
for first þai drank of þe swete, and seþin of þe sowre.   44

þan Sir dauid þe Bruse makes his mone,
þe faire coroun of scotland haues he forgone:
he luked furth into france, help had he none,
of sir philip þe valais ne ȝit of sir Iohn.   48

Þe pride of sir Dauid bigon fast to slaken,
for he wakkind þe were þat held him-self waken.
for philyp þe valaise had he brede baken,
and in þe toure of londen his ines er taken.   52
  to be both in a place þaire forward þai nomen;
  bot philip fayled þare, and dauid es cumen.

Sir Dauid þe bruse on þis manere
said vnto sir philip, al þir sawes þus sere: 56
"Philip þe valais, þou made me be here,
þis es noght þe forward we made are to-ȝere.   [col. ii]
  ffals es þi forward, and euyll mot þou fare,
  for þou and sir Iohn þi son haues kast me in care."   60

44. MS. seþin.

þe Scottes, with þaire falshede, þus went þai obout
for to win Ingland whils Edward was out.
for Cuthbert of dorem haued þai no dout;
þarfore at neuel cros law gan þai lout.   64
    þare louted þai law, and leued allane.
    þus was dauid þe Bruse into þe toure tane.

11.   THE SIEGE OF CALAIS (1347)

BY LAURENCE MINOT

Cotton MS. Galba E.ix

How Edward, als þe romance sais,   [f. 55v col. i]
held his sege bifor Calais.

Calays men, now mai ȝe care,
    and murning mun ȝe haue to mede;
mirth on mold get ȝe no mare,
    sir Edward sall ken ȝow ȝowre crede.   4
whilum war ȝe wight in wede,
    to robbing rathly for to ren;
mend ȝow sone of ȝowre misdede;
    ȝowre care es cumen, will ȝe it ken.   8

Kend it es how ȝe war kene
    al inglis men with dole to dere;
þaire gudes toke ȝe al bidene,
    no man born wald ȝe forbere.   12
ȝe spared noght with swerd ne spere
    to stik þam and þaire gudes to stele.
with wapin and with ded of were
    þus haue ȝe wonnen werldes wele.   16

No. 11. 2. MS. murnig.   11. MS. albidene.

Weleful men war ȝe, I-wis,
    bot fer on fold sall ȝe noght fare.
A bare sal now abate ȝowre blis,   [col. ii]
    and wirk ȝow bale on bankes bare.   20
he sall ȝow hunt als hund does hare,
    þat in no hole sall ȝe ȝow hide.
for all ȝowre speche will he noght spare,
    bot bigges him right by ȝowre side.   24

Biside ȝow here þe bare bigins
    to big his boure in winter tyde;
and all bi-tyme takes he his ines
    with semly sergantes him biside.   28
þe word of him walkes ful wide;
    Ihesu, saue him fro mischance!
In bataill dar he wele habide
    sir philip and sir Iohn of france.   32

Þe franche men er fers and fell,
    and mase grete dray when þai er dight;
of þam men herd slike tales tell,
    with Edward think þai forto fight;   36
him for to hald out of his right,
    and do him treson with þaire tales —
þat was þaire purpos, day and night,
    bi counsail of þe Cardinales.   40

Cardinales with hattes rede
    War fro calays wele thre myle;
þai toke þaire counsail in þat stede,
    how þai might sir Edward bigile.   44
þai lended þare bot litill while,
    till franche men to grante þaire grace;
sir philip was funden a file,
    he fled and faght noght in þat place.   48

28. MS. segantes.

In þat place þe bare was blith,
   for all was funden þat he had soght;
philip þe valas fled ful swith,
   with þe batail þat he had broght.   52
for to haue Calays had he thoght
   all at his ledeing loud or still;
bot all þaire wiles war for noght,
   Edward wan it at his will.   56

Lystens now, and ȝe may lere,
   als men þe suth may vnderstand;
þe knightes þat in Calais were
   come to sir Edward sare wepeand,   60
in kirtell one, and swerd in hand,
   and cried, "sir Edward, þine are,
do now, lord, bi law of land
   þi will with vs for euermare."   64

þe nobill burgase and þe best
   come vnto him to haue þaire hire;
þe comun puple war ful prest   [f. 56r col. i]
   rapes to bring obout þaire swire.   68
þai said all, "sir philip, oure syre,
   and his sun, sir Iohn of france,
has left vs ligand in þe mire,
   and broght vs till þis doleful dance.   72

"oure horses, þat were faire and fat,
   er etin vp ilkone bidene;
haue we nowþer conig ne cat,
   þat þai ne er etin, and hundes kene.   76
all er etin vp ful clene,
   es nowther leuid biche ne whelp;
þat es wele on oure sembland sene,
   And þai er fled þat suld vs help."   80

A knight þat was of grete renowne,
  Sir iohn de viene was his name,
he was wardaine of þe toune,
  and had done ingland mekill schame.   84
for all þaire boste þai er to blame,
  ful stalworthly þare haue þai streuyn.
a bare es cumen to mak þam tame,
  kayes of þe toun to him er gifen.   88

þe kaies er ȝolden him of þe ȝate,
  lat him now kepe þam if he kun;
to Calais cum þai all to late,
  sir philip and sir Iohn his sun.   92
al war ful ferd þat þare ware fun;
  þaire leders may þai barely ban.
all on þis wise was Calais won;
  god saue þam þat it so-gat wan.   96

12. *THE TAKING OF GUINES (1352)*

BY LAURENCE MINOT

Cotton MS. Galba E.ix

How gentill sir Edward, with his grete engines,   [f. 57r col. i]
wan with his wight men þe Castell of Gynes.

War þis winter oway, wele wald I wene
þat somer suld schew him in schawes ful schene;
both þe lely and þe lipard suld geder on a grene.
Mari, haue minde of þi man, þou whote wham I mene.   4
  lady, think what I mene, I mak þe my mone;
  þou wreke gude king Edward on wikked syr Iohn.

Of Gynes ful gladly now will I bigin;
We wote wele þat woning was wikked forto win.   [col. ii]
crist, þat swelt on þe rode for sake of mans syn,
hald þam in gude hele þat now er þarein.
   Inglis men er þarein, þe kastell to kepe;
    And Iohn of france es so wroth, for wo will he wepe.   12

Gentil Iohn of Doncaster did a ful balde dede,
when he come toward Gines to ken þam þaire Crede;
he stirt vnto þe castell with-owten any stede,
of folk þat he fand þare haued he no drede.   16
   Dred in hert had he none of all he fand þare;
    faine war þai to fle, for all þaire grete fare.

A letherin ledderr, and a lang line,
a small bote was þarby þat put þam fro pine;   20
þe folk þat þai fand þare was faine forto fyne;
sone þaire diner was dight, and þare wald þai dine.
   þare was þaire purpose to dine and to dwell,
    for treson of þe franche men þat fals war and fell.   24

Say now, sir Iohn of france, how saltou fare,
þat both Calays and Gynes has kindeld þi care?
if þou be man of mekil might, lepe up on þi mare,
Take þi gate vnto Gines, and grete þam wele þare.   28
   þare gretes þi gestes, and wendes with wo.
    king Edward has wonen þe kastell þam fro.

ȝe men of Saint Omers, trus ȝe þis tide,
and puttes out ȝowre pauiliownes with ȝowre mekill pride. 32
sendes efter sir iohn of fraunce to stand by ȝowre syde;[f. 57v
a bore es boun ȝow to biker, þat wele dar habyde.   col. i]
   Wele dar he habide, bataile to bede,
    and of ȝowre sir iohn of fraunce haues he no drede.   36

36. MS. haueuses.

God saue sir Edward his right in euer ilka nede;
and he þat will noght so, euil mot he spede!
and len oure sir Edward his life wele to lede,
þat he may at his ending haue heuin till his mede.   40

Amen.

POEMS FROM DIGBY MS. 102

13. *WHAT PROFITS A KINGDOM (1401)*

MS. Digby 102
(Sum. Cat. No. 1703)

ffor drede ofte my lippes y steke,   [f. 100*r*]
  ffor false reportours that trouhte mys-famed.
ȝut Charitee chargeth me to speke;
    þouȝ trouþe be dred, he nys not ashamed.   4
  Trouþe secheþ non hernes ther los is lamed;
      Trouþe is worschiped at euery des.
  In that kyngdom ther trouþe is blamed,
      God sendes vengeaunce to make trouþe haue pes.   8

Trouþe is messager to ryȝt,
  And ryȝt is counseille to Iustice;
Iustice in goddis stede is dyȝt.
    Do euene lawe to fooll & wyse;   [f. 100*v*]
  Set mesure in euene assise,
      The riȝte weye as lawe ges.
  And lawe be kept, folk nyl not ryse —
      That kyngdom shal haue reste & pes.   16

No. 13. *Written as prose.*

ȝif suche a tale-tellere were
   To a kyng apayre a mannys name,
The kyng shulde boþe partyes here,
    And punysche þe fals for defame.   20
    þan fals men wolde ases for blame;
      for falshed, body & soule it sles.
    ffalshed endes ay in shame;
      and trouþe, in worschipe & in pes.   24

Whanne lawe is put fro riȝt assise,
   And domes-man made by mede,
ffor fawte of lawe ȝif comouns rise,
    þan is a kyngdom most in drede.   28
    ffor whane vengeaunce a comouns lede,
      þei do gret harm er þey asses.
   There no man oþer doþ mysbede,
      That kyngdom shal haue reste & pes.   32

Whan craft riseþ aȝens craft,
   In burgh, toun, or citee,
þey go to lordes whan lawe is laft,
    Whoche party may strengere be.   36
    But wyse men þe sonere se
      By witles wille þey gedre pres.
    Or lordis medle in foly degre,
      Let lawe haue cours in reste & pes.   40

ȝit þere is þe þridde distaunce
   Bryngeþ a kyngdom in moche noyȝe:
Ofte chaunge of gouernaunce
    Of all degre, lowe & hyȝe.   44
    A kyng may not al aspie:
      Summe telle hym soþ, summe telle hym les.
    þe whete fro þe chaf ȝe tryȝe,
      So mowe ȝe leue in reste & pes.   48

I speke not in specyale
  Of oo kyngdom the lawe to telle,
I speke hool in generale
  In eche kyngdom the lawe to telle.   52
  Also is writen in þe gospelle,
    A word þat god hym-seluen ches:
Raþere þan fiȝte, a man go selle
    On of his cloþes, & biȝe hym pes.   56

A worþi knyȝt wol worchip wynne;
  He wil not ȝelde hym þouȝ me þret.
But raþere, as Malice doþ begynne,
  Quenche hit at þe firste het.   60
  ffor and ȝe lete it growe gret,
    Hit brenneþ breme as fyre in gres.
Laweles nouellerye loke ȝe lete,
    So mowe ȝe lyue in reste & pes.   64

Old speche is spoken ȝore,
  What is a kyngdom tresory?
Bestayle, corn stuffed in store;
  Riche comouns, & wyse clergy;   68
  Marchaundes, squyers, chiualry,
    That wol be redy at a res;
  And cheualrous kyng in wittes hyȝe,
    To lede in were and gouerne in pes.   72

Among philosofres wyse,
  In here bokes men writen fynde
þat synne is cause of cowardyse;   [f. 101r]
  Wel-lyuyng man, hardy of kynde;
  Wikked lyuere, graceles, blynde,
    He dredeþ deþ, þe laste mes.
  þe good lyuere haþ god in mynde;
    þat mannys counseil makeþ pes.   80

What kyng that wol haue good name,
  He wol be lad by wys counsayle,
þat loue worschip & dreden shame,
    And boldely dar fende & assayle.   84
  þere wit is, corage may not fayle,
    ffor wysdom neuere worschip les.
  Corage in querell doþ batayle,
    And ende of batayle begynneþ pes.   88

Defaute of wit makeþ long counsayle;
  ffor witteles wordes in ydel spoken,
þe more cost, þe lesse auayle;
    ffor fawte of wyt, purpos broken.   92
  In euyl soule no grace is stoken,
    ffor wikked soule is graceles.
  In good lyuere goddis wille is loken;
    þat mannys counsell makeþ pes.   96

To wete ȝif parlement be wys,
  þe comoun profit wel it preues.
A kyngdom in comouns lys —
    Alle profytes, & alle myscheues.   100
  Lordis wet neuere what comouns greues,
    Til here rentis bigynne to ses.
  þere lordis ere pore, comons releues,
    And mayntene hem in werre & pes.   104

Make god ȝoure ful frend;
  Do þe comaundement þat he bede.
þouȝ all þe world aȝen ȝow wend,
    Be god ȝoure frend, ȝe thar not drede.   108
  ffor þere-as god his frendis lede,
    He saueþ hem boþe on lond & sees,
  Who-so fiȝteþ, god doþ þe dede,
    ffor god is victorie & pes.   112

What kyngdom werreþ hym-self wiþ-ynne,
  Distroyeþ hym-self, and no mo.
Wiþ-oute, here enemys bygynne
  On eche a syde assayle hem so.   116
  þe comouns, þey wil robbe & slo,
    Make fyere, and kyndel stres.
  Whan ryches & manhode is wastede & go,
    þan drede dryueþ to trete pes.   120

The world is like a fals lemman —
  ffayre semblaunt & moche gyle.
Wiþouten heire dyeþ no man;
  God is chief lord of toun & pyle.   124
  God makeþ mony heire in a whyle,
    ffor god ressayueþ eche reles;
  God kan breke hegge & style,
    And make an hey wey to pes.   128

God made lordis gouernoures
  To gouerne puple in vnyte.
þe puple, ne ryches, nys not ȝoures:
  Al is goddis, & so be ȝe.   132
  Eche day ȝe may ȝoure myrrour se.
    Eche man after oþer deses;
  ȝoure auncetres arn gon, after shal ȝe,
    To endeles werre or endeless pes.   136

Eche kyng is sworn to gouernaunce,
  To gouerne goddis puple in riȝt.
Eche kyng bereþ swerd of goddis vengeaunce   [f. 101r]
  To felle goddis foon in fiȝt.   140
  And so doþ euerons honest knyȝt
    That bereþ þe ordre as it wes.
  The plough, þe chirche to mayntene ryȝt,
    Are goddis champyons to kepe þe pes.   144

The world is like a chery fayre,
  Ofte chaungeþ all his þynges.
Riche, pore, foul, & fayre,
  Popes, prelates, & lordynges,   148
    Alle are dedly, and so ben kynges.
      Or deþ lede 3ow in his les,
    Arraye by-tyme 3oure rekenynges,
      And trete wiþ god to gete 3ow pes.   152

What bryngeþ a kyngdom al aboue?
  Wys counseil, and good gouernaunce;
Eche lord wil other loue,
  And rule wel labourrers sustynaunce.   156
    God makeþ for his frendis no destaunce,
      ffor god kan skatre þe grete pres.
    God for his frendis maþ ordynaunce,
      And gouerneþ hem in werre & pes.   160

Good lyf is cause of good name;
  Good name is worthi to haue reueraunce.

  .   .   .   .
  Synne is cause of greuaunce.   164
  Eche kyngdom hongeþ in goddis balaunce;
    Wiþ hym þat holdeþ, wiþ hym þat fles.
  3e haue fre wille, chese 3oure chaunce
    To haue wiþ god werre or pes.   168

163. *Line lacking in MS.*

14. GOD SAVE KING HENRY V (1413)

Digby MS. 102
(Sum. Cat. No. 1703)

God kepe oure kyng, and saue the croun!　　　[f. 110*v*]

Glade in god, call hom ȝoure herte,
　In ioye & blisse ȝoure merþe encres,
And kepe goddis lawe in querte.
　þes holy tyme, lete sorwe ases.　　　　　　4
　Among oure-self, god sende vs pes.
　　þerto eche man be boun:
　To letten fooles of here res,
　　Stonde wiþ þo kyng, mayntene þe croun.　　8

What doþ a kynges crowne signyfye,
　Whan stones & floures on sercle is bent?
Lordis, comouns, & clergye
　To ben all at on assent.　　　　　　　　12
　To kepe þat crowne, take good tent,
　　In wode, in feld, in dale, & downe.
　þe leste lyge-man, wiþ body & rent,
　　He is a parcel of þe crowne.　　　　　　16

What signyfyeþ þo stones aboute?
　Richesse, strengþe, & gret bounte.
Oure townes & castels, þo reme wiþ-oute,
　þey are oure stones of gret pouste.　　　　20
　In pes þey kepe all þis contre,
　　Holynes, contemplacioun.
　God let hem neuer skaterid be,
　　And saue þe kyng, & kepe þe crowne.　　　24

Written as prose.　　　12. at *added in another hand in margin.*

By-ȝonde þe see, and we had nouȝt,
  But all oure enemys so neyȝe vs were,
þouȝ all here gold were hider brouȝt,
    I wolde set hit at lytel store.   28
  Oure enemys wolde coke þerfore
      Wiþ ordynaunce & habergeoun;
    Wynne þat, and wel more —
      Oure landes, oure lyues, þe reme, þe crowne.   32

Ȝif we among oure-self debate,
  þan endeþ floure of chyualrie.
Alle oþere londis þat doþ vs hate,
  Oure feblenes wole aspye.   36
  On euery syde þey wole in hye;   [f. 111r]
    þe stalworþe cast þe feble adoun.
  Ȝif þey wiþ myȝt haue maystrye,
    ffro þe riȝt heire wolde take þe crowne.   40

Ȝif sercle, and floures, & riche stones,
  Were eche a pece fro oþer flet;
Were þe crowne broken ones,
  Hit were ful hard aȝen to knet.   44
  Auyse ȝow er ȝe suffre þat fit.
    Amende, ȝe þat mende mown!
  Ȝe þat ben wysest, cast ȝoure wyt!
    Stonde wiþ þe kyng to kepe þe crowne.   48

To kepe þe crowne, god graunte ȝow grace,
  And let it neuere be to-broken;
ffor word of wynd lityl trespase;
  Non harm nys don, þouȝ word be spoken.   52
  Let wysdom be vnloken,
    Apert & preuyly to rowne.
  ffor non euyll, wille no man be wroken,
    But stonde wiþ riȝt, mayntene þe crowne.   56

A man myȝte be forborn
  ffer fro a kynges place;
Wolde make a kyng to be forsworn
    To lette þe lawe it most not passe.   60
    And make hym wene þat he grace,
      And holy in condicioun,
    And mayntene hym in his trespace,
      While he pykeþ þe stones out of þe crowne.   64

A kyngdom must be gouerned by riȝt,
  To chastyse false þat ar aspyed.
ffalsed and trouþe to-gydre wole fiȝt,
    Til oon þat oþer haþ distroyd.   68
    Til trouþe be fro treson tryed,
      Shal neuere be pes in regyon.
    In all kyngdomes þat man haþ gyed,
      To þe place of vertues, god geueþ þe crowne.   72

Thouȝ falsed trouþe defame,   *veritas*
  Trouþe secheþ non hernes to shewe his speche;
Trouþe of his craft þenkeþ no shame;
    He is bold, alle folk his craft to teche;   76
    And euere by trouþe stondes wreche,
      ffor wreche is goddis champioun.
    Or wreche smyte, god be leche,
      And saue þe kyng, & kepe þe crowne.   80

Loke or þyng þat ȝe begynne;
  Caste before how it wole ende,
Gostly, bodyly, what mowe ȝe wynne.
    Eche man destroyȝe his best frend —   84
    So dede fflaundres. how dede it wende?
      Of noblay þey han lore þe sown;
    Pray we god his bowe of wraþþe vnbende,
      And saue þe kyng, & kepe þe crowne.   88

81. or MS. of.

God ȝeueþ his doom to alle kynges þat be;
　　As a god, in erþe a kyng haþ myȝt.
Holy writ byd, blissed be he
　　In alle tymes þat demeþ ryȝt.　　　　　　　　　　92
　　　Men do in derk, god seeþ in lyȝt.
　　　　Synne, morþere, derne tresoun,
　　　Not may be hyd fro goddis syȝt.
　　　　To ryȝtwys Iuge, god ȝeueþ þe crowne.　　　96

That lord loueþ lityl hym-selue　　　　　　　　　[f. 111v]
　　þat ȝeueþ his blisse for sorwe & woo;
ffor þe loue of ten or twelue,
　　Make alle folk his foo,　　　　　　　　　　　100
　　And lese þe loue of god also
　　　ffor fawte of perfeccyone.
　　þouȝ he had no vauntage but of þo,
　　　He myȝte were a symple crowne.　　　　　　104

Eche a kyng haþ goddis power,
　　Of lyf & leme to saue & spille.
He muste make god his partener,
　　And do not his owen wille.　　　　　　　　　108
　　ffor god resceyueþ eche pore mannys bille,
　　　And of here playnt, god hereþ þe sowne.
　　Sette ȝoure assise in euene skille,
　　　Counseile þe kyng to kepe þe crowne.　　　112

The fadir, þe wanton child wole kenne,
　　Chastyse wiþ ȝerde & bete hit sore.
So after, þe fadyr þe ȝerde wole brenne,
　　When child is wys & takeþ to lore.　　　　　116
　　We han ben goddis ȝerde ȝore;
　　　Chastysed kyngdom, castell, & towne.
　　Twyggis of oure ȝerde we haue forlore.
　　　God saue þe kyng, & kepe þe crowne.　　　120

111. assise *supplied*.

Englische men dede maystryȝes make;
   Þurgh all þe world, here word it sprong.
Cristen & heþen þey mad to quake,
    Tok & slowen kynges strong.   124
     God let neuere werre be vs among,
      To lese þat blo of gret renowne;
     Ne neuere oure riȝt be turned to wrong.
      God saue þe kyng, & kepe þe crowne.   128

Among oure-self, ȝif fiȝt be raysed,
   Þan stroye we oure awen nest.
Þat haþ victor, wole be euel payed;
    So many good men ben lest.   132
    Ȝit is beter bowe þan brest.
     Eche man is bounden to resoun.
    Ȝe þat ben wysest, take þe best.
     Conseile þe kyng, mayntene þe crowne.   136

A comyns myȝt sone be shent,
   Wiþ-outen kyng or gouernour;
And a kyng wiþoute rent
    Myȝt liȝtly trussen his tresour.   140
    ffor comons mayntene lordis honour,
     Holy chirche, and religyoun;
    ffor comouns is þe fayrest flour
     Þat euere god sette on erþely crown.   144

Gode, lete þis kyngdom neuere be lorn
   Among oure-self in no distance!
Oþer kyngdomes lauȝhe vs not to skorn,
    And sey, "for synne, god send vengeance." 148
    God ȝeue vs space of repentance,
     Good lyf, and deuocioun.
    And god, kepe in þy gouernance
     Oure comely kyng, and saue þe crowne.   152

133. MS. berst.   149. MS. repetance.

15.   THE FOLLIES OF THE DUKE
OF BURGUNDY (1419)

Digby MS. 102
(Sum. Cat. No. 1703)

A remembraunce of LII folyes.   [f. 115*r*]

Loke how fflaundres doþ fare wiþ his folyhede!
    Durste no man dygge after trouþe wiþ no manere toles.
To wynne wrongly wele, wod þey gan wede,   [f. 115*v*]
    But werkis of wys men were cast vnder stoles.   4
Glosers counseled lordis for to take mede,
    To maken hem riche, and here lordis pore foles.
Whan þe souereyns were set here sogettis to drede,
    þe glosers skulked away, for shame of here sooles.   8
        ffalsed shal neuere ben ateynt
          Til Iuge here eche mannys pleynt;
            Redresse, & make an ende,
            Or ellys to mercy bende;   12
          Make hem kyssen & be frende
        þat were fon feynt.

ffyfty folyes ben, & two —
    Alle þo y wole mynne among.   16
To triste in trete to his fo
    þat haþ begyled hem ofte & long;
And hate hem þat telle hym so,
    And wilfully wolle suffre wrong.   20
It is worthy he smerte & be wo,
    þat of his owen skyn wole kerue a thong.
        þat chepen moche, & not han to paye,
        And wiþ his lord to homly wole playe;   24

Written as prose.

Swere moche, & not be trowed;
Boste moche, & not allowed;
Threte alle men, & neuere on-bowed:
All are folyes, þat y say.   28

He is a fool, þat werre wole wake,
   Þat may not maynten it wiþ mede,
And so moche vndertake
   Þat wot wel he may not spede.   32
And of his neyȝebour his enemy make
   ffor a straunge mannys dede;
And he þat mesure wole forsake,
   And nedles put hym-self in drede.   36
      Of mannys deþ haue no rouþe,
      But hate hem þat tellen hym trouþe;
       Loue hym þat cherische hym in synne,
       And suche games begynne   40
       Where þat he wot he may not wynne,
      But besyen hym in slouþe.

He is a fool, þat no good can,
   Ne non wole lere, but slow in dede.   44
A gret fool, y holde þat man,
   Þat of his enemys haþ no drede.
Þurgh suche foly, fflaundres be-gan;
   Of after perile þey tok non hede.   48
Hit is worthy he ete bred of bran,
   Þat wiþ floure his foo wil fede.
      And truste al in gloser charmes,
      In hyndryng in worschip of armes,   52
       And lette lawe it mot not syt,
       And conscience away flyt,
       May brynge a lord, er þat he wyt,
      Emyddis grete harmes.   56

fflaundres was þe richest land, and meriest to mynne;
   Now is it wrappid in wo, & moche welþe raft.

ffor defaute of Iustice, and syngulere to wynne,
    þey were rebell, to ryse craft aȝen craft.   60
Here lord had part of þe foly þey were wounden ynne;
    ffor-thy he les his lordshipe, & here fraunchise raft.
Here enemys lawhen hem to skorne, & seyn, "for synne,
    Of here banere of grace, god broken haþ þe shaft."   64
        When prelat is forbode to preche,   [f. 116r]
        No trewe man trouþe dar teche;
            Encresyng of temperalte
            Suspende spiritualte.   68
        What land is gouerned in þat degre,
        May wayte after wreche.

I holde hym a fool, pouȝ he be wys,
    þat spekeþ among men of name   72
þat at his wysdom set no prys,
    But skorne hym & don blame.
And he þat telleþ where peryle lys,
    And gete no þonk but harm & shame;   76
And he þat pleyneþ, y holde hym nys,
    þat get no mendys, but dowble grame.
        By þese poyntes fflaundres was lest;
        Now is it out of rule & of rest.   80
            Drede is here chef gayte.
            So eche man on hem bayte,
            þat ȝet þey honge in awayte
        Of a newe conquest.   84

He þat myȝt thryue, and nel not thee,
    Ne his owen harmes knawe,
Apert ne in preuytee,
    Serue god for loue ne awe,   88
Ne gouerne wel his owen degre,
    Ne rule hymself in ryȝtwys lawe,
Whan wyse men fro hym fle —
    þen god his grace wole fro hem drawe.   92

Þat moche wynneþ, and no-thyng wole haue,
But ȝeue it awey to nedeles þat craue,
   Aȝens conscience despit
    Borwe moche, & neuere quyt;   96
   When god for þat gylt smyt,
  What glosere can þat wounde saue?

Þat freek may wel be holden a fool,
   Þat wayueþ wit & worcheþ by wille,   100
And skippe into sclaundre scol,
   And scorne hym þat telleþ hym skylle,
And lyue in Lenton as in ȝool,
   His flesch in foly to fulfille.   104
Þouȝ þe dotard deye in dool,
   Þe ryȝtwys nel not rewe his ylle.
     Who-so wil not knowe his awen astat,
     Ne deliuere chekkys er þat he be mat,   108
      He shal haue worldis wondryng,
      And his soule hyndryng,
      And ay in paynes pondryng.
     To mende þanne, is to late.   112

Of all folk vppon fold, y fynde but foure trewe,
   Þat don here deuere dewely, and take no mede:
Syknes is oon, and sorw doþ sewe,
   Þe thridde hat deþ, and þe fierþe drede.   116
Þey clayme vs by custom, for þey oure kyn knewe, *Nota*
   And endid wiþ oure aunsetres tyl þey to erþe ȝede.
Þey spare prynce no pore, old ne newe,
   ffor þey crepe in-to his cors, and cloþe hem in his wede. 120
     Drede bryngeþ man to buxomnes;
     Sorwe of herte makeþ synnes les;
      Syknes, breþe stekenyng,
      And bowe to a bekenyng,   124
      And bryngeþ hem to rekenyng,
     Tyl deþ all redresse.

POPULAR STRUGGLES I
THE GREAT REVOLT

16. ON THE EVIL STATE OF ENGLAND (1381)

Cambridge Univ. MS. Dd.14.2

Man be ware and be no fool: [f. 312r]
þenke apon þe ax, and of þe stool!
þe stool was hard, þe ax was scharp,
þe iiij ȝere of kyng Richard.   4

17. JOHN BALL'S LETTERS, I (1381)

Stow, *Annales*

John Ball Saint Mary Priest, greeteth well all manner of
men, and biddeth them in name of the Trinitie, Father,
Sonne, & holy Ghost, stand manlike together in truth, &
helpe truth, and truth shall helpe you: *d*

now raygneth pride in price,
couetise is holden wise
lechery without shame,
gluttonie without blame,   4
enuye raygneth with reason,
and sloath is taken in great season,
God doe boote for nowe is time.   Amen.

18.   JOHN BALL'S LETTERS, II (1381)

Royal MS. 13.E.ix

littera Iohannis balle missa communibus Estsexie.   [f. 287r
                                                            col. i]

Iohan schep, som-tyme seynte marie prest of ȝork, and now
of colchestre, Greteth wel Iohan nameles & Iohn þe mullere
and Iohon cartere, and biddeþ hem þei bee war of gyle in
borugh, and stondeth to-gidere in godes name, and biddeþ   *d*
Pers plouȝman / go to his werk and chastise wel hobbe   [col. ii]
þe robbere; and takeþ wiþ ȝow Iohan Trewman and alle hijs
felawes and no mo, and loke schappe ȝou to on heued and
no mo.   *h*

    Iohan þe mullere haþ y-grounde smal, smal, smal.
    þe kynges sone of heuene schal paye for al.
    be war or þe be wo.
    knoweþ ȝour freend fro ȝour foo.   4
    haueth y-now & seith hoo!
    and do wel and bettre and fleth synne,
    and sekeþ pees and hold ȝow þer-inne.
    and so biddeþ Iohan trewaman and alle his felawes.   8

hanc litteram Idem Iohannes balle confessus est scripsisse,
et communibus transmisisse, et plura alia fatebatur et
fecit; propter-que, ut diximus, traitus, suspensus, et
decollatus apud sanctum albanum Idibus Iulij, presente   *l*
rege, et cadauer eius quadripertitum quatuor regni
cuntatibus missum est.

19.   THE COURSE OF REVOLT (1381)

MS. Digby 196
(Sum. Cat. No. 1797)

The taxe hath tened vs alle,   [f. 20v]
    probat hoc mors tot validorum;

c. þat *struck through after* hem.   d. to-gidere MS. to gidedre.
f. and *dotted for expunction after* hijs.   *Written as prose.*

The Kyng þerof had small,
    ffuit in manibus cupidorum.   4
yt had ful hard hansell,
    dans causam fine dolorum;
vengeaunce nedes most fall,
    propter peccata malorum.   8

In Kent care be-gan,
    mox infestando potentes;
On rowtes þo Rebawdes þey ran,
    Sua turpida arma ferentes.   12
ffoles þey dred no man,
    Regni Regem, neque gentes;
laddes þey were þere Cheveteyns,
    Sine iure fere superantes.   16

laddes lowde they lowght,
    Clamantes voce sonora,
The bischop wan þey slowght,
    Et corpora plura decora.   20
Maners down þey drowght,
    In regno non meliora;
Harmes they dyde y-nowght;
    habuerunt libera lora.   24

Iak strawe made yt stowte
    Cum profusa comitiua,
And seyd al schuld hem lowte,
    Anglorum corpora viua.   28
Sadly can they schowte,   [f. 21r]
    pulsant pietatis oliua,
þe wycche were wont to lowte,
    aratrum traducere stiua.   32

5. con *struck through before* hansell.
21. mareres *struck through before* maners.

Hales, þat dowghty knyӡght,
   quo splenduit Anglia tota,
dolefully he was dyӡght,
   Cum stultis pace remota.   36
There he myӡght not fyght,
   nec Christo soluere vota.

Savoy semely sette,
   heu! funditus igne cadebat.   40
Arcan don there þey bett,
   Et eos virtute premebat.
deth was ther dewe dett,
   qui captum quisque ferebat.   44

Oure kyng myght have no rest,
   Alii latuere cauerna;
To ride he was ful prest,
   recolendo gesta paterna.   48
Iak straw dovn þey cast
   Smethefeld virtute superna.
god, as þou may best,
   Regem defende, guberna.   52

20. *THE INSURRECTION AND EARTHQUAKE*
(1382)

MS. Vernon
(Sum. Cat. No. 3938)

Yit is God a Curteis lord,   [f. 411r col. ii]
   And Mekeliche con schewe his miht;
ffayn he wolde bringe til a-cord
   Monkuynde, to liue in treuþe ariht.   4

38. *An extra line added:* Sint te sua crimina lota.
44. MS. frebat.   48. MS. superna.

Allas! whi set we þat lord so liht,
    And al to foule wiþ him we fare?
In world is non so wys no wiht,
    þat þei ne haue warnyng to be ware.   8

We may not seye, but ȝif we lyȝe,
    þat god wol vengaunce on vs stele;
ffor openly we seo wiþ eiȝe
    þis warnynges beoþ wonder & fele.   12
    But nou þis wrecched worldes wele
      Makeþ vs liue in sunne and care.
    Of Mony Merueyles I may of Mele,
      And al is warnyng to be ware.   16

Whon þe Comuynes bi-gan to ryse,
    Was non so gret lord, as I gesse,
þat þei in herte bi-gon to gryse,
    And leide heore Iolyte in presse.   20
    Wher was þenne heore worþinesse,
      Whon þei made lordes droupe & dare?
    Of alle wyse men I take witnesse,
      þis was a warnyng to be ware.   24

Bi-fore, ȝif men hedde haad a graas,
    Lordes mihte wondur weel
Han let þe rysing þat þer was,
    But þat god þouȝte ȝit sumdel   28
    þat lordes schulde his lordschup feel,
      And of heore lordschipe make hem bare.
    Trust þer-to as trewe as steel,
      þis was a warnyng to be ware.   32

And also, whon þis eorþe qwok,
    Was non so proud, he nas a-gast,
And al his Iolite for-sok,
    And þouȝt on god whil þat hit last;   36

And alsone as hit was ouer-past,
   Men wox as vuel as þei dude are.
Vche mon in his herte may cast;
   þis was a warnyng to be ware.   40

ffor-soþe, þis was a lord to drede,
   So sodeynly mad Mon agast;
Of gold & seluer þei tok non hede,
   But out of her houses ful sone þei past.   44
   Chaumbres, Chimeneys al to-barst,
      Chirches & castels foule gon fare,
   Pinacles, Steples to grounde hit cast;
      And al was warnyng to be ware.   48

þe Meuyng of þis eorþe, I-wis,
   þat schulde bi cuynde be ferm & stabele,
A pure verrey toknyng hit is,
   þat Mennes hertes ben chaungable;   52
   And þat to falsed þei ben most Abul,   [f. 411r col. iii]
      ffor with good feiþ wol we not fare.
   Leef hit wel wiþ-outen fabel,
      þis was a warnyng to be ware.   56

þe Rysing of þe comuynes in londe,
   þe Pestilens, and þe eorþe-quake —
þeose þreo þinges, I vnderstonde,
   Beo-tokenes þe grete vengaunce & wrake   60
   þat schulde falle for synnes sake,
      As þis Clerkes conne de-clare.
   Nou may we chese to leue or take,
      ffor warnyng haue we to ben ware.   64

Euere I drede, be my trouþe,
   þer may no warnyng stande in sted;
We ben so ful of synne and slouþe,
   þe schame is passed þe sched of hed,   68

And we liggen riht heuy as led,
　　Cumbred in þe ffendes snare.
I leeue þis beo vr beste Red,
　　To þenke on þis warnyng & be ware.

Sikerliche, I dar wel saye,
　　In such a plyt þis world is in,
Mony for wynnyng wolde bi-traye
　　ffader and Moder and al his kin.   76
　　Nou were heih tyme to be-gin
　　　　To A-mende vr mis & wel to fare;
　　Vr bagge hongeþ on a sliper pyn,
　　　　Bote we of þis warnyng be ware.   80

Be war, for I con sey no more,
　　Be war for vengauns of trespas,
Be war and þenk vppon þis lore!
　　Be war of þis sodeyn cas;   84
　　And ȝit Be war while we haue spas,
　　　　And þonke þat child þat Marie bare,
　　Of his gret godnesse and his gras,
　　　　Send vs such warnyng to be ware.   88

POPULAR STRUGGLES II
LATER DISCONTENT

21. *THE YORKSHIRE PARTISANS (1392)*

Stowe MS. 393

In the Countrey hard was wee,   [f. 99*v*]
that in our soken shrewes should be
　　with all forto bake;

Among you fryers it is so,   4
and other orders many mo,
   whether they slepe or wake.

And yet will ilke-an hel up other
and meynteyne him als his brother,   8
   both in wrong & right;
And also will in stand & stoure
mayntayn our neighbour
   with all our might.   12

Ilke man may come & goe
among us both to & fro,
   say you sikerly.
but hething will we suffer non —   16
neither of hobb nor of Ion,
   with what man he be.

for vnkind we ware
If we sufferd lesse or mare   20
   any villan hething,
But it wer quit double againe,
and accord, & be full fayne
   to byde dressing.   24

And on that purpose yet we stand:
who-so doth vs any wrong
   In what place it fall,
yet he might als weele,   28
als haue I hap & heel,
   Doe againe us all.

16. **MS.** suffen.   18. **MS.** with what may he mery be.
21. **MS.** bethning.

22.   *A SONG OF FREEDOM (1434)*

MS. Lat. theol. d.1
(Sum. Cat. No. 29746)

ffor þou art comen of good blood,   [f. 174r]
or for art a riche man of good;
ffor þou art well loued of moo,
& for þou art a ȝong man al-soo.   4

þin ffadere was a bond man,
þin moder curtesye non can.
Euery beste þat leuyth now
Is of more fredam þan þow!   8

ȝif þou art pore, þan art þou fre.
ȝif þou be riche, þan woo is þe.
for but þou spendyte well ere þou goo,
þin song for euer is "well-ay-woo."   12

23.   *THE DAY WILL DAWN (1445)*

B. M. Addit. MS. 40166(C)

Who wot nowe þat ys here,   [f. 12v]
Where he schall be anoder yere?

Anoder ȝere hit may betyde
þis compeny to be full wyde,
And neuer on-odyr to abyde;
  Criste may send now sych a ȝere.   4

Anoþer ȝere hit may befall
þe lest þat is withyn this hall
To be more mastur þen we all;
  Cryste may send now sych a ȝere.   8

No. 23. 8. MS. Cryste. *Rest of line supplied.*

This lordis that ben wonder grete,
They threton powre men for to bete;
Hyt lendith lytull in hur threte;
    Cryste may send sich a yere.   12

24. THE KENTISH INSURRECTION (1450)

Magdalen Coll. Oxford
Charter Misc. 306

God be oure gyde,
and then schull we spede.
   Who-so-euur say nay,
ffalse for ther money reuleth!   4
Trewth for his tales spolleth!
   God seend vs a ffayre day!
   a-wey traytours, a-wey!

25. INJUSTICES AT COVENTRY (1496)

Coventry Corporation Leet Book

Wheruppon ij seducious billes wer founde i-sette vppon   [f. 278r]
þe Mynster durr in þe feste of seynt Anne, & a-noþer was
cast, etc. Wherof the tenour her-after ensuen:

The cyte is bond that shuld be fre!
The right is holden fro þe Cominalte!
our Comiens þat at Lammas open shuld be cast,
They be closed in & hegged full fast.   4
And he þat speketh for our right is in þe hall —
And þat is shame for yewe & for vs all.
You cannot denygh hit but he is your broþer,
& to boþe Gildes he hath paid as moch as anoþer,   8
They þat woll be broþer to þe Gildes or þer-to pay.

We haue no more to lose, þe soth for to say,
ffor eny fauour or frenship þe comiens with yowe fynde,
But pyke awey our thryfte & make vs all blynde.   12
And euer ye haue nede to þe Cominalte —
Such favour as ye shewe vs, such shall ye see:
We may speke feir & bid you good morowe,
But luff with our hertes shull ye haue non!   16
Cherish þe Cominalte & se they haue their right,
ffor drede of a worse chaunce be day or be nyght!
þe best of you all, litell worth shuld be,
And ye had not helpe of the Cominalte.   20
He luffeth me well þat telleth me for my goode:
"Mend þat is amysse for movyng of your mode."
On may her be a-noþer þat he shall not fynde,
But ye shall her of sum oþer what shal be þe ende!   24

POPULAR BALLADS

26. THE BATTLE OF OTTERBURN (1388)

Cotton MS. Cleop. C.iv

Yt fell abowght the lamasse tyde,   [f. 64r]
   Whan husbonds wynnes ther haye,
the dowghtye dowglasse bowynd hym to ryde
   In ynglond to take a praye.   4

the yerlle of fyffe, wyth-owghten Stryffe,
   he bowynd hym over sulway;
the grete wolde ever to-gether ryde —
   that Raysse they may rewe for aye.   8

Over hoppertope hyll they came in,
   and so dowyn by rodelyffe crage;
Upon grene lynton they lyghted dowyn,
   styrande many a stage.   12

and boldely brente northomberlond,
   and haryed many a towyn;
they dyd owr ynglyssh men grete wrange,
   to batell that were not bowyn.   16

Than spake a berne upon the bent,
   Of comforte that was not colde,
and sayd, "we have brente northomberlond;
   We have all welth in holde.   20

"now we have haryed all bamborowe schyre,
   all the welth in the worlde have wee.
I rede we ryde to newe castell,
   so styll and stalwurthlye."   24

Upon the morowe, when it was day,
   the standerds schone full bryght;
to the newe castell the toke the waye,
   and thether they cam full ryght.   28

Syr henry perssy laye at the new castell —   [f. 64v]
   I tell yow wyth-owtten drede;
he had byn a marchman all hys dayes,
   and kepte barwyke upon twede.   32

to the newe castell when they cam,
   the skottes they cryde on hyght,
"Syr hary perssy, and thow byste wyth-in,
   com to the fylde and fyght.   36

12. MS. many a styrande stage.

"for we have brente northomberlonde,
 thy erytage good and ryght;
and syne my logeyng I have take,
 wyth my brande dubbyd many a knyght."   40

syr harry perssy cam to the walls,
 the skottyssh oste for to se;
and sayd, "and thow hast brente northomberlond,
 full sore it rewyth me.   44

"yf thow hast haryed all bamborowe schyre,
 thow hast done me grete Envye;
for the trespasse thow hast me done,
 the tone of us schall dye!"   48

"where schall I byde the," sayd the dowglas,
 "or where wylte thow com to me?"
"at otterborne in the hygh way,
 ther mast thow well logeed be.   52

"The roo full rekeles ther sche Runnes,
 To make the game and glee;
The fawken and the fesaunt both,
 among the holtes on hye.   56

"Ther mast thow have thy welth at wyll, [f. 65r]
 Well looged ther mast be.
yt schall not be long or I com the tyll,"
 sayd syr harry perssye.   60

"there schall I byde the," sayd the dowglas,
 "by the fayth of my bodye."
"thether schall I com," sayd syr harry perssy,
 "my trowth I plyght to the."   64

53-56. *The first letter of the first word in each line is cut.*
54. MS. game a.   55. MS. fesaint.

a pype of wyne he gave them over the walles,
   for-soth as I yow saye.
ther he mayd the dowglasse drynke,
   and all hys ost that daye.   **68**

the dowglas turnyd hym home-warde agayne,
   for-soth wyth-owghten naye;
he toke hys logeyng at oterborne
   upon a wedyns-day.   **72**

and ther he pyght hys standerd dowyn,
   hys gettyng more and lesse,
and syne he warned hys men to goo
   to chose ther geldyngs gresse.   **76**

a skottysshe knyght hoved upon the bent,
   a wache, I dare well saye;
so was he ware on the noble perssy
   In the dawnyng of the daye.   **80**

he prycked to hys pavyleon dore,
   as faste as he myght ronne,
"awaken, dowglas," cryed the knyght,
   "for hys love, that syttes in trone.   **84**

"Awaken, dowglas," cryed the knyght,   **[f. 65v]**
   "for thow maste waken wyth wynne;
yonder have I spyed the prowde perssye,
   and seven stondardes wyth hym."   **88**

"nay, by my trowth," the dowglas sayed,
   "it ys but a fayned taylle.
he durst not loke on my brede banner
   for all ynglonde so haylle.   **92**

77. bent *added at side in another hand*; MS. beste.
85. *line repeated in* MS.

"was I not yester-daye at the newe castell,
    that stonds so fayre on tyne?
for all the men the perssy had,
    he cowde not garre me ones to dyne."   96

he stepped owt at hys pavelyon dore
    to loke and it were lesse.
"araye you, lordyngs, one and all,
    for here by-gynnes no peysse.   100

"the yerle of mentaye, thow arte my eme,
    the forwarde I gyve to the;
the yerlle of huntlay, cawte and kene,
    he schall be wyth the.   104

"the lorde of bowghan in armure bryght
    on the other hand he schall be;
lorde Ihonstone and lorde maxwell,
    they to schall be wyth me.   108

"swynton, fayre fylde upon yowr pryde,
    to batell make yow bowen;
syr davy skotte, syr water stewarde,
    syr Ihon of agurstone."   112

                a fytte   [f. 66r]

The perssy cam by-fore hys oste,
    wych was ever a gentyll knyght,
upon the dowglass lowde can he crye,
    "I wyll holde that I have hyght.   116

"for thow haste brente northomberlonde,
    and done me grete Envye;
for thys trespasse thow hast me done,
    the tone of us schall dye."   120

102. MS. foward.   104. he MS. ye.

the dowglas answerde hym agayne
   wyth grete wurds upon hye,
and sayd, "I have twenty agaynst the one,
   by-holde, and thow maste see."   124

Wyth þat the perssay was grevyd sore,
   for-soth as I yow saye;
he lyghted dowyn upon hys foote,
   and schoote hys horsse clene awaye.   128

Every man sawe that he dyd soo,
   that ryall was ever in rowght;
Every man schoote hys horsse hym froo,
   and lyght hym rowynde abowght.   132

thus syr hary perssye toke the fylde,
   for-soth as I yow saye,
Iesu cryste in heven on hyght
   dyd helpe hym well that daye.   136

but nyne thow3and, ther was no moo,
   the cronykle wyll not layne.
forty thowsande of skottes and fowre
   that day fowght them agayne.   140

but when the batell by-ganne to ioyne,
   In hast ther cam a knyght.
The letters fayre furth hath he tayne,   [f. 66v]
   and thus he sayd full ryght: 144

"my lorde, yowr father he gretes yow well,
   wyth many a noble knyght,
he desyres yow to byde
   that he may see thys fyght.   148

134. MS. for soth soth.

"þe baron of grastoke ys come owt of the west,
    wyth hym a noble companye;
all they loge at yowr fathers thys nyght,
    and the batell fayne wolde they see."   152

"for Iesus love," sayd syr harye perssy,
    "that dyed for yow and me,
wende to my lorde my father agayne,
    and saye thow sawe me not wyth yee.   156

"my trowth ys plyght to yonne skottyssh knyght,
    it nedes me not to layne,
that I schulde byde hym upon thys bent,
    and I have hys trowth agayne.   160

"and if that I wynde of thys growende,
    for-soth, on-fowghten awaye,
he wolde me call but a kowarde knyght
    In hys londe another daye.   164

"yet had I lever to be rynde and Rente,
    by mary that mykell maye,
then ever my manhood schulde be reprovyd
    wyth a skotte another day.   168

"wherfore schote, archars, for my sake,
    and let scharpe arowes flee!
mynstrells, playe up for yowr waryson,   [f. 67r]
    and well quyt it schall bee.   172

"every man thynke on hys trewe love,
    and marke hym to the trenite;
for to god I make myne avowe
    thys day wyll I not flee."   176

the blodye harte in the dowglas armes,
   hys standerde stode on hye;
that every man myght full well knowe,
   by-syde stode starres thre.   180

the whyte lyon on the ynglysshe perte,
   forsoth as I yow sayne,
the lucetts and the cressawntts both,
   the skotts fowght them agayne.   184

upon sent andrewe lowde can they crye,
   and thrysse they schowte on hyght.
and syne marked them on owr ynglysshe men,
   as I have tolde yow ryght.   188

sent george the bryght, owr ladyes knyght,
   to name they were full fayne.
owr ynglyssh men they cryde on hyght,
   and thrysse the schowtte agayne.   192

wyth that, scharpe arowes bygan to flee,
   I tell yow in sertayne;
men of armes by-ganne to Ioyne —
   many a dowghty man was ther slayne.   196

The perssy and the dowglas mette,   [f. 67v]
   that ether of other was fayne;
they swapped to-gether, whyll that the swette
   wyth swords of fyne collayne,   200

tyll the bloode from ther bassonetts Ranne,
   as the roke doth in the rayne.
"yelde the to me," sayd the dowglas,
   "or ells thow schalt be slayne.   204

183. MS. cressawtts.   199. MS. schapped.

"for I see by thy bryght bassonet
   thow arte sum man of myght;
and so I do by thy burnysshed brande,
   thow arte an yerle, or ells a knyght."   208

"by my good faythe," sayd the noble perssye,
   "now haste thow rede full ryght.
yet wyll I never yelde me to the,
   Whyll I may stonde and fyght."   212

they swapped to-gether, whyll that they swette,
   Wyth swordes scharpe and long;
ych on other so faste thee beette,
   tyll ther helmes cam in peyses dowyn.   216

The perssy was a man of strenghth,
   I tell yow in thys stounde;
he smote the dowglas at the swordes length
   that he fell to the growynde.   220

the sworde was scharpe and sore can byte,
   I tell yow in sertayne,
to the harte he cowde hym smyte,
   thus was the dowglas slayne.   224

The stonderds stode styll on eke a syde,   [f. 68r]
   wyth many a grevous grone;
ther the fowght the day and all the nyght,
   and many a dowghty man was slayne.   228

ther was no freke that ther wolde flye,
   but styffely in stowre can stond;
ychone hewyng on other whyll they myght drye,
   wyth many a bayllefull bronde.   232

ther was slayne upon the skottes syde,
   for-soth and sertenly,
syr Iames a dowglas ther was slayne,
   that day that he cowde dye.   236

the yerlle of mentaye he was slayne,
   grysely groned upon the growynd;
syr davy skotte, syr water stewarde,
   syr Iames of agurstonne.   240

syr charlles morrey in that place,
   that never a fote wold flee;
syr hewe maxwell, a lorde he was,
   wyth the dowglas dyd he dye.   244

ther was slayne upon the skottes syde,
   for-soth as I yow saye,
of fowre and forty thowsande skotts
   went but eyghtene awaye.   248

ther was slayne upon the ynglysshe syde,
   for-soth and sertenlye,
a gentell knyght, syr Ihon fechewe —
   yt was the more pety.   252

syr Iames harebotell ther was slayne,
   for hym ther hartes were sore;
The gentyll lovell ther was slayne,   [f. 68*v*]
   that the perssys standerd bore.   256

ther was slayne upon the ynglyssh perte,
   for-soth as I yow saye,
of nyne thowsand ynglyssh men
   fyve hondert cam awaye.   260

255. MS. covell.

the other were slayne in the fylde —
   cryste kepe ther sowlles from wo,
seyng ther was so fewe fryndes
   agaynst so many a foo.   264

Then on the morne they mayde them beerys
   of byrch and haysell graye;
many a wydowe wyth wepyng teyres
   ther makes they fette awaye.   268

thys fraye by-gan at otterborne,
   bytwene the nyght and the day;
ther the dowglas lost hys lyffe,
   and the perssy was lede awaye.   272

then was ther a skottyssh prisoner tayne,
   syr hewe mongomery was hys name,
for-soth as I yow saye,
   he borowed the perssy home agayne.   276

now let us all for the perssy pray,
   to Iesu most of myght,
to bryng hys sowlle to the blysse of heven,
   for he was a gentyll knyght.   280

finis.

27. THE BATTLE OF AGINCOURT (1415)

Cotton MS. Cleop. C.iv

And in Aȝyngcorte felde owre kynge favght with þe ffrenchmen [f. 24v]
þe ffryday tofore þe day of symond and Iude. & þer all þe
ryall powere of ffrensshemen come aȝenst owre kyng & his litill
meyne, save þe ffrensshe kynge, & þe Dolfyne, and þe duke of   *d*

Borgoyn, & þe duke of Barre, elles all þe lordys of ffrawnce
lay tofore þe kynge in his hy-way as he schuld passe towarde
calys, enbateylyd in iij° batayles, as þe ffrensshemen sayde
hem-silfe, þe Nowmbre of lx m¹ men of armes (& þo were þe   *h*
faireste men of armys þat euer any man saw in any plase). And
owre kyng with his litill mayne sey well he must nedys fyȝte,
or he / myght not come to Calays by þe hy way. And þan he   [f. 25*r*]
sayde to his lordys & to his mayne: 'Syres & ffelowes, þe   *l*
ȝondere mayne þenk to lett vs of owre way. & þei wil nat come
to vs, lete euery man preue hym-silfe a good man þis day, &
avant baneres, in þe best tym of the yere; for as I am trew
kynge & knyght, for me þis day schall neuer Inglond rawnsome   *p*
pay. erste many a wyght man schall leue is weddes, for here
erste to deth I wil be dyght; & þerfore lordynges, for the love
of swete Ihesu, helpe mayntene Inglondes ryght þis day. Allso,
archers, to yow I praye, no fote þat ȝe fle away, erste be we   *t*
all beten in þis felde. And þenke, be englysshemen, þat
neuer wold fle at no batelle, for aȝenste one of vs þowþe þer
be tene, þenke criste wil help vs in owre ryght. Bot I wold
no blode wer spilte, cryste helpe me, so now in þis case, Bot *x*
þo þat been cause of this trespase. when þou sittest in
Iugment, þer holde me excused tofore þi face, as þou art god
omnipotent. but passe we all now in fere, Duke, Erle, and
Bachelere; of all owre synnys he make vs sekere, Ientil Ihesu, *bb*
borne of Marye, and as for vs þou deydyst on good fryday, as
þi will was, so brynge vs to þi blisse an hy, and graunte vs
þer to haue / a place. Do & bete on ffaste.' owre kynge tho   [f. 25*v*]
bad wyþe full glad chere, and so thei dyde at þat word, lord,   *ff*
knyght, & archere. þer men myght see a semble sade þat turnyd
many on to tene & tray, for many a lorde þer ryght low lay, þat
commen was of blod full gent. By evensong tyme, soþely to say,
þer helpe vs god omnipotent.   *jj*

Stedes þer stumbelyd in þat stownde,
    þat stod stere stuffed vnder stele;
With gronyng grete þei felle to grownde,
    Here sydes federed whan þei gone fele.   4
    Owre lord þe kynge he foght ryght wele,
        Scharpliche on hem his spere he spent,

p. pay *struck through after* Inglond.
q. erste MS. r *inserted above line.*
4. fle *struck through after* gone.

Many on seke he made þat sele,
  Thorow myght of god omnipotent.   8

The Duke of glowcestre also þat tyde
  Manfully, with his mayne,
Wondes he wroght þer wondere wyde.
  The Duke of ȝorke also, perde,   12
  ffro his kyng no fote wold he flee,
    Til his basonet to his brayn was bent;
  Now on his sowle he have pete,
    Mersifull god omnipotent.   16

Hontyngdon & Oxford bothe
  Were wondere fers all in þat fyght;
That erste was glade þai made ful wrothe,
  Thorow hem many on-to deth were dyght.   20
  The Erles fowghten with mayn & myȝt,
    Rich havberke thei rofe & rente;   [f. 26r]
  Owre kyng to helpe thei were full lyght —
    Now blesse hem god omnipotent.   24

The erle of Suthfolk gan hem assaylle,
  And ser Richarde kyghle in þat stede,
Here lyves þei losten in þat bataile,
  With dyntes sore þer were thei dede.   28
  Ȝif eny man byde eny good bede
    Vnto god with good entent,
  To þo two sowles it mote be mede,
    Gracius god omnipotent.   32

Sire William Bowsere, as fovle in fright,
  Preste he þer was vpon his pray,
Erpyngham he come hym with,
  Her manhode help vs well þat day.   36

33. fright MS. r *inserted above line.*

Off ffrensshe folk in þat afray
   Thre dukes were dede, with doleful dent,
And fyve Erles, þis is no nay.
   Ther holpe vs god omnipotent.   40

Lordes of name an hunderde and mo
   Bitterly þat bargayn bowght;
Two þovsand Cot-armers also,
   After her sorow þedere thei sowght.   44
   Ten thowsand ffrensshemen to deþ wer browght,
     Off whom neuer none away went;
   All her names sothly know I nowght,
     Have mersy on hem cryst omnipotent.   [f. 26v]

Two dukes were take in þat stovre,
   He of Orliawnce & of borbon;
The Ewe, & Arthowre,
   The Erle of vendon, & many one.   52
   The Erchebisshope of sens come with ovre foon,
     .   .   .   .
   Hym failed þe wynnyng of his schon,
     Þorow myght of god omnipotent.   56

Þe fals flemynges, god ȝef hem care,
   Thei loved vs neuer ȝit, by the roode,
ffor alle here fals flateryng fare,
   Aȝenst owre kyng þat day þai stode.   60
   Bot many of hem her hert-blode
     Vnblythly bledden vpon þat bent;
   Ȝit schall þai neuer wayt Inglond good,
     I swere, by god omnipotent.   64

54. *Line missing; no gap in* MS.

28. THE SIEGE OF CALAIS (1436)

English Coll. Rome, MS. 1306

In Iuyll whan the sonne shone shene,   [f. 85r]
Bowes burgoned, and leves grene
   Gan change thaire coloures;
And fresshe floures that April made   4
Began to feynt and fade,
   Of lovely swete odours;

And faire floures grete and smale
Gan to ripe and wax pale;   8
   Than cometh tyme of labours,
To profit and worshippe wynne
In armes, so þer be not ther-in
   Vntrouthe ne false colours.   12

The Duc of Burgone, of grete pride,
Made grete assemble in landes wide,
   In flandres and Braband,
Of all the power and Chiualrie   16
Of Burgone and of Pykardie,
   Of hanaude and holland.

An C*ml* l*ti* and moo,
That were able to ride and goo,   20
   To bere spere and shelde,
And made avaunt Calais to wynne;
And alle shuld dye that were therin,
   Man, woman, and childe.   24

The wolles and the merchandise,
And other godes of grete emprise,
   Eche shulde haue a certeine;

The walles thay wolde bete adovn,   28
Tour, castell, and dongeon,
   And all shuld be made pleyne.

And thus with rede baner displaied,
With other in iij batelles araied,   32
   They come the tovn aboute;
Stately tentes anon they pight,
Large, longe, and of gret hight,
   It was a riall rowte.   36

With gonnes grete and ordinance,   [f. 85v]
That theyme myght helpe and avance;
   With many a proude pavis,
Gailly paynted and stuffed wele;
Ribawdes armed with Iren and stele,   40
   Was neuer better devyse.

So many ml cokkes to crow anyght,
And also cressettes that brenned light,   44
   Grete wonder to here and see.
How sone thay made her loggyng,
Defense of erthe in dykyng,
   Redier myght noon bee.   48

The Erle of Morteyne made a dyner,
And said, "fellowes, be of gode chere!
   And nothing haue we doute.
I trust to god to see that day,   52
That for al thaire proude aray
   fful low that thay shul lowte."

The lietanant, ser Iohn Radclyf,
That loued worshipp and dred repref,   56
   Kept full gode gouernance;

So did the Baron of Dudley,
In the Castell, the sothe to sey,
   Made full gode ordenance.   60

The lord Cameux at Boleyn yate,
The Bulwerk he did vndertake;
   At no tyme wolde he faille,
Neither late ne erly,   64
Yif any wight were so hardy
   At oones forto assaille.

At the mylkyate, ser william of Asshton,
And ser geffray warberton,   68
   With many an hardy man,
The Trumpettes lowd did they blow,
ffor the Duc sholde wel know
   The wacch whan it began.   72

The porters kept full manly   [f. 86r]
The yates open continuelly,
   To wake were they not yrke;
þe trew soudeours, bothe day and nyght,   76
Lay on the walle in armes bright —
   It was thaire hous and kirk.

The maire and burgeis were full bovn
fforto defende thaire possession,   80
   It longed to hem of right;
The worthy merchantes were redy,
At al tyme and euery skry,
   It was a ful gode sight.   84

And so did the gode comon,
That had stuffed wel the tovn
   With godes and vitaille,

83. MS. altyme.

In tovn and felde to ride and goo,   88
And alle other werkes to doo
  In al that myght availle.

The women, bothe yonge and olde,
With stones stuffed euery scaffolde —   92
  They spared no swete ne swynk;
With boilled caudrons, grete and smale,
Yif thay wolde haue sawted the wall,
  Al hote to gif hem drynke.   96

The first day the ennemys proude
Began to skirmyssh with shoutes lowde,
  But countred they were anon.
Gonners began to shew thaire art;   100
Into the tovn in many a part
  Shot many a full grete ston.

Thanked be god, and marie mylde,
They hurt neither man, woman, ne childe;   104
  Houses, thogh, they did harme.
"Seynt Barbara!" than was the crie,
Whan stones in the tovn did flye,
  They cowde noon other charme.   108

And for the duc logged hym no nere,   [f. 86v]
At the southwest corner,
  Of gonnes he had a songe;
That anoon he left his place,   112
And to the est ende he made a chace,
  Hym thoght he bode to longe.

There myght men see Archers gode
Cast away bothe gowne and hode,   116
  The better forto shote;

90. MS. In that al.   101. MS. apart.   107. did *supplied*.

The frenshe and flemmyssh were full fayn
To thaire tentes retourne ageyn,
   þey saw noon other bote.   120

And euer among an Irissh man
On his hoby that swiftly ran;
   It was a sportfull sight
How his dartes he did shake;   124
And whan hym lust to leve or take,
   They had full grete dispite.

Also an hounde that hight goby,
That longed to the waterbailly,   128
   fful swiftly wolde he renne.
At euery skirmyssh to trauaille,
Man and horse he wolde assaille,
   fful wel he cowde hem kenne.   132

And so befell, and on a thursday,
The Erle of Morteigne made afray
   At Saint Peters on the playn;
He drove hem to her tentes nere,   136
And toke many a prisoner,
   And many of hem were slayn.

And after, they come with grete Navy,
With bulged shippes ful craftily,   140
   The hauen forto haue shent,
At friday nyght; but on the morow,
Than began the dukes sorow,
   His shippes whan he saw brent.   144

And soon after, within a while,   [f. 87r]
Drawen dovn was his bastyle,
   With many an hardy man;

His men of armes were leide to grovnde;   148
And som ascaped with dethes wounde;
   But there were fewe taan.

The next nyght, or it was day,
Erly the duc fled away;   152
   With hym, they of Gaunt;
And after, Bruges and Ipre bothe,
To folow hym were they not lothe.
   Thus kept thay thaire avaunt.   156

ffor thay had verray knowyng
Of the duc of Gloucester commyng
   Calais to rescowe;
And because they bode not there,   160
In flandres he sought hem fer and nere,
   That thay may euer rewe.

O oonly god, in whom is all,
Save Calais the tovn riall,   164
   That euer it mot wel cheve
Vnto the crovn of England,
As longe as the world shal stonde,
   That noon enemys it greve!   168
                        Amen.
     Explicit.

29. MOCKERY OF THE FLEMINGS (1436)

Lambeth Palace MS. 6

And on this wise, Phelip, duk of Burgoyn, & the fflemynges, [f. 256r
departid from Caleis, and þe pycardes from þe Castel of col. ii]
Guysnes with gret shame & gret diswurship & with gret losse.
Wherfore amonges Englisshmen were made many rymes of þe   *d*
fflemmynges, among the which one is here sette for a remembraunce, that saith on this wise:

When ye fflemmyng wer fressh florisshid in your flouris
And had weth at your will, ye wolde be conquerouris
Of Caleis, þat litill toun, as it come in youre mynde.
But ye to conquere Caleis it comeþ you not of kynde.   4
Remembres on þat wurship ye wann the first day, [f. 256v
When the erle of Mortein come passing with his pray   col. i]
Before youre toun of Grauenyng, wher ye as men bold
Com rennyng on hym fersli as lyons of Cotteswold,   8
With habirgeons, & hounsculles, & rusti kettill-hattes,
With long pykes — goden daghes for to stikke the rattes,
With messis, & meskins, & eke with side Iakes
Doun vnto mydde þe leg of kanuas, lyke to sakes,   12
Stoppid al with hempen tawe, and þat in straunge wise,
Stiched like a matrace al of þe newe gyse.
Ye laid vpon þ'englisshmen so myghtily with your handes,
Til of you iij hundrid lay strechid on the sandes.   16
Ye fled þen in-to Grauenyng and wold no lenger bide,
And gaue þe erle leue to passe ouer that same tyde
In saafte with his prisoners, & lost neuer a man.
This was þe first wurship of Caleys that ye wan.   20

Remembres how ye laide seege with gret pryde & bost
To Caleis, þat littil toun. the noumbre of your host   [f. 256v
Was a hundrid thousand & fifty, to reken by þe pollis, col. ii]
As it was þat same tyme founden by youre rollis.   24
And yette for al youre gret host, erly nothir late,
Caleis was so ferd of you þey shitte neuer a gate.

Remembres how ye drowned att full see for þe nones
With shippes Caleis hauen massoned with stones,   28
And how that þe calisers hem brake the next day,
When it was lawe watir, and bare hem clene away —
Euery stikke & stone, & lafte not ther one log.
Remembres eke on Goby, the watir-bailliffes dog,   32
How he scarmysshed with you twyes vpon the day,
And among you on þe sandes made many a fray.

Remembres ye of Brugges, how ye first wan youre shon,
How ye com forth to scarmyssh vpon an aftirnon   36
With pauyses & crossebowes on saynt Petirs playn;
And how sone the Calisers made you to turn agayn,   [f. 257r
And ouerthrew you sodeynly, or euer that ye wist,   col. i]
And brought you in-to Caleis tyed fastly by the fist.   40

Remembres ye of Gaunt eke, for al youre pride & bost,
Wonnen was youre bulwerk beside youre gret host,
And slayn all that was therin; & ye that same night
ffled ouer Grauenyng watir, but go þat go myght;   44
And youre lord with you, for dreed and for fere
Of the duyk of Gloucester — & yette was he not þer!
Wel was hym might go before with pison & with paunce,
And laft behind you for hast al your ordynaunce.   48

Remembres ye picardes, at seege eke as ye lay,
Of Guysnes that strong Castel how ye fled away,
ffor ryngyng of the larum bell shamfulli in a morowe;
As ferd as þe fflemmynges, with hertes full of sorowe, 52
Ye lost there your ordynaunce of gunnes that was cheff;
To you & to al pycardis, shame and gret repreff!

Remembres now ye fflemmynges, vpon youre own shame, [f. 257r
When ye laide seege to Caleis ye wer right full to blame, 56 col. ii]
ffor more of reputacioun ben englisshmen þen ye,
And comen of more gentill blode of olde antiquite;
ffor flemmynges com of flemmed men, ye shal wel vndirstand,
ffor fflemed men & banshid men enhabit first youre land. 60

Thus proue I þat fflemmynges is but a flemed man,
And fflaunders of flemmynges the name first began;
And þerfore ye fflemmynges, þat fflemmynges ben named,
To compare with englisshmen ye aught to be ashamed. 64
Ye be nothing elles worth but gret wordes to camp,
Sette ye stille & bith in pees, God gyue you quadenramp!

Such & many oþir rimes were made amonges englisshmen, aftir
the fflemmynges were thus shamfully fled frome Caleis, & þe *h*
picardis from Guisnes fledd & gon þeire way, for drede & fere
of þe comyng of the duyk of Gloucestre, which by þat tyme was redy
at london with his power & armee to com to þe rescows of Caleis, &
to shippe at Sandwich, wher as lay redy in þe hauen iijc sailes to *l*
abyde his comyng.

In the MS. þ and y *not differentiated.*

30. SCORN OF THE DUKE OF BURGUNDY (1436)

English Coll. Rome MS. 1306

A songe made of the Duc of Bourgone.   [f. 83*v*]

O thou Phelippe, fonder of new falshede,
  Distourber of pees, Capiteine of cowardise,
Sower of discorde, Repref of al knyghthode,
    Whiche of al burgoigne (that is so grete of pryse)   4
    Thou clepist thiself duc — whan wiltow rise,
      And in pleyn felde doo mustre with thy launce?
    Se how all knyghthode thy werre dothe despise,
      Wite thyn ovne falsnes al thy myschance!   8

Remembre the, Phelippe, and haue in mynde
  How king henre the v*te*, of veray gentilnesse,
Withoute thy desert he was to the kynde,
    And alway thy socour whan thou were in distresse,   12
    Defendyng thy personne from al wilfulnesse
      Of alle thy mortall enemys, of England and fraunce,
    Wherfore thou shewedist grete vnkyndenesse,
      The which þou may wite alle thi myschance.   16

No. 30. 2. MS. cap*ne*.   16. *Line supplied from Sloane MS.* 252.

Remembre the, Phelippe, at thy begynnyng
  Whan that thy fader thurgh conspired treson,
By assent of Charles that calleth hymself kyng
    Of the reame of france, withoute grovnde of reson,   20
  Was at Motreux broght to his confusion.
    To king henry there thou did thy ligeance;
  Of lyf and land he was thy proteccion,
    Wherfore thyn ovne falsnesse causeth thy myschance. 24

Remembre the, Phelippe, what tyme and how
  To kyng henry the fyft by thyn ovne assent,
Withoute his desire, thou madest a solempne vow,
    Vsyng goddes body the holy sacrement,   28
  To become trew ligeman with gode entent
    To hym and to his heires without variance.
  Thou art false to god, by thyn owne assent,
    Whiche thou may wite al thy mischance.   32

Remembre the, Phelipp, that the yonge king
  Henre the sixt was crowned at Paryse,
Iohn duc of Bedford thyn absence excusyng,
    By souffisant warant made by thy devise;   36
  He did thyn omage as to the floure-de-lice,
    Next by condescent and true inheritance.
  This matere the lust not to aduertise;
    Wite thyn owne falsnesse al thy myschance.   40

Remembre the, Phelippe, how peple of England,   [f. 84r]
  Haue been to the euer gentil and trew,
ffor whan thou were beseged with many a thousand
    Of Armynakes, thay did the rescewe!   44
  Perfourmyng thy desire bothe olde and new,
    Euer redy thyn honeur to mayntene and avance.
  Thou moste vnkynde prince that euer man knew,
    Thyn ovne falsnesse causeth thy myschance!   48

Phelippe, thy falsnes was shewed openly
  In that thy lige lord thou woldest neuer see,
While he was in france continually
    A yere and an half to know his contree,   52
    And as a rightwys kyng there crovned to bee.
      Thou absent thiself with feyned contenance,
    Imagenyng alway cruell sotilte,
      The whiche thou may wite all thy myschance.   56

Phelippe, at Aras, thy falshed to encrece,
  Bothe of thyn avow and othes with all,
Before th'embassatours of trete of pees
    Thou shewedest thyself assoilled by a cardinal,   60
    The which was withoute power papall.
      þou did provow charles, rightwis king of france,
    fforsaking thy ligelord and frend moste special;
      Now wite thyn owne falsnesse al thy myschance.   64

Phelippe, beholde the flemmynges beside grauelyng
  How thay encountred Morteigne as he was homward;
He slow of hem hundredes, hymself defendyng;
    Beholde eke and see before the tovn of Arde   68
    How cameux distrussed grete power of Picarde;
      Wite thin owne falsnes and grete maintenance;
    Thay turned her backes as thay were coward;
      Thy falsnes is begynnyng of al thy myschance.   72

Phelippe, thurgh thy falshede and gyle,
  Bothe Parys, Pountois, and Boys vincent
Were vnwerly wonne by the lord lyle;
    And eke the Castel of Oye whan thou haddest brent,   76
    The peple thou henge by cruel Iugement;
      Thus thou began werre with treson and vengeance:
    Wherfore by right dome of god omnipotent,
      Thy treson shal ende with sorow and myschance.   80

Phelippe, thy princehode was vtterly repreved   [f. 84v]
   Whan thou tofore Calais thy tentes had pight,
And for feer of shotte thou bacward remeued;
    A gretter shame at sege gat hym neuer knyght,   84
    fforto see thy bastyle be stroied by goddes myght —
      It was thy grete trust and chief ordenance.
   Thy peple therin were slayn dovn right,
    Wite thyn owne falsnes al thy myschance.   88

Phelippe, thurgh thy prudence and reule politik,
   To let Calais of rescow and vitaille,
þou didest abolge shippes with walles of bryke;
    But whan thou knew thy purpos myght not availle,   92
    And duc humfray at Sandwich redy to saille
      To rescow Calais and doo his ligeance,
   Thou flygh away for drede of bataille:
    Neuer prince brak sege with gretter myschance.   96

Beholde duc humfray with knyghtly desire
   To meve thy courage the felde forto take;
He soght the in flandres with swerd and with fyre,
    Nyne daies brennyng, no pees did he make.   100
    Where art thou, Phelippe, whan wiltow þy swerd shake?
      Where is thy strong power and grete alliance?
   Thy land is distroied, and thou dar not awake.
    Thus endith thy purpos with sorow and myschance. 104

Conteyne thiself, Phelipp, rightwisly shamed,
   Vnderstonde thiself nothing availlable;
See thurgh cowardise thy knyghthod defamed,
    To werre ayenst god, thenk thou art not able —   108
    fforsake thy frowardnes and become stable,
      Be trew of promesse and sadde of gouernance,
   Obey thy ligelord, and be not variable
    Lest thou be destroied and ende with myschance.   112

Explicit.

31. THE DEATH OF ARCHBISHOP SCROPE (1405)

Trinity Coll. Cambridge MS. 652

Hay, hay, hay, hay,   [f. 171r]
thynke on Whitson monday!

The bysshop Scrope that was so wyse,
nowe is he dede, and lowe he lyse;
To hevyns blys yhit may he ryse,
   Thurghe helpe of Marie, that mylde may.   4

When he was broght vnto the hyll,
he held hym both mylde and styll;
he toke his deth with full gode wyll,
   as I haue herde full trewe men say.   8

He that shulde his dethe be,
he kneled downe vppon his kne:
"lord, your deth, forgyffe it me,
   Full hertly here to yowe I pray."   12

"Here I wyll the commende,
þou gyff me fyve strokys with thy hende,
And than my wayes þou latt me wende
   To hevyns blys that lastys ay."   16

Burden written as one long line. Repetition of burden after each stanza indicated by hay.

32. THE AGINCOURT CAROL (1415)
(With Music)

MS. Arch. Selden B.26
(Sum. Cat. No. 3340)

Deo gracias anglia, [f. 17*v*]
redde pro victoria.

Owre kynge went forth to normandy,
with grace & myȝt of chyualry;
ther god for hym wrouȝt mervelusly,
wherfore Englonde may calle & cry, 4
  Deo gracias!

Deo gracias anglia, *Chorus*
redde pro victoria.

He sette a sege, þe sothe for to say, [f. 18*r*]
To harflu tovne with ryal a-ray;
þat tovne he wan & made a-fray,
þat fraunce shal rywe tyl domesday, 8
  Deo gracias!

Than went our kynge with alle his oste
Thorwe fraunce, for alle þe frenshe boste;
he spared no drede of lest ne moste,
Tyl he come to agincourt coste, 12
  Deo gracias!

Than for soth þat knyȝt comely
In agincourt feld he fauȝt manly;
Thorw grace of god most myȝty,
he had bothe þe felde & þe victory. 16
  Deo gracias!

Stanzas 3 and 6 marked by a *and* b *for transposition.*
3. ther *inserted above line.*

There dukys & erlys, lorde & barone,
were take & slayne, & þat wel sone;
And summe were ladde in-to lundone,
With ioye and merthe & grete renone.   20
    Deo gracias!

Now gracious god, he saue oure kynge,
his peple, & alle his wel-wyllynge;
ȝef hym gode lyfe & gode endynge,
þat we with merth mowe sauely synge,   24
    Deo gracias!

33. THE ROSE ON BRANCH (1415)

B. M. Addit. MS. 31042

A Carolle for Crystmasse.   [f. 110*v*]

The Rose es the fayreste fflour of alle,
That euermore wasse, or euermore schall.
    The Rose of Ryse —
    Of alle thies floures, the rose berys pryce.

The rose it es þe fairest flour,
þe rose es swetteste of odoure,
þe rose in care it es comforthetur,
þe rose in seknes it es saluoure.   4
        The rose so bryghte,
        In medcynns it es most of myghte.

Witnesse thies clerkes, þat ben wysse,
Þe rose es þe flour moste holdyn in prysse;   8
Þerfore me thynke þe flour-de-lyse
Scholde wirchipe þe rose of ryse,
        And bene his thralle —
        And so scholde oþer floures alle!   12

No. 33. bur. MS. *line d precedes c.*

Many a knyghte with spere & launce
ffelowade þat rose to his plesance;
When þe rose by-tyde a chaunce,
þan ffadide alle þe floures of fraunce   16
    And chaungyde hewe,
      In plesance of þe rose so trewe.

34. *THE LILY WHITE ROSE (1486)*

(With Music)

B. M. Addit. MS. 5465

This day, day dawes,   [ff. 108*v*, 109*r*]
this gentill day, day dawes,
this gentill day dawes,
    & I must home gone.
This gentill day dawes,
This day, day dawes,
This gentill day dawes,
    & we must home gone.

In a gloryus garden grene,   [ff. 109*v*, 110*r*]
sawe I syttyng a comly quene;
among the flouris þat fressh byn,
she gadird a floure & set betwene.   4
    þe lyly-whiȝte rose me thouȝt I sawe,
    þe lyly-whiȝte rose me thouȝt I sawe,
      & euer she sang:

    This day, day dawes &c.

In þat garden be flouris of hewe,   [ff. 110*v*, 111*r*]
The gelofir gent þat she well knewe,
The floure-de-luce she did on rewe,
& said, "þe white rose is most trewe

No. 34. *Burden repeated in full after each stanza.*

This garden to rule, be ryȝtwis lawe."   12
þe lyly whiȝte rose me thought I sawe,
     & euyr she sang:

    This day, day dawes &c.

35.   THE ROSES ENTWINED (1486)
(With Music)
B. M. Addit. MS. 5465

"I loue, I loue, & whom loue ye?"   [ff. 40*v*, 41*r*]
"I loue a floure of fressh beaute."
"I loue a-nother as well as ye."
     "Than shalbe provid here anon,
     yff we iij can agree In on."

"I loue a floure of swete odour."
"magerome gentill, or lavendoure?"
"Columbyne, goldis of swete flavour?"
     "nay, nay, let be!   4
     is non of them
     that lykyth me."

    "I loue, I loue, &c."

"There is a floure, where so he be,   [ff. 41*v*, 42*r*]
and shall not yet be namyd for me."   8
"Prymeros, violett, or fressh daysy?"
     "he pass them all
     in his degre,
     that best lykyth me."   12

    "I loue, I loue, &c."

     No. 35. *Burden repeated in full after each stanza.*

"On that I loue most enterly."   [ff. 42v, 43r]
"Gelofyr gentyll, or rosemary?"
"camamyll, borage, or savery?"
 "Nay, certenly,   16
 here is not he
 that plesyth me."

 "I loue, I loue, &c."

"I chese a floure fresshist of face."   [ff. 43v, 44r]
"What is his name that thou chosen has?"   20
"the rose, I suppose? thyn hart vnbrace!"
 "that same is he,
 In hart so fre,
 that best lykyth me."   24

 "Nowe haue I louyd, &c."

"The rose it is a ryall floure."   [ff. 44v, 45r]
"The red or the white? shewe his colour!"
"both be full swete & of lyke savoure:
 all on they be,   28
 that day to se,
 it lykyth well me."

 "Nowe haue I louyd, &c."

"I loue the rose both red & white."   [ff. 45v, 46r]
"Is that your pure perfite appetite?"   32
"to here talke of them is my delite!"
 "Ioyed may we be,
 oure prince to se,
 & rosys thre!"   36

 "Nowe haue we louyd, & loue will we
 this fayre fressh floure, full of beaute;
 Most worthy it is, as thynkyth me,
  Than may be provid here anon
  That we iii be a-grede In oon."

36. FOR VICTORY IN FRANCE (1492)

Cotton MS. Domitianus xviii

A rege henrico septimo.   [f. 248*v*]

Te Rosse wolle in-to frawnse spryng —
Almythy god hym thyder bryng!

And save thys flowre wyche ys owre kyng,
   Wyche ys callyd a nobyll thyng;
Thys Rosse, þis Rosse, þis Ryall rose,
   The flowre off englond & roys owr kyng.   4

Thys apryll schowyres, wyche are ful swet,
   Hathe bownd thys rosse not ȝet ful blown;
In france he woll hys levys schote —
   hys ryȝth to conquer, hys henmyes to knowe.   8

Thys Rosse þat is of color rede
   Wyll sseke hys henmys, bothe fare & wyde,
And wyth hys bemys he woll frensse lyth —
   Sent Iorge protector, be hys good gyd!   12

God send þis flowyr wer he wold be,
   To spreyd hys flowres to his reioschyng,
In france to haue þe vyctory;
   All hynglond for hym schal pray & syng.   16

Iesu & mary, full of myȝth,
   god bo hys gyde in all hys ryȝth.
Swet sent Iorge, owr ladys knyte,
   save kyng hary, bothe be day & nyȝth.   20

2, 3. *lines transposed*.   10. MS. he*n*nys.   20. MS. savo.

37. GOD SPEED THE PLOUGH

(With Music)

MS. Arch. Selden B.26
(Sum. Cat. No. 3340)

The merthe of alle þis londe   [f. 19r]
maketh þe gode husbonde,
   With erynge of his plowe.

I-blessyd be cristes sonde,
þat haþ vs sent in honde
   merthe & ioye y-nowe.

The plowe goth mony a gate,   4
Bothe erly & eke late,
   In wynter in þe clay.

A-boute barly and whete,
þat maketh men to swete,   8
   God spede þe plowe al day!

Browne, morel, & gore
Drawen þe plowe ful sore,
   Al in the morwenynge.   12

Rewarde hem therfore
With a shefe or more,
   Alle in the evenynge.

Whan men bygynne to sowe,   16
fful wel here corne þey knowe
   In þe mounthe of may.

*The burden and first stanza are first written for two voices; then the
last line of burden and whole first stanza are repeated for three
voices.*

Howe-euer Ianyuer blowe,
Whether hye or lowe,   20
  God spede þe plowe all way!

Whan men bygynneth to wede
þe thystle fro þe sede,
  In somer whan þey may,   24

God lete hem wel to spede;
& longe gode lyfe to lede,
  All þat for plowe-men pray.

COMMEMORATION OF KINGS

38. SUMMER SUNDAY:

A LAMENT FOR EDWARD II (1327)

MS. Laud Misc. 108
(Sum. Cat. No. 1486)

Opon a somer soneday se I þe sonne   [f. 237r col. i]
  Erly risinde in þe est ende;
Day daweþ ouer doune, derk is in towne,
  I warp on my wedes, to wode wolde I wende.   4
Wiþ kenettes kene þat wel couþe crie & conne,
  I hiede to holte wiþ honteres hende.
So ryfly on rugge roon & raches ronne
  þat in launde vnder lynde me leste to lende —   8
        And Lenede.
      Kenettes questede to quelle,
      Al-so breme so any belle;
      þe deer daunteden in þe delle,   12
        þat al þe downe denede.

Denede dale & downe for dryft of þe deer in drede;
   ffor meche murþe of mouþ þe murie moeth made.
I ros & romede & sey roon raches to-ȝede;   16
   þei stalken vnder schawe, schatereden in schade.
& Lordes lenged & ladies, Leces to lede,
   Wiþ griþele grehoundes, gode to game & glade. [col. ii]
& I cam to þe game þer gromes gonne grede,   20
   & at a water wilde I wende ouer han wade
          þer was.
       I stalked be þe strem & be þe strond,
       ffer I be þe flod fond   24
       A bot doun be a lond;
          So passede I þe pas.

So passede I þe pas, priuely to pleye,
   & ferde forþ in þat frith, folk for to fynde.   28
Lawly longe I lustnede & vnder lowe lay,
   þat I ne herde hond, horn, hunte, hert ne hynde.
So wyde I walkede þat I wax wery of þe wey,
   þanne les I my layk & lenede vnder lynde;   32
& als I sat beside I say, soþ for to sey,
   A wifman wiþ a wonder whel weue with þe wynde
          & wond.
       Opon þe whel were, I wene,   36
       Merye men & madde I-mene;
       To hire I gan gon in grene
          And fortune y fond.

ffortune frend & fo, fayrest fere,   40
   ferli fals, fikel to fonde is ifounde.
þe whel ȝe torneþ to wo, fro wo into wele þat were,
   in þe ronynge rynge of þe roe þat renneþ so rounde.
A lok of þat leuedy wiþ louelich lere   44
   Mi gode gameliche game gurte to grounde;

18. MS. lenged lenged.

Couþe I carpe carpyng creftly & clere,
  Of þat birde bastons in bale me bounde
         fful bowne.   48
      Naþeles ne mene I nat nay,
      I wile ar I wende away,
      Redy resons in aray,
         Radely to roune.   52

Redely to roune, rounes to rede,
  A loueloker leuedi liuiþ non in lond.
I wolde han went wiþ þat whyt in worþlich wede,
  So ferly fair of face, tofore hire i fond,   56
Þe gold of hire gurdel gloud as a glede.   [f. 237v col. i]
  Þat blisful burde in bale me bond,
Or hire lyȝth-heued in herte I hadde hede,
  & wiþ a wonderful whel þat worþi wyȝth wond   60
      wyþ mayn.
      a wifman of so muche myȝth,
      so wonder a whelwryȝth,
      Sey I neuere wiþ syȝth,   64
         Soþ for to seyn.

Soþ to seye, sitte I sey, as my sicȝthe sente,
  a be-gyngge gome gameliche gay,
Bryȝt as þe blostme, with browes i-bente,   68
  on þe whel þat þe wyȝth weuede in þe wey.
Wyterly him was wel whan þe whel wente,
  ffor he laykyd & low, lenyng als he lay.
Loueliche lokyngges þe loueli me lente;   72
  A meriere man on molde monen I ne may
      In mynde.
      Þe gome I gaf a gretyng:
      He seyde, "sestou, swetyng,   76
      þe crowne of þat comely kyng
        I cleyme be kynde.

        60. MS. worþi wyth.

Versus.

"Be kynde it me com
to cleyme kyngene kyngdom,   80
kyngdom be kynde.
to me þe whel wile wynde.
wynd wel, worþliche wyȝth;
fare fortune, frendene flyȝth   84
fflitte forþ flyȝtte
on þe selue sete to sitte."

Sitte I say & seþe on a semeli sete,
  Ryȝth on þe rounde on þe rennyng ryng,   88
Caste kne ouer kne as a kyng kete,
  comely cloþed in a cope, crouned as a kyng.
Hey herte hadde he of hastif hete,
  He leyde his leg opon liþ at his likyng;   92
fful loþ were þe lordyng his lordsschipe lete;
  He wende al þe world were at his weldyng
      ful wyȝth.
    On knes I kyþed þat kyng: 96
    He seyde, "sestou, swetyng,
    How I regne wiþ ring,   [col. ii]
      Richest in ryȝth.

Versus.

"Richest in ryȝth, quen & knyth   100
kyng conne me calle;
mest men of myȝth,
fair folk to fote me falle.
Lordlich lif led i,   104
no lord lyuynde me iliche.
No duk ne dred i,
for I regne In ryȝth as a riche."

79. com MS. comeþ.   88. MS. rennyg.

Of riche þenkeþ rewþe is to rede & to roune,   108
 þat sitten on þat semeli sete & seþþe Wiþ sorwe þoruout sout.
And I beheld on hadde an heued hor als hor-howne;
 Al blok was his ble in bitere bales browth;
His diademe of dyamans droppede adoun;   112
 His weyes were a-weyward wroþliche wrout;
Tynt was his tresor, tente, tour, & toun.
 Nedful & nawthi, naked & nawth
     I-nome.   116
   þat gome I grette wiþ griþ;
   a word he warp & wepte wiþ,
   hou he was crouned kyng in kiþ
     and caytif become.   120

   "Be-comen a caytif a-cast,
   Kyngus king couþe me calle
   ffram frendes falle
   long, luþe, litel, lo! last.   124
   Last litel lordene lif,
   fikel is fortune, nou fer fro;
   here wel, here wo,
   here knyth, her kyng, her caytif,"   128
A caytif he was become & kenned on care;
 He myste many merþes & meche maistri.
ʒeth I say soriere, sikyng ful sare,
 A bare body in a bed, a bere I-brouth him by,   132
A duk drawe to þe deþ wiþ drouping & dare.

39.   THE DEATH OF EDWARD III (1377)

MS. Vernon
(Sum. Cat. No. 3938)

A, dere God, what mai þis be,   [f. 410v col. iii]
 þat alle þing weres & wasteþ awai?

131. MS. likyng.

ffrendschip is but a vanyte,
    Vnneþe hit dures al a day.   4
    þai beo so sliper at assai,   [f. 411r col. i]
        So leof to han, and loþ to lete,
    And so fikel in heore fai,
        þat selden I-seiȝe is sone forȝete.   8

I sei hit not wiþouten a cause,
    And þerfore takes riht good hede,
ffor ȝif ȝe construwe wel þis clause
    I puit ȝou holly out of drede,   12
    þat for puire schame ȝor hertes wol blede,
        And ȝe þis matere wysli trete:
    He þat was vr moste spede
        Is selden I-seye and sone forȝete.   16

Sum tyme an Englisch schip we had,
    Nobel hit was, and heih of tour;
þorw al Cristendam hit was drad;
    And stif wolde stande in vch a stour,   20
    And best dorst byde a scharp schour
        And oþer stormes, smale and grete;
    Now is þat schip, þat bar þe flour,
        Selden seȝe and sone forȝete.   24

Into þat schip þer longed a rooþur,
    þat steered þe schip & gouerned hit;
In al þis world nis such anoþur,
    As me þinkeþ in my wit.   28
    Whyl schip and roþur togeder was knit,
        þei dredde nouþer tempest, druyȝe, nor wete;
    Nou be þei boþe In synder flit —
        þat selden seyȝe is sone forȝete.   32

Scharpe wawes þat schip has sayled,
 And sayed alle sees at auentur;
ffor wynt ne wederes neuer hit fayled,
 Whil þe roþur mihte enduir.   36
  Þou3 þe see were rouh, or elles dimuir,
   Gode hauenes þat schip wolde gete;
  Nou is þat schip, I am wel suir,
   Selde I-seye and sone for3ete.   40

Þis goode schip I may remene
 To þe chiualrye of þis londe;
Sum tyme þei counted nou3t a bene
 Beo al ffraunce, Ich vnderstonde.   44
  Þei tok and slou3 hem with heore honde,
   Þe power of ffraunce, boþ smal & grete;
  And brouþt þe king hider to byde her bonde,
   And nou riht sone hit is for3ete.   48

Þat schip hadde a ful siker mast,
 And a sayl strong and large,
Þat made þe gode schip neuer agast
 To vndertake a þing of charge.   52
  And to þat schip þer longed a barge,
   Of al ffraunce 3af nou3t a clete.
  To vs hit was a siker targe,
   And now riht clene hit is for3ete.   56

Þe roþur was nouþer ok ne elm;
 Hit was Edward þe þridde, þe noble kniht;
Þe prince his sone bar vp his helm,
 Þat neuer scoumfited was in fiht.   60
  The kyng him rod and rouwed ariht,
   Þe prince dredde nouþer stok nor strete.
  Nou of him we lete ful liht,
   Þat selde is se3e is sone for3ete.   64

42. MS. chilualrye.

þe swifte barge was Duk Henri,
    þat noble kniht, & wel assayed;
And in is leggaunce worþili
    He abod mony a bitter brayd.   68
    3if þat his enemys ou3t outrayed,
        To chastis hem wolde he not lete.
    Nou is þat lord ful lowe I-leyd,
        þat selde is se3e is sone for3ete.   72

þis gode comunes, bi þe rode,
    I likne hem to the schipes mast;
þat with heore catel & heore goode
    Mayntened þe werre boþ furst and last.   76
    þe wynd þat bleu3 þe schip wiþ Blast,
        Hit was gode pre3ers, I sei hit a-trete;
    Nou is deuoutnes out I-cast,
        And mony gode dedes ben clen for3ete.   80

þus ben þis lordes I-leid ful lowe;
    þe stok is of þe same rote;
An ympe biginnes for to growe,
    And 3it I hope schal ben vr bote,   84
    To holde his fomen vnder fote,   [col. ii]
        And as a lord be set in sete.
    Crist leue þat he so mote,
        þat selden I-se3e be not for3ete.   88

Weor þat Impe ffully growe,
    þat he had sarri, sap, and piþ,
I hope he schulde be kud and knowe
    ffor Conquerour of moni a kiþ.   92
    He is ful lyflich in lyme and liþ,
        In armes to trauayle and to swete.
    Crist leeue we so fare him wiþ,
        þat selden se3e be neuer for3ete.   96

67. in MS. is.

And þerfore holliche I ou rede,
  Til þat þis ympe beo fully growe,
Þat vch a mon vp wiþ þe hede,
    And mayntene him boþe heiʒe and lowe.   100
    Þe ffrensche men cunne boþe boste and blowe,
      And wiþ heore scornes vs to-þrete;
    And we beoþ vnkuynde & slowe,
      Þat selden seʒe is sone forʒete.   104

And þerfore, gode sires, takeþ reward
  Of ʒor douhti kyng, þat dyʒede in age,
And to his sone Prince Edward,
    Þat welle was of alle corage.   108
    Suche two lordes of heiʒ parage
      Is not in eorþe whon we schal gete.
    And nou heore los biginneþ to swage,
      Þat selde I-seʒe is sone forʒete.   112

40. *RICHARD II INTERRED IN WESTMINSTER (1413)*

BY THOMAS HOCCLEVE

Huntington Lib. MS. HM 111

Ceste balade ensuyante feust faite tost apres que les osses   [f. 31*v*]
du Roy Richard feurent apporteʒ a Westmouster.

Where-as þat this land wont was for to be
  Of sad byleeue & constant vnioun;
And as þat holy chirche vs taghte, we
    With herte buxum lerned our lessoun —   4
    Now han we changid our condicioun.

110. Is MS. I.

Allas! an heep of vs, the feith werreye;
We waden so deepe in presumpcioun,
þat vs nat deyneth vn-to god obeye. 8

We rekken nat thogh Crystes lore deye,
The feend hath maad vs dronke of the poisoun
Of heresie, & lad vs a wrong weye,
þat torne shal to our confusioun 12
But if þat left be this abusioun;
And yit, seur confort haue I, thynkith me:
Our lige lord, the kyng, is Champioun
For holy chirche — Crystes knyght is he! 16

For why, o reuerent goostly fadres, yee
And we, your sones eek, han enchesoun
Right greet to thanke god in Trinite,
þat of his grace hath sent this Regioun 20
So noble an heed. looke vp, thow Albioun!
God thanke, & for thy cristen Prince preye,
Syn he fo is to this Rebellioun.
He, of thy soules helthe, is lok and keye! 24

What mighten folk of good byleeue seye, [f. 32r]
If bent were our kynges affeccioun
To the wrong part, who sholde hem help purueye?
A kyng set in þat wrong opinioun 28
Mighte of our feith be the subuersioun.
But eterne god, in persones three,
Hath regned dropes of conpassioun,
And sent vs our good kyng for our cheertee! 32

See eke how our kynges benignitee
And louyng herte his vertu can bywreye;
Our kyng Richard þat was, yee may wel see,
Is nat fled from his remembrance aweye. 36
My wit souffysith nat to peyse and weye

With what honour he broght is to this toun,
And with his queene at Westmynstre in th'abbeye
 Solempnely in Toumbe leid adoun.   40

Now god, byseeche I in conclusioun,
 Henri the V^e in ioie & hy nobleye
Regne on vs yeeres many a milioun,
 And where-as þat men erren & forueye,   44
 Walkynge blyndly in the dirk aleye
  Of heresie — o lord god, preye I thee,
Enspire hem þat no lenger they foleie!
  To feithes path hem lede thy pitee.   48

Amen.

41. A RECOLLECTION OF HENRY V (1429)
BY JOHN AUDELAY

MS. Douce 302
(Sum. Cat. No. 21876)

De rege nostro henrico sexto.   [f. 29r]

  A, perles pryns, to þe we pray:
  Saue oure kyng boþ nyȝt & day.

ffore he is ful ȝong, tender of age,
Semele to see, o bold corage,
Louele & lofte of his lenage,
 Boþ perles prince & kyng veray.   4

His gracious granseres & his grawndame,
His fader & moder of kyngis þay came;
Was neuer a worþear prynce of name
 So exelent in al our day.   8

No. 41. bur. MS. A a; peryns.   4. MS. prince *interlined*.
6. MS. moderis.   7. MS. a *in* worþear *interlined*.

His fader, fore loue of mayd kateryn,
In fraunce he wroȝt turment & tene;
His loue, hee sayd, hit schuld not ben,
   & send him ballis, him with to play.   12

Þen was he wyse in wars with-all,
& taȝt franchemen to plai at þe ball;
With tenes hold he ferd ham hall;
   To castelles & setis þei floyn away.   16

To harflete a sege he layd anon
& cast a bal vn-to þe towne;
þe frenchemen swere be se & sun
   Hit was þe fynd þat mad þat fray.   20

Anon þai toke ham to cownsele;
Oure gracious kyng þai wold asayle;
At agyncowrt, at þat patayle,
   þe floure of frawnce he fel þat day.   24

þe kyng of frawns þen was agast,   [f. 29v]
Mesagers to him send in hast,
ffore wele he west hit was bot wast
   Hem to witstond in hone way.   28

& prayd hym to ses of his outrage
& take kateryn to mareage;
Al frawnce to him schuld do homage,
   & croune him kyng afftyr his day.   32

Of frawnce he mad him anon regent
& wedid kateren in his present;
In-to Englond anon he went
   & cround our quene in ryal aray.   36

11. hee *interlined above* che *deleted.*

Of quen kateryn our kyng was borne
To saue our ryȝt þat was forelorne;
Oure faders in frawns had won beforne,
　　þai han hit hold mone a day.　　　　　　　　40

þus was his fader a conqueroure
& wan his moder with gret onoure;
Now may þe kyng bere þe floure
　　Of kyngis & kyngdams in vche cuntre.　　　44

On him schal fal þe prophece
þat haþ ben sayd of kyng herre:
þe hole cros wyn or he dye,
　　þat crist halud on goodfryday.　　　　　　48

Al wo & werres he schal a-cese,
& set all reams in rest & pese,
& turne to cristyndam al heþynes —
　　Now grawnt him hit so be may.　　　　　　52

Pray we þat lord is lord of all,
To saue our kyng, his reme ryal;
& let neuer myschip vppon him falle
　　Ne false traytoure him to betray.　　　　　56

I pray ȝoue, seris, of ȝour gentre,
Syng þis carol reuerently,
ffore hit is mad of kyng herre;
　　Gret ned fore him we han to pray.　　　　60

Ȝif he fare wele, wele schuld we be;
Or ellis we may be ful sore;
ffore him schal wepe mone an e —
　　þis prophecis þe blynd awdlay!　　　　　　64

39. MS. before.　　　　50. MS. all al reams.
52. MS. may *struck through before* so.　　　63. MS. ane.

42. *THE DEATH OF EDWARD IV (1483)*

Rylands Lib. Manchester, Eng. MS. 113

Kyng Edward the iiij*th*.   [f. 3*r*]

Wher is this Prynce that conquered his right
  Within Ingland, master of all his ffoon;
And after ffraunce, be very force & myght,
  Without stroke, and afterward cam hoom;   4
  Made Scotlond to yelde, and Berwyk wan he from;
    Rydyng a hontyng, hym-silff to sporte & playe?
    All men of Englond ar bounde for hym to praye.

This most dred prince that was vnder the son,   8
  Through all this wordle renewed was his name;
The dowthiest, the worthiest, withouten comparison,
  Ther was noon suche, but ye reken the same,
  Compassed the wordle, so spronge his name;   12
    And as in batell, the ffresshest I shall say.
    All men of England ar bounde for hym to pray.

Wher is he nowe, that man of noble men,
  That in his howsold kepte the ryall rowte?   16
Ther is no place in all the wordle, I ken,
  but of the substaunce he hath chosen owte.
  Hit was a wordle to se hym ride aboute
    Through-out his land, and that was day be day.   20
    All men of Englond ar bounde for hym to pray.

O noble Edward, wher art thowe be-come,
  Which full worthy I haue seen goyng in estate?
Edward the iiij*th* I mene, with the sonne,   24
  The rose, the sonne-beme, which was full fortunate.
  Noon erthly prince durst make with hym debate.
    Art thowe agoo, and was here yestirday?
    All men of Englond ar bound for the to pray.   28

The well of knyghthode, withouten any pere,
　　Of all erthely prynces thowe were the lode-sterre!
Be-holde & rede, herkyn well and hyre!
　　In gestis, in romansis, in Cronicles nygh & ferre,   32
　　Well knowen it is, þer can no man it deferre,
　　　　Perelees he was, and was here yestirday.
　　　　All men of Englond ar bounde for hym to pray.

ffy on this wordle! What may we wrecches say,   [f. 3v]
　　Thate nowe haue lost the lanterne & the light?
Oure kyng oure lorde — alas, and wele-a-wey!
　　In euery felde full redy for oure right;
　　It was no nede to pray hym for to fight;   40
　　　　Redy he was, that was here yestirday.
　　　　All men of Englond ar bounde for hym to pray.

Me thynkith euer this kyng sholde not be gon.
　　I see his lordis, I see his knyghtis all;   44
I see his plasis made of lyme and ston;
　　I see his seruauntes sittyng in the hall,
　　And walkyng among them his marchall.
　　　　What sholde I say? he was here yestirday!   48
　　　　All men of Englond ar bounde for hym to pray.

I am be-giled, for he is past and goon.
　　I mette his men wepyng in clothis blake —
Not oon nor tweyn, god wote, many oon,   52
　　Which daily waylith & sorowith for his sake.
　　Hit to endite, hit makith my herte quake,
　　　　When I remember he was here yestirday.
　　　　All men of Englond ar bounde for hym to pray.   56

Nowe pray we to god, that all this wordle hath wrought,
　　Among his aungelis this prince may haue a place;
And for his passion that vs so dere hath brought,
　　That of his paynys he may haue his grace.   60

Nowe, gracious lord, remembre well this case!
   As wofull synners, we call to the, and say,
     That we of Englond ar bounde for hym to pray.

Ye wofull men that shall this writyng rede,   64
   Remembre well here is no dwellyng place.
Se howe this prince is from vs goon, and dede,
   And we shall aftir hym sue the trace.
     Ther is no choise, ther is noon other grace;   68
      This knowe ye well — he was here yestirday.
      All men of Englond ar bounde for hym to pray.

Explicit.

POLITICAL PROPHECIES

43. GEOFFREY OF MONMOUTH'S PROPHECY

MS. Rawlinson K.42
(Sum. Cat. No. 15165)

IN the londe of more bretayngne,   [p. 104]
   Schal ben a lorde of gret renoune;
In whos tyme, As bokys seyne,
   Schal be treson in toure and towne.   4

All to destroye somme schall entende;
   And that theyre conceyte be nott soo
Off þat may sewe a dredfull ende,
   That woolle be cause of mykell woo.   8

What tyme Normandye schall be lorne,
   With ryght grete grame and dyshonoure,
Þat helde of Englonde longe beforne,
   hym schall be rewe hit with grete doloure.   12

Hym schall wante of hys astate,
    To hys garlonde a precyovse floure,
Whiche oure fore faders wyȝtlye gate —
    Cyte, Castell, Towne and towre.   16

Than by stryff & gret dyvysyon
    þat Englysshe peple schall falle Inne,
To endeless hurte & fowle confusyon,
    þen dolefulle dedys schall be-gynne.   20

Then wolle resorte in-to þat londe
    þat were lorde þerof off olde,
þer schall noȝthe be þat may with-stonde
    Hem, þat yle to haue and holde.   24

An olde man rydynge on a stede
    þat þe water of pryon schall subuerte;
To mesur a myle yif he hadde nede,
    In þat ryuer wylde and smerte.   28

Then schal Cadwaladre Conan calle,
    And gadre Scotlonde vn-to hys flocke;
þanne in Ryueres blode schall falle,
    And þanne schal perysche braunche & stocke.   32

Thanne schal Alyons Folde & falle   [p. 103]
    Ande be deposyde for euer and aye;
To ben free that nowe ben thralle
      Schall be-falle þanne ylke a daye.   36

Off lytylle bretayne lordes fele
    Schall be Ioyfulle men of thys;
Than schall bretaynes crownes dele,
    And ben then lordes where non ys.   40

Then schall Cambere Ioyfulle be,
   The myght of Cornewayle quycke anon;
Thys Englonde bretayne calle may ȝe,
   When thys tym ys commyn & gon.   44

       Explicit.

44. THE COCK IN THE NORTH

Cotton Rolls ii.23

When the cocke in the Northe hath bilde his nest, [Art. 9]
   And buskith his briddis and becenys hem to fle,
þen shall fortune his frend the yatis vp cast,
   And right shall haue his fre entree;   4

Thene shall the mone rise in the northewest,
   In a clowde of blake as þe bill of a crowe.
Then shall þe lion louse the boldest and þe best,
   þat in brytayne was born syne arthers day.   8

And a dredefull dragon shall drawe hym from his denne
   To helpe the lion with all his myght.
A bull and a bastard with speris to spen,
   Shall a-bide with the bore to reken the right.   12

A libard shall be gendred of a natiffe kynd,
   With þe sterre of bedlem shall ryse in the southe;
The molle and the mermayden mevith in mynd —
   Criste that is oure creature hath cursid hem by mouthe!   16

The Egill and the antelope shall boldly abide,
   A bridellid hors, and a bere with brondis so bright.
At sondyford, for-sothe, on the southe syde,
   A prowde prince in a prese lordly shall he light,   20

No. 44. 6. MS. crowre.   10. MS. The helpe.   13. MS. As libard.
20. MS. prest.

With bolde baronis, bernis in bassenettis, þat busshement
                                                    shal mete,
   That shall the prophecy preve that Thomas of tellis;
ffor þer shall mony a comely knyght be cast vnderfete,
   That shall make maydens to wepe that in bowre dwellis.   24

Þen shall þe day of desteny dryve to þe nyght;
   And a maiden and wife in mornyng be brought.
Þer shall mete in morowe by þe mone-light;
   Betwene seton and þe se a sorow shall be wroght.   28

The lion shall lache an hurt, and not perisshed be;
   But he shall broyde to þe best þat hym þe woo wroght.
And a man ascend on tho sterre shall fold for þat fre,
   Þe prowdest on þat prese with hale hath hytte bought.   32

The fox and the filmard and a honde shall a-take,
   And to the lion be ladde lowe to a-bide.
Bothe þe pikard and þe pye shall suffre þe same,
   And alle þe ffryndes of the fox shall fall for here pride.   36

Than shall troy vntrew tremble þat dayes,
   ffor drede of a dede man when þey here hym speke.
The townis and þe Commons of kent shall cast vp þe kayes,
   Þe busshement of bryk-hull þer-with shall breke.   40

When wormys and wedis are wasted and a-wey went,
   And ilke a segge in seson kyndly set and song,
And all right hath his rewle and falsenes is blent,
   All grace and goodenes shall growe vs among.   44

The sonne and the mone shall shyne full bright,
   That mony a day full derk hath ben,
And kepe þer cowrses by dayes and by nyght
   With myrthes mo than ony man can mene.   48

21. MS. bernis and.

þe lion and þe lionasse shall regne in pese.
   This bridlyngton, bede, bokis, and Banaster tellis,
Thomas, and merlyon, the same with-outen lese,
    They recorden and other that with prophecy mellis.   52

Then shall saxons chese theym a lord,
   þat shall rewle hem rightfully and bryng hem vndere.
A dede man shall make by-twene hem a-corde,
    And this a ferly and a grete wondere.   56

He that is ded and buryed in sight,
   Shall ryse agayn, and lyve in lond,
In confortyng of a yong knyght
    That ffortune hath chosen to be here housbond.   60

The whele shall turne to hym full ryght,
   þat ffortune hath chosen to be here fere.
In surrey shall be shewid a wonderfull sight,
    In the Cite of Babilon to bryng hem on bere: 64

xv dayes Iorney from Ierusalem
   The holy crosse shall be;
þe same bore shall wynne þe beme,
    At sondyford that degre.   68

ffor ffortune hath graunted hym the victorye,
   ffro the first tyme he armys bere;
ffor ony treson or trechery,
    Desteny shall hym not dere,   72

Till kynd of oxe to hym drawe,
   ffor euery man is wormys fee;
But he shall ende in goddes lawe,
    And in Iosephath beryed he shall be.   76

45. WHEN ROME IS REMOVED

Cambridge Univ. MS. Kk.1.5(IV)

Qwhen Rome is removyde in-to Inglande,   [f. 33r]
Ande the prest haffys the poppys power in hande,
Betuix iij and sex — who-so wyll vnderstande —
Mekyll baret ande bale shall fall in brutis lande.   4
When pryde is most in price, ande wyt is in covatyse,
Lychery is Ryffe, and theffis has haldin þar lyff,
Holy chirche is awlesse, and Iusticis ar lawlesse,
Bothte knychtis and knawys clede in on clethinge,   8
Godis fleysh and his blode swore in hethinge.
Be the yheris of cryst, comyn and gone,
ffully nynty ande nyne (nocht one wone),
þen shall sorow be sett ande vnsell,   12
þen shall dame fortowne turne her whell;
Scho sall turne vp þat ar was doune,
And þan sall leawte ber the crowne.

Betweyne þe cheyff of the somer & the sad winter,   16
ffor þe heycht of þe heyte happyne sall wer;
And eueryche lorde shall austernly werk.
þen shall Nazareth noy well A while.
And þe lilly so lele wytht lovelyche flouris   20
ffor harmes of þe harde heyte sall hillyne his ledis,
Syne speyde hime at sped and spawne in þe wynter;
All þe flowris in the fyrth sall folow hime one.
Tatcaldwers sall call on carioun the noyus,   24
And þan sall worthe vp wallys and wrethe oþir landis
And erth on tyll albany, if þai may wyne.
Herme wnto Alienys, aneuer þai sall wakyne!
þe bruttis blude sall þame wakyne & bryttne wyth brandis
                                                                    of stell, 28
þer sall no bastarde blode abyde in þat lande.

5. wyt *inserted above line.*   9. *Line supplied.*   16. MS. cheyss.

Þen Albanattus þe kene, kynde kynge offe erthe,   [f. 33v]
Vnto þe libert shall leng — leve yhe non oþir!
The lyone, leder of bestis,   32
Shall lowte to þe libert and long hume wytht,
And shall stere hume At stryff, be stremis of humber.
Þe stepsonys of þe lyonne, steryt vp at ones,
Þe leoparde sall þame stryke doune and stroy þame for euer. 36
He sall þame kenly kersse, as cryst has hume bydyne,
And þus he sall þame doune dryff, ewyne to þe ende.
ffor þai luf nocht þe lylly nor þe libert lelle,
And þai halde to þe harde, happyn as it may,   40
Ay to þe tayle of somyr tyne hir lappis.
Wytht þat sall A libert be louse, when þai lest weyne.
Ane Egle of þe est, ande ane aventruse byrde,
Shall fande flowrys to fange in þat fyrste sesoun,   44
Sterte to þe stepsonys, stryke þame doune togeþer;
To bynde bandis vnbrokyne þat salbe furthe broucht,
He sall hime garlandis gete of þe gay flowrys
At in þat sesoune spredis so fayre.   48
And all sall fawle þe foulke þat þe freke strykis.
A sely northyrune flaw sall fadyne for euer.

Hereafter on oþir syde sorow sall Ryse,
Þe barge of bariona bowne to the senkyne,   52
Secularis sall set þame in spiritual clothis
And occupy þar offices, ennoynted as þai war.
Þar tonsurys tak wytht turnamentis Inowe,
And trow tytyll of trouthe þat þe strenth haldis.   56
Þat salbe tene for to tell þe tende of þar sorow
Þat sall ourdryff the date doune to þe boke.
Þis most be-tyde in þe time — throw yhe for-suthe —
Qwhen A B C may sett hume to wryte,   60
Anon efter Ml, evene to Rewlle,

32. *A word of five letters struck through after* lyone.
34. MS. A stryff.   35. MS. stopsonys.   45. MS. stopsonys.
47. gete *supplied.*   49. MS. fawlo.   52. MS. sonkyne.

Tre CCC in A sute semblyt to-geþer,
Ande syne, efter ane 1, as þe lyne askis,   [f. 34r]
Tris X, ande ane R enterly folowande,   64
þis Is þe dolorouse date — understande yhe þe glose,
Wheroff whyll merlyne melys in his bokis.

Busk ye wyell, Berwyk, be blyth of þis wordis
þat Sant bede fande in his buk of þe byg bergh: 68
þe trewe towne vpon twede wytht towrys fayre,
þow sall Releve to þi keng, þat is þe kende Eyr.
Ande oþir burghys abowte wytht þar brade wall,
Sall wytht þe lyoune be leffe ande longe for euer.   72

46. A POLITICAL PROPHECY BY THE DICE

Trinity Coll. Dublin MS. 516

Nota·

idem vulgus Euermore schalle the [⚅] be the best cast on the dyce;   [f. 115r]

idem rex Whan that [⚀] beryth vp the [⚅] ynglond schal be as paradice.   *idem vulgus*

idem religiosi And [⚂] and [⚄] set al on oone syde,   *idem domini*

Then schal the name of the [⚅] spring vonder wyde.   *idem vulgus* 4

idem proditores [⚂] set A-side and [⚁] clene schent,   *idem bilingue*

ye schal haue a new king At a new parlement.

idem vulgus [⚅] schal vp and [⚀] schal vndur,   *idem rex*

When dede men ryse that schal be moch wondur;   8

The rede rose and the floure-de-lyce, the lockes schal vndur,

idem vulgus Yet schal the [⚅] ber the pryce, and [⚀] schal helpe ther-to.   *idem rex*

Nota.

No. 45. 62. MS. fute.   65. MS. under.

4. Then MS. The.   7. vp and [⚀] *struck through after* schal.

47. *MERLIN'S PROPHECY*

Trinity Coll. Dublin MS. 516

When lordes wille is londes law,   [f. 115r]
Prestes wylle trechery, and gyle hold soth saw,
lechery callyd pryve solace,
And robbery is hold no trespace —   4
Then schal the lond of Albyon
torne in-to confusioun!

THE FIRST UTOPIA

48. *THE LAND OF COKAYGNE*

Harley MS. 913

Fur in see, bi west spayngne,   [f. 3r]
is a lond ihote cokaygne.
þer nis lond vnder heuen-riche,
of wel, of godnis, hit iliche;   4
þoȝ peradis be miri & briȝt,
cokaygn is of fairir siȝt.
what is þer in peradis
bot grasse, & flure, & grene ris?   8
þoȝ þer be ioi & gret dute,
þer nis met bote frute;
þer nis halle, bure, no benche;
bot watir, man-is þurst to quenche.   12
beþ þer no men bot two,
hely & enok al-so;
elinglich mai hi go
whar þer woniþ men no mo.   16

No. 47. 2. the *struck through after* wylle.   No. 48. 12. MS. þursto.

In cokaigne is met & drink
wiþ-vte care, how, & swink.
þe met is trie, þe drink is clere,
to none, russin, & sopper.   20
i sigge for-soþ, boute were,
þer nis lond on erþe is pere,
vnder heuen nis lond, i-wisse,
of so mochil ioi & blisse.   24

þer is mani swete siȝte: [f. 3v]
al is dai, nis þer no niȝte;
þer nis baret noþer strif;
nis þer no deþ, ac euer lif;   28
þer nis lac of met no cloþ;
þer nis man no womman wroþ.
þer nis serpent, wolf, no fox,
hors no capil, kowe no ox,   32
þer nis schepe, no swine, no gote;
no non horwȝ, al god it wote,
noþer harace, noþer stode.
þe lond is ful of oþer gode.   36
nis þer flei, fle, no lowse,
in cloþ, in toune, bed, no house;
þer nis dunnir, slete, no hawle;
no non vile worme, no snawile,   40
no non storme, rein, no winde.
þer nis man no womman blinde.
ok al is game, Ioi, & gle.
wel is him þat þer mai be.   44

þer beþ riuers gret & fine,
of oile, melk, honi, & wine;
watir seruiþ þer to no-þing
bot to siȝt & to waiissing.   48

34. al MS. la.

þer is mani maner frute;
al is solas & dedute.

þer is a wel fair abbei,   [f. 4r]
of white monkes & of grei.   52
þer beþ bowris & halles;
al of pasteiis beþ þe walles,
of fleis, of fisse, & rich met,
þe likfullist þat man mai et.   56
fluren cakes beþ þe schingles alle,
of cherche, cloister, boure, & halle;
þe pinnes beþ fat podinges —
rich met to princeȝ & kinges.   60
man mai þer-of et inoȝ,
al wiþ riȝt & noȝt wiþ woȝ.
al is commune to ȝung & old,
to stoute & sterne, mek & bold.   64

þer is a cloister, fair & liȝt,
brod & lang, of sembli siȝt;
þe pilers of þat cloister alle
beþ iturned of cristale,   68
wiþ har bas & capitale
Of grene Iaspe & rede corale.
In þe praer is a tre,
swiþe likful forto se: 72
þe rote is gingeuir & galingale,
þe siouns beþ al sedwale,
trie maces beþ þe flure,
þe rind canel of swet odur,   76
þe frute gilofre of gode smakke.   [f. 4v]
of cucubes þer nis no lakke.
þer beþ rosis of rede ble,

49. mani *supplied.*
50. *catchword added in later hand:* þer is a well &c.
55. & *expunged after* &.   69. MS. las.

& lilie likful forto se —   80
þai faloweþ neuer dai no niȝt;
þis aȝt be a swet siȝt.

þer beþ iiij willis in þe abbei,
of triacle & halwei,   84
of baum & ek piement,
euer ernend to riȝt rent;
of þam stremis al þe molde,
stonis preciuse, & golde.   88
þer is saphir & vniune,
carbuncle & astiune,
Smaragde, lugre, & prassiune,
beril, onix, topasiune,   92
ametist & crisolite,
calcedun & epetite.

þer beþ briddes mani & fale —
þrostil, þruisse & niȝtingale,   96
Chalendre & wodwale,
& oþer briddes wiþ-out tale,
þat stinteþ neuer bi har miȝt.
miri to sing dai & niȝt.   100
ȝite i do ȝow mo to witte: [f. 5r]
þe Gees irostid on þe spitte
fleeȝ to þat abbai, god hit wot,
& grediþ, "gees, al hote! al hot!"   104
hi bringeþ garlek gret plente,
þe best idiȝt þat man mai se.
þe leuerokes, þat beþ cuþ,
liȝtiþ adun to man-is muþ,   108
idiȝt in stu, ful swiþe wel
pudrid wiþ gilofre and canel.
nis no spech of no drink;

87. þam MS. þai.   110. MS. ginglofre; ng *expunged*.

ak take inoȝ wiþ-vte swink.   112

Whan þe monkes geeþ to masse,
al þe fenestres þat beþ of glasse
turneþ in-to cristal briȝt,
to ȝiue þe monkes more liȝt.   116
whan þe masses beþ iseiid,
& þe bokes up ileiid,
þe cristal turniþ in-to glasse,
in state þat hit raþer wasse.   120

Þe ȝung monkes euch dai
aftir met goþ to plai;
nis þer hauk no fule so swifte
bettir fleing bi þe lifte,   124
þan þe monkes heiȝ of mode   [f. 5v]
wiþ har sleuis & har hode.

Whan þe abbot seeþ ham flee
þat he holt for moch glee;   128
ak naþeles al þer amang
he biddiþ ham liȝt to euensang.
þe monkes liȝtiþ noȝt adun,
ac furre fleeþ in o randun.   132

Whan þe abbot him iseeþ
þat is monkes fram him fleeþ,
he takeþ a maidin of þe route
and turniþ vp har white toute,   136
& betiþ þe taburs wiþ is hond
to make is monkes liȝt to lond!

Whan is monkes þat iseeþ,
to þe maid dun hi fleeþ,   140

116. þe *supplied*.   134. *A word erased after* monkes.

& geþ þe wench al abute
& þakkeþ al hir white toute.
& siþ aftir her swinke
Wendiþ meklich hom to drinke,   **144**
& geþ to har collacione
a wel fair processione.

Anoþer abbei is þer bi,
for-soþ a gret fair nunnerie,   **148**
vp a riuer of swet milke,   [f. 6r]
whar is plente gret of silk.
whan þe someris dai is hote,
þe ȝung nunnes takiþ a bote   **152**
And doþ ham forþ in þat riuer,
boþe wiþ oris & wiþ stere.
whan hi beþ fur fram þe abbei,
hi makiþ ham nakid forto plei,   **156**
& lepiþ dune in to þe brimme
& doþ ham sleilich forto swimme.
þe ȝung monkeȝ þat ham seeþ,
hi doþ ham vp & forþ hi fleeþ,   **160**
& commiþ to þe nunnes anon.
& euch monke him takeþ on,
& snellich berriþ forþ har prei
to þe mochil grei abbei,   **164**
& techiþ þe nunnes an oreisun
wiþ iambleue vp & dun.

Þe monke þat wol be stalun gode
& kan set ariȝt is hode,   **168**
he schal hab, wiþ-oute danger,
xii wiues euche ȝere,
al þroȝ riȝt & noȝt þroȝ grace,
for to do him-silf solace.   **172**

159. MS. monkeþ; ham MS. hi.

& þilk monke þat slepiþ best,　　　　　　　　[f. 6v]
& doþ is likam al to rest,
of him is hoppe, god hit wote,
to be sone uadir abbot.　　　　　　　　　　　176

Whose wl com þat lond to,
ful grete penance he mot do:
Seue ȝere in swine-is dritte
he mote wade, wol ȝe iwitte,　　　　　　　　180
al anon vp to þe chynne,
so he schal þe lond winne.

Lordinges gode & hend,
mot ȝe neuer of world wend,　　　　　　　　184
fort ȝe stond to ȝure cheance
& fulfille þat penance,
þat ȝe mote þat lond i-se;
& neuer-more turn a-ȝe.　　　　　　　　　　188
prey we god so mote hit be,
Amen, pur seint charite.

finit.

THE WICKED AGE

49.　THE BISSON LEADS THE BLIND (1456)

Harley MS. 5396

ffulfyllyd ys þe profesy for ay　　　　　　[f. 295r]
　　þat merlyn sayd & many on mo,
Wysdam ys wel ny away,
　　No man may knowe hys frend fro foo.　　　4
　　　Now gyllorys don gode men gye;

No. 49. 1. MS. profey.　　　4. MS. fend.

Ryȝt gos redles all behynde;
  Truthe ys turnyd to trechery;
    ffor now þe bysom ledys þe blynde.   8

Now gloserys full gayly þey go;
  Pore men be perus of þis land;
Sertes sum tyme hyt was not so,
  But sekyr all þis ys synnys sonde.   12
    Now mayntererys be made Iustys,
      And lewde men rewle þe lawe of kynde;
    Nobull men be holdyn wyse;
      ffor now þe bysom ledys þe blynde.   16

Truthe is set at lytyl prys;
  Worschyp fro us longe hath be slawe;
Robberys now rewle ryȝtwysenesse,
  And wynnerys with her sothe sawe.   20
    Synne sothfastnesse has slawe;
      Myrth ys now out of mannys mynde;
    þe drede of god ys al todrawe;
      ffor now þe bysom ledys þe blynde.   24

Now brocage ys made offycerys,
  And baratur ys made bayly;
Knyȝtus be made custemerys,
        .   .   .   28
    fflatererys be made kyngus perys;   [f. 295v]
      Lordys be led all out of kynde;
    Pore men ben knyȝtus ferys;
      ffor now þe bysom ledys þe blynde.   32

The constery ys combryd with coueytyse,
  ffor trouth ys sonkyn vndur þe grounde;
With offycyal nor den no fauour þer ys,

---

7. tre *struck through before* trechery.   13. MS. maynterys.
15. MS. beholdyn.   24. MS. bynde.   28. MS. *cut at foot of page.*
32. MS. þis blynde.   35. MS. W offycyal.

But if ser symony shewe þem syluer rovnde.   36
Þer among spiritualte it ys founde,
 ffor pete ys clene out of þer mynde.
Lord, whan thy wyll is, al ys confounde,
 ffor now þe bysom ledys þe blynde.   40

He ys louyd þat wele can lye,
 And theuys tru men honge;
To god I rede þat we cry
 þat þis lyfe last not longe.   44
 Þer werld is turnyd up so doun among;
  ffor frerys ar confessourys, ageyn a kynde,
 To þe chefe ladyes of þis londe;
  þerfor þe bysom ledys þe blynde.   48

Lordys þe lawe þey lere,

 . . . .

Iaperys syt lordys ful nere;   [f. 296r]
 Now hath þe deuyll all hys deuys.   52
 Now growyth þe gret flour-de-lys;
  Wymmonis wyttes ar full of wynd;
 Now ledres ladyn þe leward at her debres,
  for caus þe bysom ledys þe blynde.   56

Now prelates don pardon selle,
 And holy chyrche ys chaffare;
Holynes comyth out of helle,
 ffor absolucions waxyn ware.   60
 Gabberys gloson euery whare,
  And gode feyth comys all byhynde;
Ho shall be leuyd þe soþe wyll spare,
  ffor now þe bysom ledys þe blynde.   64

---

37. MS. spualte. 50. MS. *cut at foot of page.*
56. *second* þe *supplied.* 61. MS. euy. 63. MS. þe se þe wyll.
64. MS. bleynde.

The grete wyll þe soþe spare,
   The comonys loue not þe grete;
þerfor euery man may care,
   Lest þe wade growe ouer þe whete.   68
      Take hede how synne hath chastysyd frauns,
       Whan he was in hys fayrest kynde,
      How þat flaundrys hath myschaunys,
       ffor cause þe bysom ledyth þe blynde.   72

þerfor euery lord odur avauns,   [f. 296v]
   And styfly stond yn ych a stoure;
Among ȝou make no dystaunce,
   But, lordys, buskys ȝou out of boure,   76
   ffor to hold up þis londus honour,
      With strenkyth our enmys for to bynde,
þat we may wynne the heuynly tour,
      ffor here þe bysom ledys þe blynde.   80

Explicit.

50. *LONDON LICKPENNY*

Harley MS. 367

London Lyckpeny   [f. 127r]

A ballade compyled by Dan Iohn Lydgate, monke of Bery, about
[ ] yeres agoo, and now newly ouersene and amended.

To London once my stepps I bent,
   where trouth in no wyse should be faynt,
To westmynster-ward I forthwith went,
   to a man of law to make complaynt.   4
   I sayd, "for marys love, that holy saynt,

65. MS. so þe.   67. MS. eueriy.   68. MS. euer.
71. MS. falundrys; *three minims only in* myschaunys.
No. 50. 3. MS. westmyster.

Pyty the poore that wold proceede."
but, for lack of mony, I cold not spede.

And as I thrust the prese amonge, 8
  by froward chavnce my hood was gone,
yet for all that I stayd not longe,
  tyll at the kynges bench I was come.
  before the Iudge I kneled anon, 12
    and prayd hym for gods sake to take heede.
    but, for lack of mony, I myght not speede.

Beneth them sat clarkes a gret Rout,
  which fast dyd wryte by one assent; 16
There stoode vp one and cryed about,
  "Rychard, Robert, and Iohn of Kent!"
  I wyst not well what this man ment,
    he cryed so thycke there in dede. 20
    but he that lackt mony myght not spede.

Unto the common place I yode thoo,
  where sat one with a sylken hoode;
I dyd hym reverence for I ought to do so, 24
  & told my case as well as I coolde,
  how my goodes were defravded me by falshood.
    I gat not a mvm of his mouth for my meed!
    and, for lack of mony, I myght not spede. 28

Vnto the Rolls I gat me from thence,
  before the Clarkes of the Chavncerye,
where many I found earnyng of pence,
  but none at all once regarded mee. 32
  I gave them my playnt vppon my knee,
    they lyked it well, when they had it reade;
    but, lackyng mony, I could not be sped.

11. at MS. to *expunged.*   24. for *written over* ? I do.
25. coolde *later altered in* MS.

In westmynster hall I fovnd out one,   [f. 127*v*]
    which went in a long gown of Raye;
I crowched and kneled before hym anon,
    for maryes love, of help I hym praye.
      "I wot not what thou meanest," gan he say;   40
        to get me thence he dyd me bede,
        for lack of mony I cold not speede.

with-in this hall, nether rych nor yett poor
    wold do for me ought, Although I shold dye.   44
which seing, I gat me out of the doore,
    where flemynges began on me for to cry:
      "master, what will you copen or by?
        fyne felt hattes, or spectacles to reede?   48
        lay down your sylver, and here you may speede."

then to westmynster gate I presently went,
    when the sonn was at hyghe pryme,
Cookes to me they tooke good entent,   52
    and profered me bread with ale and wyne,
    rybbs of befe, both fat and ful fyne.
      a fayre cloth they gan for to sprede,
      but, wantyng mony, I myght not speede.   56

Then vnto London I dyd me hye,
    of all the land it beareth the pryse:
"hot pescodes," one began to crye;
    "strabery rype," and "cherryes in the ryse!"   60
    one bad me come nere and by some spyce;
      peper and safforne they gan me bede.
      but, for lack of mony, I myght not spede.

42. but *crossed out before* for.   43. I *crossed out before* nether.
56. MS. not be; thus (?) *overwritten on* there *before* speede.
60. MS. stabery.

then to the Chepe I gan me drawne,   64
 where mutch people I saw for to stand;
one ofred me velvet, sylke, and lawne;
 an-other he taketh me by the hande,
  "here is Parys thred, the fynest in the land."   68
  I never was used to such thynges in dede,
  and, wantyng mony, I myght not spede.

then went I forth by London stone,   [f. 126r]
 throughout all Canwyke streete;   72
drapers mutch cloth me offred anone;
 then comes me one, cryed, "hot shepes feete."
 one Cryde, "makerell"; "Ryshes grene," an-other gan greete.
  on bad me by a hood to cover my head;   76
  but, for want of mony, I myght not be sped.

Then I hyed me Into Estchepe.
 one cryes, "rybbs of befe, & many a pye!"
Pewter pottes they clattered on a heape;   80
 there was harpe, pype, and mynstrelsye.
  "yea, by cock!" "nay, by cock!" some began crye;
  Some songe of "Ienken and Iulyan" for there mede.
  but, for lack of mony, I myght not spede.   84

Then Into Cornhyll anon I yode,
 where was mvtch stolen gere amonge;
I saw where honge myne owne hoode,
 that I had lost amonge the thronge.   88
 to by my own hood I thought it wronge —
  I knew it well as I dyd my crede;
  but, for lack of mony, I could not spede.

The Taverner tooke mee by the sleve,   92
 "Sir," sayth he, "wyll you our wyne assay?"

74. comes me *corrected from* met I.   86. was *corrected from* is.
93. good *crossed out before* wyne.

I answerd, "that can not mutch me greve;
  a peny can do no more then it may."
I drank a pynt, & for it dyd paye;   **96**
  yet sore a-hungerd from thence I yede,
  and, wantyng mony, I cold not spede.

Then hyed I me to Belyngsgate,   [f. 126*v*]
  and one cryed, "hoo! go we hence!"
I prayd a barge-man, for gods sake,
  that he wold spare me my expence.
  "thou scapst not here," quod he, "under ij pence;
    I lyst not yet bestow my Almes-dede."   **104**
    thus, lacking mony, I could not speede.

Then I convayed me Into Kent,
  ffor of the law wold I meddle no more,
because no man to me tooke entent,   **108**
  I dyght me to do as I dyd before.
  now Iesus that in Bethlem was bore,
    Save london, and send trew lawyers there mede!
    for who-so wantes mony, with them shall not spede.

Explicit London Lyckpeny

51. *MONEY, MONEY!*

Royal MS. 17.B.xlvii

money, money!   [f. 160*v*]

money, money, now hay goode day!
  money, where haste thow be?
money, money, thow gost away
  & wylt not byde wyth me.

98. MS. wantynyng.   109. I *crossed out before* as.

Aboue all thing thow arte a kyng,
   and rulyst the world ouer all;
who lakythe the, all Ioy, parde,
   wyll sone then frome hym ffall.   4

In euery place thow makyste solas,
   gret Ioye, spoorte, and velfare;
when money ys gone, comfort ys none,
   but thowght, sorowe, and care.   8

In kynges corte, wher money dothe route,
   yt makyth the galandes to Iett,
and for to were gorgeouse ther gere,
   ther cappes a-wry to sett.   12

In the hey-weyes ther Ioly palfreys
   yt makyght to lepe and praunce,
It maket Iustynges, pleys, dysguysynges,
   ladys to synge and daunce.   16

for he that alway wantyth money
   stondyth a mated chere,
can neuer wel syng, lang daunce nor springe,
   nor make no lusty chere.   20

At cardes and dyce yt bereth the pryce,   [f. 161r]
   at kyng and emperoure;
at tables, tennes, and al othere games,
   money hathe euer the floure.   24

wythe squyer and knyght and euery wyghte
   money maketh men fayne;
and causeth many in sume compeney
   theyr felowes to dysdayne.   28

1. MS. thng.   5. MS. palce; *then* tomakt *struck through*.
8. so *struck through after* but.   10. MS. garlandes.
13. the MS. they.   17. wantyth yt *written above line*.
19. MS. sprnge.   25. MS. and & knyght; wyghe.
28. MS. thery.

In marchandys who can deuyse
  so good a ware, I say?
at al tymys the best ware ys
  Euer redy money.   32

money to Incresse, marchandys neuer to cease
  wyth many a sotell wyle;
Men say the wolde for syluer and golde
  Ther owne faders begyle.   36

Women, I trowe, loue money also
  To by them Ioly gere;
for that helpythe and oft causethe
  women to loke full fayre.   40

In westmynster hall the criers call;   [f. 161*v*]
  The sergeauntes plede a-pace;
Attorneys appere, now here, now there,
  renning in euery place.   44

Whate-so-euer he be, and yf that he
  whante money to plede the lawe,
do whate he cane In ys mater than
  shale proue not worthe a strawe.   48

I know yt not, but well I wotte
  I haue harde often-tymys tell,
Prestes vse thys guyse, ther benefyce
  for money to bey and sell.   **52**

Craftys-men, that be in euery cyte,
  They worke and neuer blynne;
Sum cutte, sume shaue, sume knoke, sum graue,
  only money to wynne.   56

33. MS. I cresse.   36. fath *struck through before* faders.
41. MS. westmyaster.   45. euer MS. euery.
48. MS. shale not.   50. harde *inserted above line.*
52. MS. moyney.   55. knowe *struck through after first* Sum.

The plowman hym-selfe dothe dyge & delue
   In storme, snowe, frost, and rayne,
money to get with laboure and swete —
   yet small geynes and muche peyne.   60

and sume for money lye by the wey   [f. 162r]
   a-nother mannes purse to gett;
but they that long vse yt a-monge
   ben hangyd by the neke.   64

The beggers eke in euery strete
   ly walowyng by the wey;
They begge, the crye, of them cume by,
   and all ys but for money.   68

In euery coste men loue yt moste,
   In ynglonde, spayne, and francs,
for euery man lackyng yt than
   is clene owte of countenaunce.   72

of whate degre so euer he be,
   of werteouse conyng he haue,
and wante mone, yet men wyll sey,
   That he ys but a knaue.   76

where in-dede, so god me spede,
   Sey all men whate they cane;
yt ys all-wayes sene now-a-dayes
   That money makythe the man.   80

       finis.

62. to *inserted above line*.   67. them MS. the.
76. MS. that r he.   79. ys *struck through before* yt.

The burden is indicated by money *written after each of the first twelve quatrains, and by* money &c *after each of the last eight.*

52. *HUFF! A GALAUNT*

MS. Rawlinson poet. 34
(Sum. Cat. No. 14528)

Huff! a galawnt, vylabele!   [f. 4*v*]
Thus syngyth galawntys in here revele.

Galawnt, pride thy father ys dede;
Thow hast hym robbyd, as y rede,
And clothyd the in galawntes wede —
    Huff, a galawntt!   4

Galawntt, with thy curtesy,
Thow brekyst thy hose at kne,
And with a pacche þou clowtyst Aye —
    Huff, a galawntt!   8

Thow þat thow haue a stomager þe byforne,
Thy schyrtte by-hynd ys all to-torne;
Nere thy pykyd schone, þou were forlorne —
    Huff, a galauntt!   12

Galaunt, yf þou wylt haue thy hele,
Wrap thy bryst with clothys fele;
Than mayst þou synge vylabele —
    Huff, a galauntt!   16

Butt galauntt bachelers ther be fele,
Theyre gownys be sett with plytys fele;
To schortt yt ys theyre kneys to hele —
    Huff, a galauntt!   20

So galaunt to be, yt ys noughtt,
ffor and hys purse were well y-sought,
I hold hym worse than nought —
    Huff, a galauntt!   24

11. MS. Ner were.

All a-bak he castys hys here,
ffowre enchys by-neth hys ere,
I wold hys hed were off by þe swere —
   Huff, a galauntt!   28

Theyr hosyn of red, ful close þei be,
With a whytte bulwerk abowtt þe kne;
A schrewe syȝtt ytt ys to se —
   Huff, a galawnt!   32

Galaunt, by thy gyrdyl ther hangyth a purss;
Ther-in ys neyther peny ner crosse,
Butt iij dysse, and crystys curse —
   Huff, a galawnt!   36

Galaunt, with thy daggar a-crosse,
And thy hanggyng pouche vpon thy narse,
Thow art ful abyl to stele a horse,
   Huff, a Galauntt!   40

     Huff, a galauntt, vylabele!
     Thus syngyth galauntys in theyre reuele,
       With huff, a Galauntt!

53.   *THE PRIDE OF WOMEN'S HORNS*

MS. Ashmole 59
(Sum. Cat. No. 6943)

þou þat werred þe crowne of thornes,   [f. 73r]
Fell dovne þe pryde of wommens hornes,
And suffre hem longer with longe tayles,
Ne none oþer vicyous entayles,   4

Of noþer of males ne femayles,
Ne hodes, ne tyres lyche Carrake sayle.
Lord, for þy peyneful Passyoune,
To save oure soule frome dampnacion.   8

54. THE SAYINGS OF THE FOUR
PHILOSOPHERS (1311)

Advocates MS. 19.2.1

L'en puet fere & defere,	[f. 105r col. i]
ceo fait-il trop souent;	
It nis nouþer wel ne faire,	
þerfore engelond is shent.	4
Nostre prince de engleterre,	
per le consail de sa gent,	
At Westminster after þe feire	
maden a gret perlement.	8

La chartre fet de cyre —
  ieo l'enteink & bien le crey —
It was holde to neih þe fire
  and is molten al awey.   12
Ore ne say mes que dire,
  tout i va a tripolay,
Hundred, chapitle, court & shire,
  al hit goþ a deuel wey.   16

Des plu sages de la tere,
  ore escoteȝ vn sarmoun,
Of iiij wise men, þat þer were,
  whi engelond is brouht adoun.   20

Þe ferste seide: i vnderstonde
Ne may no king wel ben in londe,
  vnder god almihte,
But he kunne him-self rede   24
hou he shal in londe lede
  Eueri man wid rihte.

1-20. *written as long lines.*

ffor miht is riht,
Liht is niht,   28
And fiht is fliht.

    ffor miht is right, þe lond is laweles;
    ffor niht is liht, þe lond is lore-les;
    ffor fiht is fliht, þe lond is nameles.   32

þat oþer seide a word ful god:
Who-so roweþ aȝein þe flod,
    Off sorwe he shal drinke;
Also hit fareþ bi þe vnsele,   36
A man shal haue litel hele,
    þer agein to swinke.

Nu on is two,
Wel is wo,   40
And frend is fo.

    ffor on is two, þat lond is streinþeles;
    ffor wel is wo, þe lond is reuþeles;
    ffor frend is fo, þe lond is loueles.   44

þat þridde seide: it is no wonder
Off þise eyres, þat goþ vnder,
    Whan þeih comen to londe,
Proude & stoute, & ginneþ ȝelpe,   48
Ac of þing, þat sholde helpe,
    Haue þeih noht on honde.

Nu lust haueþ leue,
þef is reue,   52
And pride haþe sleue.

40. MS. Anoþer is wo.

ffor lust haþ leue, þe lond is þeweles;
ffor þef is reue, þe lond is penyles;   [col. ii]
ffor pride haþe sleue, þe lond is almusles. 56

þe ferþe seide þat he is wod
þat dwelleþ to muchel in þe flod,
    ffor gold or for auhte.
ffor gold or siluer or any wele,   60
Hunger or þurst, hete or chele,
    Al shal gon to nohte.

        Nu wille is red,
        Wit is qued,   64
        And god is dede.

        ffor wille is red, þe lond is wrecful;
        ffor wit is qued, þe lond is wrongful;
        ffor god is ded, þe lond is sinful.   68

Wid wordis as we han pleid,
Sum wisdom we han seid,
    Off olde men and ȝunge;
Off many a þing þat is in londe,   72
Who-so coude it vnderstonde,
    So haue i told wid tunge.

Riche & pore, bonde & fre,
þat loue is god, ȝe mai se;   76
    Loue clepes vch man broþer,
ffor if þat he to blame be,
ffor-ȝif hit him par charite,
    al-þeih he do oþer.   80

Loue we god, & he us alle,
þat was born in an oxe stalle,
    And for us don on rode.

his swete herte-blod he let   84
ffor us, & us faire het
 þat we sholde be gode.

Be we nu gode & stedefast,
So þat we muwen, at þe last,   88
 hauen heuene blisse.
To god al-mihti i preie,
Lat us neuere in sinne deie,
 þat ioye for to misse.   92

Ac leue us alle so don here,
& leue in loue & god manere,
 þe deuel for to shende,
þat we moten alle ifere   96
Sen him þat us bouhte dere,
 In ioye wid-oute ende.

   Amen.

55. THE TWELVE ABUSES

St. John's Coll. Cambridge MS. 37

Munus fit iudex, fraus est mercator in urbe; [f. 56v]
Non est lex dominus, nec timor est pueris.
Ingenium dolus est, amor omnis ceca voluptas,
Ludus rusticitas, et gula festa dies.   4
Senex ridetur, sapiens mendosus habetur,
Diues laudatur, pauper vbique iacet.
Prudentes ceci, cognati degeneres sunt;
Mortuus inmemor est, nullus amicus erit.   8

3eft is Domesman, & gyle is chapman;
Lordys ben owtyn lawe, & chylderen ben withowtyn awe;
Wyth is trechery, & loue is lecherye;
& pley turnyt to vylanye, & holyday to glotonye.   12
Eld man in scornyng, wyse man in lesyng,
Ryche man in levyng, & pore man in losyng;
Sly men ben blynd, & kenred is onkynd;
þe ded is owtyn of mynd, for he may fynd noo frond.   16

Virtus	Ecclesia	Clerus	Demon	Simonia
cessat.	calcatur.	errat.	regnat.	dominatur.

Now men leuyn good thewis,
& holy chyrch is led with schrewys,   20
Clergie goth owt of þe wey,
þe fend among hem hath hys prey,
Symony is aboue, & awey is trwloue.

56.   ABUSES OF THE AGE, I

Harley MS. 913

Bissop lorles,   [f. 6*v*]
Kyng redeles,
3ung man rechles,
Old man witles,   4
Womman ssamles.
I swer bi heuen kyng,
þos beþ fiue liþer þing.

57.   ABUSES OF THE AGE, II

MS. Bodley 416
(Sum. Cat. No. 2315)

Vertues & good lyuinge is cleped ypocrisie;   [f. 108*v*]
trowþe & godis lawe is clepud heresie;

16. MS. owty.   22. MS. amonsg.

pouert & lownes is clepud loselrie;
trewe prechinge & penaunce is clepud folie.   4
pride is clepud honeste,
and coueityse wisdom.
richesse is clepud worþynes,
and lecherie kyndely þing,   8
robberie good wynnynge,
& glotenye but murþe.
enuye and wraþþe men clepen riʒtfulnes;
slouþe men clepen nedfulnes   12
to norshe mennes kynde.
and þus mannes lif þat shulde be holi
is turned into cursednes.
riʒtwisdom is not dred,   16
and mercy is but scorned;   [f. 109r]
lesinges and fables ben clepude good lore,
and cristes gospel but a chape.
And þus for defaute of trewe techinge,   20
men wenden to helle by many weies.
þe ioye of heuene men setten not bi,
but al bi wordli likinge.
and here-fore ueniaunce god wol take   24
on us, but ʒif we amende,
and wiþ sorwe oure synne forsake
or we hame wende.
whanne hit shal be, we knowen not!   28
þerfore turne we bi-tyme,
For ʒif we abide fort 'hadde y wyst',
þanne is al to late!

58.   ENGLAND MAY SING ALAS

Caius Coll. Cambridge MS. 71

Syn lawe for will begynnes to slaken,   [f. 50r]
& falsed for sleyth now is taken;

13. MS. norsle.

Robbyng & rewyng is holden purchas,   4
& of vnclennes is made solas,
Englond may say & syng, Allas! Allas!

59. *TRUTH IS UNPOPULAR*

Sloane MS. 2593

God be with trewþe, qwer he be.   [f. 7*r*]
I wolde he were in þis cuntre!

A man þat xuld of trewþe telle,   [f. 7*v*]
With grete lordys he may not dwelle;
In trewe story, as klerkes telle,
 trewþe is put In low degre.   4

In ladyis chaumberys comit he not,
þer dar trewþe settyn non fot;
þow he wolde he may not
 comyn among þe heye mene.   8

With men of lawe he haȝt non spas —
þey louyn trewþe in non plas;
me þinkit þey han a rewly grace,
 þat trewþe is put at swych degre.   12

In holy cherche he may not sytte,
fro man to man þey xuln hym flytte;
It rewit me sore, in myn wytte;
 Of trewþe I haue gret pete.   16

Relygius þat xulde be good,
If trewþe cum þer I holde hym wood!
þey xuldyn hym rynde cote & hood,
 & make hym bare for to fle.   20

No. 59. 3. In MS. I. 12, 16. MS. treþe. 17. MS. Relygiuus.

A man þat xulde of trewþe aspyre,
he must sekyn esylye
In þe bosum of marye,
    for þere he is for-soþe.   24

60. HOW GOES THIS WORLD ABOUT

Sloane MS. 2593

As I me lend to a lend,   [f. 33r]
    I herd a schepperde makyn a schowte;
he gronyd & seyde with sory syghyng,
    A lord, how gos þis word a-bowte!   4

It gos ful wrong, ho-so it wyst:
    a frend, ho may ken fro his foo?
to hom I may trewely trost,
    In fayth, I fynde but fewe of þo!   8

Þe soþe, me þinkyt, if I xulde say,
    trewe frendys arn fewe, with-outyn dowte;
alle half frendys, wo, wo worth hem ay.
    a lord, how gos þis word a-bowte!   12

Alle half frendys, wo worth hem ay —
    In wel, in wo, in hert, in þowth.
It must be soþ þat alle men say,
    he was neuere good frend was wroþ for nowth.   16

Now wel, now wo, now frend, now foo;   [f. 33v]
    Now lef, now þef, now in, now out;
Now cum, now go, now to, now fro —
    A lord, how gos þis word a-bowte!   20

No. 60. 13. half MS. trewe.

þe werst wytys herte of alle man kende;
  alle wykkyd tungys, ay worth hem woo!
þei arn ful fayn fals talis to fynd,
  þei gref me þus, I may not goo.   24

but god of hem þou take sum wreche,
  & a-rest hem alle be rowt;
þat false arn & fayre cun speke —
  A lord, how gos þis word a-bowte!   28

61. THIS WORLD IS VARIABLE

MS. Eng. poet. e.1
(Sum. Cat. No. 29734)

Wold god þat men myȝt sene   [f. 16r]
hertys whan þei bene,
  for thynges þat bene vn-trew.
If yt be as I wene,   4
thyng þat semyth grene,
  ys ofte fadyd of hew.

Wyll ys tak for reson;   [f. 16v]
Trew loue ys full geson;   8
  No man sett be shame.
Trost ys full of treson;
Eche man oderys cheson,
  No man hym-seylfe wyll blame.   12

Thys warlde ys varyabyll,
No-thyng þer-in ys stable,
  A-say now, ho-so wyll.
Syn yt is so mutable,   16
how shuld men be stable?
  yt may not be thorow skyll!

23. MS. faym.
No. 61. 6. MS. *faded*; *written at side* ? hew.   17. MS. me.

Whane brome wyll appolles bere,
& humlok hony in feere,   20
   þan sek rest in lond.
With men is no pees;
Ne rest in hart is, no lese,
   With few be see & sond.   24

Sythyn þer is no rest,
I hold it for þe best,
   god to be owre frend.
he þat ys owre lord,   28
delyuer vs ouȝt with hys word,
   & gravnt vs a good ende!

62. *NOW IS ENGLAND PERISHED*

Cambridge Univ. MS. Hh.2.6

Nowe is Englond perisshed in fight,   ·   [f. 58r col. ii]
With moche people & consciens light,
Many knyghtes & lytyll myght,
Many lawys & lityll right;   4

Lytyll cherite & fayn to please,
Many galantes & penylese,
Great courtears & small wages,
Many gentilmen & fewe pages;   8

Short gownys & slyt sleuys,
Wel besee & strong thevys;
Great boost & gay clothis,
Mark theym well, thei lak non otheȝ.   12

27. be *supplied*.   No. 62. 1. MS. sight.

Many fals slawnders of riches,
And yet pouerte apperith neuerthelesse;
Many beades & fewe prayers,
Many dettours & fewe good payers.   16

Small festyng & lytyll penaunce,
Thus all is turned in-to myschaunce,
Extorcion, & moch Symony,
fals couetyse with periurye;   20

With lechery & aduowetrye,
ffayned frenship & ypocrisye;
Also gyle on euery syde,
With murdre & much pride;   24

Great envy & wilfulnes,
With-out mercy or rightwysnes;
The cause is for lak of light,
That shuld be in the church of right.   28

63. THE WORLD UPSIDE DOWN

Bodl. MS. Eng. poet. b.4

Religious pepille leuyn in holynesse,   [f. 1v col. i]
    Seruiabli with-owte transmutacion.
Enuy exilid is fro gentylnesse;
    And for ypocrosye ys set deuocion.   4
    In lawe trouthe hathe his dominacion;
        All dowblenesse venquesschid bi right at þe desire;
        Stablenesse foundon, and spesialli in a-tire.

Amongge the comyns pride is now exilid;   8
    Louers vsyn no fayned countenaunce;
In knyghthod largesse nwli ys reuyuyd.

No. 63. 1, 2. *Space left for rubricated initial.*
No. 63. 3 MS. exalid is for fre.

Ho can in court fynd eny variaunce?
Prestus in litille han there suffisaunce;   12
   Conschiaunce with Marchaundice is cheffe lord & syre;
  And stablenesse foundun, and spesialli in a-tire.

Humblesse the name of rigour hath ow3t rased,
  Which grauen was in femynyte.   16
Frenchip and Kynred to-gederis ben enbrasid;
  Bovnte his sugenaunsse hathe bewte;
  Fals Raungor ys fled; and benygnyte
    Of envi hath quenchid þe sotell fire;   20
   And stablenesse Foundon, & spesialli in a-tire.

Consciens Romyng in eueri path & strete;
  Vnabelite woll take on hym no charge;
Coueitice with falshode neuyr more to mete;   24
  And playn prechorws there to sey at large;
  Aliauns put disdeyne in seruage;
    Law so parfit þat woll chaunge for no hire;
   And stabilnesse found, and spesialli in a-tire.   28

No evne Reynyngge but suche as kepith wighte;
  Favell hathe lost his tongge and countenaunce;
Parfitte trust and spesialli ow3t of syght;
  Periuri is fled forthe in-to Fraunce;   32
  Wommanhode hatyng oure aqueyntaunce;
    Freris to flatur han lost þere desire;
   And stablenesse foundon, & spesialli in a-tire.

In eche matire mede is now forsake;   36
  Lordis gamys cherished to þere availe;
Iurrours woll for-swere gold forto take;
  No fals Marchaundice sold at retaile;

12, 13. *Marked* a, b, *for transposition.*   24. MS. more to me.
30. MS. countenaunace.   32. MS. fled for forthe.
38. MS. Iurerrours.

Wiffis answerum not at þe counturtaile;   40
   All true laborerres paide daili þe hire;
   And stabilnesse foundun, specialli in a-tire.

All these lightli shold tornyn vp so dovne,   [col. ii]
   Ne were of wommen þe perfight stablenesse.   44
Ho can fynd more comfortable sovn
   Than is þere vois in eche nede & distresse?
   For þei eryn þe well of comfort & mekenesse.
     Ner the wisdomes, all we were in þe myre,   48
     And perfit stablenesse of suche as were a-tire.

CRITICS OF THE LOLLARDS

64. DEFEND US FROM ALL LOLLARDRY

Cotton MS. Vespasian B.xvi

Lo, he þat can be cristes clerc,   [f. 2v]
   And knowe þe knottes of his crede,
Now may se a wonder werke,
   Of harde happes to take goud heede.   4
   The dome of dethe is heuy drede
     For hym þat wol not mercy crie;
   þan is my rede, for mucke ne mede,
     þat no man melle of lollardrye.   8

I sey for meself, yut wist I neuer
   but now late what hit shuld be,
and, by my trouth, I haue wel leuer
   no more kyn þan my a, b, c.   12
   To lolle so hie in suyche degre,
     hit is no perfit profecie,
   Sauf seker sample to þe & me
     to be war of lollardie.   16

43. MS. lighli.   44. MS. womnen.   No. 64. MS. *written in long lines.*

The game is noȝt to lolle so hie
   þer fete failen fondement;
and yut is a moch folie
   for fals beleue to ben brent.   20
   þer þe bibell is al myswent,
      To iangle of Iob or Ieremye,
   þat construen hit after her entent
      for lewde lust of lollardie.   24

Hit is vnkyndly for a kniȝt,
   þat shuld a kynges castel kepe,
To bable þe bibel day & niȝt
   In restyng tyme when he shuld slepe;   28
   & carefoly awey to crepe,
   for alle þe chief of chiualrie.
   Wel auȝt hym to waile & wepe,
      þat suyche lust haþ in lollardie.   32

An old castel, & not repaired,
   With wast walles & wowes wide,
þe wages ben ful yuel wared
   With suich a capitayn to abide;   36
   þat rereth riot for to ride
      Agayns þe kynge & his clergie,
   With priue peyne & pore pride;
      þer is a poynt of lollardie.   40

for many a man withyn a while
   shal aby his gult ful sore;
So fele gostes to begile
   hym auȝt to rue euermore.   44
   For his sorowe shal he neuer restore
      þat he venemed with enuye;
   But ban þe burthe þat he was of bore,
      Or euer had lust in lollardie.   48

27. of *scratched out after* bable.

Euery shepe þat shuld be fed in felde,
  & kepte fro wolfes in her folde,
Hem nedeth neþer spere ne shulde,
    Ne in no castel to be withholde.   52
    for þer þe pasture is ful colde,   .
      in somer seson when hit is drie;
    & namly when þe soyle is solde,
      for lewde lust of lollardie.   56

An old castel draw al don,
  hit is ful hard to rere hit newe,
With suyche a congregacion
    þat cast hem to be vntrewe.   60
    When beggers mow neþer bake ne brewe,
      ne haue wherwith to borrow ne bie,
    Þan mot riot robbe or reve,
      Vnder þe colour of lollardie.   64

That castel is not for a kynge   [f. 3r]
  þer þe walles ben ouerthrowe;
& yut wel wors abidynge
    whan þe captayn away is flowe,   68
    And forsake spere & bowe,
      to crepe fro kniȝthode into clergie.
    Þer is a bitter blast yblowe,
      to be bawde of lollardie.   72

I trowe þer be no kniȝt alyue
  þat wold haue don so open a shame,
for þat crafte to studi or striue,
    hit is no gentel mannes game;   76
    but if hym lust to haue a name
      of pelour vnder ipocrasie,
    & þat wer a foule defame
      to haue suyche lose of lollardie.   80

64. MS. Vnde.

And, parde, lolle þei neuer so longe,
   yut wol lawe make hem lowte;
God wol not suffre hem be so stronge
   to bryng her purpos so abowte,   84
   with saun3 faile & saun3 doute,
     to rere riot and robberie;
   By reson þei shul not long route,
     while þe taile is docked of lollardie.   88

Of þe hede hit is las charge,
   when grace wol not be his gide,
Ne suffre hym for to lepe at large,
   but heuely his hede to hide.   92
   Where shuld he oþer route or ride
     agayns þe chief of chiualrie,
   Not hardi in no place to abide,
     for alle þe sekte of lollardie.   96

A! god, what vnkyndly gost
   shuld greue þat god grucched nou3t!
Thes lollardes þat lothen ymages most
   with mannes handes made & wrou3t,   100
   & pilgrimages to be sou3t;
     þei seien hit is but mawmentrie.
   He þat þis lose first vp brou3t,
     had gret lust in lollardie.   104

Ho wor ful lewde þat wolde byleue
   in figure mad of stok or ston,
Yut fourme shuld we none repreue,
   neþer of marie ne of Ion,   108
   Petre, Poule, ne oþer none
     canonised by clergie;
   þan þe seyntes euerychon
     be litel holde to lollardie.   112

And namly Iames among hem alle
  for he twyes had turnement,
Moch mischaunse mot him befalle
  þat last beheded hym in kent;   116
    & alle þat were of þat assent.
      to crist of heuen I clepe & crie,
    Send hem þe same Iugement,
      & alle þe sekte of lollardie.   120

For þat vengans agayns kynde
  was a poynt of cowardyse;
& namly suych on to bete or bynde
  þat miȝt not stand, set, ne rise.   124
    What dome wold ye hym deuyse
      by lawe of armes or gentrie,
    But serue hym in þe same wise,
      & alle þe sekte of lollardie.   128

When falsnes faileþ frele folie,
  pride wol preseyn sone amonge;
þan willerdome with old enuy
  can none oþer way but wronge.   132
    For synne & shame with sorowe strong,
      So ouerset with avutrie,
    þat fals beleue is fayn to fonge
      þe lewde lust of lollardie;   136

and vnder colour of suiche lollynge,
  To shape sodeyn surreccion
Agaynst oure liege lord kynge,
  with fals ymaginacion.   140
    & for þat corsed conclusion,
      by dome of kniȝthode & clergie,
    Now turneth to confusion
      þe sory sekte of lollardie.   144

For holy writ berith witnes,
   He þat fals is to his kyng,
þat shamful deth & hard distres
   shal be his dome at his endynge.   148
     þan double deth for suyche lollynge
      is heuy, when we shul hennes hye.
     Now, lord, þat madest of nou3t all thinge,
      defende vs all fro lollardie.   152

CRITICS OF THE FRIARS

65. THE ORDERS OF CAIN (1382)

Cotton MS. Cleopatra B.ii

Preste, ne monke, ne 3it chanoun,   [f. 62v]
Ne no man of religioun,
Gyfen hem so to deuocioun
   As done þes holy frers.   4
For summe gyuen ham to chyualry,
Somme to riote & ribaudery;
Bot ffrers gyuen ham to grete study,
   And to grete prayers.   8
     Who-so kepes þair reule al,
      boþe in worde & dede,
     I am ful siker þat he shal
      haue heuen blis to mede.   12

Men may se by þair contynaunce
þat þai are men of grete penaunce,
And also þat þair sustynaunce
   Simple is & wayke.   16
I haue lyued now fourty 3ers,
And fatter men about þe neres
3it sawe I neuer þen are þese frers,
   In contreys þer þai rayke.   20

Meteles so megre are þai made,
    & penaunce so puttes ham doun,
þat ichone is an hors-lade
    when he shal trusse of toun.   24

Allas, þat euer it shuld be so,
Suche clerkes as þai about shuld go,
Fro toun to toun by two & two,
    to seke þair sustynaunce!   28
By god þat al þis world wan,
He þat þat ordre first bygan,
Me thynk certes it was a man
    of simple ordynaunce.   32
        For þai haue noght to lyue by,
            þai wandren here & þere,
        And dele with dyuers marcerye,
            right as þai pedlers were.   36

þai dele with purses, pynnes, & knyues,
With gyrdles, gloues for wenches & wyues —
Bot euer bacward þe husband thryues
    þer þai are haunted till.   40
For when þe gode man is fro hame,
And þe frere comes to oure dame,
He spares nauþer for synne ne shame
    þat he ne dos his will.   44
        If þai no helpe of houswyues had,
            whan husbandes are not Inne,
        þe freres welfare were ful bad,
            for þai shuld brewe ful þynne.   48

Somme frers beren pelure aboute,
For grete ladys & wenches stoute,
To reuerce with þair cloþes withoute —
    Al after þat, þai ere —   52

For somme vaire, & somme gryse,
For somme bugee, & for somme byse.
& also many a dyuers spyse,
  In bagges about þai bere.   56
    Al þat for women is plesand
     ful redy certes haue þai;
    Bot lytel gyfe þai þe husband
     þat for al shal pay.   60

Trantes þai can, & many iape;   [f. 63r]
For somme can with a pound of sape
Gete him a kyrtelle & a cape
  & somwhat els þerto!   64
Wherto shuld I oþes swere?
Þer is no pedler þat pak can bere
Þat half so dere can sell his gere
  þen a frer can do.   68
    For if he gife a wyfe a knyfe
     þat cost bot penys two,
    Worþe ten knyues, so mot I thryfe,
     he wyl haue er he go.   72

Ich man þat here shal lede his life,
Þat has a faire doghter or a wyfe,
Be war þat no frer ham shryfe,
  nauther loude ne still.   76
Þof women seme of hert ful stable,
With faire byhest and with fable
Þat can make þair hertes chaungeable,
  and þair likynges fulfill.   80
    Be war ay with þe lymitour,
     & with his felawe baþe;
    & þai make maystries in þi bour,
     It shal turne þe to scaþe.   84

76. for drede of makyng wo *struck out and present line added*.

Were I am a man þat hous helde,
  If any woman with me dwelde,
þer is no frer bot he were gelde
  shuld com with-In my wones.   88
For may he til a woman wynne
In priueyte, he wyl not blynne
Er he a childe put hir with-Inne —
  & perchaunce two at ones!   92
      þof he loure vnder his hode,
        with semblaunt quaynte & mylde,
      If þou him trust, or dos him gode,
        by god, þou ert bygylde!   96

þai say þat þai distroye synne,
& þai mayntene men moste þer-Inne;
For had a man slayn al his kynne,
  go shryue him at a frere,   100
& for lesse þen a payre of shone
He wyl assoil him, clene & sone,
And say þe synne þat he has done
  his saule shal neuer dere.   104
      It semes soþe þat men sayne of hayme
        in many dyuers londe,
      þat þat caytyfe cursed cayme
        first þis ordre fonde.   108

Nou se þe soþe whedre it be swa,
þat frer carmes come of a k,
þe frer austynes come of a,
  frer Iacobynes of i,   112
Of M comen þe frer menours.
þus grounded caym thes four ordours,
þat fillen þe world ful of errours
  & of ypocrisy.   116

Alle wyckednes þat men can tell
   regnes ham among;
þer shal no saule haue rowme in hell,
   of frers þer is such þrong.   120

þai trauele ȝerne & bysily,
To brynge doun þe clergye;
þai speken þerof ay vilany,
   & þerof þai done wrong.   124
Whoso lyues oght many ȝers
Shal se þat it shall fall of frers
As it dyd of þe templers,
   þat wonned here vs among.   128
      For þai held no religioun
         bot lyued after lykyng;
      þai were distroyed & broght adoun
         þurgh ordynance of þe kyng.   132

þes frers haunten a dredful þing,
þat neuer shal come to gode endyng:
O frer for eght or nyen shal syng,
   for ten or for elleuen.   136
& when his terme is fully gone,
Conscience þen has he none,
þat he ne dar take of ychone
   Markes sixe or seuen.   140
      Suche annuels has made þes frers
         so wely & so gay,
      þat þer may no possessioners
         mayntene þair array.   144

þam felle to lyue al on purchace,
Of almes geten fro place to place;
& for all þat þam holpen has,
   shuld þai pray & syng.   148

Bot now þis londe so negh soght is,
þat vnneþe may prestes seculers
Gete any seruice for þes frers —
    þat is wondre þing.   152
        þis is a quaynt custome
           ordeyned ham among,
        þat frers shal annuel prestes bycome,
           & so-gates selle þer song.   156

Ful wysely can þai preche & say;
Bot as þai preche, no þing do þai.
I was a frere ful many a day,
    þerfor þe soþe I wate.   160
Bot when I sawe þat þair lyuyng
Acordyd not to þair preching,
Of I cast my frer cloþing
    & wyghtly went my gate.   164
        Oþer leue ne toke I none
           fro ham when I went,
        Bot toke ham to þe deuel ychone,
           þe priour & þe couent.   168

Out of þe ordre þof I be gone,
Apostota ne am I none;
Of twelue moneþes me wanted one,
    & odde days nyen or ten.   172
Away to wende I made me boun,
Or tyme come of professioun,
I went my way þurghout þe toun
    In syght of many men.   176
        Lord god þat with paynes ill   [f. 64r]
           mankynde boght so dere,
        Let neuer man after me **haue will**
           for to make him frere!   180

176. m *struck out after* In.

66. ON THE MINORITES (1382)

Cotton MS. Cleopatra B.ii

Of þes frer mynours me thenkes moch wonder,   [f. 64v]
Þat waxen are þus hauteyn, þat som tyme weren vnder;
Among men of holy chirch þai maken mochel blonder;
Nou he þat sytes vs aboue, make ham sone to sonder!   4
   With an O & an I, þai praysen not seynt poule,
   Þai lyen on seyn ffraunceys, by my fader soule!

First þai gabben on god þat all men may se,
When þai hangen him on hegh on a grene tre,   8
With leues & with blossemes þat bright are of ble,
Þat was neuer goddes son by my leute.
   With an O & an I, Men wenen þat þai wede,
   To carpe so of clergy þat can not þair crede.   12

Þai haue done him on a croys fer vp in þe skye,
And festned in hym wyenges, as he shuld flie.
Þis fals feyned byleue shal þai soure bye,
On þat louelych lord, so forto lye.   16
   With an O & an I, One sayd ful still,
   Armachan distroy ham, if it is goddes will.

Þer comes one out of þe skye in a grey goun,
As it were an hog-hyerd hyand to toun;   20
Þai haue mo goddes þen we, I say by Mahoun,
All men vnder ham, þat euer beres croun.
   With an O & an I, why shuld þai not be shent?
   Þer wantes noght bot a fyre þat þai nere all brent!   24

Went I forther on my way in þat same tyde,
Þer I sawe a frere bled in myddes of his syde,
Boþe in hondes & in fete had he woundes wyde,
To serue to þat same frer, þe pope mot abyde.   28

3. chirch *inserted above line.*   8. on *struck through after* hangen.
12. þat MS. þai.

With an O & an I, I wonder of þes dedes,
To se a pope holde a dische whyl þe frer bledes.

A cart was made al of fyre, as it shuld be,
A gray frer I sawe þer-Inne, þat best lyked me.　　　　32
Wele I wote þai shal be brent, by my leaute;
God graunt me þat grace þat I may it se.
　.　With an O & an I, Brent be þai all,
　　& all þat helpes þerto faire mot byfall.　　　　36

þai preche all of pouert, bot þat loue þai noght,
For gode mete to þair mouþe þe toun is þurgh soght;
Wyde are þair wonnynges & wonderfully wroght,
Murdre and horedome ful dere has it boght.　　　　40
　　With an O & an I, ffor sixe pens, er þai fayle,
　　Sle þi fadre & iape þi modre, & þai wyl þe assoile!

67.　FRIARS, MINISTRI MALORUM

Trinity Coll. Cambridge MS. 1144

ffreers, freers, wo ȝe be!　　　　　　　　　　[f. 58v]
　　ministri malorum.
ffor many a mannes soule brynge ȝe
　　ad penas inffernorum.　　　　　　　　　　4
whan seyntes ffelle ffryst ffrom heuen,
　　quo prius habitabant,
In erthe leyftt þo synnus vij
　　& ffratres communicabant.　　　　　　　　8
ffolnes was þe ffryst ffloure
　　quem ffratres pertulerunt,
ffor folnes & fals derei
　　multi perierunt.　　　　　　　　　　　　12

No. 67.　2. MS. minstri.

ffreers, ȝe can weyl lye
  ad ffalundum gentem,
& weyl can blere a mannus ye
  pecunias habentem.   16
yf þei may no more geytte,
  fruges petunt isti,
ffor folnes walde þei not lette,
  qui non sunt de grege cristi.   20
lat a ffreer off sum ordur
  tecum pernoctare,
odur þi wyff or þi dougtour
  hic vult violare;   24
or þi sun he weyl prefur,
  sicut ffurtam ffortis.
god gyffe syche a ffreer peyn
  In inferni portis!   28
þei weyl assaylle boyth Iacke & gylle,
  licet sint predones;
& parte off pennans take hem tylle,
  qui sunt latrones.   32
þer may no lorde of þis cuntre
  sic edifficare
as may þes ffreers, were þei be,
  qui vadunt mendicare.   36
mony-makers I trow þei be,
  regis proditores,
þerffore yll mowyth þei thee,
  ffalsi deceptores.   40
ffader ffyrst in trinite,
  ffilius atque fflamen.

    Omnes dicant Amen.

68.　THE LAYMAN'S COMPLAINT

St. John's Coll. Cambridge MS. 195

þou þat sellest þe worde of god,　　　　　　　　　　[f. iv]
Be þou berfot, be þou schod,
　　Cum neuere here.
In principio erat verbum　　　　　　　　　　　　　　4
Is þe worde of god, all & sum,
　　þat þou sellest, lewed frere.

Hit is cursed symonie
Eþer to selle or to bye　　　　　　　　　　　　　　　8
　　Ony gostly þinge;
þerfore, frere, go as þou come,
& hold þe in þi hows at home
　　til we þe almis brynge.　　　　　　　　　　　　　12

Goddis lawe ȝe reuerson,
And mennes howsis ȝe persen,
　　As poul beriþ wittnes.
As mydday deuelis goynge abowte,　　　　　　　　　16
for money lowle ȝe lowte,
　　flatteringe boyþe more & lesse.

69.　THE FRIAR'S ANSWER

St. John's Coll. Cambridge MS. 195

Allas! what schul we freris do,　　　　　　　　　[f. iv]
　　Now lewed men kun holy writ?
Alle abowte wherre I go
　　þei aposen me of it.　　　　　　　　　　　　　　4

18. flatteringe *written over* ? slakynge *struck through.*
No. 69. The fryers Complaynt *added in a later hand in margin.*

þen wondriþ me þat it is so
   How lewed men kun alle writ.
Sertenly we be vn-do
   But if we mo amende it.   8

I trowe þe deuel browȝt it aboute
   To write þe gospel in englishe,
ffor lewed men ben nowe so stowt
   þat þei ȝeuen vs neyþer fleche ne fishe.   12

When I come into a schope   [f. iiʳ]
   for to say "in principio,"
þei bidine me, "goo forþ, lewed poppe!"
   & worche & win my siluer so!   16

Yf y sae hit longoþ not
   ffor prestis to worche where þei go,
þei leggen for hem holi writ
   And sein þat seint polle did soo.   20

þan þei loken on my nabete,
   & sein, "forsoþe, withoutton oþes,
Wheþer it be russet, black, or white,
   It is worþe alle oure werynge cloþes."   24

I saye, "I, not for me,
   bot for them þat haue none."
þei seyne, "þou hauist to or þre;
   ȝeuen hem þat nedith þerof oone."   28

þus oure desseytis bene aspiede
   In þis maner & mani moo;
fewe men bedden vs abyde
   but hey fast þat we were goo.   32

23. blake *struck through and* black *added above line.*
26. them *inserted above line.*

If it goo forþe in þis maner,
  It wole done vs myche gyle;
Men schul fynde vnneþe a frere
  In englonde wiþin a whille.   36

ENGLAND'S COMMERCE

70. *A TRADE POLICY*

Lansdowne MS. 796

Anglia, propter tuas naves et lanas, Omnia regna   [f. 1*v*]
te salutare deberent.

Goo forth, lybell, and mekly schew thy face
Afore my lordes with humble countenaunss,
And pray theym all to take the to grace
In appoysayll and in cheryschyng the to avaunce.   4

ffor thow mayst expertly be provyd by prudence,
Among all discrete men hauyng sapyence,
ffor oone of þe best þat may be thought
ffor þe welth of ynglond, yf it be well sowthe.   8

ffor ther ys no reme in no maner degree
Butt they haue nede to oure englysshe commodyte;
And þe cawse þeroff I wyll to yow expresse,
The wich ys soth as þe gospell of the masse.   12

Ther ys noothir pope, Emperowre, nor kyng,
Bysschop, cardynal, or any men leuyng,
Of what condicion or what maner degree,
Duryng theyre leuyng þei must haue thynges iij: 16

Mete, drynk, & cloth to euery mannes sustynaunce.
They leng all iij withowtt varyaunce.
ffor who-so lackyth any of thyse iij thynges —
Be the popys or emperowrs or soo royall kynges —   20

Yt may not stonde with theym in any prosperyte,
ffor who-so lackyth any of thyse he suffryd aduersyte.
Wilys þis ys soth be yowre wyttes dyscerne,
Of all þe remes in þe world this beryth the lantern.   24

ffor of eueryche of thyse iij, by goddes ordynaunce,
Wee haue suffycyenly vnto oure sustynaunce;
And with þe supplusage of oone of thyse iij thynges
We my3gth rewle & gouern all crystyn kynges.   28

And paynymys also we my3th mak theym ful tame;   [f. 2r]
ffor þe cause we take no hed we be mykyll to blame.
for of all þe pepyll þat be lyuyng on grounde,
To praye & to please god we be most bownde.   32

ffor thow þei haue met, drynke, in euery kyngges londe,
Yet they lack cloth, as y vndyrstonde.
And for to determyn þat þe trouthe ys soe,
Lestyn wel to me & ye moste acord þerto.   36

ffor þe marchauntes comme oure wollys for to bye,
Or elles þe cloth þat is made þeroff sykyrly,
Oute of dyuerse londes fer byyond þe see,
To haue thyse merchaundyss into theyre contre.   40

ffrom arteyse, pekardy, henaude, & normandy,
Bretayne, fraunse, petowe, and barry,
Gasscoyne, gyon, and also aragun,
Portyngale, spayne, & nauerun;   44

Castyle, Cesyle, coleyn, & swethyn,
Pruse-londe, florence, venyse, & Iene,
Melane, catelony, and all ytally,
Bewme, hungry, greke, and gret turky;   48

And many moo londes þat I can-not neuene.
But y dar sey all þat be vnþer heuyn,
Both crystyn and hethyn of all maner degreys,
They haue nede to oure Englysshe commodyteis.   52

Therfor let not owre woole be sold for now3te,
Neyther oure cloth, for they must be sowth;
And in especyall restrayne strayttly þe wool,
That þe comyns of thys land may wyrke at the full.   56

And yf any wool be sowlde of thys londe,   [f. 2*v*]
Lete yt be of the worst, both to ffre & bonde;
And noon other in no maner wyse,
ffor many dyuerse cawsys, as y can deuyse.   60

Yf þe woole be corse, the cloth is mykyll the worse;
Yet in-to lytyll þei putt owte of purse
As mych for gardyng, spynnyng, and weuyng,
ffullyng, rowyng, dyyng, and scheryng.   64

And yet when such cloth ys all ywrowte,
To the maker it waylyth lytyll or now3tte;
The pryce ys sympyll — þe cost ys neuer the lesse:
They þat wyrkkyd soche wooll in wytte be lyke a nasse!   68

The costes into lytyll trewly at þe fulle
Ys as myche as yt were maad of þe fyne woll,
Yet a 3erde of þat oon ys worth v of þat other.
Bettyr can-not I seye, thow yt were to my brother!   72

51. and *supplied.*   59. no *supplied.*

Take hed to my lesson þat y haue schewyd here,
ffor yt ys necessary to euery clothyer,
And þe most preuayle to theym þat may be fownde,
Yf they wyll take hede þerto and yt vndyrstonde.   76

A ordynaunce wolde be maad for þe poore porayle,
That in thyse dayes haue but lytyll auayle;
þat is to sey for spynners, carders, wevers also,
ffor toukers, dyers, and schermyn þereto.   80

for in thyse dayes þer is a hewsaunce,
þat puttyth þe pore pepyll to grett hynderaunce,
By a strange mene that is late in londe
Begun and usyd, as y vndyrstonde,   84

By merchaundes & cloth-makers — for godys sake   [f. 3r]
                                    take kepe! —
þe wyche makyth þe poreyll to morne & wepe.
Lytyll þei take for theyre labur, yet halff ys merchaundyse.
Alas! for rewth, yt ys gret pyte!   88

þat they take for vjd, yt ys dere ynow of iij;
And thus þei be defrawdyd in euery contre;
The pore haue þe labur, the ryche the wynnyng.
This acordythe now3te, it is a heuy partyng.   92

Butt to uoyde fraude, and sett egallyte,
þat syche wyrkfolk be payd in good mone,
ffrom þis tyme forth by suffycyent ordynaunce
þat þe poreyll no more be putte to such greuaunce.   96

85. That *dotted for expunction before* By.
91. haue *inserted above line.*
94. MS. wyrfolk (1 *written over* r).

ffor and ye knew þe sorow and heuyness
Of the pore pepyll leuyng in dystress,
How þei be oppressyd in all maner of thyng,
In yeuyng theym to myche weythe into þe spynnyng.   100

ffor ix*li*, I wene, they schall take xij.
This is very trewth, as y know my-selff;
Theyre wages be batyd, theyre weyte ys encresyd;
þus the spynners & carders auaylys be all seasyd.   104

Yt were profytabyl also, & exspedyent for oure kyng,
And a gret awawntage of mych wynnyng,
And a gret enscherychyng to all þe comynalte
þat dwell abowte ther þat þe mynys be,   108

The wych haue yt in usage
To myne in þe erth to gete theyre sustynaunce,
þer myght be had x tymys more wynnyng
Than ys now-adayees with good gouernyng.   112

ffor and þer were a myntte ordeynyd ny þerby,   [f. 3*v*]
And a ordynaunce maad þerto sykyrly,
That all the syluer, whan yt fynyd were,
Thether schold be broȝtth and yconyd there.   116

And mony to be caryyd into a-nother place,
But oonly to be coynyd in a schort space,
Wherby þat the wyrkfolk myght trewly be payd;
Then I dar sey yt wold not be denayyd,   120

But ayenst oon man then schuld ye haue x,
for the good payment of the wyrkmen;
And the moe peopyll þat wyrk in þe mynys,
The more syluer schuld be had vp at all tymys.   124

And thus þe kyng schold be enrychyd for his parte
More than he is now, I dare playnly Ioparte,
After the rate of theyre gret wynnyng,
The wich schold be to hym a profytable thyng.   128

And thus þis lond may be enryched ageyn —
The kyng, þe lordes, and all maner of men,
Knyghtis, squyers, and all þe comynalte,
They may playnly voyd all pouerte.   132

And so to contynow owtt of heuyness,
fro penowry & nede & to be put owt of dystress,
And for to cawse owre enmyss be þis ordynaunss
To seke loue & pese withowtt varyaunss.   136

And ffull fayne þat they may be subyet to þis lond,
Yf we kepe þe woollys straytly owt of theyre hond;
ffor by þe endraperyng þeroff they haue theyre sustynaunce,
And thus owre enmys be supportyd to owre gret hynderaunce.

And therfor, for þe loue of god in trinyte,   [f. 4r]
Conceyue well these matorss, & scheryssh þe comynalte;
That theyre pouer leuyng synfull, & aduersyte
May be altratyd vnto welth, rychess, & prosperyte.   144

Here endyth þe boke of ynglysshe polysye,
That may cause all þe world yt to obeye;
Ther may no man denye but þat it ys soth,
ffor euery man must haue met, drynk, and cloth.   148
                    Etc.

126. MS. playly.

THE FALLS OF PRINCES

71. *THE SUDDEN FALL OF PRINCES*

BY JOHN LYDGATE

Trinity Coll. Cambridge MS. 600

Here folowen seven balades made by daun Iohn Lydgate   [p. 359]
of þe sodeine fal of certain Princes of Fraunce and Englande
nowe late in oure dayes.

Beholde þis gret prynce Edwarde þe secounde,   Kyng Edward
   Which of diuers landes lord was and kyng,   of Carnarvan
But so governed was he, nowe vnderstonde,
   By suche as caused foule his vndoying,   4
   For trewly to telle yowe with-owte lesing,
      He was deposed by al þe rewmes assent,
      In prisoun murdred with a broche in his foundament.

Se howe Richard, of Albyon þe king,   Kyng Richard
   Which in his tyme ryche and glorious was,   þe seconde
Sacred with abyt, with corone, and with ring,
   Yit fel his fortune so, and eke his cas,
   þat yvel counseyle rewled him so, elas,   12
      For mys-tretyng lordes of his monarchye,   [p. 360]
      He feyne was to resigne and in prysone dye.

Lo Charles, of noble Fraunce þe kyng,   Kyng Charlles
   Taken with seknesse and maladye,   16
Which lefft him never vnto his eonding,
   Were it of nature, or by sorcerye,
   Vnable he was for to governe or guye
      His reaume, which caused suche discencyon,   20
      þat fallen it is to gret destruccion.

Se nowe þis lusty Duc of Orlyaunce,   þe Duc of
   Which floured in Parys of chiuallerie,   Orlyence
Broþer to Charles, þe kyng of Fraunce.   24
   His yong hert thought never to dye,
   Bot for he vsed þe synne of lecherye,   i. Duc of
     His cosin to assent was ful fayene,   Burgoigne Iohn
     þat he in Parys was murdred and foule slayne.   28

Of Edward þe thridde, Thomas his sone,   Thomas Duc of
   Of Gloucestre duc, Constable of England,   Gloucestre
Which to love trouth it was ever his wone,
   Yet not-with-stonding his entent of trouthe,   32
   He murdred was at Caleys, þat was routhe,
     And he to god and man most acceptable,
     And to þe comvne profit moste fauorable.

Lo, here þis Eorlle and duc of Burgoyne boþe,   Iohn Duc of
   Oon of þe douspiers and deen of Fraunce,   Bourgoyne
Howe fortune gan his prosparite to looþe,
   And made him putte his lyff in suche balaunce
   þat him n'avayled kyn nor allyaunce,   40
     þat for his mourder he mortherd was and slayne,
     Of whos deth þ'armynakes were fayne.

þis duc of Yrland, of England chaumburleyn,   þe Duc of
   Which in plesaunce so he ledde his lyff,   Yrland
Tyl fortune of his welthe hade disdeyn,   [p. 361]
   þat causeles he parted was frome his wyff,   i. laumefrane
   Which grounde was of gret debate and stryff,
     And his destruccion, if I shal not lye,   48
     For banned he was, and did in meschef dye.

72. THE LAMENT OF THE DUCHESS
OF GLOUCESTER (1441)

Cambridge Univ. MS. Hh.4.12

Thorow-owt a palys as I gan passe,   [f. 89r]
  I herd a lady make gret mone;
And euer she syghyd and said, "alas!
  All erthly ioy is fro me gone.   4
  ffor I am left my-self alone,
    And all my frendys fro me thei flee;
  Alas, I am full well of wone —
    All women may be ware by me.   8

"All women that in thys world art wroght,
  By me they may ensample take;
ffor I that was browght up of noght,
  A prince me chese to be hys make.   12
  My souerayn lord thus to forsake
    It was a dulfull desteny;
  Alas to syght how shold I slake —
    All women may be ware by me.   16

"I was so hygh vpon the whele,
  My owne astate I cowd not know;
The gospell accordeth there-to ful well:
  Who wyll be hygh, he shall be lowe.   20
  Who may the whele of fortune trowe —
    It is but vayne and vanite?
  The flowrys of my medow ben downe mowe —
    All women may be ware by me.   24

"With welth, wele, and worthinesse,
  I was be-sett on euery syde;
Of glowcestre I was duchesse,
  Of all men I was magnifyed.   28
  As lucifer fell downe for pride,
    So fell I from felicite;
  I had no grace my-self to gwyde —
    All women may be ware by me.   32

"Sum tyme I was in riche aray,
  Ther myght no princes be my pere;   [f. 89*v*]
In clothys of gold and garmentys gay,
  Me thowght ther was no thyng to dere.   36
  I purchast fast from yere to yere,
    Of poore men I had no pite.
  Now ar my wittys all in were —
    All women may be ware by me.   40

"Alas, what was myn auenture
  So sodaynly downe forto fall,
That had all thyng vndyr my cure,
  Encline and croke whan I wold call?   44
  ffadyr of heuyn celestiall,
    Of my complaint haf thow pite;
  ffor now am I worst of all —
    All women may be ware by me.   48

"All women that ar ware of wark,
  My mischeue may ȝe haf in mynd;
To gef credence to any clerk;
  ffor so dyd I, and that I fynd   52
  I wrowght agayne all course of kynd,
    And lost my crede for cruelte;
  Ther may no blys my balys vnbynd —
    All women may be ware by me.   56

28. was *supplied*.   35. MS. glod.   54. MS. cuelte.

"My clerkys callyd up and downe,
  All was but mischeue that they ment;
Owre souerayn lord and kyng with crowne
  Hym to distroye was owre entent.   60
    All-myghty god omnipotent,
      He wyst full well owre cruelte;
    Loo, for such harmys I am now schente —
      All women may be ware by me.   64

"Alas, that euer I wroght treson!
  But cursyd counsell euer worth it woo.
I was mekyll agayne the crowne,   [f. 90r]
  Alas, the while that I dyd soo!   68
    My best frend now is my foo,
      My owne dere lord I dar not see;
    Alas, that we shuld twynne in too —
      All women may be ware by me.   72

"By-fore the counsell of thys lond,
  At westmynster vpon a day,
fful carefully there gan I stond;
  A word for me durst noo man say.   76
    Owre leche lord with-owtyn delay
      Was there, he myght both here and see;
    And in hys grace I put me ay —
      All women may be ware by me.   80

"Hys grace to me was euermore gayne,
  All-thow I had done gret offence;
The law wold I had ben slayne,
  And sum men dyd ther diligence.   84
    That worthi prynce of hys prudence
      Of my persone had pyte;
    Honour to hym with all reuerence —
      All women may be ware by me.   88

79. MS. hys in.

"I cam by-fore the spiritualte;
  Two cardinallys and bisshoppys fiue,
And other clerkys of gret degre
  Examynd me of all my lyffe.
  And opynly I dyd me shryffe
    That I had dolt with sorcery;
  They put me to my penance belyve —
    All women may be ware by me. 96

"Thorow-owt london in many a strete,
  Of tho that were most principall,
I went barefote vpon my fote, [f. 90v]
  That sum tyme rode there ful royall. 100
  Kyng of heuen and lord of all,
    At thyn owne wyll so mut it be;
  The synne of pride wyl haf a falle —
    All women may be ware by me. 104

"ffarewell, london, and hafe good day,
  At the I take my leve thys tyde;
ffarewell, Grenewyche, for euer and ay,
  ffarewell, fayre place upon temys syde! 108
  ffarewell, all welth in world so wyde,
    I am sygned where I shall be;
  At lerpole there must I nedes byde —
    All women may be ware by me. 112

"ffarewell, damaske and clothys of gold,
  ffarewell, velwette and clothys in grayne,
ffarewell, my clothys so manyfold,
  ffarewell, I se ȝow neuer agayne; 116
  ffarewell, my lord and souerayne,
    ffarewell, it may no bettyr be;
  Owre partyng is a priuy payne —
    All women may be ware by me. 120

92

"ffarewell, all mynstralcy and song,
  ffarewell, all worldly daliance,
ffarewell, I wote I haf do wrong
  And all I wyte mysgouernance.   124
  Now list me nedyr prike ne prawnce,
    My pride is put to pouerte,
  That bothe in englond and in fraunce
    All women may be ware by me.   128

"ffarewell now, all lustinesse;
  All worldly Ioy I here forsake;   [f. 91r]
I am so full of heuynesse,
  I wot not to whom complaynt to make.   132
  But to hym I wyll me take,
    That for us was put upon a tree,
  And in prayers wyll I wache and wake —
    All women may be ware by me."   136

Explicit.

73. *EPITAPH FOR THE DUKE OF*
GLOUCESTER (1447)

Harley MS. 2251

Epitaphium eiusdem Ducis Gloucestrie.   [f. 7r]

Souerayne Immortal, everlastyng god,
  Almyghti most mercyful, verray welle of grace,
Late nat of thy vengeaunce the dredeful rod
  Towche vs to-fore for gilt of oure trespas;   4
  How-be-it we synne, yit graunt vs tyme and space
    Oure forfetes to bewayle while oure lyf may dure,
  Sith worship, riches, and al thyng shal pas —
    Se be hym buryed in this sepulture.   8

O secrete counceyle, o divyne purviaunce,
  O nature, thy principles how hastow conveyed,
O elementes iiij sette in grete variaunce,
    Yowre stryf contynuel hath my lord downe leyd.   12
    Allas, for his lyf why ne had ye purveyed
      Hym to conserve, whiche for vs all had cure;
    But syth thy wille, lord, may nat be geynseyd,
      Have mercy on hym buryed in this sepulture.   16

Compleyne al yngland this goode lordis deth,   [f. 7*v*]
  ffor and ye considre youre causes ben right grete,
He hath with his wisdom, while hym lasted breth,
    And with his richesse made the grete hete   20
    Of oure enemyes to kele, wold they werre or trete;
      But ageyn mortalite there lith no recure;
    Now lord, syn nonother remedye may be gete,
      Have mercy on hym beryed in this sepulture.   24

Thy mercyes bene grettest, and his wag grettest also,
  Thow foryaf oure trespas and so dide he his certayne;
Of mercy and pite ther were suche no mo.
    And syth thy mercy, lord of grace, is nat bareyne,   28
    Late it be fertible to hym that dide his peyne
      To sue thi steppis folowyng the scripture
    By dauid seyde and notified ful pleyne,
      Have mercy on hym beryed in this sepulture.   32

Remembre, goode lord, that to the body of man
  Thow inspired a soule to thyne owne lykenesse,
And sythen is he turned into that thow began,
    In-to the erth, meane I (as thi-self dost witnesse),   36
    Take thyn ymage and with thy aungels dresse
      In thy perfite Ioye, euerlastyng to endure,
    Turnyng from the terestre vale, the contrey of derknesse,
      And have mercy on hym buryed in this sepulture. 40

27. MS. nomo.

Put ferre from hym the prince of derknesse,
    And take hym neere — he is thyn owne alye,
fforged of thyn hand (thow knowest it expresse),
    And nought of straunge goddis, but only of the.   44
    Although he synned thurgh fragilite
        Of ygnoraunce, as fil his aduenture,
    He denyed the neuer, conceyve his humilite,   [f. 8r]
        And have mercy on hym buryed in this sepulture.   48

Dispice nat thy part, that with thy precious bloode
    Shed on the crosse and boughte so deere,
And for the love of hir that at thy feete stoode —
    Thy moder, I meane — and Iohn that was hir feere.   52
    Whan the sharp spere went thy hert so neere,
        That thurgh thy deth thow madest vs al sure,
    Crowne hym in hevene, that in his dayes had no pere,
        And have mercy on hym buryed in this sepulture.   56

Now blessid lady, for thy Ioyes fyve,
    Specialy whan gabriel dide his glad message,
Which fest he honowred terme of his lyf,
    ffailyng neuer hardily to his vttremest age.   60
    Now shewe thy bounte, lift vp thy fayre visage
        Vnto thy sone so meke and demure,
    To defend his werk, the printe of his ymage,
        And prayed for hym buryed in this sepulture.   64

Comend hym to thi sone, as he dide the to Iohn,
    And as he was to the, be thow to hym wardeyn;
As his singuler trust was to the alon,
    So quyte the to hym, as his lady souerayne.   68
    Now blessid virgyne, of hym have no disdayne;
        He was noble in vertue as wele as in nature;
    And if he be distressed with any temporal peyne,
        Yit pray for hym buryed in this sepulture.   72

54. sure MS. *blotted*.

He was verray fader and protectour of the land,
  Ingland, I meane, that is thyn owne dowarye;
Neuer man had more ȝele, as I vndrestond,
    Ne redyer to redresse alle transgressis by and by;   76
    I dare wele say it sat his hert so ny.   [f. 8v]
      Cowde none make hym in any Ioye to endure
    Vnto his lyf passed; therfor to the I cry,
      So pray for hym buryed in this sepulture.   80

Behold of thy chirche the myghti piler stronge,
  Euer to withstande and redy to bataile;
Ageyne the chirche, enemys he wold suffre no wronge
    Vnto hir to be done, whiles he myght aught availe;   84
    ffor he hath emprised many a travaile
      Opinly, without shame or discomfiture;
    Rescow hym, therfor, whan his enemyes wil assaile,
      And pray for hym buryed in this sepulture.   88

And like as he endured with these graces thre —
  With wisdam, with riches, and with nobley —
So blessid lady, we al beseche the,
    Knele before thy sone and to hym prey,   92
    Whan of Iugement shal approche the dredeful day,
      He may be endowed beforne his figure
    Impassible, Immortal, with clerenesse lastyng ay —
      God it hym graunt buryed in this sepulture.   96

"Studye, labour, and merit for comvne wele;
  ffor reward, smal thank, or worship in recompense
Departith from me; go your wele, fare-wele.
    Sollicitith other fallen in suche diligence.   100
    Oure lord hath clepid me vnto his divyne presence,
      ffro this short lyf to that euer shal dure;
    My soule to hym I yield at my goyng hens,
      To the erth my body, as for my sepulture."   104

83. MS. suffre do no; wronge MS. *cut.*

74. *EXAMPLES OF MUTABILITY*

MS. Rawlinson C.813
(Sum. Cat. No. 12653)

Musyng vppon the mutabilite   [f. 11*r*]
   off worldlye changes & grett vnstablenes,
& me remembering howe grett aduersite
   I haue seen falle to men off highe noblenes —   4
furst welthe, and then ageyn distres,
     nowe vppe, nowe downe, as fortune turnethe hur whele,
Best is, me thinke, for mannys sikernes   [f. 11*v*]
    to trust In god & labour to doo well.   8

Wee nede not nowe to seke the cronicle3 olde
   off the romans, nor bockas tragedye,
to rede the ruyen & fallys manyffolde
   off prynces grett, putt to dethe & miserye   12
In sondrye landes, for wee haue hardelye
    here In thys lande with-In the xx yere
as wonder3 change3 seen before our eye
    as euer I trowe before thys any were.   16

Off whiche I shall reherse suche as I can —
   thoughe I In ordre sett them nott a-right.
& as I trowe a duches furst began,
   whiche Elinor off Cobeham sumtyme hight   20
or she were weddyd to that famose knyght
    off glocestur, the noble duke humffrey,
whose soll Iesu bringe to þat Ioyffull light,
    that you hym bothe humblye beseche & praye.   24

Thys ladye was soo proude & highe of harte
   that she hur-selffe thought pereles of estate,
and yet higher fayn she wold haue starte;   [f. 12*r*]
   butt sodenlye she fell, as was hur fate,   28
   & was arested, all dismayde and mate,

for sorcerye and eke for suspection
of treason wrought ageynst the king algate,
   And theruppon committed vnto prisone.   32

And after brought to the courte spirituall
  before the bisshoppes; and ther off sorcerye
founden gyltye In poyntes specyall.
    she was InIoyned In london opynlye   36
    to doo hur penaunce, And soo full petyously
      she itt perfformed; & after was she sent
    vnto a castell to abide perpetuallye.
      And soo she dyd tyll dethe awey hur hent.   40

The noble duke of somersett, Iohn,
  whome all brytayne and also normandye
hadde In grett drede (& his enemye₃ euerichon)
    for his manhode, puissance, & cheualrye,   44
    when he was weddyd & In estate most hye,
      In his best age (right as his fortune was)
    The bull to gronde hym cast cruellye   [f. 12v]
      that after soone he dyed: suche was hys grace.   48

The noble duke off whiche I spoke before —
  I meane humffrey of glocestre alsoo,
whiche off thys lande was lymyted Protector,
    & made the duke of burgoyne & muche moo   52
To flee from caleys vnto his highe honor —
vppon a tale made by a bisshoppe, a brybor,
    a wretched prest as deeffe nere as a stoune,
whiche he shulde haue harde as a confessor.   56

And to the kinge he vttered itt anon.
  wherfore att burye in a full parlyament

30. MS. socerye.
51. lymyted *written above line over letters* (mwe?) *struck through.*

by a grett lorde, or he came to the towne,
   he was arrestede by the commandement   60
off kynge henrye, for suspection off treason
thought and wrought ageynst his crowne.
      for shame and angwishe off which, Ieloussye
I-toke hym sone after, & soo lowe brought hym downe 64
   that In short while after I-caused hym to dye.

75. ARREST OF THE DUKE OF SUFFOLK
(1450)

Cotton Rolls ii.23

Now is the fox drevin to hole! hoo to hym, hoo, hoo!
ffor and he crepe out, he will yow alle vndo.
Now ye han found parfite, love well your game;
ffor and ye ren countre, then be ye to blame.   4
Sum of yow holdith with the fox, and rennyth hare;
But he þat tied talbot oure doge, euyll mot he fare!
ffor now we mys the black dog with þe wide mouth,
ffor he wold haue ronnen well at þe fox of the south.   8
And all gooth bacward, and don is in the myre,
As they han deserued, so pay þey þer hire.
Now is tyme of lent; þe fox is in the towre;
þerfore send hym salesbury to be his confessoure.   12
Many mo þer ben, and we kowd hem knowe,
But won most begyn þe daunce, and all com arowe.
Loke þat your hunte blowe well þy chase;
But he do well is part, I beshrew is face!   16
þis fox at bury slowe oure grete gandere;
þerfore at tyborn mony mon on hym wondere.
Iack napys, with his clogge,
Hath tied talbot, oure gentill dogge.   20
Wherfore Beaumownt, þat gentill rache,

63. MS. Ieloussy.

Hath brought Iack napis in an evill cache.
Be ware, al men, of that blame,
And namly ye of grete fame,   24
Spirituall and temperall, be ware of this,
Or els hit will not be well, I-wis.
God saue þe kyng, and god forbede
Þat he suche apes any mo fede.   28
And of þe perille that may be-fall
Be ware, dukes, erles, and barons alle.

76. THE DEATH OF THE DUKE OF SUFFOLK
(1450)

Cotton MS. Vespasian B.xvi

In the moneth of May when gresse groweþ grene,   [f. 1*v*]
    fflagrant in her floures with swete sauour,
Iac Napes wolde on the see a maryner to ben,
    With his clog & his cheyn, to seke more tresour.   4
    Suych a payn prikked hym, he asked a confessour.
        Nicolas said, "I am redi thi confessour to be."
    He was holden so that he ne passed that hour.
        For Iac Napes soule, Placebo and dirige.   8

Who shall execute his exequies with a solempnite?
    Bisschopes & lordes, as grete reson is,
Monkes, chanons, prestes, & other clergie
    Pray for this dukes soule þat it might come to blis,   12
    And let neuer suych another come after this!
        His interfectours blessed might thei be,
    And graunte them for ther dede to regne with angelis.
        And for Iac Nape soule, Placebo & dirige.   16

"Placebo," begynneth the bisshop of Herford.
    "Dilexi, for myn auauncement," saith þe bisshop of Chestre.
"Heu mei," saiþ Salisbury, "this goth to ferre forthe."

"Ad Dominum cum tribularer," saiþ þe abbot of Gloucestre.
"Dominus custodit," saiþ the abbot of Rouchestre.
  "Levaui oculos," saiþ frere Stanbury, "Volaui."
"Si iniquitates," saiþ þe bisshop of Worcetre,
    "For Iac Nape soule, de profundis clamaui."   24

"Opera manum tuarum," seiþ the Cardynal wisely,
  That brought forth "confitebor," for all this Napes reson.
"Audiui vocem," songe Allemightty god on hye;
  And þerfore syng we "Magnificat anima mea dominum."
  Vnto this dirige most we gon & come
    This pascall tyme, to say veryli
  Thre psalmes & thre lessons, þat alle is and somme,
    For Iac Nape soule, Placebo & dirige.   32

Executors of this office dirige for to synge,
  Shall begyn the bisshop of Synt Asse;
"Verba mea auribus," saiþ abbot of Redynge;
    "Alle your ioye and hope is come to alasse."   36
    "Conuertere, domine, yet graunte vs grace,"   [f. 2r]
      Saiþ abbot of synt Albans ful sorily.
  The abbot of þe Toure hille, with his fat face,
    Quakeþ & tremuleþ for "domine, ne in furore."   40

Maister Water liard shal synge, "Ne quando."
  The abbot of Westmynstre, "domine deus meus, in te speraui."
Requiem eternam graunte them alle to come to."
    "Þerto a pater noster," saiþ the bisshop of synt Dauy,   44
  for thes soules þat wyse were & mightty,
    Suffolk, Moleyns, and Roos — thes thre;
  And in especial for Iac Napes, that euer was wyly,
    for his soule, Placebo & dirige.   48

Rise vp, Say, rede, "parce mihi domine.
  Nihil enim sunt dies mei," þou shalt synge.
  Þe bisshop of Carleyle syng, "Credo," ful sore.

25. MS. manuum.

To suyche fals Traitours come foule endynge!   52
The baron of Dudley with grete mornynge,
   Redeth, "tedet animam meam vite mee."
Who but Danyel "qui lasarum" shal synge?
   For Iac Nape soule, Placebo & dirige.   56

Iohn Say redeth, "Manus tue fecerunt me."
   "Libera me," syngeth Trevilian, "warre the rere;
That thei do no more so, requiescant in pace."
   Thus prayes alle Englond ferre & nerre.   60
   Where is Somerset? whi aperes he not here
     To synge "dies ire & miserie"?
   God graunte Englond all in fere
     for thes traitours to synge Placebo & dirige.   64

Meny mo þer be behynde, þe sothe forto telle,
   Þat shal messes oppon thes do synge.
I pray som man do rynge the belle,
   Þat þese forsaiden may come to þe sacrynge;   68
   And þat in brief tyme, without more tarienge,
     Þat þis messe may be ended in suyche degre;
   And þat all Englond ioyfull may synge
     þe commendacioun with Placebo & Dirige.   72

THE RED ROSE OF LANCASTER

77. THE FIVE DOGS OF LONDON (1456)

Trinity College Dublin MS. 516

Colle, primus canis londonie. quinque in munere occisi   [f. 20*v*]
fuerunt. Anno domini M*e* ccccc lvj*to*

Whan lordschype fayleth, gode felowschipe awayleth.   *a*
My mayster ys cruell and can no curtesye,

No. 77. a. MS. lorschype. MS. awayleh.

ffor whos offence here am y pyghte.
hyt ys no reson þat y schulde dye
   ffor hys trespace, & he go quyte.   **4**

Grubbe, 2*us* canis:

    Offte beryth þe sone the faderis gylte.   *b*
None so gylteles as y compleyne:
   ffor ones þat y barkyd a-geynys þe mone,
With myghty force here was y sleyne.
   My tyme was come; my defenys ys done.   **8**

lugtrype, 3*us* canis:

    The tonge breketh bone, ȝit in hym is none. *c*
ffor fawte of curasse my throte was cutte.
   y cryed for helpe — y was not herde.
y wolde my mayster hadde provide my butte;
   Thys hadde y for hym to my rewarde.   **12**

Slugge, 4*us* canis:

Off folowynge aventurous, þe Iugement is Ieperdous. *d*
Wat planet compellyd me, or what signe,
   To serue þat man that all men hate?
y wolde hys hede were here for myne,
   ffor he hathe caused all þe debate.   **16**

Turne-bole, 5*us* canis:

    ffelix quem faciunt aliena pericula cautum. *e*
The blasynge starne with his late constellacion,   [f. 21*r*]
   ys pleynly determyned weyis batayle;
To soche a remedye y holde hyt geson,
   And yn rancur with-owte remedy ys none avayle. **20**

Maysterys, taketh for no grewe thewgh þat we be dede;
ffor they wylle walke be your fleke, In dyspyte of your hede.

c. MS. tionge.   18. MS. latayle.

78. *THE SHIP OF STATE (1458)*

Trinity College Dublin MS. 516

De naui vel puppe Anno domini m*l* cccc*o* lviij*o*   [f. 30*r*]
litera dominicale g.

> Stere welle the good shype.
> god be our gyde!

Our ship is launched from the grounde,
Blessed be god, both faire and sownde!
Our maryners han the shypmen founde,
    By þere taklynge will a-byde.   4
This noble shyp made of good tree,
Our souerayne lord, kynge henry.
God gyde hym from aduersyte,
    Where þat he go or ryde.   8

The shyp was charged with a mast;
Crased it was, it myght not last.
Now hath he one þat wol not brest —
    The old is leyde on syde.   12
Thys fayre mast, this myghty yeard,
Of whom fals shrewes be a-fered,
hys name of ryght is prince Edward —
    long myght he with vs a-byde.   16

The ship hath closed hym a lyght
To kepe her course in wey of ryght —
A fyre cressant þat berneth bryght,
    With fawte was neuer spyed.   20
Thys good lyght, þat is so clere,
Call y the duke of exceter,
Whos name in trouþe shyned clere;
    Hys worshyp spryngeth wyde.   24

Heading written as one line.   10. myght MS. my.
13. this MS. is.   14. MS. fere.

Thys shyp hath a sterne full good,
hem to gyde in ebbe & flood,
A-geyne þer wawes boþe wild & wode
   That rynneth on euery syde.   28
The sterne that on þe shype is sette
Ys þe duke Somerset;
ffor ragged rokkes he woll not lette
   To sterre in ebbe and eke in tyde.   32

Ther is a sayle-yeard full good and sure,
To þe shyp a grete tresour;
ffor alle stormes it wolle endure —
   It is trusty atte nede.   36
Now þe sayle-yeard, y wolle reherse,
The Erle of Pembroke curtys and ferce;   [f. 30v]
A-cros þe mast he hyeth travers,
   The good shyp for to lede.   40

The mast hath a welle good stay,
With shrowthes sure, y dare wel say,
In humble wyse hym to obey
   yf he to þem hath nede.   44
The Duke of Bokyngham thys stay is he,
Thys shrowdes be sure in thare degre;
Devenshyre, & Grey, & becheham the free,
   And scales with them in tyde.   48

The shyp hath a well good sayle,
Of fyne canvas þat woll not fayle,
With bonet iii for to travayle,
   That mekell beth of pryde.   52

33. yea *struck through after* sayle.
45. *A word* (? s...y) *blotted out before* stay.

This good sayle, y vndurstond,
The Erle of Northumberland,
Ros, clyfford, and Egremond —
    The trouþe is not to hyde.   56

Ther is a toppe þe mast on hyght,
The shyp to defende in all hys ryght;
With his foomen when he schall fyght,
    They dare hym not a-byde.   60
The Erle of Shrovesbury þe toppes name,
He kepeth þe shype from harme and blame;
The Erle of Wylchyre, one of þe same,
    That kepeth þe shyp from drede.   64

Thys good shype hath ankers thre,
Of bether mettel þer may non be,
To strenthe þe shyp be londe and se,
    When he woll stop hys tyde.   68
The furst anker, hole & sounde,
he is named þe lord beamond;
Willys and Ryveres trouþe yn þem found,
    In worship þey hem gyde.   72

Now help, saynt George, oure lady knyght,
And be oure lode-sterre day & nyght,
To strengthe oure kynge and england ryght
    And fell oure fomenus pryde.   76
Now is oure shype dressed in hys kynde,   [f. 31r]
With hys taklynge be-for and be-hynde;
Whoso loue it not, god make hym blynde,
    In peynes to a-byde!   80

53. MS. vndurston.   66. þer MS. þe.   69. MS. fust.
74. lode MS. lordes.   79. MS. whos.

79. *RECONCILIATION OF HENRY VI AND THE YORKISTS (1458)*

Cotton MS. Vespasian B.xvi

Whan charite is chosen with states to stonde,   [f. 4r]
    Stedfast and skill without distaunce,
Than wrathe may be exiled out of this londe,
    And god oure gide to haue the gouernaunce.   4
    Wisdom & wellthe, with all plesaunce,
      May rightful regne, and prosperite;
    For loue hath vnderlaide wrathful veniaunce.
      Reioise, Anglond, oure lordes acorded to be.   8

Reiose, and thanke god for euermore,
    For now shal encrese thi consolacion;
Oure enemyes quaken & dreden ful sore
    That peas is made there was diuision.   12
    Which to them is a gret confusion,
      And to vs ioi and felicite.
    God hold hem longe in euery season,
      That Anglond may reioise in concord & vnite.   16

Now is sorowe with shame fled into ffraunce,
    As a felon that hath forsworn this londe;
Love hath put out malicious gouernaunce,
    In euery place bothe fre & bonde.   20
    In Yorke, In Somerset, as I vnderstonde,
      In Warrewik also is loue & charite,
    In Sarisbury eke, & in Northumbrelande,
      That euery man may reioise in concord & vnite.   24

Egremown and Clifford, with other forsaide,
    Ben set in the same opynyon.
In euery quarter love is thus laide;
    Grace & wisdom hath thus the dominacion.   28

2. MS. stedfas.   16, 24. in *supplied*.

Awake, welth, & walke in this region,
 Rounde aboute in tovn & Cite;
And thanke them that brought hit to this conclusion.
 Reioise, Anglond, to concorde & vnite.   32

At Poules in london, with gret renoun,
 On oure ladi day in lente this peas was wrought;
The kyng, the Quene, with lordes many oone,
 To worshyp that virgine as thei ought,   36
 Wenten a procession, and spariden right nought, [f. 4v]
  In sighte of alle the Comynalte,
 In token that love was in herte and thought.
  Reiose, Anglond, in concorde & vnite.   40

Ther was bytwyn hem lovely contynaunce,
 Whiche was gret ioy to all that ther were;
That long tyme hadden be in variaunce,
 As frendes for euer that had be in fere.   44
 Thei wenten togeder and made goud chire.
  ffraunce and Britayn repente shul thei;
 for þe bargayn shul thei abye ful dere.
  Reiose, Anglond, in concorde & vnite.   48

Oure Soueraigne lord kyng, god kepe alwey,
 The Quene, & the Archbisshop of Canterbury,
And the bisshop of Wynchestre, Chanceller of Anglond,
And other that han labured to this loue-day;   52
 God preserue hem, we pray hertly,
 And london, for thei ful diligently
  Kepten the peas in trowbel & aduersite,
 To bryng in reste thei labured ful truly.   56
  Reiose, Anglond, in concorde & vnite.

Of thre thynges I praise the worshipful Cite:
 The first, þe true faithe þat thei haue to þe kynge;
The seconde, of love to þe Comynalte;   60
 The thrid, goud rule for euermore kepynge;

The which god maynteyn euermore durynge,
  And saue þe Maier and all þe worthi Cite;
And þat is amys god brynge to amendynge,   64
  That Anglond may reioise to concorde & vnite.

80. A PRAYER FOR VICTORY

MS. Ashmole 59
(Sum. Cat. No. 6943)

God all-myghty, saue and conserue owre kynge   [f. 134r]
  In all vertue to hys encrese off glorye,
Hys realme and hym by polytike levynge,
  With drede and loue to haue memorye,   4
  Of hys enmyes conquest and victory.

81. GOD AMEND WICKED COUNSEL (1464)

Bodl. MS. Lat. misc. e.85

As I walkyd my-self alone,   [f. 83r]
  Betwen the daye and the nyth,
The skye was cler, the cloudes war gon,
  The mone & the sterryes they schon ful bryȝth.   4

The dewe was sprungyn won the ston,
  Byrdes can synge from tre to tre,
The daye was komyn, nyȝth was gon,

            8

As I walkyd my-self alone,
  Besyde an halle vndirneth an hylle,
Ther herde I kynge herry the vj make his mon,
  "God amende wykkyd cownscell.   12

No. 81. 2. on *struck through after* daye.   4. MS. byȝth.

"Sum tyme lordis of thys lond sette me at gret pris,
   Swiche a prynse in this rem was þer neuer non;
I weddyd a wyf at my devyse,
   That was the cause of all my mon.   16

"Thyll her intente seyd I neuer naye;
   Ther-for I morne & no thynge am mery.
Whan sche ded syen the lorde saye,
   The duke of Glouceter was sclayn at Bery.   20

"Rychard of yorke, that lord ryal,
   He was exilyd for ȝeres thre;
Than was I leke to haue a falle,
   I clamer vpon a rotyn tre!   24

"Than sette I from my ryalte
   As angell dede from heuyn to helle;
All crystyn kynges be war be me —
   God amend wikkyd cownsel!   [f. 83v]

"O lorde Iesu, wat schuld I doo
   Withowte your grase to me inclyn,
Vpon the dredful day of dom,
   Wher euery man schul answer for his tyme?   32

"Many a man for me hath be slayn
   With bowe and axe and swerde I-drawe;
And thate I wite myn own brayn
   I-helde nowth my lordys vnder awe.   36

"Alas my awen coude neuer haue reste,
   But euer to Stryve with the cominalte;

13. MS. tyne.   18. MS. thyge.
19. I *rubbed for expunction before* whan; sayd.   21. MS. Ryc'.
24. MS. chamer.   28. f. 83v *headed* Iesus marcy.   30. MS. inchyn.
34. MS. drawe: a *superior.*   37. my *written over* nyq *struck through.*
38. *four letters* (coma ?) *struck through before* cominalte.

Alas, I badde her do her beste,
  Tyl the grase was from her & me.   40

"Now ys my por clene ourthrown,
  Wher I was kynge & bare the belle;
Than was I hye, now am I lowe —
  God amende wykkyd cownsel!   44

"Sum tyme I rodde in clothe of gold so red,
  Thorow-oute ynglond in many a town;
Alas, I dare nowth schewe now my hede —
  Thys word ys turnyd clene vppe so down!   48

"Of the bledde ryall I am kom;
  Kynge herry of Monmowthe me beforn,
He was my fadir & I his sone,
  And of qwen kateryn was I born.   52

"Now ys he dedde and leyde depe in cleye,
  And deth hath strekyn hym with his lawnse . . ."

82. *WILLIKIN'S RETURN (1470)*

B. M. Addit. MS. 19046

Nowell, nowell, nowell, nowell!   [f. 74r]
  & cryst saue mery ynglon & sped yt welle!

tyll home sull wylekyn, þis Ioly gentyl schep,
all to houre combely kyng hary þis cnat ys knyt;
  þer-fore let vs all syng nowel.

41. outhrown *struck through after* clene.
43. thane *struck through before* than; and *struck through after* now.
49. ry *and* rya *struck through after* bledde.
No. 82. 2. I o *a false start at beginning of line;* how *struck through after* to.

tyll home sull wylekyn, þis Ioly gentyl mast,   4
all to my lorde prynce, þat neuere was caste;
   þerfore let vs all syng nowel.

tyll home sull wylekyn, þis Ioly gentyl nore,
all to my lorde chamberlayne, þat neuer was for-sore;   8
   þerfore let vs all syng nowell.

tyll home sull wylekyn, þis Ioly gentyll sayle,
all to my lorde fueryn, þat neuer dyd fayle;
   þerfore let vs all syng nowell.   12

    sy amen quod Ionys.   Wyllamus 1.

83. *A REMEMBRANCE OF HENRY VI (1492)*

BY JAMES RYMAN

Cambridge Univ. MS. Ee.1.12

O good Herry, the sixte by name,   [f. 72*v*]
  Bothe of Inglond, ye, & of Fraunce,
A kyng thou were of royall fame
  And of full worthy gouernaunce,   4
  Full of mercy without vengeaunce,
    Wherfore in blisse the king of grace
    Hath grauntid the a Ioyefull place.

No. 82. *Burden written at end of poem. Poem headed* Conditor alme
siderum eterna lux &. *Repetition of burden after stanzas* 1 - 3 *indicated
by* nowel.
Burden MS. yglon; spdedyt *first* d *struck through.*
  8. MS. chaberlayne.   10. s *struck through before* Ioly.

A king thou were of grete renowne   8
  And of vertue more excellent,
XXXIX yere weryng crowne,
  By grace of god omnipotent,
  Euer in mercy permanent;   12
    Wherefore in blisse the king of grace
    Hath graunted the a Ioyefull place.

As a true knyght, both day & nyght,
  Oure sauyoure thou diddest honoure   16
With hert & myende, with wille & myght,
  In helth, in welthe, & in doloure
  Euir at nede graunting socoure;
    Wherfore in blisse the king of grace   20
    Hath graunted the a Ioyefull place.

As scripture seith, blessed they be   [f. 73r]
  That mercyfull be in worde and dede,
For they shall fyende of criest so fre   24
  Mercy also in tyme of nede.
  This vertu ay in the did sprede,
    Wherefore in blisse the king of grace
    Hath graunted the a Ioyefull place.   28

A prince thou were meke & benigne,
  Pacient in aduersite,
Wherefore thou hast a crowne condigne
  In blisse of alle felicite,   32
  Where Ioy hath perpetuite;
    In the whiche blisse the king of grace
    Hath grauntid the a ioyfull place.

In thy gesture thou were like Iobe   36
  Stedfast of feith & myelde of mode,

22. they MS. thou.

Not prowde of vesture ne of roobe,
  Ne auarous of worldely goode,
  Ne sumptuous of carnall foode;   40
    Wherefore in blisse the king of grace
    Hath graunted the A ioyefull place.

At Wyndesore, thy place natyf,
  Almyghty god in blisse aboue   44
Both vnto man, to chield, & wyf,
  Now dothe grete thingis for thy loue,
  As patently the dede doth proue.
    Wherfore in blis the king of grace   48
    Hath grauntid the a Ioyfull place.

The vertue of thy lyfe so clere,
  The whiche was had, as riche treasure,
Bothe ferre & nere, now dothe appere   52
  To yonge & olde in due measure;
  Wherefore to criest thou do thy cure,
    That he will graunte vs of his grace
    In blisse with the to haue a place.   56

THE WHITE ROSE OF YORK

84. *PRELUDE TO THE WARS (1449)*

Cotton Rolls ii.23

The Rote is ded, The swanne is goon,   Bedforde
  þe firy Cressett hath lost his lyght;   Gloucetter
Therfore Inglond may make gret mone,   Excetter
  Were not the helpe of godde almyght.   4

The Castell is wonne where care be-gown,   Roone
   The Portecolys is leyde a-down;   Somerset
I-closid we haue oure welevette hatte,   Cardinalle
   That keueryd vs from mony stormys brown.   8

þe White lioun is leyde to slepe   Northfolke
   þorowȝ the Envy of the Ape clogge;   Southfolk
And he is bownden that oure dore shuld kepe —
   That is Talbott oure good dogge.   12

The ffisshere hath lost his hangulhook,   ffawkenberg
   Gete theym agayn when it woll be.
Oure myllesaylle will not a-bowte,   Wylloby
   Hit hath so long goon emptye.   16

The Bere is bound that was so wild,   Warwik
   ffor he hath lost his ragged staff.
The Carte nathe is spokeles,   Bokyngham
   ffor the counseill that he gaff.   20

þe lily is both faire and grene;   Danyell
   The Coundite rennyth not, as I wene.   Norreys
The Cornysshe chawgh offt with his trayne   Trevilian
   Hath made oure Egulle blynde.   **Rex**

The white hard is put out of mynde,   Arundelle
   Be-cause he woll not to hem consent;
Therfore the Commyns saith is both trew and kynd,
   Bothe in Southesex and in Kent.   28

The water bowge and the wyne botelle   Bowser
   With the Vetturlockes cheyne ben fast.   Prior of Saint Iohanis
The whete yere woll theym susteyn   Excettur
   As long as he may endure and last.   32

The boore is farre in-to þe west,   Devynshire
    Þat shold vs helpe with shild and spere;
The ffawkoun fleyth and hath no rest,   Yorke
    Tille he witte where to bigge his nest.   36

85. *ADVICE TO THE COURT, I (1450)*

Cotton Rolls ii.23

ffor feer or for fauour of any fals man,
    Loose not the loue of alle þe commynalte!
Be ware and sey, by seint Iulian,
    Duke, Iwge, baron, Archebisshop and he be,   4
    He woll repent it with-in þis monthes thre.
Let ffolke accused excuse theym-selff, and þey can;
    Reseyue no good, let soche bribry be;
Support not theym this wo by-gan,   8
And let theym suche clothis as þey span,
    And take fro þeym þer wages and þer fee,
Or, by god and sent Anne,
    Som must go hens, hit may non othere weys be,   12
    And els is lost all þis lond and we.
      Hong vp suche men to oure souerayn lord,
      That euer counseld hym with fals men to be acord.

        Anno milleno domini centum quaterno
        L simplex pleno caveat omnis homo.

86. *ADVICE TO THE COURT, II (1450)*

Cotton Rolls ii.23

Ye that haue the kyng to demene,
And ffrauncheses gif theym ageyne,
    or els I rede ye fle.

ffor ye haue made the kyng so pore   4
That now he beggeth fro dore to dore —
  Alas, hit shuld so be!

Tom of say, and daniel both,
To be-gyn be not to loth,   8
  þen shall ye haue no shame.
Who will not, he shall not chese,
And his life he shall lese —
  No reson will vs blame.   12

Trowth and pore men ben appressed,
And myscheff is nothyng redressed;
  þe kyng knowith not all.
Thorow-out all Englond,   16
On tho þat holden þe fals bond
  Vengeaunce will cry and call.

The traytours wene they ben so sly,
þat no man can hem aspy;   20
  We can do them no griffe.
We swere by hym that harwed hell,
þay shall no lenger in eresy dwell,
  Ne in þer fals beleve.   24

So pore a kyng was neuer seen,
Nor richere lordes all by-dene;
  þe commvnes may no more.
þe lorde say biddeth holde hem down,   28
þat worthy dastard of renown;
  he techith a fals loore.

Suffolk normandy hath swold.
to gete hyt a-gayn he is bold.   32
  how acordeth þese to in on?

                25. MS. a kyng a kyng.

And he wenyth with-outen drede
To make the kyng to avowe his dede,
   and call hit no treson.   36

We trow þe kyng be to leere
To sell both men and lond in feere;
   hit is agayn reson.
But yif the commyns of Englond   40
Helpe þe kyng in his fond,
   Suffolk woll bere þe crown!

Be ware, kyng henre, how þou doos;
Let no lenger þy traitours go loos —   44
   þey will neuer be trewe.
Þe traytours are sworn all to-gedere
To holde fast as þey were brether;
   let hem drynk as þey han brewed.   48

Þe chaunselere þat last was hath staffes take,
Blank charters, to don vs wrake,
   no nombre of them, hit is ferd.
He woll not suffre þe clerkes preche;   52
Trowthe in no wise he will not teche;
   he is þe deuels shapard.

Þis bill is trewe. who will say nay,
In smythfeld syng he a day,   56
   and þe helpe of þe rode.
That traitours shall provid;
More reson can not be mevid;
   þer shall hit be made good.   60

O rex, si rex es, rege te, vel eris sine re rex;
Nomen habes sine re, nisi te recte regas.

87. *TAKE GOOD HEED*

Trinity Coll. Dublin MS. 432

Awake, lordes, awake & take goode hede!   [f. 69*v*]
ffor som þat speke ful fayre, þei wolde ȝour evil spede;
þouȝ þei pere in your presence with a fayre face,
And her tunge chaunged, þe hert is as it was.   4
þei seyne in þeire assemble, "it is a wondre thyng
To se þe Rose in wyntre so fressh for to spryng."
And many barked atte bere þat now be ful stylle;
ȝit þei wol hym wyrye, if þei might haue her wylle.   8
But of your fewe fomen no thing þat ye drede,
ffor þe comyns ben youres, euer at youre nede.
ȝit a seege wold be set, þe falte to take & holde,
ffor oon scabbed shepe may enfecte al a folde.   12
Trust not to moche in the fauour of youre foos,
ffor þei be double in wirking, as þe worlde gos,
Promysing feithfully obeisaunce to kepe,
But perfite loue in þeire hertis is leyde for to slepe;   16
And þouȝ þei were þe rose, or þe ragged staffe,
þei rought neuer how sone, in feiþe, þat ȝe starffe.
ffor fyre & water to-gider in kyndeling be brought,
It passeþ mannes power, be god þat me bought.   20
Nor two fases in a hode is neuer to tryst.
Beþ wele war be-fore, & þenk of "had I wyst."
ffor þei hopen & tristen to here of a day,
To se þe rose & þe lion brought to a-bay   24
With þe egel & þe bere, þat worþi be in fight.
ffrom þat infortune, preserue you god almight!
And lat not youre sauegardes be to liberalle
To your foos þat be turnyng euer as a balle;   28
And siþe fortune haþe set you hye on hir whele
And in youre comyns love, loveþ ye hem as wele.
ffor many þat were þe chayne on hir sleve

30. ye *inserted above line.*

Wold ful fayne youre lyves be-reve;   32
And som þat were þe ragged bottis   [f. 70r]
Had lever were þe stafford knottis.
But what þei mene, no man it wottis,
þerfore I counsel, eschewe þeire lottis.   36
To telle you more it is no nede,
By counsel goode ȝit take goode hede,
ffor a cristmas gestenyng, as clerkis rede,
At on-set stevyn is quyt, in dede.   40
Wherfore I counsel you sempely as I can,
Of youre disposicion telliþ not euery man.
Miche is in my mynde, no more is in my penne:
ffor þis shuld I be shent, might som men it kenne.   44
But pray we al to god þat died on a spere,
To saue þe rose, þe lyon, þe egle, & þe bere,
With al oþer lordes, trewe to youre assent;
Her sheld be euer god omnipotent.   48
                      Amen.

88. *BALLADE SET ON THE GATES OF CANTERBURY (1460)*

John Speed Davies MS.

Balat set upponne the yates of Caunterbury.   [f. 203r]

In the day of faste and spirituelle afflixione,
   The celestialle influence on bodyes transytory
Set asyde alle prophecyes, and alle commixtione
   Of iujementys sensualle to ofte in memory.   4
   I reduced to mynde the prophete Isay,
      Consideryng Englond to God in greuous offence;
   With wepyng ye, this text I fonde in his story:
      "Omne caput languidum, et omne cor merens."   8

36. eschewe h *inserted.*   No. 88. 2. D. of.

"Regnum Anglorum regnum Dei est,"
  As the Aungelle to seynt Edward dede wyttenesse.
Now regnum Sathane, it semethe, reputat best.
    For filii scelerati haue broughte it in dystresse —   12
    This preuethe fals wedlock and periury expresse —
        Fals heyres fostred, as knowethe experyence,
    Vnryghtewys dysherytyng with false oppresse,
        Sic, "omne caput languidum, et omne cor merens."   16

A planta pedis, fro the pore tylyer of the lond
  Ad verticem of spiritualle eke temporalle ennoynted crown,
Grace ys withdrawe and Goddys mercyfulle hand;
    Exalted ys falsehod, trowthe ys layde adoune;   20
    Euery reame cryethe owte of Engelondes treson.
        O falshod, with thy colored presence,
    Euer shulle we syng duryng thy season:
        "Omne caput languidum, et omne cor merens."   24

"Omne regnum in se divisum," sayethe dyuyne Scrypture,
  "Shall be desolate"; than folewethe translacione
Into the handes of theyre enemyes — Jewes arn figure.
    And now ys Englond in lyk reputacione,   28
    In wey to be conquered — truste it for sewre!
        Jhesu, for thy mercy and thy noble reuerens,
    Reforme vs to goodnesse and condicione pure,
        For "omne caput languidum, et omne cor merens."   32

Harry, oure souerayne and most Crystyne kyng,
  His trew bloode hathe flemed bothe be swerde and exyle;
What prynce by thys rewle may haue long enduryng,
    That also in moste pouert hath be long whyle?   36
    Tho bestys that thys wroughte to mydsomer haue but a myle!
        But euer mornethe Engelond for ham that be hens,
    Wythe languysshyng of herte, rehersyng my scyle,
        "Omne caput languidum, et omne cor merens."   40

14. D. heryres.   39. D. style.

Jonathas ys ded that Dauid shuld restore
  To the presence of the kyng, vnyte to make,
"Murum pro domo Israel"; presthode dar no more
    Put hymself forthe, his fat benefyce he shuld forsake. 44
    Mercyfulle God, it ys tyme thow for vs awake!
      "Mercenarius fugit," ne wylle make resistence,
    He ferethe the wolf that wolde hys bonys crake.
      "Omne caput languidum, et omne cor merens." 48

Tempus ys come falshede to dystroy,
  Tempus eradicandi the wedes fro the corne,
Tempus cremandi the breres that trees noye,
    Tempus evellendi the fals hunter with his horne, 52
    Tempus miserendi on por alle to torne,
      Tempus ponendi falsnes in perpetuelle absence,
    Thoroughe whom we syngyn bothe euyne and morne,
      "Omne caput languidum, et omne cor merens." 56

Send hom, most gracious Lord Jhesu, most benygne,
  Sende hoom thy trew blode vn-to his propre veyne,
Richard, duk of York, Job thy seruaunt insygne,
    Whom Sathan not cesethe to sette at care and dysdeyne; [f. 204r]
    But by the preserued, he may nat be slayne.
      Sette hym ut sedeat in principibus, as he dyd before,
    And so to oure newe songe, Lorde, thyn erys inclyne,
      "Gloria, laus et honor tibi sit, Rex Christe Redemptor!"

Edwarde, Erle of Marche, whos fame the erthe shalle sprede,
  Richard, Erle of Salisbury, named prudence,
Wythe that noble knyghte and floure of manhode
    Richard, erle of Warrewyk, sheelde of oure defence, 68
    Also lytelle Fauconbrege, a knyghte of grete reuerence;
      Jhesu ham restore to thayre honoure as thay had before,
    And euer shalle we syng to thyn Hyghe Excellence,
      "Gloria, laus et honor Tibi sit, Rex Christe Redemptor!"

55. D. syngyng.

No prynce, alle thyng consydered, wythe honoure
 In alle thyng requysyte to a kynges excellence
Better may lyue — serche any worthy predecessoure;
 Yet hastow, souuerayne lord, in these lordes absence 76
 Of alle thaym to a kyng ryghte resonable expens;
  Thay shalle come agayne and rekere for the scoore,
And thow shalt syng wythe vs thys verrey trew sens,
  "Gloria, laus et honor Tibi sit, Rex Christe Redemptor!"

  The deed man gretethe yow welle,
  That ys iust, trew as steele,
   With verray good entent;
  Alle the Reame of Englond   84
  Sone to louse from sorowes bond
   By ryghte indifferent iugement.

To the ryghte Worshypfulle Cyte of Caunterbury.

89. THE BATTLE OF NORTHAMPTON (1460)

Trinity Coll. Dublin MS. 432

Of all mennys disposicion naturall   [f. 67r]
 Philisophyrs wryten in euery place,
That affter the bodyes celestiall
 The Erthely body his wirkyn hase;   4
 Some tyme disposid it is to solace,
  Som tyme the contrary to hevynesse,
 And som tyme, by enspeciall grace,
  Sorow is turned into gladnesse.   8

And ensaumple here-of I take witnesse
 Of certeyn persones þat late exiled were,
Whos sorow is turned into ioyfulnesse,
 þe rose, þe fetyrlok, þe egle, & þe bere.   12

Gret games in Inglond sum tyme þer were,
  In hauking, huntyng, & fisshing in euery place
Amonge lordes with shelde & spere;
    Prosperite in reme þan reignyng wase.   16

Where-of god of his speciall grace,
  Heryng þe peple crying for mercye,
Considering þe falsehode in euery place,
  Gaue infleweinz of myrþe into bodyes on hye.   20
  The which in a berward lighted preuelye,
Edward, yong of age, disposed in solace,
  In hauking & huntyng to begynne meryly,
To Northampton with þe bere he toke his trace.   24

Now shal ye here a meruelous case,
  Allonly þorough godes ovne prouysioun;
þe berward & þe bere þei did þe dogges chace,
  And put þeyme to flight, to gret confucioun;   28
  þus a-gayne all naturall disposicioun
    To se a bere to seke his own game,
  But if it were of goddis mocioun   [f. 67v]
    þat he shuld do þe dogges shame.   32

Talbot ontrewe was þe oon dogges name,
  Bauling bewmond anodre, I vnderstonde;
þe thrid also was made ful tame,
  He was called bolde egremonde.   36
  When þe bereward come to þe grounde,
    Where he chased the forsaid leese,
  Amonge all oþer a buk he founde
    þe which was hye & fat of greese.   40

þe coriages berward put hym ferre in preese,
  To þe hunt, oure Kyng, he hyed hym ful fast;

13. games: a *inserted above line.*

The bere for all þe dogges wold not seese,
    But hyed hym sone afftre swyfftly in hast.   44
The dogges barked at hem ful fast,
    þe buk set vp his hornes on hye;
þe berward, þei cryed, þei wold downe cast,
    The bere also, if that he come nye.   48

The bereward asked no questioun why,
    But on þe dogges he set full rounde;
þe bere made the dogges to cry,
    And with his pawme cast þeyme to grounde.   52
The game was done in a litel stounde,
    þe buk was slayne, & borne away;
A-gayne þe bere þan was none hounde,
    But he might sporte and take his play.   56

But þe hunt he saued from harme þat day —
    He þouȝt neuer oþer in all his mynde —
He lowted downe, & at his fote lay,
    In token to hym that he was kynde.   60
The bereward also, þe huntes frende,
    ffell downe on kne, saying with obedience:
"Souereigne lord, thenk vs not vnkynde,   [f. 68r]
    Nor take ye this in none offence.   64

"We haue desired to com to your presence,
    To oure excuse we myght not answere;
All þinges were hyd from your audience,
    Where-fore we fled away for fere."   68
The hunt seid þo: "I wol you here.
    Ye be right welcom bothe to me;
All-way I pray you to stond me nere;
    Ye be my frendis, I may wele se.   72

57. sa *struck through after* hunt.

"Stond vp, berward, welcom be ye,
   Gramercy of your gentyl game;
ffrom you & your bere I wol neuer fle,
   Telliþe me now, what is your name."   76
   "Edward of march, I am þe same,
     Trewe to god and youre highnesse."
   þe gentyl bere seid: "with-outen blame,
     We haue be put in gret hevynesse."   80

The hunt answerid with gret mekenesse:
   "þe dogges wrought agayne all kynde,
þei labored to bryng me in distresse;
   I was þeire mayster & speciall frende.   84
   The buk ran before, þe dogges be-hynde.
     I folowed affter, I wist neuer why;
   In no place game kowde I fynde,
     þe buk and þe dogges playde by & by.   88

"A gentylle dogge wol naturally
   His mayster love & drede also;
His kyndly game if he may a-spy,
   ffrom hym belyve he wol be goo.   92
   These curre-dogges before dyd not so;
     þe buk and þey played par asent,
   They lapped a-wey the fatte me fro,   [f. 68v]
     Me to myscheue was þeire entent.   96

"And neuer to me þei wold consent,
   þe which called you euer treytours vntrewe;
Tyl now þe trewe comynerys of kent
   Be comyn with you, falsehed to destrewe,   100
   And truþe long exiled now to renewe.
     Seynt thomas I þanke, in all your right,
   þat gided you þis day, & shewid to be trewe,
     So fewe men slayne in so gret a fight!   104

74. MS. you.

"It was þe werk of god almight,
  Of mannesse power it might not be;
Gramercy, favcon, of þi fayre flight,
  þe bird from þe nest he made to fle."   108
  To london now, þat fayre cyte,
    þe hunt was brought ful reuerently;
  þe berward, þe bere, þe fawcon fre,
    Rode a-bouȝt hym full ioyefully.   112

Thorow þat cyte right opynly
  þe hunt rode, with gret gladnesse;
þe pepil reioysed inwardly,
  And þanked god of his goodenesse,   116
  That he likeþ with lustynesse
    To endewe þe hunt, oure noble kyng,
  And to remeve his heuynesse
    Which to his regall is no-þyng conservyng.   120

The egle from london was neuer remeving,
  But hovid & wayted vpon his pray;
All his delite was euer in fisshing,
  þe fisshe were closed in pyttes alway.   124
  Yit at þe last, vpon a day,
    þe fisshe drewe nere vnto þe bayte;
  Nede haþe no lawe, þis all men say,
    þe egle þerto euer layde goode wayte.   128

To skape a-way it was ful strayte,   [f. 69r]
  þe egyls birdes lay so þeyme a-bowte,
Euer beholding þe falce dissayte,
  How from þeyme all þei wold gon oute.   132
  þe egle liȝted & made hem to loute,
    þe fisshe was feynte, & litell of might;
  Ȝit iiij there were, boþe gret & stoute,
    þe which he toke all at a flight.   136

All þei had scaped vpon a nyght,
  Saue þeire skales were plucked away;

þan had þe fissh lost all here might,
  And litel ioy in watyr to play.   140
    Now god, þat madest both nyght & day,
      Bryng home þe mayster of þis game,
  þe duke of yorke, for hym we pray,
    þat noble prynce, Richard be name,   144

Whom treson ne falshod neuer dyd shame,
  But euer obedient to his souereigne;
ffalsehod euer-more put hym in blame,
  & lay awayte hym to haue sleigne.   148
  If god be with vs, who is vs agayne?
    He is so nowe, blessid mot he be;
  Of þis fortune all men may be fayne,
    þat right haþe now his fre entree.   152

Blessid be god in trinite,
  ffadir & son & holygoste,
Which kepith his seruauntes in aduersite,
  & wold not suffre þeyme to be loste.   156
  As þou art lord of mightes moste,
Saue þe kyng & his ryalte,
  And illumyn hym with þe holy goste,
His reme to set in perfyt charite.   160

Amen.

90. THE BATTLE OF TOWTON (1461)

Trinity Coll. Dublin MS. 432

Now is the rose of Rone growen to a gret honoure,   [f. 70*v*]
Therfore syng we euerychone, "I-blessid be that floure!"

I warne you euerychone, for you shuld vnderstonde,
There sprange a rose in rone & sprad into englonde,

No. 90. 1. you *supplied.*

He þat moued oure mone þorough þe grace of goddes sonde;
That rose stonte alone, þe chef flour of this londe.   4
    I-blessid be the tyme that euer god sprad that floure.

Blessid be þat rose ryall, that is so fressh of hewe!
Almighty ihesu, blesse that soule þat þe sede sewe,
And blessid be þe gardeyn þer the rose grewe;   8
Cristes blessyng haue þei all, þat to þat rose be trewe,
    And blessid be þe tyme þat euer god sprad þat floure.

Be-twix Cristmas & candelmas, a litel before þe lent,   [f. 72r]
All þe lordes of þe northe þei wrouȝt by oon assent   12
ffor to stroy þe sowthe cuntre þei did all hur entent;
Had not þe rose of Rone be, al englond had be shent.
    I-blessid be þe tyme þat euer god sprad þat floure.

Upon a shrof tuesday on a grene leede,   16
Be-twix Sandricche & saynt Albons, many man gan blede.
On an aswedynsday we levid in mykel drede,
Than cam þe rose of Rone downe & halp vs at oure nede.
    Blessid be þe tyme þat euer god sprad þat floure.   20

The norþen men made her bost, whan þei had done þat dede,
"We wol dwelle in þe southe cuntrey & take al þat we nede —
These wifes & hur doughters oure purpose shul þei spede."
Than seid þe rose of Rone, "nay, þat werk shal I for-bede!"   24
    Blessid be þe tyme þat euer god sprad þat floure.

ffor to saue al englond þe rose did his entent,
With Calys & with loue london, with Essex & with Kent,
And al þe south of englond vnto þe watyr of trent.   28
And whan he saw þe tyme best, þe rose from london went.
    Blessid be þe tyme þat euer god sprad þat floure.

The wey into þe northe cuntre þe rose ful fast he sought;
With hym went þe ragged staf, þat many man dere bought;   32

So þan did þe white lyon — ful worthely he wrought.
Almighti ihesu blesse his soule þat þo armes ought,
  And blessid be þe tyme þat euer god sprad þat floure.

The fisshe hoke cam into þe felde with ful egre mode,   36
So did þe cornyssh chowghe & brouȝt forthe all hir brode;
Þer was þe blak ragged staf, þat is boþe trewe & goode;
Þe brideld horse; þe watyr bouge be þe horse stode.
  Blessid be þe tyme þat euer god spred that floure.   40

The grehound & þe hertes hede þei quyt hem
                        wele þat day; [f. 72v]
So did þe harow of caunterbury, & clynton with his kay;
Þe white ship of brystow he feryd not þat fray;
Þe blak ram of Couentre he said not ons nay.   44
  Blessid be þe tyme þat euer god spred þat floure.

The fawcon & þe fetherlok was þer that tyde;
Þe blak bulle also, hym-self he wold not hyde;
Þe dolfyn cam from Walys, iii carpis be his syde;   48
The prowde libert of Salesbury, he gapid his gomes wide.
  Blessid be þe tyme that euer god spred that floure.

The wolf cam fro Worcestre, ful sore he þouȝt to lyte;
Þe dragon cam fro Glowcestre, he bent his tayle to smyte;   52
The griffen cam fro leycestre fleying in as tyte;
The george cam fro Notyngham with spere for to fyte.
  Blessid be þe tyme that euer god spred þat floure.

The boris hede fro Wyndesover with tusshes sharp & kene;   56
Þe estrich feder was in þe felde, þat many men myȝt sene;
The wild kat fro norhampton with hur brode nose.
Þer was many a fayre pynon wayting vpon þe rose.
  Blessid be þe tyme þat euer god spred that floure.   60

51. MS. Worcetre.

The norþen party made hem strong with spere & with sheld;
On palmesonday affter þe none þei met vs in þe feld.
With-in an owre þei were right fayne to fle & eke to yeld —
xxvii thousand þe rose kyld in þe feld.   64
    Blessid be þe tyme that euer god spred þat floure.

The rose wan þe victorye, þe feld, & also þe chace.
Now may þe housbond in þe south dwell in his owne place —
His wif & eke his faire doughtre & al þe goode he has.   [f. 71r]
Soche menys haþ the rose made by vertu & by grace.
    Blessid be þe tyme þat euer god sprad þat floure.

The rose cam to loue london, ful ryally rydyng.
ii erchbisshops of englond þei crovned þe rose kyng.   72
Almighti ihesu save þe rose & geue hym his blessyng,
And al þe reme of englond ioy of his crownyng,
    Þat we may blesse þe tyme þat euer god sprad þe floure.

Amen, pur charite.

91. TWELVE LETTERS SAVE ENGLAND (1461)

Trinity Coll. Dublin MS. 432

Yerly be þe morowe in a somer-tyde,   [f. 71r]
    I saw in a strete in london as I went,
A gentyl-woman sittyng in chepe-syde,
    Syt wirkyng vpon a vestiment.   4

She set xij letteris in order on a rowe,
    Þat I might right wele vnderstande,
Þorought þe grace of god it shal be knowe,
    Þese xij letters shal saue all Inglande.   8

A litel while if þat ye wol dwelle
    And yeue audience all vnto me,

What letters þei were, I shal you telle:
  þei were drawen out of þe a b c.   12

There was a V & thre arres to-gydre in a sute,
  With letters oþer of which I shal reherse;
3 E R E writen affter be rute,   [f. 71v]
  M S R and ff, now haue I þeyme expresse.   16

Styl as I stode with-In a litel seson,
  I construed þese letters þens or I went,
And as I conseyued be my semple reson,
  I shal telle you what þat woman ment.   20

The arris for thre Richard þat be of noble fames,
  þat for þe riȝt of englond haue sufferd moche wo —
York, Salesbury, and Warwik, þese be þe lordes names
  þat all englond is be-holden to.   24

3 for ȝorke þat is manly and myȝtfull,
  þat be grace of god & gret reuelacion,
Reynyng with rules resonable and right-full,
  þe which for oure sakes haþe sufferd vexacion.   28

E for Edward whos fame þe erþe shal sprede,
  Be-cause of his wisdom named prudence,
Shal saue all englond by his manly-hede,
  Wherfore we owe to do hym reuerence.   32

M for marche, trewe in euery tryall,
  Drawen by discrecion þat worthy & wise is,
Conseived in wedlok, & comyn of blode ryall,
  Ioynyng vnto vertu, excludyng all vises.   36

S for Salesbury, with-out any question
  Riall in his reynyng, & wise in euery case;

15. MS. 3 E G R E ; brute.

He bryngeth many maters to goode conclusion;
 Called for his wisdom pater familias.   40

W for Warwik, goode with sheld & oþer defence, [f. 75r]
 þe boldest vnder baner in batell to a-byde;
ffor þe right of englond he doþe his diligence.
 Boþe be londe & watyr, god be his gyde!   44

ff for þe feturlok þat is of gret substaunce,
 þat haþe mevid many maters þorow his mediacion,
In englond & in Wales, in scotland & in fraunce,
 He rideþ & ruleth with ryall reputacion.   48

R for þe rose þat fressh is in euery stede,
 Boþe þe rote and þe stalke ben gret of honoure;
ffro norway to normandi þeire power wol sprede,
 ffrom yrland to estland men ioy of þat flowre. 52

E for þe egle þat gret worship haþe wonne
 þorow spredyng of his wynges, þat neuer dyd fle;
þer was neuer byrde þat bred vndre sonne
 More fortunat in felde þan þat birde hathe be. 56

R for þe ragged staf þat noman may skapen,
 ffrom scotland to cales þere-of men stond in awe;
In al cristen landes is none so felle a wepen
 To correcte soche caytiffes as do a-gayne þe lawe. 60

Now haue I declarede þese xij letters acordyng
 To þeire condicions, where þei ryde or gone;
þou3 þei be disseverid, þe olde from þe yinge,
 þeire entent & purpos corden all in oone.   64

That is, to destroy treson, & make a tryall
 Of hem þat be fauty, & hurten full sore.

52. MS. ryland.

ffor þe wylle of edward, kyng most ryall,   [f. 75*v*]
    That is þe moste purpos þat we labor fore.   68

Now pray we to þe prynce moste precious & pure
    þat syttyth with his seyntis in blys eternall,
Hur entent & purpos may last & endure
    To þe plesaunce of god, & þe welfare of vs all.   72

92.   *EDWARD, DEI GRATIA*

Lambeth Palace MS. 306

    A, a, a, a.   [f. 136*r*]
    Edwardeus, Dai Gracia.

Sithe god hathe chose þe to be his kny3t
And possesside þe in this right,
Thoue hime honour with al thi myght,
    Edwardes, dai gracia.   4

Oute of þe stoke that longe lay dede
God hathe causede the to sprynge & sprede,
And of al Englond to be the hede,
    Edwardes, dei gracia.   8

Sithe god hathe yeuen the thorough his my3te,
Oute of that stoke birede in sight,
The floure to springe, & rosse so white,
    Edwardes, dai gracia.   12

Thoue yeve hem lawde and praisinge,
Thove vergyne knight of whom we synge,
Vndeffiled sithe thy begynnyng,
    Edwardes, dai gracia.   16

No. 92. bur. *one* a *supplied.*   2. his *struck through after* in.
5. lay dede MS. lade day.

God save thy contenewaunce,
And so to prospere to his plesance,
That euer thyne astate thou mowte enhaunce,
    Edwardes, dai gracia.   20

Rex Anglie & francia, y say,
hit is thine owne — why saist þou nay?
And so is spayne, that faire contrey,
    Edwardis, dai gracia.   24

ffy on slowtfull contenewaunce,
Where conquest is a noble plesance,
And regesterd in olde rememberance,
    Edwardes, day Gracia!   28

Wherfor, prince and kyng moste myȝte,
Remember þe subdeue of þis regaly
Of Englonde, fraunce, & spayn trewely,
    Edwardes, dai Gracia.   32

Explicit.

93. A POLITICAL RETROSPECT (1462)

Soc. of Antiquaries MS. 101

To have in mynde callyng to Remembbraunse   [f. 98r col. i]
    The gret wrongys doon of oold antiquitey,
Unrightful heyres by wrong alyaunce
    Usurpyng this Royaume caused gret adversitey;   4
    Kyng Richard the secounde, high of dignytee,
        Whiche of Ingeland was Rightful enheritoure,

18. MS. prospede.

In whos tyme ther was habundaunce with plentee
  Of welthe & erthely Ioye withouȝt langoure.   8

Than cam henry of derby, by force & myght,
  & undir the colour of fals periury,
He toke this rightwys kyng, goddes trew knyght,
  And hym in prison put perpetuelly.   12
  Pyned to deth, alas, ful pyteuxly!
    Holy bisshope Scrope, the blyssed confessour,
  In þat quarel toke hys deth ful paciently,
    That all the world spak of þat gret langoure.   16

Whos deth ys a very trew evidence
  To all Ingeland for the iust title & lyne,
Which for the trowthe by tyranny & violence
  Was put doun, and suspect hold benysyne;   20
  Many a trew lord then put to mortil fyne;
    Alway they have ben aboute with Rigoure
  The lynaige of kyng richard to undirmyne,
    That longe have lyved in gret langoure.   24

God smote the said henry for hys gret fersnesse,
  With a lepre holdyng hym to hys end fynally,
Next hym henry the fyfte, of knyghtly prowesse,
  Named the best of þat lyne & progeny;   28
  How-be-it he regned unrightfully,
    ȝit he upheld in Ingeland the honnour.
  Henry, hys sone, of Wyndesore, by gret foly,
    All hath retourned unto huge langoure.   32

Callyng to mynde the fals engendred treson
  And myschyefȝ þat were in hys dayes Regnyng:
The good duc of gloucestre in the season
  Of the parlement at Bury beyng,   36

20. MS. venyrsyne.   31. MS. Wydesore.   32. MS. retourne.

Was put to deth; and ay sith gret mornyng
    Hath ben in Ingeland, with many a scharp schoure,
ffalshode, myschyef, secret synne upholdyng,
    Which hath caused in Engeland endeleȝ langoure.   40

Noo mervail þough engeland hath ben unhappy, [f. 98r col. ii]
    Which hath be mysrewled ȝerys sertayne;
Scripture saith, "heritage holdyn wrongfully
    Schal never cheve, ne with the thred heyre remayne."   44
As hath be verified late ful playne:
    Where-as iij kynges have regned by erroure,
The thred put ouȝt & the right brought agayne,
    Whos absence hath caused endleȝ langoure.   48

Also scripture saith, "woo be to þat Regyon
    Where ys a kyng unwyse or Innocent."
Moreovyr it ys Right a gret abusion,
    A womman of a land to be a Regent —   52
Qwene margrete I mene, þat ever hath ment
    To gouerne all engeland with myght and poure,
And to destroye the Ryght lyne was here entent,
    Wherfore sche hath a fal, to here gret langour.   56

And now sche ne rought, so þat sche myght attayne,
    Though all engeland were brought to confusyon;
Sche and here wykked affynite certayne
    Entende uttyrly to destroye thys regioun;   60
ffor with theym ys but Deth & distruccioun,
    Robberye & vengeaunce with all Rygour.
Therefore all þat holde of þat oppynioun,
    God sende hem a schort ende with mech langour.   64

O, it ys gretly agayne kynde and nature,
    An englyssh man to corrumpe hys owne nacion —
Willyng straungiers for to Recure,
    And in Engeland to have the domynacion,   68

Wenyng þanne to be gret of Reputacion,
   fforsothe they þat soo hope, least schalbe theyre poure;
He that woold be high schalbe undir subiecion,
   And the fyrst þat schal repente the langoure.   72

Wherfore I lykken England to a gardayne,
   Which þat hath ben ouergrowen many yere
With wedys, which must be mowen doune playne,
   And þan schul the pleasant swete herbes appere.   76
   Wherfore all trewe englyssh peuple, pray yn fere
     ffor kyng Edward of Rouen, oure comfortoure,
   That he kepe Iustice and make wedis clere,
     Avoydyng the blak cloudys of langoure.   80

A gret signe it ys þat god lovyth þat knyght;   [f. 98v]
   ffor all thoo þat woold have destroyed hym utterly,
All they ar myschyeved & put to flyght.
   Than remembre hys fortune with chevalry,   84
   Which at Northamptoun gate the victory,
     And at mortimers crosse he had the honnour;
   On palme sonday he wan the palme of glorye,
     And put hys enemyes to endeleȝ langour.   88

And dreve hys adversary ouȝt of the land;
   Aftyr cam to london and was crouned kyng.
Ryght late god ȝaf hym grace to undirstonde
   The fals traytours agayn hym ymagynynge.   92
   The prophecie saith, there schal dere hym noo þinge;
     he it ys þat schal wynne castell, toune, and toure;
   Alle Rebellyous undyr he schal hem brynge,
     Willyng to hys highenesse any langoure.   96

Richard, the Erl of Warwyk, of knyghthode
   Lodesterre, borne of a stok þat evyr schalbe trewe,
Havyng the name of prowes & manhoode,
   Hath ay ben Redy to helpe and Resskewe   100

kyng Edward, in hys right hym to endewe;
  The commens þerto have redy euery houre
The voix of the peuple, the voix of Jhesu,
    Who kepe & preserue hym from all langoure.   104

Now blyssed saint george, pray the vierge Immaculat,
  to be good mediatrix, praying here sonne
That Edward of Rouen may be victorieux & fortunat,
  With all the trew lordes of hys regioun,   108
  That they may se a good way & direction
    To make peas in Engeland, þat Riche & pouer
May Ioyfully synge at the conclusyon,
  Welcom euerlastyng Ioie, and farewal langoure!   112

94.   THE BATTLE OF BARNET (1471)

Trinity Coll. Cambridge MS. 601

Gaudete iusti in domino,   [f. 244*v*]
  For now regneth ryghtwysly oure souerayn,
Trew enherytour to the crowne, hys quarell preueth so,
  Edward the fourth, by grace to attayn,   4
  With the crowne of England on vs to rayn,
    By iust tytle of hys descendyng,
  All mys-creatures to reconsyle agayn.
    Conuertimini, ye comons, & drede your kyng.   8

Conuertimini, and leue your opinion,
  And sey Credo, hyt woll noon other-wyse be;
For he ys gon that louyd dyuysion,
  Mortuus est, ther can noman hym se.   12
  Now ys Iusticia in hys owne contre,
    Prosperyng hys purpose to menteyne,
  All myscreatures to reconsyle ageyne.
    Conuertimini, ye comons, and drede your kyng.   16

Drede your kyng and your souerayn lord,
  For he ys worthy to be louyd and dred;
Hys gloryous victory bereth record
  That he ys both pacyent and sad.   20
  Of a more famous knyght I neuer rad
    Syn the tyme of Artors dayes;
  He that loueth hym nat, I holde hym mad.
    Conuertimini, ye comons, and drede your kyng.   24

Vppon Ester day befelle a pyteous case,
  Many a man hys lyfe lost in that mornyng;
"Cristus resurgens" was song with "alase!"
  "Allas!" may he syng that causyd all thys,   28
  Sorow and care causyd many a day.
    Orate pro anima, that he may com to blys;
  Ye that be hys frendys, yow prestys, to pray.
    Conuertimini, ye comons, and drede your kyng.   32

Homo proponit, oftymes in veyn,
But deus disponit, the boke telleth pleyn.

quy serra, serra.
Finis.

THE WELL-ORDERED KINGDOM

95. THE CROWNED KING:
ON THE ART OF GOVERNING (1415)

MS. Douce 95
(Sum. Cat. No. 21669)

Crist, crowned Kyng, that on Cros didest,   [f. 4r]
And art comfort of all care, þow kynd go out of cours,
With thi halwes in heuen heried mote thu be,

31. be *supplied*.

And thy worshipfull werkes worshiped euere,   4
That suche sondry signes shewest vnto man
In dremyng, in drecchyng, & in derk swevenes,
Wherwith that thei ben ware & witterly knowen
Of care and of comfort þat comyng is here-after.   8
This I sey be my-self, so saue me our lord,
Be a metyng that y met in a morowe slepe,
Hevy & hidows, y hight you, forsoth,
And the most merveylous that y met euere.   12

And ye like to leer & listen awhile,
As y may in my mynde this metynge reherce,
Sekerly and shortly þe soth y shall you shewe
Of this dredefull dreme — deme as you likes.   16
Ones y me ordeyned, as y haue ofte doon,
With frendes and felawes, frendemen and other,
And caught me in a company on corpus cristi even
Six other vij myle oute of Suthampton,   20
To take melodye and mirthes among my makes,
With redyng of romaunces, and reuelyng among.

The dym of the derknesse drowe into the west,
And began for to spryng in the grey day;   24
Than lift y vp my lyddes & loked in the sky
And knewe by the kende cours hit clered in þe est.
Blyve y busked me doun and to bed went,
For to comfort my kynde and cacche a slepe.   28
Swythe y swyed in a sweem þat y swet after;
So my spirit in a spaas so sore was y-set,
Me thought that y houed an high on an hill,
And loked doun on a dale deppest of othre.   32

Ther y sawe in my sight a selcouthe peple —
The multitude was so moche it myght not be noumbred.
Me thought y herd a crowned kyng of his comunes axe

29. swet MS. swer.   33. selcouthe MS. sere couthe.
34. MS. noumbrerd.

A soleyn subsidie to susteyne his werres,   [f. 4v]
To be rered in the reaume, as reson requyred,
Of suche as were seemly to suffre the charge;
That they that rekened were riche by reson and skyle
Shuld pay a parcell for here pouere neighbowres.   40
This ordenaunce he made in ease of his peple.

With that a clerk kneled adoun & carped these wordes:
"Liege lord, yif it you like to listen a while,
Sum sawes of salomon y shall you shew sone,   44
Besechyng you of your souerainte that y myght be suffred
To shewe you my sentence in singuler noumbre —
To peynte it with pluralites my prose wolde faile;
To pike a thonke with plesaunce my profit were but simple."
Than the kyng of his curtesie comaunded hym to ryse,
To stonde and sey what hym semed and knele no lenger.

Than he seid, "sir, crowned kyng, thou knowest well þyself.
Thi-self hast lyfe, lyme, and lawes for to keep;   52
Yif þou be chief Iustice, iustifie the trouthe;
And rule the be reson, and vpright sitte.
For that is a poynt principall — preve it who-so will —
To be dred for thy domes and dowted for thy myght;   56
For ther is neither lered ne lewed þat lyveth vpon erthe
That wyssheth after worship; his wit is full fable
But yif he wite be his werkes he hath well deserued,
And of his well doyng his dedes to deme the same.   60

"The loue of thi liegmen, that to thi lawe are bounde,
Take hit for a tresour of hem that are true,
That may the more availl in a myle-wey
Thanne moche of thy mukke þat manhode loueþ neuere.   64
The playnt of the pouere peple put þou not behynde,
For the swope and swete and swynke for thy fode;
Moche worship they wynne the in this worlde riche,

56. and dowted MS. an dowte.

Of thy gliteryng gold and of thy gay wedes,   68
Thy proude pelure, and palle with preciouse stones,
Grete castels and stronge, and styff walled townes.   [f. 5r]
And yit the most preciouse plente þat apparaill passeth,
Thi pouere peple with here ploughe pike oute of the erthe, 72
And they yeve here goddes to gouerne hem euen,
And yit the peple ben well apaid to plese þe allone.
Suche loue is on the leid of lordes and of lower,
And grete is thi grace that god hath the lent.   76

"Thi peres in parlement pull hem to-geders,
Worche after wysdom, & worshipe will folowe;
For as a lord is a lord and ledeth the peple,
So shuld prowesse in þi persone passe oþer mennes wittes: 80
The wittyest and wylyest and worthiest in armes.
All is but waste wele and he wronge vse,
And vnsemely for a souerain (so saue me our lord)
And hevy for his name that hyndred will ever.   84

"Sir, þou most be worldly wys, & ware þe betymes;
And kepe the fro glosyng of gylers mowthes,
That speken to the spiritually with spiritual tonges,
Momelyn with here mouthes moche and malys in hert,   88
And of a mys menyng maketh a faire tale,
Vnder flateryng and fair speche falsehede foloweth;
And yif they myght with her moustres to mame þe for euere,
With disceit of here derknesse þe deuell hem a-drenche! 92

"Be kende to thi clergi and comfort þe pouere;
Cherissh thy champyons and chief men of armes;
And suche as presoners mowe pike with poyntes of werre,
Lete hem wilde that they wynne, & worþyly hem þonke; 96
And suche as castels mowe cacche, or eny clos tounes,
Geve hem as gladly — than shalt þou gete hertes.
For god in his gospell asketh nothyng elles,
But oonly loue for love; and let hym be levest.   100
Also he that is stronge strokes for to dele,

Make hym thy marchall, and maner his maistre;
That for his doughtynesse men mowe hym drede,
And for his wysdom and witte the better to be ware.   [f. 5v]
Knyghtes of thy counseill, connyng in armes,
That been seker at asay, and sober to thy frendes,
Suche thou shuldest comfort be cours of thy kende,
That lede here lyves in labour for thy loue.   108
Loke þou haue suche a man that loueth not to lye,
A faithfull philosofre þat flater woll never;
For he that fareth as a faane folowyng þy wille,
Worche þou well or woo, he woll þe not amende.   112
Lere lettrewre in þy youthe, as a lord befalleth,
Whan þou to parlement shall passe þere lordes shull pere;
For to her of thy wysdom þey woll awayte after,
And though her speche be but small, þe more be here þoughtes;
For yif þou haue no science to shewe of thyself,
But as a brogour to go borowe pore mennes wittes,
That were most myscheef þat myght a lord befalle,
Ther as wyse men haue wrapped her wittes togidre.   120

"Sir, they it come to þe of kynde a kyng to be called,
Yit must þou knowe of corage what knyghthood befalleþ;
For he þat armes shall haunte, in youþe he must begynne.
Of all artes vnder heven, vse is a maistre.   124

"Sir, more-ouere be not gredy gyftes to grype;
Rather þou shalt yeve hem þat fele agreved,
So shall thy hawtesse highlich be honoured,
And prudence in thy principaltee y-preised for euere. 128
For in ensample y shall you shewe that soth is knowe:
A kyng shuld not of curtesie couetouse be holde,
For there-as couetyse is knowe in a kynges brest
Ther is corage out of kende when mukke is his maistre. 132
The condicion of a kyng shuld comfort his peple.
For such laykes ben to love þere leedes laghen alle.

105. connyng MS. comyng.

"My liege lord, of this mater y meve you no more,
But euere in your mynde haue hym þat you made,   136
And taketh a siker ensample þat crist hym-self sheweth,
Of all the seyntes in heven that for hym deth suffred, [f. 6r]
For his loue thei were so large heir lyves they lost,
And for loue of that Lord aloft now they dwelle   140
With that crowned kyng that on cros dyed;
Ther Crist in his kyngdom comfort vs euere,
And of his high grace graunte vnto vs alle
Prosperite, and pees pursue we therafter."   144

Explicit.

96. ADVICE TO THE SEVERAL ESTATES, I

BY JOHN LYDGATE

de Worde, *The Temple of Glas*

Rex sine sapiencia. Episcopus sine doctrina.
Dominus sine consilio. Mulier sine castitate.
Miles sine probitate. Iudex sine iusticia.
Diues sine elemosina. Populus sine lege.   **4**
Senex sine religione. Seruus sine timore.
Pauper superbus. Adolescens sine obediencia.

Goo forth, kyng, reule the by sapyence;
    Bysshop, be able to mynystre doctryne;   8
Lord, to treu counceyle yeue audyence;
    Womanhed, to chastyte euer enclyne;
    Knyght, lete thy dedes worshyp determyne;
        Be rightuous, Iuge, in sauyng thy name;   12
        Ryche, doo almes, lest thou lese blys with shame.

People, obeye your kyng and the lawe;
    Age, be thou ruled by good religyon;
True seruaunt, be dredfull & kepe the vnder awe;   16
    And thou, poure, fye on presumpcyon;

Inobedyence to yougth is vtter destruccyon.
  Remembre you how god hath sette you, lo!
  And doo your parte, as ye ar ordeynd to.   20

97.   ADVICE TO THE SEVERAL ESTATES, II

Sloane MS. 4031

ye that ar comons, obey yovr kynge and lorde.   [f. 2r]
  observe vnto hym love and fydelyte;
avoyde rebellyon, for certaynely dyscorde
  es rote and mother of carefvll poverte.   4
  kepe eche to other love and fydelyte.
    expell enve and slovth, moste chefe of all —
    where slovth hath place, there welth es faynt and small.

ye ryche, helpe them whyche have necessyte: 8
  eche socovr other — svche way es charytable.
no man presvme none hye than hes degre —
  a lowest place es oft moste svre and stable.
    abyde yn vertve, be never chavngeable;   12
    namely be trve to god, yovr hevenly lorde;
    thvs shall yovr lyvynge and yovr byleve accorde.

set all yovr myndes to norysshe amyte;
  for vnto a royalme the syngvler defence   16
restyth en love, concorde, and vnete,
  more than en strength or wordly opvlence.
  as for frendes love and benevolence
    es nat obtayned by batayle nor rychys,   20
    bvt by good dedes and stedfast faythfvlnes.

blynde nat yovr myndes wyth wretchyd covetyse;
  spende nat yovr ryches en prodygalte.
a meane es mesvre attaynyng nat to vyce   24
  wythyn the bovndys of lyberalyte.

No. 97.   19. MS. as for of frendes.

leve wrath, provoker of great enormyte.
  let nat blynde pryde yovr meke myndes confovnde,
  syth et so many hath brovght vnto the grovnde.   28

avoyde vyle venus and lvstes corporall,
  destrvccyon of sovle, of body, and ryches;
mankynde svbdvynge to maners bestyall.
  fle glotony whyche es bvt bestelynes.   32
  let abstynence expell from yov exces
    by ymmoderate dyet, exces, and glotony —
    man oft es mordrer of hes owne body.

bvt svche of yov as are en hye degre,   [f. 2v]
  set all yovr myndes and chefe entencyon
to se the pore have ryght and eqvyte,
  rather wyth favovr than wronge extorcyon.
  and ye that are kynge, hede of the regyon,   40
    se that eche man en maners lyve and do
    after the degre whyche he es callyd to.

and lyke as yovr rowme es moste of excellence,
  en yovr royalme to reygne wyth dyademe royall,   44
so ovght yovr lyfe be clennest from offence,
  and shyne en vertve above yovr svbgectes all.
  a vycyovs prynce es as a plage mortall,
    and fovle example to all hes comonte,   48
    occasyon to folowe hes vyle enormyte.

lyke-wyse hes lyfe establyd en vertve
  shalbe example to all hes regyon,
hes lyfe, hes maners, and vertve to ensve.   52
  et es to a prynce nye great confvsyon,
  more shame and rebvke to make transgressyon,
    than es to one of baas and lowe degre:
    the hyer hylle, man shall the farther se.   56

note well, also, how whan the hedes be
    of perfyte lyvynge and vndefyled name,
as chastely lyvynge or gyven to eqvyte,
    moste commenly the commons are the same;   60
    bvt whan the rvlers ensvyth syne and shame,
        the commons fereth the lesse ther-wyth to mell.
    for ef the hede be syke, the body es natt well.

and ye that are mynystres to god omnypotent,   64
    enforme ye other to walke the path of grace;
bvt se yovr owne lyfe be pvre and ennocent,
    en vertve grovndyd, and clere from all trespase;
    for svrely that man es en a wretchyd case   68
        whyche techyth other the way to paradyce,
        hym-selfe to helle walkynge by synne and vyce.

THE WILL FOR PEACE

98. A PRAYER FOR ENGLAND

BY JOHN LYDGATE

MS. Fairfax 16
(Sum. Cat. No. 3896)

Ab inimicis nostris defende nos criste.   [f. 199*v]

Most souereigne lord, o blessed crist ihesu,
    ffrom oure enemyes delyuer vs, and oure foon,
Vnder whos grace and vnder whos vertu
    We ben assured, where-so we ryde or goon;   4

                63. MS. for of the hele.

Now lord, that art twoo and three and oon,
  Kepe and preserve vnder thy myghty honde
    The kynge, the quene, the peple, and thy londe.

Affliccionem nostram benignus vide.

And blessed lorde, of thy benyngnytee   8
  Considre and see oure affliccion,
And lat thyn eye of mercye on vs see
  Vs to releve in tribulacion;
    And shadwe, vs, lord, with thy proteccion,   12
      And ay preserue vnder thy myghty honde
        The kynge, the quene, the peple, and thy londe.

Dolorem cordis nostri respice clemens.

And, good lord, beholde and eke aduert —
  Of thy mercy and thy grete grace —   16
Th'inwarde sorwes of oure troubled hert;
  And looke vpon vs with a benigne face,
  And lat thyn wynges of pitee vs enbrace,
    And ay preserve vnder thy myghty honde   20
      The kynge, the quene, the peple, and thy londe.

Peccata populi tui pius indulge.

Mekely foryeve the synnes olde and newe
  Of thy peple and ther grete offence;
And, good lord, vpon ther giltes rewe,   [f. 200*r*]
  And ther demerites by dome not recompence;
  But reconcyle them with thyn indulgence,
    And ay preserve vnder thy myghty honde
      The kynge, the quene, the peple, and thy londe.   28

17. MS. Thinwardes.

Oraciones nostras pius exaudi.

And, good lord, here oure orisouns
  Whan we to the for helpe clepe or calle;
Here oure compleyntes and lamentaciouns,
  And doo socour to oure offences alle;   32
    Be oure defence that noo myschefe ne falle,
      And ay preserve vnder thy myghty honde
      The kyng, the quene, the peple, and thy londe.

ffili dei vnii miserere nobis.

Thow sone of god ay lastynge and eterne,   36
  Haue mercy on vs and forgete vs nought;
And of thy grace guye vs, and gouerne,
  And reconcyle that thow so dere hast bought;
    With love and drede enbrace our inwarde thought;   40
      And ay preserve vnder thy myghty honde
      The kynge, the quene, the peple, and thy londe.

Hic et imperpetuum nos custodire digneris.

In this lyfe here and perpetuelly
  To kepe vs, lord, that thou nat disdeyne;   44
ffor alle oure truste stant in thy mercie,
  Hopynge by grace we shal ther-to atteyne.
    Thy passyon shal kepe vs oute of peyne,
      And ay preserve vnder thy myghty honde   48
      The kynge, the quene, the peple, and thy londe.

Exaudi nos criste exaudi nos criste.

Here vs, lorde, whan we to the preye;
  And here vs, lorde, in myschefe and in nede.
And Crist Ihesu by mercy vs conveye,   52

Whiche on the Croys liste for oure sake blede,
ffortune this Realme and make it wel to spede;
   Benigne Ihesu, preserve eke with thin honde   [f. 200*v*]
   The kynge, the quene, the peple, and thy londe.   56

Lenvoy

A, lorde, A-monge haue A Remembraunce
  On sixt henry, thyn ovne chose knyght,
Borne t'enheryte the Regioun of ffraunce
  By trew discent and by title of ryght;   60
  Now, good lorde, conserue him thurgh thy myght
   And ay preserve vnder thy myghty honde
   Him and his moder, thy peple, and thy londe.

Lat him in vertu ay encresse and shyne,   64
  Worthy thorgh vertu to be put in memorye,
And forgete nat hys moder kateryne,
  Where thou sittest in thy heuenly glorye.
  Yive to thy knyght conquest and victorye,   68
   And ay preserve vnder thy myghty honde
   Him and his moder, thy peple, and thy londe.

Be thow hys consaylle and hys souereigne rede,
  So as he wexeth with vertu him t'avaunce;   72
And, blessed lord, be thow bothe helpe and spede
  To alle that labouren for hys enheritaunce,
  Bothe in this realme and in the grounde of ffraunce;
   And ay preserve vnder thy myghty honde   76
   Him and hys moder, thy peple, and thy londe.

In short tyme that thow may atteyne,
  Withoute lettyng or any perturbaunce,
To be corowned with worthy corovnes tweyne,   80
  ffrist in this londe and afterwarde in ffraunce.

54. MS. fortunee.   62, 69, 76. ay *supplied*.

And yive hym grace to lyve to thy plesaunce,
   And ay preserve vnder thy myghty honde
Hym and hys moder, thy peple, and thy londe.   84
               Explicit.

99. *THAT PEACE MAY STAND*

Advocates MS. 19.3.1

Iesu, þat was borne of mare fre,   [f. 66r]
   As he hase pwower and mey best
Save all in gud prosperite,
   þat feyne wolde sette þis reme in rest;   4
And send whom luf and charite
   þat feyth were wonus among hus fast.
for, by my troþe, hit is pete
   To wytte þo pepul so sore dystrest,   8
   As þei have byn be est and west —
     Robbud and slene thoro-owt þis londe.
   All-myȝthe Iesu, os he mey best,
     lene hus grace nowe þat pese mey stond.   12

For I haue mych mervel of mony men
   þat of more myscheu wold be full feyne,
And syche as kan no resvn ken,
   þat wold þer schulde be trobul ageyne;   16
And hase hade knoleg whare and when
   how mony a gud mon has ben slene.
me thynke þat konsyons schuld hom ken
   to pray for pes with all þer mene.   20
   þat lord þat for hus soffurd pene
     And markud adam apon þo sond,
   Send luf and charete home a-geyne,
     And lene hus grace þat pes mey stond.   24

No. 99. 10. MS. longde.   14. MS. myschen.
22 *after* adam, p *blotted*.   24. *catchword*: þat pes mey stond.

And he þat more vnpes wolde haue   [f. 66v]
    With-in þis reme be dey or ny3the,
I pray to god he be not save,
    But on hym-selue þat hyt mey ly3the.   28
for þer ar mony a lydur knave
    þat in þo fylde wolde feyntly fy3th,
But trwe mens gud 3yt wolde þei have
    to Robbe and reve þem of þer rygth.   32
    Iesus, os he is most of my3th,
        send luf and charite in-to þis londe,
    þat consyons moth kepe his kandul ly3th,
        And lene hus grace now þat pes mey stonde.   36

Be mony insampuls men mey see
    þat we plese not al owre god to pey;
for hare-be-fore in yerus iij
    mych of owre welth hase wastud awey,   40
with grete darthe and poverte,
    And vnkynde wedurs be ny3th and dey,
Waturs stronke and flodus hee
    Whyche dystryde boþe borne and hey;   44
    And a-monke howr-selfe byn mony a-frey,
        be norþe and sowþe thoro-owte þis londe.
    Al-my3hty Iesu, os he best mey,
        lene hus grace nowe þat pes mo3t stonde.   48

Hyt wer grete nede to prey for pes,   [f. 67r]
    And fro all sich folys hus defende;
for, loke, sython warus be-gan to ses!
    how feire insampuls god has hus sende: 52
þo sesonabulst wedur, withowtvn leyse,
    þat euer mon sawe dryvvn tyl a nende,
And feyr on gronde kon kornus incres,
    And lyke þoro grace þat þo worde schuld mende.   56

32. MS. Robbo.

Wer luf and charite with hus blend,
   þat concions myȝth reyne with-in þis londe,
þen schulde owre trobul be at a nende,
    And I trust to god þat pes schulde stonde.   60

To pray for luf and charite
   hit was neuer so mycul nede;
for we haue lost in yerus iij
   mony duȝth mon of dede.   64
yette wolde we all trvwe men be
   And holde to-gedur when we hade nede;
with þo grace of god and owre lade
   hus thurt no nodur nacions drede.   68
   We ar yette enoo, so god me spede,
     to defende owre enmys owt of þis londe.
   þat lorde þat on a rode kon blede
     lene hus grace now þat pes mey stonde.   72

Wolde we be trwe in fylde and towne   [f. 67v]
   And all men holde a-pon a syde,
With þo ryght of ynglonde and þo cron,
   And lett no falsdam be owre gyde;   76
yf þat owr enmys wolde be boyn
   Ayenus hus for to go or ryde,
And we wolde fare with no treson,
   we schulde be abull to fel þer pride.   80
   þat lorde þat sofurd wondus wyde
     Sende luf and charite in-to þis londe,
   þat concyons myȝth among vs byde
     And lene hus grace now þat pes mey stonde.   84

And mare mylde, þat neuer hade make,
   Prey to þi son boþe dey and nyȝth,
lene hom grace seche consel take
   þat mey be plesand to god almyȝth,   88

79. MS. tresond.

And all falsdam to for-sake,
   And euery mon holde with troþe and ryght;
And þen schulde welthe and worchyp wake,
   And ful grete grace among hus lyȝth.   92
  Iesu, as he ys most of myȝth,
     lene hus grace now þat þes myȝthe stonde,
  And bryng hus all to þat bygyng bryȝth
    þer Ioy and blys ys euer-lastonde.   96

Explicit, quod heege. Amen. amen.

100. SEND US PEACE

(With Music)

B. M. Addit. MS. 5665

Ihesu, for thy mercy endelesse,   [f. 44v]
  Saue thy pepill and sende vs pesse!

Iesu, for thy wondes ffyffe,
  Saue fro shedyng cristayn blode;
sese alle grete trobill of malice & stryffe,
  & of oure neybores sende vus tydynges gode.   4

Blessed iesu!
Blessed ihesu!

Iesu, for thi, vt supra.

No. 100. *The burden is repeated, marked* Tenor.

SELECT LIST OF ABBREVIATED
TITLES CITED

ADAE DE USK: *Chronicon Adae de Usk*. Ed. by Edward Maunde Thompson. 2d ed., London, 1904.

ADAE MURIMUTH: *Adae Murimuth: Continuatio Chronicarum*. Ed. by Edward Maunde Thompson. Rolls Series 93, London, 1889.

AMUNDESHAM: *Annales a Johanne Amundesham*. 2 vols. Ed. by Henry Thomas Riley. Rolls Series 28, London, 1870.

ANONIMALLE CHRONICLE: *The Anonimalle Chronicle 1333 to 1381*. Ed. by V[ivian] H[unter] Galbraith. Manchester, 1927.

ARRIVALL OF EDWARD IV: *Historie of the Arrivall of Edward IV*. Ed. by John Bruce. Camden Society 1, London, 1838.

AUNGIER, CS 28: *Croniques de London depuis l'an 44 Hen. III jusqu'à l'an 17 Ed. III*. Ed. by George James Aungier. Camden Society 28, London, 1844.

AVESBURY: *Robertus de Avesbury: De Gestis Mirabilibus Regis Edwardi Tertii*. Ed. by Edward Maunde Thompson. Rolls Series 93, London, 1889.

BAIN: Joseph Bain. *Edwards in Scotland 1296-1377*. Edinburgh, 1901.

BAKER: *Chronicon Galfridi le Baker de Swynebroke*. Ed. by Edward Maunde Thompson. Oxford, 1889.

BISHOP PERCY'S FOLIO MS.: *Bishop Percy's Folio Manuscript: Ballads and Romances*. 3 vols. Ed. by John Wesley Hales and Frederick James Furnivall. London, 1867.

BLACMAN: *Henry the Sixth. A Reprint of John Blacman's Memoir*. Ed. by M[ontague] R[hodes] James. Cambridge, 1919.

BRANDL: A[lois] Brandl and O[tto] Zippel. *Middle English Literature (ME Sprach- und Literaturproben,* 2d ed.). New York, 1947.

BRUCE: John Barbour, *The Bruce*. 2 vols. Ed. by Walter W[illiam] Skeat. Scottish Text Society 31 with 33, 32, Edinburgh, 1894.

BRUT: *The Brut or The Chronicles of England*. 2 vols. Ed. by Friedrich W. D. Brie. Early English Text Society 131, 136, London, 1906, 1908.

CAPGRAVE: John Capgrave. *Chronicle of England*. Ed. by Francis Charles Hingeston. Rolls Series 1, London, 1858.

CHILD, POP. BALLADS: *The English and Scottish Popular Ballads*. 6 vols. Ed. by Francis James Child. Boston, 1889.

CHRONICLES OF EDW. I & EDW. II: *Chronicles of the Reigns of Edward I and Edward II*. 2 vols. Ed. by William Stubbs. Rolls Series 76, London, 1882, 1883.

CHRONICLE OF LONDON: *A Chronicle of London from 1089 to 1483* [Harley MS. 565]. [Ed. by Nicholas Harris Nicolas.] London, 1827.

CHRONICLES OF LONDON: Ed. by Charles Lethbridge Kingsford. Oxford, 1905.

CHRONICLES OF WHITE ROSE: *The Chronicles of the White Rose of York.* 2d ed., London, 1845.

CHRONICON ANGLIAE: Ed. by Edward Maunde Thompson. Rolls Series 64, London, 1874.

ENGLISH CHRONICLE: Ed. by John Silvester Davies. Camden Society 64, London, 1856.

ENG. HIST. LIT.: Charles Lethbridge Kingsford. *English Historical Literature in the Fifteenth Century.* Oxford, 1913.

FABYAN: Robert Fabyan. *The New Chronicles of England and France.* Ed. by Henry Ellis. London, 1811.

FIRST ENG. LIFE HENRY V: *The First English Life of King Henry the Fifth.* Ed. by Charles Lethbridge Kingsford. Oxford, 1911.

FLORES HIST.: [Matthew of Westminster] *Flores Historiarum.* 3 vols. Ed. by Henry Richards Luard. Rolls Series 95, London, 1890.

FLÜGEL: Edward Flügel. *Neuenglisches Lesebuch.* I Band. Halle, 1895.

FORDUN: Johannis de Fordun. *Chronica Gentis Scotorum.* Edinburgh, 1871. Eng. tr. ed. by William F[orbes] Skene. Edinburgh, 1872.

FROISSART: *Sir John Froissart's Chronicles.* 12 vols. Ed. by Thomas Johnes. London, 1808.

GASCOIGNE: Thomas Gascoigne. *Loci e Libro Veritatum.* Ed. by James E. Thorold Rogers. Oxford, 1881.

GRAFTON: *Grafton's Chronicle or History of England.* 2 vols. London, 1801.

GREENE, EARLY ENG. CAROLS: *The Early English Carols.* Ed. by Richard Leighton Greene. Oxford, 1935.

GREGORY'S CHRONICLE: *The Historical Collections of a Citizen of London.* Ed. by James Gairdner. Camden Society, new series 17, London, 1876.

HALL: *Hall's Chronicle.* [Ed. by Henry Ellis.] London, 1809.

HARDING: *The Chronicle of Iohn Hardyng ... together with the Continuation by Richard Grafton.* Ed. by Henry Ellis, London, 1812.

HEMINGBURGH: *Chronicon Domini Walteri de Hemingburgh.* 2 vols. Ed. by Hans Claude Hamilton. English Historical Society, London, 1848, 1849.

HIST. ANGLICANA: *Thomae Walsingham: Historia Anglicana.* 2 vols. Ed. by Henry Thomas Riley. Rolls Series 28, London, 1863, 1864.

HOLINSHED: *Holinshed's Chronicles*. 6 vols. London, 1808.

INDEX: Carleton Brown and Rossell Hope Robbins. *The Index of Middle English Verse*. New York, 1943.

KNIGHTON: *Chronicon Henrici Knighton*. 2 vols. Ed. by Joseph Rawson Lumby. Rolls Series 92, London, 1889, 1895.

LANERCOST CHRONICLE: *Chronicon de Lanercost*. Ed. by Joseph Stevenson. Maitland Club, London, 1839. Eng. tr. by Herbert Maxwell. Glasgow, 1913.

LANGTOFT: *The Chronicle of Pierre de Langtoft*. 2 vols. Ed. by Thomas Wright. Rolls Series 47, London, 1866, 1868.

LE BEL: *Les Vrayes Chroniques de Messire Jehan le Bel*. 2 vols. Ed. by M[atthieu] L[ambert] Polain. Bruxelles, 1863.

LETTERS FROM THE NORTHERN REGISTERS: *Historical Papers and Letters from the Northern Registers*. Ed. by James Raine. Rolls Series 61, London, 1873.

M.E.D.: *Middle English Dictionary*. Ed. by Hans Kurath. Ann Arbor, 1954 (in preparation).

MELSA CHRONICLE: *Chronica Monasterii de Melsa*. 3 vols. Ed. by Edward Augustus Bond. Rolls Series 43, London, 1866-68.

M.L.W.L.: *Medieval Latin Word List*. Ed. by J[ames] H[ouston] Baxter and Charles Johnson. London, 1934, 1950.

MONSTRELET: *The Chronicles of Enguerrand de Monstrelet*. 2 vols. Tr. by Thomas Johnes. London, 1867.

MURIMUTH CONTIN: *Adami Murimuthensis Chronica Sui Temporis*. Ed. by Thomas Hog. English Historical Society, London, 1846.

OAKDEN, ALLIT. POETRY: J[ames] P[arker] Oakden. *Alliterative Poetry in Middle English*. 2 vols. Manchester, 1930, 1935.

PALLISER: Bury Palliser. *Historical Devices, Badges, and War Cries*. London, 1870.

PASTON LETTERS: 6 vols. Ed. by James Gairdner. London, 1904.

PERCY, RELIQUES: Thomas Percy. *Reliques of Ancient English Poetry*. 1st ed., London, 1765; 3d ed., London, 1775.

POLYDORE VERGIL: *Three Books of Polydore Vergil's English History*. Ed. by Henry Ellis. Camden Society 29, London, 1844.

RAMSAY, LANC. & YORK: Sir James H[enry] Ramsay. *Lancaster and York*. 2 vols. Oxford, 1892.

REL. ANT.: Thomas Wright and James Orchard Halliwell. *Reliquiae Antiquae*. 2 vols. London, 1841, 1843.

RITSON, ANC. SONGS: *Ancient Songs and Ballads*. 2d ed. 3 vols. Ed. by Joseph Ritson. London, 1829.

ROBERT OF GLOUCESTER: *The Metrical Chronicle of Robert of Gloucester*. 2 vols. Ed. by William Aldis Wright. Rolls Series 86, London, 1897.

ROT. PARL.: *Rotuli Parliamentorum*. 6 vols. Record Commission, London, 1767-77.

RYMER: *Foedera Conventiones Litterae et cujuscumque Acta Publica inter Reges Angliae et alios*. Ed. by Thomas Rymer. Record Commission, London, 1816-69.

ST. ALBANS: *The St. Albans Chronicle 1406-1420*. Ed. by V[ivian] H[unter] Galbraith. Oxford, 1937.

ST. REMY: *Chronique de Jean le Févre Seigneur de Saint-Remy*. 2 vols. Ed. by François Morand. Paris, 1876, 1881.

SAMPSON, CAMB. BOOK OF PROSE & VERSE: George Sampson. *Cambridge Book of Prose and Verse*. Cambridge, 1924.

SCOTICHRONICON: *Johannis de Fordun: Scotichronicon cum Continuatione Walteri Boweri*. 2 vols. Ed. by Walter Goodall. Edinburgh, 1759.

SEC. LYRICS: *Secular Lyrics of the XIVth and XVth Centuries*. Ed. by Rossell Hope Robbins, 2d ed., Oxford, 1955.

SHORT ENG. CHRONICLE: *Three Fifteenth Century Chronicles*. Ed. by James Gairdner. Camden Society, new series 28, London, 1880.

SIX TOWN CHRONICLES: *Six Town Chronicles of England*. Ed. by Ralph Flenley. Oxford, 1911.

STATUTES OF THE REALM: Record Commission, London, 1810-22.

STOW, ANNALES: John Stow. *Annales*. London, 1615.

STOW, SURVEY: John Stow. *A Survey of London*. 2 vols. Ed. by Charles Lethbridge Kingsford. Oxford, 1908.

TREVET: *F. Nicholai Triveti Annales*. Ed. by Thomas Hog. English Historical Society, London, 1845.

TROKELOWE: *Johannis de Trokelowe et Henrici de Blaneforde: Chronica et Annales*. Ed. by Henry Thomas Riley. Rolls Series 28, London, 1866.

WARKWORTH: John Warkworth. *A Chronicle of the first thirteen years of the Reign of King Edward the Fourth*. Ed. by James Orchard Halliwell. Camden Society 10, London, 1839.

WAURIN: *Recueil des Chroniques par Jehan de Waurin*. 5 vols. Ed. by William Hardy. Rolls Series 39, London, 1864-91. (Eng. tr. 3 vols, Rolls Series 40, 1864-87.)

WHETHAMSTEDE: *Registrum Abbatiae Johannis Whethamstede*. Ed. Henry Thomas Riley. Rolls Series 28, London, 1872. Vol. 1.

WILLIAM OF WORCESTER: *William Wyrcester Annales Rerum Anglicarum*. Ed. by Joseph Stevenson, in *Letters and Papers Illustrative of the Wars of the English in France*. Rolls Series 22, London, 1864. Vol. 2.

WILSON, LOST. LIT.: R[ichard] M[iddlewood] Wilson. *The Lost Literature of Medieval England*. London, 1952.

WRIGHT, POL. SONGS: *The Political Songs of England*. Ed. by Thomas Wright. Camden Society 6, London, 1839.

WRIGHT, POL. POEMS: *Political Poems and Songs Relating to English History.* 2 vols. Ed. by Thomas Wright. Rolls Series 14, London, 1859, 1861.

WYNTOUN: Androw of Wyntoun: *The Orygynale Cronykil of Scotland.* 3 vols. Ed. by David Laing. Edinburgh, 1872-79.

YPODIGMA NEUSTRIAE: *Ypodigma Neustriae a Thoma Walsingham.* Ed. by Henry Thomas Riley. Rolls Series 28, London, 1876.

ZUPITZA: Julius Zupitza. *Alt- und Mittelenglische Übungsbuch.* Wien, 1915.

NOTES TO POEMS

1. THE KINGS OF ENGLAND
BY LYDGATE

Index, No. 3632. Not heretofore printed from this MS. The most popular poem in this anthology, surviving in 46 MSS.: *Index,* No. 882 (2 MSS., with 15 introductory st.); No. 444 with No. 3431 (later redaction, 5 MSS.); and No. 3632 (35 MSS. in *Index;* add 36. Bodl. 1797, f. 65*r* var.; 37. Lincoln Coll. Oxf.; 38. Ipswich Great Doomsday, pt. pr. *East Anglian,* n.s. i.38; 39. Nottingham Univ. Lib., *olim* Lyell, end-leaves; Ashburnham 140 is now Camb. Univ. Addit. 6668). *Index,* Nos. 882 (st. 16 = st. 1 here) and 3431 were printed by MacCracken, *EETS* 192.710-16, 717-22. Most texts show slight variants; later texts (e.g., Ashmole 59) add st. on Edward IV ("Long he hathe rejoysed bothe by day and nyght")*.* Cf. Bühler, *RES,* ix.47-50, and similar changes in No. 98.

4. The legendary founding of Britain by Brutus, the great-grandson of Aeneas, was first developed by Geoffrey of Monmouth. He was followed in varying degrees by later chroniclers. See Laura Keeler, *Geoffrey of Monmouth and the Late Latin Chronicles 1300-1500* (Berkeley, 1946).

39. After the fall of Acre, Richard caused the massacre of 2,600 prisoners on one day (R. Röhricht, *Geschichte des Königreiches Jerusalem* [1898], p. 576).

40. Cf. *Brut:* "And anone after, went Kyng Richard forto bisege þe castel of Gaillard. And as he rode oppon a day be þe castel, forto take avisement of þe castel, an Arweblaster smote him wiþ a quarel ... but þe quarelle hede abode stille in his heuede, & hit bigan forto rancle, þat he might nouȝt helpe him-self, ne meve his Armes" (*EETS* 131.153). Most of the other texts read Castle Chaluz.

60. despite of] notwithstanding.

73. Withoute more] without more ado.

85. in certeyn] in truth. Cf. No. 26, l. 194.

89. in sothnesse] in truth.

92. The last two st. duplicate lines in *Index,* No. 3808, Lydgate's version (dated 1426) of Calot's justification of Henry VI's claims to France; e.g., "of knyghthode moste famous"; "For which he may among the worthie nyne" (l. 96); "For to possede by enheritaunce / Crownes two of englond and of Fraunce / By true title, as ye haue hard toforne" (ll. 100-102).

96. the worthy nyne] The nine most famous historical figures: three Jews (Joshua, David, Judas Maccabaeus); three Gentiles (Hector,

Alexander, Julius Caesar); and three Christians (Arthur, Charlemagne, Godfrey of Bouillon). Frequent refs. in ME: *Index,* Nos.
1181, 1556, 2781, 3666, 3881, 4247. Also "Ector þat was off alle
knyghtes flowr," Harley MS. 2259, f. 39*v*, 9 quatrains (Furnivall,
N. & Q., ser. vii, vol. viii.22; Loomis, MP, xv.216). In 1456, Queen
Margaret was greeted at Coventry with a pageant of the Nine Con-
querors (*Index,* No. 2781).

2. SONG OF THE HUSBANDMAN, 1300

Index, No. 696. Previously printed by Wright, *Pol. Songs,* pp.
149-52 (with translation); by Böddeker, *AE Dicht.,* pp. 102-5; by
Wülcker, *Lesebuch,* i.71; by Brandl and Zippel, *ME Lit.,* pp. 134-35;
and by Sampson, *Camb. Book of Prose & Verse,* pp. 396-98.

Wright (p. 148) comments: "Edward endeavoured to call off the
vigour of his subjects from domestic sedition to foreign wars. But
the expenses dependent upon the latter only added to the many
burdens under which the English peasantry laboured; and it is now
that we begin to find the complaints of the latter vented in the shape
of popular songs." Powicke, *Oxf. Hist. of England,* iv.700, notes
that in the Parliament of 1300 "the grievances about prises, forests,
and other matters were met, so that the sufferings of the people
caused by the wars might be allayed." J. A. Gibson (London diss.,
unpub.) suggests a later date for Nos. 2, 3, 6, and 7.

The poem is unusual among songs of protest in listing specific
grievances (cf. "Jacke Upland," Wright, *Pol. Poems,* ii.16-39); for
this reason it is more effective both as complaint and as poem. It
has attracted favorable comment: e.g., *C.H.E.L.,* i.370, "one of
the notable poems of the alliterative revival;" and Oakden, *Allit.
Poetry,* ii.10, "alive with its passionate despair and sincerity of utterance."

Nearly a dozen references from this poem are recorded in *O.E.D.*
from 1300 to 1327; but others are of earlier date than those in *O.E.D.*
(e.g., lesinge, 1534; prikyares, 1362), or variant spellings not listed
(e.g., bid, bockneþ, en, launprey, sturne). The dialect is generally
southwest.

4. sawe] they do not enter into conversation.

8. þe] In the Harley MS. o and e are often indistinguishable,
while at other times clearly separated (with o open at the top).
Confusion also exists for legge (l. 45); and (in No. 4) wes (ll. 23,
124, 145, 161), lyndeseye (l. 99); wes (No. 5, l. 88); fles (No. 7,
l. 10).

     mot] must (go).

13. For other examples of "crown" verse or stanza linking, see

Nos. 11 and 38. Cf. also Medary, "Stanza linking in ME Verse," *Romanic Rev.*, vii.243-70.

15. The husbandman lists the officials who extort money from him: the hayward, a local official responsible for maintaining fences separating the common from enclosed lands; the bailiff who enforced the law; the woodward, in charge of the forest timber; and the beadle (l. 37), a warrant officer working under the bailiff. W. H. R. Cutler, *The Enclosure and Redistribution of Our Land* (Oxford, 1920), p. 22, distinguishes the hayward (responsible for the lord's grain) and his haward (responsible for the fences). Hayward in another Harley lyric, The Man in the Moon (*Index*, No. 2066), refers to the hedge keeper.

16. vs] for us.

21. swore] promised (to give what the officials wanted).

31. wondred ys wene] hardship [wandreth] is to be expected. Sampson tr. Fear is frequent.

41. hennen] hens, wk. pl. not rec. *O.E.D.*

44. borstax] *O.E.D.* gives only this example, and queries "? some kind of axe." Brandl: pickaxe (orig. obscure). Cf. ? burst (to split wood).

50. aʒeyn] against (the time that).

52. Cf. No. 9, l. 20.

53. Tr. I must venture to bribe (to the extent of) a mark or more. Alternatively, munten = to mint, coin (OE myntan).

55. þe grene wax] The seal of green wax used on Exchequer documents delivered by the sheriffs. The later "God Speed the Plough" (*Index*, No. 363) has similarly:

> Then commeth the grenewex which greveth vs sore,
> With ronnyng in reragis it doth vs sorowe Inough.

Cf. *Melsa Chronicle*, iii.191.

vnder gore] A kenning, without precise meaning (tr. in heart).

56. þat] so that.

59. Difficult: tr. The beadles have never told their giver (i.e., have never said who he was). Brandl reads fulle (possible in MS.), and so Sampson, who tr. have never suffered.

61. kippe] seize (ON kippa). *O.E.D.* equates with kepe (keep).

68. ruls] ? dung (OE hrysel); or v.<Fr. rouiller, to rust, spoil. Alternatively emend ruli (pitiable).

72. Tr. It is as good to perish right away as to labor so.

3. THE FLEMISH INSURRECTION, 1302

Index, No. 1894. Previously printed by Ritson, *Anc. Songs*, i.51-56; by Wright, *Pol. Songs*, pp. 187-95; by Böddeker, *AE Dicht.*, pp. 116-

21; and by Sampson, *Camb. Book of Prose & Verse,* pp. 399-400.

The needs of the Flemish weavers for English wool led the Count of Flanders, Guy de Dampierre, to ally himself with Edward I. Philip IV (le Bel) thereupon invaded Flanders, imprisoned its nobles, and governed the country. The harsh French rule caused a revolt, which centered on Bruges burghers under Peter de Conyng, master of the cloth-weavers, and John Breydel, master of the butchers. Having slain the French garrison at Bruges, the ill-equipped townsmen overcame the professional French armies under Robert, Count of Artois, near Courtrai. The marshland terrain hindered the heavy-armed French and made them easy prey. The battle is described in *Flores Hist.,* iii.111-12, 306-8. At this date, before the development of the native cloth industry, the English could feel sympathy for their Flemish customers of wool.

4. wednesday] The battle was fought on July 11, 1302.

13. at ene] at once.

17. fullaris] The fullers beat the cloth to clean and thicken it. Cf. *Piers Plowman,* B.xv.444-45: "Cloth þat cometh fro þe weuyng is nouȝt comly to were, Tyl it is fulled vnder fote or in fullyngstokkes."

19. Peter Conyng] conyng (Flemish) king; (English) rabbit; cf. l. 69.

30. auowerie] *O.E.D.* gives first ref. 1330, patronage. *M.L.W.L.* gives advocaria, warranty (and so Wright).

33. Sire Iakes] Cf. l. 61. *Flores Hist.,* iii.307 names Robert as Earl of Bologne or St. Paul, in the list of dead. "Commissum est igitur bellum, et ceciderunt de Francigenis comes de Artoys, comes [Iohn] de Alba Marla, comes [Iohn] de Eu, comes [Iohn] de Dru, comes [Robert] de Bolonia [l. 65], Radulphus de Neel constabularius Franciae [l. 65], Guydo de Neel marescallus Franciae, Petrus de Flote consilarius regis Franciae velut alius Achitophel, filius comitis de Henaud, ac quadraginta baneretti, cum populo infinito."

34. asemblede] he caused to assemble.

35. he] they.

pas pur pas] step by step.

36. mounde] *O.E.D.*: "it is doubtful whether *mounde* is this word in the concrete sense *'force,'* or whether, as the Fr. phrase in the context suggests, it is the F. monde (MOUND *sb.* 1) in the sense 'number of people.' "

38. basyns of bras] "This circumstance occurred on the 21st March, 1302, at the beginning of the insurrection. In the towns of Flanders, as in the boroughs of England, the people were called up in an insurrection by the sound of the church bell. There was a famous distich on the bell of Roland, at Bruges —

    Roelandt, Roelandt, als ick kleppe dan ist brandt,

Als ick luye, dan ist storm in Vlaenderlandt.

On the present occasion, the people dared not go to their bell, on account of their French governors, so they beat their brass basins: "cumque ad campanam civitatis non auderent accedere, pelves suas pulsantes ... omnem multitudinem concitarent" (Wright, p. 379).

50. dousse pers] Cf. "barouns gentil ant fre," l. 58. Cf. No. 71, l. 37.

51. eorl of artoys] The French leader; cf. Adae de Usk, pp. 108-9.

66. Tr. We will not leave alive either canon or monk.

67. anon riþt] right away. Cf. No. 4, l. 137.

68. ? so that no man lives.

69. Cf. l. 19.

70. into] as far as.

71. sesoyne] Saxony (Fr. Sessoyne).

73. y-tolde] all told.

87. fare so hit fare] happen what may.

89. Cf. Adae de Usk, 2d ed., pp. 108-9.

90. hende ant fre] A conventional formula applied to persons of noble rank.

113. pope] Boniface VIII had long been at enmity with France over his assertion of papal political power (especially in the bull *Unam sanctam,* 1302). He degraded two cardinals of the Colonna family as early as 1294 (*Hist. Anglicana,* i.49, 54; Knighton, i.291), but his successor Benedict XI restored them to their rank (Adae Murimuth, p. 6).

to rede] what advice shall you take. The verb nimen (take) is sometimes omitted in this idiom.

115. for nones kunnes mede] not for any kind of reward.

120. wel þe felle] will bring about your overthrow.

123. fot-lome] Cf. *Index,* No. 4165, l. 264: "And thus knihtshipe is acloied and waxen al fot lame."

130. Cf. Knighton, i.331.

133. prince] Edward [II] of Carnavon, since 1301; it is unnecessary to make this final st. "an addition of about 1305" (Wells, *Manual,* p. 212).

4. THE EXECUTION OF SIR SIMON FRASER, 1306

Index, No. 1889. Previously printed by Ritson, *Anc. Songs,* i.28-38; by Wright, *Pol. Songs,* pp. 212-23; by Böddeker, *AE Dicht.,* pp. 126-134; and by Brandt and Zippel, *ME Lit.,* pp. 129-33.

Sir Simon Fraser (or Frisell) was captured at the Battle of Methven or Kirkencliff (l. 91), in June, 1306, and sent to London, where he was hanged (September 7). The hatred of the enemy expressed in this poem foreshadows Minot's venom against the Scots. The piece was probably written shortly after the execution by a professional ballad-maker (cf. l. 219).

10. "These were the first instances [Wallace and Fraser] of this kind of degradation to which the bridge was appropriated, though in after ages such scenes became frequent" (Aungier, *CS* 28.32).

12. hem] for them (dat.).

18. þe waleis] William Wallace was hanged on August 23, 1305. Stow *Annales,* 1615, describes the execution: "William Wales which had oft times set Scotland in great trouble, was taken and brought to London with great numbers of men and women wondring vpon him: he was lodged in the house of William Delect a Cittizen of London, in Fanchurch streete. On the morrow being the eeuen of Saint Bartholomew, he was brought on horse-backe to Westminster, Iohn Segraue and Geffrey, knights, the Maior, Sheriffes and Alder-men of Londone, and many other, both on horse-backe and on foote accompanying him, and in the great hall at Westminster, hee being placed on the South bench crowned with Laurell, for that he had said in times past that he ought to beare a crowne in that Hall (as it was commonly reported) and being appeached for a traitour, by Syr Peter Mallorie the Kings Iustice, hee answered that he was neuer traitour to the K. of England, but for other crimes whereof hee was accused, he confessed them, and was after headed and quartered" (p. 209). A contemporary account occurs in *Chronicles of Ed. I & Ed. II,* i.139-42; later descriptions in Wyntoun, viii.2965-80; and Fordun, p. 340; Eng. tr. p. 332.

22. frysel] The contemporary form of Fraser.

25. Sire edward] Edward I.

27. The quarters were sent to Newcastle, Berwick, Perth, and Aberdeen (*Lanercost Chronicle,* p. 203 Eng. tr. p. 176).

32. hem] dat.

33. come] Mid. and Sth. forms; cf. No. 11, l. 60.

37. þryes] an intensive; tr. in every respect.

49. glascou] Robert Wishart (d. 1316), who swore allegiance to Edward I, but later supported Bruce. He was captured in 1301, released, and assisted in the coronation of Bruce. After the Battle of Methven, he was captured by Aymer de Valence, Earl of Pem-broke, and imprisoned for eight years in Porchester Castle.

50. seint Andre] William Lamberton (d. 1328), swore repeated fealty to Edward, but assisted in the coronation of Bruce (l. 65). Edward ordered Aymer de Valence to apprehend him (l. 82). He was taken in July, 1306, and kept in prison until June, 1308. Later he resumed his political activities.

51. scon] Thomas. "Þe Abbot of Scone aros, and bifore ham alle saide, þat hit was resoun forto helpe him [Bruce], and þe lande

to kepe and defende" (*EETS* 131.197). By the King's express command, all three were to be kept in iron fetters; cf. Bain, *Edwards in Scotland*, pp. 48-51.

58. "and shortly after, to witte, in the feast of the Annunciation of our Lady, in the Abbey of Scone, hee caused himselfe to bee solemnly crowned king by the Bishops of Glasgo, and Saint Andrewes first" (Stow, *Annales*, p. 209). So Hemingburgh, ii.247.

66. kyng of somere] After his adulterous marriage, Bruce said to his first wife: " 'Heri vocabamur ego comes et tu comitissa; hodie vero ego rex et tu regina vocamur.' Cui illa, 'Aestimo quod rex aestivalis sis; forsitan hyemalis non eris. Timeto autem nequando, tanquam flos agri qui hodie est et cras in clibanum mittitur, sic efforeas, ac ne pro perjurio fidei per vocabulum regnum comitatum simul perdas et regnum' " (*Flores Hist.*, iii.130).

68. kyng] dat.

73. kyng hobbe] familiar for Robert (Bruce); also used in a contemporary letter describing King Edward's displeasure at Aymer's defeat at Loudon Hill in 1307 (Bain, p. 58).

75. myhte] subj. if they might.

80. wide and far (Wright).

81. sire Edward] Edward, Prince of Wales, later Edward II; cf. No. 5, l. 73. Since Edward was ill, he entrusted the task of suppression to his son, whom he had knighted on Whitsunday.

82. Aymer de Valence, Earl of Pembroke, defeated Bruce at Methven in 1306, and was defeated by Bruce in 1307 at Loudon Hill; notable as a leader opposed to the Lancastrian earls, and ambassador for the King. He was appointed guardian for Edward II, and Lieutenant of Scotland. He died in Paris in 1324.

gentil] of good birth (not necessarily nobility); free has the same meaning.

83. huere oht] Cf. *Flores Hist.*, iii.131-32; Trevet, pp. 408-9.

89. Here the professional minstrel speaks.

91. kyrkenclyf] Battle of Methven, near Perth, June, 1306. For accounts see Hemingburgh, ii.248-49; Fordun, p. 341-42, Eng. tr. p. 334; Trevet, pp. 409-10; and *Bruce*, i. 36-45.

93. striueleyn] Stirling. Cf. No. 9, l. 13.

99. sire Iohan] John Lindsay, later Bishop of Glasgow (1323-35), active in church and politics.

105. i.e., August 25, 1306.

107. sire Thomas] Thomas de Multon, of Egremond, Cumberland, grandson of Thomas (d. 1240) who witnessed Magna Charta, fought at Caerlaverock in 1300, M. P. from 1300 to 1321; trial judge of Fraser (l. 147).

108. sire Iohan Iose] "Eodem anno, viii*vo* ydus Septembris [6], dominus Simon Frysel venit Londonias, domini Thomas de Multone,

Johannes Joce, et alii milites eum ducentes" (*Chronicles of Ed. I & Ed. II*, i.148).

114. him] Fraser.

116. Stow gives Wallace as the object of this ridicule, after early chronicles (e.g., *Chronicles of Ed. I & Ed. II*, i.139).

121. "King Edward besieged Simon Frisell in Lilyscho, and tooke him and sent him to London Tower, where he found many Scottish Lords in fetters of yron" (Stow, *Annales*, p. 210).

128. in honde] in custody. Cf. in hold (l. 132).

129. sire herbert] Of French extraction, imprisoned and forfeited his estates in 1297, and liberated under the promise of serving Edward in his Flemish war (cf. Aungier, *CS* 28.32 fn.). The fullest account of his wager is told in *Flores Hist.*, iii.133-34: "Illo quoque tempore captus est Symon Frysel in quo pendebat tota Scotorum fiducia, in tantum quod incarcerati Scoti nobiles invincibilem incomprehensibilemque illum assererent, nec illo vivente Scotos posse devinci putarent. De cujus magnanimitate praesumens, quidam Scoticus miles in turri Londoniae vinculatus, in elogium Anglorum, sed proprium dispendium, caput proprium regi dedit, quocumque die captus fuerit, amptutandum. Nomen autem hujus Herebertus de Morham, vir cunctis Scotis formosior et statura eminentior, tamen propter trinam proditionem quam regi Angliae fecerat et secundam dimissionem tertio captus, una cum patre et armigero in Turri Londoniae ferreis compedibus nexi erant. Post haec Symon Frisel ad Turrim Londoniae mittebatur ut, illo viso, voti praestiti Scotus alius recordaretur. In crastino igitur, id est in vigilia [Nativitatis] beatae Mariae, educti de Turri Herebertus et Thomas de Boys armiger ejus capitibus sunt truncati. Symon autem Frysel, propter pluralitatem proditionum quas fecerat, siccine condempnatur, a Turri Londoniae per viculos et plateas distractus ut proditor, suspensus eminus quia latro, trancatus capite ut homicida, refixusque eculeo per dies viginti, igne quoque finaliter est combustus; hujus autem caput super pontem Londoniae juxta caput Willelmi Waleys super lanceam, cunctis nationibus perhorrendum spectaculum, est affixum."

141. Tr. So I assure (you).

145. September 7, 1306.

148. sire Rauf] Ralph de Sandwich (d. 1308), knight and judge, Constable of the Tower on several occasions under Edward I, and a trial judge of William Wallace and Fraser. Cf. Aungier, *CS* 28.20-23. "Et in crastino, qui dicitur vigilia nativitatis beatae Mariae, decollati fuerunt dominus Hereberdus de Mora miles, et Thomas de Bosco suus armiger, in placea prope Turrim Londoniis, et prius in eadem Turre judicati coram domino Radulfo de Sandwyco" (*Chronicles of Ed. I & Ed. II* i.148).

149. sire Iohan Abel] Not mentioned elsewhere as a trial judge.

161. This was the procedure used for Wallace. See above, l. 115.
174. siþe] The instr. pl. is not distinguished from the sing.
181. cheepe] The Cheap.
191. sum while] at one time (Wright).
196. chil] child; d lost in sandhi.
    lokeþ] Wright lakeþ; but o clearly formed.
204. lye] ? to depend on (OE licgan). Wright glosses to wait (?).
Cf. l. 40: What does it profit to lie?
212. ate laste] at least.
218. erl of asseles] John de Strathbolgie or de Asceila, "Earle
Iohn de Athol, because he was of the kings bloud and an Englishman,
was not drawne, but hanged and headed" (Stow, *Annales*, p. 210).
He assisted in the coronation of Bruce, was captured after Methven,
executed and his head put on London Bridge. "Postea semivivus
demissus, ut majores cruciatus sentiret, crudelissime decollatur"
(*Flores Hist.*, iii.135).
227. Charles of fraunce] Charles IV (le Bel).
229. satirical: Thanks to him!
230. Tprot] an exclamation of contempt. Wright (pp. 381-82,
391) gives several further examples.
233. longe shonkes] Long-shanks, a popular name for Edward I.
Cf. Langtoft, ii.284, "le lunge jambes."

5. THE DEATH OF EDWARD I, 1307

Index. No. 205. Previously printed by Percy, *Reliques*, 1765,
ii.6-10; by Wright, *Pol. Songs*, pp. 246-50; by Zupitza, *Übungsbuch*,
pp. 158-60; by Böddeker, *AE Dicht.*, pp. 140-43; by Segar, *Some
Minor Poems*, pp. 15-18; and by Isabel S. T. Aspin, *Anglo-Norman
Political Songs* (Oxford, 1953), pp. 90-92. Three fragments in Camb.
Un. MS. Addit. 4407 are printed by Skeat, *MLR*, vii.149-50, viz.
ll. 6-12; 20-29 (omitting 24); 83-88, with four extra lines following
l. 84:

> Nou is he ded, allas, allas,
>   God ʒiue his soule rest and ro;
> Seynt Edwar and seint Thomas
>   His huerde bere ʒe þer-to.

Edward I, although seriously ill, himself led the English forces
north again, after the Scots under Bruce and his brothers had rallied
after their defeat at Methven (cf. No. 4, l. 91). He got as far as
Carlisle, where he died on July 7. His body was sent to Waltham
and on to Westminster Abbey for interment. See Hemingburgh,
ii.265-66; and Trevet, pp. 412-13.
The English is a free translation of a French song (in the same

metre) in Camb. Un. MS. Gg. 1.1, f. 489, printed by Wright, *Pol. Songs,* pp. 241-45; and by Aspin, pp. 83-86. The English rearranges some of the stanzas (1, 2, 5, 4, 3, 6, 7, 8, 10; 9 and 11 are new). Some lines are very close, e.g., 19-22:

> Le rei de Fraunce grant pecché fist,
>> Le passage à desturber,
> Qe rei Edward pur Dieu enprist,
>> Sur Sarazins l'ewe passer.   (= ll. 33-36)

and ll. 47-50:

> "Alas!" ceo dist, "comment? morist
> A qi Dieu donna tant honur?
> A l'alme en face Dieu mercist!
>> De seint eglise il fu la flour."   (= ll. 47-48)

6. Camb. of qwom þat god. Skeat inserts þat to improve metre.

9. Camb. Engelond, þou aghtes wel to knowe / Of qwom þat I þis song schal singe.

16. ber þe pris] was pre-eminent. Cf. l. 48 "ber þe flour."

27. hue] she [the heart]. Camb. it. Fr. "Outre la mere vous mandera."

28. four-score] Camb. gives seuenscore, the correct number. Edward left thirty thousand pounds for this purpose.

32. ycholde] I would (go).

33. kyng of fraunce] Charles IV (le Bel).

41. pope] "Cujus mortem summus Pontifex, reges et principes, duces et comites, ecclesiarumque praelati exterarum regionum cum populis sibi subjectis multiplici moerore planxerunt, advertentes et admirantes in tanto principe omnem hujus mundi sapientiam tam subito extinctam" (*Flores Hist.,* iii.138).

46. The Pope's lamentation appears in *Chronicles of Ed. I. & Ed. II,* ii.7-8.

54. rede & synge] a cliché applied to the church services; Fr. "commencent lur servise."

57. peyters] Poitiers; Fr. "A Peiters à l'apostoile / Une messager la mort il dist."

72. a such] Cf. mod. Fr. un tel.

75. "Ceteris interdum diversorum regnorum gentibus dolorem leviter mitigantibus, sola gens Anglicana luctus langore depressa, considerans malorum futurorum tempora, pro pallio laudis induit spiritum moeroris et confusionis" (*Flores Hist.,* iii.138).

77. pore men] commons (Wright); Zupitza poremen.

83. "Cujus bonitatis magnitudinem, aequitatis et justitiae rigorem quidam eleganti dictamine ad metros breviter sic comprehendit,

> Dum viguit rex, et valuit tua magna potestas,
> Fraus latuit, pax magna fuit, regnavit honestas"
>> (*Flores Hist.,* iii.138).

84. The last stanza is defective. Camb. completes it regularly and concludes with a half stanza, ll. 85-88. See above.

85. Camb. is clearer:

> louerd, als he was conquerur
> In ich a batayle, and hadde þe pris,
> þou ȝeue his soule mechil onur,
> And brinkyt into heuene blis.

6. SATIRE ON THE CONSISTORY COURTS, 1307

Index, No. 2287. Previously printed by Wright, *Pol. Songs,* pp. 155-59; Böddeker, *AE Dicht.,* p. 107.

The poor peasant relates his appearance before a consistory court on charges of immorality. After his graphic description of the judges and his accuser, the sompnours and the beadle, he rails at the verdict which requires he marry the woman involved (cf. *Index,* No. 3448, ll. 669-76). This poem is one of the earliest of a continuing series of attacks and satires on the venality of those concerned with administering the law (cf. Nos. 49, 50, 51, 59, 63). Oakden, *Allit. Poetry,* ii.11, comments: "Crude in style and abusive in tone, it nevertheless affords a striking example of popular satire, and it is very significant that it is written in a complicated alliterative form; there is no question of the popularity of alliteration among the lower classes even as early as the reign of Edward I." The metrical form is essentially a series of three six-line tail-rhymed stanzas, similar to that of the "Notbrowne Mayde" (*Index,* No. 467).

3. biledes] N. pr. pl. So gredes (9), unbredes (12), pynkes (25). The dialect generally is S. W. Midland; but critics often neglect the N. forms of some of the political poems. Cf. No. 8, kendles (4), werres (5); but Mid. and S. forms also occur: ascenteþ (pr. pl. 14), weddeþ (15). No. 7 is S. throughout.

4. mote] may (go).

7. on folde] in the enclosure, i.e., in the consistory court.

12. Tr. As they censure me by their book. vn-bredes, *O.E.D.* "meaning obscure." Possibly var. vmbraid (upbraid).

16. fere] i.e., mai (l. 4).

17. yt] apparently the offense.

22. heme] Stratmann: ? man, head of a family. Sampson (p. 393), hem.

> honginde] S. W. form; so mys-motinde (l. 38).

23. bales] i.e., sentence of punishment.

25. pynkes] *O.E.D.* make holes in, stab, but adds, "The meaning is uncertain." Stratmann: make figures.

38. by here euene] according to their natural ability.

41. polkeþ] ? Wright tr. put. *O.E.D.* gives first ref. for poke c. 1380.

42. clastreþ] ? clatter. *O.E.D.* "Possibly an error for that word [clatter]; but cf. Ger. *klastern* to rattle, patter, as hail, or raindrops."

colle] ? trickery. *O.E.D.* "? a conjuring trick, jugglery." Cf. Chaucer, HF 1277.

43. fayly] a failure (bankrupt). Cf. l. 77.

46. come] [he will] come; and so couren, suggen (inf.). Cf. No. 8, l. 18.

countene] the court "ot accounts" (wk. gen. pl.).

52. folht] a fool (folt), or (Wright) baptism (fullought — *O.E.D.* records fulht). The sense seems to require the former interpretation (cf. ll. 4, 16, 36).

53. hok] Stratmann quotes *Havelok* 1102: "hanged worþe he on an hok."

55. ȝeolumon] Stratmann: man dressed in yellow or bumbailiff. The beadle or court crier.

ȝeȝeþ] goes, proceeds. Not "joys" (Wright).

56. an heh] aloud.

57. Magge] dim. Margaret; Malle perhaps dim. Malkin.

61. heo beginneþ] This line may be interpreted as sing. or pl. One woman speaks ll. 62-64. hem (66) may refer to the women, as suggested by byswykeþ heo (68).

65. Tr. But I had rather.

68. Inversion of subj. and obj. for emphasis.

74. vnþeufol] Wright prints vn-thenfol.

77. Tr. And prostrate (myself) in supplication for each failure. Cf. l. 66.

83. of lyue] Off life, i.e., dead (cf. on lyue, alive). Tr. I had rather be dead than to live thus.

7. *SATIRE ON THE RETINUES OF THE GREAT, 1307*

Index. No. 2649. Previously printed by Wright, *Pol. Songs,* pp. 237-40; by Wülcker, *AE Leseb.,* i.73-4; by Böddeker, *AE Dicht.,* pp. 135-38; and by Sampson, *Camb. Book of Prose & Verse,* pp. 404-5.

The language is colloquial and idiomatic, and causes some problems. The text is southwestern from an original western dialect; cf. Oakden, *Allit. Poetry,* i.124.

3. harlotes] attendants. *O.E.D.* notes the similar use of knave (servant).

bi pate & bi polle] one by one.

5. of gonnylde gnoste] *O.E.D.,* after a long note *(Gun,* sb.), tr.

"The lackeys were gathered out of Gunnild's spark; the grooms and the pages, the varlets with their boasting, all were hatched of a horse's dung."

16. gobelyn] goblin: a mischievous demon (*O.E.D.* first rec. here).

gromene] gen. pl.

18. momeleþe] Difficult: momeleþe in the secondary meaning, eats slowly, and "moccheþ" and ruins his stomach. *O.E.D.* lists *mouch* to eat greedily, but first use in 1570; if this is an earlier usage, the meaning would fit the context.

19. for-laped] satiated with drinking, and [for-] lad, sated with the taking in of water (OE hladen) more than the sea (OE lagu). See *O.E.D.* for- (prefix 6b).

20. Tr. a dozen (such knaves] could not draw wages from dogs.

21. rybaudȝ] sing.; so he (l. 24).

rewe] *Cf. Piers Plowman,* C.ii.114 "þe dai roweþ."

22. huem] i.e., shabbes; tr. and draws þus from them.

23. sene] (it) is seen, i.e., obvious by.

24. louseth] Wülcker tr. de-louses (but first rec. *O.E.D.* 1440); tr. sets free. Shoes a shrew, ? proverb; cf. shoe a goose, gosling, gander, etc., i.e., to spend one's time in trifling or unnecessary labor.

25. capel-claweres] horse-clawers, either those who grasp the horses of the rich (i.e., attendants), or those who flatter the nobility.

27. hayfre] gen.

31. companage] relish, anything eaten with bread (not drink).

32. Tr. yet he shall grieve about the expense.

8. *THOMAS OF ERCELDOUNE'S PROPHECY*

Index, No. 3989. Previously printed by Pinkerton, *Anc. Scottish Poems* (London 1786), i.lxxviii, and repr. by Scott, *Border Minstrelsy;* by Murray, *EETS* 61.xviii-xix; by Laing, *Remains* (rev. Small, Edinburgh, 1885), pp. 401-2; and by Brandl and Zippel, *ME Lit.,* pp. 133-34.

Murray, in a long discussion of Thomas and his works, identifies him by contemporary documents as "Thomas de Erceldoun filius et heres Thomae Rymour de Ercildoun," living between the end of the twelfth and the end of the thirteenth century. The *Scotichronicon,* ii.128 (c. 1430) associates the prediction described here with 1286, when Thomas foretold a windy morrow, interpreted later as signifying the death of Alexander III. However, the prediction was linked to later events such as the murder of Comyn by Bruce in 1306 (*Bruce,* i.30) and the Battle of Kilblane in 1355 (Wyntoun, viii.4720-24). Any writer could add the label "Erceldoun" to a story; and the whole prediction on the end of the Scottish wars ("wiþ inne twenty wynter ant on") is, as customarily, deliberately vague. Consequently no date is given this piece.

rub. countesse de Donbar] Wife of the Earl of March, referred to in the *Scotichronicon* story.

2. mon] dat.

3. londyon] London. The MS. could be read loudyon (or Lothian). Murray (p. xviii) suggests "Forest may refer to the old name of Selkirkshire, or Ettrick Forest."

7. rokesbourh] Roxburgh, one of the four boroughs of Scotland.

9. bambourne] Bannockburn. Murray (p. xix): "I am inclined therefore to suppose that it was actually composed on the eve of the Battle of Bannockburn, and circulated under Thomas's name, in order to discourage the Scots and encourage the English in the battle." Followed by Brook, *Harley Lyrics*, p. 3.

11. whaty] Not in *O.E.D.*; Murray "indifferent"; Brandl emends wlaty = wlateful (base).

15. A common complaint of the moralists.

18. comen] [þis shal] comen.

9. BANNOCKBURN AVENGED, 1333
BY MINOT

Index, No. 3080. Previously printed by Ritson, *Poems by Minot* (1825), pp. 6-7; by Wright, *Pol. Poems*, i.61-62; by Wülcker, *AE Leseb.*, p. 77; by Kluge, *Lesebuch*, p. 96; by Scholle, *Quellen und Forschungen*, lii.5-6; by Zupitza, *Übungsbuch*, pp. 164-65; by Joseph Hall (with copious notes), (Oxford, 1914), pp. 4-6; by Emerson, *Reader*, pp. 160-61; by Sisam, *XIV C. Verse & Prose*, pp. 152-53; and by Douglas C. Stedman (Dublin, 1917), pp. 5-6. The language of Minot has been studied by Bierbaum, *Über Lawrence Minot und Seine Lieder* (1876); and by Dangel, *Lawrence Minot's Gedichte* (1888). See also Oakden, *Allit. Poetry*, i.106-7 (Mid-Lincolnshire).

Following an ill-advised campaign in 1327 in which the new boy-king, Edward III, and his army were out-maneuvered by the Scots under Robert Bruce, his mother, Isabella, and her lover, Mortimer, promoted the "Shameful Peace" with the Scots, whereby Edward renounced his claims to overlordship, and Scotland became virtually independent. From 1328 the truce was more or less maintained, until in 1332 Edward Balliol, the son of the late King John of Scotland, returned from his exile in France, and, with the help of those English lords who had lost their estates across the border by the terms of the "Shameful Peace," invaded Scotland. Over numerically superior forces, the pretender Balliol won a surprising victory at Dupplin Moor, largely through the disposition of his archers, and crowned himself at Scone (Fordun, pp. 354-55; Eng. tr. p. 347). Edward seized the excuse of border raids to renew the Scottish wars, and hurried to support Balliol by besieging the border fortress town of Berwick, still in the hands of the Scottish national opposition.

This is the situation preceding the events of Nos. 9 and 10. Edward met a larger Scottish army advancing to lift the siege, and, copying the encircling tactics of the archers at Dupplin Moor, decisively defeated it (July 19, 1333). The *Brut* claimed 35,712 Scots dead to seven English (*EETS* 131.288); the *Melsa Chronicle* 38,746 to fourteen (ii.370); *Lanercost Chronicle* gives 36,354 (p. 274; Eng. tr. p. 280); Wyntoun admits 10,000 Scots killed (viii.3961); Baker (p. 52) over 60,000! The effect of the victory at Halidon Hill on England's morale was immediate; spirits cast down by a chain of ill success since the great Scottish victory at the Bannock Burn outside Stirling in 1314 revived. It is this militant joy to which Minot here gives utterance. The victory is also recorded in narrative verse inserts in two prose chronicles (*Index,* No. 3539).

2. bannok burn] The *Brut* records the verses supposedly sung by the maidens of Scotland taunting their English sisters on the loss of their lovers (*EETS* 131.208):

> Maydenes of Engelande, sare may ȝe morne,
> For tynt ȝe haue lost ȝoure lemmans at Bannokesborn
> wiþ hevalogh.
> What wende þe Kyng of Engeland haue ygete Scotlande
> wiþ Rombylogh.

Fabyan (p. 420) explains: "This songe was after many dayes sungyn, in daunces, in carolis of ye maydens & mynstrellys of Scotlande, to the reproofe and dysdayne of Englysshe men, wt dyuerse other whiche I ouer passe." The refrain words make use of sailor songs and apparently refer to Edward's predilection for water travel; cf. Wilson, *Lost Lit.,* p. 213.

3. sakles] Barbour's *Bruce* (ii.178) comments on the battle:

> For throu me and my warraying
> Of blud thar hass beyne gret spilling
> Quhar mony sakles men wes slayne.

5. wele wurth þe while] good luck to the time, happy the occasion. Cf. l. 11, and No. 72, l. 66.

6. Snyder, "The Wild Irish," *MP,* xvii.711-12 lists other examples of English abuse of the Scots.

7. saint Iohnes toune] Perth, capital of Scotland, from the large church of St. John the Baptist; continued to be known under both names to the seventeenth century.

9. On the eve of Dupplin Moor, the Scots went to bed singing about the tailed Englishmen. According to one version, the Scots would turn their tails into ropes to bind them as prisoners; to another, the Scots would drag the English by their tails to the gallows. See *O.E.D.* tailand, and further refs. in Mustanoja, *Neuphil. Mitteilungen*, lv.222, fn. 2.

13. striflyn] Stirling, the Strevillyne of Barbour's *Bruce;* probably in reference to the defeat of the English by Wallace at Stirling (Bannockburn) in 1297. Cf. No. 4, l. 93.

18. bot euer] Scholle emends: for euer.

19. riueling] a rawhide boot, worn with the hairy side outward, a characteristic mark of the Scots (cf. le Bel, i.70), and so used derisively. Wyntoun (viii.4419-22) suggests it was the habitual foot-covering of the ordinary soldier, which the knights used only in great emergencies.

20. berebag] bag carrier. Froissart describes the Scots' little bags: "The Scots are bold, hardy, and much inured to war. When they make their invasions into England, they march from twenty to four-and-twenty leagues without halting, as well by night as day, for they are all on horseback ... they bring no carriages with them ... neither do they carry with them any provisions of bread or wine ... Under the flaps of his saddle each man carries a broad plate of metal; behind the saddle, a little bag of oatmeal" (i.46-47). Similarly in le Bel, i.47-48.

22. brig] Bruges (cf. burghes l. 25). Cf. *Chronicon Angliae*, p. 4: "Praelati vero totius Scotiae fugerunt in Franciam, et quidam ad summum pontificem, et remedium petierunt." So Wyntoun, viii.3653.

24. donde] Dundee. A fleet of ten ships had been sent by Philip VI of France to raise the siege of Berwick, but it was destroyed by the English fleet at Dundee (*Melsa Chronicle*, ii.365). Minot alludes to this engagement in his preceding poem, *Index*, No. 3801, ll. 15-24, 65-68.

25. betes þe stretes] pounds the pavements.

10. *THE BATTLE OF NEVILLE'S CROSS, 1346*
BY MINOT

Index, No. 3117. Previously printed by Ritson, *Poems by Minot* (1825), pp. 39-44; by Wright, *Pol. Poems*, i.83-87; by Scholle, *Quellen und Forschungen*, lii.34-36; by Hall, pp. 30-33; by Morley, *Shorter Eng. Poems*, pp. 32-34; and by Stedman, pp. 33-35.

The much later ballad of "Durham Field" also celebrates this victory (Hales and Furnivall, *Bishop Percy's Folio MS.*, ii.191-200;

Child, *Pop. Ballads,* iii.284-87). Hall prints Fr. and L. poems on this battle (pp. 112-22). For a detailed account of the battle, see *Archaeologia Aeliana,* n.s.i.271-91.

Heartened by his victory at Halidon Hill, Edward III insisted on harsh terms of submission unacceptable to the Scots. As a result, Scotland was not subdued, and, in spite of frequent English incursions, continued in a state of armed opposition. In the meantime, the hostilities between England and France broke out into what was to be the Hundred Years War. Following a series of English victories at Sluys, Crécy, and Calais (described with enthusiasm by Minot), the French King Philip VI appealed to the Scottish King David Bruce for a diversionary attack, and sent him French mercenaries. This army, after winning initial skirmishes, advanced as far south as Durham. Here, on October 17, 1346, at Neville's Cross, they met resistance in the form of a large English army under those northern lords not serving overseas with the King. The Scottish army was defeated, Bruce and many Scots captured, and Edward Balliol put back on the throne again as an English puppet.

1. Sir Dauid þe bruse] David Bruce was defeated by Edward Balliol at Dupplin Moor on August 12, 1332.

3. teched him to daunce] ironically: taught him how to fight. Cf. to lead a person a (merry) dance. Frequent in Minot; cf. *Index,* Nos. 585, l. 72; 2149, l. 58; 2189, l. 14; 3801, l. 66.

4. þe more] Stedman: "This may refer either to the battle of Dupplin Moor, in 1332, or to Neville's Cross fought on or near Bearpark Moor, 1346." So Hall, p. 88.

5. Sir philip] Cf. No. 11, l. 32.

6. þe flowres] The heraldic fleur-de-lys of France.

8. A bare] The boar, Edward III, had left them dead on the battlefield.

13. merkes] desired ends.

16. "Per Philippum de Valoys excitatus," Adae Murimuth, p. 218; and so Murimuth *Contin.,* p. 177; *Lanercost Chronicle,* p. 348; Knighton, ii.42; *Chronicon Angliae,* p. 23. The letter, dated June 20, 1346, from the hospital at Mesy, is printed in Hemingburgh, ii.421-422; and another dated July 22 from St. Denis, ii.422-23.

22. fro twede] i.e., all England, from the River Tweed, the boundary between England and Scotland, to the River Trent, which cuts across the midlands.

23. mani berebag] See No. 9, l. 20. le Bel (ii.109) numbers 43,000 light horse.

bow redy bent] W. Gilpin, *Remarks on Forest Scenery* (1791), notes: "the Englishman did not keep his left hand steady, and draw his bow with his right; but the keeping his right at rest upon the nerve, he pressed the whole weight of his body into the horns of his bow. Hence probably arose the phrase 'bending a bow,' and the French for 'drawing' one." (Quoted in Trevelyan, *Illustrated Eng. Social Hist.,* i.17).

25. waniand] The waning of the moon, considered an unlucky time to begin an enterprise. Cf. *Sax. Leechdoms,* i.320; and *Brut* on Scots' defeat in 1422 at Vernon: "But þe moste vengeance fell vpon þe proude Scottes ... So that they may say wele 'In the croke of þe mone went thei thidre warde, And in the wilde wanyende come þei homewarde' " (*EETS* 136.441).

29. ȝork] William de la Zouche (d. 1352), younger son of William la Zouche, first Baron Zouche. He entered the service of the King, becoming Keeper of the Wardrobe, Keeper of the Privy Seal in 1335, and (in 1340) Treasurer of England. In 1340 he was elected Archbishop of York. In addition to his political and ecclesiastical positions, Zouche added military. He was Warden of the Scottish March from 1346, a commissioner for raising the Northern armies, and a division commander at Neville's Cross. The *Lanercost Chronicle* (pp. 347-48; Eng. tr. p. 335) notes his fighting prowess.

31. Dorem] The Bishop of Durham, Thomas de Hatfield (d.1381), was abroad fighting with the King in France (Baker, p. 79) when informed by letter from the Prior of Durham about the battle (*Letters from the Northern Registers,* ccxli, ccxlii, pp. 385-89). Froissart (ii.188) gives him in command (with Lord Percy) of the first division.

Carlele] The Bishop of Carlisle, John de Kirkby (d.1352), was a well-known warrior since 1337 against the Scots. He certainly fought against them in 1345 (*Hist. Anglicana,* i.266; *Ypodigma Neustriae,* p. 285), but is not listed in the fighting of 1346 except in the usually reliable Baker (p. 87) and the ballad of "Durham Field," which includes him with Durham and York as battle leaders. Probably meant here are the men of these towns. Neither bishop was among the twelve English commanders congratulated by the Regent (*Rotuli Scotiae,* i.675).

34. syr dauid] Bruce and many Scots were captured; lists in Adae Murimuth, pp. 218-19; Baker, pp. 88-89; and Fordun, p. 367.

37. Iohn of Coupland] One of the commanders of the third English division (cf. *Lanercost Chronicle,* p. 351; Eng. tr. p. 341; *Anominalle Chronicle,* p. 27). He was afterwards Governor of Berwick and Sheriff of Northumberland. Wyntoun's Chronicle (viii.6266-69) tells how he took King David prisoner, but got two teeth knocked out in the capture. So *Scotichronicon,* ii.342; Froissart (ii.191-93) adds further details.

38. kend him his crede] i.e., taught him a lesson.

42. william þe dowglas] Sir William Douglas (d.1353), Knight of Liddesdale and the "Flower of Chivalry," was one of the Scot-

tish leaders in the perpetual border warfare. Among his many brilliant exploits, he effected the taking of Edinburgh and, as ambassador to France, procured naval help for his countrymen. At Neville's Cross he was in charge, with the Earl of Murray, of the second Scottish division. There he was captured, and imprisoned in the Tower of London for seven years, only securing his release by swearing fealty to Edward. On his return to his estates, he was slain by a kinsman who had assumed them during his long absence. He is the subject of the lost ballad, "The Knight of Liddesdale" (cf. Child, *Pop. Ballads,* iii.288).

48. Sir Iohn] Son of Philip VI, later John II, King of France.

50. held himself waken] allowed him no rest.

51. brede] to bake one's bread, i.e., to kill; he = Philip.

63. Durham, with the tomb of St. Cuthbert and his banner, was a popular place of pilgrimage throughout the Middle Ages. After the initial Scottish successes, David Bruce ravaged as far south as Hexham, where he dreamed he saw the ghost of St. Cuthbert foretelling disaster (*Melsa Chronicle,* iii.62). St. Cuthbert contrariwise heartened the English, bidding the prior of Hexham to take a relic, a holy cloth used by the saint, and place it on a spear and display it at the battle field. Many ascribed the victory to this unusual banner and to the mediation of St. Cuthbert (cf. *Surtees Soc.,* 15.20-23).

11. *THE SIEGE OF CALAIS, 1347*
BY MINOT

Index, No. 585. Previously printed by Ritson, *Poems by Minot* (1825), pp. 34-38; by Wright, *Pol. Poems,* i.80-83; by Scholle, *Quellen und Forschungen,* lii.30-33; by Hall, pp. 27-30; by Morley, *Shorter Eng. Poems,* pp. 30-32; by Stedman, pp. 29-32; and by Sisam, *XIV C. Verse & Prose,* pp. 153-56.

On September 4, 1346, the victorious Edward with the English army arrived from Crécy before Calais, a needed port which he thought he could speedily invest. After nearly a year, during which a blockade from the sea was made effective, the citizens surrendered on August 4, 1347. A truce was signed at the end of September, and Edward III returned to England in October. Calais was to be resettled with Englishmen and henceforth to be an English city.

3. mirth on mold] One of Minot's poetic clichés — joy on earth.

4. ken ȝow ȝowre crede] Cf. No. 10, l. 38.

5. wight in wede] valiant in arms.

19. bare] Edward III. So No. 10, l. 8.

26. in winter tyde] Edward, in spite of diminishing forces, determined to continue the siege throughout the winter of 1346-47.

"The siege went on and on," writes Edouard Perroy, *The Hundred Years War* (London, 1951), pp. 119-20. "It took all Edward's bold tenacity not to abandon it. His soldiers regarded this winter campaign, which was contrary to custom, as a scandal, and desertions from their ranks multiplied."

29. his fame is spread abroad (Sisam-Tolkein).

31. habide] not rec. with this sp. in *O.E.D.*

32. sir philip] Philip de Valois, Philip VI of France (1293-1350), and his son John, Duke of Normandy, later king (1350-1364). Sisam (p. 254) comments on John as a famous literary patron, both in France and during his confinement in England.

33. fers and fell] another cliché; cf. No. 10, l. 7.

41. Cardinales] On July 17, Philip came with an army and encamped opposite a marsh protecting the English. Instead of attacking, however, he sent two cardinals, Annibale Ceccano, Bishop of Frascati, and Etienne Aubert, later Pope Innocent VI (Hall, *Minot*, p. 85), to discuss a treaty (cf. le Bel, ii.131-32; Avesbury, p. 390; Knighton, ii.50). This relief was quite ineffective, for, as Minot says (l. 91), "to Calais cum þai all to late."

48. The negotations failing, because of English suspicion of the Papal Court at Avignon, Philip retired without offering battle.

54. at his ledeing] under his control.

61. kirtell] The *Brut* describes the emissaries to Edward: they "wenten on þe walles of þe toun, and in oþer diuers placys, as naked as þey were bore, saf here chirtys and brechys, & heldyn hire swerdus naked, & þe poynt downward, in hire handeȝ, & puttyn ropys & halterys abowte hire neckys, and ȝolden vp þe keyes of þe toun and of þe Castell to Kyng Edward, wiþ grete fere and drede of hert" (*EETS* 136.301).

62. Many editors emend to þine we are.

75. The *Brut* describes the famine; "Than þey þat were in þe toun and in þe castell byseged, seyng al þis, how þat þei hade non oþer helpe ne socour of þe Kinge of Fraunce ne of his men, & also þat her vitailles wiþin hym were spended and wasted, & for defaute of vitailles & of refresshyng þey eten hors, houndes, cattes & mys, for to kepe her trouþe as long as þey myȝte" (*EETS* 136.300).

82. Sir iohn de viene] Minot follows the *Melsa Chronicle* (iii.67) rather than the *Brut* in having Sir John of Vienna surrender the keys.

12. THE TAKING OF GUINES, 1352
BY MINOT

Index, No. 3899. Previously printed by Ritson, *Poems by Minot* (1825), pp. 48-51; by Wright, *Pol. Poems,* i.89; by Scholle, *Quellen und Forschungen,* lii.39-40; by Hall, pp. 34-36; by Morley, *Shorter*

Eng. Poems, pp. 36-37; and by Stedman, pp. 39-40.

Following the capture of Calais and the ensuing truce, the war smoldered on with limited raids and counterattacks. Early in 1352 the English got possession of Guines, a fortified town a few miles southwest of Calais, through the hardihood of an English adventurer, John of Doncaster. See Baker, pp. 116-18. This last poem in Minot's series glosses over the unsavory mercenariness of this particular incident in the Hundred Years War, and ends with the habitual praises of the English King.

3. lipard] The leopards (*lions léopardés*) of the Royal Arms of England were first quartered with the French fleur-de-lys by Edward III. Cf. Robert de Brunne, *Chronicle* (1810), p. 305: "þei sauh kynge's banere, raumpand þre lebardes."

4. þi man] i.e., Edward III.

12. Iohn of france] Cf. No. 11, l. 32.

13. Iohn of Doncaster] Believed to have been imprisoned at one time in Guines, John used his familiarity with the castle to seize both town and fortress. He then offered his loot to the highest bidder, who turned out to be Edward III. Cf. Avesbury, pp. 414-15; Baker, pp. 116-18.

31. men of Saint Omers] On January 1, 1350, Geoffrey de Chargny, the French captain of St. Omer, had tried to retake Calais by bribing an Italian mercenary in the service of Edward. But the men of St. Omer were double-crossed and themselves captured by the King, who, to show the magnanimity of his chivalry, served a great feast to the vanquished. So *Brut, EETS* 136.302-3; Avesbury, pp. 408-10; and, with some variations, Froissart, ii.239-46.

32. pauiliownes] generally tents, but here used for "standardes" or "baners" (Fr. paveillun).

34. Scholle finds this line "metrically overloaded and grammatically shocking," but there is no need to delete "ȝow."

13. WHAT PROFITS A KINGDOM, 1401

Index, No. 817. Previously printed by Kail, *EETS* 124.9-14.

2. *English Chronicle* (p. 23) notes the grumblings in 1401-1402: "And aboute this tyme the peple of this land began to grucche ayens kyng Harri, and beer him hevy, because he took thair good and paide not therfore; and desirid to haue ayeen king Richarde. Also lettriȝ cam to certayn frendis of kyng Richard, as thay hadde be sent from hymself, and saide that he was alive; wherof moche peple was glad and desirid to haue him kynge ayeen."

false reportours] denouncers.

mys-famed] *O.E.D.* first use as verb 1850; as noun 1480.

11. in goddis stede] as God's representative.

12. Cf. *Index,* No. 697, l. 6: In Euenhede Lawe ȝe lede.

15. Cf. *Index,* No. 697, l. 63: And lawe be kept, no folk nyl ryse.

17. On January 25, 1401, the Commons petitioned "q certeins Srs & autres dignes & sufficientz persones de cest Roialme feurent chalengez par les Fraunceois, par subtile ymagination de mesmes les Franceois, a quel entent homme ne sciet" (*Rot. Parl.,* iii.456).

25. "Item priount les Communes, depuis qu'il est contenu en la Graunde Chartre, 'Qe nul serra arestu ne emprisone sanz respounce, ou due Processe de la Ley:' quelle Chartre est conferme en chescun Parlement. Et ore ils supplient, q si ascun soit arestuz ou emprisonez encontre la fourme del Chartre avaunt dite, q'il veigne & appierge a sa responce, & preigne son juggement, sicome la Ley demande, issint q null tiel areste ne imprisonement soit treet en custume, en destruction de la Ley du Roy" (*Rot. Parl.,* iii.470).

33. Cf. No. 15, l. 60.

47. Cf. *Index,* No. 4005, l. 2071: "Try out the corne clene from the chaff."

49. in specyale] specially.

60. at þe firste het] at the first go.

66. "Item, Mesquerdy le xv*me* jour de Marce [1401], les Communes viendrent devaunt le Roi & les Seignrs en Parlement, & la monstrerent, Coment les Estates du Roialme purroient bien estre resemblez a une Trinite, c'est assavoir la persone du Roy, les Seignrs Espirituelx & Temporelx, & les Communes. Et en cas q'ascune division y feusse entre celles Estatz y serroit grand desolation de tout le Roialme, q Dieux defende. Et par cause q mesmes les Communes aient entenduz des aucunes divisions par entre Seignr & Seignr, & en especiale par entre le Cont de Roteland & le Sr Fitz-Wautier, ils prierent au Roy, d'ordeigner pur celle matire come meulx luy sembleroit a faire par advys des Seignrs, pur nurrir bone unite & concorde entre eux" (*Rot. Parl.,* iii.459-60).

67. in store] in reserve.

90. in ydel] in vain.

98. comoun profit] a stock phrase, frequently found in manuals of devotion and in wills, for *pro bono publico.* Cf. No. 71, l. 35.

99. Cf. No. 14, ll. 143-44.

101. Cf. *Index,* No. 3924, ll. 43-44, 52:

ȝoure tenauntes playntes ȝe mot here,
ffor þey kepen all ȝoure tresour ...
þey paye ȝoure rente to gouerne lawe.

113. "Likewise, lines 113 *et seq.* may be regarded as an allusion to the dissension among the noblemen, and to the frequent rebellions against the King. It was, indeed, the discord among the English that brought much mischief on their own country. The

Welsh profited by the civil commotions to make insurrections; the Scots renewed their incursions into England, and wasted the northern counties; the French intrigued at the English court, and began to trouble the garrison of Calais: so that, about that time, England was in fact everywhere threatened by enemies" (Kail, pp. xii-xiii).

114. Cf. No. 88, ll. 25-26.

115. Cf. No. 14, ll. 35-37.

121. Cf. ll. 145-46; also *Index*, No. 411, ll. 227-28: "þis world is a fayre nouȝt / A fals lemman þat chaunge lest."

124. toun & pyle] a poetic cliché; cf. *Index*, No. 3992, l. 139.

131. Cf. *Index*, No. 3924, l. 51: "þe puple is goddis, and noȝt ȝoures." Similarly, *Index*, No. 697, l. 19.

140. Written apparently in support of the statute *De Haeretico Comburendo* passed in 1401. Cf. *Ypodigma Neustriae*, p. 391.

145. chery fayre] A frequent symbol for the transitoriness of life; cf. Gower, *Conf. Amantis*, Pro. I.19: "For al is but a chery feire / This worldes good;" Hoccleve, *De Reg. Principum*, clxxxv.47: "Thy lyfe, my sone, is but a chery feire."

14.   GOD SAVE KING HENRY V, 1413

Index, No. 910. Previously printed by Kail, *EETS* 124.50-55.

The advice to the King, implicit in this indirect address, parallels the less concealed admonitions of No. 95. Both poems are similar to the purported words of Henry IV to his son, recorded in the *First Eng. Life Henry V* (pp. 14-16).

3. in querte] in sound condition.

4. þes holy tyme] "Easter 1413, for this piece seems to have been written under the impression of the coronation ceremonies, and besides, the poet refers to some incidents which took place about that time" (Kail, p. xvi).

7. "The conspirators who spread the rumours about Richard II. [being still alive], and who made an attempt on the life of Henry V., are the fools whose wicked plans are to be disconcerted" (Kail, p. xvi).

8. þo] the; so ll. 17 and 19.

12. at on assent] in agreement.

14. dale & downe] lowland and upland.

25. There were skirmishes in France shortly after Henry's accession. Cf. Waurin, ii.163.

35. Cf. No. 13, ll. 115-16.

37. þey] The Scots and French.

52. "Concerning the attempt on the life of Henry V, alluded to

in l. 7, 'no harm had yet been done, the offence having been restricted to those malicious reports' " (Kail, p. xvi).

57. This st. seems to refer to Henry's leniency to Oldcastle. It
may be paraphrased: A man (Oldcastle) might be removed (forborn)
far away from a king's residence (place). He would make a king
to perjure himself (be forsworn) to circumvent the law, by allowing
Oldcastle a reprieve of 40 days, so that his condemnation might not
come about. Oldcastle would also make Henry V believe that Oldcastle was in a state of grace and was holy in his religious condition,
and that Henry should defend his opinions in his sin, while Oldcastle pick the jewels out of his crown.

59. forsworn] Cf. *Index,* No. 411, ll. 217-20:

> I wolde suche a statute were,
> And þer-vpon set a payne,
> What soget wolde make his souereyn swere
> þat he tolde in counseil layne.

74. Cf. No. 13, l. 5.

77. Cf. No. 13, ll. 7-8.

85. John, Duke of Burgundy, having patched up a quarrel with
Louis, Duke of Orleans, treacherously murdered him in the streets
of Paris (1407). No. 15 continues the story to John's death in 1419.

89. Cf. *Index,* No. 3924, ll. 47-48:

> For-þy god made ȝow gouernour,
> In goddis ryȝt to deme þe dede.

93. Probably referring to John Wightlock, a leader in the early
conspiracies against Henry V (cf. l. 7).

97. That lord] Probably the Duke of Albany, who gave out that
Richard had not been slain, and promoted Thomas Ward (who
resembled the dead monarch) as the true king.

99. Cf. *Index,* No. 697, ll. 11-12:

> Noght for the loue of ten or twelue,
> Brynge not a comone in greuaunce.

106. lyf & leme] all the bodily faculties. Cf. No. 39, l. 93;
No. 95, l. 52.

113. "Apparently . . . the frequent insurrections under the preceding kings" (Kail, p. xvii).

126. blo] renown.

137. Cf. *First Eng. Life Henry V:* "And if thou keepe them thus
in subiection mixed w*th* loue and feare, thou shalt haue the most
peaceable and firtile countrie, and the most louinge, faithfull, and
manly people of the worlde, w*ch* shalbe cause of no smale feare of
thine aduersaries" (p. 15). Cf. also No. 95, ll. 65-72.

142. Cf. No. 13. ll. 99-100.

15. THE FOLLIES OF THE DUKE OF BURGUNDY, 1419

Index, No. 1939. Previously printed by Furnivall, Eng. St., xxiii.438-42; and by Kail, *EETS* 124.69-72.

John, Duke of Burgundy and Flanders, who had treacherously assassinated the Duke of Orleans in 1407 (No. 14, l. 85), himself met a similar fate at the hands of the Dauphin in 1419 (l. 62). This was considered a just retribution (ll. 63-64). While motivated by the life and deeds of the Duke, this "Remembraunce of LII Folyes" (or crimes) had general application: such acts are stupid and even criminal for any one in a high position to commit. For a full account of the murder see St. Remy, i.369-79.

2. The clergy were afraid to condemn him for his murder of Orleans.

4. cast vnder stoles] i.e., disregarded.

5. Tr. Flatterers advised lords to take bribes to make themselves rich and their lords poor dupes; when the nobles had been brought to fear their inferiors, these skulked away to avoid shame to their souls. Cf. *Index,* No. 411, ll. 73-74:

> Gloseres maken mony lesynges,
>
> Al to sone men hem leue.

8. for shame of] to avoid shame upon.

17. He trusted the Dauphin, and (l. 19) entered into negotiations with him, although some of his counsellors warned against him in this falsehood. Cf. l. 51.

19. Cf. *Index,* No. 3924, ll. 73-76:

> Who skorneþ hem þat telleþ hem wit,
>
> Is rebell to god, þat repreueþ reson;
>
> þat loueþ hym most, þat hateþ hit,
>
> Aȝenst goddis counseill cast a cheson.

33. Instead of assisting his cousin against the King of England, he made war upon him, and so promoted the cause of a stranger.

37. "He did not scruple at killing the Duke of Orleans; he even defended that deed, and openly boasted of it, and nobody durst call it a crime" (Kail, p. xxi).

51. gloser charmes] Those advising John to ally himself with the Dauphin.

59. Cf. *Index,* No. 2763, l. 60: "For synguler profyt is sotyll theft."

83. in awayte] in ambush.

87. in preuytee] in secrecy. Cf. No. 14, l. 54.

94. Cf. *Index,* No. 2088, ll. 69-70:

> And nedeles gredy þyn almes souȝt.
>
> ȝeue hem no þyng þouȝ þey crye.

95. Tr. in despite of conscience.

99. This st. alone of the Digby poet's work has a strong allitera-tion and poetic clichés (e.g., freek, folk vppon fold). It may be a conscious imitation of the alliterative revival.

100. Cf. *Index*, No. 2048, ll. 7-8:

> Gostly blynd goþ, and not neuere whidre,
> þat leueþ wit, and worchiþ by wille.

16. *ON THE EVIL STATE OF ENGLAND, 1381*

Index, No. 3306. Not heretofore printed from this MS.; added on a blank leaf near the end. MS. includes a short metrical chronicle (*Index*, No. 1105). Also in St. John's Coll. Oxf. MS. 209, printed by Coxe, *Cat.*, p. 74; by Wright, *Pol. Poems*, i.278; and by Sisam, *XIV C. Verse & Prose*, p. 161:

> The ax was sharpe, the stokke was harde,
> In the xiiij yere of kyng Richarde.

The year 1381 seems more appropriate for this complaint, in view of the repression following the Revolt, to which the quatrain may refer. In 1391 the Commons "mercierent humblement nre Sr le Roy en plein Parlement de sa bone Governance & graciouse Srie, & del grant Fervour & Zele q'il ad continuelment a son poeple" (*Rot. Parl.*, iii.283).

2. stool] The executioner's block.

17. *JOHN BALL'S LETTERS, I, 1381*

Index, No. 1791. Stow's *Annales* first appeared in 1580; it was "amended" by Edmund Howe in 1615 (the text used here, p. 294) and 1631. Reprinted by Mackay, *Percy Soc.* i.2; by Wilson, *Lost Lit.*, p. 202; and by R. H. Hilton and H. Fagan, *The English Rising of 1381* (London, 1950), p. 102.

Ball, having been excommunicated several times previously, was finally taken by Archbishop Sudbury and imprisoned in Maidstone Jail. Presumably from here he communicated with his followers by letters, some direct, others veiled. Stow also records four similar letters: *Index*, Nos. 1655, 1796 (No. 18); "John Ball greeteth you all" (a quatrain not listed in *Index*); and "Jack Carter prays you all" (prose). For Ball's use of the Evils of the Age, see Introduc-tion, p. xlii. *Index*, No. 1655 is similar.

A full account of the Revolt is given in many chronicles, e.g., *Chronicon Angliae*, pp. 285-326; *Hist. Anglicana*, i.453-84; ii.1-41; Knighton, ii.130-50.

18. JOHN BALL'S LETTERS, II, 1381

Index, No. 1796. Previously printed in *Hist. Anglicana,* ii.34. Reprinted from Stow, *Annales,* p. 294, frequently, most recently by Sisam, *XIV C. Verse & Prose,* pp. 160-61; by Trevelyan, *England in the Age of Wycliffe,* p. 203; and by Hilton and Fagan, *English Rising,* pp. 101, 103. The text occurs in other chronicles, e.g., *Chronicon Angliae,* p. 322; Holinshed, ii.749. The Royal MS., a later copy of the St. Albans Chronicle, the basis for Walsingham and for Stow, is described in *Chronicon Angliae,* pp. xxix-xxx. It precedes the letter with an explanation: "Miserat insuper ductoribus communium in Estsexia quandam literam aenigmatibus plenam, ad hortandum eos ut incepta perficerent; quae ex post inventa est in manica cujusdam suspendendi pro turbatione praefata, cujus tenor talis est."

a. Iohan schep] An assumed name of John Ball, the priest or shepherd (*schep*). A Latin poem eulogizing the dead Sudbury (Wright, *Pol. Poems,* i.227-30) ends with a list of the nicknames of the leaders of the Revolt:

Jak [S]Chep, Tronche, Jon Wrau, Thom Myllere, Tyler, Jak Strawe,
Erle of the Plo, Rak to, Deer, et Hob Carter, Rakstrawe,

Isti ductores in plebe fuere priores.

b. Iohan nameles] Another assumed name, for the protection of those involved, should the letter be intercepted.

mullere] miller; not rec. *O.E.D.* with this spelling.

e. Pers plouȝman] Langland's orthodox conclusions were interpreted otherwise by the serfs; l. 6 echoes the visions of Dowel, Dobet, and Dobest. Cf. John H. Lawson, *Hidden Heritage* (New York, 1950), p. 51.

hobbe þe robbere] Possibly Sir Robert Hales (No. 19, l. 33) or simply any robber. Hob is a familiar variant of Robert. Cf. No. 4, l. 73.

f. Iohan Trewman] Ball wishes only reliable, true men to be in his enterprise, "and no mo."

3. þe] Sisam emends ȝe.

4. "Et les ditz comunes avoient entre eux une wache worde en Engleys, 'With whom haldes yow?' et le respouns fuist, 'Wyth kynge Richarde and wyth the trew communes' " (*Anonimalle Chronicle,* p. 139).

19. THE COURSE OF REVOLT, 1381

Index, No. 3260. Not heretofore printed from this MS.; two small sheets of paper, 135 mm. by 198 mm. Variant in Corpus Christi Coll. Camb. MS. 369, printed by Wright, *Pol. Poems.* i.224-26 (collated),

and in *Rel. Ant.*, ii.283-84. St. 1, 2, 3, 7 = Corpus st. 1, 2, 5, 6;
Corpus 3 and 4 variant:

> þus hor wayes þay wente,
> > pravis pravos aemulantes,
> To london fro Kent
> > sunt predia depopulantes;
> þer was an vuel couent,
> > australi parte vagantes;
> Sythun þay sone were schent,
> > qui tunc fuerant superantes.

> Bondus þay blwun bost,
> > nolentes lege domari,
> Nede þat fre be most,
> > vel [n]ollent pacificari;
> Charters were endost,
> > hos libertate morari;
> þer hor fredam þay lost,
> > digni pro coede negari.

1. taxe] The poll tax was first voted in 1377, and repeated in 1379 and 1380-81. On May 20, 1381, the men of Fobbing and other nearby villages in Essex, resisting Thomas Bampton, the commissioner in that area, set off the revolt.

3. small] Much of the tax was diverted to the collectors.

4. The collection of the outstanding 1380 levy was bought by John Leg (*Hist. Anglicana,* i.454; Knighton, ii.130). He was later executed by the rebels.

5. yt] i.e., this misrule.

9. Kent] The first concentration of the peasants was at Maidstone under Wat Tyler, and the first town to endorse them was Canterbury. Kent was "the stronghold of the rebellion" (Trevelyan, *England in the Age of Wycliffe,* p. 211).

11. rowtes] Disorderly crowds, unlawful assemblies.

15. laddes] Men of low birth, contrasted to lords. Many of the leaders, however, were richer peasants, small merchants, poor priests, knights, and (in London) some of the aldermen. Cf. Margaret Schlauch, *Science and Society,* iv.414.

19. bischop] Simon Sudbury, Archbishop of Canterbury. As Chancellor of England, he bore the responsibility for the mismanagement and oppression of the reign, and as originator of the poll tax was especially hated by the rebels. Abandoned by the court, he sought refuge in the Tower of London, but was seized and executed.

21. maners] The manor-houses of those especially zealous in implementing repressive laws were generally destroyed, and all manorial records burned.

25. Iak strawe] One of the leaders in the revolt. He and Thomas Farringdon, a Londoner, led the rebels in burning the property of Sir Robert Hales. Straw was slain after the final dispersal of the peasants at St. John's Fields on June 15, 1381.

made yt stowte] swaggered.

33. Hales] Sir Robert Hales, Prior of the Order of St. John of Jerusalem, Treasurer of England, and therefore the man most concerned with collecting the poll tax. He was beheaded at the Tower.

39. Savoy] Savoy Palace, the newly-built residence of the unpopular John of Gaunt, at this time in Scotland. The rebels, after evacuating his family, destroyed the valuables and burned the palace (*Anonimalle Chronicle,* p. 141).

41. Arcan] Achan, who transgressed the law of Joshua by stealing valuables from Jericho (Joshua 7). Strict orders had been issued against looting, "that none on paine to lose his head, shoulde presume to conuert to his owne vse anything that there was, or mought be found" (Stow, *Annales,* p. 286, following *Chronicon Angliae,* p. 289; Knighton, ii.134-35; *Hist. Anglicana,* i.457; etc.).

46. Gower has given the classic account of how he hid in the woods for fear of the peasants, in *Vox Clamantis* (Book I, cap. xvi).

49. It was not Straw who was murdered at Smithfield, but Wat Tyler. *Brut* likewise gives Straw (*EETS* 136.337). Knighton, however, says: "Watte Tyler, sed jam nomine mutato vocatus est Jakke Strawe" (ii.137); so Holinshed, ii.736.

20. THE INSURRECTION AND EARTHQUAKE, 1382

Index, No. 4268. Previously printed by Conybeare, *Archaeologia,* xviii.26-28; by Furnivall, *EETS* 117.719-21; and by Brown, *Rel. Lyrics XIV C.,* pp. 186-88. Occurs also in B.M. Addit. MS. 22283 (Wright, *Pol. Poems,* i.250-52); and in Nat. Lib. of Wales, Peniarth MS. 395.

5. set . . . liht] despise, undervalue. Cf. No. 39, l. 63.

6. foule . . . fare] behave outrageously.

8. For the refrain, cf. *Chronicon Angliae* (p. 291): "quia, ut credimus, Deus Anglicis demonstrare voluit, quod non in fortitudine sua roborabitur vir, nec in arcu vel gladio fore sperandum, sed in Eo qui salvat nos de affligentibus nos, et odientes nos sua misericordia et pietate confundere consuevit."

20. in presse] aside.

33. Cf. *Brut:* "And yn þe v yere of King Richardeʒ Regne was þe grete Erthe quake; and þat was do generally ovir alle þe worlde, — the Wedynesday afftir Whitsonday, yn the yere after incarnacion of our Lorde Ihesu crist, ml ccc iiijxx xj, where-of alle þe peple

were sore agast, and drad long tyme aftir, for þe grete vengaunce and grete drede þat our Lorde God schewed and dede" (*EETS* 136.338).

58. Pestilens] "Possibly the 5th plague, — the Black Death of 1348-49 being the First, the plague of 1361 the Second, that of 1368-69 the Third, and that of 1375 the Fourth, while that of 1390-1391 was the Fifth — Creighton, i.206-19. But a less Plague was in 1382" (Furnivall, p. 720).

61. The *Chronicon Angliae* (pp. 310-12) gives as reasons for revolt, the growth of heresy, the infidelity of nobles, the general immorality, and the mendicant friars.

66. stande in sted] avail.

68. Proverbial; tr. we have lost all sense of shame.

79. Semi-proverbial = our life is uncertain. *O.E.D.* compares Chaucer, Merchant's Tale 272: "Youre herte hangeth on a ioly pyn." Cf. No. 39, l. 5.

21. THE YORKSHIRE PARTISANS, 1392

Index, No. 1543. Not heretofore printed from this MS.; sixteenth century, and therefore interesting for its late preservation of a popular song. Occurs also in London Public Record Office, Coram Rege Roll, printed by Hewlett, *Antiquary*, ii.203; and by Powell and Trevelyan, *Peasants Risings* (London, 1899), p. 19; headed: "Et dicunt quod predicti Iohannes Berwaldi iunior de Cotyngham et alii fecerunt quandam rimam in Anglicis verbis, et dictam rimam apud Beverle publice proclamari fecerunt die dominica proxima ante festam Sancti Iacobi apostoli [July 21], et apud Hull die dominica tunc proxima sequente [July 28], et in aliis diversis locis infra Comitium Eboracensis per diversas vices anno regni Ric. II 16, que quidem rima sequitur in hec verba."

4. you] P.R.O. this.

7. The villeins "gather themselves in great routs and agree by such confederacy that everyone shall aid other to resist their lords with strong hand" (*Statutes of the Realm*, Record Commission 1810-22, I Ric. II, cap. 6).

8. Cf. No. 86, l. 47.

10. P.R.O. wil we.

15. P.R.O. I say.

24. P.R.O. our dressyng.

29. heel] P.R.O. sel. Both phrases are clichés. Cf. *Cursor Mundi*, l. 5564, "Dright in þam sent bath happ and sele"; *Piers Plowman*, B. xx.38, "And send me happe and hele."

22. *A SONG OF FREEDOM, 1434*

Index, No. 849. Previously printed by Homer G. Pfander, *Popular Sermon* (New York, 1937), p. 49. For date see Introduction, p. xxv. These three stanzas occur in a Latin sermon by Friar Nicholas Phillipps, and are separated from one another by short commentaries. The second stanza, Pfander suggests, is a genuine fragment of a workers' song; but its context has been changed from political to religious.

9. Cf. *Index*, No. 2733 (new text: Camb. Un. Ll. 1.11, f. 32r, st. 1, 4, 2 only), ll. 16-20:

> That euer was thralle, now ys he fre;
> þat euer was smalle, now grete is she;
> now shal God deme bothe the & me
> vnto his blysse, yf we do wel.

23. *THE DAY WILL DAWN, 1445*

Index, No. 320. Previously printed by Greene, *Early Eng. Carols*, p. 77. The MS. consists of two unbound leaves, fifteenth century. The dating is approximate, but the end of the Hundred Years War seems appropriate. The return of soldiers and the formation of private armies, the continued famine conditions (e.g., 1438, 1439, 1445), and the economic turbulence of servants seeking better jobs all point to such a date.

10. John Ball had likewise complained, according to Froissart, "We are called slaves; and, if we do not perform our services, we are beaten" (v. 334).

24. *THE KENTISH INSURRECTION, 1450*

Index. No. 941. Previously printed *HMC* 8th Report, App. I, p. 267; and by Wilson, *Lost Lit.*, p. 204. The charter, a popular manifesto roughly written on a folio sheet of paper, sets forth twelve causes of England's economic distress: "These ben þe poyntes, mischeves, and causes of þe gederynge and assemblynge of us, ʒoure trew lege menne of Kent, þe weche we triste to God for to remedye, with helpe of hym oure kynge, our soveraigne lorde, and all the comyns of Ingland, and to dye therefore." Occurs also in Harley MS. 543 (Stow's chronicle), printed by Halliwell, *Archaeologia*, xxix.138; this text associated with Robert of Redesdale (ll. 4, 5. "Fals for the mone pillith / Trewthe for his talles spilethe"; l. 7 omitted). A similar proclamation occurs in Lambeth MS. 306, "writn owt of David Norcyn his booke by John Stowe," followed by No. 76. Cf. Kingsford, *Eng. Hist. Lit.*, pp. 360-62 for Cotton Rolls ii.23, Art. 7.

The insurrection was set off by the acquittal of the Duke of Suffolk in 1450, charged by the Commons with the murder of the Duke of Gloucester. The rebellion was formidable and its muster orderly. Jack Cade was the nominal leader. The rebels demanded the removal of "traitors" surrounding the King and at Blackheath were able to defeat the royal forces. As in 1381, the Londoners gave some support, along with many clergy, and the rebels were able to execute Lord Say, and his son-in-law, Crowmer, the Sheriff of Kent, both on charges of extortionate taxation. After a few days, the wealthier citizens rallied, and obtained a truce, in which, to gain time for later reprisals, a general amnesty was declared. The Kentish men went home, and Cade was eventually captured and executed. Cf. Nos. 75, 76. 85, and 86. The rising is described in the *Brut*, EETS 136.517; *English Chronicle*, pp. 64-68; *Rot. Parl.*, v.177-79; *Short Eng. Chronicle*, pp. 66-68; William of Worcester, p. 76; Polydore Vergil, pp. 82-88; *Six Town Chronicles*, pp. 130-34, 153-57; *Gregory's Chronicle*, pp. 190-94; and elsewhere, including the later chronicles, e.g., Stow, *Annales*, pp. 388-92; Grafton, i.640-643; Hall, pp. 220-22. Detailed account in B. Brogden Orridge, *Illustrations of Jack Cade's Rebellion* (London, 1869).

25. INJUSTICES AT COVENTRY, 1496

Index, No. 3322. Previously printed by Sharp, *Antiquities of Coventry*, pp. 235-36; by Harris, *EETS* 135.577-78; and by Wilson, *Lost Lit.*, p. 198.

One Laurence Saunders, an active member of the Dyers Guild, continually opposed the Corporation of Coventry, especially for sanctioning enclosures. In 1495 he was removed from the Common Council on charges of fomenting a riot. His friends and supporters thereupon wrote a bill of protest (*Index*, No. 466) and posted it. The Leet Book notes: "Mem[orandum]: þat with-in viij dayes after Lammasse there was a bill sett vppon þe north Chirch durre in seynt Mighels Chirch be some evell disposed person vnknowen the tenour wherof her-after ensueth" (*EETS* 135.566-67). In the following year, Saunders was again imprisoned, and similar protests appeared; the second is printed here. It refers to the enclosure of common lands by people of power, either the gentry or the richer freeholders who were separating from the peasant class. Saunders' feud was carried to the King's Council, where the Mayor was able to have Saunders "commyt vnto þe Flete, there to abide vnto þe tyme the kynges pleasure were knowen what ferther punysshement he shuld haue" (*EETS* 135.580).

3. Lammas] August 1.

22. for movyng of your mode] to prevent you from becoming angry.

26. THE BATTLE OF OTTERBURN, 1388

Index, No. 1620. Previously printed by Percy, *Reliques,* 1775, i.18-34; by Child, *Pop. Ballads,* iii.295; by Flügel, *Neuengl. Lesebuch,* pp. 192-98; by Ritson, *Anc. Songs,* i.94-105; by Frank Sidgwick, *Ballads,* pp. 192-203; and in other collections of ballads. For a description of the MS. see Kingsford, *Chronicles of London,* pp. ix-x.

Another (shortened) text (ll. 228) occurs in Harley MS. 293, f. 52r, printed by Percy, *Reliques,* 1765, i.18-31; and by Child, *Pop. Ballads,* iii.304. Collation: 10. Redclyffe; 16. bound; 28. they ranne; 41. Ser Henry came; 66. Henrye; 77. houered; 96. gare me oute to; 137. more; 156. with thie eye; 161. ffor yf I weynde; 193. arrowes gan vpe to; 225. elke syde; 251. ffitzhughe; 255. Covelle; 265. morowe.

Cotton MS. is about 1550, but the poem is earlier, although not contemporary. There are two important later versions:

(1) "The Hunting of the Cheviot" in Bodl. MS. Ashmole 48, late sixteenth century, printed by Hearne, *Guilielmi Newbrigiensis Historia* (1719), i.lxxxii; by Percy, *Reliques* (1765), i.1-17; by Wright, *Roxburghe Club* (1860); by Skeat, *Specimens,* pp. 67-75; by Child, *Pop. Ballads,* iii.307-10; by Flügel, *Neuengl. Lesebuch,* pp. 198-201; by Sidgwick, *Ballads,* pp. 177-89; and by others. The MS. probably belonged to Rychard Sheale, a minstrel of Tamworth; certain items are in his own handwriting. The ballad is a jumbled reworking of the Battle of Otterburn moved forward to the reign of Henry IV (ll. 90, 244), who avenges the English defeat at Homildon Hill in 1402 (l. 254). Percy identified it with the Battle of Piperdean, in 1436, between William Douglas, Earl of Angus, and the second Earl of Northumberland, the son of Percy Hotspur. A few st. borrow from the Otterburn version, e.g., ll. 123-26 = 197-200 (Otterburn); 223-26 = 241-44; 227-30 = 265-68; 263-266 = 269-72. Percy was especially fond of this version: "The fine heroic song of Chevy-Chase has ever been admired by competent judges. Those genuine strokes of nature and artless passion, which have endeared it to the most simple readers, have recommended it to the most refined, and it has equally been the amusement of our childhood, and the favourite of our riper years."

(2) "Chevy Chase," in the Percy Folio MS., printed by Percy, *Reliques,* 1765, i.231-246; by Hales and Furnivall, ii.7; and by

Child, *Pop. Ballads,* iii.311-14; also in Pepys, Douce, Roxburghe, Wood, and Bagford collections of ballads. This is the broadside version of "The Hunting of the Cheviot," and was discussed by Addison in the *Spectator,* Nos. 70 and 74 (1711), and by Sidney in his *Apologie for Poetry:* "I never heard the olde song of Percy and Duglas that I found not my heart mooved more then with a trumpet; and yet it is sung but by some blinde crouder, with no rougher voyce then rude stile: which, being so evill apparelled in the dust and cobwebbes of that uncivill age, what would it worke trymmed in the gorgeous eloquence of Pindar!"

The ballad commemorates a typical border incident already made familiar by Minot (No. 10) — a ravaging raid by a Scottish army as far south as Durham and the spirited resistance of the northern English lords.

Otterburn is described in detail by Froissart (ix.237-85) from eyewitness accounts. Taking advantage of internal faction among the northern English nobility, the Scots assembled at Yethold in the border forests of Roxburghshire a huge army, which, to confuse the English, they divided into two parts. The major contingent was to attack on the west towards Carlisle; the other, on the east, was a small striking force of 300 knights and 2,000 infantry, headed for Newcastle and Durham. This latter was commanded by James, Earl of Douglas, the Earl of March and Dunbar, and the Earl of Murray. Froissart describes this army "riding at a good pace, through bye roads" (ix.246) arriving on the lands of the Percies, which they ravaged. The English mustered at Newcastle, which the Scots attacked for two days; notable in the skirmishes were Sir Henry (Hotspur) and Sir Ralph Percy, the sons of the First Earl of Northumberland, Governor of Berwick and Warden of the Scottish Marches. The Earl of Douglas fought with Sir Henry and, according to Froissart, gained his pennon; he then marched to Otterburn where he encamped. The English, however, did not seek further battle since they believed the Scots merely a vanguard of a large invading army. When they learned the facts, a large English force, three times the size of the Scottish, hurried to Otterburn. Here the famous battle took place (1388). Froissart emphasizes "it was the hardest and most obstinate battle that was ever fought" (ix.256), and again, "Of all the battles that have been described in this history, great and small, this of which I am now speaking was the best fought and the most severe; for there was not a man, knight or squire, who did not acquit himself gallantly, hand to hand with his enemy" (ix.259). In spite of their numerical superiority, the English were defeated, and Sir Henry Percy captured. The Earl of Douglas was killed. The Scots gave Otterburn prime significance: "never since the battle of Bannockburn ... have they had so complete nor so gainful a victory" (ix.284-85).

The poem follows the chronicles closely; disregarding the embellishments, it is not too far removed from the eyewitness compilations of Froissart.

1. lamasse] August 1, the traditional harvest festival (*hlaf maesse*). The battle took place on August 19, 1388 (Froissart; Knighton and Harding differ slightly).

3. dowglasse] James Douglas, second Earl of Douglas (1358-1388), active in the border raids.

5. yerlle of fyffe] Cf. l. 101.

    wyth-owghten Stryffe] A stock minstrel kenning, one of the many in this ballad.

6. sulway] Solway Firth; apparently with reference to the other Scottish army invading the western part of England.

9. hoppertope] Ottercops Hill. The Scottish force apparently avoided the direct road south, the old Watling Street (roughly the present Great North Road), and took advantage of the protection of the fells to enter Northumberland, coming down from Ottercops by Rodeley Crag to Greenleighton (a little south of Ottercops). Nearby is Otterburn. Here the Scots had the choice of direct routes to Newcastle or Durham. The traditions of the area are preserved in the name 'Scots Gap,' within a mile of Rodeley (Rothley).

    they] the Earl of Douglas and his army.

11. lyghted down] ended their ride.

12. stage] Leland, *Itinerary,* vii.56, notes the abundance of deer in this area; cf. Chevy(ot) Chase (Hunt), and l. 53.

15. they dyd . . . wrange] Tr. They acted very unfairly towards our English men.

21. bamborowe schyre] The area around Bamburgh, to the north of Ottercops, one of the three divisions of Northumberland.

28. full ryght] directly, another cliché.

29. perssy] Sir Henry Percy (1364-1403), called Hotspur (*Hist. Anglicana,* ii.144), eldest son of Henry Percy, first Earl of Northumberland, and one of the most famous and fiery of England's military leaders, both against the Scots and French. At the age of twenty he was appointed Warden of the Scottish March (cf. Child, iii.293). He was killed at the Battle of Shrewsbury, and his body quartered as a rebel.

48. tone] the one or the other. Cf. l. 120.

57. at wyll] as one wishes.

69. "When they have well beaten each other, and one party is victorious, they are so proud of their conquest, that they ransom their prisoners instantly, and in such courteous manner to those who have been taken, that on their departure they return them their thanks" (Froissart, ix.256).

70. wyth-owghten naye] certainly.

77. hoved] remained on horseback. So Wyntoun, iii.36-37.

80. dawnyng] Percy made first contact at suppertime, and the battle was fought by nighttime (Froissart; and Wyntoun, iii.35).

91. brede] broad; *O.E.D.* lists only comp. *bredder.*

92. Tr. For the profit of all England.

94. tyne] Newcastle-on-Tyne.

96. "He could not give me my fill (of defeat)" (Sidgwick).

101. mentaye] Robert Stewart (d. 1420), Earl of Fife, third son of King Robert II, and by his marriage to Mary in 1361, Earl of Menteith; long a notable fighter in the border wars, and commanding the main Scottish forces in 1388.

103. huntlay] An anachronism, since the earldom of Huntly was founded only in 1449.

105. bowghan] Alexander Stewart (d. 1405), fourth natural son of King Robert II; by his marriage to the Countess of Ross in 1382, Earl of Buchan.

107. Ihonstone] A border family.

maxwell] Another border family; Sir John Maxwell captured Sir Ralph Percy, and for this deed was knighted by his liege, the Earl of Murray; so Froissart, ix.260.

109. swynton] Sir John Swinton (d. 1402), a Scottish soldier previously in the service of the English, who was prominent in the capture of Percy. He was killed at Homildon Hill.

111. skotte] "The illustrious family of Scot, ancestors of the Duke of Buccleugh, always made a great figure on the borders. Sir Walter Scot was at the head of this family when the battle was fought; but his great-grandson, Sir David Scot, was the hero of that house, when the ballad was written" (Percy, i.37).

stewarde] Probably Walter Stewart, Lord of Brechin, a son of King Robert II, at this time about eighteen years old. Percy suggests Sir Walter Stewart, Lord of Dalswinton and Gairlies (i.37).

112. agurstone] The Haggerston family of Berwick.

123. the] H. thy. Froissart estimated the English as three times as numerous as the Scots.

133. toke the fylde] entered the battle.

137. nyne thow3and] i.e., the number of the English.

138. cronykle] A ballad commonplace. 44,000 is the number of both Scottish armies. Froissart gives 40,000 plus 1,200 mounted knights.

151. According to Froissart, the Earl of Northumberland had remained in his stronghold of Alnick Castle, while his sons hastened to rally Newcastle (ix.246).

158. Tr. I do not have to hide the fact.

165. Tr. Yet I had rather be torn asunder (flayed).

171. In Froissart (ix.280), the playing of the Scottish minstrels mystifies and confuses the English.

183. cressawntts] Cf. Drayton, *Bar. Wars*, ii.xxiv: "The Noble Percy ... with a bright Cressant in his Guide-dome came." The silver crescent or half-moon was a well-known crest of the family. Percy (*Reliques* [1775], i.279-80) quotes from a pedigree roll (temp. Henry VII) which, having linked the family with Brutus of Troy, tells how the Percies adopted the emblem:

> In hys scheld did schyne a Mone veryfying her lyght,
> Which to all the ooste gave a perfytte syght,
> To vanquys his enemys and to deth them persue;
> And therefore the Perses the Cressant doth renew.

189. owr ladyes knyght] Frequently identified thus, but (as Child observes, iii.294) not so in any legendary. Child gives many parallels: iii.294, 520; iv.499; v.244, 297. See also Flügel, *Neuengl. Lesebuch* p. 440; and here No. 36, l. 19; No. 78, l. 73.

192. the] they. So also ll. 27, 199, 227.

199. the swette] they exerted themselves greatly.

200. collayne] Cf. "The Hunting of the Cheviot," l. 124: "with swords that were of fyn myllan" (Milan steel).

213. repeats l. 199.

216. helmes] The basinet was worn with a ventail or visor and a helm covering the shoulders.

223. cowde] did. can was used as a phonetic variant for gan (pt. tense ginnan) as a simple auxiliary; but it was early fused with can (OE cunnan), and the latter's preterite likewise became used as an auxiliary. So l. 236. See Glossary *con, gan.*

240. Iames] But syr Ihon in l. 112.

241. morrey] This family, and those of Fitzhugh (l. 251) and Harbottle (l. 253), according to Percy (i.37), were all well known in the border fighting.

255. lovell] In "The Hunting of the Cheviot" Skeat notes: "*Loumle*, Lumley; always hitherto printed *louele* (and explained Lovel), though the MS. cannot be so read, the word being written 'loūle.' 'My Lord Lumley" is mentioned in the ballad of Scotish Feilde ... and again, in the Ballad of Bosworth Feilde" (*Specimens,* p. 400). If this emendation is adopted here (this MS. is clearly *lovell*), Sir Ralph Lumley, a second cousin of Percy Hotspur, who died in 1400 fighting Henry IV, is referred to. Percy identifies the "ancient family of Delaval, of Seaton Delaval, in Northumberland."

274. mongomery] Sir John Montgomerie (d. 1398), of a very old Scottish family, Baron of Eglington and Ardrossan *jure uxoris,* brother of Sir James Douglas. He was apparently exchanged for

Sir Henry Percy; his third son Hugh was slain in this battle. According to Scottish accounts, he captured Percy; English accounts say the Earl of March. Cf. *D.N.B.*

27. THE BATTLE OF AGINCOURT, 1415

Index, No. 3213. Previously printed by Nicholas Harris Nicolas, *Hist. of Battle of Agincourt* (1833), pp. 281-82; by Wright, *Pol. Poems,* ii.125-27; and by Kingsford, *Chronicles of London,* pp. 120-122. For dialect see Oakden, i.129-30.

The ballad exists in a longer composite describing the whole campaign (*Index,* No. 969) in Harley MS. 565, ff. 102-14, erroneously ascribed to Lydgate, printed by Nicolas, pp. 301-29; and in *Chronicle of London,* 1827, pp. 216-33. It has 67 eight-line stanzas with additional refrain lines: Wot ye right well that thus it was / Gloria tibi Trinitas. MacCracken notes: "It seems to contain the fragments of earlier half-popular ballads on the subject. It is written in the style of the street, with the rhyme equipment of a poor minstrel" (*EETS* cvii, p. xlvii). An older version occurs in the (now burnt) Cotton MS. Vitell. D.xii, f. 214*v,* printed by Hearne, *Elmham's Life of Henry V,* pp. 359-75; and by Nicolas, pp. 303-25. A third text in Bodl. MS. Rawl. C.86, f. 178*r.* Yet another variant is found in printed form, *The Batayll of Egyncourt,* by John Skot, about 1530; repr. by Hazlitt, *Remains,* ii.88-108. There are several sixteenth-century ballads: see Hales and Furnivall, *Bishop Percy's Folio Manuscript,* ii. 159. For other poems on Agincourt see Nos. 32 and 33.

Critical comment includes Kingsford, *Eng. Hist. Lit.,* p. 240, "the best and most spirited of the Agincourt poems."

On his accession in 1411, Henry V faced a country still disturbed from the previous reign. The strength of the Lollards in 1414 was sufficient to cause a rebellion, in which others joined for non-religious reasons; the revolt was easily subdued, and heavy repressions followed. The Scots were threatening, and so were the Welsh. The *Rotuli Parliamentorum* (iv.15) list other domestic problems such as riots and homicides. Perhaps in an effort to take his subjects' minds away from their grievances, Henry revived the English claims to France, and demanded such exorbitant concessions that he forced on war. Having made considerable preparations, impressing soldiers and sailors, and mulcting loans (500,000 nobles, according to Waurin, ii.168) under threats of imprisonment, Henry prepared to invade France in July, 1415. Before sailing, he was fortunate to learn of a wide-spread baronial conspiracy and scotch it in time. Landing at Harfleur, Henry took the town after a month's siege, and then decided, the winter approaching, to return to England by way of Calais, a hundred miles distant. He marched along the coast to Abbeville only to find the crossings over the Somme barred; so he proceeded up the river. Once across, on the return towards the coast and Calais, the English met a much larger French army near Agincourt. The French held an area between two thickets, with their forces in three "battles" or divisions, one behind the other. The French knights in the first division tried to ride down the English archers, but those who were not shot were bogged down by the heavy rain-sodden ground and became impaled on the pointed stakes — the "peuchon aguisie a deux boutz" (Waurin, ii.210) — the English archers had foresightedly provided. The French gave way, and the third division fled without offering combat. The cost to the English was light, less than a hundred of the approximately 6,000 men. Henry returned to London in great triumph and with popular acclamation. The poem opens with a description of the French charge.

Eyewitness accounts of the battle are found in Waurin's *Chronicle,* ii.211-18, and in the anonymous Latin diary written by a priest in the train of Henry V, while "sitting on horse-back among the baggage in the rear of the battle" (tr. in Nicolas, pp. 183-300, repr. *Journal Soc. Army Hist. Research,* xii.72-4, 158-78). The concept of history prevalent in the Elizabethan period, through Stow, Hall, or Holinshed, goes back to these chronicles and ballads. Stow, for example, relying on Tito Livius and Elmham, gives a similar account to this present ballad (*Annales,* pp. 348-51). Cf. also *Henrici Quinti Gesta,* ed. Benjamin Williams (London, 1850), pp. 49-58.

b. ffryday] St. Crispin's Day, October 25, 1415.

h. þe Nowmbre] "en nombre six foiz autant que les Angelis" (Waurin, ii.207); but elsewhere (ii.205) 50,000 (five to one Englishman).

m. The priest's diary confirms: "both armies stood without moving a foot one against the other, the king determined to advance towards them, seeing that the opposing multitude deferred the charge which he had expected from them, and stood so across our route as either to break up our array, or terrify us by their number" (Nicolas, p. 253).

o. baneres] "And þanne he sayde with an hygh voyce: In þe name of Almyȝti God and Saynt George, avaunt banarer" (*EETS* 136.378).

q. Tr. Rather than a courageous man should leave his booty, sooner would I here be put to death. So *Brut:* "and prayed hem alle to make hem redy vnto þe batayle: for he wolde raþere be ded þat day, in batayle or yn felde, þan be take of his enymys; for he wolde nevir put þe rem of Engelond to no Rawnson for his persone" (*EETS* 136.377-78). Also *Index,* No. 969 (st. 46): "And lat nevere that good Reme for me be fright / Ne me on lyve this day be take."

s. mayntene] Waurin (ii.203-4) gives a speech of the King before the battle exhorting his troops that this was a righteous battle, that they should exert themselves as Englishmen so as to return to their homes, and that they had in the past a record of victories. So St. Remy, i.245-46.

bb. bachelere] "A young knight, not old enough, or having too few vassals, to display his own banner, and who therefore followed the banner of another" (*O.E.D.*).

hh. tene & tray] A commonplace.

1. stumbelyd] "but God and our archers made hem sone to stomble" (*EETS* 136.378). Also Waurin: "Et si estoient les dis Francois tant chargies darmeures quilz ne povoient eulz soustenir ne aller avant ... leurs chevaulz tumberent parmy lesdis peuchons, et eulz furent prestement occis de ces archiers ... car leurs chevaulz avoient este telement bersez du trait quilz ne les povoient tenir ne gouverner ... lors leurs chevaulz sentans le trait venir sur eulz se prindrent au fuyr arriere de leurs annemis" (ii.211, 214).

2. stuffed vnder stele] a commonplace; cf. *Gol. & Gaw.*, 200: "Weill stuffit in steel on thair stout stedis." Two thirds of the lines show alliteration (Oakden, *Allit. Poetry,* i.241).

4. Tr. When they began to feel their flanks feathered with arrows.

7. Satirical: Many a sick person he made <him> well (good) — by killing him!

9. glowcestre] Wounded in battle, but rescued by his brother the King.

11. Stock line; cf. *Melayne,* 1522: "We sall wirke þam wondis full wyde."

12. ȝorke] "The kyng þat tyme had a mys-trust in Edward, Duyk of York; and þat the Duyke well perceyuet, and come to þe Kyng, and hym besoughte that he myght haue þe vaward þat day. and þe kyng hym graunted" (*EETS* 136.554). So *English Chronicle,* p. 40. York was one of the few English casualties.

17. Hontyngdon] John de Holland (1395-1447), Earl of Huntingdon (1416), fought with the King's division; later taken prisoner in Anjou.

Oxford] Richard, eleventh Earl of Oxford, commanded the rear guard (Waurin, ii.188).

25. Suthfolk] Michael Pole, second Earl of Suffolk (1361-1415), died at the siege of Harfleur (September 18), leaving his heir, Michael, "distinguished among all the courtiers, for his bravery, courage, and activity" (*Gesta Henrici Quinti,* pp. 31, 58). The young Earl was killed at Agincourt.

26. kyghle] Listed in the Harley MS. 782 roll as dead in battle (Nicolas, p. 370); Sloane MS. 6400 lists him as providing six men at

arms and eighteen foot archers (Nicolas, p. 381). Joseph Hunter, *Agincourt* (London, 1850), pp. 37-38, states that the history of Kighley's little Lancashire contingent is as complete as it is unfortunate. One of his men died at Harfleur, two others were returned to England for sickness; and of his eighteen archers, four were slain. Kighley is also mentioned by name in a London chronicle (Kingsford, *Chronicles of London*, p. 71).

33. Bowsere] Le Sire de Bewser is listed among the nobles of England with the King, in the Harley roll. *Index*, No. 969 (st. 34) mentions Sire William Boucer.

35. Erpyngham] Sir Thomas Erpingham, in command of the archers (St. Remy, i.253). Cf. Drayton's "Ballad of Agincourt": "Well it thine age became, / O noble Erpingham, / Which didst the signal aim, / To our hid forces."

37. afray] Alternatively, a fray. Cf. No. 32, l. 7; etc.

38. The dukes of Alençon, Bar, and Brabant died; and seven counts — Blamont, Fauquembergue, Grampré, Marle, Nevers, Roussy, and Vaudemont. The *Brut* gives nine earls (*EETS* 136.379, 555). Cf. *Liber Metricus, Memorials of Henry V*, RS 11, p. 123. Following this ballad, the chronicle resumes in prose and lists the French dead.

39. þis is no nay] it cannot be denied.

41. So *Brut:* "and of gode Barons C and moo; and of worthi kniȝtis of grete alyaunce of Cote armyours, M*l* C" (other texts "a M*l* and v"; *EETS* 136.379). Similarly *English Chronicle*, p. 42; Stow, *Annales*, p. 350.

42. Tr. They paid dearly for (the battle).

43. Cot-armers] Gentlemen entitled to bear coats-of-arms.

50. The Dukes of Orleans and Bourbon.

51. Ewe] The Count of Eu.

Arthowre] Arthur, "whom the state of England had created earle of Richmonde" (Polydore Vergil, p. 13), brother to the Duke of Brittany. All the chronicles list the same five notables as captured.

53. John de Montaigu, Archbishop of Sens (Burgundy), not generally listed by the chronicles as captured. The Latin *Brut* (Lansdowne MS. 212) includes him amongst the slain (Kingsford, *Eng. Hist. Lit.*, p. 326).

55. Tr. He failed to achieve renown by a victory (cf. to win one's spurs). Cf. No. 29, l. 35. Kingsford, *Chronicles of London*, p. 305, comments: "the loss of the previous line makes this obscure. Mr. Wylie has suggested to me that it may be a reference to a wager, and cites how the Prothonotary at Mayence in 1407 bet his archbishop a pair of boots that nothing would ever make Pope Gregory XII resign. Cf. Wylie, *Henry IV*, iii.29."

57. flemynges] John, Duke of Burgundy and Flanders, refused to fight against the English and restricted his son from joining the French armies. However, many of his followers went secretly to the aid of the French; and his two brothers (the Duke of Brabant and the Count of Nevers) were among the slain.

28. THE SIEGE OF CALAIS, 1436

Index, No. 1497. Previously printed from this MS. by Klinefelter, *PMLA*, lxvii.890-94; from the Cotton MS. by Wright, *Pol. Poems*, ii.151-56; and in *Rel. Ant.*, ii.21-24. For Rome MS. see Robbins, *Neophilologus*, xxxix.131-36.

The Rome MS. is generally a better text than the Cotton. It corrects the false rhymes in ll. 51 (dred - lowte) and 164 (towne - all); avoids the difficulty of a hound playing "heigh-go-bye" by using the name "goby" (found elsewhere); and identifies the relocation of Philip's camp correctly from west to east. Cotton is occasionally superior: "boylyng cawdrens" in place of "boilled caudrons"; omission of "that" (l. 122), substitution of "and" for "of" (l. 51), both improving the grammatical construction; and correct word order in l. 90.

Nos. 28-30 are examples of the popular feelings against Philip the Good, Duke of Burgundy (1419-1467) and his subjects in the Netherlands, the Flemings. All three treat the same incident, but vary in their stress and details. For several years the English had been losing hold of their French possessions, but at the tri-power Conference of Arras in July, 1435, with unrealistic obstinacy, they refused to make any compromise with Charles VII, King of France.

The result was to encourage Philip of Burgundy to forsake his sixteen-year-old friendship with England and to make an alliance with his cousin Charles, who agreed to recognize his conquests won with the help of the English. This defection aroused much indignation in London, manifested in riots against the Flemish merchants and in violent denunciations in Parliament. By new taxes and loans, the English raised an army to invade the continent, and as an immediate reprisal tried to instigate Philip's Flemish cities to revolt. Philip replied by exploiting the commercial antagonisms of Holland against England and won support for an attack on Calais, essential to England as the wool staple and as a key town in the control of the English Channel. The siege was begun on July 9. Even before the arrival of the English army under Gloucester on August 2, however, Burgundy's attacks failed, his army melted away, and the siege was abandoned on July 25. Gloucester made a brief harry into Flanders, and returned laden with loot.

The siege is described in the *Brut*, EETS 136.572-84; *English Chronicle*, p. 55; *Short Eng. Chronicle*, pp. 81-85; *Gregory's Chronicle*, pp. 178-79; *Chronicles of London*, pp. 139-42; Hall, pp. 181-84; Stow, p. 376; Monstrelet, chaps. cciii-ccv.

Cotton variants: 2. Tres leuys & herbis grene; 3. Wyth many sonder colowris; 6. Of lusty colowris & of swete odowris; 7. And fruyte on tre both; 11. In armes so ther be no treson Inn; 19. A c l m*l* and mo; 20. That weryn all to ryd; 28. ber adown; 35. Larg & long & gret of sy3th; 43. ix m*l* cokkes; 44. And viii m*l* cressetes to bren li3th; 51. Off no thyng hav we no dred; 65. Yff any withowt wer so hardy; 67. ser Iohn ashton; 77. in harnes; 79. The burges & men; 105. To þe howsis; 107. When the stone in the stone did fly; 109. lay them; 113. west end; 122. Vppon his hoby swyftly ran; 127. that did hyeghe go by; 133. hit Byfell vpon a; 146. castell; 159. To folow after; 174. mery yngland; 175. Whils þat þis world wyll stand. The Cotton MS. adds a four-line tag:

> Lytelle wote þe fool
> Who my3th ches
> What harm yt wer
> Good caleys to lese Amen

These four lines are paraphrased in the *Libelle of Englyshe Polycye*, ll. 826-27: "For lytelle wenythe the fole, who so myght chese, / What harme it were gode Caleise for to lese."

13. "And þe Flemmynges were þen so proude and hawteyn þat they sette by none Englisshe men, but hem hade in gret despite" (*EETS* 136.572).

25. "Thei were so glad and fayn þat they shuld lay seege to Caleis, and wynne the wulles of þe staple of Caleis, and to departe it amonges hem" (*EETS* 136.572).

37. gonnes] The *Brut* (*EETS* 136.376) describes "ordynaunce" as "Gunne3, Engyne3, Tripgettis."

39. pavis] A large shield to protect both the knight and attendant who carried it, so called from its origin in Pavia.

43. Cf. *Brut*: "Flemmynges, þe nombre of an CL M*l*, and xij M*l* cartes; and ich cart had his cokke to crawe amonges the host" (*EETS* 136.576). And so Monstrelet, chap. ccv.

44. cressettes] An iron container holding pitched rope or wood to be burnt for light, usually mounted on top of a pole.

49. "And sone afterward, Edmond, Erle of Morteyn, and the Lord Camys [l. 61], Sir William of Asshton, knyghte [l. 67], And Sir Geffrey Werburton, knyghte [l. 68] ... were contirmaundit be þe Kyng ... to go thider, and strenghe þe toun till rescous myght be had" (*EETS* 136.574). Similarly Latin *Brut* (Kingsford, *Eng. Hist. Lit.*, p. 321), and elsewhere.

55. "And sone aftir, be counselle and manhood of ser Johan

Radclyffe, that tyme lieutenaunt of Caleys, the said sege was broke"
(*English Chronicle*, p. 55). He was appointed in 1436 by Duke
Humphrey of Gloucester, Captain of Calais; he was "a wurshipfull
knyȝt, and was wel-belouet amonges þe sawdiours there; for he kept
and helde A gud and open housold to who þat wolde come, and
welcome" (*EETS* 136.573).

60. Rel. pro. omitted.

61. Boleyn yate] "iij stronge bullwerkes of erthe and cley, one
att þe corner of þe Castell with-out þe toun, anoþer att Bulleyn gate,
and anoþer att þe postern be þe Princes Inne; And att Mylke gate
[l. 67] was a faire bulwerk made of breke, þat Richard Woodevile
had do make or he was discharget of his leotenauntshippe" (*EETS*
136.573).

"Roger, lord Camoys, a somewhat obscure person not known to the
peerages. He was perhaps a younger son of Thomas, the fifth lord,
who died in 1420, from whose death the title was in abeyance till
1839 ... His name occurs only in our [London] Chronicle and in
Hall, with reference to the siege of Calais" (Kingsford, *Chronicles
of London,* p. 310).

67. Sir *John* Assheton served with a lance and nine archers at
Agincourt; cf. Joseph Hunter, *Agincourt* (London, 1850), pp. 32-33.

70. "iiij Englissh trumpettes blewe vp on hye vppon Milkgate
toure, as they were wont to do euery day at þe releuyng of the
wach duryng the seege" (*EETS* 136.581).

79. maire] Robert Clidrowe (*Brut, EETS* 136.573).

92. scaffolde] generally an engine used for assaulting walls; here
apparently a catapult for counterattack.

94. boilled] C. boylyng.

106. Barbara] "but al þeire gunshot did neuer harm, thanket be
God and þe Holy Virgyn Saint Barbara" (*EETS* 136.578). Klinefelter: "The legend that St. Barbara's father was struck by lightning
when he himself assisted in her martyrdom, caused her to be regarded
as the patron saint in time of thunder storms and fire, and by
analogy, as the protector of artillery-men."

111. songe] song (transferred usage).

113. est ende] "the Duyke lay not þere but ij days, but þat he
remeved from thens ... to þe Est ende of þe toun, And þere he
pichet his tentes; for he wold ly no lenger att þe west ende of
þe toun, for cause a gune shotte thrugh his tent" (*EETS* 136.578).

114. Hym thoght] At this date, could mean either it seemed to
him or simply he thought.

121. euer among] every now and then.

127. goby] Cf. No. 29, ll. 33-35.

133. thursday] "and þe host with-in þe tentes fled out at þe
est side, and wend al þe worlde had comyn on hem: And þis was

on a Thursday; wherfore þe Flemmynges it clepit the 'Quade Thurs-
dagh' " (*EETS* 136.580).

135. Saint Peters] The plain of St. Pierre is "a myle nere out
of þe toun" (*EETS* 136.578).

141. hauen] Cf. No. 29, l. 28.

146. bastyle] Cr. No. 30, l. 85.

161. Cf. *Libelle of Englyshe Polycye*, ll. 294-96.

> For fere they turned bake and hyede faste,
> Milorde of Gloucestre made hem so agaste
> Wyth his commynge . . .

29. MOCKERY OF THE FLEMINGS, 1436

Index, No. 4034. Previously printed by Williams, *Archaeologia,*
xxxiii.130-32; by Brie, *EETS* 136.582-84; and by James and Jenkins,
Cat., p. 16. The division into stanzas follows the rubrication of
the MS. The poem roughly paraphrases and elaborates a preceding
prose account of the behavior of the besiegers around Calais. Another song against the Duke of Burgundy and the Flemings (*Index,*
No. 2657) is printed by Brie, *EETS* 136.600-601; and by MacCracken,
EETS 192.600-601. For historical note see No. 28.

1. in your flouris] in your greatest prosperity.

2. weth] Brie emends welth.

6. come] historical present.

8. lyons of Cotteswold] i.e., sheep. C. L. Kingsford, *Eng. Hist.
in Contemporary Poetry* (London, 1933), p. 22, notes: "As the
Cotswolds were a great wool-growing district, there were probably
many at Calais who hailed from thence."

9. hounsculles] ? some form of armor. Other difficulties include
messis (l. 11), meskins (l. 11), quadenramp (l. 66).

10. goden] suitable (weak form).
    daghes] daggers; cf. *dag,* to stab.

14. of þe newe gyse] of the latest fashion.

18. "The Erle þen, with his pepill, drove ouer þe havon of
Gravenyng thaire pray of bestes, att lowe water, in spite of al þe
Flemmynges, and brought hem with al thaire prisoners to Caleis,
and lost neuer a man" (*EETS* 136.575).

23. by þe pollis] by counting of heads.

27. att full see] at high tide.

28. The *Brut* gives a detailed account of the blockade of the
harbor so that Gloucester's relief ships could not land: "And when
þai had leyn þer xiiij daies, þe Duyke lete ordeyn xx shippis out
of Flaundres, wherof vj old shippes were lade with hard ston, chalke,
and brekes masont in hem with morter, to droune hem in þe haven

of Caleis, þat no shippis shuld come þer-in. And when it was full
see, about noone, þey bulgit hem, some in þe haven-mouthe, and
some be-sides the haven, to no purpos; for þei durst not tary, nor
þei had no grete leysere to droun hem, for fere of gun-shotte;
And so þei went þeire way ageyn; and on þe next day after, at
lawe water, wel was hym of þe toun þat myght bring an Ax to
breke þe shippis; and so þai did, al to peces, and broughte hem into toune, and refresshid wele þe pouer pepil; and al þe brekstones
were gyven to Saynt Mary Chirch; and so were þai al cariet in-to
toun" (*EETS* 136.579). See also Waurin, iv.176-78.

    35. Brugges] Bruges.
        wan youre shon] achieved renown. Cf. No. 27, l. 55.
    41. "They of Gaunt [Ghent] ... wend the Duk of Gloucester
had londid with his nauey þat sam nyght; wherfore þe Duk & they
of Gaunt brake vp þeire tentes sodeynly & priuely, & went ouer
Grauenyng watir þat same nyght" (*EETS* 136.581).
    44. go þat go myght] ? only he goes who was able to go.
    47. pison] armor covering upper part of body; *paunce* armor
covering lower body.
    60. banshid men] outlaws, bandits.

30. SCORN OF THE DUKE OF BURGUNDY, 1436

Index, No. 3682. Previously printed by Robbins, *Neophilologus*,
xxxix.138-40, with full discussion. Followed in the MS. immediately
by No. 28. Occurs also in Sloane MS. 252, 44 lines only, printed
by Wright, *Pol. Poems*, ii.148-49. Collation: 3. sower and distrouber;
10. Howe henry the *vth*; 14. Engelonde & of france; 16. the whiche
þou may wite alle thi myschance; 19. þat callede him self kyng;
20. withouten ground reson; 21. Motreux; 22. dedist; 24. thi falsnes;
31. Now art þou fals; 32. the which; 33. that þou yonge kyng.

    The poem divides into two sections: (1) St. 1, 9-14 refer to the
Siege of Calais, and cover the same ground as Nos. 28 and 29.
(2) St. 2-8 refer to the earlier history of Philip from 1419 to
1435, so as to emphasize his perfidy in going against the English.
After the assassination of his father, John, in 1419 (See No. 14,
l. 85; No. 15), Philip immediately came to terms with the English
(ll. 22-23), ratifying the agreement at Troyes (ll. 25-32), and
together with the English successfully fought the Armagnacs, the
adherents of the Orleans party, grouped around the Dauphin, later
Charles VII (ll. 9-16). In the years following, Philip more or less
adhered to the alliance (ll. 41-48), but ultimately in 1435 signed
a truce with Charles VII at Arras (ll. 57-64).
    The four poems on the Siege of Calais and the retreat of the

Duke of Burgundy have many resemblances among themselves and to the chronicles. For detailed examination see *Neophilologus,* xxxix.142-46. Klinefelter, *PMLA,* lxvii,.889, implies that Mac-Cracken accepts both No. 30 and *Index,* No. 2657 as Lydgate's (see also *EETS* cvii, p. xvii; *Anglia,* xxxii.283). For other poems of personal abuse see Nos. 9, 10, 12, 75, 76, and 77.

6. doo mustre] show your mettle.

36. souffisant warant] satisfactory assurance (a legal term).

43. Probably the siege of Crevant in 1423, when combined English and Burgundian forces defeated the Dauphin. See St. Remy, ii.76-79.

62. provow] a nonce-word, apparently from *pro* (in favor of) and *vow* (acknowledge). Not in *O.E.D.*

70. grete maintenance] arrogant behavior.

85. bastyle] "The seconde deuise was also accomplished, whiche was a strong bastell, set on a litle mountayne, furnished with iiij C. men and muche artilarie, whiche fortresse did let thenglishemen to issue out, when they would, to their greate displeasure and disturbaunce" (Hall, p. 183). Cf. also Waurin, iv.175-80.

96. brak sege] raised siege.

99. "And whan they were landyd att Caleys, the lordis helde ther a counsell ffryday and Satterday and Sonday; and on the Monday thei toke ther journay in to fflaundrys ward, and did moche harme in the contrey of flaunderis ffor thei brent þe tovne of popering, and many moo good tovnys and stately villagis" (*Chronicles of London,* p. 142).

105. Conteyne thiself] behave like a man.

31. THE DEATH OF ARCHBISHOP SCROPE

Index, No. 3308. Previously printed by Furnivall, *EETS* 24.128; by Greene, *Early Eng. Carols,* pp. 288-89; and (st. 1 only) by James, *Cat.,* ii.148.

The Earl of Northumberland and his son Henry (Hotspur) Percy, with other lords desirous of changing the dynasty established by Henry IV in favor of the Earl of March, were defeated at the Battle of Shrewsbury in 1403. Hotspur was killed in battle, but Northumberland was pardoned. Two years later he fomented another rising, this time openly supported by Richard Scrope, Archbishop of York, who gave the affair an aura of righteousness. Scrope issued a list of "articles" or grievances against Henry, largely centering on taxation and the impoverishment of the lords and clergy. The *English Chronicle* (pp. 31-32) tells how he "exhortid and stirid the peple to be assistent and helpyng to the correccioun and amendement of the myschiefs and mysgouernaunceȝ of the reme, hauyng in consideracioun the grete pouerte of the marchauntis in whom was wont to be the substaunce of the richeȝ of alle the land: and also the grete reisynges of taxeȝ, tallages and custumeȝ vnder colour of borowyng: and also, that due paiement be maad for the kingeȝ vitailleȝ: and that the clergie and the comune peple were not vexid ne charged with importable chargis of taxis and talagis as thay hadde longe tyme be: and that the heiris of noble men and of lordis of the lond myȝte be restorid to their enheritaunce hoolli, euery man aftir his degre and birthe: and also that suche covetous men as were of the kyngis counsel, that took away and turned to thair owen vse suche godis as were ordeyned to the comune help of the lond, and make thaym self riche withalle, be remeued and put away fro the king. Thise articles and meney othir the arche-bisshoppe made be writen in English, and were set on the yatis of the cite, and sent to curatis of the tovneȝ aboute, for to be prechid openli." Scrope was also fearful that the King might act on the suggestion of Parliament (held at Coventry, October 6 to Novem-ber 14, 1404) to expropriate church revenues. In the fighting, once again the loyalist forces under the Earl of Westmorland were vic-torious. Scrope and the Earl of Nottingham were induced to parley and dismiss their armies; thereupon Westmorland seized them. Against the opposition of the Archbishop of Canterbury and the Chief Justice, Henry packed a court to secure Scrope's death penalty and executed the cleric outside York. This was the first time a lay court had so sentenced a prelate.

3. Scrope was by many regarded as a martyr. "And anon aftir, as it was said, the king was smyte withe a lepir: for the whiche arche-bisshoppe, Almyghti God sone aftirwarde wroughte meny grete miracles" (*English Chronicle*, p. 33). And so *Ypodigma Neustriae*, p. 415. Wright, *Pol. Poems*, ii.114-18, prints a Latin poem ex-pressing the grief of the clergy for his death. Cf. No. 93, l. 26.

7. with full gode wyll] with quite cheerful acquiescence.

9. The executioner was Thomas Alman of Poppleton, who was serving a sentence in a York prison.

14. "And whenne the archebisshoppe sholde die, he saide, 'Lo! I shalle die for the laweȝ and good rewle of Engelond.' And thanne he saide vnto thayme that sholde die with him, 'Lat vs suffre deth mekely, for we shul this nyghte, be Goddis grace, be in paradis.' Thanne saide tharchebisshoppe to him that sholde smyte of his hed, 'For His loue that suffrid v woundes for alle mankynde, yeue me v strokis, and I foryeve the my dethe.' And so he dede: and thus thay deide" (*English Chronicle*, p. 33). So Gascoigne, p. 225.

32. THE AGINCOURT CAROL, 1415

Index, No. 2716. Previously printed by Stafford Smith, *Coll. Eng. Songs*, p. 9; by Nicolas, *Battle of Agincourt* (1833); by Rimbault, *Anc. Vocal Music*, No. 19; by Stainer, *Early Bodl. Music*, ii.128-29; by Wooldridge, *Oxf. Hist. Music* (1932), ii.7-9; by Sidgwick, *Ballads and Poems*, p. 45; and by Greene, *Early Eng. Carols*, p. 289. Percy, *Reliques*, prints a transcript of the Bodl. MS. from Pepys 2025 (a single leaf); followed by Burney, *Hist. Music* (1782), iii.384. Occurs also in Trinity Coll. Camb. MS. 1230 (lacks st. 3); printed by Maitland, *Carols*, p. 15; by Stevens, *Mus. Brit.*, iv.6; and (with Bodl.) by Padelford, *Anglia*, xxxvi.101-2. Collation: 13. Than went hym forth owr Kyng comely; 17. Ther lordys eerlys and barounn; 21. Almythy God he kepe our kyng; 23. and yeue hem grace with-outyn endyng; 24. þan may we calle & sauely syng. The differences, according to Padelford (p. 84), "are just such as would be expected from oral transmission."

The battle is discussed in notes to No. 27.

The celebrations on Henry's return to London were among the most sumptuous the city had ever seen. Nearly all the chronicles describe his entry and the pageants at some length: Adae de Usk, 1904, pp. 127-29; St. Albans, p. 97; Waurin, ii.223-24; Stow, pp. 350-51. The best account is in the *Brut* (*EETS* 136.558):

"And so rode he forth to London on Saint Clement day, where-as he was riolly receyuet with precession, And song 'Aue Anglorum flos, mundi miles Christi!' And when he come to London Brigge, where-as were ij turrettes on þe draw-bridge, and a gret Geaunt, and on þe turrettes stondyng a lyon and a Antelope, with many angeles syngyng 'Benedictus qui venit in nomine Domini!' And so rode he forth in-to London; and þe stretes were rially hanget with rich clothes; And in Cornhyll was made a rioll toure, full of patriarches syngyng 'Cantate Domino canticum nouum! laus laus eius, in ecclesia sanctorum!' and kest doun quyk briddes, which flawe thikke about þe Kyng. And when he come into Chepe, þe Condites ranne wyne. And on þe gret condit were xij Apposteles, syngyng 'Benedic, Anima mea, Domino!' and xij kynges knelyng, castyng doune oblays, and welcomet hym home. And þe cros in Chepe was riolly arrayet like a Castell, with toures pight full of baners, and þer-in Angeles syngyng 'Nowell, nowell!' gyvyng besandes of gold to þe kyng. And so rode he forth to Paules, where-as mette hym xiiij bisshopes; and al þe belles ronge agaynes hym; and þere he alight and went to þe hye awter. And there þei song 'Te Deum laudamus.' And from thens he rode forth to his palice at Westmynster; And after, he rode about in the land on pilgremage, and ordeynt be holy Chirch þat Saint George day shuld be kept hye and holy; and so was it neuer before þat day."

The priest's diary printed by Nicolas describes the situation into which some carol similar to this might have fitted: "And in a contiguous house behind the tower, were innumerable boys, representing the angelic host, arrayed in white, and with countenances shining with gold, and glittering wings, and virgin locks, set with precious sprigs of laurel, who at the King's approach, sang with melodious voices, and with organs, this English anthem" (p. 294). Again, similarly: "and that the tower of the conduit in the going out of Cheap towards Saint Paul's in its inscription might seem to conform with the preceding praises of the inscriptions to the honor and glory of God, not of men, it bore to the view of the passengers, this conclusion of praise, Deo Gracias" (p. 299). Unfortunately, neither this nor any of the other chronicles records the English verses.

The music (in Bodl.) is for two solo voices and three-part chorus. Wooldridge (ii.337): "probably due, in the first place, to popular minstrels, while a more skilled hand has added additional parts." Greene (p. 439): "probably the work of a cleric rather than a minstrel." This carol is historical rather than topical (cf. l. 19); but it is clearly processional. Cf. Miller, *Renaissance News*, iii.4.

bur. Deo gracias] Henry had gone on record as opposing any praises made in honor of his victory: "But that victorious and goodly Kinge suffered not those honnours to be referred vnto him, but to the laude and honnour of God" (*First Eng. Life Henry V*, p. 65).

5. He sette a sege] He lay siege (before Harfleur).

15. "Then the King of England being assured of the victorie, gaue the greatest laud and prayse to God that might be" (Stow, p. 350).

23. After Henry's exhortation on the battlefield, the troops, much encouraged, "gecterent ung hault cry en disant: 'Sire! Dieu vous doinst bonne vye et victore de vos annemis!'" (Waurin, ii.209). Similarly St. Remy, i.251.

33. THE ROSE ON BRANCH, 1415

Index, No. 3457. Previously printed by Furnivall, *Notes & Queries*, Fifth Series, xii.124; and by Greene, *Early Eng. Carols*, p. 290.

The MS. is a long collection of romances and religious stories with many shorter religious and secular items, written c. 1440 by Robert Thornton, the scribe of the similar "Thornton MS." in Lincoln Cathedral. It contains a copy of Lydgate's "Kings of England"

(No. 1). The carol is probably incomplete, for the two following pages of the MS. are missing.

For historical notes see Nos. 27 and 32.

bur. Rose of Ryse] rose on branch, a commonplace; cf. *Index,* No. 1394, l. 11: ase rose þat red is on rys; Chaucer, *Rom. Rose,* 1015; etc.

1. Greene notes (p. 439) the "strong influence from the symbolism and poetic convention of the rose as emblem of the Virgin." Cf. *Index,* Nos. 534 (rede rose of Ierico), 1032 (fairest floure), 1046 (rose on ryse most holsum of odoure); 1914; 2461 (ros Intact; blissit ros); 2610; 3536; 3603 ("þis flour is fayre & fresche of heue / Hit fadis neuer bot euer is new"); 3638; 3779; etc. For political rose symbolism see Nos. 35, 36, and 90; also the "Rose of England" (Hales and Furnivall, iii.189-94; Pollard, *Reign of Henry VII,* i.12-17):

> Our King, he is the rose soe redd,
> > that now does fflourish ffresh and gay,
> Confound his ffoes, Lord, wee beseche,
> > & loue his grace both night & day.

9. Cf. *Index,* No. 969:

> And the fairest flower in all French land
> To the rose of England I will give thee.

and *Index,* No. 927: "Her flauour excedith the fflowr-de-lyce."

16. Cf. *Index,* No. 1046: "Heyl! floure of vertu, whos feyrenesse may not fade." Also cf. No. 41, l. 24.

34. THE LILY WHITE ROSE, 1486

Index, No. 1450. Previously printed by Flügel, *Neuengl. Lesebuch,* pp. 159-60; by Bayne, *Notes & Queries,* Eighth Series, xii.385; by Furnivall, *Ballad Soc.,* vii. clix; in *Songs and Madrigals* (Plainsong & Med. Music Soc.), pp. 15-18; and by Greene, *Early Eng. Carols,* p. 294.

Nos. 34 and 35 are from the same MS., the well-known Tudor songbook, the "Fairfax MS." While some of its poems are copies of earlier texts (some by Lydgate), the majority are unique, and in their sophisticated style indicative of the very end of the fifteenth century. Consequently, both No. 34 and No. 35 seem to be reflective and reminiscent of an earlier struggle, rather than compositions of the period of bitter contest. The almost casual concern over the Yorkists, with the *chanson d'aventure* opening, the *aube* burden, and the artificial folksong series of flower names, might even suggest that a parallel poem of praise of the Lancastrians would not be out of place in the MS.

There is insufficient evidence to support the suggestion in *Songs and Madrigals* (p. xvi, fn.) that it "is the complement of the other [No. 35], and probably appeared early in 1461, when Edward IV was proclaimed King in London, though perhaps the allusion to the flower-de-luce might indicate the year 1471, when the King of France was helping the Lancastrian party." Greene's nomenclature of a "partisan" carol is similarly unsupported. It is more probable that both songs were composed after 1486, in which year the Lancastrian Henry VII married Elizabeth of York, the "comly quene" of l. 2, eldest daughter of Edward IV. (Cf. "As I walked of late by one wood side" in Percy, *Reliques* [1765], ii.259-75; Hales and Furnivall, ii.183-89). If the poem refers to an earlier period, then the queen would be Elizabeth Woodville, Queen of Edward IV, in 1464 (cf. Furnivall, p. clix).

bur. Frequently noted in other poems, apparently as a tune; cf. Douglas, *Aeneis*, xiii, Pro. 182:

> Tharto, thir byrdis singis in the schawis,
> As menstralis playing, The joly day now dawis.

also Dunbar, "Merchantis of Edinburgh," ll. 29-30:

> ȝour commone menstrallis hes no tone
> Bot Now the day dawis and Into Joun.

35. THE ROSES ENTWINED, 1486

Index, No. 1327. Previously printed by Stafford-Smith, *Coll. Eng. Songs*, No. 4; by Rimbault, *Anc. Vocal Music*; by Fehr, *Archiv*, cvi.58; in *Songs and Madrigals* (Plainsong & Med. Music Soc.), pp. 27-30; by Chambers and Sidgwick, *Early Eng. Lyr.*, p. 72; and by Greene, *Early Eng. Carols*, p. 295.

The coupling of "the rose both red & white" may perhaps be regarded as cautious fence-sitting, characteristic of the Londoners throughout the whole period of fighting, at a time when war was still raging. Such is the interpretation in *Songs and Madrigals*, that the poem was put out in 1460 as a feeler to test public opinion: "From the careful suppression of the name of the flower it may be placed in the first half of the year, before the Yorkist party had come into power by the Battle of Northampton" (p. xvi, fn.). Greene titles it "The Tudor Rose" but does not further identify it. Chambers and Sidgwick (who classify it as an amorous song) are on better ground regarding it as post civil-war (p. 342). The roses would then be Henry VII of Lancaster and Elizabeth of York, and the "prince" would be Arthur, born in 1486.

The music for this three-part song has the signature "Syr Thomas Phelyppis," who is not known otherwise as a composer. The in-

volved part-singing is a far cry from the popular arrangements of
the earlier carols, and is another indication of a late date of composition about 1500.

The list of plants includes herbs, and at least one (rosemary) to
which magical properties were ascribed. *The Oxf. Dict. Nursery
Rhymes* comments on similar lists in folk songs: "It is quite possible that the refrains are the survival of an incantation." (p. 111).

bur. In on] in harmony.

21. thyn hart vnbrace] show your feelings without restraint.

31. Cf. epitaphs on Queen Elizabeth in Balliol Coll. Oxf. MS.
354 (*EETS* ci.99-100, l. 2): Here lith the white rose in the rede
sete. Also early sixteenth-century couplet on cover of St. John's
Coll. Oxf. MS. 57, a London chronicle:

> The red rose and the wythe
> Be knyght to geder w*t* grett delyghte
> *(Six Town Chronicles, p. 60).*

36. FOR VICTORY IN FRANCE, 1492

Not listed in *Index;* delete reference under No. 2526 (Skelton's
praise of Henry VII). Previously printed by Flügel, *Neuengl. Lesebuch,* pp. 160-61; and by Robbins, *Neuphil. Mitteilungen,* lv.289-93,
with a complete discussion.

The text is added on a flyleaf in a late fifteenth- or early sixteenth-
century hand to a collection of heraldic matters (ff. 229-48), bound
up with Bernard André's official history of Henry VII (ff. 126-228).
It is obviously contaminated. The rhyme scheme of the first st. is
aaba. This is also the rhyme scheme of the third st., although rede
rhymes imperfectly with wyde and gyd. The fourth st. may have
had the same rhyme scheme originally; if so, some scribe has written
be instead of spryng (cf. the introductory couplet). The last st.
has *aaaa;* this is best taken as a modification of *aaba.* In the second
st., schote is presumably for its variant schete, and knowe may have
replaced an original mete. If this reading is correct, the rhyme
scheme is *abaa,* a modification of *aaba.* For similar songs for
Henry VIII in France, see "England be glad pluk vp thy lusty hart"
and "Pray we to god that all may gyde" from B. M. MS. Addit.
31922 (Flügel, *Neuengl. Lesebuch,* p. 161).

The invasion of France by Henry VII in October, 1492, was a
relatively minor affair, with the capture of Sluys (a haunt of pirates
preying on English shipping) the only practical result. The osten-
tatious preparation over three years was designed as proof to his
subjects that their taxes were showing results, and also as a device
for jockeying for power in the tangled international alliances between

Henry and King Maximilian of the Romans, Charles VIII of France, and Anne of Brittany. The French King was glad to come to terms with Henry, who thereby secured at the Treaty of Etaples (December, 1492) peace (with a cash indemnity) and honor.

4. roys owr] Flügel reads soydour.

37. GOD SPEED THE PLOUGH

Index, No. 3434. Previously printed by Stainer, *Early Bodl. Music,* ii.132-33; by Padelford, *Anglia,* xxxvi.104; by Chambers and Sidgwick, *Early Eng. Lyrics,* pp. 241-42; and by Stevens, *Mus. Brit.,* iv.112-13.

"The form of this song is doubtful, and it is not included among the carols collected by Greene. But the balance of evidence seems to be in favour of its interpretation as a carol ... It is possible, of course, to interpret the piece as a strophic song with chorus sections, each verse being of six lines, but as each *three* lines is marked in the MS with the symbol conventionally reserved to show the start of each verse, it is a reasonable deduction that, despite the rhyme-scheme, [ll. 1-3 are] in fact a burden" (Stevens, p. 124).

Index, No. 363 (twelve eight-line stanzas), quite distinct, has a similar refrain, "I praye to God, spede wele the plough." Chambers and Sidgwick (p. 375) note: "In *Henslowe's Diary* (ed. Greg, i.16) it is recorded that a play called 'god spead the plowe' was acted 27 December, 1593, and 5 January, 1593-94. On 1 March, 1601, John Harrison entered 'A booke called God spede the ploughe' on the *Stationers' Register* (Arber, iii.180)."

2. in honde] for our use.

5. A more sober picture is given by No. 2 and No 51, ll. 57-60.

10. gore] Difficult; the context suggests gray.

38. SUMMER SUNDAY: A LAMENT FOR EDWARD II, 1327

Index, No. 3838. Previously printed in *Rel. Ant.,* ii.7-9; and by Brown, *St. in Eng. Philol. in honor of Frederick Klaeber* (Minneapolis 1929), pp. 362-74. The main contents of the MS. are a *South English Legendary* and *King Horn,* followed by three additional lives of saints and "Somer Soneday."

Madden in *Rel. Ant.* identified the King as Richard II. Some modern scholars support Madden, dating the poem c. 1400. Brown, however, chose to interpret him as Edward II on the following grounds: (1) the MS. is of the first half of the fourteenth century; (2) many poetic words have a distinctly fourteenth-century usage,

— e.g., warp 4, griþele 19, wifman 34, weue 34, roe 43, radely 52, lyȝth-heued 59, kyþed 96, luþe 124, etc.; (3) the dialect is West-Midland (risinde 2 and lyuynde 105 are regarded as scribal introductions), possibly Cheshire or Shropshire. *Hist. Anglicana* (i.83) notes the "cantilenas pro eo lugubres lingua patria componentes" in Wales, and Brown observes "it would not be strange if others were composed in English by those living near the Welsh border ... In Wales and the counties along the border the loyal attachment to the ill-fated Edward continued even after his deposition" (p. 370). Oakden also discusses the dialect (i.116-17), commenting further that it is "a valuable link between [the short popular satires, Nos. 5-7] and the poems of the Alliterative Revival" (ii.13).

Queen Isabella and Roger Mortimer returned from Paris to Harwich in September, 1326, and were speedily joined by the forces of numerous earls and bishops. Shortly, London joined the insurgents and sacked the houses of the favorites of Edward II. The King fled westwards, but was captured in November and imprisoned at Kenilworth Castle. In January of 1327, the Parliament acclaimed his young son as Edward III, justifying its action by the charge that Edward II had broken his coronation oath. Edward II was persuaded to resign, and removed from Kenilworth to Corfe, to Bristol, and finally to Berkeley Castle, where he died on September 21, 1327, presumably murdered (cf. *Chronicles of Edw. I & Edw. II*, ii.xci-ciii; No. 71, l. 7). After his death, public opinion began to veer in his favor; and, as this poem suggests, the memory of his misdeeds receded, and he became an object of sympathy. During his imprisonment, Edward composed an Anglo-Norman poem (printed by Paul Struder, *MLR*, xvi.34-46), in which he laments the fate of Fortune which has made him "rois abatu."

10. questede] made a warning bark at the sight of game.

19. game & glade] a cliché: fun and frolic.

42. ȝe] fem. pro. sing; cf. *William of Palerne*, l. 141.

43. roe] cf. L. *rota,* wheel.

57. gloud] Brown sees in this pret., and in pl. kyngus, l. 122, slight evidence of Shropshire dialect.

63. whelwryȝth] one who turns a wheel, applied to Fortune. Cf. *Aunturs of Arthur,* l. 271: "False fortune in fyghte, that wondirfulle whele wryghte."

67. be-gyngge] ? by-going.

69. in þe wey] in its course.

80. kyngene] weak form; cf. frendene, l. 84.

91. Hey herte] great courage.

92. at his likyng] according to his wish, pleasure.

103. Tr. fall prostrate to me in homage.

105. iliche] like; cf. No. 48, l. 4.

110. hor-howne] horehound; its stem and leaves are covered with a white down.

112. Cf. *Morte Arthur*, 3296: "His dyademe was droppede downe dubbyd with stonys." Lady Fortune is described elsewhere: in *Index*, No. 3408; her wheel in *Index*, Nos. 230, 3680, *78.

121. Note the inverting of the normal stanza pattern of eight long lines plus five short into an envelope of eight short plus five long lines, "ending with a slow, dirgelike movement that fits perfectly with the melancholy scene described in the closing lines" (Brown, p. 367).

127. Cf. *Index*, No. 230, ll. 61-62: Hir whele is hir strengthe as men may fele / þat turnes summe to woo & summe to wele.

133. drouping & dare] Cf. Minot, *Index*, No. 3801, l. 9: "In þis dale I droupe and dare."

39. THE DEATH OF EDWARD III, 1377

Index, No. 5. Previously printed by Furnivall, *EETS* 117.715-18; and by Sisam, *XIV C. Verse & Prose*, pp. 157-60; from the Simeon MS. (B. M. Addit. 22283) by Wright, *Pol. Poems*, i.215-18; and by Cook, *Reader*, pp. 425-27 (ll. 17-80). Collation: 5. cliper; 13. *omits* for, hert; 15. vr; 45. wonde; 47. her bote; 67. *omits* in 75. with heore goode; 85. wolde.

Wright observes (i, p. liv): "The Black Prince, the favourite of the people, had died in the preceding year, and the crown descended upon the head of a mere child, whose subsequent reign presented a sorrowful contrast to that which was expected from his father. People in general seem to have anticipated the worst, and in the deep grief with which the death of king Edward was received, they forgot the errors of his reign to remember only his greatness and his virtues. They saw themselves on the eve of a war with France, and all their great warriors were departed. These sentiments are strongly imprinted in the melancholy tone of an English song in this collection, which has for its burthen the transitory character of human greatness and the want of durability in popular gratitude."

5. Sisam glosses: "They (friends) are so slippery when put to the test, so eager to have (for themselves), and so unwilling to give up (to others)."

15. spede] cause of success.

17. Sum tyme] once upon a time. So l. 43.

18. tour] elevated structure on deck of ship.

23. bar þe flour] excelled all others. Cf. No. 41, l. 43.

31. In synder flit] removed asunder, separated.

43. counted nouȝt a bene Beo] did not give a bean for.

47. þe king] i.e., John of France, captured in 1356 at Poitiers,, and held in England until the Treaty of Bretigny in 1360. Cf. No. 11, l. 32.

bonde] (fig.) fetters; the bondage they imposed.

52. a þing of charge] a weighty or important matter.

53. barge] a smaller sea-going ship belonging to a larger vessel.

54. Tr. which cared not a cleat for all France.

59. helm] the bar which controlled the rudder.

61. him rod] sailed.

62. stok nor strete] The allit. phrase is stok oþer ston (lit. gods of wood and stone; cf. No. 64, l. 106); here strete is substituted for ston because of the rhyme. Tr. the prince feared nothing.

63. lete ful liht] make light of, give little attention to. Cf. No. 20, l. 5.

65. Henry of Lancaster (d. 1361).

76. boþ furst and last] throughout.

83. An ympe] Richard II.

90. sarri] Sisam comments: "Prob. O. Fr. serré, sarré in the developed meaning 'active,' 'vigorous,' seen in the adv. sarréement." Cf., however, schare, groin (*pubes*).

94. swete] The allit. phrase is swynke and swete; here the equivalent trauayle replaces the first component. Cf. l. 62.

99. vp wiþ] up with, lift him.

100. Tr. May everybody uphold him.

103. If we are disloyal and inactive, so that what is rarely seen is straightway forgotten (Sisam).

105. takeþ reward Of] give a thought to.

110. Is] Simeon MS. I. *Is* used as pl.

40. RICHARD II INTERRED IN WESTMINSTER, 1413

BY HOCCLEVE

Index, No. 4066. Previously printed by Furnivall, *EETS* lxi.47-49.

After Henry IV had assumed the throne in 1399, Richard was kept in various castle prisons. In January of 1400 an unsuccessful attempt was made to restore Richard, and soon after he died. To allay suspicion that Richard had been murdered, Henry had the body brought from Pontefract to London for public exposure, and then taken for burial to the Dominican convent at Langley. The *English Chronicle* gives a full account of his enforced resignation (pp. 15-21).

On his accession in 1413, Henry V sought to reconcile his father's enemies; he restored earldoms previously forfeited to the sons of Henry Hotspur and John Holland, and he allowed pilgrimages to the tomb of Archbishop Scrope (see No. 31). In addition, he had Richard's body removed from Langley for interment in Westminster Abbey (cf. *Gregory's Chronicle*, p. 107). The major crisis of the opening of the new reign concerned the Lollards (cf. No. 14, l. 57; No. 64). Hoccleve's poem covers the early events of 1413. He praises Henry's repressive policy against the Lollards and his reburial of Richard II in the Abbey. In the same year, Hoccleve wrote a virelai praising Henry V and his actions against heresy (*Index*, No. 3402), and an address to Oldcastle (*Index*, No. 3407). Furnivall (*EETS* lxi.xx) notes that Hoccleve's adulation paid off, for in September of the same year he got a confirmation of his annuity of £ 13-6-8.

6. Cf. *Index*, No. 3402, l. 32: "Be holy chirches Champioun eek ay."

25. Cf. *Index*, No. 3402, ll. 25-27: "Strengthe your modir in chacyng away / Th'errour which sones of iniquitee / Han sowe ageyn the feith."

27. purueye] to make provision (for their defense).

39. "And also in the said first yeare of his raigne he caused the corps of Kinge Richarde the second to be taken from the earth, whome Kinge Henrie the fourth had intimulate in the Friers of Langley, and w*th* due obseruance to be from thence transported into the Abby of Westminster; where after solemne obseques for him done, was buried in Saint Peters Church in the saide Abbey on the south side of Saint Edwards shrine, by Queene Ann his wife, as he himselfe by his life had desired. Aboute whose Sepulture he founded iiij*or* Tapers to bren perpetually" (*First Eng. Life Henry V,* p. 20).

41. *A RECOLLECTION OF HENRY V, 1429*
BY AUDELAY

Index, No. 822. Previously printed by Halliwell, *Percy Soc.* xiv, pp. viii-x; by Chambers and Sidgwick, *MLR*, v.488-90; by Whiting, *EETS* 184.193-95; and by Greene, *Early Eng. Carols*, pp. 290-91. For commentary, see above editions, and Wülfing, *Anglia*, xviii. 175.

This poem, written about the time of the coronation of the ten-year-old Henry VI in 1429, harks back to the glories of Henry V who had died in 1422. In fact, the whole piece is backward-looking, although Audelay pays conventional service to the hoped-for conquest of the Near East (l. 47).

bur. perles pryns] i.e., Christ.

1. *Gregory's Chronicle* (p. 149) speaks of Henry VI as a one-year-old baby in "his tendyr age."

6. Cf. *Index*, No. 2804 (Lydgate's roundel), l. 3: "Blode of seint Edward and seint Lowys."

11. hee] The Dauphin.

14. "And þanne þe Dolfynne of Fraunce answeryd to our ambassetours, & sayde yn þis manere: þat þe King was ouyr yonge & tendir of age to make eny warre ayens hym, and was not like yette to be no gede warryor to make such a conqueste þere vpon hym; & yn scorne & despite he sent to hym a tonne fulle of teneys-ballis, be-cause he schulde haue sumwhat to play with-alle, for hym & for his lordeȝ; '& þat become hym bettir þanne to mantayne eny warre,' he sayd" (*EETS* 136.374).

15. Whiting tr. With the old game of tennis he frightened them all. The original form of tennis was played in an enclosed court; cf. No. 51, l. 23.

17. Cf. No. 32, ll. 5-8.

24. Cf. No. 33, l. 16; and for details see No. 27, ll. 43, 51, etc.

34. in his present] as a gift.

38. An adaptation of a religious cliché.

43. Cf. No. 39, l. 23.

47. A persistent aim of the English kings, including both Henry IV and Henry V.

48. halud] Chambers & Sidgwick and Greene read habud; Whiting halud.

53. Rel. pro. omitted.

42. *THE DEATH OF EDWARD IV, 1483*

Index, No. 4062. Previously printed by Furnivall, *EETS* 15.xlvi-xlviii (rev. ed.). The MS. is a copy of *The Canterbury Tales*.

This adulation is obviously the work of a devoted Yorkist, and might be compared to No. 92.

3. In 1475, by the Treaty of Pecquigny, Edward contracted his eldest daughter Elizabeth to the Dauphin, and received an annual dowry and a large tribute. His allies, the Dukes of Brittany and Burgundy, giving him no assistance, this was probably the best bargain he could hope for; but England's prestige suffered at the calling off of the invasion. Cf. Commines, Bk. iv, chap. viii; Rymer, v.65-68.

5. In 1480, the truce between England and Scotland was broken, and the Duke of Gloucester marched north to the border. Berwick opened its gates, but the garrison resisted. A revolt of the Scots against their King enabled Gloucester to enter Edinburgh. But a further doublecrossing by the Duke of Albany, the brother of the Scottish King, resulted in another change, so that Edward received

an indemnity from Edinburgh and the control of Berwick. Cf. Polydore Vergil, pp. 168-70.

6. a] This letter is clearly written and is not a careless ampersand. For Edward's love of hunting see also No. 89, l. 23; and *Index*, No. 2192 (Skelton's Lament of Soul of Edward IV), l. 63: "Where be my coursors & my horsys so hy?"

11. Tr. unless you count him (Edward).

19. Hit was a wordle] it was a great thing.

25. rose] See No. 87, l. 6.

51. Cf. *Index*, No. 1505, "The lamentacioun of ladyes for the death of King Edward the iiijth."

43. GEOFFREY OF MONMOUTH'S PROPHECY

Index, No. 1552. Previously printed by Robbins, *English Studies*, xxxviii. 259-62. The text appears on two vellum leaves, neatly and elaborately written (with space left for rubrication of initial letters); the only other English is "A craft to take pykes" and "Contra choleram." Second half fifteenth century.

Although Geoffrey of Monmouth's "Book of Merlin" (Book VII of his *Historia Regum Britanniae*) was the pattern and literary source for most of the prophecies made in Britain for four centuries, only No. 43 is a direct translation. Its lines (esp. 21-44) come from the "Lynx" or "Great Prophecy," which was frequently copied and had also an independent existence: e.g., tr. by Elias Ashmole for William Lilly, *The Worlds Catastrophe* (London, 1647), discussed by Millican, *SP*, xxviii.193; fragments in Welsh MSS., e.g., Peniarth 58, p. 77; Peniarth 94, pp. 13-14 (Margaret E. Griffiths, *Early Vaticination* [Cardiff, 1937], p. 83); and in Poem XIV of the prophetic poems in *Four Ancient Books of Wales* (Griffiths, p. 120); in the Welsh *Brut Tysilio*, tr. Peter Roberts, *Chronicle of the Kings of Britain* (London, 1811), pp. 195-96, with L.; in *Vita Merlini*, ed. John Jay Parry (Urbana, 1925), pp. 85-87; in Book III, ch. 22 (ascribed to Gildas) of Fordun's *Chronica Gestis Scotorum* (Edinburgh 1871), i.107 (L.), and iv.99; in Ordericus Vitalis, *Eccles. Hist. of Eng. & Normandy*, Book XII, ch. 47, ed. Thomas Forester (London, 1856), iv.96-103. The following are the relevant Latin lines: "Egredietur ex eo linx penetrans omnia que ruine proprie gentes imminebit. Per illam enim utramque insulam amittet neustria. & pristina dignitate spoliabitur. Deinde reuertentur ciues in insulam. nam discidium alienigenarium orietur. Niueus quoque senex in niueo [sedens] equo. fluuium peririonis diuertet. & cum candida uirga molendinum super ipsum metabitur. Calualadrus uocabit conanum. & albaniam in societatem accipiet. Tunc est strages alienigenarum. tunc flumina sanguine manabunt. Tunc erumpent armorici montes. & diademate bruti coronabitur. Replebitur Kambria leticia. & robora cornubie uirescent. Nomine bruti uocabitur insula. & nuncupatio extraneorum peribet" (Acton Griscom, *The HRB of Geoffrey of Monmouth* [New York, 1929], p. 388; also ed. J. A. Giles [London, 1844], pp. 122-23; and tr. Giles, *O. E. Chronicles* [London, 1910], p. 199; and Sebastian Evans [London, 1903], p. 176).

The elusiveness of the symbols attracted explications. One such pr. by Hammer in *Speculum*, x.1-30, and xv.409 has an ecclesiastical trend; e.g.: *"tunc flumina,* id est populus, *sanguine,* id est peccato, *manabunt,* quia maiores et minores totius Angliae sunt in peccato periurii propter libertates iuratas quas non tenuerent" (xv.409).

The English were continually afraid of the combination of the Scots and Welsh. The threat was especially immediate in the time of Edward III (the lynx; taken at other times as King John, Henry II, and Henry III). *Index,* No. 1112 ("Six Kings to follow John") uses similar framework and symbols to those of Geoffrey. See Rupert Taylor, *Pol. Prophecy* (New York, 1911), pp. 48-51.

1. more] Cf. Robert of Gloucester, l. 2223, þe more brutaine.

12. Tr. He shall rue it (*hit* nom.; *hym* dat.).

13. astate] The sense of wordly fortune almost passes into "possessions" (*O.E.D.* 1563).

27. myle] mill. L. molendinum.

29. "The prophecy of the return of Cadwalader and Kynan, which has often been said to be the invention of Geoffrey, was in Welsh long before his time ... Some of the other Welsh versions of this prophecy are undoubtedly later than Geoffrey and influenced by him" (Parry, *Vita Merlini,* p. 19; examples from *VM,* pp. 86-87; others, pp. 130-31).

"Cadwaladr was the last of the Welsh princes who held the title of Gwledig or chief sovereign of Britain. His father Cadwallon succeeded in holding the crown of Britain for a year, but was killed by Oswald in 635. His son Cadwaladr had to face powerful enemies, and in his time the country was distracted by a plague. With Cadwaladr's death the struggle for the North practically came to an end, and was decided in favour of the Angles ... After his death Cadwaladr was made a Saint and soon a legend developed that he would again return to lead the Cymry to victory" (Griffiths, p. 112).

"At what time Cynan came to be associated with the legend and who Cynan was, it is almost impossible now to tell ... It is possible therefore that the original Cynan of the legend was some old hero of the North, who lived in the sixth century ... The association of Cadwaladr and Cynan with places in North and South Wales shows that the legend must have been widespread, and probably princes of both North and South were hailed as Cadwaladers or Cynans, the long looked for deliverers" (Griffiths, pp. 114, 115, 116-17).

Geoffrey of Monmouth confused Cadwaladr with Ceadwalla, King Wessex, who died in Rome, 688; and furthermore transformed Cynan into Conan of Brittany (cf. Griffiths, pp. 117-18).

33. falle] l. 21 suggests to die by violence (*O.E.D.* 23), but there is some suggestion of be overthrown (*O.E.D.* 21b, first used 1780).

41. Such prophecies kept alive the hopes of the Welsh for success in resisting the English.

42. quycke] The Eng. substitutes myght for *robora* (oaks) *cornubie uirescent* (wax green, be quycke, *O.E.D.* 3). Tr. revive.

44. THE COCK IN THE NORTH

Index, No. 4029. Not previously printed from this MS. Printed from Camb. Un. MS. Kk.1.5 by Lumby, *EETS* 42.18-22 ("The First Scottish Prophecy"); in a composite text from 13 variants by Brandl, *Sitzungsberichte der kön. preuss. Akademie der Wissenschaften* (Berlin, 1909), pp. 1166-74; collations from three MSS. by Haferkorn, *Beiträge zür engl. Philologie,* xix.109-13. For list of MSS. see *Index;* add Peniarth 26, pp. 39-41; Peniarth 50, p. 99; and Peniarth 58, p. 18 (noted by Griffiths, p. 209). A variant appears as the second part (121 ll.) of the "Merling saies" prophecy in Waldegrave's *The Whole Prophecie of Scotland* (1603); and a L. version in Cotton MS. Vesp. E. viii, f. 132.

Several commentators on the ME prophecies have endeavored to discover the political significance of this and other prophecies; inasmuch as the prophecies are designedly obscure, it is doubtful if any such attempt can be fully successful. Little attention has been paid to the dates of the MSS., which (for this poem) start from the middle of the fifteenth and run through to the late sixteenth century. For every different dating, there will inevitably be a different interpretation; for a prophecy's only value lies in its topicality. There are many variations in the MSS. — proof that each writer was trying to allude to his own current situation. Parts of the original (not susceptible of contemporary orientation) might be left undisturbed, and other parts (suited to the times) altered or added. The 1603 print, for example, removes the allusion to Kent (l. 39) and substitutes: Al the commones of the kith, shal cast him the keyes.

Griffiths (p. 209) remarks: "This is a very difficult prophecy for which different interpretations have been suggested." Brandl identifies the poem with the Percy-Glendower rebellion of 1402, explaining the Cock (Hotspur), Moon (the Percies: cf. No. 26, l. 183), Dragon

(Glendower), Bull (the Nevilles), and Lion (Scottish king, Douglas). Taylor (pp. 75-76) tacitly accepts this equation but believes that the poem is of Scottish authorship. Murray (*EETS* 61.xxix) refers it generally to the border wars, but favors an English origin.

These editors assume a unity which this type of poem does not possess (cf. Merlin's Prophecy in Bodl. MS. Rawl. C.813, Art. 53, with mixed allusions from 1460 to 1490). The number of lines in the several MSS. varies between 75 and 139. The present text occurs in Cotton Rolls ii.23, which contains Nos. 75, 84-86, all showing a decidedly Yorkist slant and referring to events about 1450 to 1451. A prophecy in such a context could well refer to the hopes of the Yorkists against the Lancastrian lords surrounding the King and Queen (such as the prose prophecy at the end of this roll, Art. 22), and might be interpreted as follows:

1-10. Past history: the Percy Rebellion. The Cock is Hotspur; the Moon and Lion are both Percy crests; the Dragon is Glendower.

13-14. Present history: Edward, Duke of York, returns from exile in Ireland, 1450.

15-18. Some of the leaders of the opposing factions: the Lancastrians, cursed by Christ — the mole (Westmorland) and the mermaid (Queen Margaret); the Yorkists — the eagle (Salisbury) and the bear with bright brands (Warwick).

19-26. Prophecy: an impending battle between the Duke of York and his enemies (continued ll. 67-68).

27-36. Prophecy: another battle. The Lancastrians, the friends of the fox (Suffolk; cf. No. 75, l. 1), e.g., the pye (Lord Rivers) shall be laid low.

37-40. Past history: The wicked court (Troy untrue) trembled at the memory of a dead man, the murdered Duke of Gloucester, when the Kentish men attacked London (1450).

41-48. Generalities.

49-52. Obscurities.

53-76. Prophecy: Hope that Edward will be chosen king (Henry VI still reigning). The dead man here may allude to King Arthur, whose prestige is thrown to the side of the Yorkists. The new King will have a notable reign, and will go on a pilgrimage to the Holy Land, where he shall die. The text is obviously corrupt, but in order to present a typical prophecy, as little emendation as possible has been made.

1. The opening lines parallel John of Bridlington (Wright, *Pol. Poems,* i.123):

> Tempore brumali gallus nido boreali
>
> Pullos unabit, et se volitare parabit.

For Bridlington see Sister Helen Margaret Peck, *The Prophecy of John of Bridlington,* Chicago diss. (1931).

11. Cf. Thomas of Ercedoune (*Index,* No. 365), ll. 609-20; and lines from Bodl. MS. Ashmole 337 (IV), f. 10, pr. Brandl, *Thomas of Erceldoune* (Berlin, 1880), p. 130:

Then the boore and the bastard through England shall cryde [*sic*] and hold a parliament
where never was non before.
all false lawes they shall put doune
þat were used in the land,
and truthe to worke every man shall ronne,
and all England for a tyme mery shalbe.

12. bore] Camb. bere.

15. mevith in mynd] ? turn over a question (cf. *O.E.D.* move 14b). Cf. *Index,* No. *9: "the moldwarpe and þe meremayden meved in mynd."

19. *Erceldoune* lists the three major conflicts to come, between Seton and the sea (l. 526), at Gladsmoor (l. 560), and at Sandyford (l. 624). These names were regularly incorporated into later prophecies, and chroniclers seriously attempted to identify them (e.g., with Barnet, Flodden).

28. Cf. *Erceldoune,* ll. 525-26: "Then sall thay mete bathe styf and strange / Betwyx Seton and þe see."

31. sterre] MS. not distinct; *tho* is always pl. Cf. þat dayes (l. 37), theffis has (No. 45, l. 6).

32. Waldegrave: to baill shal be brought. Camb. wycht ball has it bought.

33. Cf. *Index,* No. *9, ll. 29-31:

þe fox and þe fulmard frendeȝ shall inhende
þe honde full vn hendely hent shall be þen
And led to þe lyon law to abyde.

35. pikard] barge. Waldegrave: piper; Camb. puppede.

37. Murray (*EETS* 61.lxxx) quotes from a prose prophecy: "troye vntrue yen shall tremble & quake yat daye for feare of a deade man when yei heare him speake. all thoffyceris yerin shall caste him the keyes, from vxbrydge to hownslowe ye bushment to breake."

42. Camb. And euerylk seede in his sesoune kyndly sett. The Cotton text shows the difficulty, not of explaining the prophecy, but merely of getting a correct reading which is not nonsense. Cf. ll. 73.

43. blent] *O.E.D.* blent quotes 1530, Palgrave: I blente, I lette, or I hynder. Such a meaning would be suitable here.

45. In Geoffrey, the astrological allusions are, as here, generally vague. In the fifteenth century, Waurin (i.250) was the first to interpret them as referring to the day of judgment. See Theodore Otto Wendel, *Med. Attitude toward Astrology* (New Haven, 1920), p. 4.

50. To Bede were ascribed prognostications according to the day

of the week. Cf. Migne, *Patrol. Lat.,* xc.951. William Banister is mentioned as a prophet in the *Scalacronica,* c. 1355.

63. surrey] Syria.

66. Camb. (l. 70) þe haly crosse wyne sall hee.

73. Waldegrave: Whill kinde of age till him driue.

74. fee] More generally, worms' (maggots') meat, food; i.e., man is mortal.

76. The suggestion that the King die in the Holy Land is commonplace. Cf. *Erceldoune,* ll. 641-42:

Trow þis wel, þat i þe saye:
þe bastard sall dye in þe holy lande.

Also *Index,* No. 52, ll. 45-49: to the vallie of Iehosyphat . . . shall take away his aged breath. Also prose prophecy in Harley MS. 559 (quoted Brandl, p. 124): "The which redde foxe shall steale awaye at a tyde; he shalbe buryed at Josaphathe a lyttell from Calvarye." See further No. 5, l. 28.

45. WHEN ROME IS REMOVED

Listed in *Index* as No. 4008. Delete *Index,* Nos. 4007, 4009, 4010, 4011, and emend No. 4008 as follows: Second "Scottish" Prophecy in three versions:

(A) 1. Camb. Univ. Kk.1.5 (IV), ff. 33*r* (71 ll.); 2. Nat. Lib. of Wales, Peniarth 26, pp. 129-31; 3. NLW Peniarth 50, pp. 4-7 (90 ll.); 4. NLW Peniarth 94, p. 174 (35 ll.); 5. NLW Addit 441C, pp. 49-51 (86 ll.); 6. Llanstephen 119, pp. 175-77 (95 ll.); 7. Mostyn 133, pp. 331-41 (96 ll.). Fragments: *a.* Harley 559, f. 10*r* (6 ll.); *b.* Sloane 2578, f. 44*v* (a medley of single lines written as prose); *c.* Sloane 2578, f. 67*r* (ll. 1-4); *d.* NLW Peniarth 26, p. 127; *e.* NLW Peniarth 94, pp. 167 and 262.

(B) (Begins l. 16 of A text) 1. Cotton Vesp. E.viii, ff. 21*r*-22*v* (87 ll.); 2. Sloane 1802, ff. 10*v*-14*v* (90 ll.).

(C) 1. Cotton Cleo. C.iv, f. 86*v* (14 ll.); 2. Roy. 7 A.ix, f. 4*r* (14 ll.); 3. NLW Peniarth 94, p. 257; 4. Llanstephen 119, p. 177.

A critical text of all three versions plus fragments has been printed by Haferkorn, *Beiträge zur engl. Philologie,* xix.92-102, 104-10, 112, 114-16; also A.1 by Stevenson, *Lancelot du Lak* (1839), pp. 157-59; and by Lumby, *EETS* 42.32-34; B text appears in Waldegrave, *Whole Prophecy of Scotland* (1603), (90 ll.); repr. *Bannatyne Club* (Edinburgh, 1833); and C.1 by Wright, *Pol. Poems,* ii.249.

Most of the other MSS. of the A version continue another 26 lines; the following are taken from Haferkorn's critical text (pp. 100, 102):

Elke a lede shall haue leue his lordeshipe to broke
That wyth lewte hase ben of a longe tyme.

They shall not sese of the soth (y tell þe the text!).
Ay wyll the hyght of the hete beholdyn to wynter,
Or the taile of sommer rekeueryn to chele
Or yn the end of haruyst, hote of hym-sylf,
Shall wicked dedys vndo and draw to the lyght.
But deth so derforly that sparys no wyght,
Shall gare barnys bere blame þat yett are vnborne.
This shall fall that y haue seide wythyn short time,
But when how or what dare y not tell.
The foure waterys shal waxe and wodys shall wane,
An man shall be vnman and vnman man;
The hare shall brede on the hurth stone.
Whan this tokenys is come and y-gon,
My lyue sonne, bylde thyn howse of lyme and stone,
Of lyme and stone thyn howse thow bygge,
If þu wolt walter or walwyn or ly on thy rygge.
Ffor that shall flay Scotland and Frawnce, for then
            thay waxe flich,
What tyme ther fallys too somers yn on ȝere,
Shall nothyre be sely, monke nor frere,
Person ne preste ne no regulere
Ma not be holpyn by preyere.

I prayde hym to tell what farles mo shulde falle,
And he onswoerde me no worde, but went from vs all:
How he ȝede vs fro no man cowth tell.

The Scottish characteristics of the Camb. text are discussed by Haferkorn, pp. 43-44; and by Oakden, *Allit. Poetry*, i.99: "The spelling
is typically Scottish throughout . . . . There are some traces of a Midland scribe as in the former work [No. 44, Camb. text]." Oakden
also finds (ii.263) seven distinct alliterative kennings here, and nine
for No. 44.

The third version (C), composed of single lines from (A), shows
how a short general prophecy can apply to almost any period. This
Royal variant is unpublished:

When rome remeuyd in-to ynglonde,
And ilke preste hase popis power in hand,
Betwen sixt & thirde, qwo wyll vnderstande,
Mych wer & wo sall ryse in ynglonde.
Ther sall tyde þen in a stryfe be þe stremys,
þat a northerryn flaw sall faloþe hym of humbre;
for euer þo iij sall recouer & sekyn of rewlis
þat has lyne in lent many long days.
þan worth vp walis, þat wantis no wyllis,
& help vp þat broþer with bryght hard brandes;

þer kynsmen of yrland & ledes of honor
sal spend her speris with dyntes of color,
to bryng owt of hawle þe kynde blod of [   ]
þan sall ryght rewel to lyue of herdes brutes.

Haferkorn believes that the prophecy is a composite. The original lines (16-50, 59-72) use the symbolism suggested by Geoffrey of Monmouth. The later accretions are concerned with ecclesiastical and social troubles in the second half of the fourteenth century. Such a view is supported by the independent texts of ll. 5-8 (see *Index,* No. 4006). The original prophecy was apparently Scottish in sympathy; the Camb. text, however, changes the attitude to favor the English.

1. Three MSS. head: Thys ys the laste sayinge of Thomas of Arsedon (Arseldone).

3. In the four-line fragment in Sloane MS. 2578, as in No. 46, diagrams of dice are used. The use of numbers is both in the Sibylline and Galfridian tradition; cf. *HRB* (tr. Giles, p. 198): "Then from the first to the fourth, from the fourth to the third, from the third to the second, the thumb shall roll in oil."

who-so] Tr. if any one (will understand).

5. wyt] NLW Add. wrath. Lines 5-8 appear independently in two MSS. as "Evils of the Age" (*Index,* No. 4006), and in a fifteen-line form in Lilly, *Another Old Prophecie* (Haferkorn, pp. 115-16).

6. haldin þar lyff] ? escape hanging.

8. clethinge] OE claeþan, clead. Cf. Hoccleve, *De Reg. Principum,* 506: "There may no lord take up a newe gise / But that a knave shalle the same uptake."

9. Line supplied; in all other MSS.

11. nocht one wone] Haferkorn glosses: nothing further, nothing beyond that.

13. turne] All other MSS. wyth.

15. ber the crowne] wield authority.

17. wer] Other MSS. ane werre.

18. lorde] Other MSS. And all euerwic londe ernystly be wrocht.
austernly] *O.E.D.* austere; "The adscititious *-n,* common in 14-16th c., is perhaps due to contact of form and sense with *stern* adj."

19. well] Most MSS. newly. Haferkorn expands his gloss: "Christus in anger will turn away and let the evil in the world have its course for a long time."

21. ledis] NLW Add. flowres; other MSS. leuyd.

24. Tatcaldwers] Other MSS. Cadwaladrus.
carioun] Other MSS. Caron (for Cynan).
noyus] Other MSS. noble.

25. worthe] ? to become wrathful.
wrethe] Other MSS. And worshipe here londes.

26. erth] Other MSS. And inheryt in-to Albany at here own wyll.

31. libert] Other MSS. lyly shall lende.

32. Haferkorn's composite text reads: "The lyon leder of all and lord of all this bestis." The Camb. text here changes the pro-Scottish nature of the prophecy. The lion (Scotland) will bow down to the leopard (England). His stepsons (l. 35), the Scottish lords, will be stricken down and destroyed. The English will baptize them, as Christ has commanded. This insult to the Scots would have rejoiced Minot!

33. lowte to] bow before.

libert] Other MSS. lyly. Cf. l. 31.

34. At stryff] at variance.

35. An example of homeoteleuthon; the scribe has jumped two half lines. Other MSS. (comp. text): "The stepsonnys of the lyon, stordy of hemsylf / They shall be steryde a stounde and sterte vp at onys." The scribe of NLW Add. has similarly miscopied the second half of l. 58 as l. 59.

36. Other MSS. Son strike down the bestys.

37. Other MSS. They shall kyndely kerue that Criste hath forbede.

38. dryff] Tr. And thus he will force them into subjection.

39. libert] Other MSS. lyon.

42. Other MSS. But they shull lyghtly be lowsyd.

48. sesoune] Other MSS. somer sesoun.

50. sely] Apparently corrupt (sely = insignificant). Other MSS. full, fell.

Cf. *Whole Prophecie* ("Merling saies in his booke"): "And an fellowne flaw shall fall soone after." Also Geoffrey of Monmouth, *HRB* vii: "Tunc exsurget in illum aquilo; et flores quos zephyrus procreavit eripiet."

flaw] squall *O.E.D.* first rec. 1513.

52. .bariona] Other MSS. syr Bariona ... bounde to be sonkyn. The barge of Simon Peter, the son of John (Matth. 16.17; John 1.42), i.e., the Church.

53. Secularis] Laymen(not secular clergy).

55. turnamentis] All other MSS. give the more common form, tormentys.

56. strenth] Other MSS. trewth.

64. Five texts read R, one V, one VII, and the others 2 (i.e., 1382). Haferkorn (p. 129) suggests the Arabic "2" was read as a medium length "r." As the prophecy was recopied, other years were substituted, e.g., 1387, 1482, 1535. The B version is dated 1480, although Haferkorn thinks this best preserves the original Scottish prophecy. A late variant of C is dated 1642.

65. understande] Camb. under; other MSS. vndo.

67. wyell] well (not in *O.E.D.*).

Berwyk] The border fortress, continually changing hands in the English-Scottish wars.

70. Releve] Other MSS. Shall the enclyne to the king; Shall then be left to the King.

46. A POLITICAL PROPHECY BY THE DICE

Index, No. 4018. Previously printed by Furnivall, *Thynne's Animadversions,* Chaucer Soc., Second Series, No. 13, p. lxv. This text also occurs in Trinity Coll. Camb. MS. 1157, and, with an introduction (employing the dominical letters) in Camb. Univ. MS. Ii.6.11, flyleaf; Cotton Rolls, II.23, Art.4; and Lansdowne MS. 762, f. 96r. The Dublin is the only text to gloss the throws of the dice. Since prophecies have heralded most disturbances, one might speculate (although the MSS. are later) whether this has any reference to the 1381 Revolt.

5. Camb. When dewsse putteth owght tree þen ys all schentt.
9. lockes] ? fig. prisons. Camb. The cock schall vn doo.
10. ber the pryce] Cf. No. 33, bur.

47. MERLIN'S PROPHECY

Index, No. 3986. Not heretofore printed from this MS. Occurs also in Bodl. MS. Ashmole 59, f. 78r (8 ll.), printed by Skeat, *Oxf. Chaucer,* vii, pp. lxxxi-lxxxii; and by Thynne, *Chaucer Soc.,* Second Series, xiii.xlvi. Add to *Index:* Rylands Lat. 201, f. 130r (printed in *Bulletin Rylands Lib.,* v.389); Fitzwilliam Museum 355. *Index,* No. 3943 is another version found in twelve MSS.; add to *Index:* Rawl. poet. F. 32, f. 2v; Magdalene Coll. Camb. 1236, f. 91r, printed by Robbins, *Sec. Lyrics,* p. 241. The link between the prophecies and the Abuses of the Age is seen in the parallels between this poem and, for example, Nos. 56 and 58. Cf. also *Index,* No. 2696 (printed by Bowers, *Southern Folklore Quarterly,* xv.249-50), ll. 15-21:

> Wen resone faylith & sensibalite
> Holdyth the brydle of lecherous insolenc
> And sobernes hath lost is liberte
> & to fall to lvste it doyne the reuerens
> And vice of vertue hathe an apparenc
> Missledith persons of wylfull reklesnesse
> To gret erroure of froward idelenes

The prophetic character of No. 47 is emphasized by the lines immediately following in the Magdalene MS.:

> When goneway shall on curtays call

Then wallys shall rayke & hastely ryse
Then Albeon skottlonde shall to hem fall
Then waken wonders in euery wyse
The rede londe fox shall ryse with all
    With glarynge grounde

Lucy Paton, *Les Prophécies de Merlin* (New York, 1926), p. 1, comments on the indiscriminate use of Merlin: *"The Prophecies of Merlin* has proved an elastic title. It has been given to works as unlike as the Seventh Book of the *HRB* of Geoffrey of Monmouth and the *Didot-Perceval,* to fictitious compilations mentioned in the Arthurian prose romances, to thirteenth-century prophecies in Latin, and to English political vaticinations of the fifteenth and later centuries."

2. Cf. Griffiths (p. 183) on fourteenth-century Welsh prophetic poems, listing the evils of the age.

5. Cf. *King Lear,* III.ii.91-92: "Then shall the realm of Albion / Come to great confusion." The Fool adds: "This prophecy Merlin shall make; for I live before his time." In the Dublin MS. another line follows: "A m*l* cccc lx and on few lordes or ellys noone;" then *Index,* No. 1934.

48. THE LAND OF COKAYGNE

Index, No. 762. Previously printed by Hickes, *Thesaurus,* i.231; by Ellis, *Specimens* (1811), i.82; by Furnivall, *Early Eng. Poems,* pp. 156; by Wright, *Altdeutsche Blättern,* i.396; by Mätzner,, *AE Sprachp.,* i.147; by Heuser, *Die Kildare-Gedichte,* pp. 145-50; by Morley, *Shorter Eng. Poems,* pp. 18-23; and by Cook, *Reader,* pp. 368-72 (120 ll. only). In the Kildare MS. (first quarter fourteenth century).

"The airiest and cleverest piece of satire in the whole range of Early English, if not of English, poetry" (Furnivall). The poem is a satire against monks and nuns, 70 of the 95 couplets being "devoted to the abbeys and life of the clergy" (Wells, *Manual,* p. 228). The stories of the Abbot's ruse to round up his wandering novices and the bathing episode are notable hits against the orders. On the other hand, the satire lies in the main Coquaigne tradition — but the "Order of Fair Ease" (Wright, *Pol. Songs,* pp. 137-48) is much more a clerical satire than is "Cokaygne." A. L. Morton in *The English Utopia* (London, 1952), pp. 1-34, stresses the folk background (e.g., the glass palace, the well of youth) and the peasants' utopia (abundance without serfdom, admission only to the lowest type of manual worker, ll. 177-82): "It was probably an advance that by the Fourteenth Century men were becoming conscious of this

burden .... As a result, what had formerly been so universally endured without question or hope was at last beginning to be felt as a
burden: the serf was becoming aware of his servitude and the Fourteenth Century was the great period of peasant insurrection. Out of
this situation, this *beginning* of hope, springs *The Land of Cokaygne.*
Without the hope it could scarcely have arisen at all. If the hope
had been stronger or better grounded it would not have taken shape
as a fantasy, a grotesque dream of a society wished for but not seen
as an actual possibility" (p. 15).

1. west] Paradise was placed in the east; Cokaygne in the west is
therefore heathen and anticlerical.

14. hely & enok] Elijah (II Kings 2.11) and Enoch (Gen. 5.24).

20. russin] "bite between meals"; *O.E.D.* quotes this line under
supper, but not elsewhere. Heuser (p. 143) says Anglo-Irish word.

27. This line (and ll. 29, 63) have overtones looking forward to
1381.

34. al] completely. MS. reads la, taken by Cook as interj., truly
(but *O.E.D.* first rec. 1598).

52. i.e., Cistercians, from the color of their habit (in contrast to
the regular Benedictines or Black Monks). The Carthusians and
Premonstratensian canons wore white.

53. Bowers and halls are generally in apposition; bower is the
private and hall the public part of the home. Cf. l. 11, and No. 44,
l. 24.

64. stoute & sterne] a common allit. phrase. Cf. Chaucer, Knight's
Tale, 1296: hertes sturne and stoute; *Avow. Arthur,* xii: stirrun and
stowte.

68. "The palace or hill of glass, is, indeed, a regular feature of
the earthly paradise in all mythologies" (Morton, p. 14).

69. bas] *O.E.D.* reading MS. reading har-las as hair-lace or fillet;
but quotes no other example of this spelling. The apposition of base
and capital seems more apt.

73. Spices necessary for preserving and disguising food were imported from the East and were consequently expensive.

78. cucubes] cubebs, pepperlike berries.

83. The four wells link Cokaygne to the Well of Life tradition;
cf. Morton, pp. 16-17. Cf. Mandeville *EETS* 154.113.

87. Tr. All the earth, precious stones and gold stem from them.

89. This parade of gems includes carbuncle (garnet), astiune
(astrion or sapphire), smaragde (emerald), lugre (ligure), prassiune
(chrysoprase), topasiune (topaz), ametist (amethyst), caledun (chal-
cedony), and epetite (hepatite or bloodstone). Vniune, a pearl of
large size, is not known outside of this line before 1592; *O.E.D.*
suggests here of A.F. origin. Iaspe in l. 70 is not rec. elsewhere;
Sp. & P. have jaspe.

96. The list of birds may be conventional; cf. Chaucer, *Rom. Rose,* 913-14: With popyniay, with nyghtyngale, with chalaundre, and with wodewale. See also *Owl & Night.,* 1659, *Eger & Grine,* 922, etc.

97. Chalendre] a Mediterranean species of lark. *O.E.D.* suggests that to ME writers only a name known from Fr. romances.

wodwale] The o and e in this MS. are not always clearly distinguished. Cf. No. 2, l. 8.

99. bi har miʒt] according to their ability.

102. Cf. the description in *Li Fabliaus de Coquaigne* (in Barbazan and Meon, *Fabliaux et Contes,* iv.175-81), ll.37-9:

> Par les rues vont rostissant
> Les crasses oes, et tornant
> Tout par eles.

111. Tr. There is no mention about no drinking.

119. turniþ] turns back.

125. heiʒ of mode] in high spirits.

129. al þer amang] in the midst of all, or in the meantime.

132. in o randum] in a headlong, impetuous rush. Cf. Mustanoja, *Neuphil. Mitteilungen,* lv.56-58.

166. iambleue] Morton tr. jigging up and jigging down.

169. wiþoute danger] without refusal of love.

171. Tr. as a matter of right and not as an exceptional favor.

185. Tr. until you seize your opportunity.

49. *THE BISSON LEADS THE BLIND, 1456*

Index, No. 884. Previously printed in *Rel. Ant.,* ii.283-40; and by Wright, *Pol. Poems,* ii.235-37. For date see Introduction, p. xxiv, and full discussion by Robbins, *MLN,* lxx.473-76.

2. merlyn] A prestige name, but the ills mentioned in No. 47 (q.v.) find their place here, e.g., l. 2 = l. 5; l. 1 = l. 13; and l. 4 = l. 19.

13. mayntenerys] i.e., those who improperly intervene in law suits.

14. of kynde] (as if) by right.

19. Wright glosses: "that robbers and men who only looked to their private gain were established in the place of righteousness" (ii, p. xl).

25. brocage] "The corrupt farming or jobbing of office; the price or bribe paid unlawfully for any office or place or trust, frequently mentioned as an abuse in early times" (*O.E.D.*).

26. baratur] "one who for the sake of gain raises discord between his neighbours" (*O.E.D.*) is chief magistrate of a sub-division of a county.

33. combryd] Cf. *Destr. Troy,* 11774: "To be cumbrid with covetous."

45. Cf. No. 81, l. 48.

53. Calais was now England's sole possession in France.

55. Difficult: Now leaders load the leeward to their breaking in pieces (debrise). Some meaning like "followers" would suit *leward*.

58. chaffare] that which is bought and sold.

73. Advice certainly unlikely to be followed, just before the outbreak of the Civil War again.

79. heuynly tour] *O.E.D.* (tower, I 2b) gives other examples of this epithet.

50. LONDON LICKPENNY

Index, No. 3759. Occurs also in Harley MS. 542, f. 102r ("in Stow's scratchy needle-like handwriting"); both texts printed by Hammond, *Anglia,* xx.410-19; a composite text by Holthausen, *Anglia,* xliii.62-67; and single texts by many others. See *Index* for details. Skeat, *Spec. Eng. Lit. 1394-1579,* pp. 373-76, has full notes. Harley MS. 367 is written "in a loose scrawling hand either contemporary with Stow's or a little later."

Harley MS. 542 is written in eight-line stanzas, and Hammond suggests that the version in Harley MS. 367 merely dropped a line (4, 5, or 7) of the original version, e.g., st. 1, 2, 3, 5, 7, 9, 12, 14, and 16 omit l. 7; st. 6, 13, and 15 omit l. 5; and st. 8 omits l. 4; in other st. lines are telescoped or the rhyme is changed.

The attribution to Lydgate, "one of the freaks of literature," rests on this MS. The poem is not by Lydgate; and the rubric is of interest in showing how his name became attached to any medieval poem. On the title, Skeat requotes: "Some call London a *lick-penny* (as Paris is called, by some, a *pick-purse)* because of feastings, with other occasions of expense and allurements, which cause so many unthrifts among country gentlemen, and others, who flock into her in such excessive multitudes."

An illustration of the corruption of the law courts is given in a petition of the Commons in 1455 against the Officers of the Exchequer, for taking "grete and outrageous yeftes, fees and rewardes, for doyng of thaire Offices, ayenst all reason and conscience, and their Office will not doo to the deliveraunce of your said Accomptauntz, till tyme they have suche outerageous fees, rewardes and yiftes ... to the grete hurt, oppression and undoyng of your Liege People" *(Rot. Parl.,* v.323-24).

11. kynges bench] The functions of the superior courts of common law seated at Westminster, the King's Bench and the Common Pleas (l. 22), were distinct (for criminal and for civil cases). The courts, however, would rule outside their jurisdiction should there be suffi-

cient monetary encouragement. An appeal could be taken to the Court of Chancery (the Rolls, l. 29). The poet goes from one to the other, failing to secure a hearing because he lacks money. Cf. No. 51, ll. 45-48.

16. by one assent] with one accord. Cf. No. 90, l. 12.

23. sylken hoode] The law-sergeants wore hoods of white silk (Skeat). Cf. No. 51, l. 42.

27. mvm] Not the slightest word. Cf. *Piers Plowman*, Pro. 214-215: "þow my3test better mete þe myste on maluerne hulles / þan gete a momme of here mouthe, but money were shewed."

36. Cf. No. 51, l. 41.

47. copen] to barter. The Middle Dutch form is côpen (mod. koopen), to buy; cf. cheap. The Flemings had been introduced into England to stimulate the domestic woolen manufacture (e.g., felt hattes, l. 48).

48. to reede] for reading.

51. hyghe pryme] about nine o'clock.

58. pryse] Cf. No. 33 bur; No. 51, l. 21.

59. Cf. *Piers Plowman*, Pro. 225: "Cokes and here knaues crieden: Hote pies, hote."

60. in the ryse] on small twigs.

64. In the "West Chepe" were the shops of goldsmiths and mercers, etc. (cf. Aungier, *CS*, 28.xiii).

71. London stone] "A fragment of London stone is still preserved [1880] in Cannon Street, formerly Canwick or Candlewick Street. It is built into the street wall of the Church of St. Swithin" (Skeat).

72. Canwyke] "Candlewick Street, for so many centuries the residence of the wealthy drapers, who seem to have been bound by strong ties to a spot placed beneath the protection of their patroness St. Mary Bothaw, and close beside the highly valued 'London Stone' " (Aungier, *CS*, 28.xiv)).

75. Ryshes grene] i.e., for strewing on floors.

78. Estchepe] "Eastcheap, the old Saxon market, celebrated from the time of Fitz-Stephen to the days of Lydgate, for the abundance and variety of the provisions sold there" (Aungier, *CS*, 28.xiv-xv).

82. by cock] an oath < gock < God.

83. Ienken and Iulyan] apparently a popular ballad, not identified. Cf. Coventry Myst. (*Shakespeare Soc*, p. 340): "And I wole kepe the feet this tyde Thow ther come both Iakke and Gylle."

85. Cornhyll] "hath beene inhabited for the most part with wealthie Drapers . . . [and] Vpholders, that solde olde apparell and housholde stuffe" (Stow, *Survey*, i.199).

92. Cf. *Piers Plowman*, Pro. 227-28: "Tauerners vntil hem tolde þe same / White wyn of Oseye and red wyn of Casgoigne."

95. peny] "Gascoyne wines were then to be sold at London, not

aboue 4.d. nor Rhenish wine aboue 6.d. the Gallon" (Stow, *Survey,* i.240).

107. of] with.

111. lawyers] Cf. No. 51, ll. 45-48.

51. MONEY, MONEY!

Index, No. 113. Previously printed by Halliwell, *Nugae Poeticae,* p. 46; in part by FitzGibbon, *E. E. Poetry,* pp. 173-74; by Flügel, *Neuengl. Lesebuch,* p. 140; and by Greene, *Early Eng. Carols,* pp. 261-63. For other poems deploring the misuse of money, see *Sec. Lyrics,* Nos. 57, 58, and 59; also *Index,* Nos. 1484 and 3959.

13. Greene notes the still current proverb, "Money makes the mare go."

14. praunce] Cf. No. 72, l. 125.

18. a mated chere] "with the air of one checkmated or baffled" (Greene).

20. Tr. nor provide lively entertainment, joyful welcome.

24. Tr. money is always preeminent.

35. the] they; cf. l. 67.

36. Fortescue in *De Laudibus Legum Angliae,* ed. S. B. Chrimes (Cambridge, 1942), pp. 48-49, 167, refers to the false charges against Sir Thomas Cook in 1469, in which his accuser confessed that, if again tortured, "he would accuse the same knight once more, and indeed would accuse his own father."

48. strawe] i.e., valueless.

67. Rel. pro. omitted.

72. owte of countenaunce] disconcerted, abashed.

52. HUFF! A GALAUNT

Index, No. 892. Previously printed by Furnivall, *Academy,* No. 1269 (August 29, 1896), p. 146. MS. second half fifteenth century.

"Galaunt" continued in use well into the sixteenth century, and there is a considerable body of literature on these overdressed braggarts. *Index,* No. 4255 (also in Univ. Coll. Oxf. MS. 154, flyleaf; and Trinity Coll. Camb. MS. 1157, f. 27r) presents a similar portrait. *Index,* No. 1874, also found in a new MS. in the Venerable English College, Rome (described by Klinefelter, *MLQ,* xiv.3-6; and by Robbins, *Neophilologus,* xxxix.131-36), has 32 stanzas, and an acrostic on the Seven Sins.

bur. Huff] "An exclamation attributed to a swaggerer or bully" (*O.E.D.*). Cf. Digby Myst., iii.491-506: "Her xal entyr a galavnt þus seyying: Hof, hof, hof, a frysche new galavnt!" (*EETS* lxx.73).

11. nere] were it not for. A statute of 1465 ordered the length of pikes of shoes to be kept under two inches on pain of a fine of twenty shillings. Cf. Stow, *Annales*, p. 419: "Before this time and since the yeere of our Lord, 1382. the pikes of shoes and bootes were of such length that they were faine to bee tied vp to their knees with chaines of siluer gilt, or at the least with silke laces." In 1468 the Pope issued a bull cursing "thoo that made any longe pykys passynge ij yenchys of lengthe .... And sum men sayd that they wolde were longe pykys whethyr Pope wylle or nylle, for they sayde the Popys curse wolde not kylle a flye. God amend thys. And with in schorte tyme aftyr sum of the Cordyners gate prevy selys and proteccyons to make longe pykys, and causyd tho same men of hyr crafte that laboryd to the Pope for the dystruccyon of longe pykys to be trobelyd and in grete donger" (*Gregory's Chronicle*, p. 238). Cf. *Index*, No. 4255: "With youre long peked schone / Therfor your thrift is almost don." Also *Index*, No. 3484: "She repreueþ my dagged cloþes / And long pykyd crakowed shon."

18. A statute of 1463 forbade yeomen to wear laced sleeves (*EETS* viii, p. xiv).

19. Cf. *Index*, No. 4255: "And youre schort gownys thriftlesse;" also No. 62, l. 9.

25. Cf. *Index*, No. 4255: "& with youre long here into your eyen."

30. bulwerk] Not in *O.E.D.* Furnivall suggests ruff (?).

33. Cf. *Index*, No. 2774: "He putth hys hand in hys powrs cum nichyll intus fuerat / He ffownd none þer saw godeys cowrs hoc non sibi deerat."

34. Cf. No. 62, l. 6.

38. narse] The unhistoric -n forms have been retained throughout this anthology. Cf. nabete (No. 69, l. 21), nasse (No. 70, l. 68), neres (No. 65, l. 18), nore (No. 82, l. 7).

53. THE PRIDE OF WOMEN'S HORNS

Index, No. 3698. Not heretofore printed. MS. fifteenth century. The Ashmole Catalogue links two lines immediately following st. 2:

> And never þe hyer þat þowe erte
> So moche lower beo þyne herte.

1. The first quatrain resembles the second st. of *Index*, No. 811 (Armagh MS.):

> God that berreth the crowne of thornes,
> Destroy the pryde of womens hornes
>   For his dere Passione;
> And let never har long taylys,

> That beth the Devyll of Hell his flaylys,
> Be cause of our confucione.

2. Cf. *Index*, No. 2625, by Lydgate (ll. 33-40):

> Clerkys recorde, by gret auctoryte,
> Hornes wer yove to bestys ffor dyffence —
> A thyng contrarie to ffemynyte,
> To be maad sturdy of resystence.
> But arche wives, egre in ther vyolence,
> Fers as tygre ffor to make affray,
> They haue despit, and ageyn concyence,
> Lyst nat of pryde, ther hornes cast away.

3. Cf. *Index*, No. 2285 (thirteenth-century flyleaf scrap): "Ne þi faire tail so long ne so trailende;" Lyndsay's satire on "Syde Taillis;" and No. 4093 (thirteenth-century sermon tag):

Contra mulieres ornantes:

> Who haues hornes als ha ram,
> and ha nech als a swan,
> and a midel als ha brock,
> ha tayls as he pecoch.

6. Carrake] a large ship. Chaucer's "brodder than of a carrik is the sayl" (Somnour's Tale, l. 24) suggests the extreme of fashion.

54. *THE SAYINGS OF THE FOUR PHILOSOPHERS,* 1311

Index, No. 1857. Previously printed by [B. D. D. Turnbull,] *Owain Miles* (Edinburgh, 1837); by Wright, *Pol. Songs*, pp. 253-58 (with translation); by Ellis, *E. E. Pronunciation*, Chaucer Soc., Second Series, iv.499; by Wülcker, *AE Lesebuch*, i.74-76; by Vätke, *Archiv*, lxxii.467; by Herrtage, *EETS* xxxiii.498-99; and by Holmstedt, *EETS* 182.clxxxv-clxxxvii.

Brown, in *Archiv*, cxxviii.72-76, gives the original Latin tract on the Twelve Abuses, ascribed variously to Cyprian, Augustine, and Origen, in MSS. of the ninth, tenth, and eleventh centuries. The Praefatio summarizes:

"Duodecim Abusiua sunt saeculi, hoc est: sapiens sine operibus, senex sine religione, adulescens sine obedientia, diues sine eleemosyna, femina sine pudicitia, dominus sine virtute, christianus contentiosus, pauper superbus, rex iniquus, episcopus neglegens, plebs sine disciplina, populus sine lege, sic suffocatur iustitia; haec sunt duodecim abusiua saeculi per quae saeculi rota, si in illo fuerint, decipitur et ad tartari tenebras nullo impediente iustitiae suffragio per iustum Dei iudicium rotatur" (ed. Guil. Hartel, *S. Thasci Caecili Cypriani*

Opera Omnia, Pars III [Vindobonae, 1871], pp. 152-73; also Migne, *Patrol. Lat.,* xl. col. 1079).

The first English tr. occurs in the Homilies of Aelfric (Skeat, *EETS* 94.x-xi; Morris, *EETS* 29.101-19); a fifteenth-century prose tr. ("Seynt Austyn of twelve abusyouns or mysusis") in Camb. Un. MS. Ii.6.55, ff. 64-76, and in Harley MS. 2330, ff. 100*v*. The L. is the basis of all subsequent versions of the Abuses of the Age. The more common shortened form of the sayings in the *Gesta Romanorum* version is given in No. 55.

The Sayings of the Four Philosophers are well-known in English from their incorporation as the Sexta Tabula (*Index,* No. 2167) of the *Speculum Christiani,* found in 66 MSS. (Holmstedt, *EETS* 182.xvi-xviii). An unfortunate King seeks the help of his four wise-men; each gives three answers (ll. 27-29, 39-41, 51-53, 63-68) with numerous biblical and patristic illustrations. Of the verses in the *Speculum,* Holmstedt suggests that "the person who wrote the satir-ical poem against Edward II [i.e., No. 54] either translated the sayings himself, from a MS. belonging to the same group as that from which the author of the *Speculum* copied his Latin story of the philosophers, or used a translation that had been made from such a MS., and that the satirical poem was the source of the English sayings in the *Specu-lum,* though of course not necessarily the immediate source. It is noteworthy that the sayings in the *Speculum* completely agree with those in the satirical poem, except the second and third sayings of the second philosopher which occur transposed" (*EETS* 182.clxxxix-cxc).

The traditional sayings are here preceded by a criticism of Edward II for breaking the Ordinances he had signed on October 11, 1311, recalling the Provisions of Oxford which in 1258 attempted to curb Henry III. The united opposition of the barons which had forced Edward to sign the charter broke out in armed rebellion by December, when Edward restored his favorite, Piers Gaveston. See T. F. Tout, *Place of Edward in Eng. Hist.,* (Manchester, 1936), pp. 77-84. The Abuses of the Age take on special significance in the chaotic mis-management of these years.

A twelve-line variant ("De prouisione oxonie") of these intro-ductory verses (ll. 1-16) occurs in St. John's Coll. Camb. MS. 112, printed by James, *Cat.,* p. 146; and by Isabel S. T. Aspin, *Anglo-Norman Political Songs* (Oxford, 1953), p. 62. This is probably the original text, the Auchinleck MS. omitting ll. 3, 4, 7, and 8; it may refer to the reign of Edward I, about 1306 or 1307.

> Rome poet fere et defere . si fet ele trop souent
> Þat nis noþer wel ne veyre . for þi is holy cherche ysend
> Merewele est de deu vykere . ki a tel conseil consent
> Þe man nis naȝt worþ þre eyre . þat wel doþ and suþþe went

Nostre Roy de Engleterre . par le conseil de sa gent
Wolde a nywe laghe arere . and makede a muchel perlement
Tuz y uindrent les Euekes . e le baruns ensement
And alle iswore þat þer were . and hulde taperes ytent
La purueance est de cyre io l'enteng e byn le say
And is yholde to nez þe fyre and is ymolten al away
Ieo ne say mes ke dyre mes tot y ua tribolay
Curt and laghe hundrid a syre . al it god a duuele vay.

14. tripolay] i.e., all goes to nought. Wülcker interpreted Tripoli, captured in 1289 by the Sultan at the end of the Crusades. Aspin, however, translates "something put out of order" (cf. AN v. triboler).

16. a deuel way] intensitive to strengthen away.

29. "To fight is so foolish that it is as good to flee; it is all the same if you fight or flee. Here in a moral sense" (Holmstedt, p. 265).

63. "Will is counsellor; self-indulgence, arbitrariness reigns. The O.E.D. does not record this sense of rede" (Holmstedt, p. 267).

55. THE TWELVE ABUSES

Index, No. 906. Not heretofore printed from this MS. Occurs in fourteen other MSS.; four texts conveniently printed by Brown, *Rel. Lyrics XV Century*, pp. 268-69, 345-46. For other printings see *Index*.

The English Twelve Abuses do not follow Cyprian's Latin, however, but the *Gesta Romanorum* (compiled late thirteenth or early fourteenth century). The *Gesta* has a similar framework to the *Speculum*, and introduces the English sentences thus:

"Legitur quendam Regem quondam fuisse qui habuit 4or Philosophos in regno suo; in quo regno multae plagae, multa infortunia, et multi defectus fiebant in populis. Rex autem videns se ipsum nullo peccato mortali vulneratum, mirabatur valde, et diligenter inquirebat a predictis 4or Philosophis qua de causa haec infortunia magis agebantur in tempore suo quam in tempore predecessorum suorum. Primus Philosophus dixit . . ." (Herrtage, *EETS* xxxiii.497-98; with continued discussion, pp. 498-500). Then come the answers:

The first said thus,
 gifte is domesman,
 and gile is chapman;
 the grete holde no lawe,
 and seruauntes have none awe.

The second said,
 witte is turned to trechery,

and love into lechery;
the holy day into Glotonye,
and gentrie into vilanye.

The thirde said,
wise men are but scornede,
and Wedowes be sore yernede;
grete men are but glosede,
and smale men borne downe and myslovede.

The fourthe said,
lordes wexen blynde,
and kynnesmen ben vnkynde;
dethe out of mynde,
and trewthe may no man fynde. (*EETS* xxxiii.360).

The texts of No. 55 have dropped the story framework, and the Abuses have an independent and separate existence. The Abuses are widespread throughout ME verse, and appear in many guises. So No. 17 and *Index,* Nos. 1655, adapted by John Ball; No. 45 (ll. 5-7, 51-58), No. 47, Merlin's Prophecy; and No. 96, Lydgate's Advice to the Estates. *Index,* No. 4051, a thirteenth-century version, by ascribing to Bede its ten abuses, is given a vaticinal character. Other versions include *Index,* No. 2356, Bodl. MS. Rawl. D.893, f. 75*r* (a single sheet of vellum), printed in the Introduction, p. xlii. *Index,* No. 2829 is a quatrain from a sermon collection in Merton Coll. Oxf. MS. 248, f. 146*v*, col. i:

Riȝtful dom is ouer-cast,
& trouþe is fer agon;
Soþnesse is ileyd adoun,
& riȝt nis þer non.

The Abuses also appear in an expanded version in No. 57. The Worcester text of No. 55 is the source of another expansion in quatrains (ll. 327-90) in the *Pride of Life* (Holthausen, *Archiv,* cviii.43-45); and Brown (*Archiv,* cxxviii.77) shows how "the author of the Morality made use of the English rather than the Latin text." There are about fifty distinct poems based on some variant of the Twelve Abuses.

3. ceca] So also in Worcester MS.; Ashmole MS. 750 omits. Furnivall (*EETS* viii.88) reads cera from Harley MS. — "? for certa or mera."

5. Most other MSS. read: Etas ridetur, mulier pulsatur amore / Dives laudatur, pauper adheret hvmo. Tr. "Old man is schorned, woman her wowed / Riche man ys glosed, poore man is bowed."

8. Most other MSS. read: Mortuus Ignotus, nullus amicus amat. Tr. "The dede is out of mynde / Triew frende can noman fynde."

9. Cf. "Mede in thy lande is domys man," four quatrains at end of *Catalogus Regum Anglie,* fifteenth-century MS. (*olim* Harmsworth), sold Sotheby's, Oct., 1945, Lot 1956 to Messrs. Maggs.

10. owtyn] without. Cf. *Index,* No. 4149, l. 378: "May sclawndren hys felows oute reson."

17. Cf. *Carmina Burana,* ed. Hilka and Schumann, I.i.5.

56.   ABUSES OF THE AGE, I

Index, No. 1820. Previously printed by Furnivall, *E. E. Poems,* p. 161; and by Heuser, *Bonn. Beiträge,* xiv.184. Occurs in nine other MSS., variously printed. For details see *Index.* There are slight variations in most texts. A thirteenth-century flyleaf fragment from Trinity Coll. Camb. MS. 108 is printed by James, *Cat.,* i.131:

> Ald man witles
> yung man recheles   } Aluredus king
> wyman ssameles
> betere ham were lifles

This variant in -les is a simple rendering of parts of the basic Latin list (cf. No. 54, notes). Otherwise, "the Five Evil Things are instructive merely as illustrating the extent to which the Abuses were sometimes varied or transformed by later paraphrasers" (Brown, *Archiv,* cxxviii.75).

57.   ABUSES OF THE AGE, II

Index, No. 3851. Not heretofore printed. Written in prose in a large volume of English prose devotions, including the *Mirror of St. Edmund.* Fourteenth century.

13. norshe] Cf. Trevisa, *Higden,* iv.99: "It is grete enemyte to werriours forto norsche sleuþe and leccherie."

58.   ENGLAND MAY SING ALAS

Index, No. 3133. Not heretofore printed from this MS. Occurs in the *Fasciculus Morum* (in at least nine MSS.), tempus Edward II; Bodley MS. 410 has been printed by Little, *Eng. St. in Franciscan Hist.,* p. 155, fn. 3. Little also prints a prayer for peace from the same MS. (*Index,* No. 3147) and notes: "The lawlessness of the powerful is frequently rebuked, and on this subject the English verses of the *Fasciculus Morum* attain a certain dignity" (p. 155).

Other pieces on the Abuses, found in sermon MSS., include *Index,* Nos. 592, 873, 2008, 2145, 2829, 3282, 4180.

59. TRUTH IS UNPOPULAR

Index, No. 72. Previously printed in *Rel. Ant.,* ii.165; by Wright, *Carols,* Warton Club, iv.19-20; by Chambers and Sidgwick, *Early Eng. Lyrics,* pp. 187-88; and by Greene, *Early Eng. Carols,* p. 257.

Nos. 59-61 are examples of the blending of religious, didactic and political elements into popular song. Sloane MS. 2593 and Bodl. MS. Eng. poet. e.1 are both portable books of popular carols.

8. heye mene] fine company (Greene).

22. Tr. He must seek (truth) calmly. Chambers & Sidgwick suggest emending: He must him seken besily.

24. he] truth.

60. HOW GOES THIS WORLD ABOUT

Index, No. 356. Previously printed by Wright, *Carols,* Warton Club, iv.96-98; and by Fehr, *Archiv,* cvii.50.

1. to a lend] a kenning. *O.E.D.* (land) does not record this spelling.

5. Lines 5 and 7 appear independently in a quatrain (*Index,* No. 3893): "Wele were him þat wiste / to whom he might trust." See also *Index,* No. 3892, ll. 1-2; No. 4092, ll. 4-5 (*Sec. Lyrics,* p. 101).

7. Cf. *Index,* No. 743, l. 8 (refrain): "For few be trew to tryst vpon."

11. Wo worth hem] Evil be to them. Cf. No. 72, l. 66.

16. Rel. pro. omitted.

21. Fehr omits this line, and is consequently short of l. 24.

61. THIS WORLD IS VARIABLE

Index, No. 4236. Previously printed by Wright, *Carols,* Percy Soc. xxiii.9-10; and by Chambers and Sidgwick, *Early Eng. Lyrics,* pp. 178-79.

1. Tr. Would that we could look into men's minds as they really are, for things that are false. Cf. *Index,* No. 3892, ll. 7-12: "Wol god . . . þat al men myȝt y-knowe how here hert . . . stent."

7. Cf. the poems on the Abuses of the Age (e.g., No. 57).

9. Tr. No one thinks much of modesty.

11. cheson] (will) accuse.

19. *Index,* No. 3999, l. 3: "& bromes bere appylles in euery mede."

24. be see & sond] a poetic cliché.

62. *NOW IS ENGLAND PERISHED*

Index, No. 2335. Not previously printed from this MS. (early sixteenth-century, added to a partly blank page). Occurs also in Corp. Christi Coll. Oxf. MS. 237, f. 243*v* (16 ll.; added to flyleaf), printed by Wright, *Pol. Poems,* ii.252-53 (who also prints a L. epigram on the same theme). Probably about the same time as No. 49.

2. &] Often in these contrasting phrases, *and* must be tr. *but.* So ll. 3, 4, 5, 6, 7, 8, 10, 15.

4. Corpus inserts two extra lines here: "Many actes of parlament / And few kept wyth tru entent."

5. fayn to please] much flattery (Wright).

6. Corpus inserts two extra lines here: "And many a wondurfulle dysgyȝyng / By vnprudent and myssavyȝyng."

7. courtears] Corpus reading is preferable: countenanse (show of living).

9. Short gowns and slit sleeves had long time been popular. The *Brut* notes the yearly swing of fashion in 1346: "In þis tyme, Englisshe men so muche hauntted and cleuyd to þe wodnes and foley of þe strangers, þat fro þe tyme of þe comyng of þe Henauderns, xviij ȝere passid, þey ordeyned and chaungyd ham euery ȝere diuers schappis of disgyngeȝ of cloþing, of long large and wyde cloþis, destitu and desert fram al old honeste and good vsage; & anoþer tyme schorte cloþis & stretwasted, dagged & ket, & on euery side desslatered & boned, wiþ sleues & tapets of sircotys, & hodeȝ ouere longe & large, & ouermuche hangynde, þat if y soþ schal say, þey were more liche to turmentours & deuels in hire cloþing & schewyng & oþer arraye þen comen" (*EETS* 136.296-7). Cf. No. 52, l. 19.

12. thei] i.e., gallants. The Corpus text ends here.

13. Cf. *Index,* No. 1874, ll. 127-29:

> So meche ryches in aray and so grete nede,
> So many bedes born and so litel deuocion,
> So meche fastyng for hunger and so litel mede.

63. *THE WORLD UPSIDE DOWN*

Index, No. 2805. Previously printed by Robbins, *Anglia,* lxxii.386-387; the first st. only by E. L[obel], *Bodleian Quarterly Record,* iii.220. The MS. is a fragment of two leaves, one with medical receipts, and the other with this poem. Fifteenth century, "but the verse may be supposed to be older than the copy" (Lobel).

The piece is an "Evils of the Age" in reverse: by listing what should be, it points out, by the use of a "destroying" refrain, what is not. This refrain is (from the traditional viewpoint) so obviously improbable, that by implication the other statements of the preceding six lines are likewise improbable. The last stanza clinches the ironic approach: If it were not for their wisdom, and for the perfect stability of those (women) who wear fashionable apparel, we should all be in the mire!

A comparable direct attack, mentioning similar ills, is No. 49, with which lines can be compared: 4 cf. No. 49, l. 29; 5 (17), 8 (66), 10 (27), 12 (57-58), 13 (33), 25 (61), 32 (7), 34 (46-47,) 43 (45), and 47 (54).

3. Cf. *Index,* No. 3852, ll. 18-20:

> & envy causyth gret distaunce
> both in englond & in fraunce,
> Exylyd is benyngnyte.

7. Cf. Hoccleve, *Index,* No. 124, l. 9: "Stablenes in this worlde is there none / there is no thinge but chaunge and variaunce."

18. sugenaunsse] Probably a scribal corruption for *sojournant,* a visitor or guest.

25. at large] without restraint.

40. at þe counturtale] in retort.

43. vp so dovne] upside down. This st. anticipates the later burlesque prophecies, as found in *New and Merrie Prognostication* (London, 1623), quoted by Camden, *Library,* xii.107:

> Wiues to their husbandes shall be obedient,
> In all thinges that doe themselves content.
> Nor will giue them an ill word without doubt,
> At least-wise if their tongues be cut out.

64. DEFEND US FROM ALL LOLLARDRY

Index, No. 1926. Previously printed by Turner, *Hist. of England,* (1815), iii.227-29; by Ritson, *Anc. Songs,* i.121-27; and by Wright, *Pol. Poems,* ii.243-47.

Nos. 64 (f. 2*v*), 76 (f. 1*v*) and 79 (f. 4*v*), and a few lines from the S.E. Legendary (*Index,* No. 3973) appear on five leaves preceding a C Text of *Piers Plowman.* Nos. 76 and 79 are contemporary with the events they describe (1450 and 1458). No. 64, therefore, deals with a situation already forty years old. It may be dated some time after mid 1414 and before the end of 1417. The Lollards' attempted revolt in January of 1414 had been easily crushed (ll. 37-38, 137-40), although the movement still had many adherents (ll. 43, 81-82); and strong measures were being taken (ll. 83-84). However, Sir John Oldcastle, Lord Cobham, the most important figure among the Lollards, had escaped from the Tower and was at large (ll. 68-70, 95). He was finally taken in December, 1417, and hanged and burned "for his lewdeness and fals opynyons" (*EETS* 136.386). This poem makes no reference to his death. The *O.E.D.*, quoting words from this piece, dates them 1418 (once 1450 *willerdome*).

This is the only ME poem dealing exclusively with the Lollards, although No. 13 (ll. 137-40) notes the statute *De Haeretico Comburendo* of 1401; and No. 14 (ll. 57-64) has a veiled allusion to Oldcastle's relations with Henry V. No. 40 shows Hoccleve's usual line of political and religious orthodoxy in his praise of Henry V for attacking the Lollards. *Index*, No. 3407 is Hoccleve's appeal to Oldcastle to repent.

The fullest contemporary account of the trial of Oldcastle occurs in *Ypodigma Neustriae*, pp. 438-49; similarly in *Hist. Anglicana*, ii.291-99; also in the Harley 565 text of the *London Chronicle* (London, 1827), pp. 96-98; *Short Eng. Chronicle*, p. 54; *Gregory's Chronicle*, p. 108; Stow, p. 344.

"And in the same ȝere was syr John Oldecastell, knyght, lord of Cobham, arrested into þe Towre of London. And the same ȝere he brak the prison and wente awey. And the same ȝere purposed the forsayde syr John to haue slayn the kyng and his lordes at Eltham, that is to seye the xij day atte nyght. And þt same nyght the mayere of London hadde warnyng therof. And he toke the aldermen and all the wardes of London, and made grete wache that nyght. And þt same nyght the mayre toke John Burgate, carpenter, and many oþer of the same sekt and consentyng to the forsayde syr John. And þt same ȝere the xij*e* day fell vp on þe saterday. And the Mondeday next after the Kyng whit his lordes come fro Eltham thorowe London vnto Westm. And on the morn after at nyȝth the kyng and his lordes toke the feld: for he hadde tydyng þt the forsayde syr John and syr Roger of Acton schulde be in the same feld the Wednesday next followyng w*t* xxv. M*l*. people for to distroie the Kyng and all his lordes: and the same nyȝght the Kynges men toke of hem iiij*xx* and moo of syr John Oldecastell meyne. And the friday after was forjuged of such traytours atte Westm. lxix, and led to the Tour. And the same day xij of hem weren drawe from the Towr vnto Neugate. And on the morn after were xxv moo of hem drawen from the Tour vnto Newgate, and forth all in fere vnto seint Giles; and there was made New galows for hem. And there thei were hanged euerychon: and vij of hem were brent Galows and all, and xxix henge styll on the Galowes. And the ffriday, the xix day of Janyuer, were iiij moo drawen and hanged; of wiche one was a preest þt hyght syr John Beuerley, the ij was John Burgate, the thirde a texte writer of sent Jones strete, and the iiij was a Glouer on Londen Brigge. Also the same ȝere, the xxv day of Janyuer, was a preest that hit syr Water drawen and hanged for treson: the weche preeste, as men seydon, had bought for Cobham as many bowes, arowes and other stuff as cost ix mark" (Kingsford, *Eng. Hist. Lit.,*

pp. 292-93, quoting from Harley MS. 3775 of *London Chronicle*).
12. a b c] Cf. No. 91, l. 12.
13. lolle] to speak or act as a Lollard, hence to mumble, sing in a low tone (cf. l. 81). Langland gives a false etymology equating loll with to be lame: *Piers Plowman*, C.x. 213-18:

> Now kyndeliche, by crist beþ suche callyd lolleres,
> As by englisch of oure eldres of olde menne techynge.
> He þat lolleþ is lame oþer his leg oute of ioynte,
> Oþer meymed in some membre, for to meschief hit souneþ.
> And ryght so sothlyche such manere eremytes
> Lollen aȝen þe byleyue and lawe of holy churche.

In a Latin poem (c. 1381) linking the Lollards with the insurrection, they are referred to as weeds (*lolia*) in the garden (Wright, *Pol. Poems*, i.232); so Gower in *Vox Clamantis.*
33. old castel] An obvious pun on Sir John Oldcastle; cf. l. 26.
47. burthe] the act of being born.
53. colde] fig. *O.E.D.* quotes Trevisa: "In Asturia in Spain is scarce of wyne, of whete, and of oyle: for the londe is colde."
55. solde] soiled, polluted.
74. Cf. Adae de Usk, pp. 121, 301.
94. i.e., Henry V.
99. Cf. *Ypodigma Neustriae*, p. 444 for opposition to images.
105. Ho wor] they were.
106. Cf. No. 39, l. 62.
116. hym] it, the statue of St. James. The "cowardice" of destroying an image is continued in ll. 121-28.

65. THE ORDERS OF CAIN, 1382

Index, No. 2777. Previously printed by Wright, *Pol. Poems*, i.263-68; by Brewer, *Monumenta Franciscana*, RS 4, i.601-6; and by Cook, *Reader*, pp. 361-64 (ll. 1-84 only). The poem is struck through with diagonal lines across the page.

This poem is preceded in the MS. by a Latin poem, with an O and I refrain, declaiming against the various orders. In describing the Council of London (May 19, 1382) which met to sentence the reformers, it is decidedly pro-Wyclif and attacks both friars and monks (printed by Wright, *Pol. Poems*, i.253-63; and by Brewer, pp. 592-601). The report of the proceedings is obviously contemporary. The parallel but more generalized sentiments of the English poem, its proximity in the same MS., and a similar "confession" to lend verisimilitude to its charges indicate a similar date:

Haec ego qui feceram, monachus agressus,
Per hos rasus fueram, sed nondum professus;
Sed de magnis ocreis cito fui fessus,
Et ad Christi regulam statim sum egressus.

(*Pol. Poems,* i.258)

Other ME poems attacking the friars include some scurrilous squibs (*Index,* Nos. 808, 1148); the early satire on the various orders of friars (and citizens) of Kildare (*Index,* No. 1078); the humorous fable *Lyarde* (*Index,* No. 2026) which takes up the theme of ll. 73-96; and the lengthy *Pierce the Ploughmans Crede* (*Index,* No. 663). A later poem in B.M. MS. Roy. App. 58 ("ffrere gastkyn wo ye be"), pr. Flügel, *Anglia,* xii.268-69.

The light tone of irony of the first six st. describing the contrast between precept and practice (cf. ll. 162-63) gives way to direct abuse, and the effectiveness of the poem is perhaps lessened by the sledgehammer blows against the friars' lechery and greed.

18. neres] Not kidneys, but the form with unhistoric -n used with *the* instead of *a.* Cf. No. 52, l. 38 (narse).

22. so reduced by penance (*Pol. Poems,* i. p. lxviii).

24. trusse] pack himself out of town.

35. marcerye] textiles and small wares.

37. Cf. *Index,* No. 3864; and *Sec. Lyrics,* note, p. 230.

40. Tr. Where they are accustomed to go.

44. Tr. until he has his will.

48. brewe] fig. fare.

49. pelure] fur, esp. used for lining or trimming garments.

51. reuerce] to turn back or trim (a garment) with some other material.

53. vaire] A fur obtained from a kind of squirrel with grey back and white belly, much used as a trimming or lining for garments.

gryse] a kind of grey fur.

54. bugee] budge, a kind of fur consisting of lamb's skin with the wool dressed outwards.

71. thryfe] thee is perhaps the more common idiom. Cf. No. 4, l. 190; No. 15, l. 85; and No. 67, l. 39.

76. nauther loude ne still] a poetic cliché.

81. lymitour] friar licensed to beg in a specific area. Cf. Chaucer, Wife of Bath's Tale, 9-25.

83. make maystries] play tricks.

87. gelde] geld (impotent) is first rec. *O.E.D.* 1325; gelt (castrated) not until 1440.

97. This st. is pr. by Little, *Eng. St. in Franciscan History,* p. 117: "The arguments for and against the employment of friars as confessors vary little from the time of William of St. Amour and Bonaventura to those of Armachanus and Wiclif."

107. cayme] Cain, the first murderer recorded in the Bible (Gen. 4) and hence used descriptively.

110. carmes] Carmelites.

111. austynes] Augustinians.

112. Iacobynes] Dominicans: originally applied to the French Dominicans from their first church of St. Jacques (Jacobus).

113. frer menours] Franciscans: or lesser brothers (Fratres minores), so called to signify the humility of the order. Mod. Eng. pl. friars minor.

127. The Templars had been disbanded and their properties sequestered by Edward II, on orders of the Papacy, starting in 1309.

135. The practice of replacing special paid masses for individuals by the general masses. Cf. the attack in the Latin poem (*Pol. Poems*, i.257) on suffrages or memorials at specified services ("Fratres in capitulis solent compilare literas").

141. annuels] payment for daily or anniversary masses. So adj. (l. 155).

143. possessioners] endowed clergymen. Cf. *Piers Plowman*, B.v.144; and *Index*, No. 655, ll. 73-76:

> The mownte of contemplacion strong it is to stey,
> Inhabited with possessioner and with mendinant;
> If I be a frere I may begge alway,
> Many diuerse townys frely for to hawnt.

144. mayntene] equal.

151. seruice] particular ritual services paid for by the recipient, the offertories going to the administering priest.

169. Cf. the lines quoted from the L. poem on the Council of London, above.

66. ON THE MINORITES, 1382

Index, No. 2663. Previously printed in *Rel. Ant.*, i.322; by Wright, *Pol. Poems*, i.268-70; by Heuser, *Anglia*, xxvii.302-3; by Brewer, *Monumenta Franciscana*, pp. 606-8; and by Cook, *Reader*, pp. 364-65.

Wright took this poem to be an attack on the Franciscans for their use of "pageants and theatrical shows"; similarly *Rel. Ant.* calls it "a poem against the Friars and their Miracle Plays." The descriptions, however, would seem more appropriate for wall paintings, such as appeared in the large churches the Franciscans built especially for their preaching; l. 19 describing "þer comes one out of þe skye in a grey goun" would hardly fit a dramatic performance.

The major literary interest of No. 66 is its use of the "O and I" refrain. There are fourteen other ME poems with this (or equivalent) refrain: *Index*, Nos. 412 and 1001; 1320 and 3567 (in Bodl. MS.

Don.C.13); 701 (two MSS.); 2021, 3069, 3363; 4083; *69; and 3921 ("I & E"). Heuser prints Nos. 412, 701, 1001, 2021, and 3921 in *Anglia* and discusses the form. Hammerle prints Nos. 4083 and *69 and makes comments. Three poems not listed in the *Index* are printed by A. H. Smith in *London Medieval Studies*, ii, from B. M. Addit. MS. 45869 (c.1349): "Of Alle þe witti men & wise I warne Alle i þe wache"; "Luce In hys lessoun lerede me to synge"; and "Loue hym wrouste / and loue hym brouste / Man to be hys fere."

This group of twelve poems has much in common: a standard form (septenary lines, all except one rhyming *aaaabb)*, a refrain, and generally a moral theme. They all date about the end of the fourteenth or very early fifteenth century (only the Royal MS. of No. 701 is very late fifteenth century). One of the earliest, the related sections on the Four Evangelists (No. 2021), is based on the Northern Homily Collection (Heuser, *Anglia,* xxvii.262-315).

Various theories have been advanced on the use and significance of the letter refrains. Hammerle *(Anglia,* liv. 292-96) believes that the fourteenth-century Latin poems attacking the friars, to express their excitement, took over into the refrain the vernacular expression "Ho there! Hi!" in a degenerated form "O and I" (Ho and Hi). He states (p. 293) that this expression of excitement prevails in each stanza and the English words become typical of any general mood of excitement. When this refrain appears in ME didactic poems, the expression suited to stormy fighting songs is no longer valid, and its emotional element is suppressed. Hammerle gives some later expressions which parallel the refrain (Heigh-ho, With a hey and a ho). Heuser *(Anglia,* xxvii.300) suggests "O and I" represent a form of "Ay and O" (for ever and ay), and quotes Harley MS. 2253:

> Long is ay and long is ho,
> Long is wy and long is wo!

This change is linguistically impossible. There are other difficulties in both theories: "heh", for example, does not occur as an expression of sorrow or surprise or to attract attention before 1475. It seems more simple to regard these letters simply as letters: if there were any significance there would be a tendency to retain a standard form; but as well as "O and I" there occur also: "A and I" (No. 3069, Caius MS.), "O and V" (No. 701); and "I and E," "E and I," and "E and O" *(Index,* No. 3921). Furthermore, Latin poems of the twelfth and thirteenth centuries used vowels for decoration, and Raby *(Sec. Lat. Poetry,* ii.330) quotes some examples from the *Carmina Burana:*

> a et o, o et i
> mira virtus Stephani.

and again:

> Philistei, Philistei, surgite,
> clipeos et lanceas arripite,
> i et e, i et o, hostem victum teneo,
> i et e, i et o, calvatum derideo.

Tauno Mustanoja, in *Neuphil. Mitteilungen,* lvi.161-71, reviews previous theories and presents a theory of an i-o gradation with an inherent swinging movement; "this type of vowel variation has become a symbol of a certain kind of dance movement and has developed into the well-known types of o-i refrain."

5. *Rel. Ant.* misprints the refrain, "I and an O."

18. Armachan] Richard FitzRalph, Archbishop of Armagh (d.1360), a strong opponent of the Irish mendicants.

21. Mahoun] Mahomet.

31. cart] To represent Elijah carried up to heaven in a fiery chariot.

36. faire mot byfall] may good befall (them).

37. For another attack on the greed of the friars, cf. *Wynnere and Wastoure* (*Index,* No. 3137), c.1352-53, one of the earliest examples of political satire of the Alliterative Revival.

67. FRIARS, MINISTRI MALORUM

Index, No. 871. Previously printed in *Rel. Ant.,* ii.247; and by Wright, *Pol. Poems,* ii.249-50. The Trinity MS. is a late fifteenth-century miscellany, written by William Womyndham, Canon of Kyrkeby super Algam; it includes two other English poems, *Index,* No. 806, "Augustinus de peccatis venialibus", and No. 3866, "Decem remedia contra peccata veniala."

15. blere a mannus ye] deceive, throw dust in the eye. *O.E.D.* notes "very common in 16th c."

23. Cf. No. 65, ll. 73-96.

37. mony-makers] counterfeiters.

38. proditores] traitors. From the beginning of the fourteenth century, there were sporadic accusations of treachery against friars, and the chronicles record a number of executions. Typical charges are found in an *English Chronicle* (pp. 25-26) for the year 1402. A justice says to a group of friars accused of stirring up sentiment for Richard: "Ye bith endited that ye in ipocrisie and flateryng and fals lif, haue prechid fals sermons; wherynne ye saide falsli that king Richard livith .... Also, ye with your fals flateryng and ypocrisie, haue gadrid a gret summe of money with begging, and sent it to Oweyne of Glendore, a traitour, that he sholde come and destroy Englond."

68. *THE LAYMAN'S COMPLAINT*

Index, No. 3697. Previously printed by Utley, *Harvard Theological Rev.*, xxxviii.144; and by Henry A. Person, *Camb. Lyrics* (Seattle, 1952), pp. 41-42.

Nos. 68 and 69 are written in a fifteenth-century hand, without break, on the flyleaf of a fourteenth-century *Poor Caitiff*. Added in a later hand, in the margin against No. 69, is "The fryers Complaynt." There are many scribal errors in both texts.

2. berfot] Utley notes the controversy whether friars should wear shoes, sandals, or no footwear at all. Cf. Little, *Eng. St. in Franciscan Hist.*, pp. 56-57; and *Pierce the Ploughman's Crede* (*Index*, No. 663), ll. 298-300:

> Fraunces bad his breþeren - barfote to wenden;
> Nou han þei bucled schon - for bleynynge of her heles,
> And hosen in harde weder - y-hamled by þe ancle.

4. In principio] The conventional greeting of the friars. Robinson, *Chaucer*, p. 758, suggests the sentence was "regarded with peculiar reverence and even held to have a magical value." Cf. *Jacke Upland*, par. 18 (*Pol. Poems*, ii.23):

> For ye win more by yeare
> with In principio,
> than with all the rules
> that ever your patrones made.

14. Utley sees in this line evidence of the poet's Lollard sympathy, for the Second Version of the Lollard Bible translates II Tim. 3.1-6, (...Ex his enim sunt qui penetrant domos): "Of these thei ben that persen housis." The passage continues: "et captiuas ducunt mulierculas oneratas peccatis, quae ducuntur variis desideriis," which any reformer would hold especially applicable to the friars.

16. mydday deuilis] Cf. Ps. 90.6 (Daemonium meridianum). A.V. (91.6) has "the destruction that wasteth at noonday."

18. Cf. No. 63, l. 34, and No. 67, l. 38. Also *English Chronicle*, p. 26; "ye with your fals flateryng and ypocrisie, haue gadrid a grete summe of money with begging."

69. *THE FRIAR'S ANSWER*

Index, No. 161. Previously printed by Utley, *Harvard Theological Rev.*, xxxviii.145; and by Person, *Camb. Lyrics*, pp. 42-43.

4. aposen] to bring forward objections against a theological argument.

5. wondriþ me] (impers.) I wonder.

15. poppe] Although not so rec. *O.E.D.*, poppe here seems to mean any priest; cf. pope-holy in derogatory sense in *Piers Plowman*, B.xiii.284; and No. 45, l. 2: "ande the prest haffys the poppys power in hande." Utley reads *coppe*.

17. sae] This form may be a scribal error for saie.

18. Cf. *Piers Plowman*, C.vi.56-57: "Clerkes þat aren crouned of kynde vnderstondyng / Sholde noþer swynke ne swete ne swere at enquestes."

19. leggen] Cf. *Jack Upland's Rejoinder* (*Pol. Poems*, ii.41): "thou leggist oft Goddis lawe / bot to a false entente."

20. Cf. Acts 18.3. .

21. nabete] Clerical dress. The transfer of -n from the personal pronoun to a following word beg. with a vowel is frequent in ME. Cf. No. 52, l. 38.

23. russet] coarse cloth, not necessarily reddish in color, but grey; hence with allusion to the Grey or Franciscan Friars (cf. No. 66, l. 32). The Dominicans, of course, wore black, and the Carmelites white habits. Cf. Little, *Eng. St. in Franciscan History*, pp. 59-61, for tunics.

24. werynge cloþes] articles of clothing (collectively).

25. I not] A verb (such as beg) is needed here.

32. Tr. But (they) hasten us (on) quickly, so that we might be gone.

34. gyle] The only rec. meaning "deceit" seems less suitable here than some meaning like "harm," "damage."

70. *A TRADE POLICY*

Index, No. 921. Previously printed by Wright, *Pol. Poems*, ii.282-87. For discussion see Introduction, pp. xlii-xliv; and Robbins, *MLN*, lxxi.245-48. Cf. also "The Wool Trade in the Fifteenth Century" in *Studies in English Trade in the Fifteenth Century*, ed. Eileen Power and M. M. Postan (London, 1951), pp. 39-90.

1. The first four lines come from the Envoy to the *Libelle of Englyshe Polycye* (*Index*, No. 3491), ll. 1142-45.

5. In the *Libelle* this line runs on, to hardynesse.

9. Cf. *Libelle*, ll. 88-89:

> They may not lyven to mayntene there degrees
> Wythoughten oure Englysshe commodytees.

12. Cf. *Libelle* (ll. 1153-54): "That thow arte trewe, and thus he dothe recorde / Nexte the Gospell."

20. the] they. See Glossary *þey*.

24. beryth the lantern] shows the way as a leader.

27. oone] This and l. 34 form the basis of the policy outlined in the *Libelle* (cf. ll. 99-101, 114, 123-25, 255-59, 337-38, etc.).

41. The *Libelle* mentions only some of these states: Hainault, Normandy, Brittany, France, Portugal, Spain, Prussia, Florence, Venice, Genoa, Catalonia, Bohemia, and Hungary.

53. These lines plead for regularization of the wool trade by establishing a floor for selling prices and a ceiling for the grades of wool.

55. Cf. Art. 12, Cotton Rolls ii.23: "The seconde griff is for that the woll and ffell hath course and passage oute of the Ream, wherfore all Straungers take but litell reward to bye oure Inglisshe clothe, but make hit theym selff" (Kingsford, *Eng. Hist. Lit.,* p. 363). Many of the suggestions of this poem were incorporated into legislation adopted in 1463 (and repeated in 1464), which forbade alien merchants to export wool, inasmuch as English weavers were short of raw material, and which forbad the importation of foreign woolens. "And overe this, forasmoch as the assured availle and wurship of the Wolle growyng within the Reame of Englend, the chief and principall Commodite of the same Reame, resteth in two amonges other. First, that such suffisaunt plenteth of the seid Wolle be ever abidyng and remaynyng within the seid Reame, as mowe serve resonably and competently to the occupation of the Makers of Cloth, and of all the membres and braunches therof, wherthurgh the Citees, Burghs, and Tounes of the same Reame, fallen into grete and piteous declyne, desolation and ruyne, by th'occasion of ydelnes, mowe yf God wille, be multiplied inhabitations, and restored to their auncien joye and prosperite in labour, wherby the vyces and inconveniencez of ydelnes mowe be remoeved, to Goddes pleasure" (*Rot. Parl.* v.503).

56. at the full] fully; cf. l. 69 (and *Libelle,* ll. 78, 450).

57. If poor quality wool is sold to foreigners, the English clothmakers will be at an advantage; for manufacture of any kind of cloth, "þe cost ys neuer the less" although the price for cloth of poor wool is "sympyll." And so ll. 69-72.

63. gardyng] Various processes in clothmaking (in most instances the first rec. usage in *O.E.D.*). Gardyng (O.Fr. guerder) is the dressing of wool with a comb to set fibres in order. Fullyng is beating cloth in order to cleanse and thicken it — cf. *Piers Plowman,* B.xv.44-45: "Cloth þat cometh fro þe weuyng is nouȝt comly to were / Tyl it is fulled vnder fote or in fullyng-stokkes." Rowyng is putting a nap on the cloth. Scheryng is removing the superfluous nap. The toukers (l. 80) stretched the cloth in order to finish it.

68. nasse] Several examples of unhistoric -n are found in this anthology, not rec. *O.E.D.* See No. 52, l. 38.

69. into lytyll] very nearly.

75. preuayle] benefit. Sole ref. *O.E.D.*

85. take kepe] take heed.

87. The large manufacturers forced the workers to take half their wages in merchandise. This is the mene (opportunity, device) the poem condemns. The factor gave the cloth to the worker at the inflated market price (sixpence) although its value was the actual wholesale price (threepence). The manufacturers were thereby able to increase their profits and in fact reduce the wages of their employees. In 1463, and again in 1464, Parliament passed ordinances forbidding this practice: "And also, where heretofore in the occupations of makyng of Cloth, the Laborers therof, have been dryven to take grete part of their wages in Pynnes, Girdels, and other unprofitable Merchaundise, under such price as stretcheth not to th'extent of their lefull wages, and also delyveren unto hem Wolles to be wrought by over excessive weyght, which hath dryven, and dryveth men and women into discorage of such labour; that therfore it may please unto your seid Highnes, to ordeyn and stablissh by the seid auctorite, that every man and woman Clothmaker, from the fest of seint John Baptist next commyng, pay to the Carders, Spynners, and all other the Laborers of eny membr' therof, lawfull money for all their lefull wages and payment of the same; and also delyver Wolles to be wrought, accordyng to the true pounde, and due weyght, upon peyne of forfeiture to the same Laborer, of the treble of his seid wages soo unpaied, as ofte as the seid Clothmaker refuseth to pay in that manere and fourme, to eny such Laborer by hym put to occupacion in eny of the seid membres of makyng of Cloth; and also to forfeit to the same Laborer, for every pounde of excesse and untrue weight, delyvered hym to be wrought, vi d. at every defaute ... [and all local authorities] have auctorite and power by this Ordenaunce, to here and determyn the compleyntes of every such Clothmaker and Laborer, aswell for noon paiement of the seid wages of the seid Laborers, as of the seid Forfeiture and Damagez, by due examination of the parties in that behalf" (*Rot. Parl.* v.502; 562 for 1464; similarly *Statutes of the Realm,* ii.403-7).

100. Another trick to defraud the workers. Twelve pounds of wool to be spun would be weighed and credited as nine pounds, equivalent to a wage cut of 25 percent. See above (l. 87 note) for "true pounde."

109. in usage] regularly.

119. On the other hand, the poem wants silver miners to be paid in coins to be produced at a mint near the mine, to obtain the full value of their wages. Cf. *Gregory's Chronicle,* p. 227 for changes in coinage in 1464.

139. endraperyng] weaving into cloth; *O.E.D.* has this ref. only.

71. *THE SUDDEN FALL OF PRINCES*
BY LYDGATE

Index, No. 500. Previously printed by MacCracken, *EETS* 192.660-61. Occurs also in Harley MS. 2251, f. 254*r* (H) and B. M. Addit. MS. 29729, f. 169*v* (A). Collation: 28. he in parice themferys A; 33. and that H; 42. the Armynakes H; 44. he edde H; 46. *margin* loomcerean A; 49. bourned A.

The Fall of Princes, Lydgate's longest work (36,365 ll.), c.1431-1438, lists numerous men who fell from greatness; its underlying theme

> Fortunis wheel by reuolucioun
> Doth oon clymbe up, another to discende

is part of the basic philosophy of the Middle Ages. The seven "balades" of No. 71 summarize seven examples of this theory. In spite of the absence of a descriptive colophon (with which the Trinity MS. generally heads its poems), the poem appears to be a mumming. In overall intention, it resembles Lydgate's *Index* No. 1928 (342 ll.), a "desguysing to fore þe gret estates of þis lande, þane being at London" with Dame Fortune and four attendants. Its moral, "pleasant and notable," is similar:

> A thousande moo þan I can telle —
> In-to mescheef howe þey felle
> Dovne frome hir wheel, on see and lande.

For other allusions to Lady Fortune, cf. Nos. 38, ll. 42, 126-28; 72, ll. 20-22; 74, l. 6; also *Index,* No. 2576, ll. 50-56. For a later lyric with same title, cf. Hales & Furnivall, *Bishop Percy's Folio MS.,* iii.169-73.

1. Edwarde] Cf. No. 38.

7. Cf. Baker, p. 33; followed by Stow, *Annales,* p. 227: "one night being the twentie two of September, they came rushing in vpon him sodainlie, as hee lay in his bed, with great and heauie featherbeds, being in weight as much as 15. strong men could beare, wherewith they oppressed and strangled him by smoothering. Into whom also they thrust a plummers sodring yron, being made red hot, vp into his bowelles, through a certaine Instrument like to the end of a Trumpet or glister pipe, put in at the fundament, burning thereby his inward parts, prouiding thereby least anie wound being founde in the Kings bodie, might cause his tormentors to answere for committinge open treason, and therefore suffer iust punishment."

8. Richard] Cf. No. 40.

15. Of the seven men named here, Charles VI of France was the latest to die; 1422 is therefore a *terminus a quo* for the dating of this poem.

22. Orlyaunce] Louis, Duke of Orleans, murdered by partisans of John, Duke of Burgundy, in November, 1407. Cf. No. 14, l. 85.

26. Louis was suspected of immoral relations with several noble-women, including his sister-in-law, Isabella of Bavaria, queen of Charles VI.

27. Cf. No. 14, l. 85, and No. 15.

29. Thomas] Thomas of Woodstock, Duke of Gloucester, focussed the opposition to Richard II by his condemnation of foreign policy. The Earl of Derby betrayed his intrigues, and Gloucester was arrested in July, 1397, and sent under arrest to Calais. When his case was considered by Parliament in the following September, his keeper, the Earl of Nottingham, was unable to produce the prisoner. Tait, *Owens Coll. Historical Essays* (Manchester, 1903), pp. 193-216, suggests he was tricked into a confession on promises of immunity, and then quietly killed.

35. comvne profit] Cf. No. 13, l. 98.

36. Burgoyne] See above, l. 27.

37. douspiers] The twelve great peers, spiritual and temporal, of France, supposed to represent the paladins of Charlemagne, in the romances, as the bravest of knights. The six spiritual were the Archbishop of Rheims, and the Bishops of Laon, Langres, Beauvais, Chalons, and Noyon; the temporal were the Dukes of Normandy, Burgundy, and Aquitaine, and the Counts of Toulouse, Flanders, and Champagne. Cf. No. 3, l. 50.

41. his] Louis, Duke of Orleans.

42. armynakes] The Armagnacs, who now entered into alliance with the English, former allies of Burgundy.

43. Yrland] Robert de Vere, ninth Earl of Oxford (1362-1392), hereditary Great Chamberlain of England. One of Richard's earliest favorites (cf. *Hist. Anglicana,* ii.148), he was nominated Governor of Ireland in 1385, and created Duke of Ireland in 1386, although he did not leave England. Discontent against him rising, he was accused by the King's uncle, Thomas of Woodstock (cf. l. 32), and defeated in battle in 1387. He escaped to Holland, where he learned of his sentence of death passed in 1388; he stayed in France until 1389, and then fled to Louvain. He was killed by a boar while hunting, in 1392, and three years later his body was returned to England for burial in the priory at Earl's Colne, Essex (Trokelowe, pp. 184-85).

46. He divorced his wife, Phillippa, daughter of his guardian, the Earl of Bedford, and Gloucester's niece, for one of the queen's ladies in waiting, reputedly a Bohemian. The appelation "laumer-rane," an error for "Launcecrona" (loomcerean in A), is explained in *Hist. Anglicana,* ii.160: "et aliam duceret, quae cum Regina Anna venerat de Boemia, ut fertur, cujusdam sellarii filiam, ignobilem

prorsus atque foedam; ob quam causam magna surrepsit occasio scandalorum: — cujus nomen erat, in vulgari idiomate, 'Launce-crona.' "

72. THE LAMENT OF THE DUCHESS OF GLOUCESTER, 1441

Index, No. 3720. Previously printed by Hardwick, *Cambridge Antiq. Soc. Com.*, i.186-90. A shorter version (omitting st. 5, 7-9) in Balliol Coll. Oxf. MS. 354, is printed by Wright, *Pol. Poems*, ii.205-8; by Flügel, *Anglia*, xxvi.177-80; and by Dyboski, *EETS* ci.95-96. The variations are not important. In the Balliol MS., the poem following is the parallel "Lamytacion of Quene Elyzabeth" (1503).

Jacqueline, Countess of Holland and Hainault, had married her cousin, the impotent John, Duke of Brabant, hoping to strengthen herself against her uncle, John the Pitiless, Duke of Burgundy. Her husband coming under her uncle's domination, Jacqueline fled to England. Without waiting for the results of an appeal to the Pope for annulment, she married Humphrey, Duke of Gloucester, in 1423, and was recognized as his Duchess. For this event, Lydgate wrote congratulatory verses (*Index*, No. 3718). Humphrey led a short and unsuccessful attempt to regain his wife's lands; he returned to England, leaving Jacqueline in Holland. By 1428 the Pope had found that Gloucester's marriage to Jacqueline was invalid. Thereupon, Gloucester, who had longtime forsaken her, married his mistress, Eleanor Cobham, daughter of Lord Reginald Cobham. Public opinion was hostile to Gloucester for his desertion of his wife, and women of London protested to the Lords how this act led to "suae personae, regni ruinae, et sponsalis ordinis efficaciae" (Amundesham, p. 20). Lydgate, too, wrote a poem on the misfortunes of the Countess (*Index*, No. 92; see Hammond, *Anglia*, xxvii.381-98).

In 1441 Gloucester was indirectly attacked by the arraignment of his wife Eleanor on charges of witchcraft and treason (according to Hall, p. 202). An ecclesiastical court found her guilty, and sentenced her to do penance by walking barefoot three times through the streets of London, and to imprisonment for life. Gloucester apparently was unable to save his wife this public humiliation and separation from him.

Since Humphrey was next in succession, his wife was therefore in line to be Queen. The attack on such a personage captured the imagination of the chroniclers, who report the event carefully. The present song is another result. A later ballad in quatrains, in Thomas Evans, *Old Ballads*, 1784, i.317-23, tells of Eleanor's sins, her spells and magic. This ballad was current when the *Mirror for Magistrates* was written, and the story of Humphrey and Eleanor told therein. There, Eleanor disclaims the charges; here she tacitly accepts them (See Campbell, *Huntington Lib. Bulletin,* v.119-55).

The charge of sorcery for political purposes was not uncommon during the fifteenth century, cf. Queen Joan (1419), Joan of Arc (1431), and the Duke of Clarence (1477).

7. "I have a large retinue — ironical" (Hardwick). But "wone" may be tr. possessions.

9. art] i.e., magic.

10. ensample] "A deterrent instance of punishment, or of the evil consequences of any course of conduct" (*O.E.D.*).

51. clerk] Roger Boltyngbroke, "a gret and a konnyng man in astronomye, and maister Thomas Suthwelle a chanon of saint Steveneȝ chapel wythynne Westmynstre, were take as conspiratours of the kyngis deth" (*English Chronicle*, p. 57). Bolingbroke as house chaplain was part of Humphrey's circle of scholars. Accused with them were another priest and Margery Jourdain, "the witch of Eye"; cf. *Six Town Chronicles,* p. 102.

53. course of kynde] the ordinary procedure of nature.

55. This is a well-known cliché, found in courtly love lyrics. Cf. *Index,* No. 2245, l. 2: "ther may no barn my balyes on-bynd" (*Sec. Lyrics,* p. 151).

58. "In the mene tyme, the forsaid maister Roger was examned before the kyngis counsel; where he confessid and saide that he wroughte the said nygromancie atte stiryng of the forsaid dame Alienore, to knowe what sholde falle of hir and to what astat she sholde come" (*English Chronicle,* p. 58).

60. The charge was making a wax image of the King by which his death was to be encompassed.

65. "The said maister Roger and maister Thomas as principalle, and the said dame Alienore as accessory, were enditid of treson" (*English Chronicle,* p. 58).

73. "Ferthirmore on the Satirday the xxj day of Octobir, in the chapel beforsaid, befor the bisshoppis of Londoun, maister Robert Gilbert, and of Lincoln maister William Alnewik, and of Norwich maister Thomas Brouns, to whom the said archebissshoppe of Cauntirbury, maister Henri Chichele, hadde committid his power be his commissioun because of his seeknesse to fynyshe and ende this mater, the said Alienore apperid" (*English Chronicle,* p. 59).

84. dyd ther diligence] tried their utmost (to have me slain).

90. "Wherfore she was citid to appere befor certayn bisshoppis of the kyngis; that is to say, befor maister Harri Chicheli, archebisshop of Cauntirbury, maister Harry Beaufort bisshoppe of Wynchestre and cardinalle, maister Johan Kemp archebisshoppe of York

and cardinalle, maister William Ayscoughe bisshoppe of Salisbury, and othir" (*English Chronicle,* p. 58).

92. "The said Alienore apperid and witnesseȝ were broughte forth and examned" (*English Chronicle,* p. 59).

93. "The Thursday abouesaid the said dame Alienore apperid befor tharchebisshoppe and othir in the forsaid chapelle, and receyued her penaunce vnder this fourme; that she sholde go the same day fro Templebarre with a meke and a demure countenaunce vnto Poulis beryng in her hond a tapir of a pound, and offre it there atte highe auter" (*English Chronicle,* p. 59). And similarly for two succeeding days. *Short Eng. Chronicle,* p. 63; *Chronicle of London,* p. 129; *Six Town Chronicles,* p. 115.

97. "The whiche penaunce she fulfillid and dede righte mekely, so that the more part of the peple hadde on hir gret compassioun" (*English Chronicle,* p. 60). The penance was first performed on November 13, 1441.

105. The farewell anaphora is a common ornament; cf. *Index,* Nos. 752, 763, 764, 766, 767, 4209 (*Sec. Lyrics,* pp. 122, 207-8, 212-14).

107. The Duke had a palace at Greenwich.

111. lerpole] Chester, not Liverpool, was the port for the northwest. "And aftir this she was committid ayen to the warde of ser Thomas Stanley, wherynne she was al her lif aftir." She was first sent to Chester Castle, then to Kenilworth Castle (October, 1443); in July, 1446, she was removed to the Isle of Man, but was returned to London the next year. In 1447, an act of Parliament deprived her of her dower, "considering the gret misgovernaunce of Alianore" (*Rot. Parl.,* v.135).

114. in grayne] fast dyed, scarlet.

125. prike ne prawnce] an allit. kenning, to ride (fast). Cf. No. 51, l. 14.

73. *EPITAPH FOR THE DUKE OF GLOUCESTER,*
1447

Index, No. 3206. Previously printed by Robbins, *Neuphil. Mitteilungen,* lvi. 241-49, with discussion and full notes. Occurs also in B.M. MS. Addit. 34360, f. 65*v*.

Stow, at the end of the *Siege of Thebes* in Speght's 1598 edition of Chaucer, appended a list of Lydgate's works, which included "81. Epitaph on Humphrey Duke of Glocester." This appeared as No. 139 in Ritson's list. MacCracken writes (*EETS* cvii.xi): "certainly not by Lydgate. It is a very feeble thing indeed, written in his manner, but has no MS. support for Lydgate's name, or any accordance with a known poem of his." MacCracken further notes the non-Lydgatian rhyme pattern: st. 6, abye: the; st. 9, dowarye: by: ny: I cry, etc. Vickers, *Humphrey Duke of Gloucester,* p. 390, thought the piece by Lydgate, but held no more praise for it than Mac-Cracken: "Finally, he lived long enough to write the 'Epitaphium Ducis Gloucesterie,' a piece of doggerel which almost surpasses its predecessors."

The suspected murder of Duke Humphrey in 1447 caused a sensation which reverberated several years until the death of the one considered most implicated (cf. Nos. 75 and 76) and even later (cf. No. 93, l. 37). A convenient summary of the older chronicles is given by Hall's *Chronicle,* pp. 209-10:

"So for the furtheraunce of their purpose, a parliament was somoned to be kept at Bery, whether resorted all the peres of the realme, and emongest them, the duke of Gloucester, whiche on the second daie of the session, was by the lorde Beaumond, then high Constable of Englande, accompanied by the duke of Buckyngham, and other, arrested, apprehended, and put in warde, and all his seruauntes sequestered from hym, and xxxii of the chief of his retinue, were sent to diuerse prisons, to the greate admiracion of the common people. The duke the night after his emprisonement, was found dedde in his bed, and his body shewed to the lordes and commons, as though he had died of a palsey or empostome: but all indifferent persons well knewe, that he died of no natural death but of some violent force: some iudged hym to be strangled: some afferme, that a hote spitte was put in at his foundement: other write, that he was stiffeled or smoldered betwene twoo fetherbeddes ... When the rumor of the dukes death, was blowen through the realme, many men wer sodainly appalled and amased for feare: many abhorred and detested ye faict, but all men reputed it an abhominable crueltie, and a shameful tiranny. But the publique wealth of the realme of Englande, by the vnworthy death of this pollitique prince, susteined greate losse, & ran into ruyne, for surely the whole waight and burden of the realme, rested and depended vpon him, as the experience afterward did declare." The earliest chronicles, however, make no suggestion of murder; cf. *Six Town Chronicles,* p. 66.

This epitaph, as suggested by the refrain, may have been used on a roll exhibited by the tomb at the time of the burial. Cf. *Much Ado,* V.iii.

7. Cf. *Index,* No. 769: "All thyngis passene, and so most I algate."

8. "And on the Fryday they come to Seynt Albones, and there was done his Dyryge, and on the morewe his Masse, and thanne put into a feyre vout wheche was made for hym by his lyffe, and so closed and mured vp" (*English Chronicle,* p. 118). For a description of the tomb, see Vickers, App. B, pp. 439-41.

9. counceyle] divine plan; cf. Wyclif, Ps. 33.11: "The counseill forsothe of the Lord withoute ende abit."

29. fertible] fruitful. An aureate nonce-word, not in *O.E.D.* or in *M.E.D.;* fertile first rec. *O.E.D.* 1460.

39. vale] Cf. *Index,* No. 1498, mortal vale.

59. fest] The Annunciation, March 25.

60. age] old age.

76. redyer] i.e., ne (was) redyer.

77. it sat his hert so ny] he was so seriously concerned about it. *O.E.D.* heart sb. 43.

83. Cf. Prologue to the Reader in *Fall of Princes,* 403: "That in this londe no lollard dar abide."

95. impassible] Not subject to suffering. Cf. de Worde, *Ord. Crysten Men:* "They shall be Immortal and Impassyble."

97. merit] imp. pl. deserve well. Merit as a verb not rec. *O.E.D.* until 1526, and common by seventeenth century.

74. EXAMPLES OF MUTABILITY

Index, No. 2228. Previously printed by Padelford and Benham, *Anglia,* xxxi.325-26; and by Kingsford, *Eng. Hist. Lit.,* pp. 395-97.

MS. Rawl. C.813, a collection of 29 short songs, may be dated 1530-1540. The reference to having seen "scarcely twenty years in this land wonderous changes" suggests a date for this poem not later than about 1466 (Somerset died in 1444, Gloucester in 1447; Eleanor was kept in custody from 1443 until her death in 1454). On the other hand, two words, "hardelye" (l. 13) and "lymyted" (l. 51), are rec. *O.E.D.* as only first appearing in 1553 and 1551.

10. bockas] Boccaccio's *De Casibus Virorum Illustrium,* the ultimate source of Lydgate's *Fall of Princes.*

15. wonder3] Apparently use of pl. in -s for adj. pl. for word not of Fr. origin. Cf. Wyld, *Short Hist. Eng.,* Par. 325.

19. These three stanzas summarize the longer account of Eleanor Cobham in No. 72.

25. highe of harte] arrogant.

41. John Beaufort, Earl of Somerset (1403-1444), created Duke in 1443 (*English Chronicle,* p. 60), had some earlier success in the French Wars, capturing Harfleur (1439). He returned in 1442, was appointed Captain General of France in 1443, but failed ignominiously. Soon after his return to England he was charged with treason, and banned from the court; he died in May, 1444, possibly by his own hand. The bull story is not found in the chronicles.

45. His wife was Margaret, daughter to Sir John Beauchamp. Her daughter, Margaret, became mother of Henry VII.

49. Cf. No. 73 for Gloucester. The rhyme scheme varies in these last two st.

53. Burgundy had abandoned the siege of Calais before Gloucester arrived; cf. No. 28.

54. bisshoppe] "The two stanzas on Humphrey of Gloucester are remarkable for the allegation that his arrest was due to the revelation of information obtained under the secrecy of the confessional. This is not authenticated by any other authority, and is probably only a piece of scandal, aimed perhaps at some bishop who owed his promotion to Suffolk" (Kingsford, *Eng. Hist. Lit.*, p. 395).

63. shame] "And the iij. day aftir, he deide for sorou, as some men saide, because he myghte not come to his ansuer and excuse him of suche thyngis as were falsli put on him" (*English Chronicle*, p. 63).

75. ARREST OF THE DUKE OF SUFFOLK, 1450

Index, No. 2338. Previously printed by Bentley, *Excerpta Historica*, pp. 279-80; and by Wright, *Pol. Poems*, ii.224-25.

No. 75 is followed without break in the MS. by a Latin couplet:

Gens erit australis Rector Regni generalis,

Et Regit iniuste periet quoque postea iuste.

and then immediately by *Index*, No. 1138, on the Evils of the Times, printed by Madden, *Archaeologia*, xxix.325, and by Wright, ii.225. A variant occurs independently in Bodley MS. 100 (Sum. Cat. 1497), flyleaf (4 ll.).

Public feeling, stirred up by the national disasters in France, high prices and low wages at home, private feuding among the nobles, and banditry by cashiered soldiery, turned against the Duke of Suffolk as the chief figure of the court party responsible for the chaos. He was blamed for initiating the unpopular marriage of Henry VI to Margaret of Anjou, the grant of Maine and Anjou to her impoverished father René, titular King of Sicily, the murder of the Duke of Gloucester in 1447, and for breaking the truce with France that set off the series of defeats leading to the loss of all the French possessions. This last charge is the subject of another poem in this MS., No. 84. These verses are written in the midst of this popular excitement. Parliament first indicted Suffolk on February 7, 1450 (chiefly for his loss of Maine and for alienating the Duke of Brittany), and again in March accused him of embezzlement and illegal patronage. Since no comment is made of the restoration of Suffolk to royal favor at the reassembling of Parliament in Leicester at Easter, this poem must have been composed in February, 1450.

1. fox] The Duke of Suffolk, Michael de la Pole. Cf. No. 76,

ll. 3, 46. It might be remarked that Suffolk was a writer of poetry *(Sec. Lyrics,* Nos. 187-89).

4. ren countre] pursue the scent (subj.). First rec. *O.E.D.* 1611.

5. Cf. Heywood, *Prov. & Epigr.* 137: Holde with the hare and run with the hounde (1562).

6. talbot] John Talbot, First Earl of Shrewsbury (1442), from 1436 the chief English leader in the French wars, and Marshal of France; given as hostage to the French after the fall of Rouen (cf. Stevenson, *Letters and Papers of the Wars . . . in France,* Rolls Series 22, ii.628). Later, Lieutenant of Aquitaine in 1453; killed at the siege of Castillon in the same year. The inference is that Suffolk withheld funds or supplies from Talbot, who had large claims on the Treasury for nonpayment of expenses owing him (cf. *English Chronicle,* p. 68). Cf. No. 84, l. 12.

9. don] adv.; tr. all is down in the mire. Cf. No. 11, l. 71; No. 63, l. 48. Wright takes Don(ne) as a personal name.

11. lent] "In ye which [s]ession ye commons of ye nether house put vp to the King and the Lords many articles of treason, imprission, and euill demeanour against the duke of Suffolke . . . The Queene therefore, doubting some commotion to arise, caused the said duke to be committed to the Tower, where he remained not past a moneth, but was restored to the Kings fauour . . . After this little rage asswaged, about the Octaues of Easter, the Parliament was adiorned to Leicester, whither came the King & Queene in great estate, with them the duke of Suffolke, as chief counseller" (Stow, *Annales,* p. 387). Suffolk was in protective custody in the Tower from January 28 to March 9, 1450. On March 17 he was sentenced to banishment as from May 1.

12. salesbury] William Ayscough, Bishop of Salisbury (1438), confessor to the King, clerk to the Council, murdered at the altar soon after Suffolk's death, June 29, 1450. Cf. No. 72, l. 90; No. 76, l. 19.

13. mo] i.e., more traitors.

14. begyn þe daunce] be the first in any course of action.

16. beshrew is face] Cf. Chaucer, Wife of Bath's Tale, Pro. 844.

17. gandere] Humphrey, Duke of Gloucester. Cf. Art. 7 of this MS.: "Also desirith his trewe Comyns punysshement of the fals traitours, the which contreuyd and ymagyned the deeth of our excellent prince þe Duke of Glowcetter." Cf. No. 24.

18. Gloucester's adherents were arrested with him, and taken to Tyburn. Here they were hanged, but cut down alive on orders of Suffolk who produced their pardons.

19. Iack napys] The Duke of Suffolk, a name suggested by his badge of the clog argent and chain or, such as was attached to a tame ape (cf. *CS* 67. p. 66). Cf. No. 76, l. 3; and No. 84, l. 10.

This is the first rec. of the word; *O.E.D.* suggests it was already a quasi-proper name for a tame ape.

21. Beaumownt] John, Lord Beaumont (1440), Lord Constable of England, who made the arrest of Suffolk. He died at Northampton in 1460. Cf. No. 78, l. 70; No. 89, l. 34.

76. THE DEATH OF THE DUKE OF SUFFOLK, 1450

Index, No. 1555. Previously printed by Sharon Turner, *Hist. of England* (1815), ii.169-70; by Ritson, *Anc. Songs,* i.117-20; by Madden, *Archaeologia,* xxix.320-24; by Collier, *CS* 67.72-74; and by Wright, *Pol. Poems,* ii.232-34. Occurs also in Lambeth MS. 306, f. 51r, printed by Furnivall, *EETS* 15.6-11; and by Gairdner, *Short Eng. Chronicle,* pp. 99-103; and in Trinity Coll. Dublin MS. 516, art. 15. The Lambeth text as far as l. 56 follows Cotton, with some variants; in place of ll. 57-72 it substitutes seven new stanzas; 116 ll. in all. Stow's colophon: Here folowythe a dyrge made by the Comons of Kent in the tyme of ther rysynge, when Jake Cade was theyr cappitayn (cf. No. 24).

Public opinion was against the re-establishment of Suffolk in the good graces of the court. After his appearance at Leicester at Easter, "the commons of the lower house besought the king that such persons as assented to the release of Aniow, and deliuerance of Mayne, might bee duely punished. And to be priuie to that fact they accused as principall, the duke of suffolke with Iohn Bishop of salisbury, sir Iames Fines Lord Say, Daniel Triuilian, and other whom they indited of treason, and many other matters touching the King and his commons, as it appeareth by the verdict of three inquestes, to the number of a thirtie persons, wherupon the King to appease the commons, first sequestred the lord Say, beeing treasurer of England, and other from their offices, and roomes, and after banished William de la Pole Duke of Suffolke, for fiue yeeres, who taking ship, at Ipswich in Suffolke, on the third day of May, sailed towards France but was encountred with a ship of warre, appertayning to the Duke of Excester, Constable of the tower of London, called the Nicholas of the tower. The Captaine of which barke, wt small fight entred into the Dukes ship, and perceiuing his person present, brought him to Douer Roade, and there on the side of a cocke boate, caused his heade to be striken off, and left his body with the head lying there on the sands, which corps being there found, by a chaplaine of his, was conueyed to Wingfield colledge in suffolke" (Stow, *Annales,* pp. 387-88). The charges against Suffolk are given in full in *Rot. Parl.,* v.177-82; see also *Paston Letters,* ii.146-49; Hall, pp. 217-18. Kingsford, *Prejudice & Promise,* ch. 6, gives detailed evaluation.

The poem is a pro-Yorkist attack on Suffolk and those who supported him, and is therefore valuable evidence of the clergy upholding the court (Lancastrian) party. Of the 33 names (in Cotton Rolls ii.23) of men "endited at Rowchestre afore the Cardinall of York, Bysshop of Canturbury, and the Duke of Bokyngham" (Wright, ii, p. lvii; *Eng. Hist. Lit.,* pp. 364-65), seven appear in this poem. A further nine occur in the added st. of Lambeth. The poet assigns parts of the Office of the Dead to each of these priests and peers, identifying by the first few words the various antiphons, responses and versicles, and psalms, in order as they appear in the service. The verses must have been written between May 3, the date of the murder of Suffolk, and June 29, the date of the murder of the Bishop of Salisbury (l. 19).

2. fflagrant] fragrant. L. Fragrans.

3. Iac Napes] Cf. No. 75, l. 19.

6. "And the Friday the iij day of May, he toke his shippe at Episwich and sailed forth into the high see, where another shippe callid the Nicholas of the Tour lay in waite for him, and took him. And thay that were wythynne grauntid him space of a day and a nyghte to shryue him, and make him redy to God" (*English Chronicle,* p. 69). Similarly, Kingsford, *Chronicles of London,* pp. 158-59; *Short Eng. Chronicle,* p. 66.

8. Vespers of the Dead were known as "Placebo" from the first word of the first antiphon and Matins as "Dirige" from the opening antiphon at First Nocturn. "Dirge" (l. 29) became the common name for the whole funeral office (l. 32); the "commendation" (l. 72) was the final office.

17. Herford] Richard Beauchamp, Bishop of Hereford (February 9, 1449), translated to Salisbury, August 15, 1450.

18. Chestre] William Booth, Bishop of Coventry and Lichfield (Chester) from 1447 to 1450, later promoted to York (1453), a protegé of Suffolk. His name appears in the list of Rochester indictments; and he is the subject of an alliterative attack (*Index,* No. 544) in this Cotton MS.:

> Bridell yow, bysshopp, and be not to bold,
> And biddeth yowre beawperes se to the same;
> Cast awey couetyse now ye be bold,
> This is alle ernest that ye calle game.
> The beell sire ye be, the more is youre blame.

19. Salisbury] William Ayscough; cf. No. 75, l. 12. Of Ayscough and Moleyns (l. 46), the *English Chronicle* (p. 64) says: "Thise ij bisshoppis were wonder couetous men, and euil beloued among the comune peple, and holde suspect of meny defautes, and were as-

sentyng and willyng to the deth of the duke of Gloucestre, as it was said."

this goth] L. this game gothe ferforthe.

20. Gloucestre] Reginald Boulers, abbot of St. Peter's, afterwards (December 23, 1450) Bishop of Hereford, arrested by the Duke of York on his return from Ireland in 1450 and sent to the Tower. Cf. No. 86, l. 7. The *Gloucester Annals* describe a local riot against him in 1449, "pro eo, vt dicebatur, Franciam totam pro quadam summa pecunie vendidisset" (*Eng. Hist. Lit.*, pp. 355-56).

21. Rouchestre] Williams Wellys, sometime Abbot of York, later (1436) Prior of St. Andrew's Rochester. L. Bishoppe.

22. Stanbury] John Stanbury, a Carmelite, nominated Provost of Eton, another confessor to Henry VI; Bishop of Bangor in 1447; Bishop of Hereford in 1452. A staunch Lancastrian, captured at the Battle of Northampton, died in 1474.

Volaui] Probably an error for levaui. L. omits.

23. Worcetre] John Carpenter (d. 1476), Chancellor of Oxford University in 1437, Bishop of Worcester in 1443.

25. Cardynal] John Kemp (1380-1454), Archbishop of York (1426), later Archbishop of Canterbury (1452); Cardinal (1439) and Chancellor (1426 and again in 1449); heard the charges of the Commons against Suffolk (cf. No. 72, l. 90). "A thoroughly political ecclesiastic" (*D.N.B.*).

30. pascall] L. ioyfull. Madden (p.322) observes that Easter Day in 1450 fell on April 5, and that Suffolk was indicted at the Parliament held at Leicester during the octave.

34. Synt Asse] Reginald Pecock, Bishop of St. Asaph. Although *congé d'élire* was issued on January 30, 1450, Pecock was not appointed to Chichester until March 23, 1450, and he assumed the see only on June 8. His successor at St. Asaph, Thomas Knight, was not widely known.

35. Redynge] John Thorne, elected Abbot January 7, 1446; the date of his death is unknown.

36. alasse] interj. used as n.

38. synt Albans] John Stoke, previously Prior of Wallingford, elected to St. Albans November 28, 1440, on resignation of Whethamstede. He caused a monument to be erected to the memory of Duke Humphrey. Stoke died in 1451.

39. Toure hille] No lists of the abbots of St. Mary de Graces, or Newminster, are preserved.

40. tremuleþ] trembles (with dread); an aureate form (L. tremulare) not in *O.E.D.*

41. liard] Walter Liard [or Lyhart], Provost of Oriel Coll. Oxford, Bishop of Norwich from 1445 to 1472, another friend of Suffolk. Named in the Rochester indictment.

42. Westmynstre] Edmund Kyrton, Abbot from 1440; resigned in 1462 for old age. L. Abbes of Seynt Alborghe.

44. synt Dauy] John Delabere, consecrated Bishop of St. David's in 1447; resigned in 1459; and reputed never to have visited his diocese (Giles, *Incerti Scriptoris Chronicon* [1848], p. 35).

46. The linking of these three men recalls their mission to negotiate the marriage of Henry VI and Margaret of Anjou in February, 1444. With the Beauforts they became the core of support for Margaret's court faction. Adam Moleyns, Keeper of the Privy Seal, Dean of Salisbury, became later Bishop of Chichester (1445). He was murdered on January 9, 1450, at Portsmouth; as Keeper of the Seal he was sent to pay off returned soldiers and sailors: "and so it happid that with boiste3 langage, and also for abriggyng of thair wage3, he fil in variaunce with thaym, and thay fil on him, and cruelli there kilde him" (*English Chronicle*, p. 64). Although dead, he assisted at the funeral — according to the poem. Wright misidentifies Roos as Thomas Ros (drowned in 1430), but L. correctly names him Sir Robert Roos, fourth son of William Lord Roos of Hamlake, who died December 30, 1448. Cf. Nicholas Harris Nicolas, *Journal of Beckington's Embassy* (London, 1828), pp. lxviii-lxxi.

47. wyly] L. sly.

49. Say] James Fiennes, created Lord Say and Sele (1446); fighter in the French Wars, Esquire of the King's body (1440), Warden of the Cinque Ports (1446), Lord Treasurer (1449); listed in the Rochester indictment; murdered during Cade's Rebellion on July 4, 1450. Cf. No. 86. 1. 7. He was notorious as an extortioner and as censor of all sermons preached before the King.

51. Carleyle] Bishop Marmaduke Lumley is apparently referred to here. He was translated to Lincoln January 28, 1450. Nicholas Close (d. 1452), Chancellor of Cambridge Univ. (1449), was not made Bishop of Carlisle until March 14, 1450.

53. Dudley] John Sutton, Baron Dudley, summoned to Parliament from 1440 until his death in 1487. Among those indicted at Rochester. L. omits.

55. Danyel] Thomas Daniel, Remembrancer of the Exchequer, one of the most unpopular of the King's counselors. Listed in the Rochester indictment. Cf. No. 84, 1. 21; No. 86, 1. 7.

57. Iohn Say] John Say, "esquire of London" in the Rochester lists, related to James Fiennes, speaker of the House of Commons, and attacked but not killed during Cade's Rebellion. Later became a Yorkist.

58. Trevilian] "John Trevylian, nuper de London, armiger" of the Rochester indictments, Esquire of the King's body, and one of Suffolk's unpopular colleagues. The Cornish chough of No. 84, 1. 23. Cf. *Archaeologia,* xxvii.307, 314; Kingsford, *Eng. Hist.*

Contemp. Poetry, p. 33; and Collier, *CS* 67 (who notes the family as always Lancastrian). Stow erroneously gives Daniel Trevilian. rere] elliptical for rearward (rearguard).

61. Somerset] Edmund Beaufort, Duke of Somerset (1444), Lieutenant of France from 1446, and held responsible for the English losses of Rouen and Caen. He died at the Battle of St. Albans 1458. Cf. No. 84, l. 6.

63. all in fere] all together. Cf. No. 61, l. 20; No. 86, l. 38.

68. sacrynge] consecration of the elements at mass.

77. *THE FIVE DOGS OF LONDON, 1456*

Not listed in *Index*. Mentioned in T. K. Abbot, *Cat. of the MSS.* (Dublin, 1900). Previously printed by Robbins, *PMLA*, lxx.264-68.

The identification of the dogs as servants of York betrayed by their master is not to be taken literally, although there is no question of the poem's intention to embarrass Edward. The occasion for these verses is given in Bale's *Chronicle* (*Six Town Chronicles*, p. 144):

"Item the xix day of September in the nyght tyme wer sett upon the Standard in ffletestrete a fore the duk of york being þr than lodged in the Bisshop of Salisbury place certain dogges hedes wt Scriptures in their mouthes balade wise which dogges wer slayn vengeably the same nyght."

"Colle" is the first dog (cf. Chaucer, N.P.T. 563); and is as derogatory as at least two of the other names: "Grubbe" — a short, dwarfish fellow, contemptuous, *O.E.D.;* "Slugge" — a lazy fellow. The two remaining names are obscure: "lugtrype" (? to lug or drag one's paunch) and "Turne-bole" (? a dog which turns or drives the bull, *O.E.D.* turn 25b, 1602).

a. Cf. *Oxford Dict. Eng. Proverbs:* Love and lordship like no fellowship.

b. Cf. *O.D.E.P.:* Many a one blames their wife for their own unthrift. Also: The fathers have eaten sour grapes.

6. barked a-geynys þe mone] clamored or agitated to no effect (*O.E.D.* first rec. 1655).

c. A familiar proverb. The *O.D.E.P.* gives seven quotations from 1325 to 1470.

11. butte] deliverance.

e. Cf. *O.D.E.P.,* Taverner, 1539, in L. & Eng.: Happy whom other men's perils make wary.

17. Halley's comet is frequently noted: cf., *inter alia, English Chronicle*, p. 72; *Short Eng. Chronicle*, pp. 77, 152; *Paston Letters,* i.377; Stow, *Annales*, p. 400; *Chronicles of London*, p. 166; also Lynn Thorndike, *Hist. of Magic.* iv.413-18; Camden, *Library*, xii.201-7.

21. no grewe] not a whit.

78. THE SHIP OF STATE, 1458

Index, No. 2727. Previously printed by Madden, *Archaeologia,*
xxix.326-30. In form, style, and even in phraseology, this poem
closely resembles No. 39. It is little more than a popular catalogue
of the chief figures on the Lancastrian side, compared to the several
parts of a warship, namely, Henry VI. For other ship allegories cf.
Index, No. *5; also (here) Nos. 39 and 82.

4. abyde] to stand firm (by). *O.E.D.* first rec. 1509.

9. Madden suggests an allusion to the administration under Suffolk which came to an end in 1450.

15. Edward] Only son of Henry VI, born October 13, 1453,
slain at Tewkesbury. Cf. No. 82, l. 5.

19. cressant] Henry Holland (1430-1473), second Duke of Exeter (1447) and Earl of Huntingdon, although married to Anne,
daughter of Richard, Duke of York, fought with the Lancastrians.
No. 84, l. 2 gives to John the first Duke, the badge of the Admiralty,
the cresset; the omission of the titulus, however, would explain the
two different badges.

30. Somerset] Henry Beaufort, third Duke of Somerset, executed
by the Yorkists in May, 1464, after the Battle of Hexham. Cf. No.
79, l. 21.

38. Pembroke] Jasper Tudor, half-brother to Henry VI, created
Earl of Pembroke in 1452.

45. Bokyngham] Humphrey Stafford, first Duke of Buckingham
(1444), killed at Northampton (1460). Cf. No. 84, l. 19; No. 87,
l. 34; No. 89, l. 39.

47. Devenshyre] Thomas Courtney, sixth Earl of Devonshire
(1458), captured at Towton, and slain at Tewkesbury (1471). Cf.
No. 84, l. 33.

Grey] Edmund (1420-1489), Lord Grey of Ruthyn (1440).
He deserted at the Battle of Northampton to the Yorkists, and was
created treasurer in 1463 and Earl of Kent by Edward IV in 1465.
Cf. No. 90, l. 38.

becheham] John, Lord Beauchamp of Powyk (1447), Lord
Treasurer (June 22, 1450).

48. scales] Thomas, Lord Scales, killed by the Yorkists in 1460
in attempting to escape from the Tower of London. Cf. No. 89,
l. 124.

51. bonet] an addition to the lower part of the sail.

54. Northumberland] Henry Percy, Baron Poynings, Earl of
Northumberland (1455), slain at the Battle of Towton (1461). Cf.
No. 79, l. 23.

55. Ros] Sir Henry Roos, son of Robert Roos (No. 76, l. 46),
attainted in 1461. Cf. *Rot. Parl.,* v.480.

clyfford] John, ninth Baron Clifford (1435-1461), who reputedly murdered the Earl of Rutland, the young son of the Duke of York, at Wakefield with his own hands (so Hall, p. 251). He was slain in 1461 on the eve of the Battle of Towton (*Gregory's Chronicle*, p. 217). Cf. No. 79, l. 25.

Egremond] Thomas Percy, third son of Henry, third Earl of Northumberland, created Earl of Egremont (December 20, 1449), killed at Northampton (1460). Cf. No. 79, l. 25.

57. toppe] "a platform at the head of the mast, fenced with a rail, stored with missiles and occupied by archers, etc., called more fully Top-castle" (*O.E.D.*).

61. Shrovesbury] John Talbot (1413-1460), second Earl of Shrewsbury, appointed by Queen Margaret as Lord Treasurer from 1456 to 1458; killed at Northampton in 1460. Cf. No. 89, l. 33.

62. blame] injury, hurt; but *O.E.D.* first rec. 1549, and queries.

63. Wylchyre] James Butler (1420-1461), fifth Earl of Ormonde, and, for his support of the Lancastrians, created Earl of Wiltshire (1449); fled at St. Albans (1455), but restored as treasurer in 1455 and 1458. Defeated at Mortimer's Cross, captured at Towton, and beheaded at Newcastle on May 1, 1461. Cf. No. 84, l. 29.

70. beamond] John, Viscount Beaumont; cf. No. 75, l. 21; No. 89, l. 34.

71. Willys] Leo [Lionel] Welles, sixth Baron, close friend of Henry VI, slain at Towton (1461) and later attainted.

Ryveres] Richard Wydville [Woodville], created Baron Rivers in 1448, fought at Towton for Henry, but defected to Edward, who married his daughter Elizabeth, and rewarded him as Lord Treasurer and Earl (1466). He was executed by the Lancastrians in 1469. Cf. Warkworth, pp. 7, 46; Waurin, v.580.

73. Cf. No. 26, l. 189.

77. in hys kynde] in good condition.

79. *RECONCILIATION OF HENRY VI AND THE YORKISTS, 1458*

Index, No. 3929. Previously printed by Turner, *Hist. of England*, iii.269-70; by Ritson, *Anc. Songs*, i, pp. lxix-lxx; and by Wright, *Pol. Poems*, ii.254-56. Occurs also in Cotton MS. Nero A.vi, printed (with Vesp.) by Nicolas, *Chronicle of London*, pp. 251-55.

London was traditionally Yorkist; this poem, however, is by a Londoner (ll. 58, 63) and favorable to the King. It rejoices that the danger of civil war is apparently removed, and that the Lancastrian lords (Somerset, Northumberland, Clifford, and Egremont) are reconciled to the Yorkists (York, Warwick and Salisbury). The meeting of the Great Council in 1458 was expected to be tumultuous, for all the magnates attended with large followings, and the Mayor of London kept the peace by force of arms (Fabyan, p. 634; Stow, *Annales,* p. 403). Surprisingly, a truce was reached, and the meeting ended in a procession of the rival lords to St. Paul's Cathedral on March 25 (April 5), 1458. Polydore Vergil tells of the relief of the commons: "The newes whereof made all men so gladd, as that all sortes of men every where gave by mutuall congratulation apparent testimonie of rejoysing without measure. Wherefore, to geve God thankes, generall processions were universally commaunded, and especially at London, to be solemnized with much veneration" (p. 101).

2. skill] Apparently n. used as adv. Tr. steadfastly and justly without disturbance.

7. "that all old grudges being not onely inwardly forgotten but outwardly forgiuen, should be the cause of perpetuall loue and assured amitie" (Stow, p. 403).

vnderlaide] i.e., (Love has) brought (vengeance) into subjection.

11. Henry "declared howe the Frenche men, knowing the great stirre of civill dissention within the realme, had of late enterprised to robbe and spoyle the sea coast in Kent," decided "to reconcile the duke of Yorke, and to recover the good willes of all men" (Polydore Vergil, p. 100).

21. Yorke] Arrived on January 26 with 140 horsemen. Cf. No. 84, l. 35.

Somerset] Arrived on January 31 with 200 horsemen. Cf. No. 78, l. 30.

22. Warrewik] The Earl of Warwick, detained by contrary winds at Calais, arrived in London on February 14, with 600 men in red jackets with white ragged staffs. Cf. No. 87, l. 17.

23. Sarisbury] Richard Neville, Earl of Salisbury, arrived with 400 horsemen and 80 knights and squires.

Northumbrelande] Cf. No. 78, l. 54.

25. Egremown] Thomas Percy, mentioned with Lord Clifford in No. 78, l. 55. The Lancastrians were refused admittance within the city of London, because it was rumored that Somerset, Clifford, and Egremont (whose fathers had all been slain at St. Albans in 1455) were bent on revenge. Cf. *Chronicles of London,* p. 168; *EETS* 136.525; *English Chronicle,* p. 77; *Paston Letters,* iii.125-26.

33. The account in the poem conforms to that of the chroniclers, e.g., Grafton (i.659): "for the open apparaunce, and demonstracion of this goodly concord . . . on the day of the Conception of our Ladie, in the Moneth of Marche. At which solempne feast, the king in habite royall hauyng his Diademe on his heade, kept his estate in

Procession, before whome went hande in hande, the Duke of Sommerset, the Erle of Sarisburie, the Duke of Excester and the Erle of Warwike, and so one of the one faction, and another of the other sect, and behinde the king the Duke of Yorke led the Queene with great familiaritie to all mens sightes." And so Stow, *Annales,* p. 403.

37. spariden] refrained from doing anything (right nought) likely to cause trouble.

41. lovely contynaunce] gracious behavior to each other; a common phrase, cf. *Morte Darthur,* vii.xxi.

45. made goud chire] feasted and made merry.

46. Britayn] Brittany.

50. Canterbury] Thomas Bourchier, Cardinal of S. Ciriaci in Thermes, a nominal Lancastrian supporter of a traditionally Yorkist family, negotiator between Henry and York in 1452, continued as Chancellor by the Yorkists after the first Battle of St. Albans (1455), sided with the invading Yorkist lords in 1460; died 1486. His efforts in this reconciliation are noted in the *Paston Letters* and by Stow: "At the length by the diligent trauaile, good exhortation, and prudent aduice of the Archbishoppe of Canterbury, and other learned and vertuous prelates, both partes were perswaded to come to a communication" (*Annales,* p. 403). On his tomb appear the knots and water bouget (cf. No. 84, l. 29; No. 90, l. 39).

51. An extra line, which mars the stanza pattern.

52. loue-day] "a day appointed for a meeting with a view to the amicable settlement of a dispute" (*O.E.D.*). The chronicles term March 25 (Lady Day) "dissimuled loue-day" (cf. Brotanek, *ME Dicht.,* p. 131, fn. 2).

63. Maier] Godfrey Boloinge who "kept great watch, as well by day as by night ... to see good order and peace to be kept" (Stow, *Annales,* p. 403).

80. A PRAYER FOR VICTORY

Index, No. 936. Previously printed by Robbins, *Mod. Phil.,* xxxvi.341. Actually the opening lines of the *Secrees of Old Philisoffres* by Lydgate and Burgh (*Index,* No. 935), occurring separately. The lines continue as rhyme royal stanzas (Steele, *EETS* lxvi).

1. conserue] MSS. of *Index,* No. 935 read conferme.

81. GOD AMEND WICKED COUNSEL, 1464

Index, No. 372. Previously printed by Robbins, *Neuphil. Mitteilungen,* lvi.97-99. The first nine lines are copied on f. 82v by the same early sixteenth-century hand. A later nineteenth-century hand has added a few inconsequential pencil annotations.

This poem presents the popular view of Henry VI that his troubles dated from his marriage in 1445 to Margaret of Anjou. "Fro þis tyme forward, King Henry neuer profited ne went forward; but Fortune began to turn fro him on al sides" (*EETS* 136.511-12). As with so many of these poems, there is much correspondence to the contemporary and later chronicles.

Literary parallels will be noted in Nos. 39 and 42, and especially in No. 38, ll. 121-28, where Edward II bemoans his fate in similar fashion; also "Ye that put your trust & Confydence," Balliol Coll. Oxf. MS. 354, f. 175r, "The Lamytacion off Quene Elyzabeth," *EETS* ci.97-99.

13. sette me at gret pris] esteemed me highly.

19. If syen can be taken as long ardently [of] (*O.E.D.* 1549), then sayd may be emended to saye (required by rhyme). Tr. When the Queen earnestly requested Lord Say. Cf. *English Chronicle* (p. 62): "And in the moneth of Feuerer next aftir, the x. day therof, began the parlement at saint Edmundis Bury in Suffolk; the which parlement was maad only for to sle the noble duke of Gloucestre, whoȝ deth the fals duke of Suffolk William de la Pole, and ser Jameȝ Fyneȝ lord Say, and othir of thair assent, hadde long tyme conspired and ymagyned."

20. While it was generally supposed Gloucester had been murdered, Stow notes: "his body was shewed to the lords & commons, & seemed to die of a palsey, or of an impostume" (*Annales,* p. 386). Cf. No. 73.

21. The Duke of York was appointed lieutenant of Ireland in September 1447 for ten years, but actually he was in "exile" only from July, 1449 to September, 1450.

24. clamer] MS. chamer. Cf. Palsgrave 1530: I clamer or clymme up upon a tree (*O.E.D.*).

38. Listing the evils following the marriage, the *Brut* notes "þe rebelling of commines Ageynst þer princes & lordes; what diuison Ayen þe lordes, what murdre & sleying of þame! what feldes foughten & made! in conclusion, so many, that many a man hath lost his life" (*EETS* 136.512). So Fabyan, p. 618; Hall, p. 208; Stow, *Annales,* p. 385; Holinshed, iii.208-9.

42. bare the belle] had the foremost rank.

45. Henry made several tours of England from 1446 to 1456 in an effort to restore unity. Cf. No. 42, ll. 19-20 for a similar progress of Edward IV.

47. This statement could apply either to Henry's flight after Mortimer's Cross in 1461, or, more likely, to his year in hiding from the Yorkist victories at Hedgeley Moor and Hexham early in 1464 until his capture at Clitheroe in July, 1465. During this time, "he and other liued in caues full hardly, vnknowne more than

a yeere" (Stow, *Annales*, p. 418), and "where kyng Henry was become cowde not be knowen" (*Chronicles of London*, p. 178).

48. Cf. *Index*, No. 3778: "this werlde es tournede vp-so downe."

49. bledde ryall] royal family. John Blacman, Carthusian confessor to Henry VI, described in his memoir the King's speech when imprisoned by order of Edward IV: "My father was king of England, and peaceably possessed the crown of England for the whole time of his reign. And his father and my grandfather was king of the same realm . . . and each and all of my lords did me royal homage and plighted me their faith" (James, p. 44).

50. Cf. "The Lamytacion off Quene Elyzabeth," ll. 8-9:
> Was I not born of old worthy lynage?
> Was not my moder, quene, & my fader, kyng?

82. WILLIKIN'S RETURN, 1470

Index, No. 3742. Previously printed by Greene, *Early Eng. Carols,* p. 292.

This carol is written in a large book hand of the late fifteenth early sixteenth century in a MS. of Latin proverbs, grammatical rules, and Lydgate's "Stans puer." On f. 73*v* is a note, "Thomas stanlye est possessor huius libri." If this refers to Lord Stanley, stepfather of Henry VII, it would explain the addition of this Lancastrian piece to the MS. The poem looks forward to the return of the Earl of Warwick (wylekyn) to restore Henry VI in September, 1470; the use of the "Nowel" refrain may move forward the composition nearer Christmas, after the restoration of Henry in October. For other poems with the ship allegory see Nos. 39, 78.

1. sull] shall (come).

5. prynce] Edward, Prince of Wales. Cf. No. 78, l. 15.

7. nore] Mistaken division, not rec. *O.E.D.* Cf. No. 52, l. 38.

8. chamberlayne] John Neville, Marquess of Montagu, made Lord Chamberlain in 1459, who declared for Henry; killed at Barnet. Cf. Warkworth, pp. 10-11; and No. 90, l. 53.

11. fueryn] Identification doubtful. "May conceivably be Thomas [Neville, Bastard of] Fauconberg, although he was not in fact a lord" (Chambers, *O.H.E.L.,* p. 89); nor, in fact, a Lancastrian. The other nobleman active in the restoration was the Duke of Clarence.

rub. Ionys] There is no evidence to support Chamber's identification with Edward Jones, a gentleman of the Chapel, who died in 1512; he is more likely the John Jones of Carmathen, who signed several of the items in this MS.

83. A REMEMBRANCE OF HENRY VI, 1492

BY RYMAN

Index, No. 2454. Previously printed by Zupitza, *Archiv,* lxxxix.268-69.

With Henry VII, who in fact represented the Lancastrian claims, as King, Ryman could praise Henry VI as the saintly king—his incompetence and insanity being conveniently forgotten, as well as the usurpation of his throne by Edward IV. Since there is here no hint of murder, accepted by later Lancastrians (e.g., Polydore Vergil, pp. 155-56), Chambers, *O.H.E.L.,* p. 97, suggests the date of composition as early as 1471.

12. Whethamstede's *Registrum* (i.356) notes Henry's proviso in the 1459 Act against the insurgent nobles that he might shew mercy toward them without the interposition of Parliament. Blacman, in his memoir, also records examples of his "Pietas et patientia ejus" (James, pp. 16-19) towards transgressors: "and this is plain in the case of many to whom he was exceeding gracious and merciful; for he was become an imitator of Him who saith, 'I will have mercy' " (p. 40). So in English prayer to Henry VI (not in *Index*; pr. Collier, *CS* 67.60):

> Was never man cam beforne thi face,
> Rebellion or oder yn adversite,
> Off thyn compassion commaunded them goe free.

22. Matth. 5.7.

36. Cf. Blacman: "Fuerat enim, quasi alter Job, vir simplex, et rectus."

38. Blacman describes his simple dress ("Humilitas regis," p. 14): "Further of his humility in his bearing, in his clothes and other apparel of his body, in his speech and many other parts of his outward behaviour" (p. 36).

43. Wyndesore] One of the prayers quoted by James (p. xiii) from Durham Cath. Lib. MS. V.iii.7 includes "Es wynsorie natus."

46. Royal MS. 13 C.viii is a collection of miracles presumably prepared in support of his canonization (ed. Ronald Knox and Shane Leslie [Camb. 1923]). Henry's body was buried at Chertsey, and removed by Richard III to Windsor, "because the reports of the miracles were testifying to a growth of interest in the good king which was not healthy for the dynasty of York" (James, p. 45). However, miracles were still claimed at Windsor.

54. do thy cure] apply yourself diligently.

84. PRELUDE TO THE WARS, 1449

Index, No. 3455. Previously printed by Samuel Bentley, *Excerpta Historica* (London, 1831), pp. 160-62; in *Privy Council Books,* vi, p. xxiv; by Wright, *Pol. Poems,* ii.221-23; by Collier, *CS* 67.65-68; and by Gairdner, *Paston Letters,* i.66-67.

This song, "which paved the way for the popularity of the house of York" (Wright), is in the pro-Yorkist Cotton Rolls ii.23. The latest allusion is to the fall of Rouen Castle (l. 5) in November, 1449. The charges against Suffolk came in February, 1450, but are not mentioned here. This poem, therefore, must have been written some time between these dates. It is notable for its use of badges to refer to nobles, similar to Nos. 87, 88, 89, and 90; and *Index,* No. 3529. The badge or cognizance, a figure selected from the family coat or chosen for some pertinent allusion, was worn by retainers and displayed on standards. Interlinear glossing helps identification here; but in some of the other poems the badges are occasionally confusing. Rather than direct propaganda for the Yorkists, the poem seems to reflect the dismay and uncertainty of the fluid political situation in 1448 and 1449, following the English disasters in France, just prior to the outbreak of the Wars of the Roses. The memory of the years of the great English victories is evoked by the names of earlier heroes: Bedford, Gloucester, Exeter (ll. 1-2), Shrewsbury, Fauconberg, Willoughby (ll. 12, 13, 15); the leaders of the Yorkists decline while Lancastrians flourish — Norfolk is vanquished by Suffolk (ll. 9-10); Warwick is contrasted to Daniel (ll. 17, 21); Arundel is "out of mynde." Yet Buckingham, a Lancastrian, "is spokeles"; Norris "runneth not"; and Devonshire is in the west. The final lines veer attention to Edward, Duke of York, whose future is unsettled.

1. Rote] John Plantagenet (d. 1435), third son of Henry IV, Duke of Bedford (1414), and Regent of France. His badge was the root of a tree, couped and eradicated; it decorates the Bedford Missal.

swanne] Humphrey Plantagenet, fourth son of Henry IV, Duke of Gloucester, murdered in 1447 (cf. No. 73). His badge of the swan derived from the Bohuns, Earls of Hereford, of which family his mother was coheiress.

2. Cressett] John Holland (d. 1447), Duke of Exeter (1443), Marshal and Admiral of England (1435), Governor of Aquitaine. " 'A cresset with burning fire,' i.e., a fire-beacon, is said to have been the badge of the Admiralty" (Collier, *CS* 67.65; and so Palliser, p. 307).

6. Portecolys] Edmund Beaufort, Duke of Somerset. Cf. No. 76, l. 61.

7. welevette hatte] Henry Beaufort (d. 1447), Bishop of Winchester and Cardinal.

9. White lioun] John Mowbray (d. 1461), third Duke of Norfolk (1432), a supporter of Richard of York. The badge was still used at Flodden Field. Cf. No. 87, l. 24.

10. Ape clogge] Duke of Suffolk. Cf. No. 75, l. 19.

12. Talbott] Earl of Shrewsbury. Cf. No. 75, l. 6.

13. hangulhook] William Neville (d. 1463), Lord Fauconberg *jure uxoris,* Earl of Kent (1461), fifth Earl of Westmorland, and Warwick's uncle; another distinguished Yorkist hero. Cf. No. 88, l. 69; No. 89, l. 107; No. 90, l. 36. "Among other notices of crests of Knights in the Lansdowne MS. 870, is 'Wyllyam Faulconbrydge,' probably a mistake for Fauconberg, 'the fysshe hoke' " (Collier, *CS* 67.66).

15. myllesaylle] more properly, mill-rind. Robert (d. 1452), Lord Willoughby (1409), derived this badge from his ancestors, the Beks of Eresby.

17. Bere] Richard Neville (d. 1471), Earl of Warwick (1449), the "King Maker." Cf. *2 Hen. VI,* V. i. 203: "The rampant bear chained to the ragged staff." Cf. No. 79, l. 22; No. 82, l. 1; No. 87, l. 7; No. 89, l. 12; No. 90, l. 32; No. 91, l. 57.

19. Carte nathe] The cartwheel, generally with flames issuing from the end of the spoke, the badge of Humphrey Stafford, first Duke of Buckingham (1441), a Lancastrian, killed at Northampton (1460).

21. lily] Thomas Daniel. Cf. No. 76, l. 55. The rhyme scheme of this quatrain (as of ll. 33-36) is faulty.

22. Coundite] John Norris, Esquire of the King's body, one of the officers of Henry VI.

23. Cornysshe chawgh] John Trevilian; cf. No. 76, l. 58. For another bearer of this badge cf. No. 90, l. 37.

24. Egulle] Henry VI.

25. white hard] Probably an error for white horse, the badge of William FitzAlan (d. 1487), Earl of Arundel (1438), a Yorkist. Cf. No. 90, l. 39. The white hart was the badge of Richard II and used as a Yorkist standard.

29. water bowge] Henry, Lord Bourchier, and Earl of Ewe in Normandy, created Viscount Bourchier (1446) and Earl of Essex (1461); cf. No. 90, l. 39.

wyne botelle] Not glossed in the MS. Several possibilities: a badge used by the Earls of Oxford (Palliser, p. 278); or with ref. to James Butler, Earl of Ormonde; cf. No. 78, l. 63. Alternatively, a punning ref. to Sir Robert Botyll, Prior of Knights of St. John of Jerusalem, supported in l. 30 by gloss on Vetturlockes. However the fetterlocks were used as a Yorkist standard (cf. No. 90, l. 46).

31. whete yere] Edmund Lacy, Bishop of Exeter (1420-1455).

33. boore] Thomas Courtney (d. 1458), fifth Earl of Devon (1422), a hero of the French wars, and a Lancastrian. His wife was Margaret Beaufort, daughter of John, Earl of Somerset. His son appears in No. 78, l. 47.

35. ffawkoun] Richard Plantagenet, Duke of York. Cf. No. 90, l. 46.

85. ADVICE TO THE COURT, I, 1450

Index, No. 818. Previously printed by Madden, *Archaeologia*, xxix.325; in *Rel. Ant.*, ii.255; and by Wright, *Pol. Poems*, ii.231.

This attack on Suffolk and his friends takes the form of an admonition to the King's advisers to respect the "loue of alle þe cominalte," a factor often stressed in these poems opposing the dominant court circle. In the MS. it follows the articles of impeachment. *Rel. Ant.* titles "Verses addressed to Henry VI on his friendship for the Duke of Suffolk," but ll. 14-15 imply an address to the true friends of the King.

3. Iulian] This oath, and that by Anne (l. 11), seem used for their rhyme, one of the two employed in ll. 1-13.

5. Charges by the Commons were made against Suffolk in February and March; by May he had been ordered exiled. This poem may have been an attempt to force the King to such action.

6. ffolke] Suffolk and the other noblemen associated with him. Cf. notes to No. 76.

7. let soche bribry be] Abstain from such bribery. One of the charges against Suffolk in the second indictment was peculation; cf. Polydore Vergil, "for robbing of the common Treasurie" (pp. 82-83).

86. ADVICE TO THE COURT, II, 1450

Index, No. 4261. Previously printed by Turner, *Hist. of England*, iii.155; by Ritson, *Anc. Songs*, p. 63; by Bentley, *Excerpta Historica*, pp. 360-61; and by Wright, *Pol. Poems*, ii.229-31.

This is a companion piece to No. 85, and was probably written about the same time, for Lord Say (l. 7) was indicted with Suffolk in the first months of 1450. The tail-rhyme stanzas and the use of "bill" (l. 55) indicate a popular song, perhaps for distribution in London. The abuses mentioned here are close to those listed by Cade, whose rebellion followed in a couple of months and whose demands appear in this MS. (cf. *Short Eng. Chronicle*, pp. 94-99; Stow, *Annales*, pp. 388-90; No. 24; and No. 76, Lambeth text).

1. Only the court favorites were opposed, and there was no talk of removing Henry: "We blame not all the lordys, ne all tho that is about þe kyngs person, ne all jentyllmen ne yowmen, ne all men of lawe, ne all bysshopes, ne all prestys" *(Short Eng. Chronicle,* p. 96). Similarly in 1456 (Whethamstede, i.248-49).

2. ffrauncheses] exemptions from certain forms of taxation.

4. "His dettes encreased dayly, but payment was there none; alle the possessyons and lordeshyppes that perteyned to the croune the kyng had yeue awey, some to lordes and some to other simple persones, so that he had almoste noughte to lefe onne" *(English Chronicle,* p. 79).

7. Tom of say] Probably James Fiennes, Lord Say. Cf. No. 76, l. 49.

daniel] Cf. No. 76, l. 55. Named among the traitors sought for execution by the Cade rebels: "the Lorde Saye was one, the Bysshuppe of Salysbury (No. 76, l. 19), the Baron of Dudley (No. 76, l. 53), the Abbot of Glowcester (No. 76, l. 20), and Danyell, and many moo" *(Short Eng. Chronicle,* p. 67).

8. i.e., to restore the franchises to the King.

10. chese] he shall be given no alternative.

13. Cf. Items 2 and 6 of Cade's "Complaint of the commons of Kent" (in Stow, *Annales,* p. 389); also *Six Town Chronicles,* p. 126: "So þe[r] was noo good rule nor stablenes at that tyme to greet discomfort and hevynes of the peple."

23. "For these mys-gouernaunces, and for many other, the hertes of the peple were turned away from thayme that had the lond in gouernaunce, and theyre blyssyng was turnyd in to cursyng" *(English Chronicle,* p. 79).

25. "The kyng ... owed more then he was worthe" *(English Chronicle,* p. 79).

26. all by-dene] all together.

31. "The duke of Suffolk ... hadde also aliened and sold the duchie of Normandie to the king of Fraunce" *(English Chronicle,* p. 68).

33. to] i.e., Say and Suffolk.

37. to leere] too well taught, too well informed.

42. "The Duke of Suffolke began secretly to allure his friends of the nobilitie, and priuily declared vnto them his title to the Crowne, & likewise did hee to certaine gouenours of Cities and Townes, which priuie attempt was so politikly handled and secretly kept, that his prouision was ready before his purpose was opened" (Stow, *Annales,* p. 386).

44. Suffolk was still alive in May, 1450.

47. Cf. No. 21, l. 8.

48. Cf. *O.D.E.P.* As they brew, so let them bake (drink).

49. Probably Bishop Booth, Chancellor in 1449 to Queen Margaret; he was succeeded later in 1450 by Cardinal Archbishop Kemp.

50. Blank charters] An old device; cf. *English Chronicle*, p. 163 (1398).

56. smythfeld] The traditional place for challenges to combat.

87. *TAKE GOOD HEED*

Index, No. 455. Previously printed by Madden, *Archaeologia*, xxix.340-42; and by Brotanek, *ME Dicht.*, pp. 128-29.

The dating of this poem poses many problems; and Madden, Kingsford (*Eng. Hist. Contemp. Poetry*, p. 40), and Brotanek offer different interpretations. The general import of the poem is clear: a warning to Yorkist leaders (Warwick, Salisbury, Norfolk, and York) to beware of treachery. The otherwise satisfactory date of late 1460 (before Wakefield, when York was slain), following the acceptance of Richard, Duke of York, as heir to the throne (cf. ll. 5, 29), suggested by Madden, is vitiated by l. 34. Humphrey Stafford, first Duke of Buckingham, who would lead those wearing "þe stafford knottis," had been killed at Northampton (July 9, 1460). Another possible interpretation is the short period of control by the Yorkists in February, 1454, when York was appointed Protector (l. 30). At this time all the magnates were enlisting retainers. The Duke of Buckingham, for example, had 2,000 of his badges made for distribution (l. 34); and the Duke of Somerset reputedly had spies "in every Lordes hous of this land." The Yorkists likewise were recruiting support. Perhaps the main objection to this early date is that the Lancastrians were strong enough to oppose the Yorkists openly; there was no dissembly, and Parliament did not fawn on York (cf. ll. 5-7). A third possibility is the Yorkist victory after the first Battle of St. Albans in May, 1455, after which "lordes stand in hele of ther bodies but not all at hertes ees," but dared not protest the amnesty to the Yorkists because of military intimidation, although "to the which bill many a man groged full sore nowe it is past." Here, however, the allusion in l. 5 to winter is unclear.

Another possibility is that proposed by Brotanek: from late in 1457 to March, 1458, when Lancastrians and Yorkists were seemingly reconciled (cf. No. 79). The Yorkists should beware Lancastrian promises "obeisaunce to kepe" to the expected decrees of the Grand Council; they must be sure their "sauegardes" (l. 27) or guarantees were not too mild. If this interpretation be adopted, this poem then expresses the other view of the Reconciliation, one much more in line with events to come.

6. Rose] A symbol and badge of the Yorkists. The White Rose was borne by Richard, Duke of York (*Archaeologia*, xvii.226), but

Edward made it his especial cognizance in conjunction with the radiant sun (Le Rose en Soleil), which appearing in refraction on February 2, 1461, was taken as a favorable omen before the Battle of St. Albans. *Gregory's Chronicle* describes the Londoners hearing of the approach of Edward in March, 1461: they thanked God and said: " 'Lette us walke in a newe wyne yerde, and lette us make us a gay gardon in the monythe of Marche with thys fayre whyte ros and herbe, the Erle of Marche' " (p. 215). Cf. No. 42, l. 25; No. 90, bur.; No. 92, l. 11.

7. An attempt before the end of 1456 by Somerset and Shrewsbury to kill Warwick (the bere, cf. l. 25) had failed. Cf. No. 84, l. 17.

8. wyrye] worry, kill by biting; continuing metaphor of dogs from l. 7.

9. Tr. But (I warn that) you should not stand in fear of your enemies.

11. falte] evildoers. Cf. No. 91, l. 66. Or MS. falce.

12. *O.E.D.* first rec. 1450: One scabbed sheep will mar a whole flock.

16. leyde for to slepe] Cf. No. 84, l. 9.

17. Cf. No. 79, l. 22; *Chronicles of London,* p. 168; *EETS* 136.525; *English Chronicle,* p. 77; *Paston Letters,* iii.125; Fabyan, p. 633.

21. Cf. *O.D.E.P.* To bear two faces in one hood. Also Lydgate, *Index,* No. 3823, ll. 1-2:

> Vndir your hood is but oo contenaunce,
>
> Excludid is from you al doubilnesse.

22. had I wyst] A very common proverbial phrase; for other instances see Brotanek, p. 133.

24. lion] John Mowbray, Duke of Norfolk. Cf. No. 84, l. 9; No. 90, l. 33; *Archaeologia,* xxvii.341 ("a lion rampant, argent, for the barony of Segrave").

to a-bay] to dire straits. Alternative reading: to a bay.

25. Brotanek (p. 133) interprets these lines as an attempt to set the house of York (rose) and Norfolk (lion) against the house of Neville (Salisbury, egel; Warwick, bere). But more likely a reference to the possible downfall of all four leaders by the Lancastrians.

28. Fighting between the Percies and Nevilles at Carleton in July, 1457, was arbitrated at the York assises in favor of the Nevilles.

29. whele] Cf. No. 38, l. 33.

31. chayne) The Warwick arms: the bear chained to the ragged staff — bottis (l. 33), cf. *Promp. Parv.* 26: Batte, staffe, fustis. Cf. No. 79, l. 22; No. 84, l. 17.

34. knottis] The arms of Humphrey Stafford, first Duke of Buckingham. Cf. No. 78, l. 45.

39. Used ironically: Some rash adventure or word can be repaid to us Yorkists quite unexpectedly.

40. at onset stevyn] unexpectedly, unpreparedly. Cf. Chaucer, Knt. Tale 666: "For al day meeteth men at vnset steuene."

in dede] To 1600 commonly written as two words.

45. on] by means of.

88. BALLAD SET ON THE GATES OF CANTERBURY, 1460

Index, No. 1544. Previously printed by Davies, *English Chronicle*, pp. 91-94; and reprinted by Brotanek, *ME Dicht.*, pp. 199-202.

The present location of the Davies MS. is unknown, and it may be presumed lost. This text is copied from the Camden Society printing, with three emendations proposed by Brotanek. The MS., a pro-Yorkist *Brut* Chronicle with important additions, was once owned by Stow, who drew on it very heavily for his *Annales*. From Stow it passed in 1605 to the historian, John Speed (1552-1629), and stayed in the Speed family until the nineteenth century, being last owned by John Speed Davies (1856). In that year, his son, John Silvester Davies published significant extracts for the Camden Society (vol. 64). For commentary see Introduction, pp. xxxvii.

The presence of numerous biblical quotations in Latin raises a question of the poem's effectiveness as a popular handbill; perhaps the mere act of posting would be sufficient to rouse the Kentishmen. Other similar pieces, presumably designed to influence the ordinary townsmen — not the gentry or nobility — also contain Latin lines or refrains (cf. No. 94). The parallels between this poem and Nos. 89 and 91 should be noted; since the events described here precede those of the Dublin MS., lines from these poems must be borrowed from No. 88.

1. faste] Not Lent, since the poem was written shortly before the invasion of June 28; the fast day was probably Whitsun Eve (May 31). Cf. Brotanek, p. 206.

2. influence] Cf. No. 89, ll. 3, 20.

3. prophecyes] Cf. No. 93, l. 93.

8. Isaiah 1. 5.

10. Cf. Horstman, *Nova Legenda Anglie*, i.331. For a full discussion see Brotanek, pp. 206-7.

13. fals wedlock] "The quene was defamed and desclaundered, that he that was called Prince, was nat hir sone, but a bastard goten in avoutry" (*English Chronicle*, p. 79). Cf. also *Index*, No. 2808, l. 170: "the bastarde and his meane." Also No. 91, l. 35.

17. A planta pedis] Isaiah 1. 6.

20. Cf. No. 89, l. 101.

25. Omne regum &c.] Matth. 12.25; Luke 11.17; Mark 3.24. Cf. No. 13, ll. 113-14.

27. enemyes] The Babylonians.

35. enduryng] Cf. contenewaunce (No. 92, l. 17).

37. bestys] "The erles of Shrouesbury and Wylshyre, and the lorde Beaumount, oure mortalle and extreme enemyes" (*English Chronicle*, p. 88).

to mydsomer haue but a myle] are somewhat mad.

39. scyle] Tr. repeating my reason. Brotanek retains Davies' reading style.

41. Brotanek (p. 208) suggests for Jonathas either Archbishop Kemp, the Chancellor, who died in 1454; or Bishop Lyndwood, who died in 1446.

43. Murum] Ezekiel 13.5.

46. Mercenarius] John 10.12-13. Later at St. Albans the Burgundian gunners hired by the Lancastrians were useless in battle; cf. *Gregory's Chronicle,* p. 213.

49. falshede to destroy] Cf. No. 89, l. 100; No. 91, l. 65.

50. Cf. No. 93, ll. 74-75.

52. hunter] Brotanek states that an extensive search has revealed no participant using a horn in his arms, and suggests the allusion is to the man-hunter, the Earl of Wiltshire. Cf. No. 78, l. 63.

53. por alle] Alternative reading: poralle.

58. Cf. No. 93, l. 6.

61. In the list of grievances presented by York to the Commons after his entry into London appears a charge "hit hathe be labored, studyed, and conspyred, to haue dystroyed and murthryd the seyde duke of York" (*English Chronicle,* p. 88).

62. ut sedeat] I Kings 2.8.

64. The first line of the well-known hymn by Bishop Theodulphus (Daniel, *Thes. Hymn.* i.215; and Dreves, *Anal.* 1.160). For an Eng. tr. see *Index,* No. 3872; and Brown's notes, *Rel. Lyr. XIV Cent.,* p. 247.

65. Cf. No. 91, l. 29.

66. Cf. No. 79, l. 23.

67. Cf. No. 79, l. 22; No. 84, l. 17.

69. Fauconbrege] William Neville, who had ascertained the disposition of Kent towards the Yorkists. Cf. No. 84, l. 13; Whethamstede, i.371.

73. This st. is explained by the fourth article in York's petition to the Commons: "Item, That is wolle please his sayde good grace to lyve upponne his owne lyuelode, whereopon hys noble progenitures haue in dayes heretofore lyued as honorably and as worthily as any Crystyn prynces; and nat to suffre the destroyers of the sayde

londe and of his trewe sugettes to lyue theroponne, and therefore to lacke the sustenaunces that sholde be bylongyng to hys sayde estate, and fynde hys sayde householde oppone his pore communes withoute payment, whyche nouther accordethe wyth Goddes nor mannes lawe" (*English Chronicle*, pp. 86-87).

89. THE BATTLE OF NORTHAMPTON, 1460

Index, No. 2609. Previously printed by Madden, *Archaeologia*, xxix.334-40; and by Brotanek, *ME Dicht.*, pp. 116-21. Nos. 89-91 are all in the same MS., and, says Kingsford, are "of a high degree of merit, and have a certain similarity of form which suggests that they may be the work of one writer" (*Eng. Hist. Lit.*, p. 247).

Following the events described in No. 88, Warwick, Salisbury, and March landed at Sandwich on June 26, 1460, and, joined by various sympathizers (including Archbishop Bourchier and Sir Edward Brooke of Cobham), marched into London on July 2. Salisbury (with Cobham and Sir John Wenlock) remained to besiege the Tower (held by Lord Scales and Lord Hungerford), while Edward, Earl of March, and Warwick, supported by Archbishop Bourchier, four bishops, and Abergavenny, Audley, Bourchier, Clinton, Fauconberg, Say, Scrope, and other lords, sought the king at Northampton. Owing to the treachery of Lord Grey of Ruthyn, who commanded the Lancastrian left wing, the Yorkists were able to storm the Lancastrian camp and capture Henry VI (July 10). The casualties among the soldiery were light, but heavy among the leaders — most of the Lancastrian commanders were slain (including Buckingham, ll. 39, 54; Shrewsbury, l. 33; Beaumont, l. 34; and Egremont, l. 36). Lord Scales, attempting to escape from the Tower, was recognized by London boatmen and murdered (l. 136). The triumphant Yorkists returned to London, with the captured King, on July 16. The *English Chronicle* gives a full account of the battle pp. 94-98).

This poem must have been written between the day of battle and September 8, since it lists the Duke of York as absent in Ireland (he returned to England on that date, and came to London on October 10).

The rhyme scheme, generally *ababbcbc*, at times turns into the less common form, *abababab* (ll. 17-24, 153-60). Throughout, the concluding rhyme of one stanza becomes the opening rhyme of the next.

3. Cf. No. 88, l. 2.

4. wirkyn] gerund.

7. enspeciall] first rec. *O.E.D.* 1530.

10. i.e., following the defeat at Ludlow.

12. rose] Richard, Duke of York. Cf. No. 91, l. 49. Madden incorrectly identifies as Edward, Earl of March.

fetyrlok] Edward, Earl of March, Richard's son, later Edward IV. Cf. No. 91, l. 45. Grafton notes (i.665): "After whome folowed the Erle of Marche, with the banner of his father."

egle] Richard Neville, Earl of Salisbury. Cf. No. 90, ll. 25,46; No. 91, l. 53.

bere] Richard Neville, Earl of Warwick, Salisbury's son, whose arms carry the bear chained to the gnarled trunk (ragged staff). Cf. No. 84, l. 17.

15. shelde & spere] a kenning.

20. infleweinz] In techn. sense of virtue of astral bodies. Cf. No. 88, l. 2; and Chaucer, *Troilus,* iii.618.

21. berward] Edward, Earl of March, who had joined with Warwick, the bear. In *Index,* No. 3529 (On King Richard's Ministers, 1399), the bearward represents Warwick and his son Richard Beauchamp; in *2 Hen. VI,* V.i.149, 210 the reference is to the Duke of York.

24. toke his trace] proceeded.

32. do þe dogges shame] inflict reproach on the dogs.

33. Talbot] John Talbot, second Earl of Shrewsbury, who is supposed to have introduced a race of bloodhounds into England, so named after the family. Killed in this battle. Cf. No. 78, l. 61.

34. bauling] yelping. As adj. first rec. *O.E.D.* 1594; but as n. 1440.

bewmond] John, Viscount Beaumont, killed in this battle. Cf. No. 75, l. 21.

36. egremonde] Thomas Percy, Earl of Egremont, killed in this battle. Cf. No. 78, l. 55.

38. leese] a set of three (hounds).

39. buk] Humphrey Stafford, first Duke of Buckingham, killed in this battle. Cf. No. 78, l. 45.

40. hye] with tall antlers.

fat] a techn. term in hunting. Tr. its fat (*greese*) indicated the buck was fatted (*fat*) or ready for killing.

41. coriages] courageous. ? a scribal error; not in *O.E.D.*

in preese] in the thick of the fight.

42. hunt] the huntsman, King Henry.

62. This speech closely follows the chronicles; cf. *English Chronicle:* "Whanne the feld was do, and the erles thoroughe mercy and helpe had the vyctory, they came to the kyng in his tent, and sayde in thys wyse — 'Most Noble Prince, dysplease yow nat, thoughe it haue pleased God of His Grace to graunt vs the vyctory of oure mortalle enemyes, the whyche by theyre venymous malyce haue vntrewly stered and moued youre hyghenesse to exyle vs oute of

youre londe, and wolde vs haue put to fynalle shame and confusyone. We come nat to that entent for to inquyete ne greue youre sayde hyghenesse, but for to please youre most noble personne, desiryng most tendrely the hyghe welfare and prosperyte thereof, and of alle youre reame, and for to be youre trew lyegemen, whyle oure lyfes shalle endure' " (pp. 97-78). So also Whethamstede, i.374-75; Stow, p. 409.

66. To oure excuse] to our exculpation.

68. After the defeat at Ludlow (October 12, 1459), Richard Duke of York and his younger son, the Earl of Rutland, fled through Wales to Ireland; the Nevilles (Salisbury and Warwick) and the Duke's elder son, the Earl of March, fled into Devonshire, whence they escaped into Guernsey and later to Calais.

74. Gramercy] thanks.

88. by & by] continuously.

94. played par asent] Brotanek (p. 126) glosses "sie spielten unter einer Decke" (conspired).

99. kent] traditionally Yorkist. Cf. No. 24; *English Chronicle,* p. 84.

100. destrewe] This sp. not rec. *O.E.D.*

101. truþe] Actually a common expression in the petitions to Parliament. "Pro majori observantia veritatis" is quoted by Ramsay in a petition of 1483 (*Lanc. & York,* ii.450); cf. also No. 88, l. 20.

102. right] Brotanek emends sight.

103. shewid] "The object of two connected verbs needs to be expressed only once in ME" (Brotanek, p. 126).

104. Only 300 casualties recorded, excluding the leaders. Hall, however, gives 10,000 (p. 244)!

107. favcon] William Neville, Lord Fauconberg. Cf. No. 84, l. 13.

111. "And than the Erle of Marche, and the Erle of Warwyke, with oþer lordis, brought the kynge to Northampton with myche rialte. And so the kynge with his lordis came to London, with him the Erle of Marche; þe Erle of Warwyke bare the kynges swerde" *(Short Eng. Chronicle,* p. 74). So Stow, *Annales,* p. 409.

115. "For the whyche vyctory London yaf to Almyghtye God grete lawde and thankyng" (*English Chronicle,* p. 98).

119. heuynesse] i.e., the fits of madness to which Henry was subject.

121. "And the Erle of Salysbury rode a yenes the kynge withe myche rialte; and then was called and sett a Parlement" *(Short Eng. Chronicle,* p. 74).

124. fisshe] Thomas, Lord Scales, no doubt stimulated the piscatorial imagery. Cf. No. 78, l. 48.

127. Cf. *O.D.E.P.* Necessity knows no law; also *Piers Plowman*, B.xx.10.

130. egyls birdes] The forces of the Earl of Salisbury, who had remained in London to attack the Tower.

135. The defenders of the Tower included Thomas, Lord Scales; John, Lord Lovell; Robert, Lord Hungerford; Henry Bromflete, Lord de Vescy; Richard, Lord Delaware; and John, Earl of Kendal. Cf. *English Chronicle*, p. 95; *Short Eng. Chronicle*, p. 73.

138. "But they sent the Lord Scalys a wey prevely. And that was perceyved by the shippmen, and they laide watche and toke him, and slowe him and leyde him naked in Saint Mary Overes chirche yerde" (*Short Eng. Chronicle*, p. 75). So also William of Worcester, p. 773; Stow, *Annales*, p. 409.

142. mayster of þis game] Richard's uncle, Edward, second Duke of York, had translated *The Master of Game* about 1410.

149. Rom. 8.31.

90. THE BATTLE OF TOWTON, 1461

Index, No. 1380. Previously printed by Madden, *Archaeologia*, xxix.343-47; by Parry, *Royal Visits to Wales* (Chester, 1850), p. 266; by Thornley, *Eng. under the Yorkists*, pp. 15-17 (part only); by Greene, *Early Eng. Carols*, pp. 292-94; and by Brotanek, *ME Dicht.*, pp. 138-41, with full apparatus.

Following the Yorkist victory at Northampton (No. 89), Richard, Duke of York, returned from Ireland and secured his acceptance as Henry's heir. Meanwhile, a Lancastrian army had assembled in the North, and an inadequate Yorkist force sent to oppose it was defeated at Wakefield on December 30, 1460 — York, Rutland, and Salisbury being killed (cf. Whethamstede, i.381-83). Queen Margaret brought reinforcements from Scotland to the Lancastrian lords (l. 12), and together her troops ravaged south (l. 13), and again defeated the Yorkists at St. Albans, February 17, 1461 (ll. 17-18). London was garrisoned by pro-Yorkists, and was strengthened by the arrival of Warwick's defeated army and of Edward, Earl of March, now the new Duke of York (l. 19), fresh from his victory at Mortimer's Cross on February 3. Edward was acclaimed King at a mass meeting in London on March 1 (l. 28), and assumed the crown on March 4 (Hearne's Fragment, *Thomae Sprotti Chronica* [Oxford, 1719], p. 286; repr. *Chron. of White Rose*, p. 8). Queen Margaret's army was still strong (ll. 21-22), so Edward marched north (ll. 29, 31), meeting it between the villages of Saxton and Towton, near York. On March 29, 1461, Palm Sunday (l. 62), after a bitter fight (ll. 63-64) in a driving snowstorm, Edward was victorious (l. 66). He returned to his capital and was formally crowned on June 28, 1461 (l. 72).

A detailed account of the battle, summarizing earlier descriptions, but not always reliable, occurs in Hall's *Chronicle*, pp. 255-57. An antiquarian reconstruction of Towton is given by Richard Brooke, *Visits to Fields of Battle* (London, 1857), pp. 81-129.

bur. rose] The badge of Edward IV derived from his property at Clifford Castle (cf. Ellis, *Archaeologia*, xvii.226), used for the banner of one of the Yorkist divisions. Cf. No. 33, l. 1; No. 87, l. 6; No. 92, l. 11; etc. Other Yorkist badges in ll. 46, 47, 52, 57.

Rone] Edward was born on April 28, 1442, at Rouen, where his father was then governor. Brotanek (p. 150) suggests alliterative contamination with "rone" (thicket) and quotes such kennings as "þe rose ragged on rys, richest in rone."

3. moued] Brotanek emends "mened" (bewailed).
of goddes sonde] of God's dispensation; sent from God.
4. flour] Cf. No. 5, l. 66; No. 14, l. 143; No. 36, l. 1; etc.
6. fressh of hewe] Cf. "of coomly vysage" (Polydore Vergil, p. 172); "Fort beau prince, plus que nul que j'aye jamais veu" (Commines, ed. Calmette, i. 197).

11. Queen Margaret's forces, incluaing Scottish auxiliaries, under the command of Andrew Trollope, a professional soldier who had switched sides the previous year, pillaged York and sacked many towns from Christmas to February 2.

12. lordes] i.e., Clifford, Dacre, Devonshire, Exeter, Northumberland, Roos, Somerset, and Westmorland. Cf. *Gregory's Chronicle*, p. 210.

16. shrof tuesday] The Yorkists encamped on Barnet Heath, a plateau (*leede*) north of St. Albans, on the way to Sandrich, on February 12. The Lancastrians arrived on February 17 (Shrove Tuesday), and by turning Warwick's battle array, were victorious. Cf. *Short Eng. Chronicle*, p. 172; *English Chronicle*, p. 108.

17. The casualties were light, for the Yorkists fled without striking a blow. The short Latin chronicle in this Dublin MS. (ff. 82v-85v) notes: "et in dicto anno apud fastingonge fuit bellum apud Sanctum Albanum et ibi interfecti fuerunt dux de Bonvyle et Thomas Kyrell miles cum Hugone Stanop et militibus aliis" (Brotanek, p. 151). Bonvile and Kiriel, the Yorkist custodians of the King, were, in spite of pledges of safety, killed by the Lancastrians.

18. The Londoners expected the Lancastrians to advance immediately on their town.

21. Cf. the pro-Yorkist *English Chronicle*: "The quene ... had graunted and yeue leue to the Northurmen for to spoyle and robbe the sayde cyte [London], and also the townes of Couentre, Bristow,

and Salesbury, wyth the shyrys withynne rehersed" (p. 109). Similarly *Short Eng. Chronicle,* p. 155; *Gregory's Chronicle,* p. 212; Whetham-stede, i.388; *Paston Letters,* i.541; ii.3.

27. Calys] An important assembly area for the Yorkists when in exile in 1459.

28. "It appears that Edward took possession of the Throne with the assent of the southern half of the kingdom, finally estranged from the House of Lancaster by the misconduct of Margaret's host" (Ramsay, *Lanc. & York,* ii.249).

29. March 12 or 13, 1461.

31. By March 16, Edward had assembled his forces and was on his way northwards.

32. ragged staf] Richard Neville, Earl of Warwick. Cf. No. 84, l. 17.

þat] Tr. that many must have paid dearly for.

33. white lyon] John Mowbray, third Duke of Norfolk. Cf. No. 84, l. 9. Edward IV also used this device by his descent from the Mortimers, Earls of March.

36. fisshe-hoke] William Neville, Lord Fauconberg, "hauyng the foreward, because the duke of Northfolk was fallen sycke" (Hall, p. 255). Cf. No. 84, l. 13.

37. cornyssh choughe] John, Lord Scrope of Bolton, wounded in the battle. Cf. *Paston Letters,* i.218. Not Trevilian, who bore this badge (No. 84, l. 23).

38. blak ragged staf] Edward, Lord Grey de Ruthyn. Cf. No. 78, l. 47; Palliser, pp. 299-300.

39. brideld horse] William, Earl of Arundel, who had married Warwick's sister, Joan. Cf. No. 84, l. 25.

watyr bouge] Henry, Viscount Bourchier. Cf. No. 84, l. 29. Not listed in other accounts as present at this battle. Of him, Lord Grey (l. 38), Stanley (l. 41), and Clinton (l. 42), Ramsay says: "They certainly were Yorkists, and their men may have been present" (*Lanc. & York,* ii.273, fn. 5).

41. grehound] The punning cognizance of Sir John Mauleverer.

hertes hede] Thomas, Lord Stanley, later Earl of Derby (not noted in other contemporary accounts of the battle). Sir William Stanley also used this badge. Cf. "The Rose of England" on battle of Bosworth, *Bishop Percy's Folio MS.,* ed. Hales and Furnivall, iii.189-94, l. 113.

42. harow] Brotanek, following Hunt, says the city of Canterbury. "The cause of the White Rose was upheld at Towton by a force from Bristol, which fought beneath the 'Ship,' the banner of the town, and on the same side were unfurled the 'Harrow' of Canterbury, the 'Black Ram' of Coventry, the 'Dragon' of Gloucester, and the banners of other boroughs, which sent each its contingent to the army of the

King" (W. Hunt, *Bristol,* p. 99). The arms of Canterbury bore three cornish choughs.

kay] John, Lord Clinton, who joined the Yorkists in 1459 (for which he was attainted in the same year) and fought at Northampton, bore a mullet, not a key.

43. white ship] The city arms of Bristol. Both Coventry and Bristol had suffered from the Lancastrians (cf. l. 21), and were perhaps for that reason eager to fight for Edward. Bristol outfitted a fleet which defeated Jasper, Earl of Pembroke, at Wigmore, and sent soldiers to Towton.

44. blak ram] The city arms of Coventry are now an elephant. It too assisted Edward; cf. *EETS* 135.313-19.

46. fawcon] Probably a badge for one of the companies of Edward, Duke of York. A single leaf (Digby MS. 82) gives a list of the various badges employed by the House of York (*Archaeologia,* xvii.226-27), and the falcon and fetterlock are the cognizances of the Dukedom. Cf. No. 84. l. 35.

fetherlok] Another badge used for one of the Yorkist companies. Cf. No. 91, l. 45.

47. blak bulle] A. Yorkist badge, by Edward's descent from the house of Clare: "The Bages that he beryth by the Honor of Clare ys a blacke Bolle, rowgh, his Hornes, and his cleys and membres of Gold" (*Archaeologia,* xvii.226). Madden found that in the *Rot. Parl.,* vi.93, one Ralph Vestynden received ten pounds yearly for carrying this banner at the head of one of the Yorkist divisions. Cf. also *Rot. Parl.,* v.545, 613.

48. dolfyn] Not identified.

carpis] Not identified. Brotanek (p. 146) quotes Thomas Moules, *Heraldry of Fish,* p. 77, that there exist no suitable arms which would suit this context. Perhaps confounded with the pike, the punning badge of Sir James Pykryng, one of the Yorkist leaders in this battle.

49. libert] Richard Neville (d.1471), son of Richard Neville, Earl of Salisbury (d.1460). Not identified by Brotanek.

gapid his gomes wide] opened his mouth wide.

51. wolf] Not identified.

lyte] to come (to battle).

52. dragon] Another Yorkist badge, "by the Erldom of Wolstr" [Ulster], from the De Burghs, probably used for the Gloucester contingent. Edward was in Gloucester when he heard of the death of his father and the defeat at Wakefield (December 30, 1460). From here, he raised his army which fought at Mortimer's Cross.

53. griffen] John Neville, Lord Montagu (1460), later Earl of Northumberland (1464), the younger brother of Warwick, who had lands in Leicestershire. Cf. No. 82, l. 8.

as tyte] immediately.

54. george] Perhaps Edward's brother, Richard [III]. Henry VII, after the Battle of Bosworth, offered at St. Paul's two standards, a figure of St. George, and a Dun Cow, presumably captured from Richard. So Hall, p. 423. The badges enumerated in ll. 51-54 may, of course, refer to the towns named. For example, the Leicester city arms carried a wyvern, which might be confused with a griffin. James E. Winston, *English Towns in The Wars of the Roses* (Princeton, 1921), discusses the contingents towns sent to the rival factions. His identification of the badges, however, rests solely on this poem.

56. boris hede] Richard, created Duke of Gloucester after this battle, also wore the white boar.

57. estrich feder] Another badge of Edward, Duke of York; one of the insignia of the Plantagenets, which Richard had assumed in 1448. It was displayed at Towton for one of the Yorkist companies. *Gregory's Chronicle* describes its use at St. Albans in 1461: "And be-syde alle that, every man and lorde bare the Pryncys levery, that was a bende of crymesyn and blacke with esteryge ys fetherys" (p. 212).

58. wild kat] The arms of the city of Northampton was a tower supported by two lions, perhaps (for the "brode nose") mistaken for wild cats.

59. pynon] pennon, the triangular flag indicating a knight. Previously the great lords have been listed by their individual banners.

62. palmesonday] Henry had wished to avoid fighting to keep the day holy.

vs] ? An indication of an eyewitness report.

63. With-in an owre] A Yorkist hyperbole. Polydore Vergil, for example, says the battle lasted ten hours (p. 111). See also Whethamstede, i.410; *Gregory's Chronicle,* p. 214; Hall, p. 256; and discussion by Ransome, *EHR,* iv.465. Ramsay reconstructs a graphic account of the battle (*Lanc. & York,* ii.271).

64. xxvii thousand] Other sources are similarly bloated: Polydore Vergil gives 20,000 dead and 10,000 prisoners and wounded; the *Paston Letters* (i.220) gives 28,000 dead. Ramsay (ii.278) says the total strength of each army was probably only about 5,000 men, but that the carnage was terrible. "Of the numbers engaged we can offer no estimate, but they clearly exceeded these of any domestic battle that we have recorded or shall record" (*Lanc. & York,* ii.273).

66. feld] Cf. No. 32, l. 16.

69. Soche menys] Tr. Such means (steps) has the rose taken, etc.

91. *TWELVE LETTERS SAVE ENGLAND, 1461*

Index, No. 700. Previously printed by Madden, *Archaeologia*, xxix.330-34; and by Brotanek, *ME Dicht.*, pp. 152-58. Occurs also in Lambeth MS. 306, f. 134r, printed by Furnivall, *EETS* 15.1-3; also by Brotanek, *ibid.*

This poem is a Yorkist celebration (composed soon after July, 1461) of Edward and of his reigning as King (ll. 48, 67), with a commemoration of the three other chief Yorkists responsible for this success — Richard of York and Richard of Salisbury, both now dead, and Richard of Warwick. It obviously refers to a state long before the defection of Warwick in 1467. Some of the difficulty encountered in the interpretation is caused by the use of a present tense for persons already dead, e.g., York "is manly" (l. 25), Salisbury "bryngeth" (l. 39). Hence it is possible (with Furnivall) to misidentify Edward as both Earl of March and Duke of York, and Richard as Earl of Warwick and Earl of Salisbury. The twelve letters are divided between the four lords, and identify their proper name, their title, and their arms:

Edward (l. 29), Earl of March (l. 33), with the fetterlock (l. 45).
Richard (l. 21), Duke of York (ll. 23, 27), with the white rose (l. 49).
Richard (l. 21), Earl of Salisbury (l. 37), with the eagle (l. 53).
Richard (l. 21), Earl of Warwick (l. 41), with the ragged staff (l. 57).

The Lambeth text (68 ll., at times reduced to trimeters) is much inferior, although it corrects the tenses (so York "was manely" and "reynyed"; Salisbury "was"). However, it lists initially only eight letters, then casually introduces another four only after an intervening stanza; it shows textual contamination, not necessarily due to imperfect memorizing (as Brotanek suggests, with *pater familias* becoming *patris Sapiente*), but rather to scribal illiteracy or miscopying (discrecion in l. 34 appears as eistricion; question in l. 37 becomes avision; reputacion in l. 48 becomes repetacion); it omits the essential stanza on Edward following l. 28; and finally it makes the concluding st. a conventional minstrel close with no connection to the remainder of the poem. Lambeth has unfortunately been the better known text, since it was printed in *EETS;* whereas the Dublin MS. appeared only in *Archaeologia* in 1842 and in a wartime German edition published in Halle, 1940.

A curious copying of expressions from No. 88 is seen in ll. 29, 30, 41. Cf. Kingsford's note for No. 89.

1. The *chanson d'aventure* gambit is not infrequent in these political poems. Cf. No. 38; and also *Index*, Nos. 1355, 1505.

Yerly] L. erly.

4. The robes in the statues of Richard II and Queen Anne in Westminster Abbey are decorated with emblems and the letters R and A.

11. The use of letters is similar to the "Sybilline" type of prophecy; cf. No. 45, ll. 60, 64. Brotanek (p. 161) compares an Elizabethan prophecy using the letters HEMPE (Henry, England, Mary, Philip, Elizabeth) from R. Chambers, *Domestic Annals of Scotland,* i.381.

þei were] L. they be.

12. a b c] Primer or spelling book. Cf. No. 64, l. 12.

13. V] i.e., a double V, or W, as in l. 41. L. substitutes:

They were nether A b nor S,
    Of any clarke y take wittnes,
Hit was R, w, and II ees,
    F, M, ȝ, and S.

15. be rute] in order.

19. L. And Exspoundide theim after myn owne wesdone / After the forme of Experience.

22. The twelve letters in L. are confused, hence text is altered:

A E for Edward, men wote it is soo,
    This ben the lettres of the IIII lordes names.

26. reuelacion] Brotanek quotes from Halliwell, *Archaeologia,* xxix.128, a sermon in Cotton MS. Vesp. E.vii: "And now ageine wronge, for syne be ryghte is flemed oute of the londe for ever, anno 1460. Thus it is knowen and proved of oure Lord be revelacioun in oure Lady aungelle Sibelle, quene of the Southe ... Seint Edwarde, Birgitt, Bede, Gildas, Ricardus Scrope, and many moo. Mirabilis Deus in sanctis suis. Now understond welle every man, houghe and in whome alle theis forsaide concluden and acordyn, alle in one rightefully, be inspiracioun of the Holy Gost."

29. Cf. No. 88, l. 65. L omits this st.

30. prudence] Cf. No. 88, l. 66 (applied to Richard).

35. wedlok] A snide Yorkist comment on the alleged illegitimacy of Prince Edward, the son of Queen Margaret. Cf. No. 88, l. 13.

36. Cf. No. 92, l. 14.

41. sheld] Cf. No. 88, l. 68. L. their childe & þer diffence. On f. 69*v* is a tristich on the virtues of the Earl of Warwick:

W wisdome monstrat et adventus. A bene constat.

R rightwisnes legi. W willing prospera regi.

I iust antique. K kynd est hic et ubique.

43. In L. l. 40; and replacing l. 44: The boldest vnder baner batell to abide.

45. feturlok] "The fetterlock, with a falcon inside it, was a badge of Edmund of Langley (son of Edward III.), who re-built his Castle of Fotheringay in that shape, and was consequently as-

sumed by his great grandson Edward IV" (quoted by Furnivall, *EETS* 15.xii). Cf. No. 90, l. 46.

46. mevid] L. amendide.

47. scotland] Probably in error for Ireland; MS. in l. 52 reads ryland.

48. ruleth] L. Reynyed.

49. L. frische and wol nat fade.

50. rote and þe stalke] Richard and his son Edward (IV).

51. L. þe leues do springe.

55. L. vndir þe stone.

57. ragged staf] Cf. No. 84, ll. 17-18.

62. ryde or gone] a common cliché.

63. disseverid] i.e., some are dead. Not (as Madden) some in Ireland and some in Calais.

65. Cf. No. 88, l. 49.

67. edward] Furnivall is forced by his misinterpretation to emend to Richard.

92. *EDWARD, DEI GRATIA*

Index, No. 3127. Previously printed by Halliwell, *Archaeologia,* xxix.127; by Furnivall, *EETS* 15.4-5; by Parry, *Royal Visits to Wales,* p. 265; and by Greene, *Early Eng. Carols,* p. 291-92.

This poem is probably of the same date as No. 91; certainly before May, 1464, when Edward married Elizabeth Woodville, for l. 14 refers to "Thove vergyne knight." *O.E.D.* dates 1465 (*possess,* II. 7).

5. Edward IV's accession was considered a legitimist restoration from Richard II, the three Henrys (1399-1461) being held intruders. His first Parliament (November, 1461) thanked Edward for assuming "the Reigne and Governaunce of the seid Reame, whereunto ye be rightwisely and naturally born" (*Rot. Parl.,* v.462). Cf. No. 94, l. 6; and *Short Eng. Chronicle,* pp. 170-71 for his proclamation.

10. birede in] buried from.

11. rosse] Cf. No. 42, l. 25; No. 87, l. 6.

14. vergyne knight] Edward was nineteen on his accession and unmarried. He was, however, "a lusty prince," who "attempted the stability and constant modesty of divers ladies and gentlewomen" (Hearne's Fragment, *Chronicles of White Rose,* p. 15). Thornley, *England under The Yorkists,* p. 20, quotes a Milanese letter of 1461: "It is true that he tries to afford every kind of pleasure that he can to the earl both festivities of ladies and hunting."

17. contenewaunce] continuing (as king).

21. Rex Anglie] Edward was crowned June 28, 1461. The *Short Eng. Chronicle* notes his popularity when he entered London: "On

the Thorsday the first weke of Lenten he came to London with xxx M*l* men ... and so in feld and towne everychone called Edward Kynge of Ingelond and of Fraunce" (p. 77).

22. France was already lost, and Edward was not even secure in England. In 1475 Edward claimed the crown and invaded France, but made a truce at Pecquigny in the same year. Cf. No. 42, l. 3.

23. Edward made peace treaties with Henry of Castile and John of Aragon in 1465.

30. subdeue of] Subdue is not rec. with this construction in *O.E.D.* Tr. gain control of.

93. A POLITICAL RETROSPECT, 1462

Index, No. 3756. Previously printed by Wright, *Pol. Poems*, ii.267-70.

This poem commemorates the triumph of Edward IV and gives a review of recent history as seen through the eyes of a Yorkist.

3. Unrightful heyres] i.e., the three Lancastrian kings.

9. force] During Henry's banishment, his father, John of Gaunt, died. Richard unjustly sequestered his estates, whereupon Henry returned to claim his possessions. His landing at Ravenspur recalls the invasion made by Edward IV. Gower's *Tripartite Chronicle* includes in Henry's claims to the throne, along with his right by descent and his right by popular acclaim, his right by conquest (*Pol. Poems*, i.449).

10. periury] in that (like Edward IV later) he first claimed only the restoration of his lands, and swore allegiance to the King.

12. Richard II was supposed to have died in Pontefract Castle, following the abortive rising in his name. Cf. No. 40.

13. Pyned] (he was) starved to death. So in certain chronicles: Adae de Usk, p. 42; *EETS* 136.360; etc.

  pyteuxly] Not rec. *O.E.D.* with this spelling.

14. Scrope] Cf. No. 31, l. 14.

20. benysyne] Blessing (i.e., the ecclesiastical approval given by Scrope to the rising) is held suspect. The MS. venyrsyne must be amended.

22. Rigoure] unswerving determination.

23. Sir John Fortescue, Chancellor of Henry VI, wrote a tract suggesting the illegitimacy of Philippa, daughter of Edward III's third son, the Duke of Clarence, through whom Edward claimed the crown. Fortescue later withdrew the allegation.

26. lepre] Suggested by Yorkists as divine punishment for his murder of Scrope. Cf. No. 31, l. 3.

30. Henry V's reputation was still too famous to permit his being maligned.

31. Cf. No. 83, l. 43.

37. A recurrent charge in all Yorkist accounts. Cf. No. 73.

39. Vickers, *England in the Later Middle Ages,* p. 460, quotes from B. M. Addit. MS. 4613, Edward's coronation proclamation, describing "the lamentable state and ruyne of this reaume of England ... th'oppression of the people, the manslaughter, extortion, perjurie and robberye amonge theym." He declared "that Justice, the moder of virtue, hath been long exiled," and promised "to remoeve and sette apart the seid mischieves." Cf. l. 79.

43. Scripture] Not the Bible, but John Bonif., *Lib. de furt.:* De rebus male acquisitis non gaudebit tertius heres. This almost proverbial saying is quoted by Walsingham, *Hist. Anglicana:* "De male quaesitis vix gaudet tertius heres."

46. iij kynges] The three Henrys.

54. Cf. No. 81, l. 14. "Quod secundum voluntatem ipsius reginae quasi tota negocia regni facta fuerunt per fas vel per nephas, ut dicebatur a diversis" (Gascoigne, p. 204). Also "The Quene is a grete and strong labourid woman, for she spareth noo peyne to sue hire thinges to an intent and conclusion to hir power" (*Paston Letters,* iii.75).

59. affynite] "The quene with such as were of her affynyte rewled the reame as her lyked, gaderyng ryches innumerable" (*English Chronicle,* p. 79).

67. Margaret connived with Pierre de Brezé, Seneschal of Normandy, to invade England. Cf. J. J. Bagley, *Margaret of Anjou* (London, n.d.), p. 118, fn. 1.

78. Rouen] Cf. No. 90, burden.

85. Cf. No. 89.

86. February 3, 1461.

87. Towton; cf. No. 90.

89. The defeated Lancastrians fled to Scotland.

90. crouned] June 28, 1461.

93. Almost any political prophecy could be so interpreted. Cf. No. 44, ll. 69-72.

94. castell] Cf. No. 43, l. 16.

100. Had this poem been written a few years later (e.g., 1464), the poet might have been less admiring of Warwick, who was then being described as the real authority in England; cf. Waurin, v.456-58.

105. vierge] The Virgin. *O.E.D.* lists only this ref.

106. mediatrix] i.e., the Virgin. *O.E.D.* first rec.

94. THE BATTLE OF BARNET, 1471

Index, No. 899. Previously printed by MacCracken, *Archiv,* cxxx. 309-10. Part II of the Trinity MS., third quarter fifteenth century, is a large collection of aureate religious poems, many by Lydgate; it was owned by Roger Thorney, patron of de Worde, and later by Stow. For a long narrative poem on the return of Edward and the Battle of Barnet see *Index,* No. 2808.

The Duke of Warwick, the Duke of Clarence (Edward's brother), and the Archbishop of York, complaining of the faction surrounding Edward, had crossed from Calais to England, defeated Pembroke at Edgecote Field (1469), and captured Edward near Coventry. Edward was allowed to return to London, and attempted some reconciliations. Warwick and Clarence continued to intrigue, and, after their forces had suffered defeat at Empyngham, fled to France, where they reversed their policies and made an alliance with Queen Margaret. On September 13, 1470, the Dukes landed at Dartmouth and proclaimed Henry once more King. Edward fled the country, and by October Henry was freed from the Tower. Edward, however, returned on March 14, 1471, to Ravenspur in Yorkshire, and marched southwards. Clarence defected and joined his brother, and together they entered London. On Easter Day they met and defeated Warwick at Barnet. Warkworth (pp. 15-17) and the writer of the *Arrivall of Edward IV* (pp. 17-21) both give eyewitness accounts of the battle.

This poem "presents the popular London view of Edward IV, who had endeared himself to the citizens by knightly displays and by other means hardly so honourable" (MacCracken, p. 286).

6. "Also how wrongfully and vniustly he had be, and was, dyspleased and dyseased of hys ryghte enheritaunce of the reaume and croune of Englond, by violent intrusyonne of kyng Harry the iiij*the,* whyche vnryghtefully, wrongfully, and tyrannously vsurped the crowne after the dethe of kyng Rychard his cosyn . . . he as ryghte heyre by lynealle descens from the sayde kyng Richard . . ." (*English Chronicle,* p. 99).

7. Many initially supported Edward in his claims for his duchy, but not for the throne. This poem attempts to persuade them to accept him again as king. "As to the folks of the countrye there came but right few to hym, or almost none, for, by the scuringe of suche persons as for that cawse were, by his said rebells, sent afore into those partes for to move them to be agains his highnes, the people were sore endwsed to be contrary to hym, and not to receyve, ne accepe hym, as for theyr Kynge; natwithstondynge, for the love and favour that before they had borne to the prince of fulnoble memorye, his father, Duke of Yorke, the people bare hym right great favowr to be also Duke of Yorke, and to have that of right apartayned unto hym, by the right of the sayde noble prince his fathar. And, upon this opinion, the people of the countrie, whiche in greate nombar, and in dyvars placis, were gatheryd, and in harnes, redye to resiste hym in chalenginge of the Royme and the crowne, were disposyd to

content them selfe, and in noo wyse to annoy hym, ne his felowshipe, they affirmynge that to such entent were [they] comen, and none othar" (*Arrivall of Edward IV*, p. 3). Even in London, there was considerable opposition from the poorer people (cf. *Arrivall*, p. 16).

mys-creatures] Not rec. *O.E.D.*, although the use of this prefix common.

11. he] The Earl of Warwick: "And whenne the Erle of Warwyke sawe his brothere dede, and the Erle of Oxenforde fledde, he lepte one horsebacke, and flede to a wode by the felde of Barnett, where was no waye forthe; and one of Kynge Edwardes menne had espyede hyme, and one came uppone hym and kyllled hym, and dispolede hyme nakede" (Warkworth, p. 16). Cf. Edward's report to Charles the Bold (in *Archaeologia*, xxi.16). So l. 28.

22. Cf. *Index*, No. 2808, ll. 248-49:

Noþur Alisaunder ne Artur, ne no conqueroure

No better were acompenyd with nobill men.

25. "And on Ester day in the mornynge, the xiiij. day of Apryl, ryght erly, eche of them came uppone othere; and ther was suche a grete myste, that nether of them myght see othere perfitely; ther thei faughte, from iiij. of clokke in the mornynge unto x. of clokke the fore-none" (Warkworth, p. 16).

27. Cf. *Index*, No. 2808, ll. 163-64:

Levyng behynde hym many a dede man,

Sum hurte, sum slayn, sum cryinge "Alas."

34. Cf. Thomas à Kempis, *Imit. Christi:* "Homo proponit, sed Deus disponit."

95. THE CROWNED KING:
ON THE ART OF GOVERNING, 1415

Index, No. 605. Previously printed by Skeat, *EETS* 54.524-29. The Douce MS. dates about mid-fifteenth century (on f. 12 occurs the date 1439). It contains, in addition, several secular lyrics (*Sec. Lyrics*, Nos. 199 and 205) and Latin ordinances for a coronation.

Preparations for an invasion of France had been going on for some time prior to June 18, when Henry set out from London for embark-ation at Southampton. The poet refers to the sizable grant of two tenths and two fifteenths which Henry had obtained from the Commons on November 19, 1414 (l. 63), and one of the conditions that "all prisoners were to belong to their captors" (ll. 95-96). The poet furthermore refers to the possible capture of castles (l. 97), and encourages the King to personal prowess (ll. 122-24). After the dream introduction, a cleric receives permission to speak "sum sawes of salomon." This advice covers the need to rule righteously, re-membering the value of the "pouere peple" who provide the real riches of the kingdom; giving leadership for the nobility, avoiding wicked advisers, promoting the worthiest fighters, and acquiring knowledge and ability to exercise personal leadership.

There is no need to postulate (with Skeat, p. cxxiv) that because of the allusion in l. 20 the poem was necessarily written at Southampton; no more than that *Piers Plowman* was written in the Malvern Hills. The place name simply points the reference to Henry V and the forthcoming war.

The fashion of addressing admonitions to noblemen for their moral and political improvement, which resulted in such notable works as *The Fall of Princes, De Regimine Principum,* and the *Secrees of Old Philisoffres,* produced this short political allegory, localized at Southampton on Corpus Christi Eve, May 29, 1415 (ll. 19-20). (Cf. Hoccleve's attack on Oldcastle, *Index,* No. 3407, was also written before an expedition of the King from Southampton—in August, 1413.) None of this advice is especially original, and in content (though not in style) parallels the contemporary poems in the Digby 102 series (e.g., No. 14; *Index,* No. 3924); and Hoccleve's virelai to Henry V "le iour que les seigneurs de son Roialme lui firent lour homages a Kenyngtoun" (*Index,* No. 3402). The framework of the poem not only recalls *Piers Plowman* (which it also resembles in specific lines), but *Richard the Redeles* (Index, *6), "in which the exact style and spirit of Piers the Plowman is perfectly maintained throughout" (Skeat, p. 523). Oakden, *Allit. Poetry,* ii.263, finds eighteen distinct alliterative passages here.

18. frendemen] intimate friends. Skeat emends fremde men—"lit. foreign; hence, chance acquaintances, companions to whom one is not related."

24. began] (it) began (to dawn).

27. busked me doun] got ready for sleep.

28. cacche a slepe] take a nap.

29. swyed] fell down exhausted through dizziness.

31. Cf. *Piers Plowman,* B. Pro. 13-18.

32. deppest of othre] deeper than any other.

35. Cf. *Piers Plowman,* B. Pro. 112.

36. subsidie] Taxes, mainly on cloth and skins, etc., and import duties, extended to the "tenths" and "fifteenths" income taxes.

42. Cf. *Piers Plowman,* B. Pro. 123-24.

44. Cf. *Piers Plowman,* B.iii.93-94. Saws of Solomon are quite frequent in ME verse; cf. *Index,* Nos. 3069, 3861.

47. pluralites] In contrast to singular noumbre (simple fashion) or "prose"; hence, ornamentation.

50. hym semed] seemed (best) to him.

52. lyme] The Kings power over life and limb; cf. No. 14, ll. 105-6.

53. Cf. *Piers Plowman,* B.iv.136-42.

54. Cf. No. 14, ll. 65-66.

61. Cf. *Piers Plowman*, B.iv.148.

63. the] thee

in a myle-wey] in the long run.

65. Cf. No. 14, ll. 97-100, 109-110; *Index*, No. 2211, l. 40: "Ay on þy comunes having compassyoun."

66. the] for thee; subject (they) of "swope and swete" omitted (as commonly).

71. Cf. *Index*, No. 3924, ll. 43-44: "ʒoure tenauntes playntes ʒe mot here / ffor þey kepen all ʒoure tresour."

79. Throughout, cf. the similar exhortation to Edward, Prince of Wales, son to Henry VI, in George Ashby's *Policy of a Prince, Index*, No. 2130.

82. waste wele] unprofitable prosperity.

86. Cf. *Index*, No. 3924, ll. 89-92:

Putte fro court, þat cherischeþ vys,

þat place of vertues wolde shende.

Nedeles delys, and nedeles gys,

þe wastours out of worschip spende.

89. Cf. *Index*, No. 3924, ll. 134-36:

Whan gloser & flaterer on tapetis trede,

For wynnyng þey counseled to cowardys,

Man wan neuere worschip by here dede.

91. moustres] Skeat's glosses false pretences; but musters better fits the context. Cf. *Piers Plowman*, C.vii.260.

95. poyntes of werre] warlike exercises So *O.E.D. point*, C.1, but without illustrations.

97. Cf. *Piers Plowman*, C.iv.251-53.

102. "The line is obscure, but it may mean—'and let use be his master,' or 'let habit guide him' " (Skeat, p. 532).

107. be cours] in accordance with.

118. brogour] Cf. *Piers Plowman*, B.ii.65.

126. Cf. *Piers Plowman*, B.iii.208; C.iv.266-69.

132. "There his disposition is turning aside from its trew nature" (Skeat).

134. "Those games are most liked, in which all the people who join can laugh" (Skeat).

137. taketh] "The pl. is used to shew respect, in the royal style" (Skeat).

142. Cf. *Piers Plowman*, B. Pro. 105; C.i.133.

96. *ADVICE TO THE SEVERAL ESTATES, I*
BY LYDGATE

Index, No. 920. This text comes from de Worde's first edition of

Lydgate's *Temple of Glas* (n.d., c. 1498), and also appeared in the second edition (n.d., c. 1500), in Thynne's *Chaucer* (1523), and in Stow's *Chaucer* (1561). It has been reprinted by Schick, *EETS* lx.68 (with collations); by Skeat, *Oxf. Ch.*, i.40; vii.408; and by MacCracken, *EETS* 192.707. Skeat (*Minor Poems*, p. xxix) says "Surely it must be Lydgate's"; MacCracken (p. 709) and Schirmer (p. 230) include it in the canon; Brusendorff queries Lydgate's authorship.

These two st. are preceded by a variant of the Twelve Abuses (Nos. 54 and 55), and are themselves a positive paraphrase of the Latin. Only five of the abuses remain unchanged from the pseudo-Cyprian list (Cf. note to No. 54), another (Mulier sine castitate) is slightly changed; and the whole catalogue is rearranged (cf. Brown, *Archiv*, cxxviii.74). The first st. addresses the rulers, and the second the ruled.

97. *ADVICE TO THE SEVERAL ESTATES, II*

Index, No. 4257. Previously printed by Bowers, *Southern Folklore Qr.*, xvi.223-26; and (in part) by Bergen, *EETS* cxxiv.59-60. Written in an early sixteenth-century hand on the flyleaf (not part of the original MS.) of a large copy of *The Fall of Princes*. This poem is largely a collection of typical aphorisms explaining and inculcating the medieval theory of estates or degrees.

29. venus] sexual lust. First rec. *O.E.D.* 1513.

40. "In the fifteenth century men felt themselves terribly dependent on the character that their ruler happened to possess, and they believed that the ruler's character might really be influenced by the example of virtue and vice he met in literature" (Tillyard, *Eng. Renaissance* [London, 1952], p. 68).

42. degre] A discussion of justice, based on the theory of degree, opens a declaration of Edward IV to the Commons claiming the French throne; it is a neat and official formulation: "Justice was grounde well and rote of all prosperite, peas and pollityke rule of every Reame, wheruppon all the Lawes of the world been grounde and sette, which resteth in thre; that is to sey, the Lawe of God, Lawe of nature, and posityfe Lawe . . . Justice is, every persone to doo his Office that he is put yn accordyng to his astate or degre; and as for this Lond, it is understoud that it stondeth by III estates, and above that oon principall; that is to witte, Lordes Spirituell, Lordes Temporell, and Commons, and over that, State Rial above" (*Rot. Parl.*, v.622).

63. Cf. "Si caput dolet, omnia membra languent." Parallel forms of this proverb occur in Pliny, *Ep.*, iv.22; and Seneca, *De Clementia*, ii.2.

98. A PRAYER FOR ENGLAND
BY LYDGATE

Index, No. 2218. Previously printed by Mahir, *Ein Gedichte Lydg.,* pp. 44-48; and by MacCracken, *EETS* cvii.212-16. Occurs also in Harley MS. 7578, printed in *Rel. Ant.,* i.227-28; and by Wülcker, *AE Leseb.,* ii.8-10. In Trinity Coll. Camb. MS. 601, Harley MS. 2251, and B.M. Addit. MS. 34360, the last three st. of the envoy to Henry VI are deleted, and the first st. substitutes the name of Edward IV. The Fairfax MS. (first half fifteenth century) is a major collection of Chaucer's minor poems, pseudo-Chaucerian items, and some pieces by Hoccleve (inc. *Index,* No. 3854) and Lydgate (including a copy of No. 1). The Trinity Coll. MS. (owned by Roger Thorney, 1450-1515, a rich London mercer and a Yorkist supporter — cf. No. 94; and *Library,* xii.296-97) adds a further Envoy from Chaucer's "Lak of Stedfastnesse" (*Index,* No. 3190), which satisfactorily dovetails into the whole poem.

Collation H. 2251: 1. blesful; 2. defende vs of; 5. thre two and oon; 7. Owre kyng, oure qwene, theyr peple of yngland; 8. bliesful; 17. The inward; 20. lord ay; 24. Now lord Iesu vpon her synnes rewe; 25. Where theyr demerites do nat recompence; 26. *delete* But; 27. Preservyng ay oure kyng our quene and land; 28. Goode lord Iesu vnder thy myghty hand; 29. Thow blisful lord here oure oreysoun; 31. compleynt; lamentaccoun; 32. Socoure vs crist for on vs falle; 34. And euer; 35. the land; 36. Thow goddis sone; 38. And with thi; 42. theyr peple and the land; 43. Here in this lyf and; 45. on; 46. Therto we shal; 47. passioun eke shal; 49. Both kyng; 50. Thow here vnto the; 52. thow vs convey; 56. qwene and also yngland. Envoy as for Trinity.

The poem is one of a number of official commendations which Lydgate wrote for the coronation (e.g., *Index,* Nos. 1929, 2211, and 2804); and, since it looks forward to that event, must be at least before November, 1429, and perhaps earlier (cf. l. 66). Schirmer, *John Lydgate,* suggests it has the character of a prayer in wartime, and "accordingly it was inserted in the Sunday ritual. One can imagine it spoken in church in public service" (p. 115). The Latin heads are variants of the responses in a Litany for the consecration of a church (cf. *Surtees Soc.* 27.33), and each Eng. st. is substantially a paraphrase of the Latin. The concluding Envoy is a typical Lydgatian effusion to Henry as the rightful heir to the throne.

6. The last two lines (6, 7) appear to have led a separate existence as a popular prayer tag. Dr. A. I. Doyle points out this couplet occurs in Huntington MS. EL. 26 A.13 and on the flyleaf of Corpus Christi Coll. Camb. MS. 61. In tone it is similar to another prayer by Lydgate, *Index,* No. 2156.

59. Cf. No. 1, l. 100.

60. Cf. *Index*, No. 2211, ll. 33-34: "And sith þou art frome þat noble lyne / Descendid dovne."

66. Cf. *Index*, No. 2211, ll. 103-4:

> With þe goode lyf of qweene Katheryne
> þy blessid moder in þat other syde.

Schirmer (p. 115, fn. 185) suggests that the "innigen Ton" of the address to Katherine may antedate her betrothal to Owen ap Tudor in 1425.

80. Cf. No. 1, l. 102.

99. THAT PEACE MAY STAND

Index, No. 1772. Previously printed by Turnbull, *Visions of Tundale* (1843), pp. 153-56. Advocates MS. is a very late fifteenth-century MS., a large collection of 40 items, inc. romances, saints' lives, three books of Lydgate's *Life of Our Lady*, and miscellaneous religious poetry and prose. The names of several scribes appear, including "heege," "hyheg," and "Iohn howghton."

The dating of this poem presents a problem. Certain clues are given. For three years there have been floods and other bad weathers, destruction of grain, great poverty, rioting in north and south, robbery and murder everywhere; soldiers holding back in combat only to rob the men of their own side, and many good warriors slain. During this time, negotiations for a truce have been undermined by men who profited from the confusion. At last, a truce has been arranged, and things look better: there is good weather and more grain, and although England is weak it should still be able to fend off invaders if everybody supports the King. There are two possible periods which meet most of these requirements: from 1391-1394 and from 1436/7-1440. The latter seems more likely. In the winter of 1437 there was a great frost; in 1438 great tempest and rains, severe frost, and dearth of wheat; food continued even scarcer in 1439, and by 1440 the food supply was the worst for 100 years so that grain (as in 1391) had to be imported from Prussia. In 1438 and 1439 plague and pestilence struck heavily, and the kiss of homage was abandoned because of danger of spreading infection. The judges had gone unpaid for 1438 and 1439 and threatened to resign; authority was belittled. In 1438 the Chancellor stated that justice and peace must be restored to England. The English were losing in France, and Warwick died in 1439. A conference in July, 1439 at Calais failed, but the ambassadors returned for instructions. Gloucester and the war party were trying to sabotage any such agreement, and early in 1440 they tried to indict Beaumont and Archbishop Kemp of York for peculation during the war. Since the King desired to end the war "that longe hath contyned and endured, that is to saye, an hundreth yeers and more," the negotiations were pushed; and by November, 1440, the Duke of Orleans was released to try to mediate between England and France. Cf. Polydore Vergil, p. 68; *Rot. Parl.,* v.14; Brut, *EETS* 136.470-71, 507; *Gregory's Chronicle,* p. 181; Stow, *Annales,* p. 378.

5. whom] them. Prosthetic w is found also here in pwowere, wonus. Cf. Kihlbom, *XV Century English,* pp. 162-68. Cf. swold (No. 86, l. 31).

13. Tr. For I am struck with amazement at, etc.

22. Tr. And fashioned Adam with sand (earth). Cf. *O.E.D.* upon, prep. 11. i (1553).

32. Robbe] MS. Robbo; cf. *Index,* No. 3435, f. 10r (in this MS.), for to moto. O-E confusion is not uncommon in ME MSS. So here, No. 2, l. 8; No. 4, l. 23; No. 5, l. 88; No. 36, l. 20; No. 48, l. 97. Cf. further Robbins, *MLR,* xxxv.321.

38. to pey] acceptably.

44. borne] boundary-mark; hey = hedge. Kemp Malone suggests tr. The floods played havoc with the fences, hedges, and other marks for the limits of holdings.

100.   SEND US PEACE

Index, No. 1710. Previously printed by Fehr, *Archiv,* cvi.276; by Greene, *Early Eng. Carols,* p. 296; and by Stevens, *Mus. Brit.,* iv.102. This songbook generally has late compositions. Greene (p. 443) suggests 1499, but the poem more probably refers to Edward IV's negotiations with Scotland in 1479-1483. For a similar prayer with music in this MS. cf. *Index,* No. 962: "God sende vs pese & vnite / In engelande with prosperite."

GLOSSARY

This Glossary includes those words which might present some difficulty to the reader; it is not intended to be a complete, etymological *index verborum*. Ordinarily, the first occurrence of a given form in these texts is recorded. Words or phrases requiring special comment are glossed in the Notes. Variant forms, with or without final -e, with i or y (vocalic), or with u or v (vocalic or consonantal), are generally not given separate entries; nor are plural forms of nouns without other change than -s or -n. Initial ʒ is entered following g; þ and th are entered alphabetically under t. Verbs are entered, where possible, under the infinitive.

a, interj.; ah! 60.4.

a, prep.; at 42.6; in 4.179; 79.37.

abate, v.; to destroy 11.19; pt. 3 s. *abated,* was humbled 4.92.

aby, v.; to pay the penalty for 64.42; 79.47.

abide, v.; to await 3.99; remain 4.99; 78.16; stand firm 78.4; 91.42; wait 66.28; withstand 44.17; *habide* 11.31; 12.34; pt. 3 s. *abod* 39.68.

abidynge, n.; dwelling place 64.67.

abyt, n.; gown 71.10.

aboht, See *bye.*

abolge, v.; to cause to spring a leak 30.91.

aboute, adv.; around the outside 14.17; 28.33; *abute,* on all sides 48.141; *obout* 9.15.

abowght, prep.; about 26.1.

abugge, See *bye.*

abul, adj.; disposed 20.53.

abusioun, n.; perversion 40.13; 93.51.

ac, conj.; but 48.28; 54.59; *ah* 6.7; 8.18; *ok* 48.43.

acast, See *cast.*

acese, v.; to cease from 41.49.

acord, adv.; in agreement 85.15.

acord, v.; to agree 70.36; pr. 3 s. *accordeth* 72.19; pp. *accorded* 79.8.

adoun, adv.; down 3.23; 95.42; *adun* 48.108.

adrenche, v.; to drown 4.101; 95.92; pt. pl. *dreynte* 4.98.

aduert, v. imp.; take heed 98.15.

aduowetrye, n.; adultery 62.21; *avutrie* (fig.) 64.134.

afered, pp.; frightened 78.14.

affynite, n.; kindred 93.59.

afforne, adv.; previously 1.101.

affter, prep.; according to 89.3.

afray, n.; attack 27.37; *afrey* 99.45.

afretye, v. pr. subj. s.; devour 7.8.

after, adj.; later 15.48.

after, conj.; afterwards 28.139; 42.3; 95.29.

agayne, prep.; against 26.140; 26.184; *aʒen* 13.107; *aʒens* 13.33; *aʒeynes* 3.27.

agast, adj.; alarmed 20.34; 41.25; afraid 39.51.

age, n.; old age 39.106.

agynneþ, v. pr. pl.; begin 3.38.

agon, See *goo.*

aʒe, adv.; again 48.188.

aʒt, v. pr. 3 s.; should, ought to

48.82; *ahte* 5.9; pr. pl. *aught* 29.64.

ah, See *ac*.

ay, adv.; ever 13.23; *aye* 26.8.

ailed, pp.; troubled, afflicted 10.27.

al, adv.; wholly 15.51; *all* 9.8; completely 45.49; *al* 3.39; *hall* 41.15.

alast, adv.; in the last place 4.87.

aleye, n.; alley 40.45.

algate, adv.; in every way 74.31.

alye, n.; kinsman 73.42.

alyons, n.; strangers, foreigners 43.33; *alienys* 45.27.

alliaunce, n.; union by marriage 1.65; *alyaunce*, relationship 93.3; *aliauns*, friendship 63.26.

allinge, adv.; wholly 4.48.

allonly, adv.; exclusively 89.26.

allowed, pp.; praised 15.26.

almight, adj.; almighty 89.105.

almosse, n.; alms 1.53.

almusles, adj.; alms-less 54.56.

als, conj.; as 11.21.

also, adv.; as 38.10; referring to 42.13.

alsone as, adv. phr.; as soon as 20.37.

alþeih, conj.; although 54.80.

altratyd, pp.; altered 70.144.

among, adv.; in turns 5.4.

amonges, prep.; among 3.12.

an, prep.; on 95.31.

and, conj.; if 13.15; 14.25; 25.20; 26.35; 27.*m*; 39.14; 52.22; 65.83; 75.2; 95.13; *ant*, and 3.1; 4.8.

anhonge, See *honge*.

anouen, adv.; above 3.15.

apaid, pp.; satisfied 95.74.

apayre, v.; to injure 13.18.

apert, adv.; publicly 14.54.

aplyht, adv.; in truth 4.115.

aposen, v. pr. pl.; argue 69.4.

apparaill, n.; rich clothing 95.71.

appoysayll, n.; examination 70.4.

appressed, pp.; oppressed 86.13.

aquelleden, v. pt. pl.; killed 3.79.

ar, See *here*, pro.

aray, n.; military might 28.53; 32.6; attire 41.36; *array*, estate 65.144.

are, n.; mercy 11.62.

are, prep.; before 10.58.

arewe, v.; to rue, grieve 3.11; *arewen* 7.32.

ariht, adv.; aright 20.4.

arise, See *ryse*.

arost, See *roste*.

arowe, adv.; one after another 75.14.

array, See *aray*.

arraye, v. imp.; put in order 13.151; *araye*, prepare for battle 26.99; pp. *araied* 28.32.

as, adv.; as if 45.54.

asad, pp.; satisfied 4.7.

asay, n.; trial 95.106.

ascaped, v. pt. pl.; escaped from 28.149.

ascenteþ, v. pr. pl.; assent 8.14.

ases, v.; to cease 13.21; 14.4; *asses* 13.30.

aspie, v.; to discern 13.45; 14.36; pp. *aspyed* 14.66.

aspyre, v.; to long for 59.21.

assay, v.; to sample 50.93; imp. *asay*, prove 61.15; pp. *assayed* 39.66.

assent, n.; persuasion 64.117; 87.47.

assise, n.; judgment 13.13.

assoygne, n.; delay 3.67.

assoyl, v.; to absolve 10.30; 65.102; *assaylle* 67.29.

astat, See *estate*.

at, prep.; from 72.106; to 10.17; 45.22.

at, pro.; that 45.48.

atake, v.; to overtake 44.33.

ateynt, pp.; proved guilty 15.9.

atire, n.; apparel, headdress 63.7.

atrete, adv.; plainly 39.78.

aught, See *aȝt*.

aunsetres, n.; ancestors 15.118.

austernly, adv.; harshly 45.18.

auter, n.; altar 1.42.

availe, n.; profit 63.37; 77.20; *auayles* 70.104.

availle, v.; to help 28.90; pr. 3 s. *awayleth* 77.*a*.

avance, v.; to assist 10.5; 28.38; 30.46; *avaunce*, advance 70.4.

avant, v.; to advance 27.*p*.

avaunt, n.; boast 28.22.

aventruse, adj.; daring 45.43.

aventurous, n.; hazard 77.*d*.

auyse, v. imp.; consider 14.45.

avowe, n.; vow 26.175; 30.58.

avowe, v.; to confirm 86.35.

auowerie, n.; patronage, protection 3.30.

avutrie, See *aduowetrye*.

awayleth, See *availle*.

awawntage, n.; advantage 70.106.

awe, n.; reverence 15.88; 55.10; fear 81.36; *awen*, power to inspire reverence 81.37.

awe, v.; to daunt 6.11.

aweyward, adv.; turned away 38.113.

awen, pro.; own 14.130; 15.107; *owen* 15.22.

awlesse, adj.; overbearing 45.7.

axe, v.; to ask 95.35.

bacbite, pp.; slandered 6.34.

bacward, adv.; worse 65.39.

bayly, n.; authority of an officer 6.44.

bailif, n.; bailiff 2.16; *baylies* 3.23.

bayllefull, adj.; destructive 26.232.

bayte, v. pr. 3 s.; incites 15.82.

bake, v.; to support 21.3.

balde, adj.; daring 12.13.

bale, n.; misery 2.16; 9.28; 45.4; *bales* 38.111; *balys* 72.55.

ban, v.; to curse 11.94; 64.47.

banshid, pp.; outlawed 29.60.

bare, adj.; despoiled 9.20; open 11.20; stripped 20.30.

bare, n.; boar (fig.) 10.8; *bore* 2.51; 12.34.

barely, adv.; openly 11.94.

baret, n.; distress 45.4; quarreling 48.27.

bas, n.; base 48.69.

bassonet, n.; helmet 26.205; *bassenettis* 44.21.

bastyle, n.; siege-castle 30.85.

bastons, n.; verses 38.47.

bataile, n.; army 10.8; 11.52; combat 11.31; 12.35; 27.27; *batell* 26.16; *bataille* 30.95; divisions 27.*g*; *batelles* 28.32.

bataile, v.; to do battle 73.82.

baþe, adv.; also 65.82.

batyd, pp.; diminished 70.103.

baum, n.; balm 48.85.

be, prep.; with reference to 95.9; *beo*, by 39.44; *bi*, through 48.124.

be, v.; to be 13.36; *ben* 14.12; *beo* 3.20; *buen* 4.11; pr. 2 s. *art* 22.1; *byste* 26.35; pr. 3 s. *biþ* 4.60; *es* 9.9; *is* 13.5; *ys* 88.28; neg. *nis* 48.3; *nys* 13.4; pr. pl. *ar* 14.66; *are* 13.149; *arn* 13.135; 88.27; *ben* 13.149; *beoþ* 20.12; *beþ* 2.2; *byn* 34.3; *bueþ* 4.9; *er* 9.12; *ere* 13.103; imp. *be* 16.1; pr. subj. s. *be* 3.62; *beo* 20.71; *bo* 36.18; pt. 2 s. *were* 30.12; pt. 3 s. *wasse* 48.120; *wes* 4.6; *wos* 4.18; neg. *nas* 20.34; *nes* 4.7; pt. pl. *war* 9.13; *ware* 21.19; *wor*

64.105; neg. *nere* 66.24; pt. subj. pl. *war* 10.12; *weor* 39.89; *were* 11.59; pp. *be* 89.80; *byn* 26.31; *y-be* 4.12.

becenys, v. pr. 3 s.; beckons 44.2; *bockneþ*, summons 2.16.

bede, n.; prayer 27.29; *beades*, rosaries 62.15.

bede, v. (OE beodan); to offer 9.9; 12.35; 50.63; pr. 3 s. *bede* 13.106; pr. pl. *beodeþ* 6.51; pr. subj. s. *byde* 27.29; pt. 3 s. *bad*, bade 27. *ff*; 50.76; *bed*, ordered 5.54.

beerys, See *bere*, n.

befalle, v.; to befall 95.119; pr. 3 s. *befalleth*, becomes 95.113.

before, adv.; beforehand 14.82; *beforne*, previously 41.39.

beforn, prep.; before 81.50; *by-forne*, in front 52.9.

begown, v. pt. 3 s.; originated 84.5.

bekenyng, n.; beck, gesture 15.124.

belyve, adv.; immediately 72.95; 89.92; *blyue* 3.60; 95.27.

beme, n.; the Cross 44.67; *bemys*, rays 36.11.

bent, n.; grassy plain 26.17.

bent, v. pt. 1 s.; directed 50.1; pp. dinted 27.14; disposed 40.26.

beo, See *be*.

beotokenes, v. pr. pl.; signify 20.60.

bere, n.; bier 38.132; 44.64; *beerys*, litters 26.265.

bere, v.; to wear 86.42; pr. 3 s. *bereþ*, carries 13.139; upholds 13.142; *berys*, has 33. bur.; pt. 3 s. *bere* bore 44.70; *bare*, gave birth to 20.86; wore 1.6; pt. pl. carried 29.30; pp. *borne* 89.54.

bereve, v.; to deprive 87.32.

beryed, pp.; buried 44.76; *birede* 92.10.

berne, n.; warrior, man 26.17; *bernis* 44.21.

bernen, v.; to be burnt 3.55; pr. 3 s. *berneth*, burns 78.19.

besee, adj.; busy 62.10.

besett, pp.; surrounded 72.26.

besyen, v.; to occupy oneself 15.42.

bestayle, n.; cattle 13.67.

beste, n.; animal 22.7; 44.30.

bete, v.; to strike 23.10; 27.*ee*; beat 28.28; pt. pl. *bett* 19.41; *beette* 26.215; pp. *betin* 9.8.

betes, v. pr. pl.; assuage 9.28.

bether, adj. comp.; better 78.65.

betyde, v.; to happen 23.1; pr. subj. s. *bityde* 9.12; pt. 3 s. 33.15.

betymes, See *bityme*.

betwene, adv.; in the midst 34.4.

bi, See *be*, prep.

biche, n.; bitch 11.78.

bid, n.; command 2.7.

bid, v. (OE biddan); to bid 25.15; pr. 3 s. *biddeth* 17.*b*; *byd*, commands 14.91; imp. pray 3.118.

byde, See *bede*, v.

byde, v.; to endure 39.21; maintain 21.24; remain 51. bur.; stand firm 29.17; await 26.49; 39.47; pt. 3 s. *bode* 28.114.

bidene, adv.; together 11.11.

bye, v.; to pay for 66.15; *abugge*, pay 4.63; *by*, buy 50.47; *biȝe* 13.56; *bugge* 6.44; pt. pl. *bohten* 3.3; pp. *aboht* 4.48.

big, v.; to build 11.26; *bigge* 84.36; pr. 3 s. *bigges* 11.24.

biging, n.; dwelling 9.20; 99.95; *bugging* 2.52.

byhest, n.; promise 65.78.
byhet, v. pt. 1 s.; promised 4.90.
biker, v.; to fight 12.34.
bil, n.; halberd 2.44.
biledes, v. pr. pl.; lead astray 6.3.
byleue, n.; belief 66.15; 97.14; *beleve* 86.24.
bille, n.; petition 14.109; 25.*a*; 86.55.
bymodered, pp.; covered with dirt 6.58.
bynde, v.; to make captive 49.78; pt. 3 s. *bond*, bound 38.58.
birde, n.; lady 38.47; *burde* 38.58; *briddis*, birds 44.2.
birede, See *beryed*.
byreued, pp.; taken from 4.124.
bysoht, pp.; sought 4.172.
bysom, n.; purblind 49.8.
byswykeþ, v. pr. pl.; deceive 6.68.
byþenche, v.; to reflect 4.104.
bityme, adv.; in good time 11.27; 57.29; *betymes* 95.85.
bitter, adj.; furious 39.68; comp. *bitterore*, more cruel 2.7; *bittrere*, more bitter 3.103; *bittrore* 3.134.
bywreye, v.; to reveal 40.34.
blame, n.; reproof 13.21; 15.74; injury 78.62.
ble, n.; complexion 38.111; hue 48.79; 66.9.
blin, v.; to cease 10.31; *blynne* 4.3; 65.90; pr. pl. 51.54.
blynde, adj.; undiscerning 13.77.
blisse, n.; happiness 14.98; *blis* 11.19; spiritual happiness 31.3; 72.55.
blyth, adj.; happy 45.67.
blyue, See *belyve*.
blok, adj.; pale 38.111.
blonder, n.; confusion 66.3.
blostme, n.; blossom 38.68.
blowe, v.; to brag 39.101; pt. 3 s.

bleuȝ, blew 39.77.
bo, adj.; both 6.32.
bobaunce, n.; boasting 3.29.
bocher, n.; butcher 3.93.
bockneþ, See *becenys*.
boyn, See *boune*.
bok, n.; document 6.51.
bon, n.; request 2.7.
bond, adj.; not free 22.5; 79.20.
boote, n.; deliverance 17.7; *bote* 39.84; remedy 28.120; amends 3.135.
bordon, n.; burden 2.34.
bore, See *bare*.
borwe, v. pr. pl.; borrow 15.96; pt. 3 s. *borowed*, ransomed 26.276.
boste, n.; arrogance 11.85; boasting 7.6; pride 9.8; ostentation 62.11; threat 90.21.
bot, n.; boat 38.25; *bote* 12.20.
bot, prep.; except 27.*x*; 48.10; *boute*, without 48.21.
bote, See *boote*.
bote, See *but*, conj.
bothte, adj.; both 45.8.
botouns, n.; ornamental buttons 7.26.
boune, adj.; ready 9.9; *bowen* 26.110; *bowne* 45.52; *bowyn* 26.16; *boyn* 99.77.
bounte, n.; valor 14.18; goodness 63.18.
boure, n.; abode 11.26; 49.76; chamber 3.99; 65.83; *bowre* 44.24; *bure* 48.11.
boute, See *bot*.
bowe, v.; to bow 15.124.
bowes, n.; boughs of tree 28.2.
bowge, n.; heraldic bouget 84.29.
bowynd, v. pt. 3 s.; set out 26.3.
bownd, pp.; set the bounds for 36.6.
bowne, See *boune*.
bowne, adv.; quickly 38.48.

brayd, n.; onslaught 39.68.
brak, v. pt. 3 s.; raised 30.96.
brande, n.; sword 26.40; *brondis* 44.18.
bred, v. pt. 3 s.; hatched 91.55.
brekyst, v. pr. 2 s.; tear 52.6.
breme, adj.; raging 13.62; clear 38.10.
brenne, v.; to burn 14.115; pr. 3 s. *brenneþ* 13.62; pr. p. *brennyng* 30.100; pt. pl. *brenned* 28.44; *brente* 26.13; pp. 26.19; *y-brend* 4.19.
breres, n.; brambles 88.51.
brest, v.; to break 78.11; pp. 14.133.
breþe, n.; odor 15.123.
breuen, v.; to commit to writing 6.23; pp. *breued*, briefed 6.26.
brybor, n.; briber 74.54.
bryke, n.; brick 30.91.
brimme, n.; water 48.157.
brynke, n.; bank 2.70.
bryttne, v.; to slaughter 45.28.
broche, n.; pointed iron rod 71.7.
brode, n.; brood 90.37.
brohte, v. pt. 3 s.; brought 4.176; *broght* 10.23; pt. pl. *brouȝt* 39.47; pp. 14.27; *broucht* 45.46; *brouht* 1.99.
broyde, v.; to draw a weapon on 44.30.
brome, n.; broom plant 61.19.
brondis, See *brande*.
browe, n.; brow 7.23; eyebrows 38.68.
brown, adj.; dark 84.8.
brude, n.; bride 7.26.
brugge, n.; bridge 4.10.
brust, adj.; bristled 2.51.
bud, v. pt. 3 s. impers.; behooved 10.28.
budeles, n.; beadles 2.37.
bugge, See *bye*.
bugging, See *biging*.

buk, n.; buck 89.39.
bulged, adj.; swollen 28.140.
bulwerk, n.; ramparts 28.62.
burde, See *birde*.
burel, n.; sackcloth 4.179.
burgase, n.; burghers 11.65; *burgeis* 28.79.
burgh, n.; borough 13.34; *bergh* 45.68.
burgoned, v. pt. 3 pl.; began to bud 28.2.
buskith, v. pr. 3 s.; gets ready 44.2; pt. 1 s. *busked* 95.27; pr. pl. *boskeþ*, adorn 7.26; imp. *busk*, hasten 9.22; prepare 45.67; *buskys* 49.76.
busshement, n.; ambush 44.21.
but, adv.; only 57.10; 11.45.
but, conj.; unless 40.13; *bote* 3.119; *boten*, but 6.18.
butte, n.; deliverance 77.11.
buxomness, n.; humility 15.121.
buxum, adj.; meek 40.4.

cacche, v.; to take 95.97; pr. 1 s. catch 2.61; pp. *caht*, captured 2.60; *y-caht* 4.50.
cache, n.; pursuit 75.22.
cachereles, n.; sheriff's officers 2.50.
calle, n.; headdress 6.60.
camamyll, n.; camomile 35.15.
camp, n.; combat 29.65.
can, See *con*.
canel, n.; cinnamon 48.76.
capil, n.; nag 48.32.
capped, pp.; wearing a cap 8.1.
care, n.; sorrow 5.18; 20.14; 88.60; 95.2; trouble 9.10.
care, v.; to be concerned 6.48; 49.67; mourn 11.1; take heed 2.50; pr. pl. *carieþ*, are troubled 2.9
carefvll, adj.; anxious 97.4.
carefully, adv.; grievously 72.75.

carmes, n.; Carmelites 65.110.

carp, v.; to utter 38.46; find fault with 66.12; pr. pl. *carpeþ* 2.9; pt. 3 s. *carped*, spoke 95.42.

carpyng, n.; censorious speech 38.46.

case, n.; occurrence 89.25; situation 1.83; 3.37; turn of events 20.84; 71.11.

cast, v.; to reflect 20.39; throw 28.116; pr. 3 s. *castys*, brushes 52.25; pr. pl. *cast*, set about 64.60; imp. think about 14.82; exert 14.47; pt. 3 s. threw 20.47; 41.18; pt. pl. overthrew 19.49; pp. 82.5; thrown 25.3; *kast*, put 10.60; *acast*, cast down 2.10.

cataile, n.; goods 10.26; *catel*, property 39.75.

cawte, adj.; wary 26.103.

certeine, n.; fixed amount 28.27.

certes, adv.; certainly 65.58.

chace, n.; pursuit 90.66; (fig.) change of position 28.113; *chase*, hunting 75.15.

chaffare, n.; merchandise 6.73.

champioun, n.; defender 14.78.

chape, n.; jape, idle talk 57.19.

chapitle, n.; chapter, religious assembly 54.15; *chapitre*, ecclesiastical court 6.73.

chapman, n.; merchant 55.9.

charge, n.; expense 95.38.

charged, pp.; furnished 78.9.

chaule, v.; to chatter 7.36.

chaumbres, n.; rooms 20.45; bowers 59.5.

chaunce, n.; fortune 13.167; good fortune 33.15; mishap 25.18.

chaunged, pp.; exchanged 8.11.

chawgh, n.; chough, jackdaw 84.23.

cheertee, n.; affection 40.32.

cheff, adj.; of the first order 29.53; *chefe*, leading 49.47.

cheyff, n.; height 45.16.

chekkys, n.; reverses 15.108.

chele, n.; cold weather 54.61.

chepen, v.; to buy 15.23; pr. 1 s. *chepe* 6.73.

chepyn, n.; market 2.43; *cheping* 6.82.

cherische, v. pr. pl.; encourage 15.39; imp. *scheryssh* 70.142; pr. p. *cheryschyng* 70.4.

chese, v.; to choose 20.63; imp. 13.167; pt. 3 s. 13.54; pp. *chose* 1.104; *y-core* 4.58; 5.24.

cheson, v.; to accuse 61.11.

chest, n.; coffin 1.28.

cheualrie, n.; military prowess 1.3; host 28.16; knighthood 39.42; *chiualry*, courtesy 65.5; men-at-arms 13.69; 32.2.

cheve, v.; to do homage to 28.165; succeed 93.44.

cheueuteyn, n.; chieftain 3.20; *cheveteyns* 19.15.

chost, n.; contention 2.43.

clamer, v. pr. 1 s.; climb 81.24.

clappe, v. pr. subj. pl., strike 3.15.

clede, pp.; clothed 45.8.

cleye, n.; clay, earth 81.53.

cleyme, v. pr. 1 s.; claim 38.78.

clene, adv.; completely 2.25.

clepe, v.; to call 5.71; pr. 3 s. *cleopeþ* 6.57; pr. pl. *clepe* 98.30; pp. *cleped* 57.1; *clepud* 57.2; pr. 2 s. *clepist*, proclaimest 30.5.

clere, adv.; distinctly 38.46.

clered, v. pt. 3 s.; grew clearer 95.26.

clerenesse, n.; splendor 73.95.

clerk, n.; priest 72.51; *clerkes*, clergy 5.19; 20.62; 72.91; scholars 10.14; *klerkes* 59.3;

clarkes, secretaries 50.15.
clethinge, n.; clothing 45.8.
close, adj.; tightly-fitting 52.29;
walled 95.97.
closeden, v. pt. pl.; enclosed
3.22; pp. *closed* 78.17.
clowtyst, v. pr. 2 s.; mend with
a patch 52.7.
cnat, See *knottes.*
coynte, adj.; cunning 3.45.
coke, v.; to fight 14.29.
collacione, n.; evening meal
48.145.
collayne, n.; Cologne steel
26.200.
colored, adj.; specious 88.22.
colour, n.; colors, badge 35.26;
pretence 64.64; 93.10; (fig.)
appearance 28.12.
com, v.; to come 26.50; *comyn*
59.8; pr. 3 s. *comit* 59.5; pt.
3 s. *come* 12.14; pt. pl. 4.33;
11.60; pp. *komyn* 81.7; *comen,*
born 22.1; pr. 3 s. *comeþ,*
befits 29.4.
combryd, pp.; overwhelmed
49.33.
comely, adj.; noble 14.152;
combely 82.2.
comely, adv.; becomingly 38.90.
comiens, n.; common lands 25.3.
cominalte, n.; commons, people
25.2.
comynerys, n.; citizens 89.99.
commixtione, n.; medley 88.3.
comonte, n.; commons 97.48.
comouns, n.; commonalty 13.101;
comuynes, commons 20.17;
comiens 25.11; *comon* 28.85;
comonys 49.66; *comunes*
39.73.
companage, n.; relish 7.31.
complaynt, n.; charge 50.4.
con, v. pr. 3 s. (OE cunnan); is
able 4.10; *kan* 48.168; *kun*

11.90; *kunne* 54.24; *can,*
knows 64.132; pr. pl. 65.61;
conne, can 20.62; *cun* 60.27;
kun 69.2; pt. 1 s. *cold* 50.7;
could 50.35; *cowd* 72.18;
kowde 89.87; pt. 3 s. *coupe*
4.71; 38.5; *cowde* 26.96;
knew 28.108; pt. pl. *coupen*
5.52.
con, v. pt. 3 s.; did 3.11; 4.32;
4.184; 5.12; *can* 26.185;
26.221; 81.6; began 26.116.
conceyve, v. imp.; think of 73.47.
condescent, n.; agreement 30.38.
condigne, adj.; merited 83.31.
confusion, n.; destruction 30.21;
confounding 79.13.
conyng, n.; rabbit 3.69; *conig*
11.75.
conyng, n.; scholarship 51.74.
connyng, adj.; skilled 95.105.
conschiaunce, n.; scrupulousness
63.13; *konsyons,* moral sense
99.19.
conserue, v. imp.; keep safely
80.1.
constellacion, n.; astrological
configuration 77.17.
constery, n.; consistory court
49.33; *constory* 6.76.
construen, v. pr. pl.; interpret
64.23.
conteyne, v. imp.; behave 30.105.
continaunce, n.; countenance
4.92; 65.13; demeanor 79.41;
countenaunss 70.2.
cope, n.; long cloak 38.90.
corage, n.; courage 13.85; 41.2;
gallantry 39.108; disposition
95.122.
corden, v. pr. pl.; agree 91.64.
coriages, adj.; courageous 89.41.
corrumpe, v.; to destroy 93.66.
cors, n.; body 15.120.
corsed, pp.; damnable 64.141.

coste, n.; country 51.69; district 32.12.

cot, n.; cottage 2.62.

cot-armers, n.; gentlemen 27.43.

counsail, n.; advice 11.40; 13.82; *consail* 3.18; 4.57; *counsell* 13.96; 72.73; *cownscell* 81.12; *cownsel* 81.28; *counseil* 13.80; counsel, advocate 13.10; *consaylle* 98.71; *cownsele,* deliberation 41.21; *consail,* party 1.25; *counceyle,* purpose 73.9.

counte, n.; account 2.62.

countred, pp.; opposed 28.99.

couren, v.; to crouch 6.46; pr. 1 s. *coure,* creep 6.76.

cours, n.; course 13.40; 95.2.

coustage, n.; expense 7.29.

couaitise, n.; greed 10.26; *covatyse* 45.5; *coueityse* 57.6; *couetyse* 62.20.

craft, n.; guild 13.33; power 14.75; deceit 64.75.

crake, v.; to break 88.47.

crased, pp.; broken 78.10.

craue, v. pr. pl.; beg 15.94.

creature, n.; Creator 44.16.

crede, n.; faith 72.54; lesson 10.38.

creftly, adv.; skillfully 38.46.

cressant, n.; heraldic half-moon 78.19; *cressawntts* 26.183.

cressett, n.; heraldic torch 84.2; flares 28.44.

croiȝ, n.; cross 5.31; *crois* 5.63.

croke, v.; to bow 72.44.

crommeþ, v. pr. 3 s.; crams, stuffs 7.17.

crop, n.; stomach 7.17.

crosse, v.; to hoist 1.23.

crowne, n.; pate 9.10; *croune* 9.11; tonsure 66.22; *coroun,* diadem 3.120; 10.46; *cron* 99.75.

cruelte, n.; hard-heartedness 72.54.

cuynde, See *kynde.*

cumbred, pp.; entangled 20.70.

curasse, n.; body armor 77.9.

cure, n.; charge 72.43; concern 73.14.

curre-dogges, n.; worthless dogs 89.93.

curteis, adj.; courteous 20.1; *curtys* 78.38.

curtel, n.; tunic 4.179.

curtesye, n.; courtly behavior 22.6; honorable behavior 77.1; 95.130.

custemerys, n.; customs collectors 49.27.

cuþ, pp.; renowned 48.107; *kud* 39.91; *y-cud,* known 4.24.

dabbeþ, v. pr. pl.; strike 3.85.

daliance, n.; conversation 72.122.

dance, n.; (fig.) plight 11.72.

dar, v. pr. 1 s.; dare 20.73; pr. 3 s. 11.31; pt. 3 s. *dorst* 39.21; *durste* 15.2; 26.91; 42.26; 72.76.

dare, n.; concealment 38.133.

dare, v.; to be dismayed 20.22.

darh, See *thar.*

dartes, n.; javelins 28.124.

date, n.; period 45.58.

daunteden, v. pt. pl.; subdued 38.12.

dawes, v. pr. 3 s.; dawns 34. bur.; *daweþ* 38.3; pr. subj. s. *dawe* 7.14.

debate, n.; conflict 77.16.

ded, n.; act 11.15; 12.13; 76.15; 86.35.

dede, n.; death 4.226.

dedly, adj.; mortal 13.149.

dedute, n.; delight 48.50.

deede, adj.; dead 1.22; *dedde* 81.53; *dede* 27.28; 44.38.

deen, n.; chief 71.37; *den,* dean

49.35.

defame, n.; disgrace 64.79; slander 13.20.

defamed, pp.; dishonored 30.107.

defaute, n.; want 13.89; 15.59.

defende, v.; to ward off 99.70.

defenys, n.; justification 77.8.

deferre, v.; to set aside 42.33.

degre, n.; class, station 13.44; manner 13.39; condition 15.89; *degreys* 70.51.

dey, n.; day 2.54; 99.26.

deyneth, v. pr. 3 s. impers.; designs 40.8.

del, See *dole.*

dele, v.; to apportion 43.39; give 95.101; pt. 3 s. *dolt,* trafficked 72.94.

delyuren, v.; to deliver 4.84.

delle, n.; glade 38.12.

deme, v.; to judge 4.69; 95.60; pr. 3 s. *demeþ* 14.92; imp. *deme* 95.16; pp. *y-demed* 4.161.

demene, v.; to direct, control 86.1.

den, See *deen.*

denede, v. pt. 3 s.; resounded 38.13.

denygh, v.; to deny 25.7.

dent, n.; blow 27.38; *dyntes* 27.28.

deol, See *dole.*

dere, v.; to injure 11.10.

derei, n.; violence 67.11.

derk, n.; night 38.3.

derknesse, n.; mystification 95.92.

derne, adj.; secret 14.94.

des, n.; high table 13.6.

desert, n.; worthiness 30.11.

deses, v. pr. 3 s.; dies 13.134.

destaunce, See *distaunce.*

desteny, n.; fate 72.14.

destrewe, v.; to destroy 89.100.

dett, n.; debt, due 19.43.

deuere, n.; duty 15.114.

deuys, n.; purpose 1.75; 49.52; desire 5.26; 81.15; project 28.42; testament 30.36.

deuyse, v.; to explain 70.60.

deuocion, n.; earnest reverence 63.4.

dewe, n.; moisture, pus 7.22.

dewely, adv.; with propriety 15.114.

dye, v.; to die 26.48; pr. 2 s. *deydyst* 27.cc; *didest* 95.1; pr. 3 s. *dyeþ* 13.123; pr. subj. s. *deye* 15.105; pt. 3 s. *deid* 1.49.

dygge, v.; to dig 15.2.

dyhte, v.; to attack 4.216; manage 5.79; pt. 1 s. *dyght,* prepared 50.108; pp. *dight* 11.34; put 27.r; 27.20; *y-dyht* 4.116; *dyȝght,* abused 19.35; *dyȝt,* appointed 13.11; *diht,* caused 3.5; sent 5.27.

dykyng, n.; dikes 28.47.

dilited, v. pt. 3 s.; delighted 1.53.

dym, n.; dusk 95.23.

dimuir, adj.; calm 39.37.

diner, n.; dinner 12.22; 28.49.

dirk, adj.; dark 40.45.

disceit, n.; deceit 59.92; *desseytis* 69.29.

dische, n.; dish 66.30.

dysdeyne, n.; contempt 88.60.

dysguysynges, n.; masquerades 51.15.

dispite, n.; outrage, injury 28.126.

disposicion, n.; plan, preparation 87.42.

distaunce, n.; dissension 13.41; 49.75; 79.2; *distance* 10.1; 14.146; *destaunce* 13.157; disturbance 3.26.

distres, n.; bodily affliction 64.147; *dystress* 70.98.

distrussed, v. pt. 3 s.; defeated 30.69; pp. *dystrest,* afflicted 99.8.

diswurship, n.; dishonor 29.*c.*

dyuysion, n.; dissension, discord 94.11.

do, v.; to do 14.108; pr. pl. *doþ,* row 48.153; prepare 48.160; pr. subj. s. *do,* grant 1.91; render 17.7; pt. 3 s. *did* 30.37; pp. *don,* crucified 54.83; finished 9.24; *y-don,* put 3.131.

doddeþ, v. pr. pl.; cut off 3.87.

dole, n.; grief 11.10; *del* 5.50; *deol* 5.55; *duel* 5.3; *dool,* affliction 15.105.

dolefulle, adj.; grievous 43.20; *dulfull* 72.14.

dolefully, adv.; dismally 19.35.

doloure, n.; distress 83.18.

dolt, See *dele.*

dome, n.; judgment 30.79; *doom,* authority 14.89.

domesman, n.; judge 13.26; 55.9.

dominacion, n.; control 63.5; 79.28.

donged, pp.; manured 8.9.

dool, See *dole.*

dorst, See *dar.*

double, adj.; deceitful 87.14.

douhtir, n.; daughter 1.67.

doune, n.; hill 38.3; *downe* 14.14.

dout, n.; fear 9.14; 28.51; doubt 64.85

douteþ, v. pr. 3 s.; fears 4.15; pp. *dowted* 95.56.

dowblenesse, n.; duplicity 63.6.

dowghty, adj.; valiant 19.33; *douhti* 39.106; *dughty* 10.39; sup. *dowthiest* 42.10.

dray, n.; commotion 11.34.

drawe, v.; to withdraw 15.92;

44.9; pt. 3 s. *drowe,* drew 95.23; pt. pl. *drowght,* threw down 19.21; pp. *drawen* 28.146; *to-drawe,* drawn, executed 4.9.

drecchyng, n.; troubled dreaming 95.6.

dred, adj.; overawed 13.4; revered 42.8; 57.16.

drede, n.; fear 3.48; *dreed* 29.45.

drede, v.; to terrify 15.7; fear 4.4; 20.41; pr. 1 s. 20.65; pr. pl. *dreden* 79.11; pt. 3 s. *dred* 28.56; pt. pl. 19.13; pp. 94.18; 95.56; *drad* 39.19.

dreynte, See *adrenche.*

dresse, v. imp.; place, set 73.37; pp. *dressed* 78.77.

dressing, n.; (fig.) direction 21.24.

drye, v.; to endure 26.231.

dryff, v.; to force 45.38; pt. 3 s. *dreve* 93.89.

dryft, n.; herd 38.14.

drink, n.; wine 48.19.

dritte, n.; ordure 48.179; *dryt* 7.31.

droupe, v.; to sink down 20.22.

drouping, n.; dejection 38.133.

drowned, v. pt. pl.; sank 29.27.

drue, adj.; dry 3.104.

druyȝe, n.; drought 39.30.

duel, See *dole.*

duere, adv.; dear 4.48.

duȝth, adj.; doughty 99.64.

dun, adv.; down 48.140.

dunnir, n.; thunder 48.39.

dunt, n.; dint, impact 4.47.

dure, v.; to last 73.6; pr. 3 s. *dures* 39.4; pr. p. *durynge* 79.62.

durr, n.; door 25.*b.*

durst, See *dar.*

dute, n.; pleasure 48.9.

dwell, v.; to remain dead 10.8;

abide 12.23; consider 91.9.

e, See *eiʒe.*

efter, prep.; in search of 12.33.

egallyte, n.; fairness 70.93.

egre, adj.; fierce 90.36.

eiʒe, n.; eye 20.11; *e* 41.63; *yee* 26.156; 67.15; 88.7.

eyr, n.; heir 45.70; *eyres* 54.46.

eke, adv.; also 3.32.

elinglich, adv.; sorrowfully 48.15.

eme, n.; uncle 26.101.

emyddis, prep.; amidst 15.56.

emprise, n.; value 28.26.

emprised, pp.; undertaken 73.85.

en, indef. art.; an, a 2.22.

enbateylyd, pp.; drawn up in battle order 27.*g.*

enchesoun, n.; reason 40.18.

end, n.; region 10.3.

endite, v.; to inscribe 42.54.

enduir, v.; to last 39.36.

engines, n.; engines of war 12. rub.

enoo, See *y-now.*

ensample, n.; example 72.10; 95.129; *insampuls* 99.37.

enscherychyng, n.; cherishing 70.107.

enspeciall, adj.; especial 89.7.

ensve, v.; to follow 97.52; pr. pl. *ensvyth* 97.61.

entayles, n.; fashions 53.4.

entende, v.; to purpose 43.5.

entent, n.; intention 30.29; 72.60; 90.13; attention 50.108; design 64.23.

enterly, adv.; earnestly 35.14; without exception 45.64.

entirdited, v. pt. 3 s.; interdicted 1.46.

entree, n.; right of entering 89.152.

entrid, v. pt. 3 s.; entered 1.44.

envye, n.; harm 26.46; malice 84.10.

eorþe, n.; earth 20.33; *erthe,* province 45.30.

er, See *or.*

er, adv.; formerly 2.36; before 4.89; *are* 20.38; 45.14.

ere, n.; ear 52.26; *erys* 88.63; *yere,* ear of corn 84.31.

erynge, n.; plowing 37. bur.

erytage, n.; inherited land 26.38.

erle, n.; earl 29.6; *yerle* 26.101; *yerlle* 26.5.

ernend, pr. p.; running 48.86.

erste, adv.; once, recently 27.19; *erste ... erste,* rather than ... sooner 27.*q.*

estate, n.; good condition 42.23; 74.26; *astat,* condition 15.107; 72.18; possessions 43.13.

et, v.; to eat 48.56.

eterne, adj.; eternal 98.36.

ether, pro.; either 26.198.

euch, adj.; each 48.121; *vche* 20.39; 41.44.

euene, adj.; impartial 13.12; level 45.61.

eueryche, adj.; every 45.18.

euerons, adv.; always 13.142.

eueruchon, pro.; every one 3.50.

ewyne, adv.; even 45.38.

expresse, pp.; enumerated 91.16.

faane, n.; weathervane 95.111.

fabel, n.; falsehood 20.55; *fable* 65.78.

fable, adj.; feeble 95.58.

facche, v.; to fetch 3.62; imp. *faccheþ* 3.59.

fade, v.; to wither 28.5; *fadyne,* cause to wither 45.50; pt. pl. *fadide* 33.16; pp. *fadyd,* faded 61.6.

fadir, n.; father 14.113; *fader* 20.76; *uadir* 48.176.

fay, n.; faith 4.41; 39.7.
fayly, n.; failure 6.77.
faille, v.; to give way 28.63;
pr. pl. *failen,* lack 64.18; pt.
3 s. *fayled,* defaulted 10.54;
failed 39.35.
faine, adj.; glad 12.18; eager
26.190; *fayene* 71.27; *feyne*
71.14.
fayne, adv.; gladly 20.3; eagerly
74.27; *feyne* 99.4.
fayned, adj.; false 26.90; 63.9;
pretended 62.22.
fayre, adj.; beautiful 13.147;
good 24.6; misleading 13.122;
pleasing 10.6; sup. *fayrest,*
most desirable 14.143; most
reputable 27.*i*; choicest 49.70.
fayre, adj.; beautiful 13.147;
courteously 10.16; *feir* 25.15.
fale, See *fele.*
falle, v.; to befall 20.61; pr.
subj. s. 21.27; pt. 3 s. *fel* 3.82;
fil 73.46.
falle, v.; to die 43.33; pp. *fallen,*
withered 10.6.
faloweþ, v. pr. pl.; fade 48.81.
falsdam, n.; treachery 99.76.
false, n.; falsehood 24.4.
falshede, n.; treachery 10.61;
falsehod 88.20; *falsed,* false-
ness 20.53.
falsnes, n.; deceit 64.129.
*fande*₁ v.; to proceed 45.44;
fonde, seek 5.34.
fande, v. pt. 3 s.; devised 45.68.
fange, v.; to gather 45.44; *fonge,*
resume 4.89; embrace 64.135.
fare, n.; boasting 12.18; 27.59.
fare, v.; to behave 20.78; fare
12.25; 15.1; 20.46; go 9.21;
prosper 10.59; 75.6; pr. 3 s.
fareth, acts 95.111; pr. pl.
fare, treat 20.6; 39.95.
fases, n.; faces 87.21.

fast, adv.; firmly 25.4; quickly
9.27; 72.37; vigorously
26.215; 27.*ee.*
fasten, v. pr. pl.; plight 4.41.
fastly, adv.; firmly 29.40.
fat, adj.; profitable 88.44.
fatte, See *fette.*
faute, n.; want 8.16; *fawte* 13.27;
defect 78.20.
favell, n.; duplicity 63.30.
fawken, n.; falcon 26.55.
fawle, v.; to fall 45.49.
federed, pp.; (fig.) wounded
27.4.
feere, See *fere.*
feh, n.; cattle 2.65; *fee,* salary
85.10.
feynt, adj.; cowardly 15.14; slug-
gish 89.134; *faynt,* nearly ex-
tinct 50.2.
feynt, v.; to fade 28.5.
feire, n.; fair 54.7.
felawes, n.; comrades 18.8;
companions 95.18; *felowes*
51.28.
felde, n.; country 28.88; battlefield 30.6; *fylde* 26.36.
fele, adj.; many, various 20.12;
43.37; 52.14; *fale* 48.95.
fell, adj.; cruel 10.7; 12.24;
91.59.
felle, n.; skin 7.38.
fellen, v.; to strike down 3.40;
13.140; cast down 99.80; imp.
fell 53.2.
fende, v.; to defend 13.84.
fenestres, n.; windows 48.114.
fer, adv.; far 11.18; *ferre* 89.41;
fur 48.1; *furre* 48.132.
ferd, v. pt. 3 s.; frightened
41.15; *feryd,* feared 90.43;
pp. *ferd,* afraid 11.93; 29.26;
86.51.
fere, n.; fear 29.45; 89.68; *feer*
85.1.

fere, n.; companion 6.16; 38.40; 44.62; 49.31; *feere* 73.52; *feren* 4.100; adv. phr. *in feere*, together 61.20; *all in fere* 27.*aa*; *i-fere* 54.96.

ferli, adv.; extraordinary 38.41; 38.56.

ferly, n.; marvel 44.56.

ferm, adj.; immovable 20.50.

fers, adj.; fierce 10.7; *ferce* 78.38.

fesaunt, n.; pheasant 26.55.

festyng, n.; fasting 62.17.

fette, v. pt. pl.; fetched 26.268; *fatte* 2.65.

fierþe, adj.; fourth 15.116.

figure, n.; example 88.27.

fiȝt, n.; conflict 14.129; *fyhte* 3.47; *fight*, contention 62.1.

fyȝte, v.; to fight 27.*j*; pt. 3 s. *faght* 11.48; *fauȝt* 32.14.

fil, See *falle*.

file, n.; coward 11.47.

filmard, n.; polecat 44.33.

fyn, n.; end 3.41; death 93.21.

fynd, n.; devil 41.20.

fynde, v. pr. 1 s.; find 1.16; pt. 3 s. *fand* 12.16; pt. pl. 10.43; 12.21; pp. *fun* 11.93; *funden* 11.47; founded 74.35; pt. 3 s. *fand*, received 10.20.

fyne, v.; to yield 12.21.

fynyd, pp.; refined 70.115.

fist, n.; hand 29.40.

fit, n.; shock, danger 14.45.

flay, See *flee*.

flatur, v.; to win favor 63.34.

fle, v. (OE fleon); to depart 86.30; escape 12.18; run away 26.176; 27.13; 48.127; *fleo* 6.16; pr. 3 s. *fles* 13.166; pr. pl. *fle* 15.91; *flen* 8.16; imp. *fleth* 18.6; pt. 3 s. *fled* 11.48; 28.152; pt. pl. *floyn* 41.16; pp. *flowe* 64.68.

flee, v. (OE fleogan); to fly 26.170; pr. pl. *fleeȝ* 48.103; pr. p. fleyng 48.124; 90.53; inf. *flay*, to put to flight 10.17; *flye*, flee 26.229; pt. 2 s. *flygh* 30.95.

fleh, n.; flea 7.12; *fle* 48.37; *fles* 7.10.

flei, n.; fly 48.37; *fleye* 7.10.

fleis, n.; flesh 7.38; 48.55; *fleche* 69.12.

fleke, n.; hurdle 77.22.

flemmed, pp.; banished, outlawed 29.59; *flemed* 88.34.

flet, pp.; broken off 14.42.

flyȝth, n.; contention 38.84; *flyȝtte* 38.85.

flytte, v.; to pass on 59.14; pr. 3 s. *flyt*, moves quickly 15.54; imp. *flitte*, change places 38.85; pp. removed 39.31.

flo, v.; to flay 3.69.

flod, n.; river 38.24.

floyn, See *fle*.

flore, n.; floor 7.12.

florisshid, pp.; prosperous 29.1.

floure-de-lice, n.; heraldic fleur-de-lis 30.37; *flour-de-lys* 49.53; *floure-de-luce* 34.10; *flourelys* 1.74.

flure, n.; flower 48.8; *floure* (fig.) choicest 5.66; wheat flour 15.50; heraldic flowers 10.7; 45.20; *fleurons* 14.10.

fluren, adj.; wheaten 48.57.

fol, adj.; foolish 6.43.

fold, n.; earth 11.18; 15.113.

folde, n.; (fig.) enclosure 6.7.

folde, v.; to succumb 43.33.

foleie, v. pr. pl.; play the fool 40.47.

folie, n.; foolishness 57.4; error 15.47; lewdness 15.104; crime 13.39; evils 99.50.

folyhede, n.; foolishness 15.2.

folnes, n.; viciousness 67.11.

fomen, n.; foes 10.17; 87.9; *fomenus* 78.76.

fond, n.; trial 86.41.

fonde, See *fande*.

fonde, v.; to attempt 10.9; put to test 38.41; pt. 1 s. enquired 38.56.

fonde, v. pt. 3 s.; founded 65.108.

fondement, See *foundament*.

fonder, n.; originator 30.1.

fone, adj.; few 9.28; *fune* 9.29.

fonge, See *fange*.

foo, n.; enemy 15.50; *fon* 3.130; *foon* 13.140.

fool, n.; simpleton 15.29; dupes 15.6.

for, conj.; because 7.35; 28.109; on account of 2.70; 66.151; so that 28.71; *forte*, for to 2.72; 3.6.

forbere, v.; to spare 11.12.

forbode, pp. forbidden 15.65.

forborn, pp.; removed 15.47.

foreward, n.; covenant 4.42; 10.53.

forfetes, n.; transgressions 73.6.

forlore, pp.; lost 4.86; 14.119; destroyed 2.23; undone 4.60; *forelorne*, lost 41.38; doomed 52.11.

forsore, adj.; heavily afflicted 82.8.

forst, n.; frost 4.42.

forswat, pp.; spoiled with sweating 6.70.

forsworn, adj.; perjured 9.21; 14.59.

forþi, conj.; therefore 2.64; *forthy* 15.62.

fortune, v. imp.; endow with fortune 98.54.

forueye, v. pr. pl.; go astray 40.44.

forward, n.; van 26.102.

fostred, v. pt. pl.; encouraged 88.14.

fote, n.; foot, short distance 27.*t*; 27.13; man's foot 59.6; *foot* 39.85; *fete* 64.18.

fotlome, adj.; lame 3.123.

foul, adj.; ugly 13.147.

foule, adv.; shamefully 20.46.

fovle, n.; bird 27.33.

foulke, n.; people 45.49.

foundament, n.; anus 71.7; *fondement*, foundation 64.18.

founden, pp.; ascertained 29.24; *foundon*, firmly established 63.7.

fragilite, n.; moral weakness 73.45.

fraye, n.; fight, conflict 26.269; 29.34; 32.7; 90.43; assault 41.20.

fraunchise, n.; privileges 15.62.

fre, n.; knight 44.31.

free, adj.; noble 4.82.

freek, n.; fellow 15.99; *freke* 26.229; 45.49.

frele, adj.; frail 64.129.

frende, n.; friends 15.13; *fryndes* 26.263; *frond* 55.16.

fressh, adv.; newly 29.1.

fresshest, adj. sup.; most vigorous 42.13.

fright, See *frith*.

frist, adv.; first 98.81.

frith, n.; wood 38.28; *fyrth* 45.23; *fright* 27.33.

froward, adj.; evil 1.32; 50.9.

frowardnes, n.; perversity 30.109.

fulfille, v.; to satisfy 15.104.

fullaris, n.; fullers 3.17.

fulle, n.; entire amount 2.47.

fune, See *fone*.

fur, See *fer*.

furme, adj.; first, next 6.7.

gabben, v. pr. pl.; scoff 66.7.
gabberys, n.; deceivers 49.61.
gabbyng, n.; falsehood 6.62.
gadre, v.; to join 43.30; *gedre,* collect 13.38; *geder,* gather 12.3; pr. subj. pl. assemble 3.13; pp. *gedered* 7.5; pt. 3 s. *gadird,* plucked 34.3.
gayne, adj.; well-disposed 72.81.
gayte, n.; behavior 15.81.
galandes, n.; gallants 51.10.
galingale, n.; sweet cypress 48.73.
game, n.; hunt 38.20; proceeding 64.17; pursuit 64.76; sport 3.125; 26.54; 38.19; intrigues 15.40; 63.37; mirth 48.43; *gomen* 4.194.
gamelich, adj.; sportive 38.45.
gameliche, adv.; joyfully 38.67.
gan, v. pt. 3 s.; did 27.25; 72.75; began 28.3; pt. pl. *gon* 3.53; 27.4.
garre, v.; to cause 26.96.
gaste, v.; to scare away 4.211.
gate, n.; gate of city 29.26; *ȝate* 11.89; *yate* 28.61.
gate, n.; way 12.28; 65.164; course 37.4.
gaudes, n.; tricks 9.18.
gedelynges, n.; fellows 7.2.
gedre, See *gadre.*
geldyngs, n.; horses 26.76.
gelofir, n.; gillyflower 34.9; *gilofre* 48.77.
gent, adj.; noble 27.*ii*; pretty 34.9.
gentyll, adj.; well-born 26.114; mild 34. bur.; cultivated 35.2.
gentre, n.; courtesy 41.57; *gentrie* 64.126.
gere, n.; property 50.86; apparel 51.11; goods 65.67.
gerner, n.; storeroom 7.16.
geson, adj.; barren 77.19; rare 61.8.

gestenyng, n.; feast 87.39.
gestes, n.; guests 12.29.
gestis, n.; stories 42.32.
gete, v.; to attain 39.38; find 39.110; *geytte,* to acquire 67.17; imp. *get,* watch out 9.36; pt. 1 s. *gat,* betook 50.29; pt. 3 s. won 1.75; pt. pl. 43.15; pp. *y-ȝote,* made 5.82.
gettyng, n.; booty 26.74.
gye, v.; to direct 49.5; *guye,* govern 71.19; pp. *gyed* 14.71.
gif, v.; to give 28.96; *yeve* 95.126; pr. 1 s. *gyve* 26.102; pr. 2 s. *gyff* 31.14; pr. pl. *gyfe* 65.59; imp. *yive* 98.82; pp. *gifen* 11.88; *goue* 1.103; pr. 3 s. *ȝeueþ,* entrusts 14.89; gives up 14.98.
gyle, n.; deceit 13.122; treachery 9.6.
gylers, n.; beguilers 95.86; *gyllorys* 49.5.
gyn, n.; trick 3.45; *gynne* 4.2.
gingeuir, n.; ginger 48.73.
gyues, n.; fetters 4.177.
glade, n.; joy 38.19.
glade, v. imp.; rejoice 14.1.
glede, n.; live coal 38.57.
glee, n.; sport 26.54; 48.128.
gloser, n.; sycophant 15.5; 15.51; 49.9.
glosyng, n.; flattery 95.86.
gloson, v. pr. pl.; talk speciously 49.61.
gloud, v. pt. 3 s.; glowed 38.57.
god, n.; goodness 54.65.
god, n.; property 2.11; *gud* 99.31; *godes* 28.26; *gudes* 11.11; *goodes* 50.26; wealth 39.75; livestock 28.87.
goden, adj.; suitable 29.10.
goldis, n.; marigolds 35.3.
gome, n.; man 38.67.

gomen, See *game*.

gon, See *gan*.

gonnes, n.; battering-rams 28.37.

goo, v.; to go 26.75; *gone* 34. bur.; pr. 3 s. *gase* 9.25; *ʒeʒeþ* 6.55; *ges* 13.14; pr. pl. *geeþ* 48.113; *geþ* 48.145; pr. subj. s. *go* 13.55; pt. 1 s. *yede* 50.97; *yode* 50.22; pt. pl. *ʒede* 15.118; *went* 10.25; pp. *agon* 2.3; *go* 13.119.

gore, n.; garment 2.55.

gost, n.; person 64.97.

goue, See *gif*.

gouernaunce, n.; behavior 79.17; 83.4; governing 1.46; *gouernance*, control 28.57.

graas, n.; grace 20.25; *gras* 20.87; *grace*, appearance 59.11; clemency 72.79; destiny 74.48.

graceless, adj.; ungodly 13.77.

grame, n.; harm 15.78; 43.10; *grome* 4.140.

granseres, n.; forefathers 41.5.

graue, v. pr. pl.; engrave 51.55.

grawndame, n.; grandmother 41.5.

grede, v.; to cry out 38.20; pr. pl. *gredes* 6.9; *grediþ* 48.104.

greete, v.; to cry aloud 50.75.

gref, v. pr. pl.; grieve 60.24.

greyþe, v. imp.; prepare 2.38.

grene, adj.; green, fresh 61.5.

gres, n.; grass 13.62; *gresse*, pasture 26.76.

grete, adj.; arrogant 30.70; full of sorrow 5.44; heavy 28.37.

gretes, v. pr. 3 s.; greets 26.145; imp. 12.29; *grete* 12.28.

greve, v.; to do harm 50.94; pr. subj. pl. trouble, harass 28.168.

griffe, n.; harm 86.21.

gripe, v.; to seize 4.75; 95.125.

gryse, v.; to feel terror 20.19.

grysely, adv.; horribly 26.238.

griþ, n.; peace 38.117.

gripele, adj.; handsome 38.19.

grom, n.; man 4.114; servants 7.2; 38.20.

grome, See *grame*.

groned, v. pt. 3 s.; groaned 26.238; *gronyd* 60.3.

grounde, n.; (fig.) lair 89.37; earth 70.31; *growende* 26.161; *growynde* 26.220; *grownde* 27.3.

grounded, v. pt. 3 s.; established 65.114.

grucchid, v. pt. 3 s.; complained 64.98.

grucchyng, n.; complaining 7.36.

gudes, See *god*.

guyse, n.; practice 51.51.

gurdel, n.; girdle, belt 38.57.

gurte, v. pt. 3 s.; hurled 38.45.

gwyde, v.; to conduct onself 72.31; *gyde*, lead 78.7.

ʒe, See *sche*.

ʒe, adv.; yes 6.32; *ye* 83.2.

ʒede, See *goo*.

ʒeft, n.; bribery 55.9.

ʒeʒeþ, See *goo*.

ʒelde, v. pr. 1 s.; yield 3.89; imp. *yelde* 26.203.

ʒele, n.; zeal 73.75.

ʒelpe, v.; to boast 54.48.

ʒeme, v.; to rule 4.72.

ʒent, prep.; through 5.12.

ʒer, n.; year 2.48; *yere* 23. bur.; *yheris* 45.10.

ʒerde, n.; rod 6.55; 14.114; *yard* 70.71; *yeard*, spar of ship 78.13.

ʒeueþ, See *gif*.

ʒif, conj.; if 13.97; *ʒef* 2.45; *yif* 28.65.

ʒolden, pp.; yielded 11.89.

ʒondere, adj.; yonder 27.*m.*

ʒongeþ, v. pr. 3 s.; goes 4.73.

ʒool, n.; yule 15.103.

ʒore, adv.; formerly 2.49.

ʒoures, pro.; yours 13.131; *ʒoure* 13.133; *ʒor* 39.13.

ʒung, adj.; young 3.75; *ʒynge* 3.110.

ʒut, adv.; yet 13.3; *ʒet* 5.68; *ʒit* 10.48; *ʒette* 29.46; *yhit* 31.3; *yit* 20.1; *yut* 64.9.

habergeoun, n.; habergeon 14.30; *habirgeons* 29.9.

habide, See *abide.*

hayfre, n.; heifer 7.27.

hayme, See *he.*

haysell, n.; hazel 26.266.

hald, See *holde.*

hale, n.; well-being 44.32.

halewen, n.; saints 3.118; *halwes* 95.3.

hall, See *al.*

hall, n.; guild-hall 25.5; large room 48.11; *hale* 2.35.

halt, See *holde.*

halud, v. pt. 3 s.; sanctified 41.48.

halue, n.; side 4.97.

halwei, n.; healing water 48.84.

hangulhook, n.; fishhook 84.13.

hansell, n.; omen 19.5.

hap, n.; good luck 21.29; *happes,* mischance 64.4.

happyne, v.; to come about 45.17.

har, See *here,* pro.

harace, n.; place for breeding horses 48.35.

hard, See *here.*

harde, adj.; intense 45.21; cruel 64.4.

hardy, adj.; courageous 1.37; rash 28.65.

hardilyche, adv.; boldly 3.13; *hardeliche* 3.77; *hardelye,* only 74.13.

haryed, v. pt. pl.; pillaged 26.14.

harm, n.; trouble 15.76; damage 28.105; *harmes* 19.23; sorrows 15.86; injuries 9.26; mischief 72.63; *herme,* evil 45.27.

harwed, v. pt. 3 s.; harrowed 86.22.

hast, n.; haste 29.48; 41.26.

hastif, adj.; passionate 38.91.

hat, See *hight.*

hat, n.; command 6.71.

havberke, n.; coat of mail 27.22.

haue, v.; to have 9.34; *ha* 5.69; *habbe* 3.133; *habben* 2.15; *haf* 72.103; *han* 4.11; pr. 2 s. *hastow* 88.76; pr. 3 s. *as* 8.1; *haffys* 45.2; *han* 78.3; *hase* 99.17; *haþ* 15.46; *haues* 10.46; neg. *naþ* 2.22; pr. pl. *han* 14.117; *haue* 11.75; *haues* 10.60; *haueþ* 2.14; neg. *nab-beþ* 2.59; pr. subj. s. *haue* 21.29; imp. *hay* 51. bur.; *haueth* 18.5; pt. 3 s. *haued* 10.36; *heuedest* 5.33; pt. pl. *haued* 10.63; *hedde* 20.25; *hede* 3.41; *heden* 3.131; pp. *haad* 20.25.

hauen, n.; harbor 28.141; 39.38.

hauer, adj.; skillful 6.2.

haunte, v.; to practice habitually 95.123; *haunten* 65.133; pr. pl. *haunteþ* 7.13.

hauteyn, adj.; haughty 66.2.

hawle, n.; hail 48.39.

hawtesse, n.; loftiness of character 95.127.

he, pro; they 2.2; 4.11; *hee* 4.84; *heo* 6.18; *hi* 48.105; *hii* 4.41; *hy* 8.16; *ho* 64.105; *hue* 3.21; *ham,* them 41.15; *hayme* 65.105; *hem* 2.28; *hym* 15.39; *huem* 3.86; 7.22; *hem,* themselves 15.6; *ham* 48.153.

hede, n.; attention 38.59; *heede* 50.13.

heep, n.; multitude 40.6.

heer, adv.; here 1.62; *her* 1.82.

hegged, pp.; surrounded with a hedge 25.4.

heycht, n.; promise 45.17.

hel, v.; to save from danger 21.7.

hele, n.; strength 54.37; health 12.10; *heel* 21.29.

hele, v.; to cover 52.19.

helm, n.; helm of rudder 39.59.

helmes, n.; helmets 26.216.

hem, See *he.*

hem, pro.; him 15.18; 15.92; *hym* 15.19; *hume* 45.33.

hempen, adj.; hemp 29.13.

hend, adj.; gracious 48.183; skillful 38.6; *hinde,* courteous 10.37.

hende, See *honde.*

hendy, adj.; courteous 4.147.

hene, adj.; abject 2.29.

henge, v. pt. 3 s.; hanged 30.77.

henmyes, n.; enemies 36.8.

hennes, adv.; hence 64.150.

hente, v.; to catch 4.60; take 6.71; pt. 3 s. 74.40; pt. pl. seized 10.24.

her, pro.; her 81.39; *hire* 3.7.

herbarewen, v.; to lodge 7.40.

here, pro.; their 2.2; 3.41; 13.74; 20.44; *ar* 2.27; *har* 48.69; *heore* 6.25; *huere* 3.5; 4.27; *hur* 90.13.

here, v.; to hear 13.19; pr. pl. 15.10; pt. 1 s. *herde* 2.1; pt. 3 s. 6.56; *y-herde* 3.33; pt. pl. 11.35; pp. *hard* 21.1.

heried, pp.; praised 95.3.

herygoud, n.; cloak 6.22.

heritage, n.; hereditary succession 93.43.

herme, See *harm.*

hernes, n.; corners 13.5; 14.74.

herston, n.; hearthstone 8.4.

hert, n.; hart 38.30; *hard* 84.25.

herte, n.; heart 14.1; *harde* 45.40; *huerte* 4.165.

hertly, adv.; earnestly 31.12.

het, n.; head 3.85.

hete, n.; feeling 38.91; (fig.) heat 73.20; *heyte,* heat 45.17.

hetes, See *hight.*

hepen, n.; heathens 14.123; *hepynes* 41.51.

hething, n.; derision 21.16; 45.9.

heued, n.; leader 18.g; head 3.106; 38.110; *heuedes* 3.15; 4.10.

heuenriche, n.; heaven 5.40.

heuy, adj.; grievous 70.92.

heuyness, n.; sadness 70.97; 89.6; dejection 89.80.

hewe, n.; color 34.8; appearance 90.6.

hewsaunce, n.; custom 70.81.

hi, See *he.*

hi, pro.; I 48.15; *ich* 2.1.

hye, adj.; high 81.43; *hee* 99.43; *heȝe* 4.119; *heye* 4.16; *heih* 20.77; 39.18; *hyȝe* 13.44; *hih* 1.42; adv. phr. *an hy,* (fig.) in Heaven 27. *dd*; *in hye,* in haste 14.37; *on hye,* aloft 26.56; *upon hye,* loudly 26.122.

hye, v.; to hasten 50.57; pr. 3 s. *hyeth* 78.39; pr. pl. *hey* 69.32; pr. p. *hyand* 66.20; pt. 1 s. *hiede* 38.6; pt. 3 s. 89.42.

hight, n.; height 28.35; adv. phr. *on hyght,* aloud 26.34; on high 26.135.

hight, v. pr. 1 s.; promise 95.11; pr. 3 s. *hetep* 2.15; *hetes* 9.26; *hat,* is called 15.116; shouts 6.56; pt. 3 s. *het,* ordered 54.85; pp. *hight,* was named 28.127; promised 26.116; *hiht* 2.28; *hight,* called 74.20; *i-*

hote 48.2.

hillyne, v.; to cover 45.21.

hinde, See *hend*.

hyndryng, n.; damage 15.110; disparagement 15.52.

hyne, n.; servant 6.40; fellows 2.14.

hyrdmen, n.; herdsmen 6.40.

hire, n.; reward 11.66; 63.27; 75.10.

hyrt, n.; assembly 6.2.

his, pro.; its 13.146; 15.1; 39.59; *is*, his 3.50; 4.59; 4.169; 27.*q*; 48.134.

hit, pro.; it 14.28.

hyway, n.; main road 27.*f*.

ho, pro.; who 60.6; 63.11; *hom*, whom 60.7; *ho-so*, whoso 61.15.

hoby, n.; small Irish horse 28.122.

hod, n.; hood 2.22.

hoghyerd, n.; shepherd 66.20.

hold, adj.; old 41.15.

hold, adj.; loyal 4.36; kindly disposed 64.112.

hold, n.; custody 4.132; 26.20.

holde, v.; to abide by 26.116; keep 2.11; *hald*, exclude 11.37; pr. 1 s. *holde*, consider 15.45; pr. 3 s. *holdeþ*, stands one's ground 13.166; *holt*, counts 48.128; *halt*, carries onself 2.33; profits 4.40; pr. pl. consider 2.29; *halde*, adhere 45.40; imp. keep 12.10; *hold* 18.7; pt. 3 s. *i-helde*, controlled 81.36; held possession of 43.11; owned 65.86; pp. *holde*, considered 95.130; held 41.40; *holden* 76.7; withheld 25.2; *holdyn*, gained 93.43.

hole, adj.; holy 41.47.

hole, adj.; in good condition 78.69.

holly, adv.; wholly 39.12; *holliche* 39.37.

holpe, v. imp.; help 27.40; pt. 3 s. *halp* 90.19; pp. *holpen* 65.147.

holte, n.; copse 38.6; 26.56.

homly, adv.; familiarly 15.24.

homward, adv.; homeward 30.66.

hond, n.; dog 38.30; 44.33; *hund* 11.21.

honde, n.; hand 48.137; 98.6; hands 3.7; 4.122; 39.45; *honden* 3.106; *hende* 31.14.

hondert, n.; hundred 26.260.

hone, adj.; any 41.28.

honge, v.; to hang 4.27; 49.42; pr. 3 s. *hongeþ* 13.165; pr. pl. *honge*, remain 15.83; pp. *anhonge*, hanged 4.18.

hool, adv.; wholly 13.51.

hopeþ, v. pr. 3 s.; expects 2.11; pr. pl. *hopieþ* 2.14.

hoppe, n.; hope 48.175.

hor, adj.; gray-haired 38.110.

horedome, n.; fornication 66.40.

horlynges, n.; fornicators 7.13.

hornes, n.; horned headdresses 53.2.

horsknaues, n.; horse-boys 7.3.

hors-lade, n.; horse load 65.23.

horwȝ, n.; filth 48.34.

host, n.; army 29.22; *oste* 26.42; 32.9.

houre, See *vr*.

hovid, v. pt. 3 s.; hovered 89.122; *hoved*, appeared 26.77; halted 95.31.

how, n.; trouble 48.18.

hude, n.; hide 4.163; 7.27.

hude, v.; to hide 2.22; 8.13.

hue, See *he*.

huere, See *here*, pro.

hulle, n.; hill 2.57.

hund, See *hond*.

hunte, n.; huntsman 75.15.

hure, n.; skull-cap 6.19.
hurne, v.; corner 2.35.
hurt, n.; wound 44.29; damage 43.19.
husbonde, n.; farmer 37. bur.; 26.2.

y, prep.; in 2.33; 3.16; 6.80.
ych, pro.; each 26.215; *vch* 39.20; 54.77.
ych, pro.; I 4.145.
ychot, See *witte.*
ichulle, See *sal.*
yle, n.; island 43.24.
ilka, adj.; every 12.37; *eke a* 26.225; *ilke* 21.13; 43.36.
ilkone, pro.; each one 11.74; *ychone* 26.231; 65.139; *ilke-an* 21.7.
imagenyng, pr. p.; meditating 30.55; *ymagynynge,* plotting 93.92.
ymaginacion, n.; scheming 64.140.
ympe, n.; scion 39.83.
yn, n.; lodging 3.47; *ines,* quarters 10.52.
indifferent, adj.; impartial 88.86.
infortune, n.; misfortune 87.26.
insygne, adj.; distinguished 88.59.
intente, n.; scheme 81.17.
interfectours, n.; murderers 76.14.
into, prep.; to 39.25.
yrke, adj.; loath 28.75.
yrn, n.; iron 4.111.
is, See *his.*

i-bente, pp.; arched 38.68.
y-brend, See *brenne.*
y-caht, See *cacche.*
y-conyd, pp.; coined 70.116; *coynyd* 70.118.
y-core, See *chese.*

y-cud, See *cuþ.*
i-diȝt, pp.; dressed 48.106; prepared 48.109.
i-drawe, pp.; drawn 81.34.
i-fere, See *fere.*
y-ȝote, See *gete.*
y-haht, pp.; hatched 7.7.
i-hote, See *hight.*
y-knawe, v.; to recognize 4.10.
y-laht, pp.; captured 4.49.
i-leyd, pp.; laid 39.71; *ileiid* 48.118.
i-lore, See *lese.*
i-mene, adv.; together 38.37.
y-nemned, pp.; named 4.57.
i-nome, See *nomen.*
y-now, adv.; enough 18.5; *enoo* 99.69; *inoȝ* 48.61; *y-nowght* 19.23.
i-seiȝe, See *see.*
y-styked, See *stik.*
y-suore, pp.; sworn 4.83.
i-tened, See *tened.*
y-tuht, pp.; drawn, led 4.163.
i-turned, pp.; fashioned 48.68.
i-wis, adv.; indeed 20.49.
y-wrowte, See *worche.*

iakes, n.; battle tunics 29.11.
iangle, v.; to dispute 64.22.
iape, n.; jest 65.61.
iape, v.; to seduce 66.42.
iaperys, n.; imposters 49.51.
iaspe, n.; jasper 48.70.
ieperdous, adj.; dangerous 77.*d.*
iett, v.; to strut 51.10.
ioly, adj.; mettlesome 51.13; splendid 51.38.
iolyte, n.; pleasure 20.20.
ioparte, v.; to make a wager 70.126.
iuge, n.; judge 14.96; *iudge* 50.12.
iugement, n.; sentence 30.77; *iujementys,* criticism 88.4.

iugge, v.; to condemn 3.55.
iust, adj.; lawful 1.3.
iustynges, n.; tournaments 51.15.

kayes, n.; keys 9.36.
kandul, n.; candle 99.35.
kanuas, n.; canvas-cloth 29.12.
kast, See *cast.*
kele, v.; to grow cold 73.21.
kende, See *kynde.*
kendles, v. pr. pl.; give birth 8.4.
kene, adj.; bold, eager 9.2; savage 11.76; sharp 90.56; keen-nosed 38.5.
kenly, adv.; ardently 45.37.
kenne, v. (OE cennan); to recognize 28.132; teach 14.113; know 4.135; *kyn* 64.12; *ken* 11.8; pr. 1 s. understand 42.17; pr. pl. *kenneþ,* know 6.85; pt. 3 s. *kend* 10.38; pp. 11.9; *kenned,* taught 38.129.
kennettes, n.; hunting dogs 38.5.
kenred, n.; kindred 55.15.
kepe, v.; to keep 12.11; pr. 3 s. *kepith,* protects 63.29; *kepeth* 78.62; pr. pl. maintain 2.4; *kepe* 14.21; imp. defend 14.24; pt. 3 s. *kepte* 26.32; maintained 28.57; pt. pl. *kepten* 79.55.
kersse, v.; to christen 45.37.
kerue, v.; to cut 15.22.
kete, adj.; brave, distinguished 38.89.
kettill-hattes, n.; helmets 29.9.
keuere, v.; to recover, regain 2.10; pr. 2 s. *keuerest* 3.115.
kyn, See *kenne.*
kyn, n.; kin 15.117; *kynne* 6.84.
kynde, adj.; loyal 89.60; lawful 45.30; *kende* 45.70.
kynde, n.; manner 13.76; birth 38.78; station 29.4; stock 44.13; nature 64.121; *cuynde*

20.50; *kende* 95.26.
kindel, v.; (fig.) to cause 9.10; pt. 3 s. *kindeld* 12.26; pr. 3 s. *kindels,* begins 9.19.
kyndely, adj.; natural 57.8.
kyneʒerde, n.; sceptre 4.68.
kyneriche, n.; kingdom 4.72.
kippe, v. pr. 1 s.; seize 2.61.
kirk, n.; church 28.78.
kirtell, n.; short tunic 11.61; *kyrtelle,* mantle 65.63.
kiþ, n.; native land 38.119; country 39.92.
kyþed, v. pt. 1 s.; acknowledged 38.96.
knawys, n.; low-born 45.8.
knet, v.; to join 14.44; pp. *knit.* tied 39.29.
knoke, v. pr. pl.; hammer 51.55.
knottes, n.; (fig.) main points 64.2; *cnat,* knot 82.2.
know, v.; to become familiar with 30.52; pp. *knowe,* acknowledged 39.91.
knulled, pp.; beaten 3.97.
komyn, See *com.*
konsyons, See *conschiaunce.*
kornus, n.; grain 99.55.
kowarde, adj.; cowardly 26.163.
kud, See *cuþ.*
kun, See *con.*

lache, v.; to neglect 44.29.
laddes, n.; churls 19.15.
laft, pp.; neglected 13.35.
laht, pp.; caught 3.83.
lay, n.; religious law 6.5.
layk, n.; lake 38.32.
layked, v. pt. 3 s.; sported 38.71.
laykes, n.; games 95.134.
layne, v.; to hide a fact 26.138.
lamed, pp.; (fig.) crippled 13.5.
langoure, n.; distress 93.8.
lapped, v. pt. pl.; consumed 89.95.

lappis, n.; clothing 45.41.

large, adj.; liberal 95.139.

largese, n.; munificence 63.10.

larum, adj.; warning 29.51.

last, v. pr. subj. s.; continue 49.44; pt. 3 s. 20.36.

launde, n.; glade 38.8.

launprey, n.; lamprey 2.42.

law, adj.; low 10.64.

lawhen, v. pr. pl.; laugh, deride 15.63; pr. subj. pl. *lauȝhe* 14.147; pt. 3 s. *low* 38.71; pt. pl. *lowght* 19.17.

lawly, adv.; lying down 38.29.

lawne, n.; linen 50.66.

lawnse, n.; lance 81.54.

lax, n.; salmon 2.42.

leawte, n.; fidelty 45.15; *leute*, faith 66.10.

leces, n.; leashes for hounds 38.18.

leche, adj.; liege 72.77.

leche, n.; physician 14.79.

led, n.; lead 20.69.

ledderr, n.; ladder 12.19.

lede, n.; people 3.119; *lued* 6.1; *luþe* 38.124; *ledis* 45.21; *leodes* 2.27.

lede, v.; to be foremost 13.72; guide 12.39; lead 38.18; pr. subj. s. 13.109; pp. taken 26.272; *lad*, guided 13.82; 40.11.

leede, n.; meadow 90.16.

leewe, v. pr. 1 s.; believe 20.71; imp. *leef* 20.55; *leve* 45.31; pp. *leuyd* 49.63.

leggaunce, n.; allegiance 39.67.

legge, v.; to lay 2.45.

leggen, v. pr. pl.; allege 69.19.

leye, adj.; fallow 2.64.

leke, adj.; like 81.23.

lele, adj.; loyal 45.20.

lemman, n.; lover 13.121.

lenage, n.; ancestry 41.3.

lende, v.; to tarry 38.8; *lenede* 38.9; pr. 3 s. *lendith*, abides 23.11; pt. 1 s. *lend*, came 60.1; pt. pl. remained 11.45.

lene, v. pr. subj. s.; grant 5.61; imp. 99.12; pp. *lent* 95.76; pt. 3 s. bestowed 38.72.

leng, v.; to remain 45.31; pt. pl. *lenged*, lingered 38.18.

lenyng, pr. p.; resting 38.71.

leof, adj.; eager 39.6; *leffe*, acceptable 45.72; *loue*, dear 90.27; comp. *leuere* 8.2; sup. *levest* 95.100.

leose, See *lese*.

lepe, v.; to run about 64.91; leap 4.184; imp. 12.27; pr. pl. *lepiþ*, plunge 48.157.

lepre, n.; leprosy 93.26.

lere, n.; countenance 38.44.

lere, v.; to learn 11.57; pr. pl. 49.49; imp. 95.113; inf. *leer*, to be informed 95.13.

lerede, n.; learned 6.3; 95.57.

les, adj.; false 4.34; *lesse* 26.98.

les, adj. comp.; less 15.122; *las* 64.89; *lasse* 5.76.

les, n.; lying, untruth 13.46; *leyse* 99.53.

lese, v.; to lose 14.126; 86.11; *leose* 6.65; *leosen* 2.13; pr. 2 s. *losest* 3.119; pr. pl. *leoseþ* 2.12; pr. subj. s. *lese* 14.101; imp. *loose* 85.2; pt. 1 s. *les* 38.32; pt. 3 s. 15.62; pt. pl. *loren* 3.43; pp. *lest* 14.132; 15.79; *i-lore* 5.65; *lore* 3.114; 14.86; *lorn* 14.145.

lesyng, n.; lying 55.13; 57.18.

lesinge, n.; gleaning 2.6.

lest, adv.; least 45.42.

lest, n.; least 23.6.

leste, adj.; meanest 14.15.

let, v. pr. 3 s.; shed 54.85; pr. subj. s. allow 14.125; pr. subj.

pl. 13.61; imp. 14.4; pt. 1 s. left off 4.89.

let, v.; to cut off 30.90; abandon 39.6; bar 10.18; refrain 39.70; *lette* 67.19; 78.31; circumvent 14.60; *latte* 5.35; *letten,* prevent 14.7; *lett vs,* stand in our way 27.*m*; pr. 3 s. *letes,* bars 10.19; pr. pl. *lete,* hinder 13.63; pp. put down 20.27.

letherin, adj.; leather 12.19.

lettrewre, n.; learning 95.113.

leute, See *leawte.*

leue, See *lyue.*

leue, n.; leave, permission 29.18; departure 72.106.

leue, v.; to leave 20.63; imp. 97.26; pt. pl. *lafte* 29.31; pp. *leuid* 11.78; *left,* abandoned 40.13.

leue, v. pr. subj. s.; grant 39.87; *leeue* 39.95; imp. *leue* 54.93.

leuedy, n.; lady 38.44; *ledies* 3.99; *louedis* 8.15.

leuere, adv. comp.; rather 6.65; 64.11.

leuerokes, n.; larks 48.107.

levys, n.; leaves of tree 36.7; *leues* 66.9.

lewde, adj.; ignorant 49.14; wicked 64.24; *lewed,* unlearned 6.1; 95.57.

libard, n.; leopard 44.13; *leoparde* 45.36; *libert* 45.31.

libbe, See *lyue.*

lybell, n.; tract 70.1.

lyddes, n.; eyelids 95.25.

lydur, adj.; evil 99.29.

lyen, v. pr. pl. (OE leogan); tell lies 66.6; *lyȝe* 20.9.

lyflich, adj.; active 39.93.

lifte, n.; sky 48.124.

lige, adj.; liege 40.15.

ligeance, n.; allegiance 30.22.

lygeman, n.; vassal 14.15; *lieg-men* 95.61.

ligge, v. (OE licgan); to lie 5.8; *lye,* depend on 4.204; pr. 3 s. *liþ,* lies 2.64; 3.11; 73.22; *lys,* abides 13.99; is found 15.75; is buried 31.2; *lith* 1.35; pr. pl. *leyȝen,* lie 3.42; *liggen* 20.69; pr. p. *ligand* 11.71; pt. 3 s. *lay* 27.*hh.*

light, v.; to proceed 44.20; *lyte* 90.52; *liȝt,* alight 48.130; *lyȝthe* 99.28; pr. pl. *liȝtiþ* 48.131.

lyȝthheued, n.; levity 38.59.

liȝtly, adv.; easily 14.140.

lyht, adj.; nimble 3.28; *lyght* 27.23.

likam, n.; body 48.174.

lyke, adv.; likewise 99.56.

likful, adj.; pleasant 48.72; sup. *likfullist,* most delicious 48.56.

likinge, n.; pleasure 57.23.

lykyth, v. pr. 3 s.; is pleasing to 35.6; pt. pl. *lyked,* liked 50.34; pleased 66.32.

likne, v. pr. 1 s.; compare 39.74.

lilly, n.; lily 45.20.

lymyted, adj.; appointed 74.51.

lynde, n.; tree 38.8.

line, n.; rope 12.19; lineal descent 93.18.

lys, See *ligge.*

liste, v. pr. 3 s.; wishes 1.97; pt. 3 s. chose 98.53; impers. pleases 72.125; *lust* 28.125.

liþ, n.; limb 38.92.

lyth, v.; to give light to 36.11.

liþer, See *luþer.*

lyue, v.; to live 2.6; *leue* 13.48; 54.94; *libbe* 4.12; *libben* 6.1; pr. 3 s. *leuyth* 22.7; *liuiþ* 38.55; pr. pl. *leuyn* 63.1; pr. p. *leuyng* 70.14; pt. pl. *leued* 10.65; *levid* 90.18.

lodesterre, n.; guiding star 1.92.
loge, v. pr. pl.; stay 26.151; pt. 3 s. *logged*, encamped 28.109; pp. *logeed* 26.52; *looged* 26.58.
logeyng, n.; encampment 26.39; *loggyng* 28.46.
loyne, n.; loins 3.69.
lok, n.; lock 40.24.
lok, n.; look, glance 38.44.
loken, pp.; locked up 13.95.
lokyngges, n.; looks 38.72.
long, adv.; for a long time 51.63.
longe, v.; to belong 45.72; pr. pl. *leng* 70.18; pt. 3 s. *longed* 28.81; pr. 3 s. *longeþ*, desires 4.74; *longoþ*, is unseemly 69.17.
lordyng, n.; lord 38.93; 13.148.
lordschipe, n.; sovereignty 20.30; *lordschup* 20.29.
lordswyke, n.; traitor to his lord 4.162.
lore, See *lese*.
lore, n.; education 14.116; teaching 20.83; 57.18.
lorles, adj.; uneducated 56.1; without doctrine 54.31.
los, n.; reputation 13.5; fame 39.111; repute 64.80.
lose, n.; destruction 64.103.
loselrie, n.; profligacy 57.3.
losyng, n.; dying 55.14.
losynger, n.; rascal 7.24.
lothe, adj.; reluctant 28.155.
lottis, n.; fortunes, lot 87.36.
loue, See *leof*.
louedis, See *leuedy*.
louelych, adj.; kind 66.16; beautiful 38.44; 45.20; *louele* 41.3; comp. *loueloker* 38.54.
loure, v. pr. subj. s.; look mournful 65.93.
louse, adj.; loosed 45.42.
louse, v.; to set free 44.7; 88.85; pr. 3 s. *louseth* 7.24.

low, See *lawhen*.
lowe, n.; hill 38.29.
lowght, See *lawhen*.
lowte, v.; to reverence 19.27; bow 28.54; *lout* 10.64; 89.133; pt. 3 s. *lowted* 89.59; pt. pl. *louted* 10.65.
lowte, v.; to lurk 19.31.
lucetts, n.; pike 26.183.
lued, See *lede*, n.
luff, n.; love 25.16.
luked, v. pt. 3 s.; looked 10.47.
lust, n.; sinful desire 64.24.
lustinesse, n.; pleasure 72.129.
lustneþ, v. imp.; listen 3.1.
lute, adj.; little 2.19.
lutel, n.; little 2.13.
luþe, See *lede*, n.
luþer, adj.; grievous 2.13; *liþer*, evil 56.7.
luþernesse, n.; wickedness 7.30.

maces, n.; nutmegs 48.75.
magerome, n.; marjoram 35.2.
mai, n.; maid 6.4; 31.4.
may, v. pr. 3 s.; may 10.5; pr. 2 s. *mast* 26.52; pr. pl. *mo* 69.8; *mowe* 3.99; *mowen* 4.60; *mown* 14.46; *muwen* 54.88; pt. 2 s. *mowte* 92.19; pt. 3 s. *myght* 19.45; *myȝght* 19.37; *myȝt* 14.140; pt. pl. *mihte* 20.26.
mayn, n.; force 27.21; 38.61.
mayne, n.; body of followers 27.10; *meyne* 27.d; *mene* 99.20.
maintenance, n.; behavior 30.70.
mayntene, v.; to uphold 14.63; prosecute 15.30; *menteyne* 94.14; *meynteyne*, support 21.8; pt. 3 s. *meyntened* 1.61; pt. pl. *mayntened* 39.76.
maystrye, n.; victory 14.39; *maystryȝes* 14.121; *maystries*,

tricks 65.83.

make, n.; spouse 99.85; consort 72.12; mates 26.268; comrades 95.21.

maken, v.; to make 15.6; *makyn* 60.2; pr. 3 s. *makes* 9.27; *makeþ* 20.14; *makith* 42.54; pr. pl. *mase* 11.34; pt. pl. *makeden* 3.18; pp. *maade* 1.4.

mame, v.; to render powerless 95.91.

man, n.; servant 12.4; *mon*, man 4.200.

manhood, n.; valor 26.167.

manyfold, adj.; varied 72.115.

mankled, pp.; manacled 4.122.

manlyhede, n.; bravery 91.31.

manlike, adv.; courageously 17.*c*; *manly* 28.73.

marchandys, n.; saleable commodity 51.29.

marchaundes, n.; merchants 13.69.

marchman, n.; borderer 26.31.

mare, adj.; more 11.3; sup. *meste*, greatest 3.111.

marke, pr. subj. s.; make the sign of the Cross 26.174; pt. pl. *marked*, aimed missiles 26.187.

marreþ, v. pr. 3 s.; ruins 7.18.

mase, See *maken*.

massoned, v. pt. pl.; strengthened with masonry 29.28.

mat, adj.; mate 15.108; vanquished 74.29.

matrace, n.; mattress 29.14.

maugre, prep.; notwithstanding 1.59.

mawe, n.; maw, stomach 7.16.

mawmentrie, n.; idolatry 64.102.

me, pro.; men, one 2.19; 3.46; 4.68; 13.58; *man* 8.1; 21.13; *mon* 4.3; 8.2; 20.42; *men* 11.35; 13.74; *mennes* 20.52.

mech, adj.; much 93.64.

meddle, v.; to concern oneself with 50.106; pr. pl. *medle*, contend 13.39.

mede, n.; bribe 6.29; bribery 13.26; reward 3.115; *meed*, desert 50.27.

mede, v.; to bribe 2.53.

meyne, See *mayne*.

mekeliche, adv.; meekly 20.2.

mekill, adj.; much, great 10.4; *mekil* 12.27; *mycul* 99.62; *mykel* 90.18; *mochil* 48.164; *mykell*, powerful 26.166.

mekyll, adv.; much 72.67.

mele, v.; to tell 20.15; pr. 3 s. *melys* 45.66; pr. pl. *mellis* 44.52.

mell, v.; to concern oneself 97.62; pr. subj. s. 64.8.

mende, v.; to amend 14.46; imp. 11.7.

mendys, n.; amends 15.78.

mene, See *mayne*.

mene, n.; device 70.83; *menys*, means 90.69.

mene, v.; to tell 44.48; lament 4.44; pr. 1 s. intend 12.4; pt. pl. *ment* 72.58; pp. 93.53.

menske, n.; respect 6.29.

merþe, n.; religious joy 14.2; 32.24; happiness 37.bur.; mirth 11.3; *murþe* 38.15.

mervel, n.; astonishment 99.13; *merueyles*, marvels 20.16.

mes, n.; mass, sacrament 13.78.

messager, n.; messenger 5.41; 13.9; *mesagers* 41.26.

meste, See *mare*.

mesure, n.; moderation 13.13; 15.35.

met, n.; food 48.10.

met, v. pt. 1 s.; dreamed 95.10.

meteles, adj.; having no food 65.21.

metyng, n.; dream 95.10.

meve, v.; to excite, stir 30.98; pp. *mevid* 86.59.

meuyng, n.; motion, quaking 20.49.

miche, n.; much 87.43.

myʒt, n.; power 14.90; *might* 21.12; *miht* 20.2.

mylde, adj.; merciful 31.4.

mylde, adv.; without provocation 31.6.

myle, n.; mill 43.27.

myllesaylle, n.; sail of a windmill 84.15.

minde, n.; remembrance 12.4; purpose 29.3.

mynne, v.; to recollect 15.16; mention 15.57.

myre, n.; mire, mud 75.9; (fig.) 11.71; 63.48.

miri, adj.; pleasant 48.5; sup. *meriest* 15.57.

mys, adj.; wrong 95.89.

mis, n.; wrong-doing 20.78.

mysbede, v.; to injure 13.31.

mischance, n.; misfortune 10.4; *meschaunce* 3.31; *myschaunce* 62.18; *myschaunys* 49.71.

myscheff, n.; distress 86.14; *meschef* 71.49; *myscheef*, mishap 95.119; *myschefe* 98.51; *myscheu* 99.14; *myscheues*, mischiefs 13.100.

myscheue, v.; to bring to destruction 89.96; pp. *myschyeved* 93.83.

myschip, n.; misfortune 41.55.

mysfamed, v. pt. pl.; defamed 13.2.

mysmotinde, pr. p.; misjudging 6.38.

myswent, pp.; fallen into abuse 64.21.

mo, adv.; more, further 48.101.

mo, pro.; more 13.114; 18.g;

21.5; *moo*, many 22.3.

mochil, See *mekill*.

mocioun, n.; instigation 89.31.

mode, n.; temper, mood 25.22; spirit 90.36.

modi, adj.; courageous 4.164.

moeth, n.; note of hunting horn 38.15.

mold, n.; earth 2.1.

molle, n.; mole 44.15.

momelyn, v. pr. pl.; talk ambiguously 95.88.

mon, n.; lamentation 2.1; 10.45; 12.5; 72.2; 81.11; complaint 9.27; (fig.) woe 90.3.

mone, n.; money 51.75; 70.94; *mony* 70.117.

monen, v.; to remember 38.73.

moneþ, n.; month 6.14; *mounthe* 37.18.

mony, adj.; many 20.15; *mone* 41.40; *monie* 2.14.

monkuynde, n.; mankind 20.4.

mordrer, n.; murderer 97.35.

morel, adj.; dark-colored 37.10.

morowe, adj.; morning 95.10.

morþere, n.; murder 14.94; *mourder* 71.41.

morwenynge, n.; morning 37.12.

mot, v.pr. 3 s.; may 3.101; 12.38; 15.53; 39.87; *moth* 99.35; *mut* 72.102; pr. pl. *mote* 2.5; pr. subj. s. 10.59; pr. subj. pl. *mowyth* 67.39; pt. 3 s. *most*, must 14.60; 19.7; *must* 14.65.

mounde, n.; number of people 3.36.

moued, v. pt. 3 s.; removed 90.3.

mowe, pp.; cut down 72.23.

muchele, adj.; great 3.48.

mucke, n.; (fig.) money 64.7; *mukke* 95.64.

mullere, n.; miller 18.b.

mun, v. pr. pl.; should 11.2.

munten, v.; to venture 2.53;

munte, attempt 6.29.

mures, n.; moors 4.73.

murning, n.; mourning 11.2; *mornyng* 44.26.

mutable, adj.; variable 61.16.

muwen, See *may.*

na, adv.; no 5.22; *nay* 92.22.

naht, See *nawth; nouƷt.*

nay, v.; to make denial 38.49.

naye, n.; no, denial 81.17.

name, n.; reputation 13.18; 41.7; 64.77; name 1.37; *nome* 3.90.

nameles, adj.; without reputation 54.32.

nathe, n.; hub of a wheel 84.19.

nawth, n.; nothing 38.115; *naht* 4.52.

nawthi, adj.; needy 38.115.

nede, n.; need 3.88.

nedeles, adj.; not in need 15.94.

nedes, adv.; of necessity 10.28; *nedys* 27.j.

nedes, v. pr. 3 s. impers.; needs 26.158.

nedyr, See *nowþer.*

neyƷe, adv.; near 14.26; *neh* 2.66; *neih* 54.11.

ner, adv.; never 2.59.

nest, adv. sup.; next 5.24.

neuene, v.; to name 70.49.

newe, adv.; now 5.3.

ny, adv.; nigh 49.3; 89.48.

nys, adj.; stupid 15.77.

nyþe, n.; malice 4.8.

noblay, n.; nobility 14.86; *nobleye* 40.42; 73.90.

noght, See *nowght.*

noy, v.; to afflict 45.19; choke 88.51.

noyƷe, n.; trouble 13.42.

noyus, adj.; troublesome 45.24.

nolle, n.; head 6.45.

nome, See *name.*

nomen, v. pt. pl.; took 3.21; 10.53; *nome* 4.195; pp. *i-nome* 38.116.

none, n.; midday meal 48.20.

norshe, v.; to nourish 57.13.

northyrune, adj.; northern 45.50.

notable, adj.; eminent 1.37.

noþyng, adv.; in no way 89.120.

noud, See *nowght.*

nouellerye, n.; innovation 13.63.

nouƷt, n.; nothing 14.25; *naht* 4.170; *noght* 11.55; *noþt* 8.8; *nowƷte* 70.53; *nowth* 60.16.

nowght, adv.; not 27.47; *nocht* 45.39; *noght* 10.5; *noud* 3.92; *nout* 2.11; 2.22; *nowth* 81.36.

nowþer, conj.; neither 11.75; *nauther* 65.76; *nedyr* 72.125; *noothir* 70.13; *nothir* 29.25; *nouþer* 8.17.

nwli, adv.; newly 63.10.

o, prep.; of 41.2; on 4.10.

obeisaunce, n.; compliance 87.15.

obout, See *aboute.*

odur, conj.; either 67.23.

odur, pro.; the other 49.73; *oderys* 61.11.

of, adv.; off 3.15.

of, prep.; for 50.39; in 95.2; off 65.163; with 50.107; because of 43.38; *off* 43.7.

offence, n.; disfavor 88.6; sin 98.23.

oht, n.; oath 4.83.

ok, See *ac.*

olonke, adv.; along 6.21.

omage, n.; homage 30.37.

on, pro.; one 13.56; *oo* 13.50; *oon* 14.68; *won* 75.14; neg. *noon* 28.48.

onbowed, pp.; unbowed 15.27.

onde, n.; envy 4.8.

ones, adv.; once 14.43; *oones* 28.66; *ons* 90.44; *wonus* 99.6.

onfowghten, pp.; without having fought 26.162.

ony, pro.; any 44.48.

onydyr, pro.; another 23.2; *anoder* 23.1; *anoþer* 23.5.

onkynd, See *vnkind*.

onoure, n.; reputation 41.42.

openly, adv.; plainly 20.11.

oppresse, n.; oppression 88.15.

or, conj.; before 13.39; *er* 2.68.

ordeyned, v. pt. 1 s.; made oneself ready 95.17.

ordynaunce, n.; rule of lie 65.32; military supplies 29.48; artillery 14.30; ordinance 13.159; *ordynance* 65.132; catapults 28.37; *ordenance*, device 30.86; tactical disposition 28.60.

oris, n.; oars 48.154; *nore* 82.7.

os, adv.; as 99.11.

oste, See *host*.

oþer, adv.; otherwise 89.58.

oþer, conj.; or 2.46.

ou, pro.; you 3.29; 3:122; 7.37; 39.97.

ouersene, pp.; examined for revision 50. rub.

ouȝt, adv.; in any way 39.69; *oght* 65.125.

ourdryff, v.; to delay 45.58.

oure, pro.; your 5.20.

outrage, n.; violence 41.29.

outrayed, v. pt. pl.; transgressed 39.69.

oway, adv.; away 12.1.

owre, n.; hour 90.63.

owte, n.; aught, anything valuable 42.18.

pacche, n.; patch 52.7.

payne, See *peyne*.

paynymys, n.; pagans 70.29.

palefreiours, n.; grooms 7.6.

palle, n.; fine clothes 95.69.

parage, n.; noble lineage 39.109.

parcel, n.; part 14.16.

pardee, interj.; verily 1.82.

parfit, adj.; excellent 63.27; *parfitte*, perfect 63.31; *perfit* 63.49; *perfight* 63.44.

parosshe, n.; parish 6.41.

partyng, n.; division 70.92.

pas, n.; passage 38.26.

pass, v. pr. 3 s.; excels 35.10; *passeth* 95.71; pt. 1 s. *passede*, obtained 38.26.

past, v. pt. pl.; departed 20.44.

pasteiis, n.; pies 48.54.

patayle, n.; battle 41.23; *batell* 42.13.

pavyleon, n.; tent 26.81; *pauiliownes*, banners 12.32.

pavis, n.; shield 28.39; *pauyses* 29.37.

pawme, n.; hand 89.52.

pece, n.; piece 14.42; *peyses* 26.216.

peyne, n.; trouble 64.39; bodily suffering 67.27; *payne*, sorrow 72.119; *pene*, torment 99.21.

peyse, v.; to ponder 40.37.

pelour, n.; robber 64.78; *pelers*, bandits 9.15.

pelure, n.; furred garments 95.69.

pere, n.; equal 48.22; *peres*, peers 95.77; *perys* 49.29; *perus* 49.10.

pere, v.; to appear 87.3; 95.114.

pereles, adj.; without equal 74.26.

perisshed, pp.; killed 44.29.

perpetuite, n.; endless existence 83.33.

persen, v. pr. pl.; break into 68.14.

peruenke, n.; periwinkle 4.123.

pes, n.; freedom from strife 1.79; *peas* 79.34; *peysse* 26.100.

pescodes, n.; pea pods 50.59.

pye, n.; magpie 44.35.

piement, n.; honeyed drink 48.85.

piete, n.; pity 4.25.

pyght, v. pt. 3 s.; pitched 26.73; 28.34; pp. exposed 77.2.

pike, v.; to earn 95.48; despoil 95.95; pr. 3 s. *pykeþ*, steals 14.64; pr. pl. 2.25; 7.28; *pike*, dig up 95.72; pp. *piked*, taken 2.24.

pyle, n.; stronghold 13.124.

pileþ, v. pr. pl.; rob 2.19.

pine, n.; trouble 12.20; pain 6.41.

pyned, pp.; starved 93.13.

pinnes, n.; pinnacles 48.59; brooches 65.37.

pype, n.; cask 26.65.

piþ, n.; pith 39.90.

pyttes, n.; ponds 89.124.

place, n.; palace 14.58; *plasis* 42.45.

plage, n.; plague 97.47.

playe, v.; to occupy oneself 15.24; amuse oneself 42.6; *plei* 48.156.

playnt, n.; complaint 14.110; *pleynt*, accusation 15.10.

plawe, n.; profligate indulgence 7.13.

plede, v. pr. pl.; practice 51.46.

plee, n.; game 6.79.

pleyne, adj.; razed 28.30; *playn*, candid 63.25.

pleyne, adv.; clearly 73.31.

pleyneþ, v. pr. 3 s.; complains 15.77.

pleynli, adv.; openly 1.93; 77.18.

plente, n.; abundance 1.79.

plesance, n.; will of God 92.18; pleasure 92.66; *plesaunce*, discourse 95.48.

plyght, pp.; pledged 26.157.

plyt, n.; evil condition 20.74.

plytys, n.; pleats 52.18.

po, n.; peacock 6.87.

pondryng, n.; musing 15.111.

poppys, n.; pope 45.2.

por, n.; power 81.41; *poer* 4.124; *poure* 93.54; *pwower* 99.2.

possesside, pp.; put into possession 92.2.

possessioners, n.; endowed clergymen 65.143.

posterne, n.; back door 3.46.

pouraille, n.; poor people 4.129; *porayle* 70.77; *poreyll* 70.86.

pouste, n.; power 14.20.

powre, adj.; poor 23.10; *pore* 5.77; *pouer* 93.110.

praer, n.; meadow 48.71.

praye, n.; plunder 26.4; quarry 27.34; troop 29.6.

pres, n.; crowd 13.38; 44.20; 50.8.

preseyn, v.; to press 64.130.

presence, n.; personality 88.22.

presently, adv.; without delay 50.50.

prest, adj.; prompt 11.67.

preue, v.; to demonstrate 44.22; prove 27.*n*; *proue* 29.61; imp. *preve* 95.55; pp. *preeued*, tested 1.94; *provyd* 70.5.

preuyly, adv.; privily 15.54; *priuely*, secretly 38.27.

pryde, n.; honor 26.109; ostentation 99.80; *prude*, pride 3.44.

prye, v.; to peer 4.203.

prike, v.; to ride 72.125; pr. 3 s. *prikes* 8.12; pt. 3 s. *prycked* 26.81; *prikked*, grieved 76.5; pp. *priked*, galloped 9.15.

prikyares, n.; riders 2.24.

princehode, n.; dignity of a prince 30.81.

printe, n.; divine likeness 73.63.

pris, adj.; worthy 4.55.

pris, n.; value 2.19; 30.4; 49.17;

repute 5.28; 81.13; regard 1.72; 15.73; victory 5.86; glory 4.88; 50.58; *pryce* 33. bur.; adv. phr. *in pris,* highly esteemed 4.148.

priuy, adj.; personal 72.119.

proceede, v.; to institute legal action 50.6.

prouydyd, pp.; designated 1.101.

provow, v.; to acknowledge 30.62.

prudent, adj.; sagacious 1.75.

pruest, n.; priest 6.87.

pudrid, pp.; seasoned 48.110.

puissance, n.; power 74.44.

puit, v. pr. 1 s.; put, set 39.12.

puple, n.; people 11.67; 13.130.

purchas, n.; legal acquisition 58.3; begging 65.145.

purchast, v. pt. 1 s.; became rich 72.37.

pure, adj.; genuine 20.51; *puire,* utter 39.13.

purueye, v.; to provide 40.27; pp. *purveyed* 73.13.

purviaunce, n.; providence 73.9.

putfalle, n.; ambush, trap 3.97.

pwower, See *por.*

quaynte, adj.; refined 65.94; crafty 65.153.

quake, v.; to tremble 42.54; pr. pl. *quaken* 79.11; pt. 3 s. *qwok,* shook 20.33.

quarterle, adv.; quarterly 1.74.

qued, adj.; wicked 54.64.

quelle, v.; to kill 38.10.

querell, n.; quarrel 13.87; *quarel* 93.15; *quarell,* claim 94.3.

questede, v. pt. pl.; yelped 38.10.

quic, adj.; alive 4.19.

quycke, v.; to revive 43.42.

quyte, adj.; free 77.4.

quite, v.; to prove oneself innocent 4.156; pr. pl. requite 15.96; imp. 73.68; pt. pl.

acquitted themselves 90.41; pp. requited 21.22; repaid 87.40; *quyt,* rewarded 26.172.

qwer, adv.; wherever 59. bur.

rache, n.; hunting dog 75.21; 38.7.

rade, v. pt. 3 s.; went raiding 10.2.

radely, adv.; quickly 38.52.

raft, v. pt. 3 s.; robbed 15.62; pp. despoiled 15.58.

ragged, adj.; jagged 78.31.

raye, n.; striped cloth 50.37.

rayke, v. pr. pl.; wander about 65.20.

raymeþ, v. pr. pl.; take at will 2.26.

raysse, n.; course of action 26.8.

rancour, n.; animosity 1.19; *rancur* 77.20; *raungor* 63.19.

rapes, n.; ropes 11.68.

rased, pp.; erased 63.15.

rapere, adv.; formerly, earlier 3.135; 48.120.

rathly, adv.; quickly 11.6.

rau, adj.; raw 7.8.

rawnsome, n.; ransom 27.*p.*

rebawdes, n.; rascals 19.11; *rybaus* 3.62; *rybaudჳ* 7.1; *ribawdes,* irregular or raw troops 28.41.

rebell, adj.; rebellious 15.60.

recheþ, v. pr. pl.; reach 6.39.

recure, n.; remedy 73.22.

recure, v.; to return 93.67; *rekere* 88.78.

rede, adj.; red 11.41.

rede, n.; counsel 3.113.

rede, v.; to counsel 54.24; expound 38.53; interpret 6.28; pr. 1 s. advise 26.23; suppose 52.2; read 7.1; pr. pl. expound 87.39; pt. 3 s. *radde,* read 7.11; pp. guessed 26.210.

redy, adj.; prompt 10.43; comp. *redier,* more convenient 28.48.

redles, adj.; without counsel 49.6.

redresse, v. pr. 3 s.; remedies 15.126; imp. reform 15.11.

reduced, v. pt. 1 s.; recalled 88.5.

regalie, n.; kingdom 1.69; *regaly* 92.30.

regall, n.; royal authority 89.120.

regne, v.; to reign 79.6; *rayn* 94.5; pr. 3 s. *regneth* 94.2.

reherse, v.; to relate 1.66; *reherce,* recall 95.14; pr. p. *rehersyng,* repeating 88.39.

reynyngge, n.; ruling 63.29.

reioisshe, v.; to enjoy one's position 1.105.

rekeles, adj.; careless 26.53; *rechles,* heedless 56.3.

reken, v.; to tell 44.12; pr. 3 s. *rykeneþ,* computes 7.29; pr. pl. *reken,* count 42.11; *rekken,* care 40.9; pt. 3 s. *rought* 93.57; pt. pl. *rohte* 6.17; pp. *rekened,* considered 95.39.

rekenynges, n.; accounting 13.151.

releues, v. pr. pl.; relieve 13.103.

reme, n.; realm 14.19; *reaume* 71.20; *reams* 41.50; *rewmes* 71.6.

remembraunce, n.; recollection 1.47; memory 40.36.

remene, v.; to compare 39.41.

remuy, v.; to remove 4.215.

ren, v.; to run 11.6; *renne* 28.129; *ronne* 26.82; pr. 3 s. *renneþ,* turns 38.43; pr. p. *ronynge,* revolving 38.43; *rennyng,* running 29.8; pt. 3 s. *ran* 28.122; *ronne* 38.7; pt. pl. assembled 19.11.

renewed, pp.; repeated 42.9.

renone, n.; fame 32.20; *renoune*

43.2.

rent, n.; income 14.15; profit 48.86.

repref, n.; ignominy 28.56; disgrace 30.3; *repreff* 29.54.

repreue, v.; to reject 64.107; pp. *repreved,* shamed 30.81.

rere, v.; to raise 64.58; pr. 3 s. *rereth* 64.37; pp. *rered* 5.69.

res, n.; attack 4.36; designs 14.7.

rescewe, v.; to rescue 30.44.

rest, v.; to remain 2.18.

reste, n.; freedom from disturbance 13.16; 15.80; 79.56; abode 19.45.

reþeres, n.; bullock 4.163.

reue, n.; magistrate 54.52.

reuleth, v. pr. 3 s.; reigns 24.4.

reuþeles, adj.; merciless 54.43.

reve, v.; to plunder 64.63; pt. pl. *reued* 10.24.

reverence, n.; deference 50.24.

reuerson, v. pr. pl.; overthrow 68.13.

rewarde, n.; heed 1.97; reward 77.12.

rewe, v.; to repent 15.106; regret 3.136; *rewen* 6.6; *rewe,* have pity on 34.10; *rywe* 32.8; imp. *rewe* 98.24; pt. pl. regret 28.162; impers. *rewit,* grieves 59.15.

rewe, v. pr. subj. s.; dawn 7.21.

rewyng, n.; plundering 58.3.

rewly, adj.; sorry 59.11.

rewlle, n.; ruler, measure 45.61.

ryall, adj.; noble 26.130; *ryal* 81.21; royal 41.36; *riall* 28.36.

ryalte, n.; royal power 89.158.

ribaudery, n.; debauchery 65.6.

ryþaus, See *rebawdes.*

riche, n.; mighty person 38.107.

ryffe, adj.; widespread 45.6.

rifild, pp.; plundered 9.16.

ryfly, adv.; frequently 38.7.

right, n.; dominions 42.1; rightful position 12.37; justice
62.4; *ryht* 5.77; claim 2.26;
ryght 78.15; territory 11.37;
rygth 99.32; *ryȝt*, right 13.9;
riht 1.33.

ryȝtwys, adj.; righteous 14.96;
rightwys 93.11.

ryht, adv.; very 1.93; *right*,
close 11.24; surely 93.51.

rind, n.; bark 48.76.

rynde, v.; to rend 59.19; pp. torn
asunder 26.165; *rente* 26.165;
pt. pl. 27.22.

rynge, n.; rim of wheel 38.43.

riot, n.; tumultuous crowd 64.62;
tumult 64.86; debauchery
65.6.

rys, n.; branch 2.17; 33. bur.;
48.8.

ryse, v.; to rebel 20.17; *arise*,
happen 2.18.

rywe, See *rewe*.

ro, n.; repose 2.18.

rodde, v. pt. 1 s.; rode 81.45;
pt. 3 s. *rode* 72.100; sailed
39.61.

rode, n.; cross 12.9; 39.73; 99.71;
roode 27.58.

rofe, v. pt. pl.; tore apart 27.22.

royaume, n.; kingdom 93.4;
royalme 97.16.

roke, n.; mist 26.202.

rolle, n.; roll 7.1; *rollis*, registers,
musters 29.24.

romede, v. pt. 1 s.; stretched
38.16.

ronne, See *ren*.

roo, n.; deer 26.53; *roon* 38.7.

rosse, n.; rose 36.3; *roys* 36.4.

roste, v.; to be roasted 3.69; pp.
arost 2.41; 7.8.

roþur, n.; rudder 39.36; *rooþur*
39.25.

rought, See *reken*.

rouh, adj.; rough 39.37.

rouncyn, n.; horse 3.43; 3.21.

rounde, adv.; with a rotary movement 38.43; vigorously 89.50;
rowynde, round 26.132.

roune, v.; to tell 38.52; *rowne*,
deliberate 14.54.

rounes, n.; mysterious sayings
38.53.

rout, n.; company 9.16; *rowte*
28.36; 42.16; disorderly
crowds 19.11; *rowght*, array
26.130.

route, v.; to assemble 51.9; go
on foot 64.93.

rouþe, n.; compassion 15.37;
matter of regret 71.33; *rewth*
70.88; *rouþes*, remorse 6.28.

roweþe, v. pr. 3 s.; row 54.34; pt.
3 s. *rouwed* 39.61.

rowynde, See *rounde*.

rowme, n.; space 65.119; authority 97.43.

rugge, n.; ridge 38.7.

rughfote, adj.; rough-footed
9.19.

ruȝe, n.; rye 2.68.

ruyen, n.; downfall 47.11.

rule, v.; to conduct oneself 15.90;
imp. administer 13.156.

sade, adj.; calamitous 27.*gg*;
firm 40.2; valiant 94.20; *sad-
de*, serious 30.110.

sadly, adv.; vigorously 19.29.

safforne, n.; saffron 50.62.

saht, pp.; reconciled 4.51.

saye, v.; to say 20.73; *seye* 20.9;
seyn 38.65; *segge* 4.160; *sugge*
4.62; pr. 1 s. *sae* 69.17; *sei*
39.9; *sigge* 48.21; *sugge* 4.9;
pr. 3 s. *seiþ* 2.52; pr. pl. *seyne*
43.3; imp. *sey* 85.3; pt. pl.
seiden 3.12; pp. *i-seiid* 48.117.

sayed, pp.; made trial of, explored 39.34.

sayleyeard, n.; spar for sails 78.33.

sakes, n.; sacks 29.12.

sakles, adj.; innocent 9.3.

sal, v. pr. 3 s.; shall 11.19; *sall* 11.4; *schall* 23. bur.; 26.59; *schul* 81.32; *shal* 13.16; pr. 1 s. *ichulle* 4.1; pr. 2 s. *saltou* 9.23; pr. pl. *sall* 11.18; *schull* 24.2; *xuln* 59.14; pt. 1 s. *xulde*, should 60.9; pt. 3 s. *schulde* 20.50; *sholde* 28.71; *shulde* 13.19; *suld* 10.9; *xuld* 59.1; pt. pl. *sholde* 4.66; *suld* 12.3; *xulde* 59.17; *xuldyn* 59.19.

saluoure, n.; healer 33.4.

samles, adj.; shameless 56.5.

sample, n.; warning 64.15.

sape, n.; soap 65.62.

sarsyn, adj.; saracen, infidel 1.39.

sauf, prep.; save 64.15.

saule, n.; soul 65.119.

savoure, n.; sweetness 35.27; 76.2.

sawe, n.; conversation 4.11; saying 7.15.

sawted, pp.; assaulted 28.95.

scapen, v.; to escape 6.8; *skape* 89.129; *skapen* 91.57; pp. *scaped* 89.137.

scarmyssh, v.; to skirmish 29.36; pt. 3 s. *scarmysshed* 29.33.

scape, n.; injury 6.15; 65.84.

scharp, adj.; severe 39.21; 93.38.

scharpliche, adv.; vigorously 27.6.

schatereden, v. pt. pl.; dispersed 38.17.

schawe, n.; thicket 38.17; 12.2.

sche, pro.; she 26.53; *ȝe* 38.42; dat. *hire* 38.56; poss. 38.57.

tched, n.; top of head 20.68.

schene, adj.; shining 12.2.

schep, n.; ship 82.1.

scheryssh, See *cherische*.

schingles, n.; shingles 48.57.

schipherd, n.; shepherd 10.20.

schote, v.; to sprout 36.7; imp. *schote*, shoot 26.169; pt. 3 s. dismissed 26.128.

schour, n.; squall 39.21; conflict 93.38; *schowre*, plenty 10.43.

schowte, n.; shout 60.2.

schrewe, adj.; unpleasant 52.31.

schrewes, n.; villains 10.26; rascals 21.2; *shrewes* 78.14.

scyle, See *skille*.

score, n.; charge 6.8.

scornes, n.; taunts 39.102.

scoumfited, pp.; defeated 39.60.

scrynkeþ, v. pr. 3 s.; shrinks 6.59.

scwyer, n.; squire 4.137.

seche, v.; to seek 2.63; pr. 3 s. *secheþ* 13.5; pp. *sowthe* 70.8; *soght* 11.50; searched 66.38; *soute*, pursued 38.109.

secularis, n.; laymen 45.53.

sedwale, n.; zedoary 48.74.

see, n.; sea 39.34; 41.19.

see, n.; throne 4.70.

see, v.; to see 28.52; *sen* 54.97; pr. 2 s. *sestou* 38.76; pr. 3 s. *i-seeþ*, 48.133; pr. pl. *seeþ* 48.159; *i-seeþ* 48.139; pr. subj. s. *see*, protect 4.81; pt. 1 s. *sey*, saw 38.64; pt. 3 s. 27.*j*; pp. *i-seiȝe* 39.8; *sene*, plain 9.3.

sege, n.; siege 11 rub.; *seege* 29.21.

segge, See *saye*.

segge, n.; man 44.42.

seint, adj.; holy 48.190.

seke, adj.; sick 27.7.

sekere, adj.; secure 27.*bb*; dependable 95.106; *siker* 39.49; trustworthy 95.137.

sekerly, adv.; truly 95.15; *syk-*

yrly 70.38; *sikerliche* 20.73.

sekyr, adv.; assuredly 49.12.

seknesse, n.; sickness 1.88.

selden, adv.; seldom 39.8; *selde* 4.6.

sele, adj.; good 27.7.

seli, adj.; simple 3.121.

selkeþe, adj.; strange 4.179; *selcouthe* 95.33.

semblaunt, n.; appearance 13.22; countenance 65.94; *sembland* 11.79.

semble, n.; conflict 27.*gg.*

semblyt, pp.; assembled 45.62.

semely, adv.; beautifully 19.39.

semly, adj.; good looking 11.28; *sembli* 48.66; *semeli,* stately 38.87; *seemly,* suitable 95.38.

semlynesse, n.; elegance 1.86.

senkyne, n.; sinking 45.52.

sensualle, adj.; self-willed 88.4.

sercle, n.; crown 14.10.

sere, adv.; severally 10.56.

sergantes, n.; men-at-arms 11.28.

sertayne, adv.; certainly 93.42.

sertes, adv.; certainly 49.11.

seruage, n.; servitude 63.26.

seruiabli, adv.; obediently 63.2.

seruis, n.; service 10.43.

set, adj.; fixed, appointed 2.54.

set, v.; to cause 45.60; *sett,* establish 70.93; pr. 3 s. *sett be,* value 61.9; pr. pl. *setten bi* 57.22; *set,* account 20.5; pt. 1 s. *sette,* went down 81.25; pt. pl. estimated 81.13; pp. circumscribed 45.12; *i-sette,* placed 25.*a*; *set* 29 rub.; 39.86.

sete, n.; throne 39.86; *setis,* residences 41.16.

seþin, See *siþ.*

seþþe, conj.; since 2.62; 4.18.

seue, adj.; seven 48.179.

seur, See *suir.*

sewe, v.; to follow 15.115; 43.7;

sue 42.67; 73.30.

sewe, v. pt. 3 s.; sowed 90.7.

shabbes, n.; scabs 7.22.

shadde, v. pt. 3 s.; divided 7.9.

shadwe, v. imp.; protect 98.12.

shake, v.; to brandish 28.124.

shame, n.; reproach 89.32; ignominy 3.127; *schame* 9.12; *shome* 3.121.

shankis, n.; legs 1.57; *shonkes* 4.233.

shape, v.; to cause 64.138; pr. pl. *schappe,* (fig.) obey 18.*g.*

shende, v.; to discomfit 54.95; pp. *schent,* destroyed 10.26; *shent* 28.141; punished 87.44; injured 14.137.

shene, adv.; brightly 28.1.

shitte, v. pt. pl.; shut 29.26.

shomeþ, v. pr. 3 s.; is ashamed 6.59.

shonde, n.; shame 4.189.

shone, n.; shoes 65.101.

shonkes, See *shankis.*

shotte, n.; projectiles 30.83.

shrapeþ, v. pr. pl.; scrape 7.22.

shryffe, v.; to make confession 72.93.

shryke, v.; to shriek 6.61.

shrowthes, n.; ship's rigging 78.42; *shrowdes* 78.46.

shulde, n.; shield 64.51.

shuppare, n.; maker 7.9.

shupte, v. pt. 3 s.; made 7.9.

side, adj.; long 29.11.

sydes, n.; flanks 27.4.

sigge, See *saye.*

syght, v.; to sigh 72.15.

sygned, pp.; assigned to 72.110.

syзth, n.; sight 38.64; *sicзthe* 38.66.

siker, See *sekere.*

sikernes, n.; sense of security 74.7.

sympyll, adj.; low 70.67.

syne, adv.; since, afterwards 26.39.

singuler, adj.; simple 95.46.

singulere, adv.; individually 15.59.

siouns, n.; shoots 48.74.

syre, n.; lord 6.20.

site, n.; city 4.193.

siþ, adv.; subsequently 48.143; afterwards 93.37; *syþon* 99.51; *seþin* 10.44; *seþþe* 4.187; 38.109; *seþþen* 6.79.

siþe, n.; times 4.174.

sytte, v.; to sit 59.13; *set* 64.124; pr. 3 s. *sytes* 66.4; pr. pl. *sitteþ* 6.37; imp. *sette* 29.66; pt. pl. *seten*, sat in judgment 4.146.

skatre, v.; to scatter 13.158; pp. *skaterid* 14.23.

skere, adv.; entirely 6.8.

skere, v.; to clear oneself 6.15.

skille, n.; discernment 14.111; reason 15.102; *scyle* 88.39; *skyle*, justice 95.39.

skry, n.; clamor 28.83.

slaken, v.; to diminish 10.49; *slake*, cease 72.15; become less rigorous 58.1.

slawe, adj.; slow 49.18.

sleigne, See *slo*.

sleilich, adv.; stealthily 48.158.

sleyth, n.; wisdom 58.2.

sly, adj.; wise 55.15; clever 86.19.

slike, adj.; such 11.35.

sliper, adj.; untrustworthy 39.5.

slyt, adj.; slashed 62.9.

slo, v.; to be slain 3.55; slay 13.117; pr. 3 s. *sles* 13.22; pt. 3 s. *slouh* 1.33; *slow* 30.67; pt. pl. *slogh* 9.3; *slouȝ* 39.45; *slowght* 19.19; *slowen* 3.79; destroyed 14.124; pp. *slayn*, slain 30.87; *slawe* 49.21;

sleigne 89.148; *slene* 99.18.

slouþe, n.; sloth 20.67.

slow, adj.; dull 15.44; spiritless 39.103.

slowtfull, adj.; inactive 92.25.

smakke, n.; taste 48.77.

smerte, adj.; rough 43.28.

smerte, v.; to feel pain 4.168; pr. subj. s. 15.21.

smyte, v.; to smite 26.223; *smhyte* 4.132; pr. s 3. *smyt*, destroys 15.97; pt. 3 s. *smote*, struck 26.219; cast 3.106.

snawile, n.; snail 48.40.

snellich, adv.; quickly 48.163.

so, adv.; as 4.66; *swo*, so 2.20.

sogat, adv.; in this manner 11.96; *sogates* 65.156.

sogettis, n.; subjects 15.7.

soyle, n.; country 64.55.

soken, n.; district 21.2.

solas, n.; comfort 58.4; solace 48.50; alleviation of distress 89.5.

solde, pp.; polluted 64.55.

soleyn, adj.; unusual 95.36.

soll, n.; soul 74.23; *sooles* 15.8.

somertyde, n.; summer time 91.1.

sonde, n.; dispensation 4.220; 37.1; 90.3.

sonder, v.; to disperse 66.4.

sone, adv.; soon 10.41.

sopper, n.; supper 48.20.

sor, n.; grief 6.81.

sore, adj.; afflicted 41.62.

sore, adv.; severely 14.114; deeply 26.221; with great distress 26.125; bitterly 3.136; 79.11; *soure* 66.15.

sorwe, n.; sorrow 1.26.

sote, n.; soot 3.134.

soth, n.; truth 4.14; *soht* 4.61; *suth* 10.15.

sotilte, n.; treachery 30.55.

soudeours, n.; soldiers 28.76.

souereyne, adj.; supreme 1.103; *souereigne* 98.71.

souffisant, adj.; sufficient 30.36.

soute, See *seche.*

sown, n.; fame 14.86; *sovn,* sound 63.45.

sownde, adj.; in good condition 78.2.

sowre, n.; bitter 10.44.

space, n.; opportunity 14.149; *spas* 20.85; time 59.9; *spaas,* short time 95.30.

spare, v.; to refrain from 49.63; desist 11.23; pr. 3 s. 65.43; pr. 1 s. save 2.48; pt. 1 s. *spared* 2.49; pt. 3 s. 32.11; spared 28.93.

spawne, v.; to multiply 45.22.

spec, v. pt. 3 s.; spoke 5.46.

speche, n.; plea 11.23.

spede, n.; asset 39.15; assistance 98.73; *evil spede,* ill success 87.2.

spede, v.; to succeed 3.118; further 20.93; make haste 45.22; fare 12.38; prosper 24.2; pr. subj. s. 37.9; imp. *spedeþ,* hasten 7.37.

spelle, v.; to talk 7.37.

spen, v.; to grasp 44.11.

spene, v.; to spend 2.48; consume 3.96; pt. 3 s. *spent,* wore out 27.6.

spewen, v.; to cast out 7.37.

spille, v.; to kill 14.106; waste 9.33.

spolleth, v. pr. 3 s.; robs 24.5.

spoorte, n.; diversion 51.6.

sportfull, adj.; diverting 28.123.

sprede, v.; to extend 88.65; unfold 92.6; *spreyd* 36.14; pt. 3 s. *sprad* 90.5.

spryng, v.; to proceed 36. bur.; dawn 95.24; grow 92.6; leap 51.19; spread 3.107; pt. 3 s.

sprong, extended 14.122; pp. *sprungyn,* sprinkled 81.5.

stable, adj.; trustworthy 30.109.

stablenesse, n.; stability 63.7.

stay, n.; rope for mast 78.41.

stalken, v. pr. pl.; stalk 38.17; pt. 1 s. *stalked* 38.23.

stalun, n.; stallion 48.167.

stalworþe, n.; strong man 14.38.

stalworthly, adv.; valiantly 11.86; *stalwurthlye* 26.24.

stand, n.; (fig.) resistance 21.10.

standerde, n.; ensign 26.178; *stondardes* 26.88.

stanestill, adj.; perfectly silent 9.32.

starffe, v. pr. subj. pl.; die 87.18.

starne, n.; star 77.18; *sterre* 44.31; *sterryes* 81.4.

states, n.; magnates 79.1.

statuȝ, n.; statutes 3.9.

stede, n.; place 11.43; stead 13.11.

stede, n.; steed 3.84; 10.11; 12.15; 27.1.

steke, v. pr. 1 s.; shut 13.1.

stekenyng, adj.; stopping 15.123.

stele, n.; steel armour 27.2; *stell,* steel 45.28.

stele, v.; to wreak 20.10.

steles, v. pr. 3 s.; captures by surprise 8.6.

stere, adj.; stout 27.2.

stere, n.; rudder 48.154.

stere, v.; to rouse oneself 45.34; pp. *steryt,* stirred up 45.35.

sterne, adj.; strong 48.64; *steren,* grim 9.13.

sterne, n.; rudder 78.25.

sterre, v.; to navigate 78.32.

sterte, v.; to make a sudden attack 45.45.

stiched, pp.; sewn 29.14.

styes, n.; ladders 8.6.

stif, adj.; unyielding 39.20; *styff,*

massive 95.70.

styffely, adv.; resolutely 26.230; *styfly* 49.74.

stik, v.; to stab 11.14; *stikke,* kill 29.10; pp. *y-styked,* struck through 2.42.

stinteþ, v. pr. pl.; cease 48.99.

styrande, pr. p.; rousing 26.12.

stirt, v. pt. 3 s.; hastened 12.15.

stode, n.; stud 48.35.

stode, v. pt. 3 s.; was placed 26.178; pt. pl. 26.180.

stok, n.; idol 39.62; lineage 92.5; (fig.) stem 39.82; *stocke,* trunk 43.32.

stoken, pp.; established 13.93.

stomager, n.; waistcoat 52.9.

stond, v.; to rank 1.96; endure 28.167; be stabled 10.11; *stand,* offer battle 12.33; *stonde,* stand 26.212; pr. 3 s. *stant* 98.45; *stonds* 26.94; *stont* 2.33; ranks 90.4; pr. pl. *stand,* stand firm 21.25; imp. *stonde,* stand 14.8; *stondeth* 18.*d*; pt. pl. *stode,* opposed 27.60.

stones, n.; precious stones 14.10.

stool, n.; block 16.2; *stoles,* examination stools 15.4.

stoppid, pp.; mended 29.13.

store, n.; value 14.28.

stounde, n.; moment, time 4.173; *stownde* 27.1.

stoure, n.; battle 21.10; *stowre* 26.230.

stout, adj.; fierce 9.13; arrogant 54.48; *stowt* 69.11.

strayte, adj.; difficult 89.129.

strayttly, adv.; directly 70.55.

straunge, adj.; foreign 15.34.

stre, n.; straw 2.69.

strechid, pp.; prostrate 29.16.

streinþeles, adj.; without authority 54.42.

strekyn, pp.; stabbed 81.54.

strenth, n.; legal force 45.56; *strenkyth,* strength 49.78; *streynþe* 4.77.

streuyn, pp.; struggled 11.86.

stroy, v.; to destroy 45.36; pr. pl. 14.130; pp. *stroied* 30.85.

strond, n.; bank 38.23; shore 3.6.

stronke, adj.; raging 99.43.

stu, n.; stew 48.109.

stude, n.; place 2.33; 4.35.

stuffed, pp.; well stored 13.67; padded for protection 28.40; furnished 28.86; filled 28.92.

sturne, adv.; merciless 2.33.

subuerte, v.; to turn aside 43.26.

suche, adj.; such 13.17; 25.14; *sych* 23.4; *swych* 59.12.

sue, See *sewe.*

suerd, n.; sword 3.27.

suereþ, v. pr. pl.; swear 3.126; pt. 3 s. *suor* 3.61; *swor* 3.93; pp. promised 2.21.

suffer, v.; to tolerate 21.16; pt. pl. *sufferd* 21.20.

suffisaunce, n.; satisfaction 1.103.

sugge, See *saye.*

suir, adj.; sure 39.39; *seur* 40.14; *sure,* secure 73.54.

suld, See *sal.*

sulle, v.; to sell 2.46; pr. 1 s. 2.44.

sumdel, adv.; to some extent 20.28.

sumptuous, adj.; extravagant 83.40.

sunne, n.; sin 4.166.

supplusage, n.; surplus 70.27.

sureccion, n.; insurrection 64.138.

suspection, n.; suspicion 74.30.

sustynaunce, n.; livelihood 13.156.

sute, n.; group 45.62.

swage, v.; to grow less 39.111.

swapped, v. pt. pl.; dealt blows 26.213.

swart, adj.; wicked 6.48.

sweem, n.; swoon 95.29.

sweyn, n.; man 3.24.

swelt, v. pt. 3 s.; died 12.9.

swere, n.; neck 52.27; *swire* 11.68.

swete, n.; sweet 10.44.

swete, n.; sweat 28.93; *swot* 2.20.

swete, v.; to sweat 37.8; pt. 1 s. 95.29; pt. pl. 95.66.

swevenes, n.; dreams 95.6.

swyers, n.; squires 3.75.

swykedom, n.; treachery 4.170.

swynde, v.; to waste away 2.20; *swynden*, perish 2.72.

swynk, n.; labor 2.20.

swinke, v.; to toil 54.38; pr. pl. 95.66.

swire, See *swere*.

swith, adv.; quickly 10.43; soon 95.29; very 3.36; 48.72; *suiþe* 3.125.

swo, See *so*.

swold, pp. sold 86.31.

swope, v. pr. pl.; sweep, labor 95.66.

swot, See *swete*, n.

taan, See *take*.

tables, n.; backgammon 51.23.

taburs, n.; little drums 48.137.

tadde, n.; toad 7.10.

taht, See *tek*.

tayle, n.; (fig.) end 45.41.

tayles, n.; skirt trains 53.3.

take, v.; to pay 50.13; pr. pl. receive 70.87; pr. subj. pl. take 3.14; imp. *takeþ* 18.*f*; pt. 1 s. *toke*, sent 65.167; pt. 3 s. took 28.137; pt. pl. 20.43; *token* 3.19; pp. *taken* 10.34; *tayne* 26.143; *tane* 10.66; *taan*, captured 28.150; *take* 38.18; mis-taken 61.7; *taken* 58.2.

taklynge, n.; furnishing of tackle 78.4.

tale, n.; number 4.150.

tales, n.; falsehoods 24.5; *talis* 60.23.

taletellere, n.; talebearer 13.17.

tame, adj.; civilized 70.29.

targe, n.; small shield 39.55.

tawe, n.; rope 29.13.

te, See *þo*, def. art.

tek, v. pr. 1 s.; show 2.58; pt. 3 s. *teched*, taught 10.3; *taȝt* 41.14; pp. *taht* 2.58.

telle, v.; to enumerate 4.150; pt. 1 s. *told*, paid 2.40; pp. reputed 4.148.

temed, pp.; subjugated 4.39.

tende, n.; tithe 45.57.

tene, n.; ten 27.*w*.

tene, n.; grief 27.*hh*; harm 2.58.

tened, pp.; ruined 19.1; *i-tened* 2.2.

tenour, n.; purport 25.*c*.

tent, n.; attention 14.13.

terestre, adj.; earthly 73.39.

termyne, v.; to declare 1.93.

þah, See *þouȝ*.

þakkeþ, v. pr. pl.; slap 48.142.

þan, adv.; then 10.41; 13.21; then 24.2; *þenne* 20.21.

þar, v. pr. 3 s. impers.; it is needful 13.108; *darþ* 5.80; *thurt* 99.68.

that, conj.; unless 43.6.

þat, pro.; he who 14.131; 15.93; 43.11.

the, See *þey*.

the, pro.; thee 26.102.

thee, v.; to prosper 15.85; 67.39; *þe* 4.190.

they, See *þouȝ*.

þey, pro.; they 13.30; *the* 26.27; 26.192; 26.199; 26.227; 51.35; 51.67; 70.20; *thee* 26.215;

þeih 54.47; *þai* 9.14.

þeynes, n.; thanes 4.95.

þen, conj.; as 65.68; than 5.76.

þenche, v.; to think 4.28; pr. pl. *þenk* 27.*m*; imp. 16.2; pt. 3 s. *þouȝte* 20.28; pt. pl. *þohte* 4.55; pp. *thoght* 11.53.

þer, adv.; there 3.31; *þare* 9.3; *þore* 5.55.

ther, adv.; where 13.5; 95.114.

ther, pro.; their 1.60; 19.15; 78.27; *þaire* 10.14; *þar* 45.57.

þer-ase, conj.; where 2.13; 13.109.

thether, adv.; thither 26.28; *þedere* 27.44; *thyder* 36 bur.

þeweles, adj.; destitute of morals 54.54.

thewis, n.; customs, virtues 55.19.

thycke, adv.; indistinctly 50.20.

þilke, adj.; the same 5.91; 48.173.

thyll, See *till.*

þir, pro.; these 10.56.

þis, adj.; these 2.50; 3.78; 9.26; 23.9; 39.81; *þeose* 20.59.

þo, adv.; then 3.25; 27.*ee*; 50.22; 89.69; when 3.49; 4.70.

þo, def. art.; the 10.27; 14.8; 19.11; 99.8; *te* 36. bur.

þo, pro.; those 14.103; 27.31; 44.31; 60.8; 72.98; *thoo* 93.82.

þof, See *þouȝ.*

þonk, n.; thanks 15.76; *þonkes* 6.75.

þonke, v.; to thank 6.30; imp. *thank* 20.86.

þoste, n.; dung 7.7.

þouȝ, conj.; although 13.4; *þaþ* 2.21; *they* 95.121; *thewgh* 79.21; *þof* 65.77; *thogh* 28.105; *þoȝ* 48.5; *thow* 52.9; *þowþe* 27.v.

thowght, n.; anxiety 51.8; *þoht,* expectation 4.171; *þowth,* mind 60.14.

þowþe, See *þouȝ.*

thretes, v. pr. 3 s.; threatens 9.31; pr. pl. *þret* 13.58; *threton* 23.10; imp. 15.27; pp. *þrat* 6.69.

thridde, adj.; third 1.71; 13.41; *thred* 93.44.

þryue, pp.; worthy 6.74.

þruisse, n.; thrush 48.96.

þunche, v. impers.; to seem 3.121; pr. 3 s. *þinkeþ,* 39.28; *thynk* 65.31; *thynkith* 40.14; *þuncheþ* 5.7; pt. 3 s. *thoght* 28.114.

þunne, adj.; thin 6.75.

thurgh, prep.; through 10.10; *thorwe* 32.10; *þourh* 3.44; *þurh* 4.53.

thurt, See *thar.*

tyde, n.; time, season 11.26.

tyke, n.; cur 7.10.

tylyer, n.; tiller 88.17.

tilyynge, n.; tillage 2.2.

till, prep.; to 12.40; *til* 20.3; *thyll* 81.17.

tyme, n.; lifetime 81.32.

tyne, v.; to tear, destroy 45.41; pp. *tynt,* taken away, lost 38.114.

tyres, n.; headdresses 53.6.

to, adj.; two 29.12; *too* 1.102.

to, adv.; too 9.2; 11.91; 15.24; 20.6; 86.8.

to, prep.; at 48.20; for 48.48.

to, n.; two 26.108; 69.27; *too* 72.71.

tobarst, v. pt. pl.; burst asunder 20.45; pp. *tobroken,* broken to pieces 14.50.

todrawe, pp.; destroyed 49.23; dragged 4.162; *todrowe* 4.177.

todryuen, v.; to break in pieces 3.39.

tofore, prep.; before 27.*b.*

togydre, adv.; together 14.67;

togedere 3.13.

toȝede, v.; to run towards 38.16.

toȝeynes, prep.; against 3.77.

toȝere, adv.; this year 10.58.

toknyng, n.; symbol 20.51.

toles, n.; tools 15.2.

tolyure, v. pr. 1 s.; deliver 7.4.

tolle, n.; toll, payment 7.4.

tome, adj.; tame 3.122.

toshrude, pp.; clothed 7.25.

toswolle, pp.; arrogant 6.48.

toþrete, v.; to menace 39.102.

tour, n.; tower 28.29; *towre* 43.16; tower of ship 39.18.

toute, n.; buttocks 48.136.

trace, n.; course of action 42.67; way 89.24.

tray, n.; trouble 27.*hh.*

trayne, n.; deceit 84.23.

translacione, n.; removal 88.26.

trantes, n.; tricks 65.61.

trauail, n.; hardship 1.26; 73.85.

trauaille, v.; to harass 28.130; *travayle,* pitch 78.51; pr. pl. *trauele,* endeavor, toil 65.121; pt. 3 s. *traueilid,* distressed 1.88.

travers, adv.; athwart 78.39.

tre, n.; wood 5.63.

trespace, n.; sin 14.63; breach of law 27.*y;* 77.4; *trespase,* transgression 14.51; wrong 20.82; *trespasse* 26.119.

trete, n.; treaty 15.17; 30.59.

trete, v.; to negotiate 13.120; 73.21.

trewe, adj.; loyal 89.103; *trow,* trew 45.56; *tru,* honest 49.42.

triacle, n.; medicinal salve 48.84.

trie, adj.; choice, select 48.19.

tryȝe, v. pr. pl.; sift 13.47; pp. *tryed,* set apart 14.69.

triste, v.; to have confidence 15.17; imp. *trust,* believe 20.31.

troupe, n.; pledge 20.65; *troþe* 99.7; *trowth* 26.64; *treuþe,* truth 20.4; *trewth* 24.5; *trouhte* 13.2; *trouþe* 13.4.

trowbel, n.; public disturbance 79.55.

trowe, v.; to believe 72.21; pr. 1 s. guess 74.16; imp. *throw,* believe 45.59; pp. *trowed* 15.25.

trussen, v.; to pack up 14.140; depart 65.24; imp. *trus,* make ready 12.31.

tubrugge, n.; drawbridge 4.201.

turment, n.; affliction 41.10.

turn, v.; to proceed from 9 rub.; *turn agayn,* retreat 29.38; *torne,* lead 40.12; pr. subj. pl. *turne,* reform 57.29; pt. 3 s. *turnyd,* changed his course, went 26.69.

turnement, n.; torment 64.114.

tusshes, n.; tusks 90.56.

twyes, adv.; twice 29.33.

twynne, v.; to part 72.71.

vche, See *euch.*

vnabelite, n.; inability 63.23.

vnbynd, v.; to set free 72.55.

vnblythly, adv.; unpleasantly 27.62.

vnbrad, adj.; obscure 6.13.

vnbredes, v. pr. pl.; censure 6.12.

vnder, adj.; defeated 9.18; subordinate 66.2.

vnyte, n.; harmony 13.130.

vnkind, adj.; ungenerous 21.19; inclement 99.42; disloyal 89.63; *unkuynde* 39.103; *on-kynd,* degenerate 55.15.

vnkyndly, adj.; improper 64.25; unnatural 64.97.

vnneþe, adv.; with difficulty 39.4; 69.35.

vnpes, n.; dissension 99.25.

vnryghtewys, adv.; dishonestly 88.15.

vnsele, adv.; wretchedly 10.27.

vnsell, n.; unhappiness 45.12; *vnsele*, unfortunate person 54.36.

vnþeufol, adj.; vicious 6.74.

vnwerly, adv.; unexpectedly 30.75.

vpo, prep.; upon 2.1.

vpright, adv.; in justice 95.54.

vr, pro.; our 20.71; *ovre* 27.53; *houre* 82.2.

vsyn, v. pr. pl.; employ 63.9; *vse*, practice 51.63; pt. 3 s. *vsed* 71.26.

vttremest, adj. sup.; extreme 73.60.

vuel, adj.; evil 20.38.

uadir, See *fadir*.

vanite, n.; worthless thing 72.22.

vauntage, n.; advantage 14.103.

venemed, v. pt. 3 s.; corrupted 64.46.

verrey, adj.; true 20.51; *verray* 28.157; *veray* 41.4.

vertu, n.; distinction 1.99.

vetturlockes, n.; heraldic fetter-locks 84.30.

vexacion, n.; disappointment 91.28.

victor, n.; victory 14.131.

vyhte, n.; fighting 4.224.

vylabele, adj.; to be desired 52. bur.

villan, n.; scroundrel 21.21.

villiche, adv.; vilely 4.199.

vylte, n.; disgrace 3.91.

vitaille, n.; provisions 28.87.

uoyde, v.; to avoid 70.93.

vonder, See *wondur*.

wache, n.; sentinel 26.78; *wacch*, night-watch 28.72.

wade, n.; weed 49.68; *wedis* 44.41.

wag, n.; reward 73.25.

wayke, adj.; inadequate 65.16.

waylyth, pr. 3 s.; avails 70.66.

waiour, n.; wager 4.131.

waissing, pr. p.; washing 48.48.

wayte, v.; to expect 15.70; inflict injury on 27.63.

waiteþ, v. pr. 3 s.; shows 2.17.

wayueþ, v. pr. 3 s.; forsakes 15.100.

wake, v.; to keep guard 28.75; stir up 15.29; awake 99.91; *waken* 26.86; *wakyne*, rouse 45.28; wake up 45.27; pr. 3 s. *wakeneþ*, awakens 2.71; pr. pl. wake 21.6; pt. 3 s. *wakkind*, stirred up 10.50; pp. *waken*, been diligent 10.33.

walkes, v. pr. 3 s.; spreads 11.29.

wan, See *whan*.

wan, See *win*.

wan, adj.; pale 3.72.

waniand, n.; waning of moon 10.25.

wanton, adj.; naughty 14.113.

wappen, n.; weapon 10.32; *wapin* 11.15.

war, adj.; vigilant 4.102; 65.81; 81.27.

war, v. imp.; beware of, guard against 9.6; 76.58.

warant, n.; pledge 30.36.

wardaine, n.; commander of the garrison 11.83; *wardeyn*, guardian 73.66.

ware, adj.; careful 16.1; 20.8; aware 26.79; 95.7.

ware, n.; goods 3.86; (fig.) 6.90; commodities 49.60.

wared, pp.; expended 64.35.

waryson, n.; reward 26.171.

wark, n.; trouble 72.49; *werke*, business 64.3.

warny, v.; to warn 4.17.

waron, adv.; whereon 4.159.

warp, v. pr. 1 s.; throw 38.4; pt. 3 s. uttered 38.118.

wast, adj.; ruined 64.34.

wat, pro.; what 81.29; *wet* 4.204; *weht* 4.40; *whet* 3.113.

waterbailly, n.; customs official 28.128; *watir-bailliffes* 29.32.

wawes, n.; waves 39.33; 78.27.

waxyn, v. pr. pl.; grow 49.60; 66.2; pt. pl. *wox* 20.38.

webbes, n.; weavers 3.17.

wed, n.; pledge 2.45; *weddes* 27.*q*.

weddeþ, v. pr. 3 s.; marries 6.88; pt. 1 s. *weddyd* 81.15; pt. 3 s. *wedid*, gave in marriage 41.34.

wede, n.; armor 10.37; clothes 15.120; *wedes*, dress 38.4; 95.68.

wede, v.; to go mad 15.3; 66.11.

wederes, n.; storms 39.35.

wedis, See *wade*.

wee, See *wo*.

weht, See *wat*.

weye, n.; way 13.14.

weye, v.; to consider 40.37.

weys, n.; manner 85.12.

weythe, n.; weight 70.100; *weyte* 70.103.

welde, v.; to win, enjoy 6.64; *wilde*, dispose of 95.96.

weldyng, n.; command 38.94.

wele, adv.; well 9.5; *weel* 1.66; *weyl* 67.13; *welle* 3.135; *wel*, much 14.31; quite 11.42.

wele, n.; success 11.16; prosperity 15.3; *weole* 2.66; wealth 6.27; *wele* 20.13; 54.60.

weleful, adj.; prosperous 11.17.

wely, adj.; artful 65.142.

wellaywo, interj.; alas 22.12; *weylaway* 3.8; *weylawo* 3.112; *weleawey* 42.38.

welle, n.; fountain 39.108; source 42.29; *willis*, wells 48.83.

wellyuyng, adj.; upright 13.76.

welth, n.; possession 26.20; prosperity 74.5.

welwyllynge, n.; friends 32.22.

wende, v.; to depart 65.173; go 5.36; take place 14.85; turn 13.107; pr. pl. *wendeþ*, tamper with 6.13; pr. subj. s. *wynde*, leave 26.161; imp. *wendes*, go 12.29; pt. pl. *wende* 3.35; pp. *went* 38.55.

wene, v.; to think 12.1; pr. 1 s. suspect 61.4; pr. pl. *weyne* 45.42; *wene*, think 86.19; *weneþ* 2.10; pr. p. *wenyng* 93.69; pt. 3 s. *wende* 4.127; pt. pl. *wenden* 4.11.

wepe, v. pr. 1 s.; weep 2.66; pr. p. *wepeand* 11.60.

wer, See *whare*.

were, n.; doubt 48.21.

were, n.; confusion 72.39; war 10.50; 11.15; 13.72; 45.17; *werre* 1.52; *werres* 95.36; *warus* 99.51.

weres, v. pr. 3 s.; decays 39.2; pr. pl. *were*, wear 63.49; 87.17.

wery, v.; to curse 9.23.

werre, v.; to make war 73.21; pr. 3 s. *werreþ* 13.113.

werrey, v.; to make war on 1.18; pr. pl. 40.6.

werteouse, adj.; worthwhile 51.74.

wet, See *wat*.

wete, See *witte*.

weth, n.; spoil 29.2.

weue, v. pr. 3 s.; moves to and fro 38.34.

whan, adv.; when 1.87; *wan* 19.19; *whon* 20.17.

whare, adv.; where 9.7; *wher*

20.21; *whore* 10.19; *wer* 36.13.

wharepourh, adv.; whereby 3.7.

what, pro.; that 43.9.

whedre, conj.; whether 65.109.

whel, n.; wheel of Fortune 38.34; *whell* 45.13.

whyl, conj.; while 39.29; 39.36.

while, n.; time 9.5.

whilum, adv.; formerly 11.5.

whissheþ, v. pr. pl.; wish 6.86.

whoche, pro.; which 13.36; *wych* 26.114.

whore, See *whare*.

whose, pro.; whoso 2.11; 4.14; 7.11.

wyde, adv.; abroad 23.2; wide open 64.34.

wyf, n.; woman 81.15.

wifman, n.; woman 38.34.

wight, adj.; courageous 10.37; 12. rub.; 27.*q*.

wyȝth, adv.; directly 38.95.

wyȝtlye, adv.; bravely 43.15; *wyghtly*, nimbly 65.164.

wyht, n.; person 4.138; *whyt* 38.55; *wight* 28.65; *wyȝth* 38.60.

wikked, adj.; wicked 12.6; difficult 12.8.

wilde, adj.; temptestuous 38.21.

wyle, n.; ruse 51.34.

wilfulnesse, n.; purposeful acts 30.13; perversity 62.25.

wilys, conj.; while 70.23.

will, n.; desire 65.179; acquiescence 31.7; will 9.34; 29.2; self-will 54.63; *wil* 2.23.

will, v. pr. 1 s.; will 12.7; pr. 2 s. *wylte* 26.50; *wiltou* 9.21; *wiltow* 30.5; pr. 3 s. *wel* 3.120; *weyl* 67.25; *wil* 13.155: *wille* 14.55; *wl* 48.177; *wol* 13.57; *wolle* 15.20; *woolle* 43.8; neg. *nel* 15.85; *nyl*

13.15; *nule* 4.3; pr. pl. *wol* 13.70; *wolleþ* 4.84; pt. 1 s. *wolde* 38.4; *wald* 12.1; pt. 3 s. 10.10; pt. pl. 12.22; *wolde* 13.21; neg. *nolden* 3.86.

willerdome, n.; willfulness 64.131.

willis, See *welle*.

win, v.; to recover 10.22; conquer 10.62; *wynnen*, win 5.40; *wynne* 14.31; earn 13.57; gain 14.83; get 15.3; profit 15.59; succeed 15.41; *wyne* 45.26; pr. pl. *wynnes*, dry 26.2; pt. 3 s. *wan*, won 11.56; got 41.42; recovered 42.5; pt. pl. *wann* 29.5; *wan*, gained 10.33; pp. *wonen* 12.30; *wonnen* 11.16; *won*, conquered 11.95.

wind, n.; breath 9.33; (fig.) empty talk 14.51; 49.54; wind 38.34; *wynt* 39.35.

wynde, See *wende*.

wynde, v.; to turn 38.82; imp. 38.83; pt. 3 s. *wond*, caused to turn 38.35.

wynne, n.; pleasure 6.78; *wunne*, gain 4.167.

wynne, v.; to get at 65.89.

wynnerys, n.; profiteers 49.20.

wynnyng, n.; profit, gain 20.75.

wirchipe, v.; to honor 33.10; pp. *worschiped* 13.6.

wirking, n.; deeds 87.14; *wirkyn*, influence 89.4.

wysloker, adv. comp.; more wisely 3.119.

wysse, v.; to teach 5.38.

wit, n.; wisdom 13.85; *wyth* 55.11; *wyt*, sense 6.45; mind 39.28; *wytte* 59.15; intelligence 49.54.

wite, v. imp.; blame 30.8.

wyte, v.; to guard 4.211.

wyterly, adv.; undoubtedly 38.70; *witterly* 95.7.

with, prep.; among 11.64; from 28.149; with 13.168; *wid* 54.26; *wytht* 45.33.

withholde, pp.; defended, preserved 64.52.

witte, v.; to know 48.101; 99.8; *wyte* 4.142; 6.35; *wete* 13.97; pr. 1 s. *wate* 65.160; *wot* 50.40; 72.123; *ychot* 4.49; pr. 2 s. *whote* 12.4; *wost* 2.39; pr. 3 s. *wot* 15.32; 23. bur.; 48.175; *wottis* 87.35; pr. pl. *i-witte* 48.180; *wote* 12.8; pr. subj. s. *wyte* 72.124; *witte* 84.36; pt. 1 s. *wyst* 50.19; pt. 3 s. *west* 41.27; *wiste* 4.158; 60.5; pt. pl. *wist* 29.39.

wlonke, adj.; splendid 6.27.

wo, n.; misfortune 12.12; *wee* 2.71; *woჳ,* wrong 48.62.

wod, v. pt. 3 s.; waded 4.100.

wode, adj.; raging 78.27; mad 15.3; *wood* 59.18.

wodwale, n.; woodpecker 48.97.

wolles, n.; wool 28.25.

wombe, n.; belly 4.121.

won, See *on.*

won, n.; course 2.5.

won, prep.; on 81.5.

won, v.; to dwell 9.23; pr. pl. *woniþ* 48.16; pt. pl. *wonned* 65.128.

wonde, v.; to hesitate 10.10.

wonder, n.; surprising occurrence 28.45; 66.1.

wondes, n.; wounds 27.11.

wondrede, v. pt. 3 s.; wandered 7.33.

wondryng, n.; amazement 15.109.

wondur, adv.; very 20.26; *wonder* 23.9; 27.11; wondrous 20.12; *wonderჳ* 74.15; *vonder,* far 46.4.

wone, n.; custom, habit 71.31.

wones, n.; dwelling 65.88.

woning, n.; dwelling 12.8; *wonnynges* 66.39.

wont, adj.; accustomed 19.31.

wonus, See *ones.*

worche, v.; to work 2.5; *wirk,* cause 11.20; pr. 2 s. *worche,* act 3.119; pr. 3 s. *worcheþ,* works 15.100; pr. pl. 6.89; imp. *worche* 95.78; pr. p. *wirkyng,* embroidering 91.4; pt. 3 s. *wroght,* inflicted 27.11; *wrouჳt,* acted 32.3; pt. pl. *wroght,* practiced 72.9; pp. *wrout,* made 38.113; y-wrowte 70.65.

word, n.; renown 11.29; news 3.107.

word, n.; world 60.4; 81.48; 99.56; *werld* 49.45.

wordle, n.; world 42.12; marvel 42.19.

worschipe, n.; honor 13.24; *wirschip* 10.32; *worchip* 13.57; *worship* 73.98; *worshippe* 28.10; *wurship* 29.5.

worþi, adj.; estimable 13.57; becoming 15.21.

worþinesse, n.; merit 20.21; pomp 72.25.

worþlich, adj.; excellent 38.55.

wote, See *witte.*

wounden, pp.; involved 15.61.

wowes, n.; walls of house 64.34.

wox, See *waxyn.*

wrake, n.; vengeance 20.60; 86.50.

wrappid, pp.; beset 15.58.

wraþþe, n.; anger 14.87; *wrathe* 79.3.

wrecched, adj.; wretched 20.13.

wrecful, adj.; full of revenge 54.66.

wreche, n.; vengeance 14.77;

60.25.

wreint, pp.; accused 6.33.

wreke, v. pr. subj. s.; avenge 12.6; pp. *wroken* 9.4; *wrokin* 9.5.

wretche, n.; wretch 9.21.

wrethe, v.; to goad 45.25.

writ, n.; legal document 2.39.

wroght, See *worche*.

wroth, adj.; angry 12.12; sorrowful 27.19.

wroþliche, adv.; wrathfully 38.113.

wrout, See *worche*.

yate, See *gate*.

ye, See *ȝe*.

yeard, See *ȝerde*.

yee, See *eiȝe*.

yelde, See *ȝelde*.

yere, See *ere*.

yere, See *ȝer*.

yerle, See *erle*.

yeve, See *gif*.

yheris, See *ȝer*.

yif, See *ȝif*.

yode, See *goo*.

INDEX OF FIRST LINES

First lines beginning with articles "a" or "the" are listed under
the article

Number

A dere God what mai þis be	39
A man þat xuld of trewþe telle	59
Aboue all thing thow arte a kyng	51
Allas what schul we freris do	69
Alle þat beoþ of huerte trew	5
And save thys flowre wyche ys owre kyng	36
Anoder ȝere hit may betyde	23
As I me lend to a lend	60
As I walkyd my-self alone	81
Awake lordes awake & take goode hede	87
Beholde þis gret prynce Edwarde þe secounde	71
Bissop lorles	56
Calays men now mai ȝe care	11
Crist crowned Kyng that on Cros didest	95
Euermore schalle the six be the best cast on the dyce	46
ffor drede ofte my lippes y steke	13
ffor feer or for fauour of any fals man	85
ffore he is ful ȝong tender of age	41
ffor þou art comen of good blood	22
ffreers freers wo ȝe be	67
ffulfyllyd ys þe profesy for ay	49
Fur in see bi west spayngne	48
Galawnt pride thy father ys dede	52
Gaudete iusti in domino	94
Glade in god call hom ȝoure herte	14
God all-myghty saue and conserue owre kynge	80
God be oure gyde	24
Goo forth kynge reule the by sapience	96
Goo forth lybell and mekly schew thy face	70
ȝeft is Domesman & gyle is Chapman	55
I loue a floure of swete odour	35
I warne you euerychone for you schuld vnderstonde	90
I-blessyd be cristes sonde	37
Ich Herde men vpo mold make muche mon	2